THE JOURNALS

John Fowles was born in 1926. His books include *The Collector*, *The Aristos*, *The French Lieutenant's Woman*, *The Ebony Tower*, *Daniel Martin*, Mantissa, *A Maggot* and *Wormholes*. He lives in Lyme Regis.

Charles Drazin is an editor and writer, whose previous books include *In Search of the Third Man* and *Korda: Britain's Only Movie Mogul*.

ALSO BY JOHN FOWLES

John Fowles

THE JOURNALS
VOLUME I

EDITED AND WITH AN INTRODUCTION BY
Charles Drazin

V

VINTAGE

Published by Vintage 2004

4 6 8 10 9 7 5

Copyright © John Fowles 2003

John Fowles has asserted his right under the Copyright,
Designs and Patents Act, 1988 to be identified as the author
of this work

First published in Great Britain in 2003 by
Jonathan Cape

Vintage
Random House, 20 Vauxhall Bridge Road,
London SW1V 2SA

Addresses for companies within The Random House Group Limited
can be found at: www.randomhouse.co.uk/offices.htm

The Random House Group Limited Reg. No. 954009
www.randomhouse.co.uk/vintage

A CIP catalogue record for this book
is available from the British Library

ISBN 978 0 099 44342 1

Penguin Random House is committed to a sustainable future for
our business, our readers and our planet. This book is made from
Forest Stewardship Council® certified paper.

Printed and bound in Great Britain by Clays Ltd, St Ives plc

Contents

Illustrations

All photographs are from the collection of John Fowles and are reproduced
by permission. Photograph no. 27 is by Terry Spencer.

These disjoints are for my wives, Elizabeth and Sarah.

Introduction

This volume of journals commences rather abruptly in 1949 during John Fowles's final year at Oxford. John had actually kept a journal long before this time, but considered it had little worth beyond revealing the considerable depths of his immaturity. 'What a distance separates me from 1946,' he would write of one of these old diaries. 'The entries are so naif and puerile that they frighten me.' He marvelled at comments that revealed himself to be as 'inarticulate as a dummy' and asked, 'Shall I ever overcome my past?' The entries that the final-year student at Oxford made just three years later do not reveal a notably mature person, but they do mark the moment when John first seriously began to consider his place in the world. They mark too the point at which the wish to become a writer had firmly crystallized. Henceforward, it would be his chief ambition.

The reasons above help to explain why this first volume of John's published journal begins where it does, but to appreciate it more fully requires a brief look at the past that John felt he had to overcome.

John Robert Fowles was born on 31 March 1926 in Leigh-on-Sea, Essex – a small town at the mouth of the Thames, some thirty-five miles from London. His father, Robert, belonged, in John's own words, to 'one of the generation whose lives were determined once and for all by the 1914–18 War'. He had trained to be a lawyer, but the death of a brother at Ypres and then of his father, who had a young family from a second marriage, left him with their dependants to support and forced him to take over the management of the family tobacco firm, Allen & Wright Ltd. Every day he commuted into London and, weighed down with responsibilities, was 'careful not to offend the mores of the two worlds he lived in, suburbia and business London'.

The parents of John's mother, Gladys May – John and Elizabeth Richards – had come to London as a young couple from Cornwall. During their early years in the capital John worked as a draper and his wife Elizabeth was in service but, as John swiftly progressed to become chief buyer of a large London department store, they soon joined the ranks of the new middle classes. Their daughter was able to enjoy a comfortable upbringing in Chelsea, before moving with them to Leigh-on-Sea during the First World War. It was here that she would meet and marry Robert Fowles in 1925. As in the case of so many other middle-class women of her time, Gladys May sought fulfilment in the role of wife and home-maker. Cheerful and talkative, she looked after a small but pleasant 1920s semi-detached house at number 63 Fillebrooke Avenue and doted on her son, who would remain an only child until the arrival of a sister, Hazel, some fifteen years later.

John Fowles enjoyed a happy and secure – if, in the absence of any siblings, a sometimes rather solitary – boyhood. He attended Alleyn Court preparatory school in nearby Westcliff-on-Sea, where both his Uncle Stanley (Gladys May's brother) and Aunt Eileen were teachers. Here he showed an aptitude for both learning and sports, but his chief passion – encouraged by his Uncle Stanley – was for nature. With his friend Mackie, another teacher at Alleyn Court, Stanley would often take his nephew on nature expeditions into the countryside outside Leigh-on-Sea, looking for caterpillars that lived on the sloe bushes in the Thames estuary marshes or hunting lappet moths at Paglesham, a village a few miles to the north. 'I adored accompanying them,' John recalled, 'sitting with them in a pub. Ever warm and goldening evenings.'

In his first published essay, 'Entomology for a Schoolboy', written when he was twelve years old, the future author of *The Collector* gave an account of how to trap moths by smearing a mixture of honey and beer on a tree. Through his life, this love of nature would remain as central to him as the subsequent pursuit of literature.

In 1939 John won an exhibition from Alleyn Court to Bedford School, a public school that had a reputation for preparing boys for service in the Empire. After a cocooned childhood in Leigh-on-Sea, this strange new school, where he was boarding for the first time, was a shock. He missed home and had to endure the merciless teasing of the other boys. After a miserable first year – at the instigation of a mother who hated to see her child so obviously unhappy – John took a term off from school, which coincided with his family evacuating to Ipplepen, a Devon village halfway between Newton Abbot and Totnes.

In Ipplepen, John lived with his family in a cottage that belonged to distant relatives, and the knowledge that his grandparents had come from Cornwall further contributed to his sense that the move to the West Country represented a homeward journey. Over the years this identification has grown only stronger, so that today John takes particular pride in his Cornish ancestry and feels an enormous kinship with the West of England school of writing, of which he considers himself a member.

Although John would return to Bedford for the spring term of 1941, he passed every holiday in Ipplepen until his last year at the school in 1944. It was a marvellous haven, which gave him the opportunity to pursue his love of the countryside. His tutors in country life were a retired army major in the village – Major Lawrence – and a carpenter, B.W. Brealey, from the nearby village of King's Teignton.

Major Lawrence ran the local unit of the Home Guard and, a keen fisherman, held the record for the largest salmon ever caught in Norway, but he stood out most in John's memory for his command of the art of poaching. Expeditions with the Major would often involve furtive forays into farmers' fields in the pursuit of rabbits or pigeons. 'He taught me how to creep,' commented John, in summary of his influence.

More correct, BB, as John came to know Brealey, used to take him wildfowling. Over fifty years later, John regrets his participation in such a cruel sport, but none the less remembers it as one of the greatest experiences in his life. Getting up at dawn, he and BB would set out with BB's Irish water poodle for the lower marshes of the River Teign. Here they would wait for the Flight – the return of the birds from their night-time feeding grounds – passing the hours with esoteric conversations about shooting etiquette or shot-size. The challenge was to know how to wait, since the time of the birds' return was incalculable. Suddenly, almost faster than you could anticipate, they were upon you and then, in a flash, out of range again.

John could hardly have been further removed from the war. While most of Britain had to put up with rationing and raids from the Luftwaffe, the Fowles family enjoyed the peace of the countryside and feasted on the produce of the neighbouring farms. 'I still can't think of those years except in terms of cream and butter,' John would later recall, 'and an acid little bit of guilt.'

John's boyhood years were ones of sharp contrasts – the comfortable, sheltered upbringing in Leigh-on-Sea and the rude shock of boarding school; the rural idyll of Devon and the war damage which he saw every time he journeyed back to Bedford for a new term. The marvels of the one world must have helped him to endure the disappointments of the other.

Knowing that there was this wonderful countryside to return to at the end of every term made it easier to face the difficulties of school life with more equanimity, to buckle down and to apply himself.

An image that John uses in his journal is that of the caddis-fly larva, which builds around itself a tough protective casing out of whatever surrounding material happens to be available. At Bedford, John built his casing out of sporting prowess, academic achievement and respect for the system. He won a place at Oxford to read Modern Languages. He became Captain of Cricket and Head of School, responsible for imposing discipline on 500 boys. But although he acted as an efficient upholder of authority, privately he had qualms about the show of convinced rightness that his role required. He used to think of the Nazi bombers that raided Bedford Station. 'I became increasingly aware of the opposition between what the Nazis were doing to us and what I had to do to countless younger boys at the school.'

Outwardly the representative of authority but inwardly a dissenter, this Head of School with an uneasy conscience wore the trappings of his office like a mask. The tug between the conventional middle-class values of his upbringing and his own inner sense of injustice was a catalyst for the sort of writer John would become.

He went on from Bedford to join the officer training corps of the Royal Marines in late 1944. After basic training at the Royal Marines camp at Deal, he was posted to Plymouth and then, as an instructor in charge of training commando units, to Okehampton camp on Dartmoor. It was a posting liable to defer any further searching questions, since it returned him to the countryside he loved – where teaching commando units how to live off the land involved the sort of pursuits that he in any case regarded as his favourite pastimes. Indeed, at the end of his compulsory service, he would feel enough in sympathy with military life to regard the choice between staying on in the Marines and studying at Oxford as a real dilemma. A visit from the Socialist mayor of Plymouth, Sir Isaac Foot, helped to decide the issue. Only a fool would choose a military career, the mayor advised him when he confided the matter.

John went up to New College, Oxford, in 1947 to read French and German, but soon dropped German to concentrate on French language and literature. Regretting his inability to read German today, he recalls an intense distaste for the *lieder* evenings of the German faculty as the reason.

Here was another sharp contrast – from the discipline and order of military life to the intoxicating liberty of Oxford, where, apart from the weekly tutorial, you could do pretty much what you liked. It was a place where, free of responsibility, you were left to find yourself – a quest that must have seemed all the more pressing to a generation that had just experienced wartime service.

John's self-discovery involved a revolt against not only the institutions he had previously helped to uphold but also his own family. The birth of his sister Hazel, so many years younger than himself, had opened up a gulf between his needs, on the threshold of adulthood, and those of his parents, who now had a young child to care for. His father's decision at the end of the war not to stay in Devon but to return to the house in Leigh-on-Sea only further deepened his sense that what mattered to him did not matter to his parents. The sudden flood of experience that Oxford encouraged served to make them, once and for all, firm symbols of all that was regressive in his life.

Swiftly he was discarding the old skin of the public school boy and the Marines officer. The future lay in new friendships, new ideas and new places. In April 1948, he visited the south of France for the first time when as one of a party of Oxford undergraduates he went on a month-long cultural exchange trip to Aix-en-Provence, as guest of the city of Aix and the university of Aix-Marseilles. He travelled down with an old schoolfriend, Ronnie Payne. Just after the war, when so few people travelled abroad, this first largely carefree contact with the south was magical. 'We had to attend the odd lecture,' Payne remembered, 'but it was a jolly really. There were endless *vins d'honneur* and the town was full of pretty girls coming up to university for the first time.'

One night the two were sitting in the Deux Garçons café on the Cour Mirabeau, when a member of their student party came up to them in a pair of old army shorts and asked if they would like to join him in an aperitif. Fred 'Podge' Porter had joined the army at the beginning of the war and had served out in the Far East. Now he was studying French at St Catherine's. Over ten years older, he was married with a young daughter. Podge soon impressed his two fellow students with a teasing, sardonic manner. He was a 'born mischief-maker' Payne recalled. 'We rather liked his cynical disregard, his mocking almost everything in sight.' A convinced Marxist, in the years to come he would become John's close friend and, with his wife Eileen, helped to encourage his radical views – a new family in Oxford to replace the ideologically unsound one in Leigh-on-Sea.

That summer of 1948 had something of a fairy-tale quality. After playing host to the group of exchange students from Aix-Marseilles, who made the reciprocal trip to Oxford in July, John and Ronnie Payne travelled back to the south of France. They stayed in the Mediterranean port town of Collioure, close to the Spanish border, and found temporary work picking grapes. John stayed on after Payne returned to England at the end of August.

Some days later, hitch-hiking outside Banyuls-sur-Mer just to the south of Collioure, he was given a lift by an elderly millionaire from Lyons, M. Jullié, and his young woman friend Micheline Gilbert. M. Jullié invited him to join the crew of his yacht the *Sinbad*, which was harboured at Collioure.

Micheline, who had been in the Resistance during the war and had a husband in Paris, was left-wing and a woman of passionately expressed ideas who over the next few weeks would give the young Oxford student a crash course in the ways of the world and how best to engage with it. He fell in love with her, but, as he later recalled, 'The only reward I received was to be allowed to become something of her confidant and her butt: what the Resistance had really been like, why she loved both her Parisian husband and the gentle millionaire (and could never love me – and how ridiculous and sentimental my transparent near calf love for her was); her feelings about life, the impossible naïveté of the English, the monstrous selfishness of her bourgeois compatriots.'

The summer ended with the yacht being taken up the coast to its winter berth at Le Grau du Roi in the Camargue. The cook for the journey was a young Danish woman called Kaja Juhl, who was happy to become John's lover for the length of the voyage, introducing him to yet another new area of experience.

So ended an extraordinary summer of initiations. The long vacation of the next year was just as memorable. With his ex-Marines and Oxford friend Guy Hardy, John joined an expedition of ornithologists to the Finnmark region of Norway. Organized by the Severn Wildfowl Trust, their mission was to catch and bring back some Lesser White-fronted geese to the Trust's sanctuary at Slimbridge and to report on sightings of the very rare Steller's Eider Duck. Neither of these tasks was achieved, but the weeks spent travelling through Arctic tundra and fir forests provided as much material for the future novelist as the Mediterranean adventures of the previous year.

An isolated farm in the northern Finnmark made a particularly deep impression. Located on the Pasvik river near the Russian border, 'Noatun' was run by a retired engineer called Schaaning who lived there, dozens of miles from any other human habitation, with his wife, niece and nephew. It was 'a splendid setting for real tragedy,' John noted at the time, 'with something fixed and inevitable in it, like the ancient Greek.' Years later, he drew on the situation to create the character of Gustav Nyaard in *The Magus*, the educated farmer who looks after his mad and blind hermit brother Henrik as he waits in the wilderness to meet God.

In those consecutive student summers lay two poles of experience – the warmth, culture and civilization of the South; the cold emptiness of the extreme North. Together they marked a faultline in John's character, which could value the glorious humanist achievements of the one, yet feel equally drawn to the pristine solitude of the other. Noatun had the irresistible but dangerous pull of a Circe's island for him. 'Peace, peace and stillness,' he wrote of the place. 'The kind of quiet that can be traced back to the eternal absence of man – no one has ever been here since the beginning. This is the world minus man. Sometimes the silence is frightening, as when I waded back one dusk from fishing and felt the uncanniness of all that absence welling up into the personification of loneliness and inhumanity.'

Written just a few weeks before the beginning of this published version of his journal, these words belonged to a sensibility that could appreciate the extremes of human experience, but often struggled to cope with the comfortable in-between. Leigh-on-Sea, where John had grown up, was in reality a very pleasant little town close to London, but the more he discovered the world beyond the more he found its ordinariness stifling.

The events of those two summers helped to reveal his vocation. The chief theme of this first volume of John's journal is his struggle to become a writer, not just a published writer nor a bestselling writer nor even a critically acclaimed writer, but the best writer he could be according to his own exacting standards. The journal offers enormous insight into the high emotional toll of such an ambition as well as the nature of the apprenticeship required.

Literary success did not come early, but a formidable determination and inner confidence sustained John through all the self-doubt, disappointments and hardship that his goal entailed. The all-consuming passion and effort he poured into the task have an almost epic quality. While other writers have been content to climb Parnassus in their imaginations, it is somehow typical of John that he should have trekked across the Argive Plain and climbed the mountain for real.

But this journal also reveals a close relationship between literary inspiration and autobiographical experience. Alain-Fournier, the writer of one of John's most treasured novels, *Le Grand Meaulnes*, once commented that all he was good for was to make up stories, and to have them happen to him. John's journal suggests that he must often have thought the same thing. It chronicles a life not passed in an ivory tower, but one caught up in more than its fair share of dramatic incident.

Determined to be true to himself, John throws himself into pursuits with whole-hearted, unsparing devotion, whether he is striving to become a writer, exploring a foreign country or falling in love. One of the journal's most appealing qualities – although it is often leavened with a compensating sense of irony and absurdity – is this unreserved, total engagement. The writer observes none of the discreet veils or conventional compromises of life, but – mercilessly frank about his own and everybody else's failings – scrutinizes the world with a penetrating honesty.

This does not mean that he is immune to self-delusion. Indeed, his very fallibility and emotional vulnerability lend a poignancy to the quest for self-understanding that the journal chronicles. In spite of the extraordinary widening of horizons that John experienced during his Oxford years, the character who sets forth into the world stands out as a deeply shy individual whose loneliness makes him scorn but also love with an extra intensity. His responsiveness to environment is striking. The young man who after leaving Oxford teaches for a year at the French university of Poitiers, is an uncertain loner prone to despondency, but with his arrival on the beautiful Greek island of Spetsai he experiences a spiritual blossoming that recalls something of the joy the unhappy schoolboy must have felt suddenly to discover the Devon countryside.

The island, with its fir forests and beaches and the mountains of the Peloponnesus in the distance, was another domain to cherish. When many years later John read *Le Grand Meaulnes* for the first time, he must have done so with an extraordinary sense of recognition, because this story of the boy who finds, then loses an enchanted domain had, more than once, been his story too.

Indeed, in the journal, John passes through a series of domains. Arriving in Spetsai, he begins to teach at the prestigious Anargyrios and Korgialeinos school, but prefers to spend his time wandering Robinson Crusoe-like over the island, exhilarated to find 'a jewel, a Treasure Island, a paradise'.

At the end of the school year, touring Spain with a group of French students whom he had first got to know at Poitiers, he falls deeply in love with Monique, one of the members of the party. He recognizes in her 'a shadow of the perfect woman', although she is too much of an ideal ever to win in reality. He sees in her a 'glimpse of another world', but does not declare his love. As the tour group's charabanc crosses burning plains and wends its way over the high sierras, he aches with his longing for an unobtainable dream, far too bewitched by this *princesse lointaine* to appreciate the great cathedrals and Moorish palaces of Spain.

He returns from Spain feeling 'more remote, more isolated than ever'. But back in Spetsai to teach for a second year, he finds himself attracted to Elizabeth, the wife of a new English teacher. He warns himself that he mustn't become in any way involved with her: 'The one place where an eternal triangle might be intolerable is on an island.' But fate draws them together.

After years of struggle back in England, the triangle is eventually resolved, but the impression of his life passing through a series of domains continues right to the very end of the volume, when, now a successful author, he escapes to the south coast town of Lyme Regis, the domain in which, forty years later, he still lives.

The extremely forthright nature of this journal makes it important to stress the often wide gulf between John's perception of a situation or character and the objective reality. A diary is a place where you can write the things you dare not say in public, a place where you are free to vent your anger, frustration and prejudice, no matter how unreasonable those feelings might be.

In editing these diaries, a chief concern of mine was to respect this freedom of thought. I made a conscious effort not to censor them in any way, but it was impossible not to have qualms about many passages that were bound to upset people, and I thought it was important that John should have the opportunity to consider whether there were any comments that he regretted and wished to remain private.

From our resulting conversations it quickly became clear that there were many comments he regretted, but he had made them and, however foolish or wrong or hurtful they might seem now, the vital quality of the journal was to record how he had felt at the time.

The decision to leave such comments, even when they tended to be particularly hurtful to his closest friends – who after all were the most readily available victims – stems from his deepest instincts as a writer. It is worth quoting from the diary itself to convey just how much this principle of total truth matters to John. Soon after he fell in love with his first wife Elizabeth, he wrote: 'She has asked me not to write about her in here. But I could not not write, loving her as I do.' He concluded: 'What else I betrayed, I could not betray this diary.' Fifty years later, he has not changed his mind.

In a recent article the novelist William Boyd wrote, 'No true journal worthy of the name can be published while its author is alive. Only a posthumous appearance guarantees the prime condition of honesty.' The case of John's journal seems to me to stand in contradiction. The best guarantee of honesty was always his unwavering determination to remain faithful to what he had written.

A far bigger threat to this journal's integrity has come from the need to condense for publication two million words (the equivalent of about twenty good-length novels). In cutting down to a publishable length, my aim has been not to gather together a compendium of 'best passages', but to distil an essence of John's character, interests and attitudes over time. A huge challenge has been to do justice to the extraordinarily wide range of his interests, most of which have been pursued with as much emotional energy and seriousness as he has devoted to his writing. John once referred to his various selves as 'the John Fowles Club'. Its members – to mention just a few – include a poet, an ornithologist, a naturalist, a traveller, an extremely accomplished gardener, an indefatigable local historian, a musician, a cinephile, a collector of old books and a critic who customarily writes detailed and highly perceptive analyses of just about everything he has seen or read. If many of these personalities have made a more fleeting appearance here than I would have wished, it is important to remember that they all remain valued members of the club even if it is John Fowles the writer who takes centre stage.

This journal amounts to a barometer of a person changing, maturing – and sometimes regressing – through his experience of life. Immediately apparent to anyone reading the original diaries is their powerful narrative quality. The wish to preserve this quality has more than anything else dictated the cuts that have been made. John the neutral observer of other people and places has been pared down in favour of bringing out his own story. The criterion for selection was the degree to which a person, episode or subject could be considered to provide insight into character or help to carry the narrative forward.

The process of distillation gives a focus and direction to diaries that had seemed so loose and disconnected that John called them 'Disjoints'. With the benefit of hindsight, an editor is able to find a pattern in the material that the writer, who could chronicle his life only as it unfolded, was not in a position to appreciate. However appealing this narrative coherence may be, it represents a simplification.

This condensed version of the journal, with its emphasis on the significant episodes and achievements in John's life, risks making him seem more brooding and intense than he really was. While here he tends to be caught up rather quickly in one drama or another, the reader of the unabridged diaries will appreciate that in fact he found plenty of time just 'to stand and stare'. Many wonderful accounts of his travels abroad, for example, were omitted because they were a departure from rather than a continuation of the central narrative, but in themselves they count among some of John's happiest and most valuable experiences. So it should be borne in mind that while this published journal has sought to be representative, it does not presume to be definitive. Only the full-length diaries can be that.

In his short book *The Tree*, John compares his novel-writing to taking a path through an unknown wood. He makes the point that 'woods and forests are in fact subtler than any conceivable fiction, which can never represent the actual multiplicity of choice of paths in a wood, but only one particular path through it.' This strikes me as a useful analogy for my role as an editor, which has been to take one particular path through the forest of the many paths that I might have chosen. Anyone who wishes to appreciate the entire forest, must consult the complete, unedited diaries, which have been entrusted to the safe keeping of the Harry Ransom Humanities Center in Austin, Texas.[1] In John's own words, 'That is where my ego, my self, for what it is worth, will lie.'

The original diaries from which this first volume has been drawn were almost entirely handwritten in a small, occasionally impossible-to-decipher hand, but this edition does not signpost the doubts of an often illegible text. It seemed to me that to do so would be to disturb the

---

[1] There is also a copy in the library of Exeter University.

journal's tremendous readability. Instead, I have quietly excised the more impenetrable confusions or, in the cases of extreme illegibility, taken a guess at what seemed to be the most likely word. The knowledge that serious scholars who wish to make their own efforts at decipherment can do so by consulting the original diaries encouraged me to take this practical rather than academic approach.

By the same token, I have tried to be as sparing with footnotes as possible. John's own voice is so strong that anyone else's risks being an irritating distraction. I have resorted to such notes only where to omit them seemed likely to raise even more distracting questions. Yet some questions that the reader may consider important remain unanswered. This is most notably the case with respect to the many stories, plays and poems that John wrote long before he became a published author. Most of these early works were destroyed and, although their names are preserved in the journal, so many years later John cannot recall what they were about. Although such omissions are to be regretted, we can perhaps console ourselves with the thought that finally this volume is not a catalogue but one man's journal, in which it is foolish to expect complete tidiness.

The last novel John Fowles published was *The Maggot* in 1985, nearly twenty years ago. Such a big gap may suggest the end of a writing career, but it is worth remembering that he took fifteen years to write *The Magus*. For John, a novel is not written to a timetable but emerges out of a complex brew of thoughts, which observes its own unpredictable pace. Over the past two decades there have been many events in John's life to stifle this brewing process from bereavement to personal illness, but his sense of being a writer has remained as strong as ever.

To an extent, the diary itself supplanted a future novel by becoming the major literary preoccupation after the death of his first wife Elizabeth in 1990. At this critical stage, it provided the obvious means to look back over his life, to attempt the self-understanding that was an important aim of the novels themselves.

As the deadline for this first volume loomed, I asked John what he hoped its publication would achieve. We were sitting in his writing room, the edges of his desk charred black with the marks of innumerable cigarettes, which it occurred to me could probably be carbon-dated all the way back to *The Collector*.

'The diary will really try and tell people who you are and what you were,' he answered. 'The alternative is writing nothing, or creating a totally lifeless, as it is leafless, garden.'

The words brought out how intimately related the diarist and the novelist were.

Many years ago John spoke of the novel as conveying not any philosophical propositions or scientific truths but instead 'feeling truths'. This journal has the same quality, containing the paradox of fiction that to do justice to one kind of truth is often to do injury to another.

Indeed, the connection between his fiction and life is so strong that John himself has suggested that his journal might best be thought of as another novel. If the process of writing fiction has involved fabricating a series of masks behind which his personality has taken shelter, then the two volumes of this journal provide yet one more mask, drawing not on a particular incident or period, but on a whole life from adulthood to old age. 'This is why I think the diaries – or the 'disjoints' as I call them – are very truly the last novel I have to write.'

This volume is the first part of that novel. It ends with a young writer achieving huge success, but choosing to live apart from literary society. In the second volume we will discover what he made of his self-imposed exile.

Charles Drazin,
July 2003

Part One

Oxford

63 Fillebrook Avenue, Leigh-on-Sea, 11 September 1949
This so dull life, mingled with hate and annoyance and pity. No attempt
here at method or speed. The housework drags on all day – cleaning,
hoovering, dusting, making beds, sewing, washing-up and so on. No one
ever sits down before suppertime. It is wrong, but the smallness of the
rooms and the house is so noticeable now. The nursery stuffed full of
things, always untidy; the dining-room dark and gloomy – only the
lounge is tolerable, and one never lives there. The cloistered life with
no one to talk to, no one to laugh with – here I am like a hermit, and
quite unnatural. An absolute craving for new faces, new meetings, new
places. I would tell them so much, but a curious obstinacy prevents this.
Always an air of mulish hostility.

24 September
Two beautiful things. A big, spacious sunset sky – elegant and not ostentatious, but curiously in the east, to the west nothing but a bank of low,
dark clouds. The end of a Spergularia in the microscope – like a minute
green saturn.[1] A tiny shining ball with a ring of gauzy skin around it.
Also the sails of some Thames barges half-hidden by mist. A curious
thing. About to throw a piece of screwed-up paper into the yellow jug
which serves as waste-paper basket, I said to myself, 'As much chance
as you have of being genius.' It fell into the jug without a murmur, a
20 to 1 chance, at the least.

Another day of silence, listening to other people's trivialities – a dreadful
hour at night when all the completely banal information gained from
a visit of relatives is repeated and reviewed. Two mathematical impossibilities I should like to see. One, a graph of the words spoken by me
each day over a year – the rise and fall would be eye-opening. Near zero
here, and normal everywhere else. Two, a count of words spoken by my
mother and myself – David and Goliatha!

The visit by unknown relations is frightening, slightly, to the ego, and

---

[1] A plant, known as the sea or sand spurrey, which grows in sandy regions and
salt marshes.

being. I feel awkward, not because I feel superior, but because I feel that they feel I am. Probably oversensitivity. But they are definitely not at home with me.

Trying to get at oneself is a continual unwrapping – each new skin decreases steadily in beauty and value after it is exposed. Always the seed of truth, the maximum fulfilment of self, appears to be just beneath the next layer. Plainly there is no end to this unwrapping, but the sensation is damping.

Being a poet, divining beauty, is like divining nature – a gift. It does not matter if one does not create. It is enough to have the poetic vision. To see the beauty hidden. As I did tonight, hearing someone whistle in the distance as I stood by an open window. I felt all kinds of moods of streets at night, of walking with loved women, of the dark blue and whiteness, and the strange, magical desertion of streets at night. I felt it all *exactly* in a moment, such a rush of impressions that they can hardly be seized. Algernon Blackwood: 'To feel like a poet is not to be a poet.'[1] True, yet, poetry, making, is not necessarily the printing of words. It is a philosophical outlook, an epicureanism, a hedonism.

25 September
3 a.m. Beautifully played New Orleans jazz, with clarinet in low register, and very jazzy tuba and cornet. Bessie Smith singing. This sort of stuff has in it the germ of music that will last.
  Op. 55. Splendidly vigorous, with some of the secret lyricality of the last quartets.[2]

Writing fever. Can't get any university work done. Full of ideas for 'Cognac' and full of frustration at not having the time to do them. 'Cognac' must aim at being popular, with art overboard. The idea came all in two hours last night and this morning.

30 September
Another appalling half-hour of talk. When screaming was close. Talk of the utmost banality, on prices of mattresses, on Mrs Ramsey's daughter who married a doctor in Montreal. A few comments are made

---

[1] Blackwood (1869–1951) was a British writer of supernatural fiction. Affectionately known as the 'Ghost Man', from the 1930s he enjoyed a very successful second career broadcasting his stories, talks and dramas on BBC radio.
[2] At Oxford, JF had become a great admirer of Beethoven. Here he is referring to the 'Eroica' Symphony (No. 3 in E Flat Major).

on poetry. So hopeless to try and explain. They would never understand. No mention of art can ever be developed in case we are 'highbrow' – God, how I hate that word! No philosophy is mentioned, without Thomas Hardy and Darwin getting dragged in. It is *la mère*. Her attitude to conversation is one of complete alertness. I must break in, and I must say something – and in she breaks and says something, whether she has any knowledge, real opinion or not. It is with great difficulty that I can keep my oyster silence. But I must not hurt. With *le père*, it is partly a defence; modernity is ignored, age is suspicious of invention.

I feel violent with 'hate' against this bloody town. Least violent, now, against the geographical situation (once I longed for Devon), most against the way of life, and then the people who allow it to sap all the beauty of life out of them. All my sympathy goes out to the boy who ran away to be a bullfighter. I'm sure he must have 'felt' the complete horror of this place. This town can have as much horror mentally for a sensitive person as a blitzed city may have, physically, for a turnip. It is the unsociability, the not-knowing-anyone, the having-no-colour, that kills. No interesting people to talk to, no sincere people, no unusual things to do.

Then there is 'niceness' as a standard of judgement – God, how I hate that word, too! – 'a nice girl', 'a nice road'. Nice = colourless, efficient, with nose glued to the middle path, with middle interests, dizzy with ordinariness. Ugh!

Oxford, 6 October
Reread some early poems. All bad. It is like seeing oneself in a film walk naked through a crowded street.

But then to feel oneself unfolding, like a flower.

7 October
Lunch with Guy Hardy and Basil Beeston and a serious Pole.[1] In the Kemp. I cannot concentrate on those with whom I happen to be. Always there are more interesting people at the next table. Beautiful women to be watched. G and BB seem so set up in the world – they sit on a terrace by the sea and I drift past, watching them, jealous, unhappy. Yet I have the jewel. I may drift to even-more-to-be-coveted terraces, and land.

*

[1] Guy Hardy and Basil Beeston were two of JF's closest friends at Oxford, who shared his interest in wildlife and nature. Guy Hardy was at Corpus Christi and had travelled with JF on an ornithology trip to Norway (see introduction, page xiv). Basil Beeston was reading Engineering at New College.

Immortality is a convention, a white elephant. A futility. There is no
logic in planning for it. No enjoyment, no beauty can come out of it.
All life should be designed to be contained within life. Within the closed
circle. Outside the theatre, the bouquets won't be seen. The turnip who
gains fame in his life, and lives, has an immense superiority over the
poet who becomes famous after his death, and obscurely exists.
Immortality is the gravestone of the spirit. What use is the gravestone?

5 November
Guy Fawkes night. A great crowd of people, vaguely contented at shaking
off the discipline of the world as it is. The undergraduates form the
largest part, for the most part just watching, with a few active spirits
shouting, calling, singing, making speeches. A certain air of forcedness
about all these crowds. Fireworks shooting up, and people exploding
away from them when they land. The police and the proctors standing
ineffectively. Buses moving slowly, cars being rocked and thumped.
Many climb up the scaffolding around the Martyr's Memorial,[1] then a
vague move is made to the Taj Mahal restaurant where there is a man
climbing up, men shouting, and a solid mass of people. Water out of
the windows.

Basically one cannot help feeling contempt for all this *canaille*, noisily
and offensively drunk yet not doing anything positive. Most of them
posturing in a ridiculous manner. A good many girls, who seem the
most genuinely excited.

To a certain extent there is a vast good will that can be sensed; roughly
everyone is together and enjoying themselves, with the police and the
proctors symbolizing all kinds of emotion and, ultimately, the determinism
in life. GH and BB both enjoy themselves, and look for some means to
manifest their lawlessness. I have absolutely no desire to do anything else
but watch, wanting to be everywhere and see everything, observing
people's faces. Roger Hendry[2] is like me but not so finely 'set', for he has
to pretend to a certain lawlessness which isn't innate in him at all.

Too many of the faces are vacuous and want filling.

The sight of the girl in green, about whom I wrote the Hospital story,
with a thick well set-up young man, is distressing. Above all the sight of
the moon, nearly full, in a clear night sky, not particularly cold, after a
dull, rainy day. I wanted very much to see one of the people who climbed

---

[1] A monument erected in Oxford in 1841 in memory of the Protestant leaders
Cranmer, Ridley and Latimer, whom the Catholic Queen Mary I had burned at
the stake after a trial for heresy in 1554. It is situated in St Giles outside Balliol
College.
[2] Roger Hendry was a friend and contemporary of JF at New College. He read
Greats and introduced JF to the music of Beethoven.

the Memorial fall down to his death. The indrawn breath and sudden laugh would have been most effective.

12 November
A self-searching night at the Podges[1],' with Faith.[2]

Faith, a curious kind of extrovert, conversation-dominating, with the same strident rise in pitch (when she wishes to break in on top of anyone else) as M. Confidential, bold, tomboyish – revealing about her monastic father, whom she says worries her greatly at times.

Podge and Eileen are a perfect duo; in harmony or perfect discord.

During this evening (having felt ill all day, with a certain amount of pain) I keep very quiet and feel unable to assert myself in any way. Not particularly self-conscious and oversensitive but lacking more than lost colour. Two mes: ego, thinking with and at tangents from the others, full of the right words, curious ideas and so on; and the alter ego, not being able to break into the discussions.

An empty walk home with Faith, yawning myself and she whistling and singing.[3] I feel a vague need to explain myself, and also to know what she is thinking. A wet, warm, windy night.

I can feel more concretely a philosophy of life on occasions like these. To be persuasive, to watch and analyse, externally; internally, to record and create. It is absolutely necessary to remain balanced; that is, never to become submerged completely – always to have the intention of creating beauty for others, however reduced this infusion into action and society becomes. Theoretically I want to become a core receiving prehensions, being moulded by them, yet remaining pointed in the one direction, towards creation of beauty. I can't pretend that this is a natural attitude; it leads to compression of feeling, to a dangerous bottling of the need to express, an overtense introversion. The advantages are 1. the forming-house for creation (although some kind of objectivity and

---

[1] The 'Podges' are Fred 'Podge' Porter, and his wife Eileen. Podge, whom JF had first got to know during the spring of 1948 on a visit of Oxford students to Aix-en-Provence, was studying French at St Catherine's College. After graduation Podge became a teacher at Magdalen College School in Oxford. Twelve years older than JF and a confirmed Marxist, he was a close friend and an important influence in shaping JF's radical views.

[2] Faith Faulconbridge, who was studying English at St Anne's, had been one of the students on the 1948 Aix-en-Provence trip. After Oxford, she became a teacher and sculptress, and married Christopher Tolkien, son of the author and Oxford don J. R. R. Tolkien.

[3] 'Home' was La Maison Française, then at 72 Woodstock Road. The Maison had been founded by the Universities of Oxford and Paris to encourage co-operation between researchers, lecturers and students from the two institutions, and every year provided board to a number of undergraduates and scholars.

self-criticism must be obtained), 2. that the final axion *is* one of external expression in fame through beauty created. It is creation which acts as a safety-valve, as well as being the ultimate purpose. The essentials are constant attention to practice of the means and a self-confident devotion to the end.

I think that this is the nearest I can get to self-fulfilment, considering, as I do now, that everything is purely relative, and that no beauty is immortal. I can see little point in immortal fame; yet can believe in the human illogic of doing good by the creation of beauty, even though it will only be temporarily existent. (Not forgetting the time-space question, when nothing that has existed can disappear.) Must *strive* after living glory; it is unnatural to push, but it is necessary.

We also talked of the parent–child relationship.

The crux is when the bridge of realization is reached. The otherness of parents, their separate personality, their defaults and often their inferiority. A solid link of respect should be maintained (E)[1] – but respect can't come when the 'truth' (however false) seems to be clear. One's parents seem inferior 'x' and nothing can make them respected 'y'. Only hypocrisy and convention. It's like being C of E when there is no faith. Eileen's interesting theory that this break is good for creating individuals; that happy families are those when the children have failed to 'personalize' or 'separate' their parents and so become submerged within the family 'soul' with unrealized individuality.

Going through a long period of self-discontent; no faith. Fair certainty that several of the projects, especially the plays, are good, but impossibility of long concentration and doubt about powers of technique and realization. Moreover, the consciousness that nothing will be done for at least a year. And at times the deliberate withdrawal from the world becomes too much of an effort to permit any surety.

21 November
The constant quantum of self-estimation and the temporary urges to write which must die away because there is no time to canalize the inspiration. Sense of waste.

JW.[2] Dapper, impeccable, and fairly well off. Conventional and sociable, but without great originality except for a certain facility of wit. Easy to get on with. Not strikingly dressed. Slightly French in manner, not thoroughly English (brought up for some years in France).

---

[1] i.e. Eileen Porter.
[2] Here and in the paragraphs that follow JF gives character portraits of some of his fellow residents at the Maison Française.

GH. Ex-RAF – still a flyer in the OR.[1] Self-possessed, insensitive, often unintentionally rude because of his certainty in self. Intelligent, but apparently not imaginative. His egoism is annoying, partly because it is not fully conscious on his part; it is not deeply objectionable, but annoying. A question of limited assurance, but still assurance. No one sensitive is ever assured. Well-liked by others.

RF. Religious, obtuse, wet. Wishes to be a schoolmaster. Earnest worker, never relaxing. Constantly a Boy Scout badge in his lapel. Bad French accent, with many stupid remarks. Naïve to an infuriating degree. Reliable, always willing to help. Keen on amateur photography; no sense of art, of beauty. Insensitive.

PW. The most interesting character. An ex-POW, with a brilliant Oxford career. President of French class and OUDS, editor of *Isis*. A very quiet and silent little person, chubby-faced, with dark glasses always. A problem because his past and his present silence seem to suggest hidden depths, which may or may not exist in truth. By no means infallible or intolerant – an excess of diplomacy, never impolite, brusque or outspoken. Sense of humour; well-chosen opinions and remarks. Listened to deferentially. Today, revealed a little about himself to me for the first time since I met him, i.e. his shyness in discussion, which he confessed.

MLG. An easy character. Provincial Provençal, but with no great meridional traits, except a certain quickness of temperament. Great sense of humour; polite and very conventional. Not basically a prude, yet unapproachable externally. No warmth of relationship, such as one might find in an English girl (without any implication of love).

HF (Henri Fluchère).[2] Small, temperamental, Provençal. Sense of humour, excellent conversationalist, with sophist and sophisticated dissertations on literature. Unprepossessing appearance – a certain foxiness, slyness, which is misleading. Excellent but badly pronounced English.

3 December
Feature of twentieth century – the mass of authors; difficult to rise above a struggling welter. Need for order; genius is crowded out, stifled. It is pleasant to think of some perfect state where only the official writers may write. Increased education means increased tyroism in the arts – everyone tries their hand. Need to find a striking individuality.

Cycling along a wet road under a sky full of scudding clouds, with a full moon shining through them with a variety of strange effects, pinknesses,

---

[1] Officer Reserve.
[2] The then director of the Maison Française.

opaque masses. The wind very strong from the west. A feeling of momentary jubilation, being at one with nature, and sensing the good fortune of being human, the leading actor standing out from the harmonious background. This is a rather eighteenth-century sentiment, but one which is full of happiness for those that can still *genuinely* feel it. Everything related by love within the whole, a pantheistic joy. Science and civilization are encroaching on this relationship between man and nature, but the irreducible element of comparative immortality prevents any kind of total conquest. The sky remains. Feeling such a moment is like looking back into the Promised Land.

Three days running, a red ladybird lands on my desk in spite of the cold weather. The superstition still vaguely makes itself felt.

The question of intimacy in style – the objectivist always writes for a potential reader other than himself; he is never half alone and *chez soi*, never getting to the rock-bottom of things, for the style affects the expression. The subjectivist writes purely for himself, egotistically saying a thing in the way which seems to himself best to express exactly his own view of it. All creation tends to one of these two poles, which are, very approximately, classical and romantic. This is an interesting test to perform on all memoirists and diarists. What if the greatest combines the two qualities?

The vital thing is time. It is the fundamental problem of life, around which all metaphysical speculation ought to turn. Time as a notation, as a measurement, is valueless, an artificial invention. The important thing is the becoming, the dynamism.

Some arts use time more than others. Painting, sculpture, present a more or less static object. Poetry and music, the cinema, a fluidity absolutely reliant on time for effect. The miracle of photography, challenging time, fixing.

Death is simply not becoming, a loss of fluidity. The loss of the element of presence. Death kills time and enthrones, enhances place.

Life is the gift of consciousness of time. A gift which, once it has been given, cannot be rejected. Awareness is becoming. There is a continual awareness of presence.

Could death punish by stopping enjoyment and awareness, which are the benefits of time, and reward by changing time?

Awareness can give our highest imagined happiness. We cannot imagine timelessness and unawareness as a higher happiness, since they are conceptions unrelated to our present condition.

Given the *gifts* of awareness and time, it is futile to pursue timelessness, like the mystics. The gift of awareness must be fully enjoyed, since it is the highest potential in the present condition. This belief is necessary, though not absolutely true. It has relation truth.

Absolute happiness is timelessness and unawareness, but imperfect organisms cannot apprehend absolutes.

Leigh-on-Sea, 16 December
Spasm of hate. Trying to listen to Mozart 465 Quartet, when M[other] seems, almost deliberately, to spoil it. Mounting unease and fury and sense of martyrdom. Partly the fury is the fact that all (fundamentally and now in this incidental environment) is arid to them, and all reproach creates a guilty conscience. Finally (in the middle of the third movement) the decision that the decorations should be put up: 'Everyone else has put them up. The Farmers have put them up.' We are out of line, horror! Father, up till now, a passive spectator, infuriates because he remains passive, i.e., instead of saying, 'Whenever! It can wait,' he mumbles, 'Better get it done,' and starts fiddling about with the streams of coloured paper. Partly I feel this is to annoy the highbrow in me. I switch off the wireless, and help in a savage, couldn't-care-less way. For some time I feel willingly that I could like killing them. When they remonstrate about burning some barren strips of holly, I find joy in burning it deliberately, to show that I think it nonsense and that hanging Christmas decorations is for me a duty, not a pleasure. Hazel[1] begins to cough and cry, she is ill. I feel an accession of pity, and in a way the spirit of Christmas immanent in the decorations, though only very vaguely, releases my fury. I help carry coal to light a fire and so on. F scorches a hole in his new flannel trousers against an electric fire. I cannot help laughing when he tells me this. A thing I inherit from him – amusement at minor pains and misfortunes. It is the point of absurdity which pricks the situation, and the progress of the evening ends up on a Beethoven sonata and the feeling that an ugly series of incidents have resolved themselves.

This atmosphere of tension is frequent here at home, being mainly caused by the confined space, living all the time in the same small room, when all relationships have to go on the level of the LCD, i.e. M, on the level of triteness and mundanity. My sympathy goes towards F now. The difficulty for me is correlating the mood – dutiful and necessary attitude which is to be adopted and the actual attitude I have created at Oxford. There is a wide gap between the two milieux. In the intellectual and aesthetic sense I have developed out of the rest, yet I have to try and conceal that in order to make life livable. Always present, too, is the guilty knowledge that financially I am a passenger in a leaking ship.

---

[1] JF's much younger sister, born in 1942, fifteen years after him.

Hazel is an interesting test-object for egotism. Financially it is to my benefit that she should not exist. I don't feel particularly jealous that love should be diverted from myself to her, but annoyed and pitiful that she should swallow up the affection of such old parents. I pity her because she will grow up in an old-fashioned way, with antique views and a conventional cliché mind. Her only hope of being modern is that she is left an orphan, or that I distract her away. Also she is a sister, my family; but the disparity in age destroys all close love and family sense. She merely seems like a small pet. But the change will come when she is fifteen, or at the most by the time that she is twenty. Then I shall, perhaps, be a middle-aged failure in need of rejuvenation, *et la voilà!* But now, at present, she seems to threaten all the peaceful old age of the two people whom I must wish to see happy. She is a Fowles, nervous, intelligent, *sans* intellect, *sans* culture, I see it all coming. Also she is weak in health and there will be trouble. I realize that they, *now*, could not be happy *otherwise*. But it is the *now* and the *otherwise* which jar. To me it seems they would have been happier in another set of circumstances, where they had little but their own comfort to consider. Admittedly having to be parents to youth makes them artificially younger, but that does not make me happier. And the child H twists the dagger in the wound when she says, 'John's my father, you're my grandfather and M's my mother.' With a kind of diabolically inglorious perception.

Writing a poem is like standing on some shore and saying, 'I shall row to that enchanting island over there.' But when I start rowing, the joy of the action makes me lose all sense of direction, and of course eventually one returns always from where one set out, plus experience, but minus perfect success, which is unattainable. And when, later, I look back over the route, the rowing which was joy, it seems ridiculous, petty.

Beauty of Leigh marshes. The wasteland, the wilderness, the sanctuary. The narrow ugly line of Canvey Island, a thin, distant bar with the square blocks of houses, low clumps of trees. Canvey Beck, the deserted point. The Hadleigh hills, graceful and English, soft and solid, and the thoughtful ruins of the castle. The smug, impersonal town, with its rows of similar houses. Old Leigh, with its spikery of masts and patterns of boat's hulls, with character. Southend pier, beastly like the railway line, scarring the sea as the other scars the land. The Thames, flat and magnificent.

The mud-flats, all distance and middle-distance, and no nearness. The desolation of the sea-walls and the saltings. Only winter is congruous. The austere birds, the meadow-pipit, the curlew and the redshank the perfect soloists and inhabitants. Aloofness and wildness. When the wigeon whistle all the town recedes into oblivion. Their spirit transcends all its badly constructed material.

The constellations of black stars, the moving skeins of gulls and curlew flying out to sea in the distance, against a yellow western sky. A sunset, a red, tawny sun sinking into the golden, ragged tops of a low, heavy layer of blue clouds, miles and miles away over London. The excited chattering of flocks of small waders as they follow the edge of the ebbing tide, an insight into a society as far removed as that of Mars. Hearing them is like some sight of a fabulous planet. The pleasure of fighting the wet and the cold, and feeling animal and strong, elemental. Of being alone on a difficult quest, with all the lights of those in comfort twinkling ashore.

The smell of the tide and the islands of reeds in the flat water. The two trees.

The pleasure of knowing a place intimately. The run of the tide, the guts, the runnels, the kinks in the walls, the mussel-bed, the places to hide.

29 December
Confused Christmas with many petty worries and malaises. Unpleasantness of small children. Stupidity of adults. Impossible to talk with, unless it is mundanities. All a bit puzzled and embarrassed by me. I want to be myself to them, but the slightest move in that direction leads to puzzlement.

Sensitivity is one of the easiest diagnostics of the quality of humanity. No one truly sensitive can hurt another human being.

Adrift, waiting for a current, or a view of land which isn't a mirage. So many abstract -isms, so many real and minor troubles now. So many little mice scratching, when there should be dragons to kill. Being in a cell and searching for a loose brick; and if it was loose, would my future commit itself? Here I have to make life into a prison, and lock the door upon my real self. It is a kind of suicide for reality. For if only what is, is real, then the what I feel I would unrestrainedly be, in other circumstances, is a ghost. Hate for this town, its cheap, shoddy travesty of life.

2 January 1950
A girl in Southend High Street, cheap, sloppy. But pretty, and curiously, afterwards, I realized with a touch of Lawrence about her. I tolerate Southend High Street; it has a certain brassiness and individuality of character which is refreshing.

Hazel, at tea: 'I suppose you were all sitting here at tea, facing the fire like this, before me, when I was in heaven.'

*

Another phase of vague illness again; like sleeping in a haunted house and *not* seeing the ghost. This morning I escaped the *miaiseries* and walked along the path between Chalkwell and Old Leigh. A raw, dull day with a wind and all-pervading greyness. The tide full in, and the sea faintly grey-green, ugly. Few people about; at sea the hulls of the small yachts and motorboats wintering at their moorings. No birds but sea-gulls, resting silently on the sea, or uneasily flying up. The fishing fleet moved out of Leigh into the gloom of the east coast, smacks painted grey and green, with their crews on deck. I envied them for their free life. Old Leigh is a single narrow street, with salty, muddy houses, still retaining strongly the character of fishing and *naïveté*. The railway line, in this case, preserves the community – its special nature. Past Old Leigh, the cockle-sheds, a dark line of huts. The boat-building shed. The begin-ning of the sea-wall, the corporation dump, the loneliness. In a sense all nicely divided and gradated. A bleak sort of affection is possible.

5 January
A whim to go afar. To Canvey Island, up the sea-wall to Shell Haven.[1] A pale, cold, half-fine day; obscure blueness and insistent clouds, general bright blue-greyness, making in the morning the grass very green and the water grey and ruffled, an aqueous brightness every-where. Later the weather settled into a cold, windy dullness. This part of Canvey isolated, overrun by rabbits. I meet a friendly man, with a red face, carrying an old sack bag with a bottle in it. One of the few countrymen left. Then on into a wasteland of rubble-dumps, with to-and-fro lorries, cranes, wharves, distant oil-tanks. One or two houses deserted, forsaken; few birds. A strange part of the world. It seems so deserted in contrast with the oil-shipping atmosphere given by the tanks. I don't pass a soul. The creek here is wide, bleak and impersonal, another world from Old Leigh.

Past the oil-tanks home, they seem without men; past a white house set in a few shrubby trees, with one room lit on the top floor, past and around a deserted army camp, full of huts, towers and desuetude, back into the myriad-housed centre of Canvey. All bungalows and jerry-built, yet full of television aerials. The people, this centre, seem to ignore the desolation and harshness of the rest of the island east, with its hundreds of acres of grassland and marshy drains. Like the heart of the lettuce.

Denigrating effect of Oxford, like a pin balloon-pricking. Essential un-friendliness. Thirst for purpose and duty. Complete doubt as to future and literary ability. Depressing Schools results – either failures or successes.

---

[1] An oil refinery and storage depot built by the Shell oil company at Canvey Island on the north bank of the Thames estuary.

All day walking about, seeing tutors, meeting people. A wet, warm day. The pavements at night remind me of things I have forgotten, summer somewhere and feeling very happy – a curious smell, very West wind, blossoming from them. Nostalgic; and above the nostalgia a layer of unhappy what's-the-good-ness, being sensitive, feeling, living in the past, when the present is what it is. Here is the home of rivality, of comparisons. *Chacun pour soi*, socially, academically. Everyone has assets beyond me.

Chekhov's *The Three Sisters*, listened to on a grey, dull Sunday, when I feel alone, as always on Sundays. Deeply enjoyed. So many things felt. The optimism wrung out of the mass of pessimism, the absurd *fardeau* of life. 'There is no happiness; only the longing for it.' 'My soul is like a piano, whose key has been lost.' Frustration, ennui, acceptance. Chekhov knew how out of the sisters' misery, so typical, so universal, so timeless, would come the beauty, the joy and tragedy, catharsis, the strangest help. Basically, a realization of man's position in an indifferent world, the glow of full consciousness vaguely felt. Masochism, pity for the general through the individual, the general being incomprehensible, non-existent except through the individual. Tragedy should create pity, should broaden, deepen, emancipate the sympathetic imagination into a realm where the consequent will to creation, action, can be realized; should create ghosts with the will to climb into real life.

19 January
News that the specialist has diagnosed my illness;[1] relief, sense of vindication, slight regret for the past state, masochistic. Not altogether an ill wind; so many depths would have been unplumbed. Suffering is essential to know oneself. Introspection. A return to normality is not altogether a blessing.

Splendid evening light over afternoon London, gilding quite literally everything with beauty. I have never felt so sensitive – in all directions, in all objects, sudden apprehensions of subtle charms. The River Thames a beautiful pale glowing blue, the concrete of the normally off-white bridges, a pink-gold soft opal. The sky intense, tinged turquoise.

Curious interstate of a dream – an exact continuity. I dreamed I was exactly where I was, lying in bed in the home, waiting for the nurse to come and inject. But in the dream someone was also waiting and the lights were on (actual time 4 a.m.), and an announcer had just said on

---

[1] The diagnosis was amoebic dysentery. Soon afterwards JF was admitted to a nursing home in London.

the wireless that someone called Ray(mond?) Noble was going to play
the piano. When the nurse came in actually, she came in in the dream.
For once I didn't seem to wake immediately.

30 January
Three nurses here, strong types in the subtle distinction category.
One a full big-breasted strong girl whose body smells, whose approach,
with a bright smile and a bright remark, is healthily sexual, like a
barmaid or a Scandinavian (she is blonde). Her natural element and
position is bed and open-limbed. Two, a mousy, unobtrusive, small,
flat-cheeked girl, feminine and unsexual, with a certain gentle prettiness. Shy and unassertive in approach, a faint, conversational smile.
All her life in a minor key, in the background, negative, though not
without its charm of faintness. Three, better, a year older, trim-figured,
good legs, nice breasts, quite a pretty face, tinge of Jewishness.
Practical, aloof, cold. Suggestion of sexuality, but carefully locked
away. The best-uniformed. Self-contained, indifferent to all but the
quick, efficient execution of the job. Smart office-girl, gin-and-orange
type. Interesting to have them on a voyage, or to sleep with them all,
not particularly from desire, but better to be able to classify and distinguish them.

The tissue of life. The pain and embarrassment of the cure; its apparent
unsuccess; the boredom; the frustration, sexual and adventurous; the
three young nurses; the mad old senile women, vaguely heard, never
seen, phantasmagoria from outside; the dull, little room, the empty
bed, the green chair, the china Alsatian climbing up the green steps,
the insufficient wireless, the silver half-hunter wall-engraved; the unattractive meals; the routine, the bed being made; the ugly patch of
garden out of the window; the occasional golden light (Claude) in the
sky. The parental visits, the prompt retreat into the shell, the banalities, the poses, the indifference, the guilt of ingratitude. The withdrawal
from life, from reality, from responsibility, like a toad in his flower-pot
by a busy walk. Like a bee still in his honeycomb cell. Waxed, silent,
indifferent, falling into a despair, self, groping back into the cave so
that no one is at the mouth of the cave to deal with passers-by. Only a
voice shouting out of the darkness, angry at being disturbed, back over
my shoulder.

Extraordinary inversion of sickness. Because I feel myself no better, a
kind of compensatory masochism, not so much a psychologically whining
self-pity as a tight-lipped stoic self-dramatization, arises. The tragedy of
the vague illness and its vague effects on life become real, and the sense
of difference, the growing away from the normal world is universal. Most

of my day-dreams are violent reactions into a hard, active, adventurous, romantic life; I become lost in them more easily in a stagnant situation like this. Some are the ideal fulfilment of past or future potentialities, more often, naturally, the latter. Others are outside even the realm of potentiality. This placing of the ego in a tragic (or again a day-dream tragic, a potentially tragic) frame, though pernicious, cannot be willed away. It's like a leak in a boat; for a long time one can keep pace, then it wins. Baling is done in two ways – by an effort of will, by concentration on externals, both periodic things. The natural self-interest will always win through, though again it is equally periodic, even when there is no will to persist. As always, it opens doors into gardens and storeyards of self-realization.

Writing it down and reading it, objectively, make it seem all false.

3 February

Dostoevsky, *House of the Dead*.[1] The calm objectivity, the coolness of it all. Immolated. Also the monotony, greyness, illuminated by his super-journalistic spirit. 'The passionate desire to rise up again, to be needed, to begin a new life, gave me the strength to wait and hope' . . . 'though I had hundreds of comrades, I was fearfully touchy, and at last I grew fond of that laziness' . . . 'and sometimes I bless fate for sending me this solitude, without which I could not have judged myself like this'.

His prison was like this illness of mine, a barrier from freedom, a thing to be hoped past, imagining freedom a much more real thing than it is. In such a situation there are only two loopholes, hope, or if that is impossible, like his old Russian Believer, martyrdom; glorification and suffering through abject humiliation.

12 February

Long, vague period of dreaming and frustration, dull despondency. Work in spasms, conscious of the irresponsibility of such a habit, and the certain penalty. Universally ambitious, and nothing to aim at. A psychological claustrophobia. No literary inspirations, and that way no self-faith. Living half of each day in a dream. Usually of some Provençal farm where the masterpieces grow like grapes on the vine. Antithesis to this quiet, drily inhabited little house in a grey and bourgeois suburb. Not that I hate the bourgeoisie here except in as much as I have to form part of it. Find distraction in Herodotus. Other ages, other manners; but fortunately the same powers of imagination. The future

---

[1] Published in 1861, *House of the Dead* was a fictionalized account of prison life in Siberia, which drew on personal experience. A decade previously Dostoevsky had served a sentence of four years' hard labour.

seeming definitely to assume a forbidding shape. No set lines. And all around other people are springing up, marrying, mixing, loving, quarrelling, being. I vaguely drift on the time point, with no volition to leap out. Then this illness shows no sign of being cured, when everyone feels it should be. Myself, I begin to grow indifferent to it. Here also, the absolute friendlessness is a little saddening. Not one visitor in three weeks of nursing-home. *Tant pis!* I can support it, but unnaturally. The immense gap between child and parents also is ridiculous and tragic, unnecessary and inevitable. The innate sensitivity only makes things more felt in secret. No common ground at all. I too proud and abstracted to want to talk trivialities, to discuss the deep, loved things (because I have to formalize them to make them be understood – I hate having to descend to explain the heights where I feel at home), they too absorbed, too *enfoncé* in the minute details and facets of the *vie quotidienne.* Even if both sides made a sincere effort to attain a *rapprochement,* the disparity would still be the same. Even the smallest external noise infuriates me during music; they always treat it as secondary to food, conversation, paper-rattling, or Hazel. The difference in environmental norms accounts for much – a boarding-school, an officer's mess, a university, all have led me into a much wider plane than twenty-five rather introvert years in the same quiet household, where the class has slipped.[1]

Long period of *détente,* which I so much want to leave. I feel as if I am running face on to a windward shore, ugly cliffs, with my one gap offering salvation, Scylla and Charybdis narrow. Perhaps it would be better to be wrecked, lost in the way of an existence of mediocrity. Yet I must regard a year in France as a continuation of the *détente.*[2] The thing to concentrate on there are the two plays. The stories are all too occasional. The torture is the slow one of seeing youth, *première jeunesse,* spring, slip past untasted, unexplored. I would seize any chance of some extraordinary experience – exploration preferably. Here, life is only one truth complete. No extra-spiritual enjoyments. Physically on the bedrock of mundanity. Worst of all, no attempt at escape. One can sit and write about the necessity for will, for *élan vital,* but actual experience crumbles to dust.

---

[1] The family tobacco firm, Allen & Wright, had been struggling for many years and the Fowles family had to accustom itself to a life of reduced financial means.
[2] Through his tutor at New College, JF had been offered the opportunity to take up a year-long post as a *lecteur* in the English faculty at the University of Poitiers.

2 March

Fascination of listening in the small hours of the morning to Election results. The constant interruption of the music and the numbers counted floating out of the loudspeaker. Interest grows like a child's interest in a match boat-race in a gutter. The Liberals play a magnificent spoiling game. The Conservatives creep up, stealthily. A dull, wet night.[1]

A mixed day. At home with the Election *à l'arrière-fond*, unsettled, queasy at setting out in the world again. Nerves temporarily out of control. Then meeting TS at Paddington and travelling with him. At the MF I find it difficult to adopt a new role – the old one of reserved coldness still clings, an old shell. At table I find it impossible to talk lightly, although speaking better French than the others. Afterwards, in a spasm of insouciance, rather desperate when so much work has to be done, I went with Guy to the Experimental Theatre Company, Chekov's *The Bear* and Fielding's *Tom Thumb*. Played in a small uncomfortable hall, on a tiny stage, with a resultant atmosphere of intimacy which is excellent. Rather over-acted, and both pieces far from faultless, but an enjoyable evening. It is unfortunate that Merlin Thomas[2] should be there, and more that he saw me. Feeling a small boy guilt. The faint charm of Oxford was in the theatre, the glow of a young and intelligently human society. Walk home through the wet, warm, rain-shining streets with GH. The Woodstock Road is solemn and full of ghosts. Girls stand saying goodnight outside Somerville. We talk and the distance passes unnoticed. Strange, sociable Oxford. Where everyone is received and everything is moderate, where extremes and the essential knowledge are rarely discovered. The great sturdy mass of creatures of tradition balances the boat of the present.

Stomach bad again. Disgust with body; even with mind. I can return out of my body, separating myself from it objectively, and I would like to do the same thing with my mind. Could I leave my mind as well? Can the mind be left and walked beside, walked away from?

7 March

Sudden pain again in prostate. It always jabs when I slow up my pessimism. Today I have felt more than usually happy, so it had to return.

[1] The General Election took place on Thursday 23 February 1950. Counting in 267 mostly urban constituencies began after the polls had closed, and the results were announced on the radio through the night. When the votes of the remaining constituencies were counted the following day, Labour's landslide majority was reduced to a slender one of just six seats.
[2] JF's French tutor at New College.

I see no end to this. I have never felt cured, after the period in the
nursing-home. If I had been really cured, I should have felt it intuitively.
The mental will to get better has never been present, because the mind
knew the body was still ill. So?

9 March
Another day of illness. Impossible to eat. Trying to force food down is
a torture. So joy-destroying. From time to time I have an excess of
sorrow that I can't justify myself to these people. At dinner everyone
was gay and laughing, the candles were alight. The dinner was excellent. They talked of various things and, because I say nothing, must
think me wholly heavy and stupid. But I wanted violently to be sick,
and it was all I could do to sit at the table, let alone smile and make
witty conversation. I feel upset at estranging people who fundamentally
would like me. The desire to shine in society is an egotist one, but to
renounce it is unnatural. People do not understand renunciation.
Sometimes they admire it, but they never understand or fully sympathize with it. All this social and psychological trouble springs out of the
basic, physical deficiency – I haven't sat down and enjoyed a meal for
two years. I can say that without exaggeration. Always there was nausea,
or no appetite – capable of eating, but not of enjoying. That, combined
with the general weakness and faintness, drains the positive aspects of
life away. Even the conscious act of ignoring or minimizing the illness
brings no solution – in itself it is a form of hypochondria. In these
things self-pretence is hopeless.

The imagined truth dominates all. I am beginning to find it difficult to
remember the time when I felt completely fit and well. When I walked
out on a spring day and felt life like the sap in the trees. When I could
drink myself sick without danger, when I could eat twenty times what I do
now. I write this in the hope that one day I shall be able to look back and
smile. But now I have no faith at all in the possibility of such a day coming.

26 March
Lately have had many ideas and thoughts, but no desire to record. A
gentleness, an unstiffening of the creative will. One happy mood, cycling
at night past Keble; this has happened before, so there must be a sprite
near by. And then another time, a night wind, cold and steely, blowing
in the strangely deserted Banbury Road, giving a sudden sharp impression of loneliness, of having blown all round the world without touching
a single human. The wind of a world without men, without life. A middle-
aged woman chasing a small black dog up the Woodstock Road, calling
more and more desperately 'Roland, Roland', apparently without avail.

*

Depressed at not knowing at all what I am, or shall be. The want always to write, the feel of duty about work, conflicts, doubts, chaos. Contempt for eminence in a profession. Something better than that. All these clever dons and clever undergraduates add up to nothing for personal immortality. They don't seem to be sensitive about this. They accept their limits, which is monstrous. One would imagine them always striving, with their fine brains, to immortality. Instead they accept their niches. The secret is never to accept minute-to-minute, day-to-day occurrences. To be always searching, always dissatisfied.

There are empty futile moods where hope, self-satisfaction and above all will are absent. A petulant ennui, a sense of individual uselessness.

Two causes for hate. Being born into an age and place where the civilization has been crowned, and now is a decadent monarchy. Thus France culminates in her seventeenth, us in our sixteenth, Germany in her eighteenth to nineteenth, Russia in her nineteenth, Italy in her twelfth–fourteenth–fifteenth (and Rome). Coming at the tail-end, one has no chance. It is impossible to surmount the barriers inherent in the age. Secondly, to be destined to the most limited and perishable of arts, literature. Pictorial art and music both last longer and appeal more widely. Poetry is the most confined of all. To write it is an art of self-denial. The only hope is a great new American culture.

For a moment today I thought that I was thinking in time with the music; a sudden double jump in my thought corresponded exactly with a double upsurge in the music (Schubert 8th). Could music be inter-related with sound-nerves and so pulse perhaps with intuitive force in the brain? Why does some music create especially aware and creative moods in me? Perhaps some electro-magnetic connection between the sound-waves, the emotions arising out of certain notes, the stimulation in the particular (my literary) sphere.

Beethoven's genius is a particular sensitivity to universal reality (with joy and pain as basic themes, life and death), crystallized in an attitude intuitively chosen to express most absolutely that comprehensive sensibility. There is no religious emotion. It is pure fundamental emotion, deeper than religion. Human emotion.

Excellent study of Beethoven by John Sullivan.[1] Objectively romantic.

I cannot stop reading his life, the fascination of positiveness, his dominant genius. Even reading descriptions of the last quartets makes me

---

[1] *Beethoven*, Penguin, 1949.

melt for the feelings he has aroused in man. He died exactly 123 years ago yesterday.

D. H. Lawrence, *The Virgin and the Gipsy*.[1] Queer, naïve, tremulous writing. Flashes of childish hate. Psychological inconsistencies, a dream- or insane world. Astounding 'feel' for countryside. Yvette, an almost Pre-Raphaelite maiden. The gipsy satyrnine, elemental, full of natural desire. All of the characters are distorted, almost surrealist.

D. H. Lawrence, *St Mawr*.[2] Different from the last, fuller, more rich and coloured. Symbolism of pantheistic nature, creative urge (= St Mawr). All the characters are again supernaturally distorted. Brilliant portrayal of landscapes – the ranch description is magnificent. Many pathological touches – yearning for the South, hate of 'middle' (i.e. bourgeois) civilizations which do not possess, or destroy, all finer perceptions of nature. The artist, the poet (in the widest sense of 'poet') against the normal universe. L can't integrate himself with reality. He sees reality so acutely, with so many nuances of mood and feeling and underlying philosophic content, that he inevitably forces himself (or is forced) into a position different from those who see reality in the normal not very acute – even obscure – way. He doesn't himself seem to realize this fundamental cure for his split with society. Very little pity for the 'middle' civilization. The line of descent to Aldous Huxley is clear. As a stylist, the roughness and romanticism, the decadence in his expressions, will date quickly. Too many *longueurs*, too many too rich sentences.

Lunch with Connie Morgenstern.[3] An unusual personality. Her eyes are almost abstract, faint blue or pale blue-grey, almost meaning nothing. They give nothing away. When you talk to her they shift a very small amount continually, with an impression of vagueness, of disinterest, of rootlessness. She has little bursts of enthusiasm and amusement, but usually periods when it is difficult to talk with her. She always seems to be wishing she were somewhere else, in another sort of life or body.

Scott Fitzgerald, *The Great Gatsby*. Most impressive – far and away the best novel I have read for a long time. Much better than Huxley or

[1] Discovered after Lawrence's death in 1930, this short novel tells the story of Yvette, a clergyman's daughter, who, longing to escape from the stifling social convention of her world, falls in love with a gipsy.

[2] Written in 1925, *St Mawr* is the story of an an American girl Lou Witt, who after many years in England, brings her stallion, St Mawr, to a ranch in Texas. Here she experiences a vitality that she was unable to find in Europe.

[3] Girlfriend, and later wife, of JF's New College friend Michael Farrer (see note 1 on page 24).

Waugh. He has their satire but seems to get right down to the bottom of it – a question of environment and heredity and civilization. The futility and tragedy, self-realized by the characters, i.e. Daisy and Jordan, is inevitable. Gatsby is the only character out of the age, who steps in and tries to conquer, and of course fails.[1] The story is as subtle, inexorable, concise and restrainedly objective and *profoundly* tragic as a play by Racine. Gatsby tries to attract the age by the age. A subtlety is the subjective frame used – one knows that this is part Scott Fitzgerald as he is, and part seen objectively by his genius. Thus everything is slightly distorted – or better, put on the same level – by his semi-blinded vision, i.e. he in a way accepts the age, because he is in it, and this gives him a sympathy, only a superficial one, but still sympathy for his people and their dilemma. Basically of course, he is against, he condemns. But there is that pity which is missing in *Antic Hay* and (in a different key) in *Brideshead Revisited.* Also a very supple, easy and in some ways poignant style; flashes of beautifully felicitous sensation of mood (the first entry into the Buchanans' house). All his tense scenes are finely handled. This is much more durable stuff than Lawrence. Another aspect – the classic faithful love-affaire with unrequited love and tragic ending. There is a quiet immense and not too simple, not too complicated fatality in the way the story unfolds. Strongly constructed, architecturally.

Brayfield. April 1 weekend. A long cross-country journey, with not very attractive black and green landscapes. Some old county towns with ugly small-factory suburbs. Interesting series of passengers, little glimpses of other people's lives. Three strange Lithuanian or Slav men who come together on the bus, and then sit very far apart, without speaking, without talking to each other. They all have fat tanned faces, new gaberdine mackintoshes and hats whose brims are turned up all the way round, which makes them look vaguely stupid. This combined with their strong, heavy faces makes them ominously, coarsely brutal. They get off the bus separately, but meet together on the kerb. They look like Chicago thugs, almost inhumanly merciless and unscrupulous, idiotically out of place on a country bus route. One of them looks out at a passing pretty girl in a deadly material calculating sort of way – not a look of admiration,

[1] Jay Gatsby and Daisy Buchanan were in love before the war, but Daisy wouldn't marry Gatsby because he had no money. Many years later, she is in a loveless marriage with the rich but dull Tom Buchanan, and Gatsby is a wealthy man with a mysterious fortune who throws lavish parties in his Long Island mansion. When Gatsby discovers that his neighbour Nick Carraway is a distant cousin of Daisy, he persuades Nick to arrange a meeting with her. Still in love with Daisy, Gatsby tries to persuade her to leave Tom, and the tragic events that follow bear out Nick's warning to Gatsby that 'You can't repeat the past.' Jordan is Daisy's girlhood friend.

nor of sexuality, but pure brutish interest, like a thinking bull. The conductors call me 'Sir' – and no one else.

Brayfield, a large house on a large estate, a kind of Brideshead, ruined by the army in the war, now derelict, useless, the house of another age. There are ugly huts of corrugated iron and brick dotted about over the park, which festers with similar eyesores. The house looks out over a hill down to the River Ouse and the small and nicely isolated village of Newton Blossomville, and a long line of uphill country beyond.

Michael F a curious phenomenon.[1] County, but in some strange way unscrupulous about keeping to strict county standards (like Major Lawrence).[2] Long, lean-faced, blue eyes, fair hair, with a mock *naïveté*. Responsible, the young squire. He goes to church in his two parishes, twice on Sundays, so as to be the dutiful churchwarden. This annoys Constance. A very charming person, with apparent (often feigned) interest in all you say. Extremely polite, without ever seeming so. Very thorough way of clearing his nose after blowing it; quite an operation, each nostril receiving comparatively prolonged attention. Listening to a Third Programme satire: 'Jolly funny! But if you chaps hadn't been laughing, I should have thought it all serious.' Typical of the mock *naïveté*. He has a very flexible way of being his age. A wide range – sometimes the boy of 20, at others the serious, worried with responsibility man of 30–35.

Roger Pierce – affable, pleasant, like a cocker spaniel, a well-bred one. Also, like M; the half-anti-high-brow *naïveté*. But on the whole more intellectual than M. Keen on fishing. He wears a very old coat and torn trousers well. A good social person, sound and tolerant, fairly deep without being complex.

Constance heavy-eyed but happier. Efficient in an inefficient way. Full of little moods. Being a guest with them, one is made to feel almost at once that one is not a guest. Work has to be done, and shared. The best of things (food, etc), does not go to one, unless it should happen to be by chance. No conscious effort to please. On Sunday they ride off and away in the afternoon. They do not feel responsible in the old (or possibly just middle-class) close way – where host and guest are linked every minute of the day by a kind of faked intimate convention.

---

[1] Michael Farrer, who had studied Agriculture at New College, had graduated a year before JF and was now managing the family estate at Cold Brayfield in North Buckinghamshire after the death of his father Major Denis Farrer. Through his mother Joan, a sister of the 2nd Lord Redesdale, he was a cousin of the Mitford girls.

[2] Major Lawrence was a retired army officer who lived in Ipplepen, when the Fowles family were living there during the war. He befriended JF and, among various country pursuits, taught him how to poach. See introduction, page xi.

Characters. M's sister B, tall, slim, corduroy trousers and tweed coat, fair straggly hair, with sharp, determined features, a little hard. Horsey. Always busy feeding or cleaning out. Her husband, ex-Russian, Colonel Paul Rodzianko, thick, heavy, tall man who speaks broken English, has a bushy colonel's moustache, and has apparently still the serf complex. A famous show horse trainer. Annoys the Fs because he won't help clean out the stables, etc. They obviously think him rather a fraud.[1]

Mrs Farrer,[2] a sharp-minded and -tongued late-middle-aged lady, still active and interested. Still rather the 'grande dame'. Religious and practical, and incurably well-bred. With strange eyes, blue and rather lizard-like, which she uses a great deal when talking. She must have been very minxishly pretty when she was young. Too clever and sharp to have a son as naïve as Michael pretends to be. She is like her younger daughter and R (whom C dislikes for his egotism).

Lassie. A curious blue- and black-eyed Welsh collie. Her eyes have a strangely remote look. Affectionate. Scared-stiff of the ewes. Much too much of a pet in a farmer's house.

Dick. A thick-necked rather self-consciously (because we are all younger) proud good farmer. Financially shrewd, and plainly in the game for money as much as anything. Not county, with slight accent and roughnesses of language. His wife, shrewd also, self-possessed, with a little air of possessiveness as regards C as if she wants me to know how close she is to the Farrers – which makes me suspect she would judge people rather harshly on purely snob grounds.

The house is locked up, weather-beaten; even the façades seem musty. Remnants of garden, of flowering shrubs.

On Sunday morning I go for a long walk in the country to a wood on the estate. Past a nice old church at Newton, along an uphill road, where the wind is cold and strong and it begins to drive rain as a shower comes. A beautiful April day, astringent, with spring coming, the country going green, with flowers – violets, primroses, celandines – in the hedges. A distant, flat landscape, with smoke-grey woods, red houses and mist-green fields, the whole mottled with sunlight and cloud. A large sky, white cloud and bright blueness, in the dark-grey intervals where the showers are raining. I chew the honey out of white violet flowers, and walk with Lassie, pleased that she follows me, a stranger. The wind is cold, the road deserted, everything sharp and

[1] A White Russian, Rodzianko had been Edward VIII's riding instructor and trained the Irish show jumping team. Michael had an older sister Barbara, but it was actually his sister Joan (known as 'Robin') who was married to Colonel Rodzianko.

[2] i.e. Michael's mother, Joan Farrer (née Mitford).

clean and expectant. I feel happy sheltering out of the rain under a
straw rick especially when I continue on to the wood, exultantly drying
in the blue burst of sunshine which follows the rain. The wood is
deserted and I walk quietly down the paths, listening to birds, feeling
so content to be in the real country again and alone, after so long. I
still feel the old pantheistic sympathy, the feel that I know everything
that's going on, the delight in little things, little scenes, in the ever
changing atmosphere of each second. A great tit's cap, brilliantly glossy
and iridescent in the day's brightness. Jays screeching, a missel-thrush,
robins, singing. Fragrant blossoms, Clumps of primroses, and the sweet
taste of violets.

A feudalism still survives, an ambiance of country-old respect for the
main family. All the villagers know the big house and 'Mr Michael'. 'Mr
Farrer' still means the *père*, some time dead. It is impossible to imagine
communism invading an atmosphere like that.

Basil B. Full of intimate details of a seduction he managed over the
weekend. A kind of cock-crowing, full-bellowing satisfied smugness.
His virility is proved by it; he causes envy and admiration, and yet it
is a mixture of egocentric pride and psychological sadism. The question is (when I feel hostile to his 'confession') why exactly does one
dislike these revelations? Is it pure jealousy and envy? Or a kind of
prudishness, a subconsciously offended morality (subconscious
because one, or I, would do the same thing without any qualm)? Is
one naturally hostile to intimate confessions when they come from
friends, because they open new and unknown vistas where before it
was imagined that everything was known? The faith of previous accumulated knowledge is shaken by the need to adapt it to the fresh
circumstances. In this case, too, I could not help feeling that B was
exaggerating, if not indeed totally inventing – a kind of seducer's
licence, like the traditional fishing story.

Impossible struggle between wanting to write and think, and having to
do all this abominably unnecessary philology and other work, which
resolves itself in a struggle between a guilty conscience and a willing
acceptance of the challenge – and out of the struggle comes my indecision and doubt.

Peter Nurse.[1] Schools-conscious. Continually asking me questions, and
answering them for me. Has all the characteristics of a certain first.

---

[1] Peter Nurse was studying Modern Languages at Magdalen. He did get a first
and, after postgraduate studies at Oxford, became a lecturer in French at
Queen's University, Belfast, and then at Kent University.

Spends all his time talking shop. Knows all the critical answers. I hate
people who are academically sound, who accept the futility instead of
resenting and rejecting it.

Constance. Tea and walk around Oxford. She is looking especially
striking, younger than usual. She has a curious magnetic attraction for
me, yet I don't feel at all in love with her. It's just comfortable and
pleasant to be with her. Even being silent with her is without strain. Her
quaint moods and the sullen, handsome way she looks when she isn't
doing anything in particular.

Leigh-on-Sea, 6 April
Flowering of spring, happiness, lightness, joy and certainty of self.

Infuriating evening in a way, although I don't feel particularly annoyed.
The Ninth is played. Mother counts her stitches aloud and rattles the
paper. Father goes to sleep. I feel sick and sad that something which
penetrates right into the heart of me runs off their backs like water off
a duck's. Complete separation of feeling. More and more comes this
sense of divorce with the world. Sorrow for the world's insensitivity and
insufficiency and pride in my own awareness and intellect. And again
sorrow that the world doesn't want to be raised, but that the effort to
lift it up must be made. Atlas is eternally needed.

Quai des Brumes.[1] Beautifully made film. Simple tragedy of sordidity.
Kafkaesque despair. The really beautiful profile of Michèle Morgan. A
hundred subtle and striking touches, with a wonderful theme tune,
simple and nostalgic and dramatic. Being here, there had to be sniggers and laughs in the audience – some of them quite literally didn't
seem to understand anything about it at all. During the kissing scenes,
whispers behind: 'This is a bit of all right,' and a woman saying, 'We
oughtn't to have brought him.' They laughed at the end, when the dog
strained on the leash to get away from the cabin. It is terrible to think
of so many people so incapable of imagining or feeling tragedy. The
English are naturally averse to catharsis, to *sensibilité*, to the enjoyment

---

[1] Made in 1938 by the director-writer partnership of Marcel Carné and Jacques
Prévert, *Quai des Brumes* was a fatalistic and symbol-laden story of doomed love
which captured the mood of pre-war France. Jean Gabin plays an army deserter
who falls in love with a girl (Michèle Morgan) in Le Havre, the port where he
is hiding from the police. After killing the girl's ill-intentioned guardian (Michel
Simon), who is mixed up with a group of gangsters, he tries to get passage on
board a ship leaving Le Havre, but is killed by one of the gangsters before he
can make his escape.

of tragedy. They are afraid of emotion. I hate the damned condescension of Basil G,[1] who says of the film 'one of them things about life in the raw' – in an amiable, tolerant, amused sort of way, as if life in the raw is something of a joke, and not real compared to the silly, conventional routine of a suburban semi-man-about-town. The average Englishman can't imagine, and can't feel, and even if he does, is too inhibited to ever show either quality.

9 April
New word to describe how I felt this morning – perferridity. Life seemed to be rushing past – whole phases of existence and awareness tumbling out, pressing on each other's backs to get past me, through me and out of me. Spurs of doubt, of assurance, near-crises of nerves, faintness, sense of illness and death. The sudden desire for normality and an afternoon's golf. By the 14th hole I feel tired and relaxed – some kind of physical labour is necessary for me.

Symptom of this morning. It suddenly seemed to me that my heart was beating like a sledge hammer – a pulsating, terrible, audible thump, thump, thump. I didn't know what to do. I felt faint, horribly ill. I went in the garden, smoked a cigarette. Went back into my room. By keeping calm I traced the thumping sound to the clock – the noise produced by the pendulum. I get too convolute here.

12 April
Strange uneasy state I'm in. Literally no work done in this vacation, so that a Third or Fourth, and probably a fail, is bound to ensue. I keep on saying, I must fail, to keep free, to give my real self a chance. A Second would certainly mean oblivion. Teaching history, not making it. Money, money, money. If only there was enough money for two years' peace. Time to think, time to read, time to slowly, unpressedly, create. I see myself now failing, being penniless and getting work somewhere on a farm, a ship – I don't know. And fortunately don't much care. Oxford's been sucked dry.

Sudden shock of seeing a very pretty girl, after a round of not very interesting golf on a dull, heavy afternoon. So out of place, so unexpected. An auburn-haired, minxish little slut, dressed in a long dark-azure blue corduroy coat, with black semi-ballet-slipper shoes on – the black shoes, a few inches of stocking, the blue coat, the auburn mop of hair, short-cut as is the style. She walked affectedly, rather awkwardly, as if she wasn't used to walking anywhere. A bright flame in the dull London Road of

---

[1] Basil Glover, a neighbour who lived across the street from the Fowles family in Leigh-on-Sea.

little shops, sooty houses and ugly advertisement hoardings. In me she arouses a queer sort of aching pain, a sureness in the heart – almost the perfect girl to be purely sexual with. She is the unfulfilment of spring, spring unseized.

Oxford, 18 April
Drinking with John Lee.[1] A very sound earthy, Rabelaisan type. No finesse, and no wetness, no insincerities. In Whites'. The polyglot, on-the-fringe clientèle – socialists and literary and seedy, a few semi – demi – *mondaines*, bar-sitting, looking round. One, a pretty, sharp little girl, keeps on looking at the door, though not waiting for anyone – impression of waiting for something symbolical to arrive. Kafka feeling. Upstairs, a blonde with a green dress, deeply split, young, silly, drinking too much, making eyes, exclaiming, laughing with her men. Somehow so sparse of real pleasure and joy. For her, drinking in a smart bar, talking with vaguely raffish men, smoking, doing nothing, just existing, seems to cause an ennui below the surface, a vague sense that life isn't being fully realized. Probably a naïve, sincere, natural approach would upset her veneer of lacquered calm and conventionally smart-barish behaviour.

Jour de Fête. Fine French film.[2] Almost documentary background of French provincial village-town. Rich, accurate atmosphere. Tati, a long, individual, gawky clown.

25 April
Snows. Very cold, and all the trees in bloom. Strange mood in the air, the wintry feeling of a new age, a new system of seasons coming.

26 April
Illness is coming back. I feel possessed, malignly. I understand the medieval superstition – if only I could believe in a spiritual imagination, even of a miracle at Lourdes. But I know it is only a germ or some physiological abnormality. I can't escape the body by romance. There is nothing spiritual.

In the afternoon, we walk in the Parks. A bright, warm, day. People in bright clothes, punts, swans, mallards on the pond. One brood of six fluff-ball ducklings. Shaughan, a young red setter, undisciplined, sinuous, aristocratic, bounding and running all over the path, the grass, sniffing

---

[1] A fellow student of JF who was studying PPE at New College.
[2] Made in 1948, *Jour de Fête* was directed by and starred the French comedian Jacques Tati as a village postman.

people, chasing other dogs, fluid, never immobile. A little boy in bright red trousers, and a small girl in a bright red coat, looking at the dull-green, sun-shot river, with a bunch of yellow celandines in her hand. There is a *pretty* quality in park scenes; the statuesque background of trees, paths, greenness. Then the moving dots, the various-coloured dresses, the dogs, the perambulators, the children. The flashes of bright, crude colour, the bright reds and blues, are the decorative blobs, the Dufy element – it is all simple, naïve, pleasant. A park is a pleasure. The paths lead nowhere, are no short cut, so everybody is walking for pleasure. Fast walking is a sin.

Basil tries to help a small boy fly a toy glider. Because it isn't heavy enough, he puts sixpence in a clip on the nose. The sixpence falls out on the grass and is lost. He explains carefully to the boy how to fly it, why it flies, why it doesn't fly well at this moment. Then throws it himself and breaks it. I, and Peter Malpas, can't help laughing – the little boy wants to cry. It is cruel to laugh, but there is a humour in the second. Basil kneels down, talks, explains, gives the little boy a shilling. The father comes up, Basil talks more, all is well.

Basil is immensely *correct* in all his nuances of action and behaviour, like a skilful fencer with life and personalities. Polite and charming, crude, always at the right moments. Unconsciously people surrender to his expertise in the petty relationships of life, his *savoir vivre*. He possesses adequately, or well, practically all the social attainments.

Also we saw a hornet in the road, a big yellow buzz. It settled over a drain, a fat, broad, powerful wasp-like creature. I rode at it on my bicycle, but it escaped down a hole in the drain-cover, and flew up as I passed over. A fearsome brute.

These days mean nothing. One exists, one is happy, one is sad. No more, no positive gains from them. No setting of these days in eternity, no setting them in a fire of glory. That's the great fault of Oxford – one slips, one slides, gently, easily, comfortably into an unworried indolence, where all the days are old gold and every point is blunted. It's almost as if there was a filter around the town which sieved out all the sharp anxieties and extreme joys of existence.

3 May

Podge Porter comes in in the evening, and tells of the break-up of his marriage.[1] His calmness and cynicism implied are strangely incongruous. He treats it impassively, without crying or breaking in any way. His attitude to life is a queer mixture of realism and cynicism, a compound of natural and artificial disappointment in the face of

---

[1] In the event, Podge and Eileen continued to remain married for many years in spite of severe strains.

things. He is a sharp anti-romantic, a pricker of balloons. Eileen he likens to Orestes, dangerously impotent. He lacks the touch of heart, but is such a pleasantly astringent, real character. Intelligence and bitterness and a sense of humour make a good trio. He introduces all these realities, these domestic and financial worries, these cosmological reflections on the absurd in trivial things, with an amusing mock air of showmanship. His ultimate use of the Socratic method – faint ignorance – positive, attacking, destructive criticism, form valuable assets in any friend. His sort are few and far between, though he'd be the last to agree.

6 May

The swifts – i.e. full summer – arrived this afternoon. Flying around in the low-cloud mist.

8–9 May

Lucien Jacques – a small-faced insignificant little man with grey hair and beautifully soft and meek hazel eyes. A very mild and wise gentleman-peasant. Simple and fresh. Intelligent. Knows Matisse. For several years he was a shepherd in Provence. He has that air of calmness and peace, of animal intelligence and meekness, which only an intensely human nature saturated in wild nature – flowers, scents, landscapes, countries – can give. A delightful person. I can't think of anyone who made such a charming impression so quickly.[1] Such a relief after the impatience and cynical worldliness of a Fluchère. A quiet, human person. Pleasant to all the world. He strikes one as being a simple lover of life, yet profoundly, not naïvely, simple – the great thing is his peace. How striking it is when you strike these people who have achieved their peace.

9 May

Lucien Jacques. Today confirms yesterday. Admirably set in his world. Intelligent, humble, with little flashes of self-pride. Favorite composer – Mozart. He's known H. G. Wells, Gide, etc. Such a remarkably adaptable person. He speaks very quietly and slowly, but people stop and listen to him. His words are simple, sometimes a little bizarre, *pittoresque*. It is extraordinary how he brought the sun with him – these two days have been completely bright. Quite literally no cloud for forty-eight hours. He has the Midas touch. Fat, pudgy sensitive hands. Incessant smoker. He has a

---

[1] The son of a cobbler, Lucien Jacques (1891–1961) became a painter, writer and poet. His wide literary acquaintance included Jean Giono, with whom he translated Melville's *Moby Dick* into French. After the war he lived for several years with shepherds in the Lure mountains.

way of sitting which is entirely relaxed, round-shouldered without
seeming unpleasant or slouched. When he eats, he holds the knife and
fork firmly, peasant-wise without thinking of the environment – whereas
we tend to hold the knife in a line with the forefinger, his is held at an
angle, clumsily almost. He sat in the garden this evening, in the setting
sun, back against a tree, the beret over his eyes, his knee raised, one
arm rested on it with drooping wrist, the other leg straight out, the
whole pose redolent with neat and – although he must be fifty – adolescent ease. A pose you couldn't learn except by being a shepherd for
seven years, sitting in excessive heat and watching your flock, for weeks,
for months. Sitting like that he looked as if he could sit for ever. Around
his eyes he has wrinkles through constant smiling.

I hate May fine weather. It's too perfect. Absolute beauty, happiness is
always imperfect. Near the summit, but not the summit.

18 May
The first day of summer, a dreadful day. A pale blue sky, white fluffy
clouds, no wind, heavy, a dull brightness everywhere. *Mundane* fine
weather. Too many ugly flowers ostentatiously blooming, and people look
depressed. Heaviness is inherent in most English summer fine weather.

Talking with Merlin Thomas about the future. I feel guilty and ashamed
and a little bit resentful that I have *chosen* to do badly. When I told him
that I daren't do well, he pooh-poohed it and said, 'I put you between
1 and 2, on the borderline.' That is so unlikely that I can say nothing.
I wanted to tell him all about this great bout of denial, but it is usually
impossible. I do not look forward to the revelation, either with him, at
home, or elsewhere.

Villon. How he stands out in the literary forest! Stark, black, dramatic,
naïf and finished at the same time, morbid, ironic, gay, self-pitying, always
muscular, nervous, contorted. Tense. There is no relaxation, no interlude
long enough to break the strain. In literary stature he's very thin and very
tall. There is no fat to waste away, only a tough, irreducible core.[1] No *false*
romantic qualities, no softness or sentimentality (he's at the opposite end
of the scale from Wordsworth, who is for the most part reliant on softness

---

[1] François Villon (1431–after 1463) fled Paris in 1455 after killing a priest.
Imprisoned several times afterwards for violent crime and theft, he composed
his *Ballade des pendus* under sentence of death. His other surviving work consists
chiefly of *Le Lais* (or *Petit Testament*) and *Le Testament* (or *Grand Testament*), which
offer an account of his turbulent life. His verses were often in a satirical vein,
but as notable for their sincerity and deep human sympathy.

and sentimentality for his effects. W is not half as immortal as V, but his medium, romanticism, is much harder to work in).

All one evening feel purposelessness like a fog around me. Fog which won't ever lift. I reread the *Pandaras* play and see so many defects, *longueurs*, that it makes me yawn. The essential is to try and try again, and aim at the essence of one's imagination and creative intelligence, which lies always just ahead, in a new world around the corner. The vital core alone; what will both penetrate the reluctant future, and dazzle the present.

Bump Supper. Written tonight 1.15. A masculine medieval orgy. Drink, drink. Shouting, marching, lawlessness. I remember stabbing at a fence with iron bars. Sitting in the far corner of Hall. Too tired now.

Tutorial with Harding.[1] Oxford the imperturbable. He is intolerably slow and exact, meticulous. A sleepy, soft, profoundly unemotional sort of voice, but with no drawl, no engaging qualities. Dry as a desert. Another little man there – he comes almost exactly in the 'little man' category of insignificance – had a notebook with a white label pasted on the cover and the words 'Eighteenth Century Literature' carefully written on. Each letter must have taken some time to write, because the bars and curves were thick, made by many parallel strokes of the pen. There were little flourishes – but nothing exaggerated. The psychology of someone who wastes his time drawing in letters like that is of a retarded schoolboy nature. I was interested to imagine myself in his place, decorating with such ease. Such an unimportant function. It was as difficult as imagining myself in Patagonia. Anyhow, such people should be banned from action.

28 May
In a sunny spell – the day fitful, cloudy – at 10.21 this morning a bottlefly with an emerald abdomen settled on the grey and black sunlit sill of my window. I could write a poem. Instead I wish to record it. At 72 Woodstock Road, 10.21 a.m., May 28, 1950, in short sunlight, a small fly with a green belly. *En fais ce que tu veux.* I wish to record; each trembling, infinitesimal point of light which makes the whole symphonic illumination of life.

To be precise, I should say, schoolboy-fashion, 72 Woodstock Road, Oxford, England, this world, this system, this galaxy, this cosmos. And just as we think of one cosmos, I think of several, all expanding and all approaching. The interpenetration of cosmi! Like spokes of wheels, as interpenetrating and mutually destroying.

Weekend of no work again. In the evening out with Basil Beeston, John Lee. The morning, it's Whit Sunday morning, I had an awful head and

[1] i.e. F. J. W. Harding, a lecturer at New College.

a taste of acrid futility, both in my mouth and my mind. The dull, drab
despair of a hangover. The futility of it. The futility of my futility. I hate
myself for having done things I myself despise. I sat and tried to work,
listened to the wireless, thought, dreamed, hated it all. On a morning
like this one could kill oneself in a sudden fit, out of pique, knowing that
it would be regretted afterwards. Sad and depressed with the vague infla-
tion and deflation of moods which go with drinking, the feeling that it
is a (I hate giving myself to anything, including alcohol) second-best thing,
a waste of time. That one could be so much better occupied otherwise.

I try and exist, be existentialist, enjoying the second for the second,
but something nags all the time, the suspicion that there might be an
essence I have missed. Also there is always tomorrow and yesterday. For
as long as we know so much about them, it is impossible to shut oneself
up in today. The past is a judge and standard for the present. Real pleasure
in a moment in itself, but the afterglow depends on the insight it has set
against the past. And the future is a test-ground for the dreams we elect
to create. A cupboard for ideals, belittling all present actualities.

Lying in the garden most of the day. Hot, lazy day. Many people about;
Constance came to tea, slim and silent and secretive as usual. We sat on
a rug, and sipped China tea, talked a little. I felt contented, *bien*. Later
we went to the Podges. We sat in the garden and I played with a kitten
whose eyes were sea-green or mauve, depending on the angle. The Ps
were abnormally cynical, but showed their usual facility for plunging
quickly into metaphysics and philosophy and life and art. They are expert
at heightening the subject. We talked about careers and sincerity. They
refused to believe that I could become a farm labourer without intellectual malaise. I felt in me hardening this vague resolve to experiment
with my life, to try and be ideally honest and sincere. That is my only
chance, use it as well as you know how, savour it. It's no good working
for an examination which will lead to a safe career and stagnation. That
is a solution open like a door which must not be entered. Despise the
chances into safety, that's the true solution. They kept on talking about
bald facts. Thank God I still am young enough to mould hard facts,
having no responsibilities to hamper me in the work. The evening was
useful, for although I didn't say much, as usual, I could generally crystal-
lize my own feelings. I felt violently convinced of free will, that I was
prepared to accept my own beliefs and act by them. I am sure I want
to choose my own way of living, that is, to write. That I want to be as
free as possible, in order to give the artist in me elbow-room.

2 June
A tutorial from Harding yesterday was hell. Two hours of completely
useless lesson. Two hours so appallingly wasted that they seemed like two

years – a real sin, pure vandalism. His slow, uncertain manner of talking, searching for words. He fiddles with his spectacles or his shoelaces while he tries to think of something to say. He respects platitudes, stresses obvious points. There are long silences in his delivery, so long that it becomes ultimately embarrassing, infuriating, amusing. A complete lack of live sympathy towards a work. Academic dehydration. No sense of humour. He has an irritating way of heightening his stress, expanding, oiling his voice, or words or sentences of conventional appreciation and admiration. As if he isn't forced by genuine admiration to speak so, but rather by convention, purely and simply. My head was splitting, cracking with frustration. I was bowed and furious, tense and het up that such a baby should be a tutor. The others kept stony, non-committal faces. Outside I saw two people walking suddenly stop and clutch each other with desire, kissing intently. Her hand slipped over his head. As Harding drowsed and drifted on, I dreamt of her lips in Queen's Lane below.

8 June
The daily hell and paraphernalia of Schools. It means getting up early, putting on subfusc and white tie, carrying gown and mortarboard, entering the building, climbing up the stone stairs, into the great room with the bent figures, and then writing, writing, writing. Each night cramming frantically for the morrow. Moods of elation, braggadocio, humour, despair, fatigue, delirium, depression. Now I am in it, I take it seriously and surprise myself with the amount I manage to drag up out of the past. It is impossible to resist the excitement of beating the examiners. But now I shall fall between two stools. Intelligent, but lazy.

14 June
Schools. Today I did the most difficult exam and passed it. A relief and a feeling of smug jubilation. No one could have done less work than I have, or deserved less credit. I have had luck, and my method of intense work just before that examination is, I am sure, the right one. Every night I crammed really hard, and have had no difficulty with questions. What a farce and terribly bad test of a person it all is! Ridiculously inefficient. It is mainly a question of memory. On Flaubert, for instance, I had one question. One question to test so much reading! Fortunately I have taken it all in the spirit of a farce, as if it was a game to be played – as well as possible. Taking Schools seriously must be misery indeed.

16 June
E. M. Forster, *Howard's End*. A slightly insipid, uncharming book. A queer, feminine, faintly fusty flavour. As if written by an intelligent rabbit. Unpleasantly weak little moral, philosophical, psychological and metaphysical difficulties. Comparative felicity of style, but no really striking

descriptions. Some of it is a little *sensible*, romantic. It may be true, but
I don't like its inconclusiveness and cynicisms. An atmosphere very
slightly soft, overmellow, sickly.

19 June
Last day of Schools. A difficult exam, which I did badly. Afterwards I
felt half good, half bad. It is almost an anti-climax, but not quite. A
great relief after the end of an unpleasant period. A new sense of liberty
and freedom, and purposelessness.

20 June
In New College garden on a sunny, breezy afternoon, reading *Wuthering
Heights*. It is immensely refreshing to read narrative without symbolical
or psychological asides halting the progress. A pretty girl came into the
garden in a beach-dress, pulling her skirt right up, bare-shouldered,
lying on her back against the grass bank. Enter Isaiah Berlin,[1] fat, cosmopolitan, unpleasant by conventional English standards, and slim, very
fair-haired, young James Joll. Both in dark suits. They cavort around the
corner, where the girl is, her head covered by a small cape, look sideways at her, talk about her, smile amusedly and smugly. I try and think
how, exactly, and realize it is monastically. Like monks seeing a shepherdess bathing. I have a vision of Isaiah B disappearing like a porpoise,
with his owl's head, big eyes and fleshy lips looking back reluctantly as
he sank, passed into the deep, dark-green shade under the chestnuts.
For a moment he was uniquely satyric.

21 June
Interesting evening, the Podges, and a minor film director friend,
Stephen? He is tall, almost aggressively unconventional, young for his
age (35–7ish), with a tremendous naïf enthusiasm for Communism. He
denied this, but his left wing was so far extended that 'socialism', in such
an attitude, is a euphemism. Bitter against the middle-classes (from which
he came). Admitted himself as a born revolutionary, speaking of it as a
natural accomplishment, like skating or swimming. Hate of America,
Capitalism, Toryism. A dangerous, narrow, intense person. Rootless and
destructive. The Podges, as usual, cynical and gaily, absurdly pessimistic.
Eileen has a way of cutting through posturing which is refreshing. Being
with them, after a week of idling, self-centred amusement and indulgence, was like a cold shower. Talked of war, of economics, of the chances
of existence, survival. Adult, serious pessimism. Like a sudden bar of
black across the thin bow. I said nothing, was passive, listened, and felt

---

[1] The celebrated philosopher and political theorist, then a Fellow of New College,
was JF's 'moral tutor', responsible for offering guidance on personal matters.

aloof, wise, profounder than they. And listening to the Communist, felt the truth of Voltaire – '*cultiver notre jardin*' – unalterably true in times of disrupted existence like the present. That means, be self-centred without being selfish, be and live self-contained, help where needed, be tolerant, be content, be mediocre, philosophize, and enjoy nature and simplicity. And never, never commit oneself over ideals. *Martyrdom is never worthwhile*. Latitude of mind is more important than longitude.

As I left, they gave me a keepsake, *Juno and the Paycock*, and wrote in the flyleaf. The kindness touched me: whatever our divergence of views, I feel in complete – in the best sense – sympathy with them. They are among the people I would least like to see disappear. Basil Beeston has the common-sense, similar nature; Roger Hendry has the train-power; Guy Hardy the charm. Podge and Eileen manage to combine all these. I think of them as one personality.

Most of day with Basil at Minster Lovell. We painted the views. I was too impatient and too bright as usual. Used too many crude colours. Later did a cubist view of the same site.

Leigh-on-Sea, 27 June
I have seen too much pleasure these last few days. Basil *is* an excellent companion, but he drowns my better self. Too much self-enjoyment with him. I have written no poems, nothing, for a long time. Yet my life is full and, except for that, happy. *Life must be empty to create*. I feel myself in a vacuum, between two worlds here at Leigh. Oxford behind, having done its best and worst by me. I feel a new physical self growing – stoutish, tanned, round adult-faced, with the top outside creases of the eyes drooping, down-angled with good humour and crinkled smiling. A new hedonist, more assured, more dominant and assertive self. Yet I am feeling profoundly immoral, as if my acceptance of no absolutes has gradually sapped the base of my sense of justice, fairness, duty and respectability. At this time, too, the news of the Korea incident overshadows faintly the vivid events of personal existence. The Americans have gone in, and are even being killed this moment. War is rubbing hands.[1]

---

[1] After the defeat of Japan in 1945, the Korean peninsula was divided into two zones along the 38th parallel, the north occupied by the Soviet Union and the south by the United States. In 1949 the US occupation ended and the Republic of Korea was established in the south. But on 25 June 1950 a North Korean force of 135,000 men launched a massive attack across the 38th parallel with the intention of reuniting the peninsula. President Truman committed US forces to South Korea's defence and two days later, on 27 June, the UN Security Council passed a resolution recommending that its members help South Korea 'to repel the armed attack and to restore international peace and security to the area'.

29 June
Brayfield: pleasure of doing hard work again, sensing the strain and the
rhythm of manual labour. The responsibility of driving a horse and cart
through two or three miles of lanes. I felt like a test pilot on a new
plane. My hands are very soft. Blisters come off the pitchfork handle in
next to no time. Swallows nest all round the house – in a slit in the
stables, in the roof of the potting-shed. Happy, beautiful, glossy, azure-
singing creatures. Twelve turtle-doves sprang out of a green-yellow field
of clover and charlock, giving a beautiful impression of black-and-white
fan-tails splayed down, and bronze backs. A wayside-trimmer, man with
a scythe, who carried a stone in his belt behind him, an especially
designed leather belt. The way the haystack was put up, commented on
by everyone, passers-by and all. The sense of a closely knit community.
MF knows apparently everyone, adults and children. Newton Blossomville – jerry-built name! – has nine more inhabitants now than in the
Domesday Book.

Countless minor ills attendant on the new life. Blisters, cuts, bruises. I
have lost all sense of physical stress and strain, long endeavour. They
all, in their ways, criticize me; the criticism of the countryman, happy
and pleased to criticize. Frank and Jack, the one dour and complaining,
a real groaner, the other more humorous, still complaining, but with a
twinkle. They all hark back to the old days, the time of their own heyday.
Catastrophe today. I led the cart with a full hayload out of the gate and
caught it in an unseen hawthorn, which tilted the cart, capsized it, throwing Trooper, the carthorse, off his feet. Shock and panic. Trooper struggled. I held on to him. The others ran back. There was a frantic scuffle
for a few minutes, trying to get the chains off. Dust and flying hooves.
Luckily, no damage. I got off with a scratch. Michael almost laughs about
it – he overrides temper and obstacles with extraordinary – almost
debonair – ease.
    M the long-legged, thin, upright bundle of energy. Continually on
the go. Stops moving at eleven, is at it again at five-thirty in the morning.
Walks all over the place, probing, looking out, making sure. 14–16 hour
day. 'I'm too tired to get anything done for myself – reading, let alone
writing.'

6 July
Work and tiredness drug all the finer side. One notices things, remembers them a few moments, how to transmit and write them down, then
they go. The veins of all this are dirt and strain. Constant muck and
constant labour. The routine of feeding and cultivating is inexorable,
always nearly out of control. There are fine moments. The goslings,
stupid and always panicking, follow-my-leader, with minute wings and

twinkling legs. The two hounds, Goddess and Gordon, always hungry, mangy, lanky, searching, familiar yet aloof, with no sense of discipline.

Michael Farrer is a curious intro-extrovert character. He is cheery, polite, and charming to all the world, yet he never wants to penetrate intimately into another person's thought or character. All his solicitude is to do with minor matters. He has his well-defined personal vocabulary of slang – fancy way of creating names for conditions – Henry Chillington = chilled cold. I am Wellington, for no reason at all. Also 'operation pigfeed', and so on. The Fs have a strange unsentimentality to life. Only very occasionally does the crust crack and the real human show. M says almost the same things to everyone, treats them all with a sort of bluff, trampling good nature. He has no sensitivity apparent at all towards other people, but his rough blows are so wrapped around with charm that they can't hurt, at the most push almost harmlessly. He and Mrs F talk and have little polite exchanges of presents, as if they both know it is only a game, not real. Exaggerated pleasure in giving and receiving. Constance is often given sentiments she very rarely has: 'Constance was awfully pleased, sends all her thanks . . .' etc. Michael covering up for her.

Constance talking horses and show-jumping, repeating herself, being horribly authentic. I sit and smile and say nothing, and get very bored and irritated. I hate horsiness. Treating animals and athletic girls like toys, the sweat-and-sawdust fraternity. It seems so absurd treating and discussing such topics with universal seriousness.

17 July
The hard deadening routine at Brayfield. This has slipped altogether out of control, because I have been always too tired to do anything about it. This agricultural existence, undermanned and staffed, is too intense and rushed to suit any but the human animal. There's no time for anything else. Michael can take it. He doesn't appear to need the relief, the contrast of any kind of intellectual or artistic life. It's all work and no play. My day varies, but roughly 7–9 chicken- and calf-feeding, and the geese; 10–1 hay-making, or sugar-beet-hoeing; 2–5 the same; 5.30–7 feeding, egg-collecting. But somehow the day never seems ended till about 9 o'clock. One day I worked from 6 a.m. to 9 p.m. with only two breaks – one hour for breakfast and half an hour for tea. At times all the countless jobs and the fatigue get on top of me, and I have to fight hard to prove the point of working. But it has acted as an excellent purge from Oxford – hard labour, recontact with the country, the feel of closeness to the true life. The animals dying and being born, the sense of a continuity beneath all the incidents; the torch carried on, regardless of the manners of falling out. I couldn't live all my life at this continual hard pressure. Existence becomes a mockery. One does voluntarily what

it would need a convict camp to enforce otherwise. There are compensations. I enjoy tractor-driving. The tractor is a kind of big and expensive toy.

Two episodes I remember particularly, one pleasant, one not. One was a ram lamb which was maggot-struck, eaten all over the back by maggots, so that they had crawled through the skin into the inside. It was a terrible thing. We put it in a dusbin of Jeyes fluid and bathed it; nearly a quart of maggots came out. Later, I tried to pick the maggots out with forceps from the holes they had eaten into the flesh. The lamb died half an hour after having the bath. A ram in a dreadful thicket. The senseless cruelty of such a death is appalling. Bitter, absurd existence. The other was a pile of old honeycombs in the disused railway carriage; they still retained the rich, luxury aroma of long-past honey, a hot, subtle, heavy, velvety honey-waxy sort of scent, toned down by fustiness, age and airlessness. A scent like a still nostalgic backwater, full of memories, emotional and physical. Of richness and luxury, country healthy luxury, of the spacious golden age. One of those very mellow and evocative scents.

Feeding piglets by bottle; the strange tenderness one feels for them. Their mother had no milk. They died one by one from weakness. They scuffle and squeal and seek warmth avidly. Their eyelids and lashes and minute feet are rather beautiful, shell-delicate. Sheep-dipping. I fixed, improvised a bath, a sheet of iron and some hurdles. One fine morning we pulled the fifty sheep through. Tiring work, because they had to be bathed, being too big and unwieldy to be immersed otherwise. We got soaked. The village policeman watching laughed, and called me 'old man'. He's supposed to be very strict. He's young and evidently wants to get on.

The sameness of the days is inescapable. They merge in a sinister way, like hidden doors, so one doesn't know where they were. One gets to know fields and animals and people and becomes absorbed by the drift of the current, stagnant, forgetting how to weave out of the current. The country is its own clock.

Korean situation overshadowing all. I feel indifferent and apathetic to it. I'm convinced Communism is best for S. Korea, and also that it is the worst possible thing for ourselves. If only the relativity of it all could be seen by both sides. In some ways for the Communists it is a crusade.

Viva. One is shepherded into a room of Schools. Five dons, two women, three men, sit around a table, three at the head, two at the side, like a naval court-martial. One by one, we walk up and speak with them. I only had a few minutes, speaking in French. Reading the last speech of *Phèdre*.

Chandler, *Farewell, My Lovely*. The usual slick, original, spell-binder. Soon back to the relentless routine of it all. The makeshiftedness.

20 July

I felt ill all day. A bit sick and a bit faint. Nausea. But had to work hard. In the morning dug a pit to bury a pig in; it reminded us both of digging a shit-trench, and that we might soon have to be doing that. Michael saying 'I don't know what I shall do about the farm if war breaks out' – as if staying to work it was impossible. His conscientiousness is remarkable. Yet I mildly despise him for it. I can't help feeling that his long hours of work, his stubbornness, his sense of duty, both in parochial-public, and in private, things, all indicate a mind which has seen so far and no further. Excellent part in the community. But it remains for the unattached like me to be left.

Tony. A little fair-haired boy with dark eyes and a good knowledge of birds. Shy, simple, not quick, but not a fool. Not town-precocious, but country-wise. His parents are very poor. Fine potential human. The same thing occurs to me when I see that Lord Lake gives £350 annual subscription to the Oakley hounds. How I hated that! Dozens of rich farmers and herdsmen giving money to the hunt. I should destroy hunting like a plague if I had the power. All that money should be directed to small boys like Tony, so that they could afford hooks and gut to fish with, and binoculars to watch birds with, and books to read.

23 July

Beginning to feel again my 'touch' with wild things. The secret is slow, very slow movement, and the cultivation of an intuitive sense; and developing the continuity of awareness in observation. Not just at odd times, but always. I watched a water-rat swimming in a pool of water-lilies, a sniffy enwhiskered creature, gentler and more amiable in appearance than the common rat. It swam about the pool without hurry, efficiently, not lazily. Swallows singing; I could never praise the sound enough.

Helen Sanders. A heavy, black, squarish creature, with a thick uncouth voice. A minor *contretemps* arose. I was left alone with her this morning for an hour. I didn't speak to her. I was reading, there was a concert of music, she would have bored me. Later, when they thought I was out, I heard her complaining that I hadn't said a word to her all the time.

To myself I say, *'Je m'en fous.'* I'm not interested in her; the thought of kissing her is repulsive. But all my motives seem bad. It is self-centred in the extreme. Rude and embarrassing to her, intolerant of faults which are probably inherited. But I don't care and I'm content to be independent and sincere. But modelling action on reaction is impossible in society.

This episode is a terrible period of *détente* – my intellectual and creative self stands absolutely still. I stagnate. I do my work, exist. Don't create.

26 July

Letter from Podge, to say I have a Second at Oxford. Great sense of joy. I had half expected it. No one will believe me when I say I did no work. But it shows how the system can be foiled by intelligence and sudden effort at the right time. I got through on the few intense hours of work each night before the examination. It seems such an unimportant thing, like a foreign travel visa in comparison with actually being abroad.

29 July

A strange mixed dream. I was alone with Constance in the cottage at Brayfield, and there was the faintest hint of electricity between us – a tension and embarrassment. If she'd come, I should have been powerless. But I dreamed instead. I was in a hotel bar, where I went with a man, a friend. There was a girl leaning against the bar, drinking, alone, who didn't turn round. My friend talked with someone, and suddenly the girl turned to me and said: 'Are you going to have another one?' I was shocked by the direct approach and said brusquely, 'No, I only wanted one.' But later we were walking together down a corridor. There were other people. Later I realized it was *la petite Suedoise* whom I met and so liked on the Copenhagen ferry.[1] Curious use of nostalgic past memory to express present frustration.

31 July

Letter from Curtis. Poitiers is open. Future smiles.

1 August

Unusual depression of father. The Korea war threat, business affairs. How terribly life has nagged at him. Hundreds of minor circumstances, and he unable to make the big cut, the final slash. The environment is like a leech. It forces everyone back into themselves. No freedom of action or thought, no whimsy, no exuberance, no sincere mutual relationship. Only a tissue of suburban conventions. A dry, precise, mouse-like, mole-like rut. He cannot be persuaded to risk the financial reefs of a change. Any anchorage is better than none. But a new, safer, healthier place would rejuvenate like a spring morning. The way he walks around the garden, ditting and dabbing, just

---

[1] This encounter probably took place during the long vacation of 1949, when JF travelled to Scandinavia as part of an ornithology expedition. See introduction, page xiv.

looking. The garden full to impossibility, and yet he talks of a half-acre garden as 'colossal great place', 'immense', and so on. He is as difficult to flush as an old pheasant. He can always find new cover, new obstacles, new pretexts. An almost humorous way of assuming the very worst about everything. It is terrible also to see him so without interest in anything. No hobbies, no outside interests. The reluctant snail. I wish very much that I could have a car for a fortnight. I could find a new world for him.

Butler, *The Way of All Flesh*.[1] I found it heavy-going. Too much middleway tolerance and wisdom, too thorough, too mild, too humdrum, too objective. Yet the passage on how we ought to live more as animals, enjoying the present, and ignoring all but the immediate past and future, has impressed me. In it I find much of my own present vaguely self-centred, vaguely existentialist manner of living. I ought not to go to France. But I go. Improves more as one reads it. Definitely a major novel. Shades of Fielding. The great fault is the lack of fire, of life, of an ever-present soul. The soul died as the book was written. It smells like a classic, and ought to be read in a classic edition. So thorough, so assured and controlled. The very antithesis of Lawrentian style.

1–31 August
The holiday in France 1 Aug – 31 Aug.[2] As holidays go, not a success. A variety of reasons. Dissympathy with the others. If I'm not being sometimes intellectual, highbrow, I feel depressed.

Then France has lost its freshness for me and I haven't found its profundities as yet. I've got over the novelty of the first taste, and haven't achieved the grateful familiarity of the old customer.

I wasn't very well, and couldn't write. I felt bottled up.

I don't like travelling so far and so fast. I like vegetating.

Financially I ought not to have gone.

---

[1] Published in 1903, a year after Samuel Butler's death, this semi-autobiographical novel follows the fortunes of Ernest Pontifex, who seeks to escape the restrictive influence of his immediate forebears and to return to the simplicity of his great grandfather, a village carpenter. Cf. JF's autobiographical essay *The Tree* (Vintage, 2000), p.14, where he writes: 'My great-grandfather was clerk to an attorney in Somerset, and I think his father was a blacksmith. I like having such very ordinary ancestors, but my father, being only a generation away from the great rise out of immemorial West Country obscurity into well-to-do mercantile London, did not.'

[2] JF drove through France to Andorra and back with a couple of friends, stopping off to camp along the way.

2 September
Frightful depression this town brings on me. The sedentary, cloistered, inward way of life. I sit about all day, trying to think, plan, write, all the time only dreaming. I feel frustrated by my poverty, which seems to threaten to cut me off from the future. I feel myself growing old, yet have no great pleasure, no experience. An introvert, dwarfed existence. Living with people to whom I can scarcely talk, and they my parents. No common subjects. All the old trouble. Sexual frustration. The feeling of irresponsibility, drift, weightlessness. Twenty-four and no job, no prospect of success. Aimlessness and futility. And now I feel I can't make the effort to escape. It is a mistake to go to Oxford without money. One sees a promised land and can't afford it. One ought to work and earn money and be able to afford a life of one's own, a physical life, a wife, a car, a home. My life is wasting, wasting, wasted. Here, even depression is only a mediocre gutless thing. The gutlessness of life.

12 September
Haydn. Op. 772. F Quartet. Elegiac simplicity of third movement. There is something strangely naïve and lovable about Haydn. Never very clever or very intense like Beethoven or Mozart. He is rather sad, or rather gay, always interesting, never harsh. Elegant domesticity.

I have a new way of keeping butterflies. Take the wings off the body, gum them to a strip of paper and then enclose them in a cellophane envelope. The work is without any point scientifically. A collecting of odd specimens – a sort of souvenir addiction, which I try and combat with other things. But here there is beauty. One works with beauty. The wings are so beautiful. Especially the pale-green opalescent sheen on the wings of the Chalkhill blue – a pale washed blue suddenly flaming into this strange remote iridescence.

15 September
James Grieve. A very aristocratic apple. One of the best for texture and flavour. I enjoyed picking a boxful this morning; tall, pale-green, white-green going to yellow-green apples, some going red. Most of them were clean.

Homer, *Iliad.* So great and vast and mythical that it is almost beyond criticism. The astounding thing is the kind of tolerant amusement with which Homer sees both men and gods. He is above both of them. All the actions and episodes are stylized in a neat, clean manner. Very highly stylized, a kind of vase-painting stylization. But there are touches of humanity and brilliant metaphors here and there. A love of simple objects and their elementary shapes and qualities. The effect of Homer's humanity is one of irony – he presents the hero (in which can be counted the gods) alongside all their faults. They are constantly betraying their own perfection. Like mimers whose masks keep on slipping. In fact the creator of heroic mythology seems to be laughing at it all at the same time. Another point is the humour. A sense of humour which can survive 3,000 years is of astounding vitality – i.e. the games scene, where Achilles is taken in by Antilochus' obvious flattery and Agamemnon's unwon prize.[1] Achilles is objectively seen, and portrayed more black than white. An impossibly self-conceited bully. His only redemption is the short speech in the final Priam scene.[2]

Diomedes is another cocksure lout. As usual Odysseus is the engaging character.

One feels sorry for the Trojans as a rule. The Greeks, except Nestor and Odysseus, are rather heavy and sulky and egocentric.

23 September
Wildfowling on Leigh marshes. A cold day with a high wind. The marshes absolutely deserted except for the mussel-picker. The sky massed with clouds. A fine sunset. And the thin line of jewels, diamond, emerald, ruby, orange lights of the illuminations, four miles away across the mud, extending along the Southend front and up the pier. It was pleasant to sit in the darkness, with the incoming tide lapping and creeping onwards, meaning danger, the unset sunset behind, the steel-cold wind, the cries of redshanks and dunlin and ringed plover, and the bright lights of civilization a long way off. It is the same feeling that one gets on a mountain-top, looking down on the villages and towns of the valley. The delight of isolation.

I had some promptings about the ethics. I shot a curlew, which fell wounded a hundred yards away. I ran up to it. It was crying in a feeble, puzzled way, and tried to flap off.

From this two conflicting emotions. Pleasure, at having outwitted and

---

[1] In a running race at the funeral games for Achilles' fallen comrade Patroclus, Antilochus, the son of Nestor, takes the last prize after Odysseus and Ajax. Within the hearing of Achilles, who is giving out the prizes, Antilochus comments how the only Greek capable of defeating Odysseus is Achilles. Pleased with this praise, Achilles gives him an extra half-talent of gold. The final event in the games is the javelin competition, but when Agamemnon stands up for the competition, Achilles says everyone knows how he is by far the best javelin-thrower there is and gives him the prize without the event taking place.
[2] Priam begs Achilles to allow him to fetch back the body of his dead son Hector in exchange for a ransom. Moved, Achilles agrees and tells him that he will restrain the Greeks from fighting for as long as he needs to mourn his son.

caught a very wild creature. That came first, immediately. Then, thinking, sorrow at having wounded it, doubts about the justice of it.

Absolutely, there can be no doubt. It is wrong to shoot. Hunting and killing give pleasure, cause pain. It is the animal which is so excited by the chase. I wonder if it is a sublimation for sex. It would be interesting to know.

Then can an animal feel pain and reason it? Has it any self-consciousness? Is pain increased by self-consciousness? Guided partly by instinct, is pain only a form of acute danger reflex, with no special implications of suffering?

25 September
Alan Fowles.[1] Tall and cadaverous, pale in the face, round-shouldered, he walked across the other side of the street from me. He wore an old brown overcoat, red-brown, and a dark-brown trilby, and walked into Chalkwell Park, cold and wintry and deserted, with the grey Thames in the distance. What a terrible life. He walks with his eyes fixed in front of him, as if he is afraid of seeing anyone, or dulled, stunned by the poverty and monotony of his existence. Even his ears seem flattened back, like a poor dog too starved, too whipped. It suddenly seemed terrible to me that he was my half-uncle. I begin to visualize my grand-parent that side. He spent all his money and spawned like a rabbit. I imagine him self-indulgent and self-righteous. From him comes that streak of self-pity and weak will, that dull miserable powerlessness to act which seems the curse of the male part of the family. A kind of timidity and sensitivity about change, about trying to climb. An abnormal contentment with lot.

He was on the other side of the street, and so I didn't speak to him. And I felt ashamed. Partly because his life had been – through no fault of his, the fault is an appallingly *pure* hereditary one – so feeble and without colour, so flat, dull, drab, grey. And he must have been imagi-native enough to have felt some of the waste, the terrible desert of it. Partly because I am animally ashamed to have him as a relative.

E. M. Forster, *Passage to India*. A great novel, but somehow it doesn't satisfy. It doesn't communicate. Forster creates a kind of dry barrier of objectivity. Everything is seen through a glass. Structurally I thought the last part an anti-climax. The narrative travels, fast and absorbing, till the end of the caves. The last episode is muddled, and the ending almost trite. What he has done so well is the view of Anglo-India. His method

---

[1] One of the children of JF's paternal grandfather by his second marriage (see introduction, page viii). JF recalls him as a man of 'no gifts at all' who failed to find any kind of a career.

is on the whole gentle objective satire, as if he says to himself, 'I shall paint them in a satirical manner, as if one is ultimately uninterested in the matter.' There is no personal bitter element. He tries to see both sides too much; because he hasn't the stature of an Olympian. He never saw a daemon, not even the tail of one, and there are flashes of the intelligent rabbit again, as in *Howard's End*. His style is not supreme, sometimes a little gauche, or inelegant, or over-romantic, 'dated'. I hate those clever, wise generalizations aside, which interrupt the reality and create the puppet atmosphere, which is all wrong. He is too finickety and feminine, almost too academic, too bourgeois-humanist, look-at-me-I'm-not-condescending.

Chap 14. 'Most of life is so dull that there is nothing to be said about it.'[1] Typical clever aside. But also this sums up a trait in EMF – one feels that he is pessimist and disillusioned and that he can only write by an effort of will, and that his credo is rather that of Mrs Moore in the caves, an empty one.[2] He never sounds eager. Usually reluctant. Perhaps he realizes that he lacks the final touch. On the whole it is a carefully observed, brilliantly conducted, historical social document. Not a novel, and not a work of art except as a piece of documentation.

Father. His absolute listlessness, disinterest in life. He spends the whole day staring out of the window, doing the crossword, walking about, money-jingling, making a fuss about a hundred minutiae, which are his only barriers against complete nullity. It is terrible when one has lost all desire to have interest.

2 October

Sudden fit of black depression. A lovely, cold windy day. But oh the dull endlessness of the town and the people and the buildings and the moods. Money is at the root of it all – with no money one can't afford friends, male or female. I can't go and see them. They can't come here. I can't afford to know a girl. I can't afford anything, clothes, books, records, anything. I sponge here. I should be working, but I hate work and a fixed confine. I have no energy to get things typed, to attempt publishing. I have no will to get out in the world.

Here I know no one. I haven't spoken a happy, spontaneous word since I came back here in Aug. There's no spontaneity in the few things I say. They are all thought out, deliberate. I almost forget what talking is.

---

[1] The opening words of chapter 14.
[2] Frightened by an echo during her visit to the caves, Mrs Moore was filled with a sense of despair, and emerged with the conviction that 'Everything exists, nothing has value.'

And I see all this reflected in F. He spends all his time groaning and mumbling and sniffing and coughing, in a kind of dreadful psychological hypochondria. He casts a dull, funereal gloom over everything. All his intonations have the groan as their basis.

Then there is the complete lack of any sign of affection or family love. I can't believe it's all come purely out of my own reserves. I don't know why I'm emotional and dreamy and sensitive below and dry and cold and reserved on the surface. Something must have put the crust there. Something hardened me. I put all the blame on this travesty of life in the drab suburb of an ugly town. Most accept the pattern. They may complain, they may even genuinely feel. But they accept. Because I don't accept, yet I've got to live in it, I form a hard crust. I live by all the conventions, masks with nothing behind.

I've seen other worlds to compare this with – that's the stab of realization. Comparison. Knowing how others live.

And there's no way out. I write and I write and I know I never write well enough. It's only the fact that I still glimmer with the hope that one day I may write well, it's the only thing that keeps me sane. Or keeps me still rebellious. I wouldn't go insane – the crust's grown too thick. I'd just sink back into the rut. Get a job, and become a Fowles, an ordinary mortal, oblivious of ordinariness and doubly careless about mortality. That seems impossible now. But I may one day accept oblivion.

I've partly written the depression away.

In the peak of it, as I was cycling home from golf, I had to pass a small boy holding a ball ready to throw at another boy. As I got near him, he suddenly raised his arm and shouted at me, 'Get out of the way, you.' He said it with a peculiar violent harshness and hatred in his tone. He had a Southend accent – 'Ge' ou' mer wäi, yew' – and the air of a bully in embryo. I was feeling so sad that I just stared at him without saying anything. He was just an ill-bred little lout with the lout's genius for saying the cruel thing clumsily at the right time. Some hostile god might have been in him, Homer-fashion. Somehow the action was so typical of the crudity and coarse ignorance of this jerry-built town, that I almost felt the whole place had found a voice. It was diabolically well timed. And the advice is implicit in the relationship between the two worlds, my minute individual one and their giant sprawling suburban one.

6 October

The ridiculous situation of Allen and Wright, where a manager can steal £300 in the year and nothing be done. His name is Wood. He has a mistress, besides his wife, and so presumably needs money. He runs the handling of orders and all trade. He runs the shop. It's not known whether he takes money or goods, but the profits are always less than they should be. This year it is about £300. And there is no direct proof, so no case can be proved. Also, he is a skilled manager and has the business at his fingertips. He knows the ropes, how to order, how to sell. If he went, sales would drop. It's a terrible situation, where a man like him can control all the laws of morality. Where he's got absolutely the whiphand. F wants to sit under it, has to sit under it. It's the old story of the servant who knows he is indispensable and takes every advantage.

9 October
Death of Sheila.

A sudden illness, a paralysis of the hind limbs with complications in the liver. This day – the vet came to destroy her at 9.30 p.m. – was harrowing. She could not move, and was in pain whenever anyone tried to shift her. We put her in the cupboard under the stairs. There she sat and whined gently, with a terrible – truly terrible – look in her eyes. A terrible fear – she was always a strangely timid, sensitive dog – of the unknown, this dreadful and painful punishment; a bewilderment; an agony at the danger of it, the leaving of life; and a kind of soft luminous frenzy at being unable to communicate. Her eyes seemed extraordinarily large and soft, her ears lay back and she looked up, suffering, suffering, and we were appalled at the impossibility of communication. It was as if she was looking at us across a great abyss, which we had never seen until this moment; and gradually she seemed, as death became inevitable, to be looking at us from, and belonging to, another world. It is not so much the pain which is so shattering, but this dull incomprehension. To see her sitting there, shivering and sniffling, with her great eyes watching us, and we watching her, and our voices and the intensity of her effort to understand, to make us understand.

The vet was a little man with a curious rictus smile, and a way of speaking as if he was not really convinced that we believed him. Very earnest and anxious. In some ways a clown with his seriousness and little quirks of humour. A way of saying small things in an important manner. He did his best, his ignorant best. It is a uniquely difficult science.

The whole house was upset. Hazel at first tried to make it lighter than it was, and then, towards the end, tried to prevent us hearing her cry by shutting doors. Then she broke down when the vet was coming to destroy. Such a tiny tragedy, but so large in the small circle of a closed existence. She has become so much a part of life; her presence at mealtimes, her bouts of playfulness, her having to be put out at nights. The eyes and 'sweetness' of her, the gentle humanity of her. One was spoilt, treated indulgently.

Because of her astounding good nature. No dog was ever gentler. She had a sweet dignity, a playfulness, an aristocratic repose, an aloofness outside the home, a feminine timidity, though a proper doglike anger

towards mice and cats. Most charming of all, she was never bored by
one's advances.

I treated the whole incident with outward nonchalance and coldness.
One can only be dry-eyed about a dog. A dog is a dog, and that Sheila
should have become almost – to Mother and Hazel – a member of the
family is only a reflection on their way of life. But loss of animals is a
strange thing. It is less restrained and almost as deep as human loss. I
put my arm around her when she was crying with pain and willed fiercely
that she should relax, and her poor wracked body did sag slowly, very
slowly, with frequent jerks awake. But it is at such moments when one
is doing one's spiritual utmost to understand and sympathize and soothe,
that, even though it is a complex human dealing with a domesticated
beast, one gets a sense of the Franciscan universal sympathy, the poignant
fraternity of existence.

To us also, come from Poole,[1] she was a sort of link with Devon, with
Ipplepen and all the happiness I had there. Especially Poole, with that
fine old couple. I remember seeing the puppies in the barn, and the
difficulty of choice.

I helped the vet carry her corpse out after he had killed her. It was
in a sack, which we threw into the boot of his car. Already she was a
memory. Still poignant, when I felt her still warm bedding, and picked
up her collar, and saw some of her hairs on the mat, and remembered
and remembered and knew memory is a thing which fades, and she's
gone for ever.

11 October
The race against time with the *Pandarus* play. I can't be certain of it,
having it so close to me all the time. The fault is that it is too topical,
too connected with present thoughts and fears. And too wordy.

A new view on my parents, which embraces all their faults – or better,
the qualities they lack. They have no sense of style. They can't tell a
stylish jug from a pretty jug, they don't feel the style of things, of a book,
of a piece of music, of a meal, of a flavouring, of life. It is the same as
lacking aesthetic sensibility, but goes deeper, is more comprehensive as
an observation. It is, in fact, the great criticism of suburbia. It lacks altogether the sense of style – it has conventional and very restricted ideas
of beauty and above all of 'prettiness' – but no ability to see style in
spheres outside the arts. Every little movement is style. Even pure nature
has its style. There are varieties of style in landscape, in the shape of
flowers, in the flight of birds.

---

[1] Poole was a small farm near Ipplepen owned by a couple called the Hills.

14 October
H. James, *Roderick Hudson.* Something about James bores me. A long-windedness. A disembodiedness. But perhaps it was my mood – one should never judge a book till it has been read three times, and at intervals.

15 October
An excellent wireless documentary on the finding of the mother of Aesop's tomb. There is something immensely exciting and romantic and poignant in the thought that they found in her cosmetics box an instrument 'pointed at one end, to clean the nails, and round and flat at the other, to press back the cuticles'. Such a fact makes time lose all its horror. Yesterday's death is the same as the death of 5,000 years ago. How the ancient Egyptians 'live' still! Really through their immensely vital art. They seem like exotic yet intimate neighbours.

Finish *Pandarus.* This is the third writing, and the first one with any structural strength and 'set' language. The difficult is to get the language hard. I feel pleased it is finished. A lot of polishing and pruning remains. Some of it is too sentimental. Too high-flown. But there is some good theatre. I shall never get it in in time.

24 October
A tubby little taciturn old man, seedily dressed, rather like a shrewd toad, came today to buy clothes. He turned them all over expertly and thoroughly. And offered me thirty-five shillings. Thirty-five shillings for a suit, two coats, a pullover, a shirt, all in good condition. I refused the offer. He pulled out a pound note and a ten-shilling note, as if the sight of so much money would make me lose my head. I refused again, and he hopped quietly away.

Herodotus.[1] Finished after six months. Very, very much enjoyed. The great and superb thing about him is his humanity. That he was gullible and inaccurate and undignified are to me added enhancements, especially as he has none of these faults to any excess. One is struck by his curiosity, his

---

[1] Born in Halicarnassus, in Caria, in 484 BC, Herodotus, 'the Father of History', describes in his *History* the war between the Persians and the Greeks in the early years of the fifth century BC. Although he is often criticized for his lack of historical rigour, his account stands out for its sympathetic good will and an encyclopedic interest in other cultures. Besides the historical details of the war, he also writes at length about the customs, manners and legends of the many places he visited in the course of his extensive travels. He died at Thurii in about 420 BC.

love of minor incident, and at times an almost super-temporal amusement of human foibles. His work abounds with themes fairly crying out for modernization. A vast orchard of ideas. Again and again the essential *essences* of humanity are rubbed in; but on the other hand he has the spiciness and exoticism of a strange and barbaric past. I have marked the important passages; important because they are amusing, aesthetically pleasurable, or interesting, revealing. More often than not the so-called important history – the dry facts of the case – are boring and valueless except to the historian. It all depends on whether you think it is more important to know where X was on a certain day, or what he ate. I think the latter is far more important. The loveliest book is the one about Egypt. The first four are better than the last five, and if I had to prepare a complete edition, I should choose them entire. The translation is undoubtedly a 'classic', as 'classics' go. The most original quality in Herodotus – his mixture of academic objectivity and charmingly irrelevant quaintness.

25 October
Indecision about *Pandarus*. At times some of it seems superb. Then at others it seems terrible. And now it is really too late to do anything about getting it in. I feel I can never become sufficiently objective. If I carry myself away with a piece of writing, I distrust it when I wake up. Mainly because the words act as keys to the original inspiration and instead of creating in themselves, I know they are only stepping-stones to the other shore.

I begin to feel that my chief virtue from the creative point of view is my sharp sense of criticism, a flair for *faux tons*. At the moment I can't apply this at all successfully to what I write. But I think I shall eventually be able to encompass that duality. T. S. Eliot seems to me to be pre-eminently a creator by self-criticism. His greatness is due to the particularly acute sensitivity of his critical faculties, not to the ease with which he can temper his positive urges by this negative value.

Father – who has no aesthetic sense – attacks all questions of aesthetics as a matter for disputation. He says, 'That is the greatest symphony so-and-so wrote,' and in the statement there is an implicit challenge. Never a quiet remarking enjoyment, a mere expression of personal pleasure.

28 October
For three days a terrible rush to try and get *Pandarus* typed out. But the effort will fail. It has to be handed in by Nov 1st. I can't type fast enough, and at the same time I know it isn't 'set' as it should be. Over all the hurry I feel a kind of dull distress, as if yet another chance of proving myself by external standards has been allowed to pass. There is always

the tempting possibility, however remote it may seem, of gaining sudden fame. Yet I must have the will to withhold. Living in such isolation as this, quite literally encased inside my profoundly monotonous *vie quotidienne*, I can only rely on the certainty of my own judgements. And since they are obviously only capable of a very limited objectivity, I have to be *absolutely* certain of their validity before I can venture outside. The faintest impression of softness, of false values, must be sufficient to condense. And *Pandarus* is full of weaknesses. *Even I* see that. In poetry it is easy. One must create and destroy in oneself, *in oneself only*, until the ruins achieve a certain height fit to be built from. There is a parallel in the growth of coral to above the surface of the sea. Poetry now being an uncommercial art, at least one can keep it pure, unalloyed with more temporal considerations. Economy of output is the salient characteristic of the pure poet. Villon and T. S. Eliot spring to my mind. Not Shakespeare, not Dante.

But in a novel or a play the decision is much more difficult. The Devil is dressed up in the guise of 'Get published at any cost'. There's a tremendous desire to betray oneself, be one's own Judas, for gold, actual or metaphorical. In a way I feel content that *Pandoras* won't be tested, put 'outside', since it would only be there with my reluctant consent. But the proposal of withholding much longer is desperate and frustrating. Especially as I have let the career side of my life slip and slide away. The inside gains at the expense of the outside.

Part Two

A Year in France

Part Two

A Year in France

Crossing to France. Uneventful, except for one incident. That a pretty tomboyish Swedish girl was in my compartment at Victoria. I smoked outside in the corridor during the journey to Newhaven. In the hope that she would come out. But she didn't. On board the boat I saw her standing at the side of the bar. I went and got a drink, and she actually moved up beside me. And still I hadn't the courage. I moved back to the side of the bar, watched her out of the corner of my eyes, and noticed that my hand was shaking. What a terrible state to be in. I think, in all sincerity, that I would have spoken then. But at the crucial moment, just as she was four feet from me, and taking her first sip of her drink, out of the blue came the voice of an American.

'Well, that's starting pretty early.' As she turned: 'You shouldn't do that till you get to France, you know.' She smiled a little. 'Are you Scandinavian?'

'Yes.' And away they went, a Jewish-looking American, and a Hellenic-looking cosmopolitan youth of eighteen. He wore a check shirt of bright red, had thick lips, a slim body, sallow skin and a worldly, absurd and corrupt manner. They went conversationally away. I listened for a few minutes, envying the slickness of the American technique, the way he could carry it off before a whole crowd of men, and say in a loud voice: 'I've been to fifty-two countries and never seen one like France.' Even if he said twenty-two only, it was still outrageous. And again: 'I found Athens like a little Paris.' I don't know why – and this isn't so isolated a thing as the accosting frustration – I and most Englishmen flinch slightly at such boasts, especially when they are situated at the very beginning of an acquaintance, before familiarity can compensate for the falsely struck notes. I went through a few minutes' bitter self-examination while all this was going on. I stared at the livid green sea washing against the harbour pillars as we drew away, and found the consolation of a parallel in the frigidity of the colour, as without passion as jade. (Jade is a quite passionless colour. Faint relationship with jaded?) Two elements struggled. I analysed my sexuality and its desuetude, and consoled myself with the thought that my role was that of the artist-observer, inward loquaciousness and outward calm and denial and silence. In many ways I believe this conflict between reality and the artificial dream of my

character is better unresolved. That is, if I got to the state where I was
not only sexually satisfied, but managed to turn outwards, to 'extrovert'
the inward loquaciousness by speech and immediate action, I think the
happiness inside me would detract from any artistic aims I might be
envisaging. I certainly would not see as much.

At Paris, Peter Nurse.[1] A strange person. Almost as soon as I saw him,
in his room at the Ecole Normale, he showed me a copy of Miller's
Tropic of Capricorn and read out to me one or two of the juiciest extracts.[2]
He talked of his liberty about women. He could bring anyone he liked
in, and keep her till any hour. And practically all the evening he was
harping on the same theme. He told me how many times he had copulated with his fiancée each week at Oxford; how he was going to Germany
to a girl, with whom he could sleep, for Christmas – he seemed quite
unaware of the still – even in 1950 – rather shabby ambiguity of this;
how he had once paid a pound to two women in Montmartre to put
on a lesbian act – this he described in some detail; how two French
contraceptives he had used with his fiancée had broken, and of the fears
that had worried them afterwards. And a good many other things. All
this to me, whom he doesn't know very well. I could only think of a
handful of reasons: one, that it was a case of frustration trying to talk
itself into the longed-for state; two, that he had misjudged me, and
thought me as a hard and experienced person in sex who must be
rivalled; three, that he was desperately anxious not to appear academic,
the young don. I think the last reason is most likely. If it was a genuine
and straightforward expression of his mental outlook on sex, he must
be a strange scholar. He will be a somewhat unique don at Oxford. Who
will perhaps become notorious, but I don't think celebrated. He is very
thorough and intelligent, but not super-thorough nor brilliantly intelligent. More it is a natural 'flair' for languages. Oh yes, another possible
reason – he has been very ill – possibly his attitude was vaguely devil-
may-care, *demain nous serons morts.* Curiously enough it didn't absolutely
anger me, drive me into a cold temper – as Basil Beeston has once or
twice with this much more obviously cock-a-hoop manner – but almost
attracted me, and I even managed, without too much distaste, to throw
smut back at him. There was something naïve and sincere about it.
Admittedly Paris is a terrible aphrodisiac. The odour of cheap tobacco,
garlic and expensive scent in the bistro. The suavity and oiliness and
richness of the older men, the leaping, swaggering virility of the younger.

---

[1] See note on page 26.
[2] Henry Miller's sexually explicit and autobiographical novel about an American
artist's adventures in Paris was published in France in 1934, but remained banned
in Britain and America until the 1960s.

The unashamed sexuality of the women, with their clothes sense and their sharply anti-utilitarian femininity. The night life. We drank at the meretricious Dupont café. We were stalked by a little blonde, with dark eyes, and slightly corrupt, sophisticated features, her blue dress was cut very low. One could sense her breasts perfectly willing to leap out. She behaved in a flamboyant, excited way, as if she was going on benzedrine. She talked broken English. We sat in a corner and by adroit movements, one with a quite brilliant tactical sense, she contrived to get within a yard of us, and made faces at us, and spoke her loud English. I was profile, and Peter faced her out well enough. One day he will have her. She talked of English cigarettes, which I was smoking, but her only direct remark to us was after she had said (to a young man who had tried to put his arm around her) *Je n'aime pas les pédérastes.'* She then said to us: *'Vous comprenez? Comprenez?'* There was something febrile and shallow about her which made me pity her in a vague way.

When I got back to my hotel, an evil intention made me look on top of the wardrobe. There were three pornographic magazines there. One (French) fulfilled its purpose, but I noted that the flagellant and homosexual passages didn't stimulate me in the least. Something gained!

2 November
La Toussaint.[1] To Poitiers. I met my future employer[2] and felt myself rather reluctantly being affable and complimentary to him. He is breezy and active and impatient, proud of Poitiers, rather excited by me, although I could see he thought me a little slow during the periods when I was observing him from inside. He was very anxious to be kind and do the right thing. And I liked him quite well in spite of the difference in temperament. We met various people, saw the churches, the faculties, the main street, drove out to get a panorama of the town.

It was badly blitzed in the war – a 300-plane raid which took place in 22 minutes. The only raid, but a terrible one. And we, the English, did it. I expressed conventional regrets, but felt absolutely indifferent. I even thought it vaguely amusing. *Absurde* in the Camus sense.

My room is small, third floor, giving down a steep slope of ugly roofs to the road, the marshalling yard, across to the hillside opposite, loosely stuffed with new and rather crudely unattractive houses. Not a good view, but a view. The room is bare, unattractive except for a magnificent Turkish rug used as a bed-cover and a rather pretty – pretty can be used justly here – pink wallpaper with a floral pattern. I can't help wondering over the disparity of a perfumed block of naptha in the lavatory – the system, *ça va de soi*, doesn't flush properly – and the niggardly

---

[1] All Saint's Day.
[2] Professor Martin, head of the Faculté des Lettres.

bowl and jug of cold water which has to do to wash in. French houses are so illogical in their domestic arrangements.

The landlady, Mme Maleport, is blonde, forty, rather reserved. A hinted oddity by Martin is that she comes of good family, and that her sister lives in rich style around the corner. Yet Mme M is running a *couture* business. I have seen one quite pretty, one pretty girl, here. I feel I might do worse that way. The place is full of vague possibilities; I can people my empty mirror on the wall with the figures of a dozen unknown and unmaterializable girls and women drinking and making themselves up. This is the best part of an adventure – the start of it. But I mustn't accept that.

Yesterday, I mentioned to PN that the reason why I wasn't doing a thesis was that I wanted to write a novel. And then he said, 'What sort of novel?', and suddenly I was embarrassed and unnatural. I made some rather silly remark about doing a Kafka theme in a Joyce manner. A very silly remark, in fact. I couldn't bring myself to be more precise. Till I do, my style and my themes will be full of coynesses and falsities.

The Cité Universitaire restaurant – bright and new, with a gay hunting mural, medieval in scene. The food quite adequate, but always cold. I suppose my stomach will eventually get acclimatized. After five meals I still have not talked to anyone. They all talk so fast and seem so well situated in groups. So that as an odd particle, I don't know where or how to fit in. These first few days have been an anticlimax. I know no one and Martin has left me alone. A routine of gaps between the meals at the Cité. My impression of Poitiers is of rather a grey, *closed* town. One feels there is a secret, but it is hidden. Other cities, Paris, Oxford, Edinburgh, Stockholm, Copenhagen, are essentially open. I have seen the English *assistante* here. She is ugly. The peeling of the dream to the core of reality has begun.

Un cortège civil. A rather delightfully gay little carriage, with an arch of mauve flowers over the embowered coffin. A procession of people in black, but not in the least funereal, talking and chatty; two soldiers – it was the funeral of an *ancien militaire* – in khaki greatcoats and blue-and-gold *képis*. Martin whispered to me in rather a shocked manner, '*Cortège civil!* That is not at all usual. There are so many priests, you know.' But it was all a charming picture, enclosed and dwindling away down the perspective of an old Poitiers street, shuttered with light-grey *volets*, with Norman blue slate roofs, and the subtly monotonous variety of the plain plaster façades, on one side of the street bright with pink golden afternoon sunlight, on the other in transparent shade. A harmony of greys and blacks and light amber, and blues. In a walk about the town with Martin, I began to feel its charm diffuse me, to permeate gently, like all good, *old* things. Old things, by their age, can never really strike. If they do, they lose in amiability, because the fact that they strike means that they have something violent and monstrous hidden in their nature.

6 November

Two Germans in the Cité Universitaire. *Boursières.*[1] They both spoke excellent French, and were to all appearances perfectly pleasant. The people at the table treated them normally. But it must need courage on their part to play with only just quieted hornets.

7 November

Those sudden and dreadful moments when one stands outside one's life and despises it. I think the most frightening moments of all. When for a moment one loses one's grip on self-faith, and sees it fall. It's like dropping a valuable old glass. Almost instinctively one snatches at it to catch it back. I suddenly thought, What am I doing here in this obscure little French town, wasting a year doing nothing? When I ought to be starting a job in England, fighting, entering the world. I sit like a recluse and am frightened by the world. The only people I have spoken to are the two Germans, and they spoke to me first. I admire one of them his good French, his thoroughness, his eagerness to learn. He seems so anxious to go to lectures on French literature. I don't want to go to them. I'm not interested any longer in the history of French literature. Now there are only books I want to read. And I don't really seem to want them. I feel myself slipping, slipping, slipping. With only my hopes of becoming a writer to cling to, and they dwindling as every month goes by, and I still feel afraid to try my luck, and afraid to try it before I am certain of myself.

Why do I waste these best years of my life in this silly little city? With not even enough money to enjoy what there is to enjoy in it. Each day the gap between my dreams and reality, my ambitions and my acts, widens. I live torn between them. I can't talk to people, because, with them, I am the person of my dreams, and there is no point of contact.

Yet I catch the glass. It doesn't hit the ground. I think, what is twenty-four? I'm too young to judge. I have the blend – the sensual flesh and the oversensitive mind. Some artistic good is bound to come of it. Some has come. One has to accept the frustration and martyrdom, such as it is.

I saw the English *assistante* again today. She is not ugly.

---

[1] 'Grant-holders.'

9 November
Today, when I came back after dining at the Cité I found that the lights in my room had fused, so I went down to the room of Madame. Monsieur is away, *en voyage*. I knocked boldly. '*Entrez.*' And I realized a new phase had started. Till now, a knock on the door has been always followed by a scuffle to the door, and I have not been allowed more than a peep. But I was allowed in today for a second. Vision of ironing-boards, cutting-boards, bits of clothes. I had a little idea that I was expected. Madame wore an expensive perfume, and it seemed to me that the fuse wasn't burnt. But I might be mistaken. In any case, as she was mending the fuse, she suddenly asked me if I liked dancing. Her apprentice-girl has a dance coming soon, and wants to learn English. With deprecations, I submit. Tomorrow we are to be introduced. Plainly I have fallen, or am falling, on my feet. As usual my imagination seized on this and twisted it a hundred ways in ten seconds. That is the trouble. I anticipate all joys before they arrive. Today I am boiling over with the need to create, to express. I feel in control, galloping on a powerful horse, the world. I met Léaud this evening, an interesting Celtic man, a Limousin.[1] I told him I was writing a novel. I can't hold it in any longer.

11 November
The introduction to the girl has not come. As usual, I imagined too many miles beyond reality.

A terrible evening, full of the self-reproaches of solitude. Far more psychologically than physically ill. Today I haven't spoken a word to a soul; I said one or two words at lunch – the minute necessities such as 'Pass the bread, please' and 'Thank you'. This evening I just couldn't face another silent meal among the thousands of chattering French monkeys. So I walked down to the baker's on the corner. The streets were wet, I passed a pair of lovers, gay music came out of some of the houses, and there was an air of celebration in the town. Happily the baker's was still open. My voice nearly broke with emotion at being greeted by the baker and asked what I wanted. I bought six croissants and a bar of chocolate. And I went home. Everyone was out.

13 November
I can see that the work here is going to be pretty tantalizing. It is difficult to be impartial, or effective when there are mixed classes of ugly and beautiful. It is going to be difficult to be charming and interesting. Fortunately beauty is rare. Real beauty seems so far non-existent. But

---

[1] Léaud was a fellow teacher at the Faculté des Lettres.

two attractive women, and one brassy, twiggyish type who would do admirably on a dark night.

A new idea for synchronizing my poetry and the novel. A system of foot-notes, signs, so that each poem can refer to a point in the story – can elucidate that point, but not be necessary at all in the novel. A kind of optional gloss, commentary. This could integrate literature in a new way. It is wrong to divide the genres off arbitrarily.

17 November
Lectures here are rather ridiculous. I talk in a loud, slow voice and write names on the board. They don't seem to understand at all. Unless I laugh at my own jokes, I get no following.

During the babel of lunch-hour it was announced that we should all stand for a minute in memory of students killed in the war. I was surprised at so much silence and solemnity so soon present. The French are volatile, but they can go black as quickly as they become colourful. Outside there was a babel of voices waiting for the second *séance*, which spoilt the effect, but even so.

I met an American student here and have him in for a few drinks.[1] He is ex-Harvard, very slow-speaking, serious, keeps on talking about intel-lectuals and intellectual life, and culture. Tells me several times that he is gauche and ignorant. Plainly an immensely thorough and painstaking person, being, I think, just a little overconsciously the American in Europe. James would have loved him. So full of plans – he intends visiting the Near East, Greece, Italy and Sicily for Christmas, a week's opera at Vienna, a quite fabulous person. Such richness and freedom made me sneer at him, especially when I soon saw that his aesthetic desires were far beyond his capacity. The very slowness and imperfection of his expression revealed his physical inability to feel the brief instantaneous impact of real beauty. He talked of learning about art, as if learning was the key to feeling. In music he seemed more fulfilled, yet he spoke of Beethoven's 11th. But that was his only fault, though a grave one. To be fair to him, the age and beauty and multi-farious subtleties of Europe must be stunning, especially since his nature is slow and hesitant. He reminded me of a smooth, round ready-made ball. Although he wasn't boastful, he said that 'I did pretty well at Harvard'. He said it exactly as if it was the polite due, but nothing to brag about. It was what most Englishmen would like to have said, but not said. The complete roundness of the American; no cavities, indentations; and

---

[1] The American student's name was Charles Gaisser, a Harvard history graduate, from Oxford, Mississippi.

no protuberances. The perfection of the middle way. Speaking with him I felt both individually and racially more mature. Life isn't factory-made, nor only in a printed book with lavish photographs.

25 November

Dance, given by a Brigitte Ruel. Mme Ruel, cold, *soignée*. M. Ruel, successful businessman, slim, exactly debonair. It lasted 7–3 in the morning. I was bored and ill at ease the whole time. I dance so badly that it was impossible to keep any partner for more than two dances. And then there was nothing to talk about. More and more I am becoming reluctant to talk trivia. I can't be bothered to fill all the vague gaps in the disinterest. I bore people because they all bore me. There were only one or two girls there whom I thought attractive. I am beginning to see that either I shall be poor and lucky and marry the sympathetic genius who will understand me – she will have to be a genius to penetrate all the wrappings, or I shall be rich and able to buy attractions. Sensual women here are physically beautiful. I despair of ever finding the perfect match. She would have to be so complex, so complex.

The dance was held in a drawing-room. About twenty couples. But it was all dislocated, schoolgirlish, without real warmth.

I stood apart. Several couples came past, stared at me, smiled faintly, and I would hear the word '*Anglais*', which didn't worry me much. I felt dry and aloof and dully frustrated.

I stood apart. Tangos, paso dobles, jazz. Sometimes I shuffled round. My partners were polite or bored or frightened. I have to talk when I'm dancing to distract from the clumsiness of my steps.

I came back through the rain, having had to fight a battle with an inferiority complex. All I have against it is the vague faith in my future greatness. I feel so flat and dry now that I can't even write well. I drank a lot, but water off a duck's back. For a time I was warm. By 1 o'clock I was stone sober again. I feel as if I have been watching a great many chances go by, as if a great hope has gone for ever, as if my character has stiffened, can no longer be altered. I am forced for ever to stand outside, watching, watching, and never joining in, never finding the consolation I seek. I stood apart. I think of K.[1] I didn't love her. She loved me for a short time. That's the rub of it. I will never meet anyone I don't stand outside. No one will ever make me surrender my position and enter their heart and body.

I stood, stand, apart. I am finding it increasingly hard to enter even my own body. Every action, every word, is judged by this dreadful, eternal, me. The slightest '*faux ton*', maladroitness, failure, is noted. The slightest

---

[1] i.e. Kaja Juhl, a Danish girl with whom JF had an affair while in the south of France during the late summer of 1948. See introduction, page xiv.

clues of reaction in others are seen. Everybody who speaks to me is dissected, analysed, and closely watched for his response to my positive actions. There are two egos in me: the one, emotional, love-starved, unattractive, taciturn; the other, cold, cynical, aloof, constantly detracting.

26 November
Sunday. Bach recital in the Cathedral. Cold and dank. The *Grand Orgue* was completely successful in destroying all the joy in Bach. Thundering and growling and rampaging, as delicate and clear as an elephant playing a spinet.

1 December
Heavy night with Charles. I let up on myself, and the big smack came at once. Dear God, always waiting. We played billiards, drank beer in the Café de la Paix, and then, not feeling tired, went round to a smart little café in a backstreet, and drank whisky till 6 in the morning. I just slipped gently down the slope, and spent from 6.30 till 12 in the morning being repeatedly sick. I don't think I've ever had worse bouts of retching. In between I sincerely wondered whether life was worth going on with. Sitting on the floor with a bucket between one's knees, one has one's doubts. About everything. Slept fitfully from 12 till 5.30. Having successfully managed to stumble to the telephone and cancel the day's engagements. From then on gradually slip back into the stream of life. At 5.30 I even feebly smiled, and carefully noted the time.

I don't think I shall drink as much as that again for a long time. My stomach is allergic to alcohol. What the head desires, the heart refuses.

Flicking about on the wireless. Queer, disjointed fragments of sound, of music, jingoistic, impersonal, personal, full of moods, *nostalgie.* Nightclubs, soft flowers, soft lights. Piano music, space in a great room. Spanish music, pungent, bitter. Polyglot languages, atmospherics, fadings, halfheard things. Things which repel and a flick of the finger destroys for ever. Things which do not interest, equally dismissed. And here I feel I'm missing life equally. Only hearing it through a wireless. I spend too much time doing nothing, waiting, sitting, drinking coffee, playing billiards. Being bored. When I can't write. Slowly the great me is slipping. I shall never be a truly great writer. The effort necessary behind a production which satisifes. I have to write everything ten times, and still it isn't right. And this being at Poitiers is a profound waste of time. A drab, sleepy old town which is out of the current. Stagnant. I can't find anyone here that I really can approach. More and more I feel alone. Odd people have meant something. The Podges above all. Guy, Basil, Roger. I have lost them all. And none of them ever knew me. But with the Podges I felt happiest. A multiple feeling – all this is futile, but it needn't be futile, but it is futile. A kind of ghastly ping-pong match between two lethargic protagonists within myself.

Terribly depressing effect of the international news. War seems close, universal chaos, an absolute deadlock, where every man wants one thing and the force of nature wants another. And it's the other which is conquering. This slow trundling impact of two vast organisms sliding downhill against each other. The inevitable crash at the very bottom. Sickness everywhere. For the first time a crisis is beginning to have a personal effect on me. There seems to be so much pain and cruelty and stupidity and pointlessness. I knew that before, but never saw it directly, never felt it as a direct impact. I want to write and can't write. I waste my time in the Café de la Paix, because I must mix with my fellow-men and rediscover a little faith. I crave for laughter and forgetfulness with them. It is a craving. With this new awareness I couldn't stay alone. So I play billiards and drink coffee and make jokes, and watch time pass as if it was valueless.

8 December
Charles and I went round to the bar again at midnight, but with the determination not to get drunk. Later when we went home, I had a most strange ornithological experience. It was three in the morning, the town absolutely silent and deserted and under a slight dank mist. A few street lights. Suddenly I became aware of countless thin voices, the unmistakable whistle of redwings. Everywhere. In the sky. On the roofs of the houses. A curious cry they have; a very thin, high-pitched, *glistening* whistle; an inbreath; there is a definite tenuous, glistening quality about them. I kept on thinking of the adjective 'glistening'. Like a sudden small gleam of old silver in a dark room. Strange, remote, beautiful sounds. Then, as I stood in the middle of the square of the *préfecture*, there came the unmistakable whistle of a cock wigeon, and an abrupt thrill shot through me. Hardly anything in art, nothing in nature, except possibly a woodlark, could have given me such an immediate excitement and joy. The effect of hearing that wild, romantic whistle in the middle of a grey, silent, inland city, was like an electric shock. So absolutely unexpected, and so full of special meaning for me; that I, of all the 60,000 people here, should have heard them. I stood for half an hour in the square. It was very cold and very still. In all that time, not a car, not a soul passed. And gradually realization dawned. The sky was full. I would have given anything to have known exactly what was there; to see daylight come as suddenly as if it had been switched on. I heard green plovers time after time, a golden plover flew around the square, as if lost, and so low that I almost felt I could see it. Redwings everywhere. Then sensual cries I did not recognize. Continual thin squeaks and vague rustlings. Then a vast rushing, such as only a really big team of wigeon make. They must have

been comparatively low. For some reason a huge migration rush must have been going on, and I had stumbled across it. Why at Poitiers nobody knows. I went to my room. It was about 3.30. I opened my window. An immediate inrush of redwing whistles. Green plovers. I stared out over the railway marshalling yards. Suddenly out over the railway was a sudden inrush of wigeon whistles, as if they had recognized the still-lighted station. A little later, more whistles. In the end I became frozen and went to bed.

I felt profoundly that I was a link between two worlds. That I, standing on my balcony and listening to the wigeon whistling, belonged to a wilder, more mysterious world than anyone else in this whole city.

And I felt sad and frustrated that it was immeasurable, that I could never transmute the intensity and the magic of such an experience. It is magic only because I have spent so much time bird watching and hunting wigeon.

A very wonderful experience, vastly heightened by its absolute unexpectedness. All today I looked up in the sky, but saw nothing.

Mozart concert: local players. Not particularly enjoyable. A curiously built conductor in tails, a tall man who seemed broader round the hips than across the shoulders. From the back he looked exactly like a cockroach. The pianist in the concerto was exactly like a guineapig. He seemed worried all the time, frightened. Every time he finished playing, he looked up with immense relief, as if he had just finished some violent physical exercize. Much more memorable as a guineapig-and-cockroach, than as a Mozart, concert.

Can't write. I want to, but never seem to have the time. But if I don't find the time now – with only seven hours' work a week – I never will. At long last I'm near the edge of the waterfall. I must get *The Revolt* finished by next summer.

17 December

A longish period of creative constipation. It was a mistake ever to come to this town. The life is dead. There are interesting people, but they take so long to get to know. The social instincts of the provinces are almost non-existent. A lack of spontaneity. A closing-up like a sea-anemone. And then there's my impossible ego, which is itself like a sea-anemone, only flowering in solitude, shrinking and disappearing when touched. I don't know why everybody bores me so intensely. Only occasionally am I not bored. If I try and make conversation, I am usually driven out of myself in two sentences. A person talks, but my real ego is gone. I listen to the others talking, and marvel at how they can accept the boredom, and keep on talking because they feel they ought to be talking. The most desperately boring are the French people. Not only can I not understand the nuances of their wit, but even if I do, I have to admit that it is insipid. The most terrible are the girls in my conversation classes. If I meet them elsewhere they look sheepishly at me, and I ignore them. Increasingly now, if I dislike a person, I ignore them. Or sometimes when I know them, I ignore them out of perversity. CG has become friendly with a girl, Ginette – not unintelligent, not unpretty – who I could have approached, but didn't. And now, because he is getting into her (very much like a punter to geese), I feel jealous. And I can hardly speak to him. And twice today I have stood by her – once she deliberately hurried to be at the door at the same time as me – and twice have cut her dead. It annoys them that I hardly ever shake hands. I feel like cutting away.

20 December

Solitary. I have been feeling solitary for several days now. All my American friends here are going away, have gone away. The shops are gay, the streets full of people shopping, and I have only the prospect of Christmas alone. I am bad at solitude. But I console myself that the experience will be good for me. Life as an instrument for literary creation is nonsense, but I have to believe it is reason. I say too many cruel things when I'm with people. It hurts them, and they don't understand or like me.

The Americans are very depressed and slightly frightened about the international situation.[1] Elsewhere the people seem ignorant and apathetic. The French have caved in. They don't care any longer what happens elsewhere, as long as it doesn't happen here. The war is so close now that it can't be ignored. One reason I don't write is that it seems useless. Not only would everything change, but everything would be destroyed. There's nothing like war for making things old-fashioned, giving new visions. And I feel poor. Today is very cold, and my overcoat – the one I got at demobilization – is not thick enough to keep out the cold. I have only one pair of brown shoes. My money dwindles, and I can't afford new clothes. My poverty is only very comparative. Millions and millions are really poor, piteous, suffering. I just have dreams, and have been educated above reality. Never quite managed to bridge my gap. No merger.

But all this, I believe – it is my only faith – is temporary. One day my prince will come. Therefore my situation, even if it was far worse than it is, could never be extreme. It is only after years and years of trying

---

[1] The war in Korea was going very badly. In November 1950 Mao Tse-tung had ordered the massive intervention of Chinese Communist forces on the North Korean side. Overwhelmed by vastly superior numbers, the UN Forces were forced to withdraw to a line well south of Seoul.

that one can say, 'Failure!' Then I shall be on the extreme edge.

I walk down a foggy road, expecting a turning to a new road, a new life, world. Only when my legs begin to give under me, and the road drives on without turning. Only then.

21 December

'My Kingdom for a Corkscrew'. New type of short story. Written in one evening, 8–1. I could hardly keep awake at the end, but it is better to do it all together like that, without a break. I had felt it in me all day. I thought it was going to be a long-short story, but it was this instead. About 4,000 words.

22 December

I was asked to a party given for an engineering student who had just finished his examinations here. I didn't know him very well, nor any of the people who were with him. I got asked via some American friends, and therefore I was on the fringe. For a long time I felt external, unwanted. We sat round a long table and drank wine and champagne and ate *galettes* and cakes and tangerines, and smoked a lot. The evening was very slow to warm, but finally it became quite convivial. Mainly because of a strange girl. She was Spanish, with a chignon, rather pretty with dark skin, very dark eyes, and negroid but not coarse lips. A deep, mysterious person. Her forte was fortune-telling by cards. Her stage-sense, and her mixture of seriousness and *taquineries* were perfect. You could see that everyone was a little frightened by her. They blushed and trembled slightly, and tried to make jokes. Undoubtedly, she was a skilful reader of physiognomy. It is not the cards, but the face. She rather frightened me, because her analysis of my character was penetrating. She said I was *'de bonne coeur, de très bonne coeur, mais infiançiable'*. That I often had periods of depression. *'Vous avez souvent le cafard.'* That in matters of love, I was *'indifférent'*. *'Vous avez beaucoup souffert.'* *'Votre moral est bas.'* Then, *'Vous marierez une dame de très bonne situation, une dame d'un certain âge. Elle sera riche, très riche.'* *'Vous êtes très honnête, très droit.'* All of that was – except for the marriage, which is possible enough – true. I said nothing, and was very impressed. I am sure she had seen it all in my expression.

She interested me very much indeed, both as a woman and as a *tireuse de cartes*. I think I could do card-fortunes as well. It is only a question of intuition and observation, and the art of generalization.

It is a pleasure, because one can say what one likes of people – and people like being limelighted – behind the pretext of seeing it in the cards. One can believe in the cards to a certain point, assign them fixed values, and always use them – that is for entertainment, to most people. But the major part is psychoanalysis, both rational and intuitive.

After having been silent all the evening, I managed to establish a certain position by – at the time – witty remarks.

Because the cards advertised '. . . *une dame de très bonne situation,*' *'Une princesse?'*

'Vous voulez un mariage avec la princesse Margarète?'

Very casually, *'J'y pense.'*

'Une dame d'un certain âge.'

'*Ah. Pour avoir une jeune femme, quelle carte faut-il choisir?'*

'La dame de coeur.'

Regretfully, *'Mais je ne la savais pas.'*

All these got big laughs.

Three things I forgot to mention about the fortune-telling. *'Vous n'avez pas une grande volonté.'* That was the only thing I rather doubted. *'Vous êtes très doux, très, très doux.'* And then she said *'Voulez-vous demander une question?'* One asks the question to oneself, chooses four cards, and then she says 'Yes' or 'No'. I asked, 'Shall I be a great writer?' and she said, 'No.' Then she said, *'Vous pensiez que j'allais dire "oui", n'est-ce pas? Vous étiez presque certain.'* She was absolutely right.

Christmas Eve

Christmas Eve. I was frightened of being alone, and did things which I normally wouldn't have done. Fortunately there were some others also alone. The practice in France is to have the great celebration after midnight mass. A young man with a sense of fellowship invited us all to the Cercle Catholique. I didn't know where it was, and spent rather a desperate half-hour walking round Poitiers to try and find it. I looked it up in the telephone directory and it said Boulevard Jeanne d'Arc. And that turned out to be a desolate back street, which had been badly bombed. It was dark, full of rubble and ruined houses. A few cars passed. I felt completely solitary, the feeling magnified by the day. After about ten minutes searching a man appeared who knew where the Cercle was.

When I got there, I found a group in a kind of monastery waiting-room. Hard chairs, holly, a noticeboard, a table, a crucifix on the wall. Sitting around the table was a very mixed bag. Two or three French, a Catholic priest, myself, several Iranians, Syrians, Iraqis, a Turk, and a negro whom everyone called 'Ivory Coast'. There was wine – one glass each, tea without milk, and a slice of cake. And singing. From 9 to 11.30 we spent in singing. I enjoyed it. It was an astounding mixture. One of the Iranians, a champion wrestler, sang in a husky monotone, impassively, with slight smile and a rasp in his voice. An Iranian sang brilliantly in Arabic, very attractive rhythmic tunes which were apparently scandalous, because all his compatriots roared with laughter when he sang and when he tried to explain in French what the words meant. There was one marvellous little thing about a gazelle which had been wounded in love but which tottered gaily through a forest. All the time the young organizer was singing in-between, in Spanish, Basque, French, Czech, Polish. He had a very good voice and was happy to sing. I was clamoured at. So I told a joke, which only the French understood, and even they looked as if they had heard it before. In the end I sang English songs with the young organizer, and a French girl sang a song in Bearnais dialect. The *père* sang a sentimental song, very well. Then at 11.30 it was time for mass.

I and the young organizer led the Middle East colonies to the Cathedral. But the service there wasn't very striking. The bishop was elsewhere. So we filed out. It was bitterly cold. I noticed how the cantor's breath steamed in the air as he sang. We ran, laughing and jostling passers-by, as far as Notre-Dame la Grande. That was packed out, but the service seemed no better. We were squashed into a corner and saw very little of what went on. It was like having a bad seat at the opera. The singing (and organ) was bad.

Home at 2 o'clock. Having killed the fated hours without too much pain and self-degradation. One degrades oneself sometimes in the effort not to be lonely.

Christmas Day

A very cold, grey day. No wind, a complete greyness everywhere, including my own heart. I got up at eleven, dressed and shaved, read two letters from home. A letter and a card. The card was from Basil B. I thought I had lost him. This was the only Christmas aspect of the day. Then at 12.15 to the little backstreet café where we sat; shredded celery and cold beetroot, a raw thin steak, mashed potatoes, seven dried figs, a glass of water. Everyone there was slightly depressed and sad, even though to most of them – the Middle Easterns – Christmas means nothing. I only felt a kind of numb depression. Faintly sad, and rather cynical. After twenty years' unshaken belief in the glorious climax of this day, it is difficult to accept it as an ordinary twenty-four hours. As I write I can see a train at the station. It has just drawn in. Hardly anyone descends. Otherwise it is a train at a station, any day of the year. After this gay Christmas dinner, I drank coffee with two Germans in the deserted Café de la Paix. A few people crossed the Place d'Armes outside, but not many. It was the time when everyone was having dinner, *en famille*. All there felt very strongly a sense of being ostracized, of being outside the town, though in the centre of it. The Germans attacked the inhospitality of a town which could allow twenty foreign students to be on their own at Christmas. 'At home, people would compete for the honour of inviting them to the Christmas festivities.' I wonder. A small provincial town is a closed circle anywhere. Poitiers is not in any sense an enterprising, lively town. It drifts in and rests on its laurels. Dust-covered leaves. But we were all bitter. Perhaps not entirely without justification.

On the other hand all this is not absolutely without light. I get a certain bitter joy – and it *is* a perverse pleasure – out of being alone, on the outside. There is a pleasure in being unhappy, outside. And it is the *only* way to 'know thyself'.

I knew good would come out of the lion's carcass, honey out of being solitary. I wrote what is, I think, the best poem I have ever written. It came vaguely out of a water-colour painting I did a few days ago. A red flower beside a lonely road in a desolate winter landscape. It is roughly on the human condition, and its misery, and the artist's consolation. I think I shall call it, 'That the one wild rose should grow' after one of the lines.

Someone asked me out to supper tonight, but I refused. Why, I honestly don't know. I suppose I didn't want to seem alone, unasked anywhere. Partly that and partly the perverse pleasure of being alone.

27–30 December
L'Aiguillon-sur-Mer. A little fishing-village of one-storey houses set in a vast bare landscape of unhedged fields, marshes, ditches and dykes, and sea. The people small, tense and vital, but very reserved. Dark Celtic-looking people, cruel and critical, with weather-tanned faces.

It was snowy weather; we left Poitiers at 7.30, arrived at L'Aiguillon about one o'clock. A long cold journey, first of all, cramped up in a little van. We stopped at Fontenay-le-Comte to buy *'permis de chasse'* for La Vendée. In England you walk into a Post Office and buy your gun-licence; here you have to struggle through a series of unrelated formalities.

We got to L'Aiguillon. A comfortable, warm hotel, good food. We had oysters at lunch. I had never tasted them before. Hitherto I have always pretended that they didn't agree with me, because to be twenty-four and not tasted an oyster seems distressingly green. I liked them immensely, and they agreed excellently with me. We had other shell-fish, and mussels, which I didn't like so well. Then there was a ray cooked *au beurre noir* – a butter sauce with a caramel flavour. The ray is slightly glutinous, but good. Then grey mullet in plain butter sauce, quite as good as trout, and fried dabs.

The first evening I shot a pochard drake, and that was all, except for one or two small birds. The gun was a sixteen-bore, and didn't suit me at all. Apart from anything else, it is cruel. Firing at long ranges, you wound more than you kill. But the French have no idea of ranges and shot-power.

We went out each morning and evening for the flight. At least there were thousands of duck about. The very first morning we shot geese, white-fronts, very high but making a magnificent gabble as they flew over many hundreds of feet up. We saw plenty of them there, and never got near a shot. I wasn't sorry. If I ever kill one, I'd rather do it with my own gun. But everything was wild and unapproachable.

We went out in a small boat and killed waders. Including two avocets. What incredibly lovely, gracious things they are! One of the most elegant creatures of creation. Even in the one pert line of their upturned beak there is a sophisticated elegance almost unequalled in any other bird.

I refused to fire at them, and I wished the others hadn't. To see them flapping feebly in the water, in the mud, was seeing so much beauty thrown down the drain. More and more I feel the terrible symbolism, the blood complex, of hunting. Chernot, the professional fowler, held a wounded curlew, letting it cry, so that others might be attracted, and I suddenly felt furiously angry with him for being so insanely cruel. But such a feeling expends itself at once. One can't fight the multiplicity of the world. And the joy and the agony lie in the same reality.

The others wouldn't kill what they shot. They seemed to me to enjoy holding birds in their hands and watching them still kick. Undoubtedly as a race they (the French) are more cruel. And when you magnify a small thing like that from an individual to a whole nation, it shows a great streak of cruelty. The English love of sportsmanship, for all its conventional and snob aspects, is fundamentally a hate of cruelty. Most Englishmen kill as quickly as they can.

We had two trips out to sea in a boat. I got very, very cold, and didn't enjoy it very much.

I enjoyed the flights. It is such an extraordinary experience, hearing hundreds of wings surging along in the darkness, the whistling and gurglings of wigeon, the quacking of mallard, curlew, geese. The strained senses, waiting for the hurtling shapes.

At the very end I stalked two shelduck and shot one. It was badly wounded and fell on to a little spit of land. I regretted it. It couldn't be found, although we all searched for it. It was a miracle to know how it escaped. But it did. To misery.

I got a little tired of talking French all the time. None of the others knew any English, so that I felt isolated from them. I can express myself easily now, and even start to think in French, but I can't be humorous and fantastic as in English. The French haven't the baroque sense of fantasy.

At the end I developed a heavy cold. Punishment and justice. But I enjoyed the four days immensely. What I remember above all is the oysters and the thousands of duck in the flights, and the high passing of the year.

1 January 1951
Wildfowling fever. I can think of nothing but wildfowling. I spent all
today writing a long letter to BB[1] about the trip to L'Aiguillon. Living
each incident again. I begin to see increasingly in it a kind of symbolism.
It is a kind of poetry and at the same time a most desperately exciting
sport.

1 Jan. The start of the New Year. A kind of milestone. I wonder what the
country will look like at the next. Whether I shall fall by the way *en route.*

Writing all the time. I cannot deny that the short-story medium suits
me. Creation is a period of complete happiness. Everything disappears
in the present world except the pen or the typewriter, the things on the
table, and I am standing at a doorway between two rooms, the one dark,
the other full of light, and fascinating conversation, and fascinating
people. And the miracle is – in all objectivity – how they do actually live
and talk in other ways from those which one had planned. And sometimes they get excited, and I am left behind, so that I can't remember
all that they have said, and feel disappointed when I have to sit and try
and remember.

Passing a lorry with bright headlights one night. As it flashed past,
dazzling me, leaving me in darkness, I thought, at the very moment
when it passed, that I might be dead, that it might have crashed into
me, and I walking in on death. Corollary. I have lived long enough.
From now onwards, it is expressing life in better and better fashion; and
not finding it.

Destroying old manuscripts. A sad, difficult and necessary task. Usually
the themes were all right, but the treatment terrible. One, a ghost story
of a shape in black at the window, another of a man who seduced a girl
in a wood but left her at the vital point, one worth remembering.

Sunday 7 January
Sitting about in a café most of the day. People bore me profoundly and
desperately. There is one girl (G) who is beginning to interest me frac-
tionally.[2] She attacks me all the time, and I attack her, and we're not
bored while we're doing it.

Thoughts on a book about population.
    That statistics and economic intentions bore me. I am not interested

---

[1] i.e. B. W. Brealey. See introduction, page xi.
[2] 'G' was Ginette Marcailloux, one of the students who attended JF's lectures.

in whether the birth-rate is declining or not, and it does not worry me that the author of the book should deem it serious. All I know is that I should like to have a wife and family, but financially and psychologically it is impossible. It doesn't worry me very much that the race is disappearing. In any case it's nice to think of a very small world, sparsely populated. Either a world where man had completely dominated the machine, a world of spacious, organized comfort, or a return to congenial pastoral simplicity – self-support. Either would be preferable to the present sardine-tin fantasy. The secret of life is the pursuit of pleasure, which lies in beauty. And beauty is always simplicity, even in the face of apparent complexity. Great art is having an impeccable sense of space. Bare details, silences, only mysterious, sweet syntheses. Room.

Feel ill, and spend whole evening playing dice with Ginette and Phil. Ginette, dark, vivacious in a not too gleaming way. With fine dark malicious eyes. We are always attacking each other. She treats with a certain mock respect our student–lecturer relationship. Philip, tall and ginger-haired and quiet and thoroughly reliable. Quietly intelligent. He will almost obviously become a good University professor. I taught them liar's dice. We played till midnight, and I won fifteen francs, or fourpence. It is good to be together for an evening – to be together in the deep sense, shutting out the outside world.

14 January
Sewing a tear in my mackintosh. It is beginning to fall to pieces. I don't like darning. It is like undressing an ugly woman. Revealing poverty.

I have made a tacit arrangement with my alter ego (artist) not to write for a week. To take a week's holday from my ambitions. And I have done nothing but a minor poem. But it gives me an uneasy conscience, and I feel as if I am stabbling myself in the back.

A new hat. A nylon American-style *imperméable*, light khaki. It cost thirty shillings, which was more than I could afford, but I got easily that amount of pleasure from it in the first night (yesterday) when it rained hard, and I went out with Pat and J and Phil and my head was dry and I was highly conscious of wearing a smart new hat. And pleased about it.

Weekend with André Brosset at Thouars.[1] He is a strange person, massive

---

[1] A student at Poitiers, Brosset had been on the wildfowling trip to L'Aiguillon and shared JF's countryside interests. Thouars, a small town to the north of Poitiers, was where several of JF's students lived.

and strong, rather taciturn, but amiable, with a Rabelaisian sense of humour and flashes of eccentricity. He reminds me rather of a badger. Superficially rather slow and heavy. But he is – besides being an excellent naturalist – a widely read person, knowledgeable on art, a fair painter, and a much wiser and shrewder person than he seems.

The family is of peasant-smallholder origin, the salt of the earth. The mother massive, dignified, with shrewd, kind eyes. The father blunt, bluff, shrewd. They are all shrewd, even the small girls. A vast family – nine or ten; all rather of the same heavy build. Living in a middle-sized house, dilapidated, untidy, dirty.

The family is rich, has got on greatly in the world, workshop to big factory. The house is full of oddments – good spinning-wheels and old furniture, expensive curios, crucifixes (whence the big family!), what-nots, souvenirs, an extraordinary mixture. Another son who is a speleologist had recently found a Neolithic earthenware pot practically intact. A fine, solid, simple shape. Very suitable for the Brosset family. A very finely shaped object. I handled it, and realized that it was several thousand years old, and I believe it is the first time I have handled such an ancient thing. I was moved.

The food was excellent, rich and plentiful, and no shortage of wine. We had a huge Sunday dinner – a vast meal with several wines to drink, and a dozen to table. I ate too much and felt very good, full of bien-être. We discussed politics and I had a vicious belief that I was making a good impression, and there was plenty of bonhomie. There's more reason than one for drinking wine at Communion. It's a pity it's only a sip there.

The same day we went to Aigenton, a village near them, to try and catch a polecat – by trapping. We stayed with A's grandparents. A very old couple – nearly ninety – in an old, tumble-down cottage. The old lady is very fine, with quick, humorous eyes of extreme simplicity in a wrinkled, time-worn face. She wore a black dress and a kind of white-lace headdress. Her husband of the same height as she, with the same gentle and humorous expression – a kind of simple twinkle in their eyes. He had a fine white moustache with upstanding bristles. They made a very fine old couple, the perfect Darby and Joan. After we had set the traps for the polecat we had supper with them. They said little, supped their soup, and twinkled quietly at us.

We visited the traps for the polecats early next morning, after having discussed literature and art into the night (A and I) and generally explored each other's character. The first trap was empty. The second had a tame cat gone wild in it, which took some killing. It wasn't dead when we left it. A heavy, fat animal. A pretended to be annoyed, but I think he was secretly pleased to have taken something at least.

Then back to Poitiers, across the wide, flat plains of Poitou, in a very lovely mood. The day was windy, with rugged clouds, and great stretches of bright blue sky. The countryside full of colour, brilliant and soft and washed with the night's rain. It was as if Corot and Constable and Sisley had co-operated to turn out a perfect landscape. (Curious how early Corot is always windless, Constable always with a soft breeze). Sisley, blue skies. Constable, softness and light. Corot, clarity, clear forms. The Poitiers plain is full of little valleys, rivers, small villages, old bridges, mills, lines of bare poplars.

17 January
Distractions of this time. I want to paint more than I want to write, which is serious. Because I could never get much further than the style of pastiche, and it is only a side-lane from what must be the main road of my development. The only consolation is that one comes back out of the side-lanes always a little wiser.

And then I am drifting vaguely into love (G), as usual with a meridional beauty. She is one of the few pretty girls here; with black hair, a finely shaped mouth, brilliant red in a pale face. I can't describe the meridional Greek-Latin complexion – there is a kind of opaqueness; it is rather like very pale amber, or alabaster. And her eyes are large, dark brown, with very white whites, and very expressive. Her figure is a little too heavy, but only very slightly so. She is not very beautiful, but she is more than quite pretty. Above all, she is interesting. Intelligent, and our intelligences go well together, always mocking and teasing, but knowing when to drop the masks. The only difficulties are that I have no *jeune premier* charm. And physically I can't hold a candle to the most plain of film stars. And also she is an entomologist, and collects moths, and as long as I am the principal or one of the principal moths, I don't mind. But after that . . . But she is alive, which makes her almost unique in Poitiers.

19 January
Interview with a Jesuit father. I was approached to see whether I would speak English with the boys. I said, no, not every week, but doing it once, I wouldn't mind. A meeting was arranged at the famous Collège St Joseph. It is a building with a small insignificant front, and vast buildings hidden behind. Very Jesuit. We passed through a number of corridors, sad and dreary, up some stairs to the corridor of the fathers. A long gloomy passage of closed doors, with rows of tall cupboards in-between.

The French student who accompanied me knocked on a door, and we went into a long dark room devoid of all life and comfort. Dusty and dirty and disused. A vast bookshelf of books with dull backs. A table littered with papers. A stove in the middle of the room, with ashes on the floor around it. Disorder everywhere. An atmosphere of must. In a kind of alcove was an unmade bed, and pyjamas, pale blue-striped.

The *père* offered me cigarettes, French or English. I was surprised that he should smoke. His ashtray was a mound of stub-ends. He smoked his cigarette to the last possible moment, like a peasant, holding it pinched in his thumb and fingernail.

We entered into negotiations. Before I knew where I was I was talking for an hour a week, and had my head in the snare of another. But I jumped back, and started haggling over the first hour. I have six hours of work only a week at the Faculty, but didn't want a free day blotched by this additional effort. Then came the question of payment. He said that the college was poor, etc, and after a lot of preliminaries, it came to the point where he offered me a free lunch each week, in return for my services. I didn't think much of this, and it must have been a little obvious. But I accepted, not very graciously.

The *père* was a small, thin man with glasses, wearing a shabby habit, nervous and shrewd. His eyes and his glasses were the only things alive in the room. His bargaining was hard, and I didn't quite like the sense of a cunning transaction, the lever on my good nature, when a simple appeal would have been better. The very fact that payment was the last detail discussed struck me as being a stroke of diplomacy, and religiously cunning.

But on the way home I thought that I was perhaps being mean. At least teaching boys English is some sort of aid to international comprehension. Yet I can't accept the fact that I am only an atom and should do an atom's work. I feel my powers lay on me greater, deeper social duties. That spending two hours a week talking English to the boys of an obscure provincial Jesuit college won't satisfy me. I want to influence thousands of people, not dozens. Teaching is only a thing to fall back on, the cushion. A cushion of mediocre ideals for the common man. But I think I will do the two hours. I shall hate it, but it is something for the dim cause. Perhaps it is poetic that it should be in a Jesuit college.

English club. A long speech by Martin. His reference to the necessity for 'rubbing shoulders' drew a big *double entendre* laugh because we all know what sort of a man he is. *Chasseur de jupons*. He always takes girl students by the arm.

Sequel of Jesuit affaire . . . Martin was shocked that I had entered into negotiations with them. The systems never mix. Evidently I have my good excuse. All my good intentions will slip – one must admit, unmanned – down the drain.

The necessity of holding aloof from the mundane literary life. It must be very assiduously avoided. To be a critic, to always be reading and examining other people's creations, destroys one's own impulses. One drains away all one's resources in a kind of eunuch pleasure (not eunuch. I can't think of the exact word. It's terrible when that happens. Illicit? artificial? Something like that). It's lying sleeping every night with the woman you love without touching her. And then one day when you move close and want to take her, you are impotent. A fresh approach, an approach from outside, is impossible.

25 January
Ill. And I have an all-night dance ahead. *Bal des Lettres.* I don't know what the illness is. Whether it's love, or hunger, or too much medicine, or influenza, or lack of sleep, or dysentery. Whatever it is, it's nasty.

Bal des Lettres – a noisy student affair, with a good Latin American band. I filled myself up with pills, took three cognacs and put on my best blue suit, and went. With Ginette and Pat and Phil. All the evening I groaned about having to dance, but once there I enjoyed it as much as anyone. I danced with Ginette practically all the time, and we developed a kind of sexual cuddle-step which we employed for all rhythms. It was hampered by the number of my pupils present, who fixed me with a beady eye if they saw me too close to Ginette's hand. Dancing with her I was completely happy, because we have both a sharp sense of rhythm, and she is not afraid to cling tight.

We left just after three, all four of us together. There was a cold mist over the deserted town. We split and I took G home, but when we were there, I suggested we walked further. Because I wanted to kiss her and hadn't got the courage at that point. But she had been rubbing my fingers ever since we left the dance-hall. We wandered through several streets, empty and dark, and became closer and closer and still didn't touch mouths. Finally down a dark street I caught her and kissed her and all went well. At first she said, 'But why?' We kissed for a long time. She asked me several times whether it was premeditated or not. And then said, *'Bizarre. C'est bizarre.'* We walked back home kissing and playing through the deserted streets. She has fine eyes and a nice mouth, and a beautifully soft complexion. A very interesting face. She kept on biting my hand.

I came home at five to write this, feeling gay and happy.

I'm not deeply in love with her. She has some faults. But for Poitiers very few.

28 January
It is a strange thing how even being in love cannot satisfy. There is always another field beyond the hedge. She came to my room today before supper and after supper, and I turned on the wireless and left the lights

off, and we lay on my narrow bed and kissed. Sometimes her face is
very serious, as if something terrible is happening. Her face is as broad
and wide as it is possible to be without being ugly. The sweetest moments
are when she stops teasing. We mentally fight each other, all the time.
But there are moments when she relaxes, and I feel myself psychologically as well as physically succumbed against. When we are in public, we
have our secret, and are deliberately cold and monosyllabic to each
other, and we enjoy this acting immensely. I look at her and analyse her
physical faults. In profile she is often extremely pretty. In full face, nearly
ugly by flashes. And yet even when I feel surfeited with kissing her, with
holding her, there is an unanalysed something which I can't seize. It is
a soul of sorts, a more than the mere sum of. A kind of tender realization, a link. Because mentally I can't criticize her. She is intelligent,
quick, 'fine'. Gallic. And our minds go together. So that underneath all
the physical maladjustments, there is a steady current flowing between
us. More sympathy than love. I think that the perfect love would be at
the point where no mental criticism is possible.

There is a kind of undertow in ordinary life. I can't eat with any
enjoyment. I can't write or read. With me, the intensity of experience
destroys all hope of creation. I must have the calm after the storm, as
today. We had lunch together and drank coffee in the Café de la Paix.
Then walked through several streets aimlessly but happily, although it
was a grey, cold Sunday. And parted, with the delicious reluctance of a
voluntary abstention.

With G. We went after dinner to the Café de la Paix, with the others.
There were about ten there, three Americans, a Canadian, two dreadful
English girls, one or two French people. The talk was desultory, the
atmosphere heavy. I was bored stiff. The English girl opposite to me
horrifies me. She is plump and mousy and conventional. She can't
believe I'm as evil as I'm painted. If I describe myself to her as publicly
disinterested and academically irresponsible, she only smiles in an
embarrassed way, and disbelieves me. Of course, she is right to disbelieve
me, but – in spite of her being pejoratively conventional – such behaviour shows an ignorance of the elementary conventions of conversation. It is terrible how the English girls here lack finesse – part of it is
the accursed tradition of games and fair play. Good conversation consists
of smiling dishonestly and nuances of hypocrisy, gossip, maliciousness
and scabrous details. A continual teasing and attacking. That is how
Ginette and I talk; only very rarely are we serious. She says, *'Je ne fais
jamais des compliments en publique.'* That is a secret to success. But the
wretched dowdy English plough steadily and lumpishly through their
cliché subjects and cliché phrases.

Ginette seemed crushed by it all, and suddenly got up and left. I

followed her, although I hesitated. She said she needed fresh air. She
was cold, upset.

We wandered through the streets of Poitiers. She gave me her hand
and gradually we warmed, and started to laugh and snatch kisses as we
walked. It was like a flower opening out after a frosty dawn, in new
sunshine. We climbed the hill out of Poitiers on the road to St Benoit.
Looked back at Poitiers, on its slope studded with lights. Then we were
in the real country, bare and deserted, on a long road between bare
trees. We kept on kissing, and playing. It was very cold, with a sharp
wind and a nasty damp mist. Yet we were like children, ridiculously
happy. She told me of some past affaire of hers, and I talked of mine.
Of Kaja, and of another I invented. We walked back to Poitiers in a kind
of golden lassitude, through the damp dark night. It was a mood impossible to recapture. Something of a miracle. The oldest miracle, yet none
of those others in the café could have effected it so strangely and
profoundly. I wrote a poem about it, but failed.

But writing this, I have an exciting idea for a short novel.

30 January
After we had finished work, we came back to my room and lay in each
other's arms. I had two feelings – one, that the first hot tenderness and
thrill of having her was already disappearing. She keeps on saying, *'Nous
nous embrassons trop,'* and she is right. Surfeit breeds disgust. But the
other feeling is a kind of compensatory and more pervading warmth;
of intimacy and companionship; a very faint premarital taste of domestic
comfort.

At first the feeling of disgust was strongest. Not disgust so much as
disinterest, or the first promptings of disinterest. But then later when
we were walking together down to the student restaurant, I suddenly
saw her in a new, more extended way. She asked me what I was thinking
about, and I couldn't explain, except that my conception of her was
transforming, so that when I thought I had seized her, it was only the
shadow of my own amorous desire. Yet I realized dimly that the body
causing the shadow was close at hand. And would always be close at
hand, just as I would be only clutching the shadow always. Two people,
however intimate, only know each other's shadows.

I wondered about marrying her. Our love isn't a *'grand amour'*. At the
moment it's no more than a strong sympathy. But it seems admirably
mutual, although I fear the moment at which I might discover that she
loves me because I am one of her professors and a member of the
country whose language she studies. I wonder if it would be possible to
love anyone purely, without the adulteration of their attractive qualities.
I doubt it. Love must rest on something. I think of G as she would think
of her, of her uglinesses, her faults, of her distance from the vague ideals

which I have had. That is the problem; to swallow, to bridge the gap between one's ideals and reality. My ideas are – or to me seem – not wholly fantastic. They are based on the possible projection of my literary talent into a famous future, where my wife would be similarly beautiful, famous, intelligent. Not G. But should I take what reality offers? At some point there is always a place where one must accept the necessity of return. The peak is like Everest, unreachable. Once the slope towards one's ideals has conquered, one must descend the best one can. And that might be G. In literature the great climbers are Mallarmé and Flaubert – they are the Irvines and Mallorys of the highest endeavour. How the use of such metaphors dates. In a hundred years, 'Irvines and Mallorys' will need a footnote).[1]

31 January
First strain. (I examine all these things clinically. I believe I always would, with any woman). She eats at a different table from mine as a rule, and left before me. I thought she had gone away home without waiting. But she was in the Café de la Paix. Meanwhile I had invited another girl to have coffee. An intelligent girl, of good family, with a round unusual face, and magnificent thick black eyebrows. We sat near G, at the next table, ostensibly with her, but she was hideously dark and sullen, as only a meridional can be black. I talked in English with Moira, the girl with eyebrows, but G wouldn't join in, and I left without her. I think she was rather more upset than I was.

A meeting (via Dominique and André) with a mad Marquis – the Marquis d'Abadie. He is a ripe-looking man of sixty with a heavy, pompous face, which needs a wig, but which has a mane of white-grey hair instead. He is a rich aristo of old family, notorious in the district. His three interests in life are collecting birds, especially their droppings, dirty stories, and publicity signs. A curious mixture of petty schoolboyishness and gestures in the *grande manière*. His diary is full of little notes about his collection of bats, like a boy boasting of his birds' eggs. He was well dressed – he is rich. His lips are thick, fleshy, and his general expression vaguely decadent and unhealthy. We met in the Café de la Paix, and he told us dirty stories in a loud voice, interminably, with the mechanical impetuosity of the extrovert who dandles the scabrous. Several of them were anti-English; he wanted to bait me. They were all

---

[1] This entry was written two years before Sherpa Tenzing and Edmund Hillary successfully conquered Mount Everest. The most famous previous expedition to the mountain had occurred in 1924 when the climbers George Mallory and Sandy Irvine set out from their high camp for the summit, but lost their lives in the attempt.

disgusting. 'An Englishman wanted to bathe. So he went in naked. But two pretty girls came and sat near his clothes. He was in a desperate fix. He didn't know whether to cover his front or his behind. But in the end he saw a way. He caught a large jelly-fish and clapped it over his loins, and then left the sea, walking sideways past the girls. One of them turned to the other and said: "Look at that man! What a charming dream he must have had!"' That was one of the less disgusting ones. The Marquis came to Poitiers because his mistress lives here. He has had a good number, apparently. He described his present concubine as *'délicieuse; elle est si charmante à ma femme et mes enfants.'* He invited us to meet him on Thursday, at his château.

First strain clearly established. I waited for her after dinner. We went up the lighted way, which was a kind of symbol. We were silent and awkward. She was, I think, playing a part, although she may have felt genuinely cut. I had gone down to dinner in a particularly happy mood, however, and it was now my turn to suffer. I started to try and thaw her, but with great unsuccess. I was unnatural and a little hurt and angry. I said I was sorry for the café incident. She said she couldn't see that there was anything to be sorry about, and that of course I could do strictly what I liked about other girls. It was a cliché atmosphere of dissatisfaction. She looked at my face as if it disgusted her, and sang to herself in the way people sing when they want to appear untense. I became too solicitous in my attempt at touching her. And even started to chase her psychologically. But she was adamant. I thought she was probably half acting, half serious. I was very interested in the curious perversity of our attitude. The way it is when two things won't fit, and they keep on touching and drawing apart and jamming together with ever more strength. It could easily be made into a definitive break.

But the course of true love, etc . . . Consolations are that I think she suffered as much as I did and probably more, because of the recording machine in me which is prepared to accept pain in order to gain experience and variety of information. I like to think of her crying on her bed. There is a not unpleasant sadism in the situation. A mixture of masochism and sadism – deliberate estrangement, the expectation of reconciliation.

We shook hands coldly and she said, 'Till Monday, then.' That is five days. I'm going away tomorrow, and she on Friday, home. That was an ominous note. I think she was glad of the abstention. She is frightened of the way things are going.

Writing this, it still hurts. A not undelicious unhappiness.

I write too much. It is a kind of self-abuse.

1 February
I saw G at lunch, but not to speak to. She looked extremely serious and
unhappy, and I was pleased to walk out early with Dominique and André.
Our eyes met once. Hers were desperately unconcerned. We did not
smile. Desperately was the right word.

I left lunch early with D and A because we were invited to go to the
château of the Marquis d'Abadie. It is Chercorat, near Magnac-Laval,
about 80–90 kilometres away. We set off in high spirits in D's car, a pre-
war Opal of very imperfect condition. One of the front tyres had a large
hole in it. However, after twenty-five or so kilometres, it was one of the
rear tyres that blew. We were miles from anywhere, and changed it with
an even more dilapidated *roue de secours*. This got us to the nearest garage,
at Lhommaize, where the repairs were done by a German mechanic. He
was still at work at two o'clock, when we had our rendezvous at the
château of d'Abadie. Eventually we set off. *En route*, something flew up
against the windscreen. D said he thought it was broken glass on the
road. We went gaily on. When we got to the château, we found one of
the headlights had fallen off. I started laughing, and had to find an
excuse to cover up my mirth. Finally, coming back, we found the rear
light wasn't working, and stopped at the same garage in Lhommaize.
The mechanic tried to mend it, but all he succeeded in doing was putting
his spanner through the glass and smashing it. *Jour néfaste!*

But the journey there was very fine, through pleasant countryside,
cold but sunny, rather like a crisp, autumn day. The trees all seemed
russet, the sky was Sisley blue, and the distant stretches of plain and
forest seemed pink and Antwerp blue. The tone was Augustan, golden.
The villages were colourful, old, with flat, *méridionel* roofs. Near
Chercorat we passed through pleasant wooded valleys, blue and fresh
in spite of the bare trees. The Marquis received us. His château is a
smallish country house, rather in ruins outside, but well enough kept
up in the interior. We were shown his collections. Thousands of birds,
eggs, fossils, reptiles. They bored me very quickly. The only living thing
there was a pleasant little brindled cocker spaniel bitch. Nothing will
persuade me that, except for the scientist-born, collecting is not a sign
of an inferior and insensitive intelligence. By the engravings and pictures
which he had I could see that he hadn't good taste. A person of good
taste – paradox as this may seem – could not be a collector of living
things. He also showed us his collection of dirty stories. Some six or
seven hundred, neatly indexed, with cross-references. And a pornographic *Mémoires d'une petite comtesse* which he was writing.

He also gave us copies of some of his works. Pamphlets on bird
ornithology, on district legends, and so on. *Au fond*, he is provincial, a
minor man of regional scientific letters.

We took tea with the Marquise. They are both unconventional, and

very similar to the county type in England. We drank tea in an elegant
dining-room, and then, because we looked hungry, she rang for a loaf
and an old jampot of brawn, which we hacked up and munched. She
apparently took a liking for me, because after a quarter of an hour she
asked me to come and stay with them for several days at Easter, and talk
English to her daughters. According to D they are very pretty. I expressed
incredulity and amazement and gratitude. I think it was just a whim. *On
verra.* The Marquis talked openly of his mistress before his wife – *une
petite amie* – but he took André aside to fix a rendezvous with her for
the Saturday. And he gave D a letter to take to her. I think he is not
unpleased that the situation is so well known.

At home. And not without thoughts of G. But already that is less
painful. Strain repaired. At lunch she came to me and asked me how
yesterday was. I felt delightfully the conqueror, although I did not exact
hard conditions. I had intended to be cold to her, but that was impossible. We had coffee together, and our eyes told us we had forgiven each
other. Then we went to the museum. We were the only people there,
and found a little bedroom where we kissed. It was a bedroom exhibiting
period peasant furniture. We kept on kissing and holding hands round
the rooms. The feeling of *bien-être* was wonderful for both us us. A relief.
She had to catch a train home afterwards, but the glow remained. I
painted all day. One bad big painting, which I shall destroy, although
it took four hours. And then a better small one in the evening – one
hour.

4 February
G back. She came to my room before dinner. We were both tired, and
made love in a kind of delicious stupor. I kissed the whole length of
her arms. She is quick to reject my intimacy beyond a certain point, yet
the repulsion is reluctant. Already I feel that we have reached the limits
of the vanity of kisses which can be created without real intimacy. I can't
stop criticizing her entirely. I feel her provinciality from time to time.
Yet when I left her after dinner – we both had work – it was with an
ache at not being able to spend the evening with her. Sometimes I find
it difficult to talk with her. Especially in public. Daylight destroys fantasy.
And as she says, we lack mutual insomnia. We have no base. Even now,
we trace back each stage in the development of our love, as if it was
ancient history.

I wander about giving titles to works – perhaps in many ways, it is more
honest to quite simply number them; as musical opus. I think I shall do
that. By dates, years. 1950 A, B, C. With poetry there is more excuse for
titles. They are an inherent part of the creation. Sometimes.

*

Madness. It started to rain after dinner. I was with G. But I wanted to be with her, and suggested we walked. In pouring rain. I had already a bronchial cold. By the end I was coughing and had a pain in my chest. It was ridiculous to have done it. But I was happy. If I had enough money, I don't know. I might. So many problems would be solved. Walking through the wet streets with her, I feel intensely together, shared and sharing. And yet she says that she never knows whether I am sincere or not. That is my fault. I never know myself even. And now I shall be ill. She showed me an amusing problem:

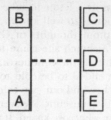

Five houses, on the banks of a river. The only link is by D, a ferry. E is a girl, engaged to A. B loves her, but without being loved in return. C is an old man. D operates the ferry. One day E decides that she must see A at once, for an urgent reason. She goes to D, who is not there, and so passes to C. She asks him his advice. He says that the river is in flood, and dangerous, and so advises her to stay at home. But she finds D and asks him to take her across. He looks at the swollen river, and says, all right, but only on condition that you give me all that you have on you. She agrees. He ferries her across, safely, but leaves her completely naked, without a stitch of clothing. E goes to A's house. But he is not at home. At a loss, she seeks shelter with B. B relishes her, and asks her to sit down with him. He offers her no clothes, but does not touch her. A comes to see B, finds his fiancée naked with another man, and furious, breaks off the engagement.

In what order do you respect these people? Who are the most admirable? The answer is the value of the symbols – A = morality and conventionality; B = sense of adventure; C = reason; D = materialism; E = love. My choice was EBCDA.

It is a test of character in a way. Obviously it needs elaborating.

12 February
With G to a play in the Jesuit college theatre. A matinée, and unremittingly mediocre. Musset's *Caprice* and Anouilh's *Antigone*. It was absolutely without distinction. More interesting were two small boys in front of us, very much in love with one another. They put each other's arms over each other's shoulders, and I saw one of them kiss the other's ear.

Perhaps they were ten, not more. Innocent and fraternal. Then back home with G. We are falling heavily. Now, when we are together, we feel a kind of languour and softness coming over us, a dark sympathy which blots out the rest of world. We say of each other that we are completely 'abruti'. It is more expressive than any English term. It is the resurgence of the animal. Not pejorative. A stupor, coma of closeness, when we both surrender. She said that I had dropped the mask. It is true. My only thought was of each second of being with her, like the period between lying down in bed and going to sleep.

Later we went dancing, at the student centre. All the dances there are in more or less darkness, drowsy, sensual. We danced together all the time, hugged close. I was very tired, and had a headache but, rocking along with her in plastic unison, I felt myself disembodied. Or rather re-embodied. For once, the full conquest of the body.

This is evil, retrograde. The domination of the future by the past. The couples dancing seemed drugged. Kissing, clutched tight. G and I left in a kind of intense mist of love, and wandered through the cold streets, serious, as if we felt ourselves falling literally, and forlorn at the position. Yet always falling further.

If I had any money, I would be thinking of marriage with her. Happily, I have no money.

I collapsed into bed at 2.30 and slept like a log till 1.45. And still feel tired.

I spend all the evening correcting a prose for G. She has to hand it in to Léaud, and wants it to be a good one. It is dishonest and valueless for her. I am indifferent, morally. It is flagrant cheating, but if she wants illegal help from me, she can have it. Tomorrow I shall be going through it with Léaud, and shall have to pretend that I haven't seen it before.

13 February

Curious and amusing incident. I was lunching with G, next to the window. Looking out, I suddenly saw a green and yellow parrot fly around the corner of a wall twenty yards away. I exclaimed, 'Good God, a parrot.' G laughed and refused to believe me. It was one of those terrible situations where one is certain and yet cannot convince. When one is the only witness. And then suddenly a woman came round the corner, carrying the parrot in her hand. I crowed with joy. Someone else sitting at the other end of the table said, 'Oh, didn't you know, they keep a parrot in the kitchen, below.' Il faut croire.

Graham Greene, The Man Within. A fantastically bad book. A pair to E. M. Forster's Where Angels Fear to Tread. Romantic and full of bad writing. Conventionally turbid and turgid. The hero is a cad with a golden heart, the period uneasily historical. So many faults of motivation and style encourage me. The only significant trait is the disgust with the body which still continues. Of shabby priesthood. Otherwise it is astonishingly old-fashioned and novelettish. But at least he got it written. By this age of mine.[1] And I am still a century off being satisfied.

15 February
Behindhand with this. I jot things down in order to expand them at leisure. Comes leisure, and I can't find the jottings; which makes me furious.

Book-marking. I have been marking Greene's *Man Within* and now Faulkner's *Sanctuary*. It is very enjoyable to be able to analyse and dissect, and keep highly responsive. And one learns what the pitfalls and the cunning tricks. G is full of the former, F of the latter. Some people scream against marking a book. That's only because they are incapable of knowing a work of art when they see one. Or because they are afraid to give themselves away by their comments. No one would think of marking an expensive and beautiful edition.

G. Several times lately she has shocked me by her bad taste. I wonder if I could ever meet anyone who didn't shock me that way sooner or later. I don't like it when she speaks in English; her accent is affected, with superfluity of h's and drawled syllables. At other times I feel intensely in love with her. Already we are reaching something of the domestic bliss stage. The first glamour has worn off. The next stage is in bed. She is too virtuous for that, I am frightened of entanglement. I don't believe she is my intended. I like it when she is lying in my arms and I tickle her. She squirms and succumbs and I find myself much stronger than her. That sounds naïf. The emotion is simple. In many ways I wouldn't mind her as a wife; at least she would fulfil all her functions adequately, and leave me time to create, create, create.

17 February
Dominique and the Marquis. He went with him and his mistress to Thouars, to help collect bats for d'Abadie's collection. Afterwards they had a meal in a restaurant there. It appears the M was disgusting. According to D, he took his mistress's leg and put it on the table, and proceeded to fiddle under her skirt, to the horror of the waiter. And the Marquis described how he had been shaving in his bathroom and his daughter had entered and undressed before him preparatory to having a bath; how she was

---

[1] Set in the early 1800s, *The Man Within*, Greene's first novel, told the story of Francis Andrews, who flees a band of smugglers and falls in love with the woman who gives him shelter. It was published in June 1929 when he was twenty-four.

well-made and pretty, and he was embarrassed by her. These stories come
from D, an unreliable source, but they ring true. A corpulent and decadent old man, wasting his life, amoral, hedonist, unhealthy.

Reading a French book on *l'art anglais*, it strikes me that I have learnt
all about France in England, and now vice versa. Objectivity increases
interest and love. I like the sense of isolation in France, of mild exile.

G's bad taste. I am finical about it. But when she talks in English with an
affected accent, it makes me furious. That anything I could love could be
so ugly. She started talking like that as we left the AG tonight. I walked on
in silence and she felt that I was angry. That way she is sensitive. Later we
were alone and she begged and begged me to tell her what it was. After
some not unpleasant hesitation, I told her why. In many ways I am prepared
to experiment with her because I could stand a separation. More and more
I see faults in her. Provincial faults, and I am a snob to see them. But one
can't love where one doesn't respect. She was very subdued about my criticism, and then affectionate. It cleared the air, I suppose. I drank two beers,
and we became warmer. 'In her weaknesses lies her strength.' I suppose
that applies even to faults. At least G has the intelligence of her faults, as
one has the courage of one's conviction. Tonight she did all the chasing,
complimenting me on my new haircut, my pullover, my looks. In the end,
when we walked for a few minutes around the streets before going to our
respective beds, I kissed her a little. I do believe someone is in love with
me. Was, at any rate, for this one evening. I felt objective.

   12.15. Immense, sharp squall. I thought the window was going to
break in, and the house collapse.

21 February
Ginette. Warmer and warmer. Yesterday I slowly started to caress the
skin below her neck, and finally achieved her breasts. Her face was
intensely serious, but she was more than willing. When we make love
she looks sad and I laugh. Women take it all so desperately earnestly.
But now I have to think. Obviously from here, from her bare breasts, I
can see the last slope. And this is the gate where comes the great decision. If only it didn't entail so many complications. With me it is the
flesh. My spirit is hardly there at all. I feel cynical and immoral about
her, because I don't love her profoundly. All I want is the gratification
of my own body – a main part of that gratitude is of course the mutual
aspect of it. La Rochefoucauld.[1] One gives pleasure for the pleasure of
giving. If I caress her nipples it is because I can join in her sexual

---

[1] In his *Maximes*, François La Rochefoucauld (1613–80) asserted that cases of
apparent virtue or selfless feeling generally hid some selfish motive.

pleasure. It is strange that skin is almost the only thing from which we can derive great tactile enjoyment. I love the soft plasticity of her skin, the unblemished, faintly perfumed quality of it. Soft round depths.

And yet it is not only the body. I feel a sense of relationship, of connectedness with the world, which I can dimly remember from the time of Kaja. I am not deluded. The world is completely indifferent and time rolls on, but none the less the refuge of affection and sympathy is a beautiful myth. All the more poignant because it is a myth. I wrote a poem the other day explaining how for one moment I refused to believe that the myth was not reality. For a vague moment I almost did deceive myself.

How ridiculously arbitrary time is. When I think of half an hour with her and half an hour waiting for a train. What nonsense to think that the half an hour is any link at all. Time is an obscure example of man's innate puritanism. The more complicated and inhibited he becomes, the more time-conscious.

26 February

A terrible day. G came to me for all the afternoon. I did a very bad aquarelle of her. Of course we kissed and made love. Later I undressed her to the waist. Her breasts are large and firm. She kept on groaning – *Je t'en prie'*, *'laisse-moi'*, *'pas plus'* – but at the same time clung and beseeched. A warm, strong body. I became very excited. It is a kind of sensual indulgence which we are both unable to resist. Somehow I am never fully identified with it. I keep on standing back, and seeing her extended body and her closed eyes, and thinking of her only as an instrument, not as another human being. When she tries to tell me how serious it all is for her, I feel that she is lying, because of my own feelings. But also I begin to feel a sense of guilt. That I am making her jump in where I can swim and where she will be drowned. The heavy somnolent solemnity of her eyes and visage, watching mine between kisses.

The terrible part of the day was afterwards, when we went to the AG for dinner. I found that I was in great pain, the pit of the stomach. I had promised to go with G to the weekly dance. But I felt very ill. I went home alone and lay on my bed, my knees drawn up – that way I got some relief – and smoked. And reflected. I don't know what the trouble is. Perhaps too much caressing and too little real satisfaction. Or stomach trouble, dysentery, appendicitis. I don't know. It doesn't much matter. All that struck me was the speed with which my happiness was knocked out of my hand. A kind of ironically divine coincidence. For some time now I have been aware of pain in my genitals. I know it is because G and I are too intimate, yet not intimate to the point of satisfaction. I know I am a hypochondriac, yet it seems to me that the pain is incontrovertible. I seemed destined to waste my time and suffer. And I hate all this self-pitying.

I went to meet G, later, at 10. Dominique was with her. I refused to go and dance. So we all three went and sat in a café, and were miserable. G and I morose and silent. I not in pain, but uncomfortable – D insisted on talking and reminiscing. Silence frightens him. Then sadly we went home. I to write this.

Now I think appendicitis. So I write. One never knows. It might be the last. That doesn't worry me. Death is quite immaterial, and it is at least absolute in all this damned jungle of relativity and isolated phenomena.

At least one gets an enhanced view of the value of each episode. Convinced of relativity, things become more separate, more distinct. And now, with the pain stirring dully away inside me, I feel almost crushed that I can remember her standing in the middle of this same room, her underclothes around her waist, and her breasts stretched taut. A kind of erotic relief from the present; a certainty to put against all the vague threats of the immediate and distant future. She has given me that, for which I am sincerely grateful. The hell of it is that I must repay her true love by insincerity. And yet sometimes I wonder. I feel closer to her than to anyone else I have *ever* known. Even Kaja.

Until tomorrow, silence here.

Tomorrow. How exaggerated all that seems. I still feel ill, but in a dull, disengaged sort of way. In a kind of interregnum, yearning and not unhappy at being unhappy. But yesterday did seem terrible at that time. Because of the excessive physical indulgence, a kind of bright red flower on the grey deceptive stem of my last year or two's celibate life; and because of the simultaneous pain, and all the misty phantasmagorias which follow it like vultures. Mainly it is a purely physiological concern about my sexual condition, combined with the impossibility of really testing it. For, in spite of all, I cannot be immoral. Yet. My morality is inherited. It takes some time to know really one's inherited characteristics. Once known, they are conquered. They may still exist, but they can always be executed. To know oneself is to pass judgement on one's ancestors.

28 February

G and I have coffee sometimes with Marie-Thérèse Cochard, a slim little slip of a girl, fresh-faced, with a bad scar on her forehead, and rather mischievous, very faintly neurotic eyes. Like all very small and pretty women, fragile and doll-like; she is sharp and intelligent, with a rather fine, resonant voice, and nervous hands.

We sat in a café and giggled and discussed seriously for a long time.

They wouldn't believe me when I said that platonic love was only a kind of foreplay, titillation, a playing with fire. I wonder how many true platonic love affairs there have been; where neither side has wished more intimacy, had erotic daydreams, been at times miserable at the discord of mind without body. Platonic love is like the moment before sitting down to a good meal, the mingling of hunger and expectation. But it can't exist there always. Some time starvation sets in, and the food gets cold. G liked this simile. She is always using the word *astuce*; sentimental and sexual ambiguities please her.

Then they agreed with me that some foreigners can be nearer to one than one's own countrymen or women. The obvious example for me is Ginette. Even though there is the language trouble, that is nothing besides the general communication problem. With G I feel the same, I can say almost anything I like; and know that I shall be understood in the deeper sense, once the words have been comprehended. There is always that tradition in the French, the delight in minute analysis of the sentiments, in speaking of oneself, and speaking in the frankest, but not the loudest, terms. With so many Englishwomen I feel out of touch. Constance Farrer is practically the only one with whom I felt at home, and she was curiously enough almost inarticulate, a brooding rather than an active sympathy.

I went back with G, after we had taken M-T home, to another café, and we went on talking, of ourselves. She said that I was always attempting to isolate myself. That even when she felt intimate with me, there was something which escaped. I suppose she senses my cruel objectivity to all experience, even though I try and conceal it from her. She said that with some people one felt immediately that they bared their souls. But to me that only means that they do not usually know themselves. I don't 'give' myself because I am so bewildered at my own complexity, at all the depths I know exist yet have not sounded. That sounds immodest. But all I want to say is that my self-analytical apparatus (perhaps over-encouraged by this diary) is sufficiently perceptive for me to be aware of my own vast and labyrinthine personality. I can't explain it, and I have a hate and fear of anyone else trying to do so. All my life I shall resist outside interference, simply because of my own uncertainty. It is a paradoxical attitude, a proud humility. Perhaps self-knowledge is the only infinite, and its non-achievement the only absolute. It seems to worry and fascinate G, as if I was always hiding myself from her. But I hate moral undressing. It is much more fundamentally embarrassing than the physical taking off of clothes. None the less, even to explain all this to G was a kind of revelation, a stripping off. It is in such revelations that intelligent people enjoy their intellectual life most; and intelligent people are where you find them. Intelligence and sympathy are the most cosmopolitan of qualities, and cosmopolitanism one of the great stairs to an upper storey of humanity. Brotherhood of the mind and spirit, and damn the racial blood.

So we talked, softly buried in ourselves. Skirted marriage. I said I would never be unfaithful without telling my wife first. A dangerous remark, when the recipient might possibly become that unlucky person. I am beginning to feel a real need and tenderness for G. Sometimes I see her in flashes of ugliness, squat and Jewish-looking, with her rather vulgar vehemence and affectations in speaking with others (but never with me), and her meridional accent. At other times she seems melting with a sweet romantic softness, soul sympathetic and body desirable. And I am not sure that all really beautiful things have not that variable nature, in a sense reflecting one's own self.

A happy evening, made vaguely, dully poignant for me by a slight but constant ache in my prostate. There is a cog loose in the sexual machinery. Damn the body.

1 March
An ice-cold day of brilliant sunshine, clear as glass, a mountain day; and the town teeming with people, cars parked everywhere, country-people in their dark suits, Sunday best; all because it is *la foire de la mi-carême*.[1] Faintly I resented this intrusion into *my* town of all these people, all this movement, and talking, jostling crowds down each street, the cafés full. Also it was like a summer day, except for the heat. And I hate summer. For me it means hay fever and dysentery and discomfort, listlessness, a continual battle with the body. The winter is my season. I like the world to be dark after dinner. And G today kept on saying: 'How lovely it is, how summer-like; how I love summer.' For the first times the cafés had outside tables. And I felt a vague stirring, resentment in my heart and stomach.

2 March
G. This weekend she spends at home. I miss her. There is an ache, a grey prospect. Curiously at 10 to 6 – her train was at 6 – I looked out of the window, and there far below, to the left, she was crossing the rainy station-yard. I can only see a small part of it, and it seemed to me a more than coincidence that I should go to the window at the beginning of just the right ten seconds. She passed out of sight, and I felt sad. And happy to have someone to be sad about.

5 March
Style. One of my great faults is my changing style. Revising the Andorran story, I can sense the constant changes, a series of pastiches. I have tried

---

[1] The Mid-Lent Fair.

to level it out. Even so, the shadows of DHL and James flit through the background. Now, Faulkner also. But I am beginning to wonder whether it is such a fault, whether a ubiquitous style is necessarily good. In a series of incidents, it is not always the same style that presents them best. Each event has its unique style, its best presentation. I don't see what is wrong with writing in a variety of different styles. Some things are best treated by Joyce, others by Greene. To each sequence his own expression. I feel this more strongly in art. Particularly over a painting I have just done. A desert landscape, low foothills, a distant, vague city. Vast clouds looming diagonally. All that more or less realistically. Then in the foreground two cubist figures, in black and white and carmine, posturing. I can't see any dissonance. The picture has faults, but not on the count of homogeneity.

G. She has been away for three days. She came to my room. We lay on the bed, kissed. Were happy. Went to dinner. Then suddenly she became silent, sulky, completely withdrawn. I tried to draw her out, without success. I thought, and said so, that she was acting to herself; that she had had a movement of sadness, and allowed it to run all through her, with a not uncommon masochism. I explained it by saying that she had stumbled, and then let herself fall. She replied, 'I never act to myself.' But everyone does, though perhaps not to the extent I do. I was sure she was acting. But suddenly she produced a tear. And her eyes were red. Acting to that point made me change my mind. I believed her and even felt embarrassed by such an intensity. She would not tell me why all this mute suffering happened, except that she had felt terrifyingly alone. Alone for ever. This seemed to me self-dramatization, still does. But there is the evidence of the tears. We walked to her home, and she wanted, or pretended to want, to leave me. But I persuaded her to come with me, to walk. It was a sharp, moonless, brilliantly clear night. We went down to the bombed quarter of Poitiers, walked in the ruins, stood beside the train-tracks. There's romance in night trains, I said. Walked along the river. Saw a rat run along the road in front of us. Stopped on a wide bridge and looked at the stars, and the dark, silent water. The town seemed deserted. The night crisp, scintillating, almost laughing at the dull world below. As if all the sky was mysteriously alive. I pointed out Orion, the Dragon, the Dog. And Orion's sword, although I said that it was his penis.

And she said, 'Who thought of that?'

'The ancients.'

'The ancient English,' she answered.

Nearer than she knew, because I had only just noticed it, and invented the ancestry. But I can't be the first to have noticed it. It's much more likely than the sword. We crossed back over a footbridge into the town, stood there silently a long time, her head buried in my overcoat, close, mute. A kind of gentle unassailable dumbness. There was a grey trail of mist, and tall black poplars. We were lost in a sort of unison, deep, satisfying, yet poignant. Always the current of time, the passing. Walked on. Hung together again against a fence, in shadow, lost, touching. In all ways except our own, ridiculous. Two people embracing on a cold night in a deserted sidestreet. Yet you go into sanctuary where you find it.

10 March

Redwings. A still, warm night, low cloud. A curiously eerie sound, that thin shimmering whistle. Everywhere I go I seem to hear it. Tonight I was almost frightened by it, as if it was something supernatural, demonic, stalking me. At night it is the awareness of another universe, birds flying in the darkness, invisible. With redwings it is above all the cry, so thin and forlorn and remote, unattached. The cry is more important than the bird. In fact the bird ceases to exist. A stream of faint whistles. There seemed to be a good many this time. I think some were resting on the house-tops. No northerly movement perceptible. Two reasons for night flying: safer – no hawks, men; and town lights? I don't see why birds shouldn't have a memory like human beings.

11 March

Several days' depression. Futility of this year here. Virtually I have written nothing, and I am going stale. The old amoebic colitis trouble is coming back: liver pains, terrible constipation, prostate trouble, blushing, psychological malaise – the mind is tragically dependent on the body, for better and for worse. I seem to get all the worse. I should be looking for a job, for next year. But I haven't done anything about it. I want to swim, yet I stand shivering on the edge. Everyone in the university here goes away for Easter, but I can't afford it. And when people say, 'I don't know how you can stay at Poitiers all the time,' I am not anxious to say, 'But I can't afford to go away.' I'm not really embarrassed about poverty. But I find it difficult to live on thirty thousand a month here. Especially as my landlords ridiculously overcharge me. My bill averages 5,000 fr. a month. That, for a small room and no running water, is much above the normal price – about 2,000. They (the Malaperts) are smug, crepuscular people whom I dislike and despise. They feel it, perhaps. I am the cow to be milked dry. Madame has been ill, but I refused to buy her flowers. God damn the Malaperts in all the Poitiers. And I drift from day to day, doing nothing. Painting stupid little pictures, making love to G, doing the minimum preparation for my university work, and unable to write. I have half a dozen things half finished. I reread them, and feel depressed. They are all invariably mediocre.

And I can't still accept the terrible fact that I am only a mediocre

person. Yet I know it. And daren't acknowledge it. For several days I
have had an absolute certainty about that. I have no will, no burning
necessity to write. After a few pages I get tired, bored with myself. And
there is the split between painting and writing. I spend hours fiddling
with water-colours when I ought to be writing.

I don't know. I'm wasting my life. No money, no ambition.

13 March

G. More and more we are together. Now we have ceased to tease each
other, except very softly. Alone, there comes an immediate warmth, an
'*euphorie*'. And more and more I feel lost without her, because our affection is the only thing in which I can any longer believe. Even in myself
I have no longer faith. Only in this liaison established is there reason.
Physically I criticize her. That way I cannot blind myself. She is warm,
nubile; but not beautiful. And I see her growing old quickly, fat, with
the Jewish, Mediterranean strain coming out in her. I see her in all sorts
of conditions – whenever they entail 'chic', she disappoints me. She has
all the D. H. Lawrence qualities, heart and soul and heat, humanity,
intelligence and simplicity when it is needed, the qualities of peasant
stock, but no aristocratic traits. And aesthetically I need a little aristocracy, a little carriage, fine-bred beauty. Socially it would hurt me to marry
a peasant, but at least I would be ashamed of being hurt. (Theoretically
I damn all class differences. There are only three classes: the sages, both
wise and intelligent, sincere, and simple and cultured; the intelligentsia,
intelligent and cultured; and the non-intelligentsia, stupid and simple
(even though vicious) and uncultivated. A question of heredity and
opportunity. That there can be any class distinction other than by intelligence seems to me a fundamental fault in any civilization. Plato's is
the only Utopia.) I think it would do me good to marry G just for this
one reason. That I should then limit myself, and achieve a certain
humility which is lacking at the moment. Shed some of my aristocratic
dream-projections. For example, I have day-dreamed of seducing
Princess Margaret. I suppose many men must have done that. For unattached men she must be an obvious evasion out of solitary reality. That
is an extreme example of the tendency. To imagine a future in the most
aristocratic (aesthetically and socially and artistically) of worlds. In G I
would have a certain platform, a ledge reached. From there I could start
new explorations.

All this gives me melancholy. My poverty puts her right out of reach,
for a year at any rate. And I can't face an engagement. A long, protracted
cooling off, hundreds of miles apart. And I am afraid of not being
certain. That G is really the one and only. And she also virtually the
first. But now I feel that my life is a running the wrong way against the
nap, and that with G all would be magically smooth. No. But what I

feel, intuitively, irrationally – it is wanting to live with someone, to share myself. I am getting too heavy to support my own weight. Education, in the broadest sense. The vast multiple universe drawing out the individual as he grows up becomes a succubus. One of the reasons people marry at the first quarter-century is that in that span they begin to feel the crushing multiplicity of the world's reflection in themselves, and they feel they have to shed it. They can't face the world any longer alone. A little, I feel that, now. And G, with her sympathy and warmth, is an oasis. That she is French means nothing. I am an artist, and owe more to and respect France as much as my own country. We understand each other deeply in any case. And there is the intrigue. The other day we talked of sleeping together. I admitted I wanted her. But she refused to give. '*Pour moi c'est une chose si serieuse. Je ne le pourrais pas.*' And I felt almost relieved, although I want her. We caress too much. But there are so many complications, and I admire her virtue. Because it is not conventionality. We discuss everything. But a respect for the sentiment of love, which is essential in the good human. For love and libertinism are not the most profound solutions. To oppose them is not purely sentimental. I say that, knowing I have not the will myself to resist being a libertine, if opportunity arose. I would sleep with G tomorrow if she offered herself. But I admire her refusal more than I could have welcomed her acceptance. Nor is it a question of marriage. Marriage is only a legal convenience. As metaphysical religion, with strict religious sense, it is nonsense; as ridiculous as baptism or confirmation. But there is a truth in the religious symbolism. Do not commit adultery, the closed circle. Once again a willed and voluntary respect for the sentiment of love. There are two ways of finding love; by making experiments, having the maximum amount of affaires and finally settling on the most piquant and promising. But any such liaison risks a new transformation. An experimental attitude to love. The other way is to refuse to give until the day when one gives absolutely. Then one gives not only the gift, but all the previous abstentions. In a way it is much more daring than being immoral. Immorality no longer has a panache, and this is putting all one's eggs in one basket.

This respect for the sentiment of love is entirely lacking in many people. It is modern, slick, almost normal, to sleep together when the affaire is where G and I are. Hundreds of girls are picked up each night in dance-halls and copulated with afterwards. But it is copulation, animal, a function, uninhibited but weak-willed. To abstain is inhibited, but willed, in our case. Much more will than inhibition. The respect for an animal sentiment is a form of self-control. If any attack is to be successfully launched on cynicism (which in our absurd and purely relative worlds is the natural, spontaneous and therefore, in 1951, prevalent reaction), it must be from the truth of this respect for love. A belief that out of love can come more than pure physical enjoyment. But the only real –

though poignantly temporary – sanctuary. The one true hope.

All this is *ex cathedra*. For me, personally, artificial. I haven't the moralist's backbone. But I can try and push the practice some way toward the preaching.

An old man, walking painfully, hobbling, on two sticks, with a stained, drooping white walrus moustache, a frayed black coat. A very old, decrepit man, crossing the rain-wet road outside the Café de la Paix. And we inside, two, young, rubbing our thighs in secret, side by side – drinking our after-lunch coffee.

16 March
G. We separated today for a fortnight. It will be a sort of test. Lately I have been in one long fit of depression, rolling below the waves like a porpoise, poking up occasionally in gay and comic anti-climactical moods, but most of the time sick. She pulled me out of it, gave me something to believe in. Increasingly I have been pouring myself out to her, a rather self-dramatized representation, but in the main sincere. The incredible relief of a confession. I have tried to explain my solitude, the abysm between myself and my parents.

The University restaurant closes today. There was a notice: 'Student tickets not accepted anywhere else.' For me that means a serious financial problem, as I shall have to buy cheap meals elsewhere. I certainly shan't be able to go away. I have only 10,000 francs until next payday, and at the very cheapest, 5,000 of that will be lost on meals. Economy, economy.

Last night I wrote a little story about the Café de la Comédie. Very short and bare. I shall make it Opus 1, purely in order to keep a track on things.

17 March
A Saturday. Terrible sense of loneliness, mainly by anticipation. I ate a supper of two hard-boiled eggs, 50 grams of paté, and a hunk of bread (69 francs in all) and a cup of cocoa. I have nowhere to go in the town. A dreadful thirst for company. Yet often when I am with people, I wish I could be alone. And I can't settle down to work, to write.

The concept of humidity in tragedy. It is almost in the nature of tragedy to be damp, vegetal, lush, morbid, brooding. That's what the Greeks have uniquely. A parched, sun-dried tragedy, without water, where the only liquid, the only mobile element, is blood.

T. S. Eliot. How infuriatingly irrefutable all his opinions are. He is a

kind of touchstone for all creation. He is, in style, the logical conclusion to Flaubert and Mallarmé. But yet he has never dared to step off
his own pinnacle on to that of the great men of genius. He has never
given his heart. In literature he will always be the cold phenomenon of
stone. Perhaps a kind of Malherbe for the failure.[1]

21 March
After lunch today, the grey clouds disappeared, and the sun came out
in a bright blue sky. To the east – there was a faint easterly breeze –
appeared gigantic cirrus formations, very high and mysterious, like
rippling towers, or a many-fingered hand groping across a whole half
of the sky. The day was fresh, but the sun very warm; a delicious combination. So I went for a walk. To rediscover the country. Along the valley
of the Boivre to the *grottes de la Norée*. It is a quiet, but not uninhabited,
little combe. Today it was all green and sparkling with water, because
the Boivre was in flood and had spilled over the meadows. The road
was along the bottom of the valley, which is criss-crossed with alders and
poplars.

I started at three, and by five, when I was home, exhausted after five
miles' walking, the clouds had spread intermittently in long streaks all
over the sky. A vast, classical, washed appearance. I met women and children with branches of violets, cowslips, celandines. Along the river
clumps of kingcups. Celandines are a perfect example of nature being
artistic rather than natural. They burst open with a kind of minor *joie
de vivre. Soleils d'or*. The perfect marginal emblem for the pattern of
spring. Simplicity and *bon goût*.

I felt vividly aware of everything, full of sympathy, happy. To be artist
and naturalist is the perfect blend. The one supplies the deficiencies of
the other, and together they augment the pleasure.

It was really nature's day. But an old peasant-woman with a huge sack,
bending, tearing up the spring grass with her hands, and stuffing it
inside. It reminded me of the pathetic sight of people in tiny suburban
gardens cutting their little patches of lawn with scissors. One gets a sense
of poverty in passing French houses which is unknown in England, and
they still do work which seems the work of the extreme poor. There is
still a kind of *ancien régime* hovel-and-scrape atmosphere about the
average French country village. Almost a feudal serfdom. None of the
sturdy, honest, cleanliness of the English, with the puritan self-respect
and prosperous illusion of independence. A more charming aspect of
the villages here is their Roman past – the flat meridional roofs, and

---

[1] François de Malherbe (1555–1628) became official poet to Henry IV, remaining
in favour under Louis XIII and Cardinal Richelieu. He gained a reputation as
a purist who preferred the intellect to the emotions.

the sienna and ochre semicircular tiles. These roofs have a kind of ruddy, massive heat inherent in them. A faint tinge of the Orient, which strikes a faintly exotic contrast in the fresh green countryside, more Norman or English than Mediterranean.

For me those two hours in the country were a kind of escape from exile. I was born in a town, have lived most of my life in towns, yet. Just yet. The strange thing is that I don't have to get out of the towns very often. Just once in a while I feel bottled up, and I explode out into the country. And then I always realize that I am returning home, because I am among living things that I know. When I hear a blackcap in the vallée de la Boivre,[1] it is the same blackcap that I heard one morning nine or ten years ago, in a holly-bush, when I was riding, near Marldon in South Devon. All the times I have ever heard blackcaps are like the times I have ever met one friend. And so for all species of all living things, except humans. Where we can distinguish individuality, we are more generally alone among strangers, although more particularly happy when among friends. For me a walk in the country is a walk among old friends.

That seems sentimental. Naïf, pastoral. An eighteenth-century pantheism. But I feel it very strongly, and very strongly that it is one of the sentiments which is not false, in any age. Nor is it irrelevant.

Food. I eat at the Chandron d'Or, a little restaurant in a sidestreet here. For 150 francs one eats quite well; if I have a *'demie de blanc'* I think I am eating well.

22 March

How alone I feel, once again. In this town I know no one. A few people to say *'Bon jour'* to, and to pass on. There is no one here I can go out to meet. No one to invite me to their homes. All I have found here is Ginette. The trouble is my coldness. All the preliminary stages of friendship bore me. Unless I can get close to people I am lost; frozen and bored. I hate it when I have to think of something to say, to be amusing, to smile. The only person with whom I know how to be insincere is myself. And then I bore people by my own account. *Tant pis.* Poitiers is a town full of the living dead, in any case.

Writing the 'Unit One' play till two in the morning. About 7,000 words today – the whole of a first draft of Act II. Exhausted. The idea came on the 15th – I have not wasted time, for once. Full of ideas, I'm full, for it. But I have learned not to be too happy too soon. A two-act

---

[1] A river valley to the south of Poitiers.

play. Now complete. Now for a related prologue which I have sketched out.

Easter Sunday, 25 March

A cold, windy day. I cycled out to Ligugé, to hear Vespers in the ancient church.[1] A very big congregation, a mixture of sightseers and villagers. I like the rather casual atmosphere of all Catholic services; the way people talk and not to each other, and watch – rather than take part in – the proceedings. They are less submissive than a Protestant congregation.

As it was Easter, the monks came in procession from the monastery. A white brother with the mitre, two other brothers, the abbot, enormous and full of a pompous dignity – very impressive – with two monks holding his train, the officiants in gold and white, and the train of black fathers. Many of them were very tall. As they passed slowly by, they gave a strange impression of mystery and power. Many of them have cultivated expressions; the expression of a man of the world *d'un certain âge.* Yet the tonsure and habit reduces them all to the same age, the same purpose. One of them especially, a tall, stout man of sixty, had exactly the appearance of a rich businessman, or a general. The service was long, full of their complicated ritual and plain chant. The abbot had a strange throttled voice, as if he was singing from the bottom of a great bottle up into the narrow, remote neck of his pursed mouth.

They filed out in all their full ceremonial robes, the abbot in his mitre, holding his crosier, stopping and blessing people, most of all children, and giving his ring to be kissed. A very magnificent figure with a heavy jowl and eyes of great weight, iron-grey. The very image of the power temporal and celestial personified in one person. It's not often that I have the sensation of being completely crushed by another personality.

31 March

My twenty-fifth birthday. I meant to write a lot here. But the OUDS[2] have arrived from Oxford, a lot of fuss, and I haven't had time to do anything. These special days lose their specialness if one is alone. It needs two to create a myth, even that of the quarter-century.

This last month I have started to write a new form of poetry. Very sparse, taut, old words, phrases, precise, correct, with occasional very small bursts of rhyme and music. Mallarmé was right about the vast importance of spacing, the salience. Economy and salience. Now I must find a suitable

---

[1] Ligugé is a small town eight kilometres south of Poitiers. Its sixteenth-century parish church is part of the Abbey of St Martin, which was founded in 361.
[2] i.e. the Oxford University Drama Society.

prose style. Voltaire, Swift. In painting I am going the same way, against prolixity, gamuts of colour. All this is a weeding-out of the inherent sentiment, the fat, the padding, in me.

1 April

G. How soon I can forget her. In a fortnight I can almost forget to need her. I feel very little excitement at her coming back. I like the being unattached, solitary, unhappy but ambitious. I don't believe I could be capable of marital fidelity with G. Today I met a very pretty girl, the daughter of one of the biggest bank managers here. Curiously enough she has made me think a lot of G, and always unfavourably. She sent me a birthday card on the 31st – kind of her. But what a terrible card. Silly without being silly enough to be amusing. Yet if she had the looks of the banker's daughter, I believe I could forgive her anything. Beauty covets *beaucoup*. At the most cynical, a reserve tank.

The OUDS. I had to take some of them out to lunch. How they bored me – the bright young things of Oxford. Still bright, still young. An odious little grammar-school boy, David Thomson, posturing, bespectacled, puky. In describing a production he used the word 'Helpmann-esque' three times, tilting back on his chair, and glancing sideways to see if it had registered. A tall, fat girl, inclined to wobble with laughter, full of slang, actor's shop. A Jew, young and strong and smooth. Out of environments I have quitted. They seemed appreciably behind. Tony Richardson, the producer here, is tall and nervous and excitable, rather like an overgrown child in many ways. Not artificial. A weak mouth and face, but intelligent, attractive eyes.[1] Simon Lee, a slim, energetic, but rather feather-brained *régisseur.* I like him. Rather quick-silvery, temperamental, changeable, naïf and childish, enthusiastic. He seems to know a lot of people. Talks all the time. Somehow I don't altogether trust him. Engaging, not viciously dishonest, but untrustworthy by lack of concentration.

The electrician's mate is a scruffy young man, always dirty and badly dressed. Exceedingly uncouth, always talking electricity and lighting technique. A mouth with prominent teeth and lips, like a rabbit's. I was rather surprised to learn that he was Lord Roseberry's second son. Viscount Primrose. He has an expensive new car here, in which he transported all the electrical gear from England. But anybody so outrageously reacted from his rank would be difficult to imagine.

I went with them to another theatre – in the Jesuit college – to try

---

[1] Tony Richardson (1928–1991), then in his last year as President of OUDS, would recall the tour in his memoirs: 'In the provinces we played huge theatres where I made an introductory speech in French so extravagant and hyperbolic – *"Nos coeurs toq-toquent ensemble"* – that everyone thought I was drunk.'

and find a dimmer for their lights. We arrived in the middle of a Passion
Play. While we were arguing backstage, Jesus Christ came off and was
presented as such. We were busy arguing and only nodded at him,
whence some divine disfavour. He went off in his wig and his nightgown
in a huff.

Afterwards, made chase after the dimmer, trying to find the director
of the theatre at Poitiers. I went to about twelve different addresses and
at length ran him to ground in the Garde du Commerce. No dimmer.
But his name, Brémont, and the French for dimmer, *la rhéostat*, are
surely graven for eternity on my heart.

3 April

Windfall. After being confined to Poitiers for financial reasons during
the holidays, I found that my pay-check today had jumped 7,000. And
later, that I was owed a retrospective 28,000 for the last few months.
What jubilance a little money gives. I immediately bought the *Poésies
complètes* of Valéry.

Also I went to see about my future (as if the future was a thing to go
and see about). As always, my saleability is reduced to nothing after a
few practical questions. All I have is good French. But at this bureau at
least, the man, Marion, was pleasant and sympathetic. Not like the efficient and impatient John Tanner of Oxford. You can't kick people about
like a football. Marion promised to introduce me to a *grand commerçant
de vins*. I now see myself agent for a cognac firm. I wouldn't mind that.
OUDS still here. The things they want. A living parrot, two pairs of
midwife's forceps, a wicker fruit-basket. In many ways I enjoy seeing them
for this short time. It is a kind of re-entry into the idiom of another existence. Continually saying the unusual and the outrageous. Among the
non-Oxfordians that seems affected. With them one 'knows the form'.

The OUDS play Webster's *Duchess of Malfi* in the medieval Palais de
Justice. Very spectacular – the robes against the stone, the darkness of
movement. An obscure, morbid play. Some of it is melodrama, but the
language is always more elevated. The production was rather precocious,
ebullient, almost too clever. But it is much better than the normal professional touring company in France. I thought that Ferdinand, Hugh
Rickson, and the Cardinal, Nigel Davenport, were the most accomplished.

6 April

G. A curious effect of the Oxford visit has been to put her in perspective. All her provincialisms. Now I dislike her for the very things which
pleased me – lack of elegance, the black humour of the meridional,
Provençal accent. What irritates me is her constant petty jealousy about
other girls. Allusions to them, and the most acrid criticism when she

thinks I don't mind. She wants us to be boxed away from the rest of the world. The me-or-them attitude. I can't stand that, and her lack of urbanity. Physically she begins to disinterest me. Rather, I feel cloyed, stifled. And she dresses badly.

We spent the whole of one evening walking about the backstreets arguing. I was bored and cold and in the end started alternately soothing and provoking her. Her attitude was one of anger at having to follow me. 'If you think you can leave me (i.e., for a day when the OUDS were here) and then have me follow you again just when *you* want' . . . and so on, ad infinitum, ludicrously. It seemed to me all such a waste of time, childish, nagging and bickering about nothings.

Part of the secret of sympathy is to know when to drop the mask. We both wear a mask of irony, and we never let it fall at the same time. The art of timing is essential in marriage. To know when to undress, morally and physically. It is an art G lacks altogether. She expects to be chased in her black moods, all the way. If only she could get the idea of so far, but not all the way. One reaches a point where the chase ceases to be worthwhile. And where cajoling won't get the gun off its rack.

12 April
Feeling of guilt at my work here. To one of the lectures I am meant to give this term, no one came. I have only a handful of people at the conversation groups. In spite of my cynicism I feel ostracized, slighted. It annoyed me that Léaud had to advertise my lectures as his own. I am much too ego-centred to be a good educator.

15 April
A tour of some Loire châteaux. A lovely spring day, warm and fresh at the same time, without clouds. The charabanc was full of foreign students, mostly English girls, Americans. G came with me. The English girls sang almost without stop from the moment we left to the moment we came home.

I don't like tourism. My appetite for beauty is like that for food; it soon gets blunted. Perhaps that is why I can't do sustained creative work. Also the blunted appetite acts as a splendid selection committee. By the time we got to Azay, only the very best was good enough to make me look twice. In that I find an argument for creating against my disinclination, but I am not sure that the analogy is constant.

That night a cavalcade. All the town *en gala*. A procession of many bands, normally of boys and appallingly bad, with various tableaux, mummers. Poor in quality, but rich in spirit. Poitiers is so bare of entertainment that people are almost pathetically willing to laugh and clap at the most amateurish of antics.

Later with G, on one of our nocturnal walks. We dived down a dark deserted alley, and started to caress and clutch. The other day she let me caress all of her legs and eventually all of her. She kept on repeating, 'Tu n'as pas le droit,' but she was unable to resist. In the dark alley I lifted her skirt and started to caress her again. That is something animal, a reversion, which I can't prevent. A complete contrast from my normal life, all my education, from being a gentleman or an Englishman. Later, in the bright moonlight, leaning on a wall beside the river, we talked for an hour or more about ourselves, skirting marriage. We have come to the crossroads. Either we drift apart or we sleep together. Spring and the full moon and our bodies torture us. A nightingale sun in the distance. I would sleep with her if she gave me the chance. But I don't want to forge a bond which would be unbreakable. Sleeping together is bound to create fears, obligations. About a wife I am ambitious. And yet sometimes G seems perfect. A bed-partner and a comrade and French, and with whom I can discuss anything. I think that if I had the money I should marry her, and dispense with my ambitions. For they are only temporal, of the flesh, and at some point I must settle on those of immortality.

2 May
G. Things are getting impossible. We alternate between fits of intimate tenderness and physical desire, and periods of tension, disgust and bad temper. All yesterday we were together, happy, warm. She had tea with me, we lay on the bed together, read some of my Disjoints from Collioure.[1] Afterwards we went to the cinema, to see an Ophüls film. We walked home in the pouring rain. The drops spattering on the umbrella, her arm on mine, close, warm. A day with a kind of soft glow.

Then at lunch, she suddenly got up and left, and afterwards she wasn't in either of the usual cafés.

This time it was all my fault. At table I spoke all the time with Philip, and suddenly she stood up and left. I'd been brusque, and she'd asked about my morning, and I didn't ask about hers. And then I gave a book I'd promised her to another person. For me one of the proofs of intimacy is that you can be silent, that you can seem to be elsewhere, talking with other people, but the fact that you are side by side is enough, and *you* know that everything else is exterior.

I was wrong about the book. I ought to have followed her quickly out, but I was slow to react. Or rather slow to analyse my own guilt.

Then there is the French. It is so difficult being delicate, when each phrase has to be planned, constructed.

---

[1] Collioure was a coastal town in the south-west of France that JF visited in the summer of 1948 (see introduction, page xiii), and 'Disjoints' the word he used to describe his diaries.

It makes me feel miserable. There is a sort of joy in it, though. A dryness.

I am an egoist. She says I only love her, caress her, for my own pleasure. That is almost true. I feel no external devotion. Yet I don't know if this La Rochefoucauld cynicism is real or relative.[1] Do other people analyse themselves like me, harshly?

Even the harshness of my cynicism and self-nihilism is a sort of affectation.

Always my aesthetic sense troubles me. It intrudes and dominates all departments of my thought, my dreams, my actions. G isn't beautiful enough. I am worth more than that. She doesn't like music. Has little knowledge of art. Doesn't dress well. Is temperamental, assertive (She says *'Ce qu'il te faut, c'est une caniche.'* That's true. Because I've been so unloved, I want to be truly loved, even my faults). She refuses to accept the inferior role of woman. She argues the toss. The wise woman doesn't give a damn about the toss. She knows it doesn't really matter.

But she's pleasant, solid, warm, affectionate, stable; vulgarity almost becomes a virtue in her. She'd be a pillar.

But can I accept the chains? There is also the question of cutting one's losses. But I can afford to wait.

Even if I wanted to, I have no money, no position, no hope except nebulous.

What she hates is the way I change from private hot to public cold. For me the public is something to guard against. When I find privacy, I treat it as such and do what I like. She never believed Englishmen could be so warm in their caresses. To her it must seem like a kind of dishonesty, this duality. A hypocrisy.

But for me it is more natural to be cold in public than warm in private. That is the fault of my temperament and upbringing.

Added to that, I have an artificial sense of time. Everything seems relative to me. I can be warm with her one day, and cold the next, because that is in the true nature of the occasions. They seem to me unrelated, no proof or guarantee of anything past and present *in themselves*. I am not so concerned with the general tendencies. I tend to live second by second, or buried in the past.

I know I can't expect other people not to be hurt or disconcerted. Some days I speak to people, others I walk past them without looking at them. I can't understand why, myself, except that it seems more natural and more sincere. Perhaps it's more lazy. Too lazy to make the pretence.

I'm not prepared *invariably* to oil the ball-bearings. There isn't much

---

[1] See note on page 89.

oil in me. I hate giving myself. It's having a stiff spike, a high opinion of myself, supported on the constantly rendered props of my day-dreams. Yet when I humble myself like that, I admit the effort of humiliation. There is no end to my self-pride. It is very sensitive, easily wounded, easily discouraged, but there is no end to it.

I suppose it is something to be aware of.

I keep on having periods now when I can't write. And I have a desire to throw it all up, to go and carve out a financial career, become rich if I can, and taste all the arts. To spend the rest of my life being a factor, instead of trying to create new tastes. The truth is, I am tired of being the future artist.

I am beginning to live in a marital state of mind. I spend a very great deal of my time trying to decide whether I want to marry G or not. I don't know if it is a problem which should be decided in my subjective states of affection – when we are close, surrounded by loneliness – or in my objective coolness. At a dance last night I couldn't help thinking how many more girls were prettier than her. Partly that is staleness, a reaction. But with how many of them could I achieve anywhere near as interesting a state of mental intimacy – camaraderie?

I had my haircut today. Seeing my face in a barber's mirror always has the same effect on me. I get an inferiority complex about my looks. I seem heavy and stolid and very ugly. And I think I'm lucky to have her at all. If we married, it would be an April marriage – showers and bursts of sunshine. As long as the showers wouldn't develop into a constant storm.

Preoccupied with new thoughts about my creation – I want to begin with a more or less fixed general attitude.

It seems to me Kafka and Camus mark a boundary. They have cut through to the bone, laid bare the one truth. The absurdity and hope-lessness of things. The end of immortality. Whatever we do is only tempo-rary. The only sort of 'afterlife' that could exist is on the time-space level – a repetition of the life in which we seem conscious. In fact even after death we can't escape from the limitations of the life we seem to have lived.

With this lack of hope, accepting the wretchedness of the position, all we can do is to try and make things less wretched. That comes under the term 'espoir'.

In other words we choose 'art for the Weltanschauung's sake' – it is evident that the world and life are philosophically futile. The point is established.

Now, art to amuse, and art to relieve. That is in the realm of the fantastic and the romantic, the beautiful, the strange.

But each of these new 'espoir' creations is an apostrophe – i.e. 'the

world is futile, but . . .' In other attempts no effort at denying the full
horror. Torches in a black cave. The cave is not dismissible. It exists
behind and beyond all torches.

12 May

Wasting my time here. I ought to be writing frantically. But instead, it
is spasmodically. I have virtually no pupils; not more than a dozen a
week except at the one big lecture.

Whirling with ideas and themes, but never getting anything done.

I spent four hours one evening sitting under a wall by the river, where
there is a small park, making love to G. She let me caress all her body.
All rather wild, feverish, pointless. On the damp, cold grass, with the
trains rattling over the nearby railway bridge, and the new moon sinking
out of sight. We discussed marriage at the end, after midnight, cramped
and exhausted and frozen.

I shall never have any money. If I leave G for a month, I shall have
the desire to marry her. If only writing was just a matter of work, routine.
If I don't want to write, I can't. If I force myself, I only have to destroy
what is written.

I shall have to get a job school-teaching, and hope for the best. But
expecting the worse.

At twenty-five I have created nothing that I can venture to publish. All
of it is derivative, or faulty in technique or conception. I don't know
what I want to be. Nor can I be individual, reconcile all the diverse
ambitions that I feel. And the tide is creeping, inexorably. Soon I shall
have no money, and shall be forced to find work. Everything I create I
move away from, often in the very moment of creation. It is illogical
that I should have such an unshakeable optimism about the future.

How slowly experience moves. To have to wait so long to be moulded.

19 May

Sometimes my ideals turn round and bite me. After dinner G and I went
down to Poitiers Plage, a riverside *biergarten*, hired a rowing-skiff, went
down the river. She wore an ugly pair of openwork shoes, which clacked
as she walked. But the river was peaceful, green, slow, running through
fresh gardens. A still, blue evening, fresh and lush. We sat in the *biergarten* afterwards. It was cool, dark, with a full moon rising, and we
only people there. Then we went to Blossac park, where there is a fair.
Hundreds of people, trade stands. All that crushed me, and her terrible
streetwalker's shoes. There was an open-air revue, third-rate local artists,
people standing and gaping, mediocrity surrounding mediocrity.

As we left, I saw the full moon caught in the top of a tree; and started
to feel desperate, frustrated, determined to sulk. All the shabby stalls –

the illuminations and the waste paper and the spent air of the fair, the shoddiness. Her shoddy shoes. Poor girl, not her fault.

And then I bought nougat I didn't want at an outrageous price at a flashy stall. Avarice came into it. We clacked home under a clear indigo sky, moon-washed, with bright stars in the gaps between the houses. She started to ask me what was wrong. I can't stand it. And when she takes my arm, just at that wrong moment. And the clack-clack-clack. And all I want to do is to stand on an immense hill, miles from any city, get out there among the stars, away and away and away. Anything away from the present.

G had to suffer. When I think that they clack because she puts iron tips on the heels to economize in leather.

Afterwards she said, 'It's just like a poet, an attitude. Artificial.'

But that only adds to my external mute fury. Of course it's artificial. I have no rational reason to dislike her shoes.

This was an aesthetic disgust with my situation here. It came almost as abruptly as an attack of nausea.

The lid rattling on the kettle.

June
Lunch at the Jesuit college.

The lector read his piece at a fantastic rate, spurting at the end into meaninglessness. I was shocked by the immediate laughter and outbreak of conversation. He himself smiled as he came down from the lectern. It was Friday, and so fish. But strawberries, and two sorts of wine.

I was shocked to see the boys smoking. And the easy way they talked to the fathers.

Two of the fathers joking together like schoolboys.

It is an enormous building, with a charming park beside the river.

All the time I am there, I am conscious of being prejudiced against them; all the anti-Catholic nonsense of a Protestant upbringing; and I feel like an explorer, daring and rewarded, to be among them. Even though I know I am being what I despise – excessively English.

Robert Bresson, *Journal d'un curé de campagne*.[1] A remarkable film. Quite inordinately gloomy. Not a magnificent despair, but a study in depression. No gaiety, no relief, very slow developments, with many things only half said. Kafka, Pascal and the early Russian cinema. The profoundly miserable face of the young priest is unforgettable – but the way it is played, one can't help wondering if it isn't miserabilism and masochism

---

[1] Made in 1950, the film follows the disillusioning experience of an idealistic young priest who leaves the seminary to take up his ministry in an unwelcoming and largely hostile country parish.

that keeps him (and many martyrs) going. Such complete and all-pervading seriousness and agony is not natural. People could not ima-ginably be so penetrated with dolour. This is an extreme case, a psychological misfit. The treatment is of a high order, without being very original in anything except the silences on the soundtrack. I don't think I have ever seen people leave a cinema so silently. Essentially a Catholic film.

The film was introduced by a Dominican father, who gave a kind of pulpit commentary. In the style so dear to the culture of the French provinces, interminably and conventionally describing what is already known and evident. But he looked magnificent in his cream-white robes against a sage-green curtain. There were murmurs, yawns, but on the whole people listened to him. Poitiers is one of the few towns where that can still happen.

G and I are continually falling out nowadays, under the shadow of the inevitable separation in a fortnight's time.

The other day I explained that I did not think I was capable of completely loving any woman, but I could love several as I now love G. I could indeed love some women more than her. But never completely. The reason I gave was that I loved myself, above all my future, uncre-ated self, too much ever to be able to give myself completely. I explained egoism was not a quality I enjoyed having; it's not easy to be uniquely one thing, when I can imagine most of the other things.

With G I love her sufficiently to marry her tomorrow, if I had the money. But I shan't have the money for several years. In that interval she can become petrified for me, and I can meet another with whom I find and reach the requisite warmth and sympathy. I know that this impossibility of complete love in me means that I depend on time. I couldn't love G absent. The only possibility is that in two years' time I am still alone, and she is still alone, and we could begin again where we left off.

The strongest part of me is the part I never divulge; a mixture of the ego of my ambitions and my best capability, ruthlessly determined to achieve its own fulfilment. The device, 'Forget the past and achieve the future.' I ought never to marry, but I shall.

Two days ago she kept on crying. She said, 'There's nothing to be done about it, I love you more than you love me.' I didn't pretend that that wasn't so, although I explained that the fault in me was inherent, general, and not particular, and love is one of the things where the will plays no part. A willed, insincere love in inviting ruin between two sensi-tive people like ourselves. Artificiality shows up at once. We have Geiger counters, tap the wheels continually.

She said, 'It makes me almost believe in God. It's the exact reverse of Paris.' (She had become unofficially engaged with a young law student, but broke it off – from her side.) 'I never understood till now what he suffered.'

I felt guilty, unhappy, tried to console her. But even in that I was only eighty per cent involved. In any contact with the external world, I am only partly involved. And the highest that part can be is around the level I am with G. Always the rest of me withholds and watches.

Schizophrenia. Or priggishness of an esoteric kind?

8 June

G. My profound hypocrisy with her. Psychologically I play her like a tired ball, experimenting, risking, showing off. Because now I am beginning to plan and formulate a *nouvelle* about her, or around her, I treat her more as the character in the novel than as her real self. The novel necessitates a 'sad' end – an end of separation, that is, which presents no sadness to me (sadness is a romantic hypocrisy) – and so I prepare and indulge in melancholy for our departure. She ought to blow me up with dynamite. I feel myself a monster, because now, when we are together, we are no longer (for me) real, but characters in an unwritten novel. I am beginning to realize that I have become faintly detached from real life, in my efforts to observe it objectively, to *solve* it. I don't believe I wish to regain terra firma; and the drift in this sea of complex self-analysis is away from the terrestrial contact, the sincere and unquestioning, the *blindly* giving relationship with my fellow-man or woman.

She says, 'I wish I had never met you. If only I had known all the suffering I should have.' I answered every experience is valuable. She: 'But what is the point, when it all ends in the *néant*, this irrevocable separation?' You can deny the point of life, and defend suicide, by the same reasoning. The *néant* will come. It is what one can do in the waiting which counts.

But I understand the vast difference between us. Continuing the metaphor above, she is still on land, *in* experience, suffering or joyous. I suffer and enjoy as well, but also I am at sea, can see the suffering and joy, the passing show.

I said to her, 'You must try and forget me. But I don't need to forget you. For me you will be past experience.' What I meant was that the artistic, seaborne me was outside terrestrial suffering. This duality, schizophrenia, is a sort of benediction. I have, and she has not, grace. In as much as one can be romantic and proud about such things, it is the exalted privilege of the poet-artist. The seer.

Difference between an artist and a non-artist. For the latter human beings and their relationships are sharply defined, positive, one-dimensional. For me they are full of transparencies and opacities, hypocrisies, mysteries. All this complicated by the sensitivity of my own reflecting apparatus, and its multiple reactions; its capacity for inviting hypotheses, for transposing into the artistic and fictitious world.

15 June

G. She never asks for anything; conversely always has to be wheedled. Her parents are anti-clerical, and she was never baptized even. I believe prayer is a valuable habit to form in a child. The habit of asking. Absolute independence would drive charity out of the world. Most of the softest moments are moments of giving, and to give one has to ask and be asked. B. W. Brealey resembles her in this; but it is a quality more proper to a man.

The other day she was almost bitterly sarcastic when I said I called the Jesuit priests 'Father'. It only seems polite to me. I don't believe in the army, but I should address an officer by his rank. The respect due to parallel worlds.

Today she questioned whether there was any point in our writing to each other when we parted. I said it seemed more natural. She answered, 'Your letters are always so elaborate, *récherchées*. You write as if there had never been anything between us.' That is true. I hate subjective emotion on paper, especially shared paper. My parents made me believe that all emotion is bad taste. And my education. But they were right. Except that they went too far. Emotion exists and must be let out. But in private (here), or objectively, or transiently. In everyday unrecorded contacts. It is not a thing to read, to transmit by letter.

But the real reason is her bitterness about the parting. Increasingly she is bitter, critical of me. She said, 'What is the use of writing when we are parting for ever?' I answered, 'To soften the death.' She cynically affects a sharp cut; but I think she will change her mind.

She: 'I don't see any point in writing.' I: 'In that case, although I am quite willing to write, I will wait for a letter from you.' She (emphatically): 'I *never* write first.' Feminine cul-de-sac.

17 June

Last day with G. For the first time in some weeks we were 'together'. All the afternoon in my room, a sandwich in a café, and then a stroll to Blossac. There we sat under a heavy grey sky, mute. There seemed nothing to say. I tried to make out that it was not definitive. She told me not to be hypocritical. I had to be frank; I think there is only a faint possibility that we shall meet again. I was pervaded with a soft not unpleasant melancholy. I look forward to liberty. The solitude will follow.

Later, we went to the Sully nightclub. Then down to the little park by the river. Home. I didn't know what to say when we said goodnight. In that situation 'never again' was not conceivable. I think I laughed.

It seems impossible that the torture could be broken.
Separation as imaginable as death.
End of an epoch.
Written 2.30 in the morning. I suddenly regret not having taken her,
kept her, married her.

I have a train to catch in three hours' time. *En route* for Brittany. It's
when I come back that the hell will come.

5 o'clock. Heavy rain. Grey limbo. Partition.

Brittany.
A long journey up, many changes, undistinguished country. And I
had terrible hay fever, was tired, still stunned by the separation.

Also appalled by a meanness which I perpetrated yesterday. I felt
that I had to give her a present. But I left it until the last moment, undecided. Just before the shops closed on Saturday I bought the
Confessions of Rousseau in an exquisite edition. That night, before going
to bed, I read some extracts, was magnetized. The next day I kept on
putting off the presentation until there came a time when I knew that
I was not going to make it. Partly it was because I knew she was not
going to give me anything; I found an opportunity to look in her bag
and make sure of that; and therefore I was afraid of making her
conscious of deficiency. And I knew she had no money. Such sensitivity
is probably ridiculous. I think we were both the same, not wishing to
give and not receive, not from any bare or selfish reason, but because
of the tender and mysterious embarrassment which pervades all last
moments.

One day I hope I shall find out.

I think of G almost continually. Every pleasurable moment, I imagine
it shared; every woman I compare to her. With the English the result is
terrible.

Objectivity with the family. We met with the utmost lack of demonstration, as if I had just been away for a night, instead of eight months.
All the convention is trivial, mundane, *quotidien.*

I have a hatred of saying what I do not sincerely. Speaking to destroy
silence is a vandalism beyond my powers of self-control. What the English
lack is the spirit of exaggeration, of *'astuces'*, teasing, attacking, being
ironic.

Mont St Michel. Maggot-struck. Completely spoilt by the commerce
of souvenirs, of money-grabbing merchants. I was furious at the prices.
F has a Panglossian attitude to everything; determined to make the best.
He found everything cheap, fine quality. Driven into opposition, and by
nature, I criticized everything. But there were times when I curse the
objectivity, the eternal attitude of criticism. When I should like to

simulate the enthusiasm, the insincere pleasure. But the moment I start acting, I criticize that, and shame myself into silence.

Mont St M is best from a distance, like Carcasonne. The magic diminishes as one approaches. The Abbey is still wonderful, especially the cloisters, and the Gothic interiors.

But all those people trailing round after the guide, what does it mean to them? I think nothing. A name to be ticked off. As for architectural periods, the spirit of an age even in its architecture . . .

The evening platitudes in the hotel drawing-room . . . stifling . . . and the sad, weary downfall of the English middle-class stress. What they all speak is common ground – rationing, dogs, children, illnesses. All departures away from common ground dwindle into silence. The cause is probably insularity, being driven in on each other. The belief in the master race, dear to, and unconfessed by, every Englishman.

Immense desire to sink back into French, tease and be shocking with G. Turning over a plate, seeing 'Limoges', knowing what a pang is.[1]

The impossibility of our family unit. Where people are not certain whether Hazel and I are brother and sister, or father and daughter. They live on her level.

F talking in a loud voice one night. 'I wrote some short stories last winter.' I was profoundly embarrassed, doubly so when Hazel asked, 'What did you call them?' and some other people near by smiled.

Return to Poitiers, a grey, wet, cold morning. The room, memories, a sad little letter from her.

> *J'attends mes parents Dimanche, et je suis presque contente de quitter Poitiers, j'ai veçu quelques journées horribles; n'avoir rien à faire, et surtout n'avoir envie de ne rien faire; rester impossible à l'A.G. sous les regards ironiques ou apitoyés, éviter les endroits où nous allions parce que tout en'y parle de toi; bref, me sentir dans le plus total isolement, tout cela n'est pas très drôle.*[2]

The wireless was set where it had been the last day we had been together. There was a packet of books I had left.

For once I feel miserably in want of something.

---

[1] Limoges, about eighty kilometres to the south-east of Poitiers, was Ginette's home town.

[2] 'My parents are coming on Sunday and I'm almost pleased to leave Poitiers. I've had some awful days, with nothing to do, and above all with no desire to do anything; finding it impossible to stay at the A.G. under the pitiless, ironic stares, and avoiding the places where we used to go because everyone talks of you; in short, feeling myself to be in the most total isolation. Not funny at all.'

*

Thinking of the nature of the final speech I would write for a tragedy of Socrates, I started to cry. Without formulating the words, or even the thoughts. But of the intensity and poignancy of them.

6 July

Sudden violent faintness in my room. I nearly fell to the ground. A Jesuit father was there, arranging for me to take examinations with his pupils. I had to push him almost out of the room, and then collapsed on a chair. He must have thought me extraordinary; strange how animals seek solitude for their sickness. Three hours afterward I still feel faint, fuzzy, with a growing pain in my back, which means either jaundice or a chill.

I have never fainted in my life; but I have never been so near to doing so as I was this afternoon. I missed dinner. Now I am beginning to start a fever. It gave me a sharp shock, because so unexpected. Just as I am highly sensitive to life, so am I to death. In a few minutes I was plunged in an acute and black depression. My imagination foresaw all sorts of possibilities, a sudden death, a long one, hospital, funerals, my parents coming from England, Ginette. And over all the bitter feeling that I had not fulfilled anything; not only not, but nowhere near it.

I cannot see a photograph of myself and imagine myself not there to see it. The fear of death condenses the past. I remember the moment when I left all that seemed to be expected from a head of a school, a Marine officer, and started to hack my way out, sideways, to heights I couldn't then see for the jungle. All the false tracks, mistakes, *naïvetés*, discoveries, resolutions – where I still am, but also beginning to see the heights. I must have disappointed my father terribly. What he wants is a good job, security, a future; and all I want are chimeras.

This year I have grown. Solitude – in exile geographically and socially – is essential for me. Everyone does in Rome what the Romans do, and I should be contaminated. People ask me what I do here now that the university is finished. I say 'read', or occasionally 'write'. And I know what they think – that slow, aloof person is too stolid to have any hope as an artist. But I am proud of what I am. The pmassive attitude is the only attitude today.[1]

I had planned to meet Ginette at Bellac next Wednesday,[2] and now I know the irony of all anticipation. Always before journeys which are important, I am ill. But this time it is different. I shall be ill on Wednesday.

---

[1] Reading these words in 1993, JF explained them as follows: 'Pmassive, both passive and massive, was a rather puerile neologism I used – too much – at this time. I meant suffering, but stoic, firm as a rock in spite of all.'
[2] The town, which was on the road between Poitiers and Ginette's home town of Limoges, served as a convenient meeting-place.

On Friday she goes away on holiday, and there will be no more chances.
Thank God for her. If one can inspire love in only one person, it is
consolation. Consolation which I need, since my parents have left me,
long ago.

All this week I have been thinking of Spitsbergen.[1] It has been hot,
dry here. I have thought of birds, flowers, summer in snow. Above all,
solitude. I have constantly imagined myself going there, living a life of
pure solitude and happiness. I need a place with a magnificent desolation, out of this world. A presentiment of something which, now,
frightens me.

If I died. I think of all the arrangements. I should like all my books to
go to Ginette. They are all I have. Souvenirs to the few friends who remain
– even they seem remote. Perhaps something would be dragged out of
all the papers, projects; I can hardly write, think, drugged with sleep.

8 July

Restored, a little shaken, and weak, to life. The doctor diagnoses a mild
sunstroke. Rousseau – *Je puis bien dire que je ne commençais de vivre que
quand je me regardais comme un homme mort.*[2] *Confessions*, p. 225. He had
far more reason than I have to think himself dead. Although an increased
awareness, inclusiveness, means an increased awareness of death.

10 July

I went to Bellac to meet Ginette. Two hours across the gentle, wooded
Poitou and Limousin country, in hot July sunshine, to a sleepy town on
the crown of a large hill, and far away, a blue ripple of hills like Dartmoor,
the Monts de Blond, attractively and atmospherically distant over a
rumpled carpet of wooded hills in between.

The pleasure of seeing her again was great. Affectionately, I call her
sometimes '*une caniche*'; and the pleasure I had was a magnified version
of the pleasure one has of seeing a pet dog, the reassurance that one
can still command a unique esteem. I do not see that I should despise
a doglike affection because I am incapable of it myself, too *méfiant*. In
point of fact, I would like to achieve it.

An interminable journey back home in a *train omnibus*. In my carriage
was a woman of fifty or sixty, in mourning-dress. She kept on nervously

---

[1] In the summer of 1949 JF joined an expedition organized by the Severn
Wildfowl Trust to confirm sightings of the rare Steller's Eider Duck in the
northern Arctic. Spitsbergen is an island archipelago in the Arctic Ocean, which
JF often talked about – although did not actually visit – during this ornithological trip (see introduction, page xiv). The tales of its exceptional solitude
made a deep impression on him.

[2] 'I can truly say that I only began to live when I pictured myself as a dead man.'

hitching up her dress and revealing her knee. If she hadn't been so old
and so ugly, I should have said she was making advances. But I believe
it was because she was wearing black nylons for the first time, and she
hadn't got over the novelty.

11 July
Tour de France. It came through Poitiers today, a caravan of lorries,
jeeps, motorcycles two or three hours long. Almost every product was
advertised. The whole town turned out to watch. The cyclists were almost
an anti-climax when they came. In a brilliant, febrile flurry, all in one
minute or two. Bright-coloured jerseys and shimmering wheels. People
clapped but there was very little cheering.

20 August
Yesterday, a Sunday, I returned from a fortnight's holiday in Switzerland,
the Austrian Tyrol and Bavaria. I went expecting to be disappointed,
and was completely enchanted. Yesterday evening was like the abrupt
cessation of a music in which I had been completely lost, and I felt
sadder about a separation than I have felt for many years. Only two
occasions equal it. When I was very young, and fell in love with a girl
in Norfolk. I was thirteen or fourteen, and can still remember sitting
in my bedroom at 63 Fillebrooke Avenue with an intolerable – because
it seemed at that age irrational and inexpressible – melancholy in my
heart. When I left Aix-en-Provence, and sat all night in the train from
Marseilles to Paris aching with the movement away.[1] I wrote a poem
which at least was sincere, if otherwise bad. In that case it was a kind
of multiple love which was broken – a love for Provence, for the South
and all its physical and psychological implications, and a vague love for
all the girls with whom I had inexpertly flirted – they had remained
simply *camarades*. But in my imagination a tender kind of *camarade*, and
they were unusually beautiful. In both cases the conditions were the
same – a new landscape, an unfulfilled and vague sexual love, a brief,
harshly terminated period.

A kind of corporate, inclusive love. All the others in the group were
from Thouars or Poitou; most of them had known each other from
childhood. They were more like a family than a group of young people.
The average age must have been about nineteen; I was one of the oldest
there. Psychologically I was, or could be, younger. Before I went, the
only person I knew was André Brosset. He was the very antithesis of the
general spirit of the group. The freshness and the gaiety, the simplicity
and the sentimentality, the spontaneity. From time to time there was a

---

[1] JF is recalling the summer of 1948. See introduction, page xiii.

kind of sparkling surge which lifted us all into a kind of momentarily eternal youth. There was always the shadow of time, the *movement* of the charabanc. But that only stressed one of the great truths – that all which is eternal lacks poignancy. As a holiday, the conditions were variable, there was bad weather, bad camping conditions, faults in the organization. In retrospect they seem only a series of minor obstacles immediately conquered by the exuberant happiness and homogeneity of the group.

Life in a charabanc is like the life in a ship. You are inescapably together, a body of individuals. A kind of vehicle for psychological analysis, a magnifying-glass. All the faults and the virtues, the charms and the uglinesses, are enlarged, revealed. Whether the mixture is good or bad, you are in the mixture, and partake of it. The mixture here was like a grapy wine, fresh and heady.

The group was divided (by the *jeunes*) into *vieux* and *jeunes*. All the freshness and the enchantment lay with the latter. Monique Baudouin, the youngest and most exuberant, with a strange rhythm of bubbling dynamism, flashes of *enfant terrible* and a Betty Hutton, and completely collapsed repose; a voice like alcohol, hoarse, husky, continually breaking; a genius for singing in discords, for the deliberate *gaffe*, for the timing of her bricks and *bons mots*; dark, alive eyes, a mischievous smile, pigtails tied in string, a round, tanned face, round-cheeked, beaming, faintly Red Indian, but essentially Latin. French. On the brink of womanhood, and beneath all the fun, she had a kind of provincial innocent simplicity which I found very charming. I think she was probably the most intelligent girl there. She had a way of pretending to be shocked by *gauloiseries* which was more subtly *gaulois* than the *gauloiserie* itself. Saying '*Dégoûtant personnage*' several times when someone was telling stories, and pretending to block her ears. Her love of rich cakes; to see her eating a cream cake was the image of all carnal desire. A special kind of shyly excited, tremulous smile, half delight and half fear, when she had said something exceptionally terrible. Perhaps the most attractive variety of woman, the wit and the tomboy, but always the woman. I can't imagine anyone resisting for long that raucous, uninhibited voice, jumping from tenderness to burlesque, from discord to harmony, soprano to contralto, but always vigorously individual. And all that in a schoolgirl. The result of a freer, more generous, more carnal, perhaps more decadent society than that of England. In a way Monique represents a large part of what foreigners love in France.

The others were less striking, but all with the unexpected grace and freshness. Titi, *la sylphide camuse*, supple, athletic, modern, in pale-blue, three-quarters-length canvas trousers. With a wide indulgent mouth, and the strange pug-nose. Nanni Baraton, with a *Mater Dolorosa* face, dark eyes, and a kind of inner melancholy; rather silent and aloof, with a kind of studied grace when she danced; magnificent black hair, reaching down her back, tied with red ribbon; a way of casting her eyes down in modesty. A beautiful figure, small waist, wide hips, full breasts and a large head. But in an old-fashioned way; not the narrow, sophisticated beauty of today. Armèle, faintly Jewish, very soft and gentle and peaceful, quietly eating cakes and listening to the others. She was engaged to Nanni's brother, Jean-Paul. Brigitte, *fille du peuple*, exuberant, but faintly coarse, and with already blousy good looks. Faintly tired, a perpetual air of the morning after. Françoise Brosset, sharp, intelligent, a shrew. Françoise de Bordeaux, plump and blonde, with a strident meridional accent which convulsed everyone every time she spoke. A tubby, kind face, always smiling, faintly tomboy, full of life. Her Nordic appearance and her accent were violently incongruous. Jacqueline, who ran all her words together in a kind of lazy current, with short black curly hair, a faintly porcine face (not ugly), and black trousers. Josette, a *poule* in embryo, pert, sharp-breasted, trim and continually occupied with her *toilette*, with her effect. Very young, but already sophisticated in a shallow, superficial way; the *demi-mondaine* in miniature; a kind of sulky, libidinous quality. I can be bought, but only at a price: corrupt. Yvette, her pretty, anaemic friend, faint, pale, dainty, weak, without intelligence or will, an ephemeral clinger.

The older girls were less attractive – Claudine 'Coco' Baraton, with heavy eyes and the rather weary look of a bloodhound, but full of energy, small and very strong. She was in a sense the foster-mother of the *jeunes*, their choir-mistress and *maîtresse de ballet*. Colette, a faded blonde with sad face, always singing, plunged in the community, wherever there was life, conversation. A kind of leech, trying to destroy some sadness of her own life. Probably because she had missed love. She was perhaps twenty-eight years old, and sucked the youth of *les jeunes*. Apparently she was very beautiful when she was young. But she lacked femininity, was a kind of Nordic lesbian woman lost in a climate of normal love. Generous, anxious to help, to give, to join in – a sort of spiritual Girl Guide, and I, like most individualists, hate that spirit. Marinette, ugly, with more money than the others. Marie Challet, without sex. Ginette Poinot, a silent, shy girl, with a beautiful mouth, elegantly curved, and strange transparent grey eyes – a look of faint reproach, of incomprehension, as if she was vaguely expecting to be hurt. Madeleine Narvelle, the *parfaite femme d'intérieur* – for whom men are things to be fed and tended; as if all life was cooking meals in a doll's house.

The men. Michel Godichet and Jean-Paul Baraton, two students from Paris, uninteresting to me because they were pleasant and normal. They and André's brother, Paul, belonged to the *jeunes*. Paul was a kind of favorite spaniel, lazy but lovable, and caressed by everyone. He had a way of looking sorry which would have got him out of any trouble. I envied

him his lack of inhibition, his ease. When I think of my own solitude at
that age, I realize how much I lost in having no brother, no sister, no
fixed home town, no society in which I was known, no 'set'. Jacques, *un
jeune egoiste imberbe.*

Les vieux. Jean-Claude Jouteau, a small thin person with a thin moustache, a talent for imitation, and a certain wit. He was the jester of the
group, something of a courtier, prepared to be cruel in order to be
amusing. He was dishonest in his personal relationships. He always said
something calculated to please the person to whom he was talking, a
kind of ubiquitous hypocrisy. If things went wrong, he always expressed
a kind of public indignation, a generous objectivity. I should say Jouteau
was impotent; there was something stunted in him. *Un renard de La
Fontaine,* engaging but untrustworthy. Tinard, a tall, ascetic person with
a Chinese face, and a large hooked nose. An eccentric, but with something of a cultivated eccentricity. He kept on wandering off on his own,
disappearing. Rather a precious way of talking; his conversation
proceeded by *boutades,* outrageous statements and ingenious justification. I felt his mind was a kind of complicated labyrinth without much
exterior meaning. Laffont, the ass of the group. Without a sense of
humour, and with an impossible desire to brag, to be the man of the
moment, the experienced campaigner. A kind of amateur Don Juan,
caressing the girls whenever he got a chance. He pretended to be an
experienced voyager, read the map, gave instructions, advice, ordered
people about. The kind of bully who deceives no one. I felt sorry for
him; he had a hernia. He kept on twitching his nose sideways, screwing
up his mouth, a kind of nervous tic. And he wrote hundreds of postcards, for a reason only too easy to guess. He told us that his mother
had given him a list to send, and I can see plainly that his faults are
inherited. Coarse and ostentatious. Richard, the sergeant-major of the
group; somebody who has never been fully demobilized. In spirit he was
a Scotch puritan; an invalid, yet hard, painstaking, finding a pleasure
in the difficulties of life. He insisted on a strict schedule, on camping
out, on cooking his own meals, on the unpleasant aspect of each situation. A kind of pessimist for pleasure. Hollow-cheeked, dour. Not
without a sense of humour, but of the military kind, shouting phrases
of German, being wrily ferocious. A deliberate, schoolmasterly way of
talking. Slow and suspicious. The only reason that he didn't show his
dislike for me was that the good non-commissioned officer doesn't have
favourites. He was angry that some of us had minor *affaires de coeur.*
Apart from language, I am French and he is peculiarly English. Paul
Challet, with whom I shared a tent for most of the trip. I recognized
the type at once, the first-class commando. Medium height, honest eyes,
simplicity, a sense of humour, unlimited endurance, an ability to live on
the edge of existence. He is a speleologist, and for that one must possess

a peculiar kind of courage and nervous force. He was naïve, not very cultured, possessed more common-sense than intelligence. I suspect that he must lack imagination. A lack of imagination seems to me an essential quality in a speleologist. He described to me a passage a kilometre below ground where the cave was so narrow that he had been able to move only three yards every fifteen minutes, centimetre by centimetre. The thought of doing that makes me almost sick with horror. And the knowledge that if one loses one's light, death is virtually certain in a labyrinth of subterranean corridors. He spoke of the magic of finding fantastic caves which no man had ever seen before. Of stalagmites, stalactites, waterfalls; but all that doesn't seem to me a sufficient recompense. There was about Challet a kind of animal hardness and self-sufficiency, and that automatically precludes sensitivity. None the less, a very likeable, dependable person, the ideal expedition member.

The two chauffeurs, Max and Marco. Marco (Marc Girard) was a kind of clown, brittle and tireless, like a marionette. A fine driver, full of care and concentration; but when he was not driving, full of laughter, continual clowning, an Ariel to the Prospero of André. With large eyes, and well-marked eyebrows, a mobile mouth, and the gestures of the clown. He had a genius for getting things cheap; a kind of engaging dishonesty. Very much the type of the fighter pilot. A mixture of skill and irresponsibility, of risk and authority. I didn't altogether like him. In a way he is a product of the mechanical age, a cavalier of the machine. I hate machines and their slickness. He had an affair with Josette, and an aristocratic and snobbish remnant in me deplores the fact that a driver can flirt with a passenger. Sometimes he seemed to me to go out of his way to be popular and generous. Perhaps I class that as a fault only because I am incapable of doing it myself. He did a great deal outside his contract to make the trip go well.

André (le Président as he was called) reminds me above all of a bear; of a badger. A massive, reserved creature, sagacious, tolerant, but very well able to maul. A month younger than me, he has already the air of a vieux tigre, heavy, brooding, rumbling. He has the head of a Lloyd-George, a Clemençeau, an Einstein, a Schweitzer – square, ponderous, with a strong jaw and a tight but expressive mouth, heavy eyebrows. Massive, slightly bowed shoulders. The authority he had over the group was astounding. Whenever he spoke he was listened to in silence. He had a talent for public speaking which surprised me, and power of admonition which would be hard to equal. An immensely difficult person to know. Sometimes he refuses to speak. His interest in natural history and the arts corresponds with my own specialities. His taste is shrewder, but not so catholic as mine. And I feel myself far more cosmopolitan, whereas he is rooted strongly in his native lair, although in a sense living in a different world from his brothers and friends. In a way he must seem a freak at Thouars, very little understood. A natural leader, just as Richard's a natural NCO. I should think his career is politics or philosophy. I think he resembles me in being a dreamer, a drifter. He vegetates. But I find him an impressive, individual character, of an equal stature to mine. I often wish to impress him, which is very rare with me. And if I felt a sentiment of guilt with Ginette, it was because of him.

Ginette Poinot. I had a bizarre affaire with her. She was between the *jeunes* and the *vieilles*, a curiously aloof, inscrutable little person, with an enigmatic and slightly ironic smile. She hardly ever spoke. A trim figure, and a pale freckled face, too narrow to be beautiful, but not without charm. She was probably the best-dressed girl there, perhaps because it was the first time she had been camping. It was also the first time she had been abroad, and the first time, I believe, that she had ever left her parents. For some reason she always kept close to me. The others, exuberant and noisy, seemed to frighten and disgust her. She was very timid and inexperienced, and completely without intellect, culture and coquetry. A very pale and remote person. Yet she was warm enough when her reserve broke down. But still she didn't speak. In spite of spending so much time with her, I really knew nothing about her, except that her parents were strict and that Thouars bored her. She sold furniture in her father's shop. We slid slowly into a kind of temporary love. I don't think anyone had ever kissed her seriously before, and she was stunned by the surprise a little, of having accepted a foreigner, and in such a short time.

Perhaps I was at fault. I liked her, was puzzled by her, enjoyed going out with her, kissing her, but I could not stay long beside someone so without conversation. I felt proud at having collected rather a rare flower, at having beaten the other men at the most important of games. When we held hands in the car, I crowed inside like a cock, and laughed at the way the other *vieilles* incredulously watched us out of the corner of their eyes. The young people were more natural about it.

3 August
We joined the charabanc at Poitiers. A grey, uninteresting day. A girl grinning a welcome at me out of the back of the coach: later I was to know it was Brigitte. I felt out of place in all the noise and the singing and the excitement; and I was surprised by the girls, who were prettier than I expected, and more numerous. We camped at a place not far from Nevers beside a canal. It was cold and damp. André made a speech, which was disciplinary and witty at the same time. I was surprised that he had the talent for that sort of thing; there was a kind of general introduction, each one of us stood up in turn, and all the torches were trained like a spotlight. I hate that sort of public attention. They insisted that I pronounce my name. 'John Fowles,' I said. 'John Fowles,' they

repeated, and went on repeating with a kind of mock sanctity and prolongation of the syllables. All through the voyage it would come back from time to time, and one of the girls would start chanting it, Monique later confessing that she had not slept a wink all night thinking about it. They sang a chorale under the faint stars. There were fireflies in the grass. I kept close to Tinard. We were both a little intimidated by the ebullience of the others. The chorale in the night was like a fountain of fresh water. Eating sardines by torchlight.

I did not sleep much. I had not got used to sleeping under canvas, and in a sleeping-bag; but it was the only night of insomnia I had.

4 August

We travelled all day to the Swiss frontier into country increasingly mountainous and interesting. Into the Jura, forest and rain and moist, deep valleys and mountains out of sight.

I began to notice Ginette Poinot, she was wearing a black ski-suit with green trouser turn-ups, which accentuated the slimness of her figure and her pointed breasts. She was monopolized by Richard, but I could see that he bored her with his earnestness. The Alps appeared in the sunset in the distance, the snow on their upper peaks orange and pink, afire. A splendid ending to the day, which had been rather dull otherwise.

5 August

Geneva in the morning. I shaved in a mountain torrent, and remembered Norway, the Marines, all the past times I had shaved in cold water and in the open air. It is inconvenient, but not without pleasure.

Geneva reminded me rather of Stockholm and Copenhagen, clean and open and sparkling. Swans in the water and gulls in the air, bright gardens and the people strolling in brilliant sunshine. In the distance the dark green barrier of the Jura. We walked out on the mole to the great fountain, a solid white column like a giant obelisk;[1] the sheets of spray and the rainbows. The cigarette-shops.

We lunched at a little town on the shores of Lac Leman, with Mont Blanc in the distance. Later, Chillon, Montreux, Lausanne. It is all very beautiful, but I dislike the crowds and the element of tourism, and regret the complete and savage isolation of the N. Norwegian fjords. We camped a little before Neuchâtel, in a disagreeable organized camp. In the evening we strolled to a little nearby town with a floodlit castle gateway. Ginette and I separated from the others and she told me a little about herself, nervously.

---

[1] i.e. the 'Jet d'Eau', which rises 140 metres into the sky.

6 August
In the morning, Berne. A town of arcades and coloured statues. We climbed the cathedral tower and admired the distant mountains. The cathedral was ugly. The Swiss and the Swedes have no taste. The transition from Switzerland to Austria accentuates this. There is more architectural beauty in a town like Hall than in the whole of Switzerland. The Lac de Thun, Interlaken. A vulgar town, cosmopolitan, in a magnificent setting. We camped at Brienz. The mountains were steeper, more Norwegian. In Brienz we found a wood-carving shop, full of souvenirs and statuettes, yet there was nothing beautiful there. Some things that must have been exceptionally difficult to carve; but beauty isn't difficulty.

7 August
I swam in the early morning. It was cold and I didn't enjoy it. It is a purely *conventional* pleasure; *if* you swim in the morning, you *must* enjoy it. We saw Lucerne under a sullen sky. Alpine swifts round the tower of the wooden bridge. We camped near the Lac de Zug. It was a wet, drizzling evening, with grebes and coots calling in the reeds. Paul and I pitched our tent away from the others. We had dinner all together in a *gasthaus*. The girls sang, danced, Nanni played the piano, someone brought us wine. When we got back to the camp, the girls went on singing in the rain: indefatigable harmony.

8 August
Zurich in dull weather. We had lunch in a railway buffet. *Saucisse de Saint Gaul*, white and tasteless. We travelled into Austria, the mountains under cloud, in intermittent rain, yet the car kept happy. Somebody always seemed ready to sing. The little *cliques* began to sort themselves out, people began to mix, to thaw; a kind of spontaneity, a lack of stiffness, altogether French and so un-English. We wanted to sleep at Feldkirch, but there was no accommodation. At last we found that, in the ballroom of a mountain village. The men slept on stage, behind the curtain, the girls in the auditorium. A flood of jokes. We had supper, there was a German who sang in a romantic high-pitched tenor: 'Der Tannenbaum', 'Die Forelle', and 'Lili Marlene'. After supper he – with some friends – and the girls sang alternately. He spoke English a little and a distinct atmosphere of *entente cordiale* grew between us all. At the end he gave me a highly emotional message to translate into French. I think he was a little disappointed that I only muttered a few syllables; but music says more than words.

Going to bed under a shower of giggles and gallantries. '*Les Gaulois sont sur la scène.*' Jouteau telling Françoise de Bordeaux not to tickle, fooling with the curtain. I was embarrassed by all the lack of inhibition,

but underneath all the words the actions are as innocent as an English
vicarage teaparty. Gradually I was thawing out under the charm of *les
jeunes*. A kind of second adolescence, *baigné dans la jeunesse*.

9 August
Arlberg Pass. Cold and wet, but we saw the mountains. On to
Innsbruck in the rain. Once again we camped in a ballroom, but this
time it was an outdoor one enclosed in glass. A deluge of *astuces*. It
is strange, the difference in French and English table manners. An
Englishman always waits until everyone is served before starting;
usually chooses the smallest portion; waits to be asked. The French
simply take and eat what they want. Above all, none of the fancy knife-
and-fork play.

Hall, a charming old eighteenth-century town, rococo and Mozart-
ian, enclosed in the mountains. Rather like the music of Mozart, supreme
elegance in a wild, chaotic world. That evening we saw Tyrolean folk-
dancing in a local nightclub, danced ourselves. It is time I learned to
waltz. I see Richard has a *tendre* for Ginette. Out of devilment mainly I
make her go home before the others, with me.

10 August
In the evening, we went up by *téléferique* to a refuge on the Patscherkofel
Mountain. A noisy meal in a small dining-room; far below, the lights
of Innsbruck. I told card fortunes for the first time in my life, and
amused people. I gave Monique two lovers after her marriage, Brigitte
a career similar to that of Ninon de Lenclos,[1] and Laffont a few home
truths. We slept in a dormitory, all together, not without an overture
of giggles.

11 August
The most memorable day of the trip. We climbed to the top of the
Patscherkofel. The weather improved rapidly and we began to have
splendid views. We descended the mountain on foot in hot sunshine,
Claudine setting a furious pace. One of the best mountain days I can
remember spending.

12 August
To Innsbruck. It did not impress me very much as a town, although
the Maria Theresa Strasse must be one of the world's most beautiful
streets with the background of mountains and the glimpse of the

---

[1] Anne (known as 'Ninon') de Lenclos (1620–1705) was famed for her affairs
with some of the most distinguished men of her time and presided over a literary
salon that included La Fontaine, Racine and Molière.

Goldene Dachl at the end.[1] In the evening we went to a rather artificial dance programme. I walked back to the camp alone with Ginette. The others take our isolation more or less for granted by now.

14 August

Through the North Tyrol to Germany. Deep wooded valleys, small mountains, and in one place a chain of brilliant emerald-green jade lakes. The nose of the boat has turned; a certain melancholy set in. Into Germany. Plainly Germany did not lose the war. Things are expensive but plentiful. We camped on the edge of Lake Constance, at Langenargen. Ginette and I went to a floodlit hotel, and drank on the terrace, looking out over the lake inundated with moonlight falling in strange patterns through the infrequent clouds. Somewhere out on the lake there was a boat playing music. We walked slowly home. I did not touch her, although I could feel the current of sympathy coming strongly out of her silence.

15 August

We remained at Langenargen. In the morning I saw two hobbies hawking for insects over the reeds – incredibly swift, agile creatures, turning and twisting like super-charged kestrels. There were also green and common sandpipers. In the afternoon we went out on the lake across to the Swiss shore. I sat for a time beside Nanni. We paddled our feet in the water. I never felt so clearly the freshness of the girls, a kind of springlike and virginal innocence, yet with all the signs of corrupt womanhood already inherent. Nanni is perhaps the most beautiful girl here; for me, a touch of incest. She resembles my mother as a girl. A softness and shyness, a demureness rare in modern times. Nanni jitterbugs well. The effect is strange – the clipped, convulsive movements and the demure graceful gestures. Her dance is the pavane; yet there was something very attractive in the jitterbugging. When the girls looked out over the lake and sang in a kind of pianissimo, there was something wistful, lost in their eyes, which I wanted desperately to but could not capture. The lake was calm; the German boatman described the height of every mountain and the identities of each hamlet, methodically, like a Baedeker. On the way back I talked with a German businessman, very gemütlich and apologetic about the war. He gave me two cigarettes. But that did not conceal the fact that he was nothing but a fat well-to-do businessman from Stuttgart, who had been little troubled by the war.

---

[1] Built in the heart of the old city of Innsbruck, the Goldene Dachl (Golden Roof) is a two-storey spectator's box from which the emperor Maximilian I used to watch court entertainments. Designed by Nikolaus Türing the elder in 1594–6, its eye-catching roof is made up of 2,600 gilded copper shingles.

Later we went swimming; Ginette and I went out in a canoe, and then on a *pedalo*, along the quiet shores of the lake. In a bathing-costume I could see that she had rather a remarkable figure, very slim and well-made, a ballerina's figure. I also learned that she was interested in ballet-dancing and the harpsichord. But she had never heard of Scarlatti, and had never seen a ballet. We went to a dance. There were thirteen girls and I was the only man. It was in a distinctly bourgeois hotel. I had on ragged clothes, but managed to work up enough contempt for the Germans to carry them. But I could not dance to the sort of music they were playing, and passed an embarrassing hour or so surrounded by expectant females. I danced once. I walked back with Ginette under a bright moon. I knew that she was waiting to be kissed and, because of that, abstained.

16 August

Through the Black Forest, which disappointed me, to St Blasien, a quiet town with an ugly and enormous dome on its church. We had a cheerful dinner in a crowded *gasthaus*. I drew cards again. There is only one principle in telling card fortunes – to be as rude as possible and as outrageous.

I stayed on after the others with Ginette; walked back to the camp with her through the deserted town. We went beside a little church stream, and I kissed her. The moon, the running water, the pine-trees, a slight mist. She was without experience, nervous and excited; little sniffs of laughter, as if she was being contemptuous. I asked her what went on in her head; nothing, she said, it's empty. I believe that was the truth. She had a timid, frightened look all the time, yet she was having what she wanted. Certainly she was not simply afraid of resisting, because she came back for more. Besides, at the first sign of distaste on her part I should have stopped. Contempt frightens me more than anything else in the world. In the night it was very cold.

17 August

To Lake Titi. We rowed out on the lake, held hands. I suppose the hand-caress is old-fashioned, but it has an infinite and subtle variety for people who are still sensitive enough. Freiburg. A beautiful cathedral, with some of the most magnificent glass I have ever seen. We crossed the Rhine, and everyone was sad to be home, and then suddenly gay. Through Colmar to Munster, where we camped in a kind of park and drank a Bodensee wine which was the driest thing I have ever tasted. Ginette and I went into the town. In a café we found a mechanical wonder, a pianola incorporating a violin: a weird and wonderful machine which played violin sonatas and variations with a kind of continuo of rumbling and obscure machinery. Later we wandered through the moonlit park.

She was more natural, warmer, but still inarticulate. Incredibly slim; I could almost encircle her waist with my two hands. She lay against me half asleep, a sort of soft contentment on her face.

18 August
Over the Vosges, a perfect morning. They impress me more than the Black Forest. Travelling all the time. A *cassis* at Dijon. In the evening we spent an hour at Vézelay: one of the loveliest little towns I have ever seen, a single street leading to the magnificent church.[1] Extraordinary capitals and tympanum. One capital of St Peter waking up from a dream with swollen eyes, and another person beside him smiling slyly. The power of the nave. It has almost as much uplift as the Gothic. André and I climbed to the tower, a fine view over the Morvan, woods and valleys. A countryside to revisit. We camped at Clamecy. At night was a *parade aux flambeaux* with the *pompiers* producing some particularly noisy and discordant music. Everyone happy. A brilliant moon. Ginette and I spent a long time lying under a canal bridge. It was cold and uncomfortable, but neither of us wanted to separate. In a way I saw ourselves cast in the roles of the characters in Laclos. The evil marquis and the innocent Cécile.[2]

19 August
Home. I dozed most of the time, everyone was subdued. I dreaded a sentimental goodbye. I gave Ginette a sprig of heather. A few minutes later she presented me, embarrassed, with a pine-cone. I pressed her hand, and we drove through Poitiers. By an extraordinary chance it started to rain. When we all got out of the charabanc at the station there was a sudden violent shower; we crowded into the hall of the station. They sang 'Auld Lang Syne'. Fortunately I met the *père préfet* of the Jesuit college and did not have to join in. We all shook hands; Monique was crying and one or two of the others. We stood around, not knowing how to part. I stood beside Ginette and whispered, '*Méfiez-vous des Anglais.*' She smiled faintly. They got in the charabanc. I blew a kiss to Monique. Jouteau and I watched them drive away.

---

[1] A hilltop village of about 500 inhabitants overlooking a Burgundy valley, Vézelay is famous for its Romanesque abbey church, the Basilique Sainte-Madeleine. Containing what were believed to be the remains of St Mary Magdalene, the church remained an important site of Christian pilgrimage until 1280, when it was discovered that the bones belonged to someone else.
[2] The 'evil marquis' is Valmont, who in Choderlos de Laclos's letter novel *Les Liaisons dangereuses* accepts the challenge of his accomplice and correspondent Madame de Merteuil to seduce and corrupt an innocent young girl, Cécile de Volanges.

A news vendor behind us said, 'One of them's crying.'
Jouteau said, *'Mon Dieu, ça me coupe la parole.'*
We climbed up the steps to the town together. I asked him up for a drink. I stood at the window hoping to see the charabanc climb the hill opposite, but they must have already gone. Jouteau and I discussed the holiday. Then he left, and I was alone again. I became suddenly aware of the lack of friends in my life, the need each one of us has for sympathy. I sat in my chair, and seemed to be still rushing down across France. They had performed a sort of miracle; made me believe I was charming. I knew myself well enough to know that I am anything but that.

The deserted room – I had done most of the packing – was terrible, silent. I did not know how to begin to write. The multiplicity, the concentration of those golden fourteen days seemed to me impossible to reproduce. I was only conscious of my impotence before time; my only consolation, the poignancy of the situation. Now, two days later, they already seem incredibly distant, faded, desiccated remains, absolutely gone. Already I forget, and begin to accept the oblivion. Perhaps it was because they were Catholics; they treat religion gaily, as a pleasure more than a duty. They even laugh about it, and about the national anthem and king and country. We are so stern and unbending about such things. Also their singing and the dancing of the girls – I enjoy the simplicity, the spontaneity of amateur singing, which is good but not perfect. A kind of pleasant roughness, a greenness, in the singing. I felt very sharply my own lack of entertaining ability; I include no party tricks. I want to learn the guitar, I must see about it this winter.

The songs they sang – two I liked especially – 'La Chanson des Marais' and 'Les Mariés de Notre Ville'. Monique singing a burlesque of 'Froufrou, Froufrou' with tremendous gusto, carrying us all away. The force in her rolled r's was enough to make the window-panes tremble. There is a psychological hint in the difference of English and French speech – the force and clarity of French, energetic and extrovert; the slurred, mumbled effect of English, lazy and introvert.

22 August
An attempt to snatch at the time again, catch it before it fades, disappears. All the time I am remembering and realizing that what is past is past. Poitiers is grey, cool, autumnal, empty of life. But there is traffic, the trains in the station, the noises of the workmen building the houses below my room – all that suggests work, duty, the mechanical rhythm of life. I cling desperately to the fourteen golden days. In a sense they simplified me, ironed me out. I am too sophisticated, involved, reticent, cosmopolitan, intellectual. They took me back into an old, more natural self.

*

Ginette Marcailloux came to spend the day with me. She questioned me about the other Ginette, whom I had vaguely mentioned in a letter. I lied to her, I could not tell the truth. She had come all the way from Limoges to say goodbye. We spent most of the day embracing on my bed. The sun had turned her skin dark brown and she had never seemed prettier to me. We lunched with Philip. A glass of wine made her talk incessantly, which annoyed me. In the afternoon, after some passionate kisses, she asked me if I had nothing to say. Then we went over all the old problems – how much she loved me, wanted to marry me, how much she regretted having met me, the hell of loving someone more than he loves you, and so on. The woman's interior theatre. I took it all coolly. I believe that she thought she had a chance of forcing my hand, and persuading me to commit myself.

But I have never concealed my intentions to her. I don't want to marry yet. In any case, in my present financial climate, it is impossible to think about marriage. And the love that conquers all is not for the intellectual. I repeated what I had already said; that I liked her very much and didn't consider that our separation was a final break; that I still had a vague ideal about marriage which I knew would dissolve sooner or later, and might well leave me only too glad to accept her. Six months of England could make me mad to have her. I said so. 'Then you only want me if you are unhappy,' she answered. 'That's egotism.' I said I thought that it was also frankness. One of the great uses of love is to help surmount obstacles. I could marry her and be reasonably happy. She is the person most to my taste whom I have met, but I believe I *could* be wildly happy.

We said goodbye in the station – a little dryly, apologizing to each other, tenderly cold. I hate separations. The train was a long time waiting. We pressed hands, I waved, turned my back, and yawned. It felt good to be free again, and not obliged to imagine myself a cynical brute.

23 August
Even a fortnight away from writing and I feel the rust in the wheels – stiffness of vocabulary, make-do phrases, a variable gap between the truth in my head and the speech in my pen.

24 August
Last evening in Poitiers. I am glad to leave, to move on, although I have nowhere certain to go. I dread being fixed, in a certain career, enclosed. Yet within a month I shall be that.

This year is a year partly wasted. I'm beginning to realize that I cannot write to publish because I've not yet achieved a mature style. I have not written much here. Perhaps the spring is drying.

A dull, depressing city, but France. I am now certain of at least one thing, that I love France. I do not want to go back to England, I want to stay here. I don't regret being always taken for an Englishman. I haven't the desire to become French. Perhaps no one can enjoy France like an Englishman: accepted, but with all the background of the opposite pole with which to make comparisons. There is no doubt that the French live more completely than the English. As a human being without race, I cannot help preferring the gusto and the simplicity of the Gallic love for life. France is for individuals, England for good citizens. I hate to leave, but I need a year of exile *in* Britain. For now I begin to believe that I was born in the wrong country.

29 August

After four or five days back in England, I know which country is mine. I cannot stand the mediocrity and the uniformity, the universal adaptability – which is here. The tired eyes of England. I travelled to London with a sort of numbness in my mind. There were crowds of English holiday-makers returning from Paris and I felt myself violently foreign to them. Leaving France was intolerable, impossible.

My trunk had not arrived at London, so I had to spend a day there. I went to the Festival of Britain.[1] I arrived early and joined a queue, a vast, orderly line of people. There were two policemen to control several hundred people. I thought of the French, ebullient, individual, undisciplined, needing an army of *gendarmes*. The queue was along the Thames. It was high tide, beginning to ebb, a grey, cold sky; and the Houses of Parliament looked tired, fussy. Only the strokes of Big Ben consoled me for my own country. The Festival I saw in a morning, skimming through it. All the cleverness and the practicality and the didacticism I found rather repellent.

In the afternoon I walked through Regent's Park to the Zoo. The Park was silent, as if it were the country, with colourful flower-beds and hordes of sparrows. I had not been to the Zoo for perhaps fifteen years, but it seemed the same. I found the cages and the animals sad, especially the waders and seagulls.

Then home down the dirty, dreary Southend line. A cold wind at Chalkwell station. There were soused mackerel for supper. Everything seemed like a soused mackerel; drab and full of small bones.

---

[1] Intended to lift the spirits of the nation after years of post-war austerity, this nationwide Festival, in which 18 million people took part, was held between May and September 1951. It was, in the words of Herbert Morrison, the minister who oversaw the project, 'the British showing themselves to themselves – and the world'. In London, the centrepiece was the South Bank Exhibition, with its newly built complex of arts buildings.

My father in a decline, physical and psychological; he breathes a kind of damp, desperate mist over the house, only increased by M's forced gaiety. He has adopted to an extraordinary degree the view that all is for the worst in the worst of all possible worlds. Every aspect of life is judged by its most pessimistic possibilities. He enlarges disadvantages, finds a thousand means of dodging happiness. Now he adopts an air of great age, walking in a bent way, groaning and grunting all the time. If only we knew more exactly the financial situation, but he only speaks of it in vague terms. I should go and see Sassienie.[1] But this climate saps all will, all spontaneity, and I feel myself already sinking back into the old apathy. When one drags painfully through each day, on a tissue of conventions, silences and hypocrisies. In his case, it was the war. When he came home (from the front and the Occupation) in 1920, the war and the loss of his father induced a nervous crisis – he could not even hold a teacup. In 1923 he was psychoanalysed. And the Freudian explanation was that he had lost his mother at the age of six and had never acclimatized himself to his young step-mother. The millstone of the business, a luxury trade in an age of slumps and restrictions, official or economic, had worn him out. He has a punctiliousness that must make responsibility a torture. And he was brought up in a rich home, lived with well-to-do people, still has friends and connections in a richer stratum of life. He regrets all that and has now an obsession about other people's riches. I see only one solution possible; that I win a football pool.

Instead of writing applications for jobs, working for the translators' examination, I do nothing. I cannot imagine myself working in a routine post. I do not care what happens, as long as it is in no way certain. I want to go abroad again, to live in a solitary place, an island, in the snow. To get away. I wasted my time today reading a book on Spitsbergen;[2] I shall go there as soon as I can. It is not England I hate, but the English civilization.

Henry Miller – talking of a Greek poet, Seferiades – 'his poems were becoming more and more gem-like, more compact, compressed, scintillating and revelatory.'[3] I also.

Chekov, *The Cherry Orchard*. A strange plotless play, without beginning or end. The characters seem mysterious, unreal, but their mood I recognize at once. It is the mood of this town – the ubiquity of futility; the

---

[1] Sassienie was the family's accountant.
[2] See note 1 on page 116.
[3] Henry Miller, *The Colossus of Maroussi* (New Directions, 1941), p.47.

genteel descent into oblivion, where no one is capable of saying what their heart says.

1 September

Galsworthy, *The Forsyte Saga*. A massive piece despite the inferior detail. The outlines are impeccable, the balance exact. Only the style, some of the soliloquies especially, seem to date. I don't like the whimsical satire. Satire should never be anything but bitter. Of course it is all artificial – the interweaving of the family, the coincidences. It is not only technically necessary – so as to be able to keep disparate characters in view – but desired by the reader – he wants to know how the characters react, intermingle. I suppose it is the most popular novel of the first half of the century. In any case, I can remember it being talked of in the family before the war: a unique literary distinction.

4 September

The family makes an expedition to Canvey Island. To the Lobster Smack, an inn on the sea-wall, facing the shipway and the Kentish coast and the complicated organization of the machinery at Shell Haven.[1] Silver tanks, cylindrical and linked by girders, smoke, chimneys. We ate lunch on a little mole jutting out from the sea-wall. The day was heavy, very listless, a grey, tired sky. A shoal of porpoises rolled lazily by; there were common terns fishing. We did a long walk back along the sea-wall. Father insisted on coming and about half way was crippled by sciatica. The rest of the walk was done in slow stages, wih a continuo of reproaches, recriminations and groans. Eventually I got a taxi to help him over the last stage. Once we were home he seemed better.

No one hates the country more than my father, yet he insists on doing things which he does not like. Above all he lacks the courage of his pleasures; in fact his main pleasure lies in denying himself pleasure. He almost goes out of his way to suffer.

5 September

A letter from Ginette (Marcailloux). Only now do I know what it is to be without her. Her letter was particularly just and dignified, such a letter as I could never write – from the heart, and I write always from the brain. But she held out her hand, in spite of her reproaches. If I had the money I should go and marry her. The lack of money nags at me; yet I cannot bear the thought of routine work, with only a fortnight's holiday a year. I must have leisure-time.

---

[1] See note on page 14.

14 September
Journey to London to take the examination – with three hundred others – for OEEC translators;[1] but the important thing for me was that I had recurrent bursts of poetic inspiration. That has occurred to me more than once on Chalkwell station. It is well situated to evoke the phenomenon – or perhaps it is the effect of any journey into the unknown. Such moments are immensely consoling; not because of themselves but because in coming they show that there is something extraterrestrial, outside-willing, inspirational, in writing poetry. The very fact that these moments cannot be controlled, induced, is a kind of guarantee of individuality, a confirmation of my own opinion of myself. A mysterious ability to set all the complex but automatic machinery in motion, and produce the fragments of amber. They say every faculty will be artificially bred one day; but the poetry faculty will be the last tamed.

A period of prolonged psychological constipation. I must find work. I sit here day after day waiting for some miracle, my dreams becoming more and more removed from reality.

17 September
Two letters in the same post, from the two Ginettes. That coincidence pleased me enormously.

20 September
Two observations on myself. I lack virility. The essential thing in virility is action; a continual decisiveness, a clear-cut independence of movement. But sensitivity needs a delicate climate; the softer one is, the more sensitivitized one becomes. That part of me, the soft, the tender, the stagnant, is neutral, sexless; there is a parallel with the eunuch. It is only incidentally that I make use of my masculine properties: strength, endurance, independence . . .

I cannot discuss things here, at home. Every moment I am aware that I am twenty-five and not paying my way; jobless, a burden. I fight shy of discussions, arguments, because that fact seems to me to enter every one of them; to be an unanswerable weapon in my father's hands. Another might baulk; but I have a great deal of patience for minor discomforts.

The photographs I took on the Tyrol holiday arrived today. The warmth had gone, it was like seeing yesterday's meal rehashed. Only

---

[1] The OEEC was the Organization for European Economic Co-operation, established in 1948 to co-ordinate efforts for Europe's recovery under the Marshall Plan.

Monique Baudouin really came through – a gay, mocking, tender vivid-ness, a sincerity of mood, natural grace. An unfadeable personality.

Philately. I have been selecting some things for sale. A curiously pure form of collecting, almost collecting as an abstract, the pure essence. The only interest I find in it is financial, the romantically high sums attached to little bits of badly printed paper. I need the money now I cannot afford to spend anything at all. It is terrible never having a reserve for the dry periods. Poverty is like a friend who amused one once, but I'd like to cast off now. I try the pools. They are worth the stake if only for the dreams, the standing a chance.

Ginette Poinot: she sent me violets and a small rose pressed between the pages of her letter. *'Je vous écris du jardin, et une rose miniscule se penche vers cette feuille – peut-être a-t-elle reconnu un ami? Je vous l'envoie. Heureuse fleur!'* She writes in a very old-fashioned, conventional style, full of flowery phrases and euphemisms; rather eighteenth century, and faintly charming. I threw the flowers in a waste-paper basket and sent her back a feather from a redshank's tail.

1 October

Interview with the British Council: a pleasant, cordial atmosphere, where I did at least feel they wanted to help me. Not like the recent cold and rather hostile quarter of an hour at Unilever's. I spent an hour and a half between various people. The most fascinating vacancy is at a school on a Greek island, Spetsai, south of Athens.[1] I can hardly dare to imagine myself successful there, yet already I have dreamed all about and around the place. There is another job in Brazil, and a third at Baghdad. I heard this morning that the translator's job at Paris in the OEEC was no use. I failed the preliminary examination. Besides these there is the British Museum.

To take the Greek job would be madness. It has no future, except lotus-eating. But I know that I should take it at once, if I have the chance.

Election. This is more apathetic than the 1950 one. But now it is a choice between Tory romance and Socialist practicality. The Tories offer

---

[1] The Anargyrios and Korgialeneios College. Established through the bequests of two wealthy expatriate Greek benefactors, the Spetsai-born tobacco baron Sotirios Anargyros (1849–1918) and Marinos Korgialeneios (1830–1910), the school had been modelled on the image of a traditional English public school. It opened in 1927 under the headmastership of an Englishman, Eric Sloman. 'The best families send their sons there, to train them up as statesmen,' wrote Lawrence Durrell; 'the result always seems to be much the same – instead of statesmen, they become politicians, a very different sort of animal.'

nationalism, the Empire, freedom of enterprise and so on; the Socialists increasing uniformity, the death of the *ancien régime* individual. As a social unit, I shall vote for the Welfare State. I vote for what I think best for society. A Tory world, obviously, would most benefit me; but I am still young and poor enough to vote against my own corruption.[1]

14 October
Pat Fowles (my half-aunt) was married today; I refused to go to the wedding. I dislike weddings, wedding atmosphere, wedding wit in wedding speeches. The Fowles family were apparently annoyed. I dislike family gatherings. Mother spent the whole of the rest of the day going over each detail, what everyone had said, what she had said in reply. Indefatigably trivial, like a placid stream, or a top which needs only an occasional flick to keep spinning.

The new suavity. A kind of disinfected amiability of exposition, peculiar to young intellectuals and dons. Merlin Thomas (my tutor at Oxford) is an example. There are frequent others on the wireless. They strike a balance between being very modern and well-informed, and explaining things, talking in a familiar, careful, colloquial way. Their aim is urbane vulgarization. They speak on a level with the man on the street, never down to him. They never enthuse, or if they do, they always follow with a trite comment, or a light joke, as an anticlimax. That is their self-insurance. They don't want to sound committed over emotion. Perhaps something to do with logical positivism and the scientific outlook. Something I must avoid. It is better to be cantankerous and committed than charmingly intelligent and non-committal.

20 October
Waiting for the decision of the selection board about the Spetsai job. I cannot bear to hope, yet I have a sort of feeling that I might be successful. It could mar or make me, but only in the one sense (direction). I might go only to stagnate. Here, at home, I am quite shameless about living off my parents. At the moment I am writing fairly regularly. I should have *Drag* finished by the middle of next month, and a 1951 diary by 1952. But this latter is a much vaster effort. I can write *Drag* almost at full writing speed, without pauses. In the other I have to deliberate between every sentence.

*

---

[1] After a long five-week campaign, the General Election took place on 25 October. The Labour government was defeated and the Conservatives, under Churchill, were returned with a seventeen-seat majority.

Making a bookshelf today, I was amused to catch myself thirsty for immortality. I have made it very strong, consciously, so that it will last. It gave me pleasure to be building something which will perhaps outlast me; the wood – from the old wooden mantelpiece recently taken down in the nursery – is heavy oak. And as I write this – in bed – it has just struck me very vividly that someone must have made this bed. It is thirty or forty years old, and all the furniture in the room. That is all furniture is, *au fond*. Unsigned monuments, perpetuities of absent hands.

1 November
I received a letter this morning to say that they have recommended me for the post at Spetsai. It is exactly a year today from my arrival at Poitiers. I received the news calmly, almost coldly. Not even the news that I was the Son of God would have disturbed me unduly, I believe. I could play poker well; but my heart sings. Yesterday I went to a Civil Service competitive selection board and I think I did well there. There was a job in the dockyard school at Rosyth – virgin territory, inculcating some rudimentary culture into the apprentices. A safe job with a future; or there is the BBC possibility. I ought to stick to that. But I fall for the exotic.

8 November
Webster, *The White Devil*. A very powerful writer. His poetry affects me very strongly – it has a wild and weird quality, an almost mad talent for fantastic similes and metaphors. A daemonic writer, I think of him with Lautréamont, Hoffman, Poe, Faulkner. Above all, I think, Lautréamont – they both strike me as being deliberately what they are. It is not so much a subconscious morbidity as a deliberate presentation of an exotic world: a vivid imagination in a cool head. There I find myself also, I read Webster like a brother. And there is a lot to be learnt from his prose-poetry mingling. Some characters speak naturally in verse.

In *The White Devil* it seems to me Flamineo is the key character – Vittoria, Medici, Brachiano are all evil in their ways, but they are less motivated by passions of the body, desire for revenge, the animal instincts. Without Flamineo, the play would be merely a struggle between magnificent animals. Flamineo has his motives of self-advancement, but they are only for the play. He is a Figaro-type character, who has an extra dimension – he lives *outside* the play as well. The dark, profound cynic, who sees through his own motives even when he obeys them. A complete objectivity means that he is without any absolutes, even of evil. He *knows* he lives in a world of pure chance. He is a far more profound character than the others – like Bosola in *The Duchess of Malfi* – and in reading at any rate seems to me to tower over all the other players. He is certainly most of all the mouthpiece for Webster.

The Duchess of Malfi. I think inferior as a play to *The White Devil*. The

Duchess has not the brilliancy, the colour, of Vittoria. And Bosola is not so black and sardonic a masterpiece as Flamineo.

I like a comment of Charles Lamb *à propos* of Webster's imitators: 'Their affrightments are without decorum.'

Tourneur, *The Atheist's Tragedy*. This doesn't stand beside Webster's dark other world, his 'black lake'. Already a tinge of the moral and the mundane which drags the violent action down to melodrama. Also his language is not dramatic like Webster's, and not nearly so picturesque. *The Revenger's Tragedy*. Incomparably better than the foregoing. It is difficult to see how they could come from the same hand. But still not on the level of Webster. Vendice is a fair-sized character, but the others have no depth. Castiza is a hideous prude. One or two cleverly contrived scenes, but the final blood-bath is impossible. Could anyone see this on the stage without laughing?

'Virginity is paradise locked up.'

12 November

Politics. I have to register a change in my own views, of which I have been for some time perfectly aware, but too lazy to analyse or admit. That is to say, I no longer believe in democracy. That doesn't mean a shift from socialism. Albert Camus said in a broadcast the other day that one was socialist *par simple décence*. That seems to me admirably put. If one has any pretensions to being intelligent then one must assume a certain international and moral objectivity. It is plain that very nearly two thirds of the world is living at a low standard, lower than we have here in England. Socialism is *their* obvious salvation. Free enterprise is an ideal solution – if men were ideal. But we have, if we are frank, to admit they are not. They need controlling. Communism goes to an extreme; socialism is the middle way. The fact that the Tories have got back has made me think. They have got back purely on emotional grounds. People want an economic gamble and the beating drums again. It seems to me that only one in a hundred people are fit to vote in this country; in many countries one in a thousand would be nearer the mark. People here have cast their votes on issues like Abadan and Egypt without any semblance of objective understanding of the pros and cons of those situations.[1]

---

[1] Abadan was the centre of the oil industry in Iran. An international crisis occurred when in May 1951 the Persian government nationalized the assets of the British-run Anglo-Iranian Oil Company and expelled its foreign staff. Egypt was disputing the existence of the Canal Zone, a strip of territory flanking the Suez Canal which British troops occupied. In October 1951 Egypt announced its intention to abrogate the Anglo-Egyptian treaty of 1936, under which the Canal Zone had been created.

So many people here vote for themselves or their ways of life. Many intelligent people in the upper layers – the professions, sciences, arts – vote Tory to keep the order going. Plainly no one above or below certain incomes should vote. They will be too biased.

What I dream of is an oligarchy of left-wing intellectuals, who are cold and dispassionate and scientifically philanthropic, who could do something about all the causes of ignorance – the violently partisan press, which *en masse* is all right; but most people only read one and the same paper day by day. It is easy to be drugged by one point of view. Constant dripping . . . And then a modern vote is valueless. I know beforehand here that Channon will be elected,[1] I know he does not in the least represent my views, I shall never speak to him or influence him (the fact that I can is such a minute possibility as not to be worth considering in defence of the system – there are so many practical drawbacks). In my case the MP is a particularly bad one. He never speaks in the House, which is perhaps fortunate as he is a fool, and Southend is as near being a 'rotten borough' as it is possible to imagine. I have no say in the government of my society. A one fifty millionth is not enough. All I can do is dream of the city-state.

The more I think, the more I am determined that the need is for a city-state world. Division and re-division, until one can live in a community again: knowing everyone, meeting one's neighbours frequently, and having a direct say in the government.

Laski, *Faith, Reason and Civilization*.[2] A very lucid, impressive book, it seems alive; some memorable phrases. A dangerously clear, well-informed and persuasive mind. I think this would be a book the future will remember, however spasmodically. It half convinces and confirms me. The only trouble is that the USSR does not seem, now, what Laski presumed it to be. The Christians eventually betrayed themselves; and

[1] Leigh-on-Sea was in the constituency of Southend, West. The Conservative MP and diarist Henry "Chips" Channon (1897–1958) had held the seat since 1935. His son, Paul Channon, would succeed him as the constituency's MP after his death.

[2] Harold Laski (1893–1950) was Professor of Political Science at the London School of Economics from 1926 to 1950. In *Faith, Reason and Civilization* (Victor Gollancz, 1944), he argued that the future of the post-war world lay with the 'Russian idea'. Just as Christianity had revitalized civilization after the fall of Rome, so the socialist revolution in Russia would bring to the West a new age of progress, based on a more just and rational system of social equality. The book was not well received. George Orwell criticized Laski for turning a blind eye to 'purges, liquidations, the dictatorship of a minority, suppression of criticism and so forth'.

so have the Communists, and much quicker. But his points: the decay of all revealed religions, the undeniable justice of the theoretical communist state, seem to me essentially right. It was an important book for me.

It is a sad fact that this book has been taken out of the public library only twice in eighteen months.

Full of sap for several weeks. I live here, never going out, with all the company of my imagination to keep me amused. I used to have periods of restlessness. But now I believe I could stay forever inside myself.

20 November
Tea with the Nobles.[1] Platitudes, old meals rehashed. I felt external, uncouth, daemonic, Beethovenish. Hazel (my sister) at the end got down on the rug, and started smoothing the nap with her hand. I wish I could have done the same.

6 December
A letter from Ginette Marcailloux. Short, cold, depressed and depressing. She has not written for some three weeks. For her, all is over, dry bones. It is true our letters are becoming cooler, humdrum; end is inevitable.

The Bible. I chanced to start reading some of the last Old Testament prophets the other day. A revelation of poetry; superb language and imagery. It is a mistake to imagine that the Bible is the same in all languages. The English translation is a work of great genius; it should be to us what Homer was to the Greeks.

Wildfowling at Leigh. At home a heavy raw mist settled over everything. I walked offshore out towards the sea. Gradually the mist thinned, and things became clear. The mud-flats stretched far, still slightly veiled, full of their strange obscure magic. In the distance I saw a fisherman picking up mussels. A wind sprang up and chased all the mist away. And the sky became more beautiful than I can remember seeing it anywhere, on any previous occasion. A clear, luminous green-blue, blue shimmering with green, soft and bright and shining. There were a few wisps of amethyst-like clouds, pink and faintly blue-white. In the west, over Canvey Island, very low, was the sun, extraordinarily magnified and distorted in a massif of clouds on the distant horizon. When it finally sank out of sight these clouds became fire-red and black, but they were small and very far away. The sky appeared paler and greener; now green shimmering with blue. The half-moon began to outshine; and Jupiter near

---

[1] E. P. Noble was the headmaster of JF's preparatory school, Alleyn Court.

by. It was bitterly cold. I walked right out to the main channel. A trawler with two men aboard, one steering, hunched up with the cold, the other sorting cockle-sieves, ran down from Canvey back against the tide, beating into the little waves. I stood and watched the creeks filling, the wind singing in my gun-barrels. There were curlew and redshank in the distance. Leigh and Westcliff seemed many miles away, wreathed still in mist. Leigh church rose strangely out of it; a clump of poplars stood up like the parapets and towers of a distant castle, of Carcassonne.[1] Everywhere the sky, in pools, in creeks, above. Like half a transparent duck's egg. I wounded a curlew, and held it under my foot in a creek to drown it. I watched its death-struggles dispassionately under the divine sky.

I shall leave all the poetry I have written here when I go to Greece. Now I am trying to prune, to cut down. But a poem so rarely seems to me wholly bad. There are always lines, turns, ideas beneath the rubbish. I shall have to leave a lot of 'ore' behind; tough material. It would be easy if one was certain of death; one could be ruthless, destroy all but the best. But as it is, I like to have a stock of material.

A letter today from Geoffrey Fletcher in Holland; he is doing well.[2] Every time a contemporary meets with material success, I am discomforted. Yet with my philosophy of life now, no amount of contemporary, practical fame would satisfy me. Not even the practical administration of the whole world would be enough. My enemy is oblivion; everything else expands from that. My attitude to life; my lack of interest in ordinary people; my interest for the famous; my contempt for contemporary artists; my fear of growing stale, or blunt; my sacrifice of any careerist future I might have had; this miserable dependence on my parents; this withdrawal from society and its kindred comforts.

26 December

There has been little to record these last four or five months; my existence has been virtually monastic. I have felt little of the horror that this place (Leigh-on-Sea) used to inspire in me. I once thought that I was unhappy here because I could imagine myself so vividly in so many other situations; now it seems to me that I am happy – or rather content not to revolt – for exactly the same reason. My imagination is a counterweight, an outlet, which I can control: it is no longer a mere wild

---

[1] The fortified medieval city of Carcassonne in southern France boasts three kilometres of double ramparts and forty-eight towers.
[2] Fletcher, who had matriculated in the same year as JF, was a Classics scholar at Queen's College.

universe of the day-dream. To organize one's imagination is a vital step before creation; to learn to assess its products. Everything new, every new pleasure, new vista, is not necessarily good because it is new.

If I was killed now, there are two or three short stories and some 15–20 poems which might resist time for a little. All the rest is immature, often rubbish.

Greece seemed at first romantic, much to be desired; now, close at hand, ominous and full of pitfalls. A letter from a master already there suggests that conditions may be far worse than I can imagine. It would indeed be rare if I was to find my niche; unless the life is very ideal, I shall certainly stiffen against it, as at Poitiers, and do myself no social good. I shall not find a Ginette again.

I suppose it is a stupid thing to do; to turn one's back on all the obvious openings. But if one is certain of being a poet (Greek sense) then one can only refuse the safe and the obvious. You cannot expect a cat to jump in the pond; nor a poet into the neutral. I hate waiting on the springboard; packing, buying odds and ends, rushing, foreseeing contingencies, calculating, being in a very all-consuming whirl. I hate movement; I like being in new places.

Part Three

An Island and Greece

2 January 1952

In a taxi up to Athens – a vast sprawling suburb between Piraeus and the city – unmetalled side-roads, dilapidated houses, palm-trees. Then we passed some orange-trees laden with glowing fruit in sunshine. Such small things are more important than all the vast monuments, so often seen before. I found the British Council, met Ball, the Educational Representative: a bespectacled, balding, brush-moustachio'd civil servant, frigid and unhelpful. He sent me off to find my new colleagues at a hotel near Omonia Square.

The next two days spent in Athens with Sharrocks and Pringle, mainly drinking and hearing their accounts of the school. Pringle is fortyish, mildly alcoholic, choleric, well-read but unwise. He talks about literature by means of his reading, by what other writers and critics think; a series of cross-references. I do not excel in such atmospheres. One can only join in by adding other cross-references; a personal opinion does not count. Pringle's eyes are unpleasant, beady, buried in flesh. His fingernails long and filthy. He has schoolmastered in India, in the Sudan, and elsewhere. A rather forlorn failure, professing an admiration for the Roy Campbell–Hemingway attitude of revolt.[1] And touchy about that admiration, which I mildly mocked. He told me a mass of stories about the school – its atmosphere seems decidedly strange, a constant intriguing between masters for popularity with the headmaster and with the boys. The boys without discipline, uninhibited in their curiosity, their affection or their hate. A kind of laboratory, hothouse atmosphere, where eccentricities are enormously exaggerated.

Sharrocks is tall, good-looking in a pale aesthetic way – he could carry the lily well down Piccadilly – and very suavely soft-spoken – a discreetly cultured accent with one or two Lancashire lapses – '*wan*' for one. He appears to know Athens and Greece well, with many friends. Pringle said he lacks devil; he has stayed at Spetsai longer than anyone else post-war,

---

[1] Born in South Africa in 1901, Roy Campbell made a reputation for himself as a poet, memoirist and satirist whose targets included the Bloomsbury Group and the poets Auden, Day-Lewis and Spender. He shared Hemingway's taste for travel and adventure, but supported the opposite side during the Spanish Civil War. His professed enthusiasm for Franco's Nationalists in the long poem *Flowering Rifle* (1939) attracted heavy criticism for his supposed Fascist views. He died in a car crash in Portugal in 1957.

because he is adept at maintaining his balance here. He is apparently a *poète manqué*. He seemed to treat Pringle with considerable expertise, by the difficult means of never disagreeing with him.[1]

Athens is not a pleasant city at first sight – a gigantic city, uneasy, full of movement, irregular hours, rich people – and between Omonia Square and Constitution Square, very few poor. The women are beautiful, and very feminine – the mannish, mousy face does not seem to exist; nor does the classical Greek; but the Turkish element is visible everywhere – full cheeks, oriental and languorous, expressive eyes, full lips, open and pouting. All the women are soft, look as if they would yield; none of the modern equality-*ergo*-sexlessness. So many Greeks have a beautiful smile with the eyes – a warm, inviting smile; *sympathique*. The language I cannot understand at all – it is soft, lisping, hard to catch, full of *ee* vowel sounds.

I went up to the Acropolis one grey afternoon. It was oppressive, muggy in the city, with a kind of dirty slime on all the pavements, which I found as slippery as ice. I walked down past the vulgar modern cathedral, and headed vaguely towards the Acropolis, through an older, poorer quarter – a street full of butchers' shops with rows of skinned lamb and greengrocers with glowing heaps of oranges – still leafy – and other fruit. A man in rags, with bare feet and carrying a large sack, passed, chanting and staggering from side to side. I worked my way up through low white houses with tiled red and ochre roofs on to a road which led upwards under the Acropolis wall. But it was, so a boy told me, not the right road. I went down again on to the main road up to the Propylaeon.[2]

I do not know how to describe my reaction to the Acropolis – everything in it I have seen so often before – in books, photos, paintings. Yet I had not the least idea of the ensemble of the setting, which is everything. The Parthenon is so powerful, on its short slope, or from below, glimpsed over the wall. Brooding, timeless. But I found it all so sad, so *past* – it was cold, raining, there were only a handful of visitors, a few

---

[1] Denys Sharrocks would become a close friend of JF. He had been brought up in Southport, where he went to the King George V Grammar School and, then, after war service in the RAF, completed his studies in language and literature at Liverpool University. He began to teach in the English department of the Anargyrios and Korgialeneios College in 1948.

Although JF wasn't aware of it at the time, Kenneth Pringle had in fact just been sacked from the school for having had homosexual affairs with one or more of the boys. The headmaster had asked Sharrocks to escort Pringle from the island to Athens and at the same time to meet and bring back the new teacher.

[2] The roofed gateway to the Acropolis.

photographers blowing on their hands. The Parthenon looked a pale russet colour against the grey-black slopes of Mount Hymettos. The beautiful vaselike sections of distant perspective between any two columns. Especially looking down the east colonnade, northwards, at two cypresses framed in the vase-opening.

The sky was grey-black tangled with clouds. It was very cold. I watched the city below, the old Byzantine churches, the ancient Agora, the Hephaesteion.[1] The sky cleared over the Peloponnesus – bright golden clouds, silver reaches on the sea, blue-green rifts of clear sky over the dark blue mountains. But all that was a long way off – on the Acropolis it drizzled, and the wind was very cold indeed.

The beautiful Erectheion – the Parthenon is not beautiful, any more than a man can be beautiful – feminine, graceful, poised.[2] The huge city at one's feet, commanded.

I walked down back to the hotel, disappointed at not knowing what to think about the Acropolis – it aroused no vivid reactions in me.

That night we drank too much – Pringle got cantankerous and dogmatic and finally drunk. S (Sharrocks) was non-committal and sober. I had nausea, was annoyed by Pringle's pugnacity, and wanted to go to bed. But it seemed Pringle was unstoppable. We ended up in a nightclub near the hotel and there dragged out an expensive two hours. The place was largely occupied by businessmen – 'papas' as Pringle called them – and two or three décolleté hostesses, who were pulled about, danced with, and also drank champagne. An uglier and more colleté hostess sat with us, or with Sharrocks, who non-committally accepted her. Pringle got angry with her, and shouted at her to go away. He had fits of laughter when the tears ran down his cheeks. I watched the antics of the businessmen and the abandon of the girls; one of then had jet-black hair with a blue sheen, a heavily rouged and very pretty face, and broad supple hips. Four or five of the businessmen were trying to win her.

At last we got away at half past four. Sharrocks and I had a boat to catch at eight for Spetsai. Pringle had the room next to mine; after some fumbling he managed to get the key in the lock and get in. Then a cock outside began to crow, and Pringle started to shout at it. 'Crow away; cock, cock, crow away . . . Crow away.' And he went on droning this for minutes: 'Crow away . . . Crow away.' That was the last I heard of him.

---

[1] A small temple on the western edge of the Agora at the foot of the Acropolis, built around 450 BC and named after Hephaestus, the god of fire.

[2] Built as a shrine to Athena and Poseidon-Erectheus and containing the tomb of Cecrops, the legendary founder of Athens, this temple was finished in 395 BC. Standing on the northern edge of the Acropolis, it is considered to be one of the most perfect examples of ancient Greek architecture.

A strange, failed, stunted yet violent personality, he had written several novels, travelled, and plainly drunk a good deal. His writing is crabbed and mean, and not very expressive – if one can judge by the letter he sent me. A highly emotional person – with no sense of objectivity, easily offended, faintly malignant, yet with flashes of intelligent and real perception.

I awoke at 6.30, feeling foul. Put out my hand for a sickness tablet, and knocked them off the shelf so that they fell down the plug-hole of the wash basin. It had no grating, and they were gone. I was lost. I called the maid, who called a porter, to see if it was by the inspection hole in the piping – but no. It had gone. I would be sick.

But I wasn't. We got a taxi to Piraeus, and got aboard the little motor-vessel which runs to Poros and Spetsai – once Ciano's yacht.[1] I went down to a cabin and lay dozing for four hours. It was a lovely day and we passed through superb scenery. But I lay in the dark cabin, paying for the sin of not having resisted the Pringle in things. I came on deck in brilliant sunshine as we ran into a bay, the sea bright blue and sparkling – a bay with a small white-washed village at one end, Hermione.[2] Brilliantly white houses in a small plain, barren mountains behind, and to the left a soft promontory covered in pines.

Half an hour later we came to Spetsai – a largish village on the north side of the long green island; the snow-covered Peloponnesus in the distance, the coast of Argolis ochre and red and smiling a mile to the north, and several bare islands miraculously poised like tops (a mirage) over the scintillating waves.

These island villages are incredibly white and clean, clustered small cubes, crystallizations at the foot of the pine-covered slopes, on the blue water's edge. At Spetsai a small boat took us ashore to the quay. I met two masters, was much stared at. We went off to a small backstreet restaurant; a Spanish-looking guitarist came in and sang a series of Greek

---

[1] Galeazzo Ciano (1903–44) was an immensely rich Italian Count who had served in Mussolini's government as foreign minister and was also his son-in-law. After the Axis defeats of 1942, Ciano urged a separate peace with the Allies, and Mussolini eventually had him put on trial and executed for treason.

[2] The islands of Poros and Spetsai are on the south side of the Saronic Gulf, just off the north-east coast of the Peloponnesus. The boat from the Piraeus would have stopped off at Poros, then Hermione, a town on the Peloponnese coast, and finally Spetsai. JF's description of the imaginary island of Phraxos in *The Magus* accurately sets the scene: 'Phraxos lay eight dazzling hours in a small steamer south of Athens, about six miles off the mainland of the Peloponnesus and in the centre of a landscape as memorable as itself: to the north and west, a great fixed arm of mountains, in whose crook the island stood; to the east a distant gently-peaked archipelago; to the south the soft blue desert of the Aegean stretching away to Crete.'

songs. Greek music has affinities with Spanish Andalusian and Arabic music, and of course, Turkish. A very particular, aromatic, discordant music, full of dropping notes, broken rhythms, oriental intonations. He sang in a clear, strong tenor, to a Greek just back from America who was drinking a good deal of retsina with some cronies, and who finally danced in the Greek-Turkish way up and down the aisle between the tables. The guitarist improvised a song about him, full of sly digs which were greatly enjoyed.

We went to the school. I did not expect such huge buildings. Five large blocks, several storeys high – wide, unfurnished corridors, with bare stone floors everywhere. There is a resonance when one speaks; a church, a morgue, a prison. My room is some 30 × 30 feet, sufficiently furnished.

The school is in a park by the sea, which one can hear on the shingle. The garden is full of cypress and olive-trees. There are hibiscus in bloom. A well-equipped gymnasium, a football pitch, tennis courts, even two fives courts! A school which is a dream, superbly situated and equipped for four hundred boys. But there are only one hundred and fifty, and they are dwindling in numbers. So many things could be done here – an international school, a co-educational one. Sharrocks thinks any change is hopeless.

I met the deputy headmaster – a pleasant man with crinkled eyelids and an honest smile. We ate with some of the boys. I speak no Greek, the other masters speak no English, so I could talk only to Sharrocks.

8 January [1]
I went for a short walk in the morning. It was very cold with a choppy sea blowing up against the shore. I saw two kingfishers sitting on the strand, least expected of birds; a kestrel, and what looked like choughs; and several other birds. And there were many flowers. Sharrocks says there are no birds here – but there seem to me great possibilities. The variety of natural life excites me – the natural historian has a profound advantage over all other men. When I pass through a new country, the birds and the flowers and insects mean – from the point of view of my own pleasure – as much to me as the people and their artificial world. They form a kind of ubiquitous sanctuary.

I went down with Sharrocks to Spetsai to buy some utensils – we ate fried cuttlefish – very pleasant – fat olives and chips, and drank beer in a small restaurant with a moth-eaten stuffed buzzard hanging from the ceiling. The people seem so friendly; amicable – able to be friendly.

---

[1] Looking back through his diaries forty years later, JF would comment, 'I think we may call this early January entry the genesis of *The Magus*.'

Today I met most of the rest of the staff – as yet they possess no characters, but only the nicknames I base on their unpronounceable Greek surnames.

I sat at a table with seven boys for supper – a Cretan on one side of me who was nearly inarticulate, and a Turk on the other who spoke fairly well. But it is going to be difficult to keep up a thriving conversation for a whole term on a vocabulary of a hundred or so words.

The plunge has been taken; the work seems, from the point of view of hours, easy. Four teaching periods a day, total three hours, and two duties a week, total five, which makes twenty-three hours a week. I cannot complain. The boys are ebullient, spontaneous, and eager; more feminine than English boys. I saw a newly arrived (from holidays) boy kiss a friend on the cheek. The older boys show more affection to the junior than an English boy would dare. Facially, and in habits, one might almost be in England.

The boys, however, cannot discipline themselves; there are no organized games; and the day of seven periods followed by two and three-quarter hours' homework is too much. The teaching methods appear antiquated. The school needs reorganizing. Partly it is the lack of a University tradition like Oxford and Cambridge in England, or the Ecole Normale Supérieure/Sorbonne in France. There is no core of cultured masters. Here they seem to know their subjects, but to have few outside interests, and little except gossip in common. Rather like village school-masters in England.

But the island is a jewel, a Treasure Island, a paradise. I went for a long walk up into the hills inland – through the pine-trees, up stony goat-tracks in a cold bright silence. It was a perfect cloudless day with a small wind from the central Peloponnesus; with almost the warmth of a warm March day in England. The pines are loose, shapeless, small and scattered, so that the views are rarely impeded and often superbly framed. A sea of these pines is a sea of round tops like cork-oaks. What is strange in the hills is the silence; no birds (yet they are everywhere in the school); very few insects; no humans, no animals; only the still silence and the brilliant light and the blue sea below, with the Argolian plain and its small central mountains opposite. A purity and simplicity of emotion, a kind of quintessential Mediterranean ecstasy, pervade the air; the air infused with pine-resin and winter sharpness and the brine from far below.

I saw no one for a long time; one or two shepherds called in the distance – sound carries fantastically. A small boat chugging out to the daily steamer anchored off the village sounded a few hundred yards away. But it was two or three miles. I passed an astronomy station, strangely isolated in this hill-forest. On another hill further east I could see a monastery looming white among the black cypress-trees which guarded it.[1] The view became more and more beautiful at each new stage in the climb. Opposite, Argolis, like a relief map, indented, edged by small bays with pink-orange cliffs and further inland, dark green pine-woods. But these woods are so open, so airy, that there is no sense of the sombre, the far North. You *can* see these woods for their trees; and they are a relief – a sanctuary from the hot, bare plains. Argolis appears well inhabited – one or two white rashes of village, and a regular speckling of isolated farms and cottages. Only the central mountains are barren and uninhabited. To the right, the beautiful islands around Hydra, and Hydra itself blue and pale-green and pink, floating in the veronica-blue sea. Massy islands, with bluff peaks, and big cliffs and escarpments, but balanced together in the distance. All the colours are vivid, but soft, pastel without being furry, aquarelle yet solid.

To the right, over the bay of Nauplia, the big mountains of the Central Peloponnesus – snow-covered, like pink clouds low on the horizon, glittering faintly in the oblique sunlight. Far hills, cliffs, villages, and the vast carpet of the sea.

I climbed up and up and came on to a rough road, and found myself on the central ridge of the island, bathed in sunlight, an undulating sea of pines falling to the southern coast, which is much more deserted than the north, and has only a few cottages and a villa or two to populate it. The sun was over Sparta; the sea between Spetsai and the Peloponnesus glittered brilliantly, variegated by small ruffling breezes. A fire far below, near a cottage, sent a column of smoke straight up into the air; but up where I was there was a small, cold breeze tempering the warm sunlight. Near by I saw a man, the first I had seen, cutting faggots. Two more men appeared riding donkeys. One of them stopped by me and stared at me and smiled, and said something sharply. He wore a stained pale blue beret and ragged trousers; his face was linseed-oil brown, like an old cricket bat, and he had a good black moustache. He repeated the same phrase as before. I stammered something. He stared back. '*Anglike,*' I said.

'Ah!' he nodded, half shrugged, kicked at his donkey, and rode on without another look at me. His companion drove the other donkey, minute under a mountain of pine-branches, past me, with a friendly '*Kal' emeras*'.[2]

'*Emeras,*' I said, and went my way.

I walked along the road for a while. I walked through a small brake, and a woodcock flew off from under my feet. A lizard scuttled away. It

---

[1] The monastery of St Nicolaos, which is also the island's cathedral, sits on a hill just outside Spetsai town. St Nicolaos is the patron saint of Spetsai and all seamen.
[2] 'Good day.'

was very warm, airy; I struck off the road and came to a cliff facing west-
wards. I sat on the edge of it, on a rock, and the world was at my feet.
I have never had so vividly the sense of standing *on* the world; the world
below me. From the cliff, successive waves of forest fell down to the sea,
the sparkling sea. The Peloponnesus was absolutely without depth or
detail; just a vast blue shadow in the path of the sun; even with field-
glasses, no details could be seen, except in the snowy mountain-tops.
The effect was weird and for a few minutes I felt incomprehensibly
excited as if I was experiencing something infinitely rare. Certainly I
have never seen so beautiful a landscape; a compound of gloriously blue
sky, brilliant sunlight, miles of rock and pine, and the sea. All the
elements, at such a pitch of purity that I was spellbound. I have had
almost the same feeling in mountains, but the earth element is missing
there – one is exalted and remote. Here the earth was all around one.
A sort of supreme level of awareness of existence, an all-embracing
euphoria which cannot last long. At the time I could not define what I
was feeling; the impact and uplifting had made me lose myself. I was
suspended in bright air, timeless, motionless, floating on a sublime
synthesis of the elements. Then there was the fragrant wind, the knowledge that this was Greece, more than that, the spark which lit ancient
Greece; and very strongly, the memory of all those grey streets, those
grey towns, that *greyness* of England. Landscapes like this, on such days,
advance men immeasurably. Perhaps ancient Greece was only the effect
of a landscape and a light on a sensitive people. It would explain the
wisdom, the beauty and the childishness; wisdom lies in the higher
region – and Greek landscapes are full of higher regions, mountains
over the plains; beauty in nature in every corner, a *simplicity* of landscapes, a purity which exalts a similar purity and simplicity; a childishness because such beauty is not human, not practical, not evil – and
minds fed on, surrounded by, such a paradise must become its dupes,
intensely attached to it, and after the initial offering of worship (the
Golden Age) they must be creatively sapped by it. One created beauty
to supply a lack of it; here there is plenitude. One does not create; one
enjoys.

Such fragments make good shoring.

I walked back towards home; thinking of Treasure Island. The sun
fell, gilding the crests; the valleys were green, gloomy. I came to a valley
full of the tinkling of goat-bells. There were twenty or thirty of them;
the goatherd called regularly, '*Ahi! Hia!*' and gave a fluty, penetrating
whistle. I glimpsed him making his way down through the trees,
surrounded by goats, a tall man in dove-grey trousers, patched very pale
grey at the knees, and a black coat. I hurried down the path to catch
up with him, but I caught sight of a small plant by the side. I fell on
my knees, and incredibly, there was an early spider orchid in bloom

before me, a little thing some six inches high, with one large flower, its blotched purple lip insolently outspread, hooded by the pale green sepals, and the green bud of a second flower. I knelt down and took the details, the goatherd forgotten and his goats tunkling fainter and fainter away. Now it was getting dark; the mountains looked dark blue, the Argolian countryside black. The air was cold. I walked swiftly down the goat-tracks, as there was still a good way to go. At last I stood on a bluff from where I could see the school. It was studded with anemones, little plants three or four inches high, pink and mauve, nodding in what slight breeze there was.

I tumbled down through the olive-terraces, past a ruined farm, and on to the road, which led to the school in a few minutes. I think one of the most satisfying walks I have ever made. Once one knows the background, I think the school is best seen as a kind of necessary evil. But such a day – vision – dwarfs pedagogy and all things pedagogic. In the evening after dinner I had coffee with Sharrocks and Hippo[1] and the Cockroach, who chattered away at nothings. The Hippo said he had 'a delightful walk in the town, where we had a very good time'. Shades of the great – they live on the island and do not see it. The miracle will not repeat.

But meanwhile we pale Northerners may still be slightly wrought upon.

Kesseris, 5B. 'I like to make an archaeologist, and to light some ancient men with strange perspicacities.'

12 January
An incredibly soft, brilliant moonlit night; colours stood out plainly; the sea was opaque; a symphony of white houses and black cypresses. It being Saturday, and the afternoon occupied with a particularly Kafkaesque masters' meeting. The main disputation was about some boys who had spent a night on Poros gambling and drinking instead of returning straight to the school from Athens. Any small item of school business has to be debated by all the masters in plenary session. Today there were two camps – the lenient, liberal school and the conservatives out for blood, the latter faction headed by the arch-Jesuitical Timaigenis, the theology master, a reeking Tartuffe. The headmaster opened the debate with the striking words, 'We are not allowed to punish boys, but we must think of a punishment for these.' He acted like a temperamental granny throughout, mainly bursting out against any master who

---

[1] The 'Hippo' was a nickname for Potamianos, a Greek master who taught English.

cast adverse reflections on the school discipline. Sharrocks said that most
of the boys regarded the public school 'court' as a farce. 'Ah,' said the
headmaster, 'but that is how we all treat courts in Greece.' The whole
atmosphere is mad.

It being Saturday, we had a meal in Spetsai, at a café where a fine
guitar-player was playing. Surrounded by cronies, a Sancho Panza type
of figure, sly, malicious, a brilliant improviser and wit. The café was full
of fishermen and local tradesmen. We drank retsina, which as yet I don't
like – yet feel it is Greece, and must be liked – one of the minor obstacles – and ate a big meal of chips and lamb chops and liver. The guitarist
sang about us, we bought him and his table beer. A raising of glasses.
A tall, fat old caique skipper in a blue cap sang a duet with him; sang
in a high tenor, passionately, with quavers, his face upraised and his
throat vibrating, like a bird singing. A youth sang also, in a strong,
melancholy tenor.

It was a relief to escape from the school, although it is not as bad as
I expected – grim, but not terrible. The boys are ebullient, irrepress-
ible, but as charming and affectionate as they are hateful. In class they
all talk, they whisper, are continually jumping up, raising their hands,
asking questions, laughing. Silence here is a comparative thing. Yet much
of the trouble is eagerness. They want to learn. The masters are far
worse – a gutless, uncultured lot of old women, uneasily perched on
the system of hard work and repression.

The grounds of the school are studded with pines and cypresses,
through which the veronica sea appears even more blue. One of the
loveliest of shapes, the cypress; black flame, obelisk or fountain. A
common weed in the garden is an Oxalis with vivid citrus-yellow flowers
which only open in sunshine. They nod on fragile, graceful stems, in
their hundreds, humanly.

The strange marble resonances of these stone buildings. Every sound
is magnified, hollowed, echoed and becomes institutional – prison,
morgue, hospital, school, barracks. Wirelesses produce weirdly remote
sounds. Each floor is divided in three lengthwise, so that the central
corridor is as wide as the rooms that flank it – and all the sounds gather
in it. As I write, a woman is singing in Arabic on someone's wireless –
and the music sounds doubly exotic, remotely resonant, from afar, past
ages, nostalgic, sad, like dead beauty.

This afternoon there was a football match. The pitch is good. The
boys wore shirts of yellow and black, and red and white stripes. They
played with brio, unscientifically – on the red ochre earth they made
lovely patterns, as they ran after the ball, which was light and bounced
high, uncontrollably. It was a championship match between two forms,
and all the school was there to watch on the concrete grandstand, and
many people from the village as well. The boys had toy trumpets,

whistles, shouted. We, the masters, sat on a kind of royal dais in the centre of the stand, watched the game, and the line of cypresses beyond, and the white school blocks; and beyond them the mauve-blue channel, and the Argolian hills in the late afternoon light, where Mycenae and Tiryns and some gems of history are hidden in the blue, still shapes, and under the white and pink few clouds. The schoolish activity seemed antlike in such a setting; games, a prostitution of real action. School discipline, organization, prefects, referees, white lines, goalposts, a scar, scum on the everlasting.

A new English master arrives today – Egyptiadis – an old man with grey hair shaven almost bald, so that he looks likes a wrestler or ex-convict. A bull neck, wide mouth, few teeth, massive body and polite manner. He has lived in the States for nineteen years and speaks English well. And apparently many other languages. He spoke to us in several; proud of being multilingual, although his knowledge of other tongues seems mainly a matter of memorized extracts. He struck me as being something of a rogue. And no doubt his parrot-like repetition of odd fragments of prayer and proverb in many languages will soon become very boring. Unfortunately he has the room next to mine.

Tamarus, Class 4: 'Slippers are the shoes of the night.'

Potamianos – a young sprig of smugness, with protuberant lips, downy cheeks and curly backswept hair; the air of an enthusiastic young innocent, the pride of the seminary. He is very thick-skinned, and transparently self-interested. He has got a corner in the English extra-tuition market; he naïvely tells us how all the boys love his teaching methods; and criticizes nice old Egyptiadis.

Today he came up to me in the common-room and asked how I 'propose to affront (sic) the problem of being without women on the island'.

'I shall use goats,' I said.

'Is that what you go into the hills for?' he asked. My botanical interests puzzle him deeply.

'Of course,' I said.

'You know,' he went on, 'before I left Piraeus I spent two hours with a woman in a hotel. I did it four times in two hours. I have done three times before, but never four.'

'Indeed,' I said.

'Papiriou (the gym master) and I want a girl here from Athens,' he said. 'Would you like to join us? My girl would come. All she wants is a room and food. And Dokos, the music master, would join us, and perhaps Mr Sharrocks, so it wouldn't cost much if we all shared.'

And he looked at me like an amateur 50–50 Rousseau, innocent and vicious, inquiring. I kept him playing for nearly half an hour. Heard all his love life. 'My dream is a widow,' he said very seriously. 'With widows one reaches more far.'

He told it all to Sharrocks later; an offensively dense young man, who imagines himself of the world. Later he was singing in the music-room; not a vestige of musical knowledge; but droning away like an undiscovered Caruso overconscious of his destiny.

This latter *soirée musicale* was enlivened by Egyptiadis, who insisted on giving imitations (a hollow whistle into cupped hands) of an owl, an American train and, of all things, the Eton College boating-song. Dokos, a balding, bespectacled, brown-faced clown of a man, played fragments of *Rigoletto*, dance-tunes, Greek popular airs, *La Traviata*, Strauss and finally Boieldieu, whom he seems to regard as the apogee of West European music.[1] He plays with a kind of thumping brio, very far from perfectly as regards notes, and I suspect he must have worked at some period in a busy restaurant, against a continual invasion of noise on his music.

I am beginning to understand the peculiar flavour of existence here. The complete lack of contact with the outside world; I have not read a newspaper since I came here; no doubt one could get news broadcasts, but I have no desire to listen to them. I read a *New Statesman* the other day, and it seemed suddenly and mysteriously in perspective, rather affectedly intellectual; the criticisms especially seemed to me the lucubrations of unbalanced young know-alls, undergraduate stuff. The whole *NS* world, which so recently I found pleasantly esoteric, almost a clique – a county cricket team whose averages I cultivated – now seems a minor planet, and faintly grotesque, a narrow small heart of a small narrow faction who live in North London and Oxford and Cambridge – and nowhere else. My geographical remoteness would not, I should have thought, affect my inner standard of values. I thought they were proof against physical removals. But environment makyth man.[2]

The frustrations of a prison existence – a prison without even the benefit of more or less solitary cells, since one's room is a very insecure sanctuary, penetrated by masters, bells, boys' shouts and voices, and intolerably institutional in its furniture and ambiance. Yet the prison is purely artificial – the lovely island, the lovely sea is all around, a minute away. Yet the school seems (when one is inside it) to have poisoned the whole scene. Outside, it dwindles, disappears, in a few steps. Yet few of the masters appear ever to go out – occasionally they go into the village, but never into the pine-forests. No attempt to escape.

---

[1] François-Adrien Boieldieu (1775–1834) was the leading composer of opera in France at the beginning of the nineteenth century.

[2] The motto of JF's Oxford college, New College, was: 'Manners makyth man.'

And yet there is so little privacy here – especially in the boys' blocks, where the life is much more that of the officer messing in with his men.

A hypersensitive perception of the absurd and humorous. Sharrocks and I spend most of our time in private together laughing. The other masters are so uncultured, so childish and transparent and insular in their motives that one can only laugh. Yet things happen here which make us laugh, and they are not funny – except on Spetsai. Partly the whole presence of this ridiculous great mock-British school on a gem-like Aegean island is intrinsically absurd. One has to laugh. And being English gives one a peculiarly objective standpoint from which to mock foreigners. We are uninteresting, but stable. Foreigners have no fixed standpoint, unless it be of purely private interest. They dart, move about, change. But we are set on one point, moral, democratic, wise, governing and governable, indulgently adult; and the rest of the world is precociously juvenile.

Arapangis, Class VIA: 'I have some more to say, but time is not enough. The bell rings.' For whom the bell –

18 January

I went into town with Hippo today to see about getting a *permis de séjour*. He has a way of boring into one as he walks, and my progress to the police station was very much between the devil and the deep blue sea. It was a grey day, but the mainland and islands to the east were of a beautiful *silent* dark grey-blue colour. The sea was a satiny grey, very calm. The Hippo regaled me with anecdotes mainly smutty – how he had been riding a she-donkey and a he-donkey mounted her. 'So I got off and ran away – I was very much scared.' And he described in detail the forcible mating of a stallion with a mare. 'Very interesting.' He says everything so earnestly, beseeching credulity, that one can hardly keep a straight face with him. He sang all the time – Italian opera, *The Merry Widow* and so on. A clown, a Candide.

We had an amusing half-hour with the Chief of Police in his office, laboriously filling out the vast forms. He made very heavy going of all the English names. He was a lugubrious character with sleek black hair and the face of a jaundiced bloodhound, wearing an old British Army khaki greatcoat with two large silver stars on each epaulette. He wrote heavily, in red ink, with a scratchy pen. When we came to the question, 'Religion?', I promptly answered (determined to be absurd in the land of the absurd), 'None!'

'But you must have a religion!' said the Hippo.

'No,' said I.

'He's not got a religion,' said Hippo in Greek to the Police Chief.

That worthy looked at me then back at Hippo, and spat out something.
'Well, look here,' said Hippo, 'he says you must have a religion?'
'But I haven't.'
'Well look here, you've got a Christian name?'
'Yes.'
'Then you must be a Christian.'
I was unable to confound this triumphant piece of logic. I shrugged and said firmly, 'I haven't a religion.'
Hippo said something to the Police Chief, who looked at me, scratched his head, and suddenly burst out laughing.
'What the hell's he laughing at?' I asked.
'He says he's never heard of anyone not having a religion. He thinks it very funny.' I had bargained for a little provincial awe of the declared atheist, but not laughter.
'Tell him I was a Protestant, once,' I said resignedly. 'Tell him to write down "Protestant (once)".'
And so it was written. When the form was filled up, the Lieutenant asked me for six or eight photographs.
'Six or eight?' I asked. Hippo discussed this point with him.
'He says six or seven, but six will do, and he'll get them himself from the photographer.'
The Greeks are mad.
That same night Sharrocks and Egyptiadis drank a bottle of my brandy. Greek brandy is sweet and weaker than cognac, and the level drops correspondingly faster. Still, it was a cheap price to pay to hear Egyptiadis thundering out an endless variety of hymns, Turkish and Greek songs, novelty numbers, national anthems and lines from the *Iliad*, to say nothing of the quotations and proverbs. He got mildly excited, and his voice rang through the building. There were voices in the corridor, murmurs. The headmaster has the room above mine. He must have felt the tortures of the damned. Egyptiadis sings bass and tenor, very powerfully, and even a whisper in these stone rooms resounds loudly.
He drinks brandy neat, and at a gulp. In return he has offered us some superb Turkish Delight, made at Syros, and also a Turkish cake called *kata*, a kind of walnut *paté* inside a crisp shortbread envelope.
Egyptiadis has a very humble dutiful approach to teaching here. He constantly tells us how proud he is to be our colleague; writes down everything so as not to forget it; conscientiously answers every bell – where most of us come late or not at all to meals. The other day he was in my room when a boy came to say that he was meant to be teaching. He had mistaken his free period. He rushed out of my room and I saw him running in quick glides, so evidently shocked and eager to get to the teaching block. Grotesque, because he is a massive, portly figure,

normally dignified and slow in his movements, and pathetic in his anxiety. Far more the latter than the former.

All his life seems to have been work; conscientious labour and learning. He does not smoke, and declares himself able to abstain from anything. A dry, frugal character, clean but garrulous, almost parsonical, in the least likely of bodily forms.

In the morning following my epic interview with the Police Chief, I went in again with Hippo to be photographed. A clear, sparkling morning, with the hills and islands brilliant and soft in the breezy sunlight. We sat in the photographer's and haggled about prices. He wanted to charge us more than Athenian prices, which are already outrageous. At last a more or less agreeable compromise was arrived at. We went outside and I stood in a striking pose in the village square. The photographer suddenly seemed struck by grave doubts.

'He thinks the photos may be too small for the Police Chief,' said Hippo. 'He may want bigger ones – more expensive.'

'For Christ's sake,' I said, laughing, 'surely he knows by now what size the police use.'

Hippo talked.

'It depends on the form,' said Hippo.

'Let's go to the Chief of Police,' I said. So the three of us trooped through a door with a faded sign, across a garden with some small oranges on small trees, up the steps to the police station. The Chief of Police seemed little pleased to see us. There was much haggling and disputing. I smiled constantly in the background, reserving the bombshell till the end.

'Tell them to send the bill to the school,' I said.

'The school!' The Chief of Police and the photographer looked at each other, shrugged and agreed with surprising meekness. We went out into the square, the photo was taken.

Then Hippo and I went and sat at a little table on the cobbles above the small harbour. We sat under a pine-tree, by the line of ancient cannons, warm in the sunshine, eating cakes. The sea was dark blue, Hydra and the rest pink and ochre and olive. A big caique was pitching and rolling out of the lee of the island.

And I had a mild hangover.

A good night's drinking in the village. Sharrocks and I went to the local cinema to see a film about the aborigines of Australia – *Bitter Springs*. The aborigines were good. The audience was not large – six. The soundtrack was in English although I did not discover that for some time after the film had started. Lengthy gaps for the changing of reels rather broke one's concentration.

Later we went to Lambris. Sharrocks and I went to join four of the waiters. One of them, who was sitting in the back room with Dokos, the music master, was celebrating his name day. A vast dish was set in the middle of the table – fried liver and some kind of entrail, thin segments of orange and cheese-balls – from which we each speared the morsel we wanted, Arab-fashion. Sharrocks and I, having the prestige of foreignness, had pieces speared for us and delicately held out for us to bite from the fork – a charming habit. The Greeks have a graciousness which is unsurpassed; among themselves they appear greedy and egoistical. The boys at my table snatch what they need; they take the best portions; and when there is a second helping, the first boy will take far more than his fair share before he passes on the dish. Sometimes he will take the whole lot, and the others seem to regard it as normal. There is something callous, un-Christian in the Greek temperament. They do not renounce; and they respect chance. If you have, you hold on; if you have not, you are ridiculous and not in the least pitiable.

Yet with foreigners they are polite, charming and, in their way, patient. In any case, to laugh at the misfortune of others is less hypocritical than the customary English conventional sympathy; and I am not sure it does not give one a better weapon against one's own setbacks. Here all one can do is shrug, laugh and suffer in silence, and get better as soon as one can.

There was a continual clinking of glasses. Everyone became more or less amiable and intoxicated. The guitarist Evangelakis came in and fenced with Dokos about an engagement at the school. Dokos started to show off academically, and started talking about the history of music and his own wide knowledge of it. The little guitarist, who has more music – humble though it may be – in his little finger than a thousand Dokos's, listened to it all with a kind of sulky patience. The waiters and ourselves got the guitarist to start playing – once started he went on – a popular song, bawdy, melancholy, sentimental and brilliant improvisations which had all the waiters and Sharrocks in fits of laughter. His speed of versifying was miraculous. Dokos made one or two weak improvisations, but without a pause the guitarist answered back and much better. Nothing seemed too difficult for him. Dokos, a little sour at the guitarist's success, and ourselves. Sharrocks is a very skilled performer indeed at the social game – not a champion, but a very good person to have on or at one's side. Unruffled, diplomatic, amused and amusing; socially supple, which they all are here – masters, servants, boys . . . I cannot keep up at this high level – sometimes I fall, sag, am silent, walk out.

They sang Greek songs with closed eyes, swaying, with passion. Some of the broken rhythms affect me as Catalan music does – very deeply. At half past one we came away, and walked down the road beside the sea, which was pounding the rocks. Back through the drizzle and spray to bed and stupor.

I said last night that two more evenings like that, and I could die for Greece. Two more hangovers like this, and I shall. Retsina goes up to the head and this morning I have a splitting headache – blinding lights and jangling bells. I sat for an hour nursing my head, then took a Veganine pill and felt better. I strolled out on the strand and watched the sea beating angrily up on the beach. The sea was every shade of Antwerp blue – sun-stained, tipped with white. A superb windy day.

In the afternoon I went for a long walk to the end of the island, along sheep-tracks on the cliffs. I did not see a soul; it was windy, but mild. The cliffs are a tangle of furze and pines and weather-carved rocks. At every pace magnificent glimpses of the bright jade-green sea below. On the barer patches were clusters of bright blue muscari hyacinth – Oxford and Cambridge blue. At one place I find a large scattered colony of spider orchids, with bigger, fatter flowers than I have previously seen. Very few birds live on these cliffs. It is the north side of the island, rather cold, deserted, ominous. The cliffs are tall and steep, and the coves enclosed. One bay with a big grove of cypresses is especially beautiful.

I remember one moment of enchantment. I had been walking for hours through the trees above the sea, not seeing a soul, and the sea, being rough, was empty of boats, and then suddenly I had a kind of flash of vivid perception of the marvellous, the poetic – a tissue of the legendary, the enchanted forest, the spirits of places, nymphs in groves, partly French and medieval, partly Greek and classical, partly my own dreamworld. I stood in a glade, looking uphill at some densely obscure pines, almost aware of a new world.

Then I walked home, fast, through the trees, and again, although I was now on the road, saw nobody. But I heard a weird cry, which I thought must be some shepherd, until I was standing directly below it. I threw a stone into the tall cypress from which the call came, and a small owl flew out in the twilight. Mr Scops, I presume. The invigorating solitude had cleared me of my hangover.

Papiriou, the games master, the champion hammer-thrower of Greece – a sulky, muscle-bound athlete, beginning to run to fat. He is very body-conscious, continually throwing out his chest, flexing his muscles and so on. He slaps one on the back, and his approach is pugnacious, and usually lewd. He is genital-conscious as well, and incredibly lacking in tact and *savoir faire*. Or perhaps he does it because it is quite evident no one will pick a fight with him. His chest is diabolically hairy and his left eye is blinded, giving him a rather unsatisfactory expression. He is very sensitive about it, and usually wears dark glasses. The virile brute incarnate; he sets my nerves on edge.

*

The boys in the top form were talking today about the Communists. They had some very gruesome stories about the Civil War.[1] Stammanoyatis said that they dug out the eyeballs of their prisoners and kept them in tins to send to Moscow; that they executed their prisoners by chopping off their limbs one by one. He described how he had seen mothers embracing the decayed corpses of their children. I was a little incredulous, but such is that streak of callousness in the Greek temperament. Perhaps it came mainly from Turkey, but one of the additions of Christianity to the philosophy of ancient Greece is precisely of the lacking quality of compassion. These boys are so bitterly anti-Communist that it frightens me. They call Plastiras – who is mildly left-wing – a Communist.[2] When I asked them to name the four people they would most like to destroy, they said Stalin, Mao-Tse-Tung, Vishinsky[3] and Plastiras.

The horror is in their own lack of comprehension. They have seen only the violence and cruelty of their own Communist countrymen. Because of that they are scared of any reform – and Greece needs reforming. At some future date the peasants will burst out again and the same bloody battle will be fought. The same situation in Spain, in Iraq, Persia, Italy, Egypt – masses of oppressed peasantry who are not being relieved, gently, democratically, but only oppressed more violently, more frantically. And with a younger generation like this – the 'cream' of Greece – solidly reactionary, there is no hope at all.

Spider orchids. I have found them scattered all over the island. Aloof, bizarre plants, with a rich brown lip, tinged gold and purple in sunlight, and delicate yellow-green wings. They grow singly, or in twos and threes, rarely more than two flowers on a plant. I have kept one in water for over ten days, painted it, and looked at it a great deal. They give me

---

[1] The restoration of the Greek monarchy in September 1946 left the country bitterly divided. In December 1946 a Communist-dominated Democratic Army of Greece (DAG) was formed out of the nucleus of the wartime resistance movement ELAS and, operating out of the mountains, it conducted a guerrilla campaign against government forces. The conflict was marked by enormous brutality on both sides, with many villages destroyed and civilians killed. By the time the war had ended with the defeat of DAG in August 1949, over 80,000 people had lost their lives. The Greek Communist Party (KKE) remained banned after the return of peace.

[2] The then Greek prime minster General Nikolaos Plastiras (1883–1953) was leader of the National Progressive Centre Union Party and had formed a coalition with the Liberals.

[3] Andrei Vishinsky (1883–1954), who gained notoriety during the 1930s as the chief prosecutor of the Great Purge trials in Moscow, became the Soviet Union's foreign minister in 1949.

great pleasure. Upside down they have a weirdly expressionistic resemblance to a human face – a neurotic clown.

At table the favourite topics are those which border on the obscene. The boys, especially the fat little Cretan, Kabella, are constantly giggling and stammering things out to me which would gain them instant expulsion in a British school. If I get angry, they will talk in Greek; if I look shocked, they will tease me; so all I can do is laugh. Yesterday, the prefect at my table, a son of a former minister of labour, handed me the following joke which he had written out on a piece of paper.

> Hotelkeeper (to honeymooning husband, the morning after): How
>   did the whole thing go?
> Husband· Very well. I liked the hole, and she liked the thing.

> 'A very good joke,' he shouted from the bottom of the table.
> 'Very good indeed,' I agreed.
> 'Mr Potamianos told it to me,' he said.
> I tried to look amused.

On my left sits Asymakos, a tall, handsome boy with an olive complexion, lustrous eyes, very long lashes and a generally girlish manner. He spends most of his time fluttering his eyelashes at me, and asking me what marks I shall give him. He and the Cretan have vilifying contests. According to the Cretan, Asymakos seduced the maid at home last year; one can hardly blame the maid. As for A, he says that the Cretan boy (aged sixteen) spends all his time with 'bad womens' in Athens. Kabella has kindly offered to show me the night life of Athens, and the prefect has suggested that I visit him in Salonika, where he has a Buick and a Jeep and plenty of girls at his disposal.

A visit to the barber's. Here, one is a king; and for my benefit the complete haircutting ritual was performed. Pomading after pomading; everything disinfected and re-disinfected; constant brushing away of small hairs; brilliantined three times. Artistic snippetings. An acolyte, a youth in a monkey-jacket, stood beside the barber and handed him scissors and combs and atomizers as needed, like a nurse attending a fussy surgeon. At one point he handed the barber the wrong thing, and he was brushed impatiently aside. After a while, I had to resist a furious inclination to laugh. It was good service carried to the point of worship. The gods must giggle. But what a change from the frigid attitude of democratic England, where the barber works like a machine. It is not a base servitude to do a service pleasantly. It does not imply that the server is inferior to the served. And one pays with pleasure, not because the law demands it.

The guitarist Evangelakis. He came to our table, and talked. A humble, timid, yet faintly shy person. He sang one or two songs at the end; and then one which he said he didn't often sing. A strident, painful, intense song, somewhere between a Spanish lament and the Negro 'blues'. He told me afterwards that it was his mother's song, one which he associated with her death, since it was about hospitals and doctors dressed in white. The guitar accompaniment was particularly savage, discordant, melancholy, and he sang with closed eyes and a serene, almost ecstatic kind of force, bursting the words out, prolonging them, quavering. One of the school waiters, Dionysos, who was sitting with us, had the – not the nerve, the impermeability – to yawn. A very vicious yawn; Dionysos is a nice, easy-going fellow, but he seemed to represent the unmoving, immovable callous stupidity, the blindness of the masses, faced with real sincerity and beauty. The poor little guitarist saw him stifle his yawn, closed his eyes again, and went on singing his heart out.

3 February

A savagely windy Sunday; the sky kept almost clear of clouds and the sea was magnificent, steel-blue and jade, torn at by the wind. The white waves galloped up the strait and hurled themselves at the shore or went raging out and onwards towards Hydra and Dokos and Trikera,[1] blurred in an embattled mist. The air was cold; the wind coming off the Peloponnesus snows. The cypresses bent their tips supply and their bodies hardly at all; aristocratic trees, with the old courtier's elegance in bowing. In the morning I had a duty period for two hours, when the boys studied. It was a top room overlooking the strait and Argolis opposite and Didyma crowned with small clouds. The wind roared at the window; the shutters rattled; and the sunshine outside, in the wind, was tremendous. Poor imprisoned innocents.

In the afternoon I walked up the leeward side of one of the cultivated valleys which run inland from Spetsai village. It was wide, full of sinuous terraces, accentuating the contours like a woman's dress; of narrow bands of green young corn; rocks; the crests pine-covered. A shepherd wandered along with his flock in the wind and sunshine; all the fruit-trees are blossoming; the terraces are powdered with pink and white dust; black stems under the flowers. I came up into the wind on the central ridge. It was blowing straight from the Peloponnesian mountains which were shrouded in storm-clouds; the sea glittered. I stood

---

[1] Three islands in the Saronic Gulf to the north-east of Spetsai.

by a ruined cottage, shimmering in the sunshine. I walked down the central road which gives one superb views on both sides, till I came to another ruined house enclosed by a wall. I climbed in to look at it. There were some huge blood-red anemones there, drowned in the wind. Then down a track to Spetsai, past some cottages overlooking the curving terraces and the flowering trees, with the brilliantly white houses ahead and the blue channel, and the golden-green coast of Argolis and Didyma[1] darkly behind. I walked through the back of Spetsai – crowded cottages; masses of fruit-blossom and hedges of prickly pear; the houses are all spotlessly white and the streets clean. I came finally to the harbour. The sun had disappeared, but over Hydra and Dokos, dark blue in the dusk, were a few puffed white clouds, pink and orange and very distant. I walked back to the school, beside the sea which was still dashing over the wall across the road.

Realism. I am trying to write a Maughamesque short story; it is as necessary to be able to do that as it is for an artist to have mastered the art of drawing.

6 February
Death of King George VI – people keep on coming up to me, and gleefully announcing the sad news. When I came into dinner, all the boys at my table looked at me with a joyful smile, and the prefect said, with a broad grin, 'The king of England is died.' I think they were faintly surprised I was not in black, and weeping.

The death of a king no longer touches the particular, except in as much as it is a milestone, the end and the beginning of epochs. This king had no characteristics – a neutral, insipid personality. The modern king is a constitutional nobody; his only chance of being remembered is by his personality.

Now we shall be flooded under with obituaries and salutes to the glorious new Queen, with a drawing of parallels and general smugness. But Elizabethan ages, and the conditions in which they could arise, are done with; now only political epochs, and this Elizabeth is a prig, a throwback, a second Victoria.

Why does the first surprise announcement of death usually produce a smile?

Egyptiadis. He is teaching me Greek. This afternoon I knocked on his door. There was no answer. I went away. Later, when I saw him, I pulled

---

[1] A mountain on the mainland about thirty-five kilometres north of Spetsai.

his leg about sleeping. He was quite hurt about that. Some two hours later he burst into my room.

'Mr Fowles, I know why I was not in my room when you knocked this afternoon.' He has a very precise, determined way of speaking, brooking no opposition, and making no elision. He always tries to get a verb into his sentences; the professional language teacher's hate of monosyllables. 'Now I know why. I went away to defecate.' He pronounced 'defecate' in his strongest and most determined way.

He is an original. He has an alert, bouncy way of walking, like an athletic fat lady; with small steps, yet quickly. His whole figure, massive, with long arms and an ample belly, is gorilla-like, while his shaven head, bull neck and swollen eyes given him an air of the rascally old ex-wrestler. He always shaves at night, and goes through the day with a silvery grizzle over his chin and throat. He always wears the same tie – a silk one with scarlet and grey stripes. He has two shirts, which are always tightly buttoned at the neck – this can be seen because his tie is invariably loose – and two suits, one old, one new; the latter made, he tells us, for his appointment here.

All his life seems to have been one of renunciation. He is more ascetic than many monks, abstemious, thrifty, moral, a tremendous worker. Born at Ankara, he was educated in an American mission, emigrated to America, and worked there for nineteen years in a variety of posts – as accountant, labourer, civil servant, drugstore attendant, night engineer. He says he made no friends; did not smoke; did not even drink coffee. After work, he returned home and studied. Always language; his memory is remarkable. He is trilingual in Greek, Turkish and English. His French is good. And he has smatterings of German, Spanish, Arabic and Italian. Before the war he decided to leave America and come home. He had saved money and wanted to marry. A marriage was arranged. He came home, bought a house, and the marriage was consummated. He talks of it as if marriage was a business deal. Now he has his wife, a daughter and his home in Nea Ionia, an Athens suburb. During the war he gave clandestine English lessons; after the war he taught privately, and was – according to his own stories – the ace translator of the British Police Mission.

He is the perfect master – obedient, unquestioning, full of ideas and enthusiasm, and highly punctual. As soon as a bell rings, he dashes off to meet its summons. He goes ten minutes early to meals in order not to miss grace. At all his duties, he is ten minutes in advance. He is always talking about grammar, teaching methods, what he is going to do in the future.

Above all he is a quoter, with a vast stock of fragments from many writings in many languages. His literary knowledge and interests are minute. He spends most of his free time correcting and reading the school book on English. He likes conversation, mostly in the form of quizzing – the origin of names, difficult points of grammar, rare words. If you know the answer, he is faintly hurt. He knows many songs, and when he is singing it is impossible to interrupt.

We are not without suspecting this paragon. He praises his own virtues and especially his abstemiousness, not in a boastful way, but with a kind of Socratic sagacity, with a humble sense of rightness. He judges everyone by himself.

'Why do the boys here talk in class?' he says. 'When I was in class, I only wanted to learn and to hear what my teacher said. I did not want to speak to my neighbours all the time. I had nothing to talk about.'

He talks much of himself; not as an extrovert does, with self-conscious exhibitionism, but as an introvert who has seen little but his own industry and life of abstention, and so has not much else to talk about. There is a shrewdness in his smile; at times he shakes with a high-pitched laugh, and his face wrinkles like a crying baby's, but with merriment. Sometimes he seems obtuse; he does not understand new methods. In class he is stern, unsmiling, and his emphatic, almost explosively correct pronunciation of English becomes so exaggerated that I find it hard to understand. He speaks German like a car backfiring; his Arabic is terrifyingly glottal; whilst his French, though very correct, is without any musicality; like a Mozart symphony played by a brass band.

There must be some flaw. Certainly, he likes cognac, and likes it neat; and he drinks it with expert gulps, and for a moment, the normal vacancy of his face disintegrates, and his eyes cloud over. At such moments he reminds me above all of a toad who has just swallowed a fly. Permitting himself a blink, and the faintest shade of satisfaction.

He has a glorious inconsequence in conversation, normally interrupting its flow with some totally irrelevant quiz or reminiscence. Today I was walking back at dusk with him from the school. A robin flew on the path just before us.

'Look at that robin,' I said. It flew away.

'A frog, did you say?' he asked. I felt that if I had said that frogs have wings he would have believed me. He has no interests outside his languages. He can recite the Linnaean system in Latin, but he does not know the commonest flower. He spoke then as if robins and frogs were metaphysical things, without any established entity, words in a dictionary.

Glimpses like that into his fantastic universe compensate for his less endearing qualities – dogmatism, obtuseness and simple morality.

11 February

A superb day. The weather like a new razor; a cloudless sky and a steel-cold wind, ultramontane, the mistral. It came straight off the Peloponnesus, over the sea, ruffled and Trinidad blue, or Antwerp blue.

The air was brilliantly clear, and the mountains stood in a great snowy line across the sea, the snow growing pinker and pinker as the sun moved west. The sky absolutely pure, invigorating, windswept; and yet it was the coldest day I have had here. Mount Didyma, opposite the school, seemed only five or six miles away. In the evening it took on a glorious purple-blue tinge and the sky behind was lemon-blue, very pale green, rosaceous, and still astoundingly clear and transparent. The coast was silver, the cliffs burnished red ochre, the trees green and timelessly golden.

Today this supremely beautiful landscape seemed to me to be almost unreal in its perfection. It produces a tonic effect on me. The day, for some reason, was full of minor annoyances. And I did not feel well. But just one glance out of a window, or as I crossed the garden, at the magnificent petrified comber of mountains seemed to blast, to cut all petty human things away. I felt a kind of aesthetic exhilaration, a mental exuberance and keenness of perception, a complete environmental euphoria.

I was in Sharrocks' room, listening to the news from England. Grey, chill, methodical, uninterested. All that world, as I stood at the window, staring out at the deep blue sea and the sunlit wind-tossed olives and those incredibly perfect mountains – all that world seemed minute, twisted, pettily inflated, the life one sees when one turns a stone up. And this bright perfect landscape, the upper side, I a lizard in the sun.

Yesterday Sharrocks and I went for a long Sunday walk, through the backstreets of Spetsai, which is much more extensive than it appears from the sea. Through alleys of worn rock, over small dry gulches, across small swards, past the uniformly brilliant white houses with their shuttered windows and sun-drenched air. It was very windy. The trees softened the lines and edges with their misty blossom, pink and white. We passed some lemon-trees laden with fruit. Near the western end of the village, in a grassy square, we came on a shepherd sitting with his sheep around him, brown and white rams and clean, gambolling lambs. The sun shone down through the almond-blossom, accenting the charcoal blackness of their stems. There were ruined houses around, and piles of rubble. A beautiful pastoral vignette. We went to another grassy square where there were children dancing. They laughed when S took photographs. They came around us, clamouring, with bright eyes and quick mouths, and the boys with heads shaven bald, in the village fashion – a detestable one.

Spetsai is full of ruined houses and vacant lots. It is built haphazardly, up the banks of dry streambeds, facing in all directions. As one goes in and out of the houses, along the paths, there are constant small vistas. The whiteness of the walls is entrancing; every other colour has a raised value thereby – blue, ochre, the green grass. They become softer and more intense at the same time.

The eastern end of the island is less natural, less rugged, less lonely than the west. There are meadows and orchards and vineyards and even some small fields of sprouting corn. The small island of Spetsopoula, even more of a Treasure Island than Spetsai, with wooded slopes and a central ridge, blocks out the southern distant coast of the Peloponnesus. To the west the sea, one or two small islands dropped therein, and somewhere just under the horizon, the Cyclades. We turned inland to a small estate owned by a friend of S. A small villa tucked away among olives and cypress. The owner was away, but the garden was full of small blue irises, and on the terrace there were geraniums and carnations and stocks and bougainvillea in flower. We came away, past a fowl-run, where the hens and one very majestic and very cowardly white cock stood in the shade, statuesque, immobile, watching us sideways, for all the world like the painted figures and heads in some Giotto or Carpaccio crowd.

We climbed up to the monastery, an ugly group of buildings – though redeemed by their white, cypress-guarded brilliance – and from the terrace absorbed a beautiful view down through the olives and almond-blossom to the gentle curve of Marina Bay and the dark woods of Spetsopoula. A high point over the sea; a lovely place to be buried. The sun was setting and we came down a path to the village; beside the path were another sort of iris, with three splashes of deep green-black, black iridescently green, on their glaucous green flowers.

Suddenly the wind blew cold, and clouds banked up to hide the sun. We went along the quay of the old port, full of tossing caiques and swaying masts and bitter wind. All the bright colours of the hills, the geranium reds, the greens, the blues, were muted. The far slopes of Didyma were still golden, golden against the inky black clouds beyond. The quayside, the alleyways, became bleak. The white houses looked grey. We went into the village church – the most important of the sixty-five chapels on Spetsai – a dense, incense-drenched atmosphere of icons and tapestries and ornate candlesticks; a cavern of Byzantine bric-à-brac with the red lights of the lamps glowing evilly in the darkness.

Later we went to the café of the moth-eaten buzzard[1] and sat there talking and talking till midnight. It is at the moment occupied (in the military sense) by a film unit. They all more or less speak English. A very handsome male star, *un très brave cavalier*, with the smiles and manners of a faintly effeminate profile. An enthusiastic young mongrel of an assistant cameraman, voluble and American in accent. Two or three fine old priests – the film is partly religious – in their Orthodox

---

[1] The café was called Lambris.

Greek robes and with nobly bearded Socratic faces. A young man with a quite other beard, a distant echo of St Germain des Prés. A tall, journalistically dressed young artist, who had the perfect classical noble profile, and a very pleasantly fresh, shy manner. He was really more handsome than the star. Evangelakis the guitarist came in and played, showing his paces before the film company. He was at his improvising best – with a tremendous speed of invention. The producer of the film sat at a central table with a strained, grimly uninterested expression. Evangelakis danced, his fat, short figure delicately stepping and revolving with the rhythm, his arms out sideways, balancing, his fingers snapping out the time, his mouth spitting out wisecracks at each turn. Some of the local fishermen danced; three of them did a kind of drunkards' dance, with a delightful very slow tipsy rhythm, their arms around each others' necks, and the end man at each chorus appearing to fall to the ground and just being saved, at the last moment, by his comrades. A very athletic performance. Then another man came out in the space we had cleared and did some dance which entailed somersaults over a chair. The artist drew cartoons of S, who looked like an intellectual turnip with Fascist tendencies, and myself, who looked untidily Aryan and faintly like the Duke of Windsor, and Evangelakis, who is already a caricature of nature.

The dancing in Greece is spontaneous and often skilful. In fact, in male company in a Greek café where there is music there seems to be a point where it is as important to be able to do some dance as it is, at a similar point at a pub in England, to tell a dirty joke. Not that Greeks do not tell dirty jokes; but Englishmen never dance.

We were charged over £3 for our evening; at least twice too much. A less pleasant aspect of Greece. Our walk back to the school was doubly unpleasant; the bill angered us, and an icy wind off the mountains cut right through to our spines.

A very typical letter from Ginette Poinot. A kind of provincial faded grace and formal language. She is a natural letter-writer. Not one quarter as vivacious or quick-witted as Ginette Marcailloux, but incomparably more graceful in putting her thoughts, her love and her dreams on paper. I enjoy writing in reply.

'Partout dans la ville, sur les terrasses des collines, des fontaines, nuages, flocons d'arbres en fleur.' I admire my own last words.

She wants me to go with the *famille thouarsaise*[1] to Spain next year. I am quite eager to do so; the journey would be good, and she, good enough company. But I feel some sense of responsibility – my only

---

[1] i.e. the group of young students, mostly from Thouars, with whom JF had the previous year toured Switzerland, the Tyrol and Bavaria.

morality now being in personal relationships – of keeping her hoping
– however much I destroy the possibilities; *'Je ne veux pas voir développer
une amitié chaleureuse en amour désesperé, nourri de brefs rencontres et longues
tristesses.'*

Elsewhere I spoke of *'une énigme à la jolie taille'.*

*'Je ne veux point vous faire mal, mais non plus vous charmer au point où
vous oubliez notre situation et les plusieurs distances qui nous séparent.'*

It seems that the *'famille'* had some plan of giving a concert to raise
funds to get me to France if I could not afford the fare myself. I am
touched to have touched, and somewhat bewildered; to be frank, incredulous, but eager to believe.

24 February

I went off alone for the day, walking. A pure, cloudless, dreamlike day.
I walked for miles – and did not see a soul. The centre of the island is
strangely still, devoid of anything but plant life, aboriginal. I clambered
up the steep slopes, through the solitary valleys with their pine-woods,
over the brilliantly blue sea. The mountains in the Peloponnesus were
very clear, standing close across the ten miles of gulf, with their snows
magnificently white against the pure blue sky. The whole atmosphere
was dazzlingly clear and sunny; so perfect a day that I felt strangely
uneasy, almost dissatisfied. I had lunch on a bluff facing the west; the
whole of the central Peloponnesus stretched out before me. The gulf
between seems unreal; a stretch of glittering blue sea swamped the
mountains opposite. A tortoise scuffled across the stones; I tried to feed
it, but all it wanted to do was to scuffle slowly away. The wind was warm,
the air scented by hundreds of grape hyacinths, humming with bees. A
raven croaked high overhead. I was thirsty and an orange was doubly
good. After lunch I took off my shirt, and lay under a pine in the sun
and warm wind, drowsing, close to the earth, elemental. I felt erotic;
sunshine and bare skin have that effect on me. Sun-worship must have
had an erotic basis; the man who fell in love with the sun.

This landscape, on the westernmost high hills of Spetsai, must be one
of the loveliest in this world. One can so arrange it that by a turn of
the head one can include Hermione and Didyma in the panorama, and
then Greece is like a naked woman, giving, as much as a landscape can
to one human, all her secrets. This is the land of the *Odyssey,* of the
wander and effort of the ancient Greeks. Blue seas, pine-trees, and snow-
capped mountains; all like iced wine; catalytic, redolent.

I went down through long sunny slopes to a bay which is lovely even
in this island of lovely bays.[1] The two headlands embrace the distant

---

[1] This is Agia Paraskevi, Holy Friday Bay, where JF set *The Magus.*

Peloponnesus; a grove of pines run down to a long track. A small chapel and a cottage stand out, dazzling white against the trees. A herd of goats, small, black and agile, with tinkling bells, grazed along the edge of the sea. Outside the chapel I saw the goatherd's long cloak and his wallet. A very lonely paradise.

I came home, a long climb and travest round the central ridge, feeling tired to exhaustion. Didyma was glowing mauve and purple, then indigo against the Ionian blue sky. I heard the school bell ring for preparation, still two miles away. Then came voices from the village, the children singing as they danced.

Later, I went into Spetsai to meet S for supper. He read out bits of a *New Statesman* and its editorial criticizing the Royal Funeral.[1] Politics and kings seemed far. We went to Lambris, listened to Evangelakis and others singing, watched the film actors with four Athenian tarts, drank beer and half a bottle of cognac which the owner gave us, and finally returned far from ready to face the week.

This perfect country and climate – today is the third completely cloudless day of a divine spring. This flawless natural world is small, only a narrow layer of cream on the deep milk of reality. A terrible dissonance between the landscapes and the modern Greeks. They are blind, lost in their tiny mole-runs.

The ludicrous unreality of all the *oraisons funèbres* and pompous praise for the late King and new Queen. The necrophilous lingering over all the funeral arrangements; the criticism of the ceremony – criticism has become so ingrained a feature of the modern world that nature itself will soon be criticized – and the declarations of devotion. Most silly of all, the parallels with the great Queen Elizabeth. England was a family then, vigorous, but still a hierarchy; people did not mind looking up. Now the world is a hive of individual units; they look levelly; have no family national love for a monarch. If the monarchy remains, it is because the lives of the masses are so colourless that they welcome the chance of any sublimation. And the crown is a psychological anchor, a break – a sea-anchor. It keeps us dragging safely back.

---

[1] On 16 February 1952 under the heading, 'The Queen's Opportunity', the *New Statesman* wrote that the 'peremptory order for national mourning was both intrusive and silly'. It expressed the hope that the new monarch would 'seize the opportunity to sweep away the old order at Court and substitute a way of life which matches the times they live in and the aspirations of peoples they rule'.

1. John Robert Fowles, aged thirteen

2. John and Gladys May Fowles at Stonehenge, *c.* 1935

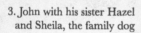

3. John with his sister Hazel and Sheila, the family dog

4. John in uniform, *c.* 1944

5. John with *vin et pain*, Paris, 1948

6. Paris 1948

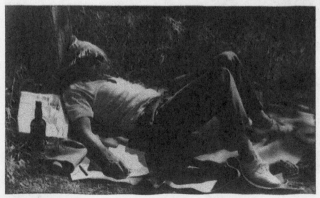

7. 1950: 'How I got a second at Oxford.'

8. The Anargyrios and Korgialeneios School, Spetsai, Greece

9. Members of staff of the Anargyrios School, John Fowles on bollard

10 John Fowles, headmaster Gerandopoulos,
Denys Sharrocks, 1952

11 John in his room at the
Anargyrios School, 1952

12. Monemvasia: 'The beard begins.'

13. John, Elizabeth and Roy Christy, Spetsai

6 March
Spetsai is more than a match for the diarist. The days slip by like eels,
especially when the weather is fine. Things happen, I meet people, I
teach, I play tennis, and nothing gets done. No month in my life went
with the speed of this last February. These last few days have been
Carnival – Apocryas.[1] All the school was decorated, the walls of the
dormitories and dining-room with gay figures and streamers, and everything else spruce and clean. Spetsai was full of rich parents and pretty
sisters. The weather perfect. Sharrocks and I were patronized by the
Govanoglous, a rich couple who spoke excellent French, and who
seemed very cultivated beside the rest of the rather *nouveaux riches* Mamas
and Papas. The President, Chairman of Governors, Sotiriou, came and
did a tour of inspection of the dormitories. A little old white-haired
man, very feeble and decrepit, hobbling along with a stick; the inspection was almost military. The boys stood to attention by their beds while
Sotiriou and his entourage crept past, poking at the boys' lockers and
making polite remarks of commendation. Another pompous little fellow
of fifty or sixty, dressed in ginger tweeds, with a military moustache, took
the role of adjutant. After came the headmaster, the vice-master, the
housemasters and the lengthy procession of masters, prefects and
parents. All would have been well, but for the pace set by Sotiriou, a
kind of funereal crawl, which reduced the more frivolous of us to helpless laughter.

On Sunday morning we sat in sunshine by Spetsai harbour, watching
the *un*usual gay throng, drinking beer. That afternoon there was a football match, followed by a founder's commemoration ceremony. The
whole school formed up before the statue of Anargyros.[2] Shuffling of
feet, sniggers. A boy was sent to get a chair, so that the wreath might
be laid over the great man's statue's shoulders. The chair is put in place.
All is well.

'The wreath,' shouts the headmaster. No sound. The wreath has been
forgotten. A small boy rushes off to get it. Shuffling of feet, sniggers.
The small boy reappears, carrying a large wreath of laurel leaves. The
headmaster stands with the wreath, bewildered. He has just realized that
the old boy who is meant to lay the wreath is not there. Shuffling of
feet, sniggers. A posse of old boys is seen running down the wrong path,
lost. Shouts. The old boys lose their heads, and come dashing up through
the bushes, over the flower-beds. Laughter. Angry shouts from the gym
master. Silence. The chief old boy hastily straightens his tie, smooths
his hair, is given the wreath.

[1] The Greek Orthodox version of Mardi Gras, Apocryas begins every year on
the Sunday before Clean Monday, which marks the start of Lent.
[2] One of the two founders of the school. See note on page 135.

'Atten . . . tion!' shouts the gym master.

Everyone is facing the school and the statue. On the school flagpole the flag of Greece begins to slowly rise. All is well till half-way, when it jams. Small tugs, it is lowered slightly, jerked up. But it is jammed. Everyone bites their lips to stop laughing.

The old boy looks at the headmaster, the headmaster looks round; shuffling of feet, sniggers. The senior old boy moves forward to lay the wreath. Apparently he does not realize what the cheer is for. He lays the wreath at the foot of the statue, and steps gingerly back to his place. Some of the boys laugh.

The headmaster and the old boys stand looking at each other; the headmaster makes a motion with his hat. The old boys look at one another in an embarrassed way. The silence becomes unbearable. Everyone had expected everyone else to make a speech.

It is the gym master's finest moment.

He blows his whistle. The boys start talking and the parents move. A crisis is averted.

The headmaster says, 'Good!' The old boys bow. Everyone smiles secretly. The gym master blows his whistle again. The boys march off, laughing and talking. The headmaster pulls out a small boy and gets him to set the wreath on top of the statue. The old boys try not to look ashamed.

The ceremony is over.

Only Anargyros himself rose above the absurdity. His idealized stone head, humane, far-seeing, indulgent but noble, gazed whitely out above the ridiculous crowd. The head of a great idealist, almost a dreamer. His dream is so far from being fulfilled; but stone has patience.

The statue, incidentally, is nothing like his photograph; but the facts say that the inner man must have had features almost as fine as the statue.

10 March

The best day of the carnival was the last, when we went by caique across the channel to the mainland village – a very dirty one – of Porto Kheli. A brilliant day, with the Peloponnesus clear as a bell, the water dancing, and the sky quite cloudless. We went to a small tavern outside the village and had lunch under a carob-tree; a very Greek meal with white carnival loaves, shrimps, great succulent Kalamata olives, large winkles, onions, lettuce and *halva* to finish with; ouzo and retsina to drink. S and I were at a table with some parents. There was Greek dancing; everyone danced, in a ring, to a decrepit gramophone set at the tavern door. A great deal of laughter, sunshine, a small breeze. The smaller boys flew kites; somebody picked a great bunch of dark red anemones and stuck them in a glass among the debris of our meal. They stood all day alive in the breeze, most ancient Greek of flowers.

20 March

Time goes too fast; I have been in bed for a week with flu. I haven't felt ill at all; but I don't feel like plunging back into the furnace as long as I can stay here. Moral laxity. Thank God nothing commits me in this school. I can devote all my time to my own problems. It is almost an ideal solution. The maximum of money and pleasure for the small amount of work I do.

Excursion to Spetsopoula, a delightful small island, a mile to the south-east of Spetsai – barely inhabited, a minature gem of an island. Sharrocks and I went for a long walk round its southern side, along steep cliff-tops, eroded and sloping to the rocks, with a calm swell on the sea and the Peloponnesus stretching for miles in the distance. Hot rocks, brilliant sea. We went along a grassy path, bordered with wild pink gladioli and bright yellow mint-bushes; there were constellations of small white lilies and a delicious little wild onion, with the neat small name of triqueterous leek. We came to the high point of the island, a chain of groves surrounded by terraces, terraces suspended over the sea. Always the sea in these islands – or rather not the sea, *thalassa*. I saw a hoopoe, a jaunty cinnamon, black and white jay perched on a white rock. A little later there was a ferocious flapping of wings, and a peregrine falcon flashed past down the cliff. All these cliffs, these groves, these hills, terraces and pines, this sea and sky, all these are like a paradise, a totally new discovery. Every day new flowers, new birds. The landscape is there for anyone to enjoy – but that is only one dimension. The birds and the flowers are the speech, movement and dress on the bare lifeless body. Without natural history, the world is only a fraction seen. I felt this strongly with Sharrocks, putting myself in his place, not knowing any flowers, any birds. To him, as to so many, they are meaningless hieroglyphs.

We came back past an isolated farmstead surrounded by green meadows and several small ponies. A rather Irish scene. The masters and their wives had lunch in a large villa. We all sat round a long table, with the headmaster being grannyishly jovial at the head. It was a long, pointless meal. Outside the sun shone superbly on the lovely island; but we stayed cooped up in the dining-room, nibbling endlessly and exchanging schoolmasters' wit. Dokos, the music master, a sallow balding bitter little man, very jealous and vain, and fancying himself as a clown, got up on a chair and did his one-armed conductor's baton act – putting a finger out as a penis and holding the baton while he blew his nose. Sharrocks and I were fairly astounded; there were four or five masters' wives present and also one or two important parents, a rather dowagery woman and her husband. But they all laughed, although some were nervous and one, to her eternal credit, had the courage to look disgusted. It says much about Greece that such a trick in such company can be performed. Dokos later told some dirty stories, all over the line for even the broadest social lunch in England. Not *gaulois*, but just dirty. I can't stand the mixture of the oriental and the bourgeois in Greece – a kind of unholy marriage between the Arab and the Swiss. Egyptiadis sang his party songs and was shamefully teased by the others. His eyes had that fixed small Turkish smile which means: 'I hate you for eternity.' He gets a good deal of attention, and for that reason Dokos and the Hippo tease him in a bitter, malignant way.

On the whole, a day when Greece and the modern Greeks struck one of their most strident discords.

5 April

Karageorgis, 4A. A slender, faunlike child with a shock of black hair, slanting long-lashed eyes, and a small pretty mouth. He never seemed quite present – one moment gazing obliquely away into some weird distance, the next eager and irresistible. He lives at only two tempos, very slow and very fast. Small things react terribly on him: an amusing nothing makes him grin with delight, like a flower – a wonderfully charming spontaneous smile – whilst any setback infuriates him. Today he had some questions in a test which he could not answer. After looking very solemn and blank for a while, he suddenly stood up, came to my desk and slammed the paper down on it, and walked away. I called him back. His whole body was tense, outraged, his eyes anguished; I suddenly realized he was crying. Perhaps something sadistic drove me to be angry with him. It seemed such a vicious squall for so small a cause. He said he had not had time to do any revising. I told him to get out. He stood in a kind of mute young rage, almost unable to move. I tore up his paper, and told him that he would not swim for a whole week. He ran back to his desk and flung his head on his arms, face down, and began to sob. The others went on writing. Ten minutes passed. I wrote some more questions on the board. He looked up, his eyes still red, but suddenly in sunshine. He came to me and asked if he could try again. He picked up the torn pieces of paper and copied out what he had written before, and answered the other questions. By the end of the lesson he was smiling and explaining things I said to the others. Later in the break, when he was playing with some other boys, he suddenly briefly looked up, gave me a brilliantly happy, excited smile, and waved, then back to his tug-of-war. The spirit of April aged thirteen; needless to say, I did not punish him.

Here, at the end of term, I am increasingly aware of the dormant homosexual in me. I enjoy being with certain boys, have too many eyes for them, speak to them too often. It does not worry me; in fact, some of the young boys here, caught in that last budding year when their sexlessness makes them only more feminine, are very beautiful. Mischievous and exuberant and full of a green innocence like spring birdsong or fruit-trees in blossom. Sometimes I feel as if I am in a river of tenderness dangerously near to overflooding. Not that I could ever, I now believe, be swept away into allowing myself to seduce them. This is a thing of the spirit with me; to admit, indulge, since I see no evil in it, but not extend.

Common-room farce. Today the Hippo and I started to translate the dramatis personae of *A Midsummer Night's Dream* into Greek, for the summer-term play programme. All went well till we came to Bottom, and I explained the meaning here was more anatomical than anything else. The Hippo said that the only Greek word was very coarse.

'What do you say when you want to indicate it?' I asked him.

'A periphrasis. The lower part of the back, or the top of the leg. Something like that.'

I started to laugh. The theology master came in; the Hippo asked his advice. Timaigenis was outraged. He said something and shot out of the room, to reappear a moment later with the headmaster, talking volubly with him and pointing at me as if I was unclean. So began an argument which went on for nearly an hour. To translate 'Bottom', or not to trans-late 'Bottom'? The deputy head came in, we all gave our points of view, other masters joined in. It was unanimously decided (with only myself withstanding) that 'Bottom' was a filthy and obscene term.

'It suggests terrible things in Greek,' said the Hippo. 'Terrible things.'

But not only was 'Bottom' untranslatable; all the other names of the Athenian herdsmen were doubtful. There were the boys' parents to think of; Mr Vrakas is not going to like it if his son is 'Pig-faced' (Snout). So in the end it was decided to do nothing, but leave the names in English.

The headmaster looked profoundly worried by the whole thing. His parting words were: 'We mustn't make the play seem funny.' He has a horrible surprise coming.

After this highly (and typically) puritanical teacup storm about the abominable name 'Bottom', that same night blossomed out into one of this school's maddest paradoxes. The Sixth Form gave an end-of-term party, to which ten or twelve masters (including the Old Man) were invited. The boys decorated a room and rigged up a band platform on which four of them played music. And then, with the headmaster's smiling approval, they began to dance together. The tall boys took out the pretty ones; they danced sambas, tangos, foxtrots, close and with every sign of pleasure. Some were just enjoying themselves normally, and some others, it seemed to me, abnormally. These were friendships suddenly practised as liaisons. I thought it all slightly distasteful and very amusing, after the morning's show of purity.

Further characteristics of modern Greece; the drinking-water and sewage-pipes run side by side; their mental sanitation, disinfected one minute, and stinking the next, is bewilderingly naïf. Every Greek seems to possess two quite unrelated persons inside him.

11 April

A term all but completed. At the present pace, I shall not fall out for a while. A growing dislike for the masters, the school system, and the public character (Tartuffe) of the modern Greek, is counter-balanced by my love for this superbly lovely landscape, the loneliness of this island, where often I walk for hours and see no living thing at all except plants and insects – even birds are rare – the climate and my liking for some of the boys. They have a precociousness, a cynicism which gives them a slightly *faisandé* quality; something corrupt in even the most innocent. The cherubic pink face of the small English boy does not exist here; the devil has had his say; a touch of the faunlike, and much worldly wisdom.

The boy on my left at table, Glaros, 'Seagull' (a highly appropriate name – extremely beautiful to look at, in nature less pretty), intrigues me perhaps more than any other. He has been to America, and so acts as my interpreter; or we simply talk to each other. A tall, slim boy, very dusky, certainly with oriental blood behind him, since his face has perfect Arab female beauty. Very dark expressive eyes, a soft, full red mouth, warm brown skin, eyelashes of incredible length and curve and a general air of *Arabian Nights* allurement. He talks all the time about girls; discusses the other masters quite openly with me and criticizes the school. The other day he even told me that he didn't believe in the Orthodox religion. He is very precocious, self-centred, temperamental, and hopelessly out of place in such a cold narrow room as this school.

15–30 April

Easter holidays. Much needed, not so much consciously, as unconsciously; not until now, when I am back again, can I see that I was becoming in almost all ways insular.

I went to Crete, with Sharrocks. Keeping a diary was difficult. I never find myself capable of much more than jottings and one or two key phrases – keys, only too often, to empty rooms. The immediate rendition is only too often an ornate key-phrase, a kind of trap, a siren, misleading one into superfluous labyrinths. If one waits, the perspectives come; if, at the moment of writing it down, there are things which struck one at the time as being important and noteworthy and which are now forgotten, then memory has merely sorted things out. *Raturer le vif,* one's own best critic.

And then Sharrocks and I are both shy of our literary ambitions; we spend a great deal of time talking about writers and writing. His world is, in fact, almost wholly literary. But we show each other nothing, never discuss our own work; and to write in the other's presence would be tantamount to inviting an almost – so inhibited are we about *that* – obscene intimacy. There is a very close parallel between the self-conscious virgin and the intending young writer who has not published – tormented, deceitful and paralytically shy. In fact what very few notes I made were scribbled in the rare moments I was out of his sight. At least those rare moments when I both wanted to record and was out of his sight.

11 May
This term is different from the others. A new routine – school from eight till one, and sleep in the afternoon. Every day before lunch I swim. The weather is sultry, the sky usually half-veiled with thin clouds, the grass yellow, dust and parched earth. There are occasional breezes, but they are hot and unrefreshing. At night the air is stifling, and I am plagued by mosquitoes. The days seem heat-drenched, dry, lifeless – existence seems dull. The mountains are invisible, always hazed over. I long for rain, thunder, a chill in the air. Sometimes I seem to be only half-conscious, sunk, drugged. I have done no writing, written no poetry. The days burn on and out, on and out, remorselessly, like a third-degreeing arc-lamp.

For an hour each day I swim, with the underwater mask. That makes life tolerable, a time of daily stimulus. The minute shock of entering the water; then the drifting over the rocks and the seaweed, through the weird translucent other-world of sea-urchins and starfish, blue sand and dark crannies, green vistas and pink jelly-fish; a theatrical world, above all of the ballet or the silent cinema, where every movement is graceful, unmotivated. There are many kinds of fish – the commonest are a kind of angel-fish, varying from the size of a penny to some as big as a dinner-plate. They swim in flocks, grey silvery discs with a black spot near the tail. They even follow me, especially when I overturn rocks, like robins attending a digging gardener. There are long striped fish, all kinds of ugly, grotesque rock-fish, strange little bright red and bright yellow blennies, splendid fish with long bright emerald bodies and blue fins and tails. Green ones with orange wings and spots. One princely little creature with six legs and comparatively huge fanlike fins of brilliantly iridescent azure. Large pearly fish like salmon, with mournful eyes, who swim round and round me if I try and chase them, so near yet never quite in reach. I fear the octopus and the sharks. Only one or two people are lost each year in Greece from sharks, but it is difficult to forget them – something fascinating, something frightening in floating over deep valleys and ridges of blue-green water. Rocks in the distance often look like motionless bodies, lurking, waiting.

Mitso, the school postman, was turning over the letters today to see if we had any post from England. There was a large envelope addressed

to a master who left the school before the war. I glanced at it and saw
the word *Bedford*. It was, in fact, an Old Bedfordians' magazine,
addressed by some weird chance to this school, though Noel-Paton
left in 1930-something. I read the magazine. Re-entry into a forgotten
room; old names, memories. I am still not reconciled to Bedford; wish
to forget it. I enjoyed my last years there. But they retarded me two
years. I did not begin to grow up till my last year at Oxford. All the
atmosphere of the magazine seemed to me out of date, frowsty. A naïf
Victorian world of schoolroom values, old-tie sentimentality – there
was news of many of my contemporaries. They seem still unemancipated, engaged in Old Bedfordian activities, still clinging together. An
illusion, or 99 per cent of it; but I prefer the complete cut-off, the 100
per cent isolation.

14 May
Five destroyers and two submarines appeared mysteriously off Spetsai
yesterday evening, and cast anchor. The Greek fleet on a cruise. Ominous
shapes in the peaceful straits.

Henry Miller, *The Colossus of Maroussi.*[1] A vigorous tough style; but I don't
like the continually exuberant enthusiasm – in the end it sounded like
a vicar trying to warm up a deadly teaparty. But Miller's view of the
modern Greek is so different from mine that I wonder which of us is
right. I think I am, but perhaps I have got too certain of my own vision.
At the moment I find it hard to find anything good in the modern
Greek at all. Miller at least causes a re-examination.
  'Greece is now the only paradise in Europe.' Greek landscapes are
like Mozart's music. Miller paints with the tube and a splayed thumb.
But my own style seems insipid beside his.

23 May
A Milleresque moment. I went today up into the hills – burning sunlight,
bright breeze and a dazzlingly brilliant atmosphere. Everything inland
is parched, stone-dry – only the blue-mauve thyme plant and a kind of

---

[1] In 1939 Henry Miller (1891–1980) travelled to Greece to see his friend
Lawrence Durrell. During a visit to Athens, Durrell introduced Miller to the
writer and raconteur George Katsimbalis, a larger-than-life figure who lived in
Maroussi, a northern suburb of Athens. *The Colossus of Maroussi*, first published
in 1941 by the Colt Press in San Francisco, is an affectionate portrait of
Katsimbalis, and an account of the travels that followed when Katsimbalis offered
to show Miller around Greece. Miller, who fell deeply in love with the country,
wrote of 'an enthusiastic, curious-minded, passionate people', and delighted in
their 'contradictoriness, confusion, chaos – all these sterling human qualities'.

dwarf yellow gorse in flower. But the pines give shade. No birds, few butterflies – a multitude of wasps, bees, flies, grasshoppers. The sky was swept cloud-clear, the corn straw-ripe. On the opposite side of a small valley three girls began to sing with a tremendously powerful rhythm and stridency. Not like any singing I have heard elsewhere, in complete accord with the dryness and brilliance of the air. Part song, without subtlety, undertones, shadows – songs for an open sunburnt hill. They sang at full stretch, incredibly violent, young sun-priestesses, the mother-cult. Before they sang I could not have believed any sound could have fitted in with that landscape. Then they gave it all a voice. They walked down a path to a rock-cistern; walked back again. One of them had bare brown arms, with black hair. I could not see whether she was pretty or not. I had field-glasses, but preferred not to use them. She lifted her skirt up to her waist, to let the sun shine on her petticoat. I heard them singing still half an hour later. From a great distance.

June
Maupassant, *Miss Harriet.*
Reading Maupassant I felt a wave of helplessness come over me. No writer is more brilliant in the most difficult of techniques – realism. I cannot hope to ever equal the mastery of such men.

Here I do nothing. The Greeks contaminate me with their egocentricity, their long glissade through sunshine into stagnation. Sunburnt stagnation, that is life here. I have the time, but no will to use it. Dissatisfaction with all I do, have done.

The boys, the masters, the system, they all grate on my nerves. I am turned by them full of spleen, contemptuous and *je-m'en-foutiste*, bitter and enraged, ready to lash out at anyone. Small things, incidents upset me ridiculously. The only thing puritan left inside me is my sense of time – it has taken the place of an unhappy conscience. Now the passage of time agonizes me. The worm in the lotus bud.

4 June
Beautiful days. Hot sun, no clouds. The sky is acutely blue, the sea delicious. The school's annual beanfeast is approaching, a whirl and chaos of rehearsals, costumes, new timetables, endless lists of things to do.

One day I went along the coast to a Byzantine bay, the sun like a comet, a wind, the cliff slopes completely deserted. No birds, no animals; few flowers, few butterflies. Even the reptiles seem to have gone. This is when one notices the island's lack of water. The trees mean shadow, there is vegetation, but it is sparse, burnt. Now only thyme blooms profusely; I found also a colony of tall bright-pink centaury; geranium stars under the carob-trees. The bay was empty, emptier than the sky.

There is a small ruined mill at one corner of the beach. I swam, watched the fish, swam out of the bay to where the bases of the cliffs fell in steps mysteriously and frighteningly away into the indigo depths. To float over the underwater precipice gives one a birdlike sensation. I ran on the beach, threw stones, stood in the sun. It seemed for an hour at the most. But there was no sign anywhere of anything human. I walked back quickly to school, to be in time for lunch, drenched in the elements. I found I was two hours late.

Walking into Spetsai. The mountains at dusk are a feline deep grey-blue, luminous against the lemon-blue pale radiance of the clear sky. Over the Peloponnesus, fiery red wisps of cloud above the black sea of the mountains. The sea breeze-ruffled, the islands ethereal, grey, pink, pale blue, mauve. The hibiscus are blood-red outside the dazzling white cottages. The village children play down the road, the older women sit and talk by their doors. We pass a crone, a bent old creature, in black with a faded blue blouse and a grey headscarf, clutching three huge unripe lemons, the colour of the western sky, to her bosom. A moment's superb impression, unpaintable, but magnificent. Small girls in red at the sea's edge.

We sat at George's, a small taverna looking across the sea to Mount Didyma, and watched the landscape disappear in night. Ate fat small fried fish, many olives, a cucumber, and drank beer. Did not speak much.

There was a rehearsal of the French play in the open-air theatre – Molière extracts. Everyone was there to watch it, under the stars. People stammered out bits of French. The boys laughed to see other boys dressed as girls. One beefy boy, become Argan,[1] stopped the show for two minutes, standing where he had entered, in purple velvet, flushed and rather angry. The play was badly done. Good for schoolboys, but Molière needs professionals more than most.

Then the choir sang – marching songs, patriotic songs, school songs. They all sounded alike. Dokos, the music master, conducted with vigour. As he flapped his arms, his coat went up and the shiny seat of his trousers flashed out. Everyone sniggered. '*Il a de belles fesses,*' I said to the physics master. The shiny patch flickered in and out, mesmerizing us all. Then there was a Mozart sonata, some Haydn, '*Plaisir d'Amour*' on two squeaky violins. The theology master talked in a low voice; he is a die-hard Byzantinist, and must disapprove of Mozart.

I asked Glaros how he and his friends liked the evening. 'I don't know,' he said. 'We were asleep.' He is an attractively sophisticated, blasé little siren of thirteen. I have him next to me now at meals all the time. He at least can talk English fluently; he is mischievous, extremely pretty,

---

[1] Argan was the hypochondriac of the title in Molière's play *Le Malade imaginaire.*

possesses unbounded contempt for the school, and makes me look
forward to meals. I hesitate even here to say that I am in love with him.
But if he for some reason is not at table, I feel revealingly disappointed.

A strange, rather beautiful dream. I was staying in the country, in some
house in a peculiar situation. In a neighbouring house, some miles away,
there was a girl who wanted to hear from me. I could not go and see
her. Somebody, an old man, her father, kept on ringing me to send a
message, not for her sake, but some other reason – because when one
day an aeroplane flew over, he allowed me to say (to whom?) that it was
taking my message. I remember watching through field-glasses in the
direction in which the girl's house lay. I saw a blonde woman (Kaja)[1]
in a red mackintosh and gumboots, followed by a man, who seemed to
me to be a rival, since I felt jealous, and angry. Then news came that
the girl had killed herself. The next thing I remember was sitting at
table one day, when Dionysos, one of the school waiters, came. 'She
wrote a poem about you,' he said. He was holding a large sheet with
many printed stanzas. I felt a sudden surge of pleasure. I do not recall
feeling any sorrow for her death. The sheet of paper seemed to become
a book which Dionysos handed me. It was a strange volume, full of
surrealist photographs and printing tricks. The title was a silly play on
words. I can't remember it but the author was A. C. Count Rendered.
To my intense regret, I saw that the date was 1916. I smiled sadly, thinking
it was a joke. But when I began to read the book I saw that it was
curiously printed, each page seemed covered in a cream wash – and I
felt that this was renovation. Sometimes the page appeared black or with
designs and print almost indecipherable below the renovation mixture.
But others were clearly inked in above the wash, and there were photos
which showed clearly that 1916 was not the true date. Suddenly I came
on a photograph of a girl's head of extreme beauty, a perfectly classical
face, with high cheek-bones and a wide expressive mouth. It resembled
Marlene Dietrich or perhaps Garbo in the rather sad expression. Also
Constance Farrer, but far more beautiful; the hair was long, framing the
face. She was smiling happily. The next photograph I remember was
one of her much sadder, staring out of the picture while above her
floated a tissue-like death's head. Finally there was a picture of me, but
my mouth seemed non-existent – the whole of the lower part of my face
flat and featureless. Underneath was a caption – something like 'The
Garden Boy' or 'My Garden Love'. Something to do with a garden
seemed to run all through this book of remembrance. The frontispiece
was strange – a kind of drawing of a glass window behind which a white

---

[1] See note on page 64.

face was grinning. On the window was written in large letters
'PAPADOPOULOS, A MOI LA REVANCHE!' (An interpolation – via
Dionysos – in the main current of the dream?)

The interesting thing for me in this dream was seeing the girl's face.
At once I knew her, felt a sweet romantic sorrow in the knowledge that
she was dead. But it seemed to me when I woke that I had known her
very well – but where? Obviously not in my life (unless C F and Brayfield).
Perhaps in some other dream. I have had some other dream about her
which I cannot remember.

10 June
The summer 'At Home' of the school, three days of parent-infested hell,
is past. An incredible amount of hand-shaking, hypocrisy, intriguing,
mealy mouths. The school marched down to the harbour to greet the
Neraida, bringing the Committee[1] and the main batch of proud parents.
On the quay, the boys, all in white, were drawn up in two lines through
which the newly-landed had to walk like newly-weds. The more deferential masters – that is to say, all the Greek staff – crowded round each
important personage; an oriental scrimmage for the great one's momentary hand-clasp. A multitude of oily smiles and false joviality. The
pomposity of the Greek high official and the sycophancy of his inferiors
are emetic. It makes me feel furious and farouche.

A long weekend of ceremonies, richly dressed ugly women, gross grey-
suited fathers. Our parents seem all the same, bourgeois, *nouveaux riches*,
hideous to talk to. There are exceptions; Papa Veziroglou, a delightful
walrusy doctor, bubbling over with wit and good humour. Another fine
old man with a very young son, the two of them touchingly in love,
absorbed in each other, the old man strangely wistful, and even the boy
silent, almost sad, with emotion and contentment. But the others are
foul. Molière and Mozart were never so much pearls before so many
swine.

There was a gym display, the stadium packed with people. Everyone
stood up for the Greek flag to be hoisted. Its halyard snapped at half-
mast and to the general horror, and my delight, the flag collapsed into
the dust below. The Committee members – we were in the royal box
– seemed furious, the boys were paralysed, the headmaster almost in
tears. Another flag was hastily got and tied to the bottom of the mast.
My only regret was that the flag never reached the top. It was a huge
thing and the mast was as thin and whippy as a fly-rod. I am sure it
would have snapped most divertingly. The boys went through their
routines, but halfway through the athletics the Deputy Prime Minister,

---

[1] The school's board of governors.

Venizelos,[1] arrived. Everything was stopped, dislocated, the band played their ridiculous flouncy little march of welcome. The great man, about five feet tall, walked across the field like a dictator on holiday with a posse of celebrities behind him. A red-faced, sandy-haired little person, full of political hand waves, curt political smiles and a bluff political manner. A child of four could see he was inflated, a puppet, a nonentity. There was some luke-warm applause, one or two enthusiastic shouts. Everyone despises Venizelos. They know he lives by his father's prestige and the vested interests that back him. Yet it is so typical of Greece that he is tolerated, a 'great man' in spite of his obvious pettiness. He has arrived, he is consecrated. What a man is in Greece is nothing beside where he is.

Sharrocks and I met the writer Katsimbalis that night for a few moments. He is the Colossus of Henry Miller's *Colossus of Maroussi* – a bad book, I now think, and more than ever after seeing Katsimbalis.[2] He seemed falsely bluff, a self-conscious conversationalist, trying to impress. A stout, hale man of sixty or so, with a white-grey halo of hair, khaki trousers and a walking-stick. A vaguely military appearance, a stage joviality. Miller's portrait of him seems about as accurate as his Poros.[3]

He was with the Tathams, the director of the British Council at Athens and his wife. A tall convention-bound very English Englishman – somehow one knew he had been a housemaster at Eton before he said it – with a horsy upper middle-class giantess of a wife. An affected, intelligent, ginny woman, who evidently despised him. He was pipe-smoking, the senior officer chumming up with the subalterns. I didn't altogether dislike him; he is lucky in having such a filthy wife to be contrasted with. A career couple, celebrity snobs, but influential, so I betrayed myself and was a good public schoolboy and hearty sportsman. Literature didn't seem to take with them.

Our play – mostly my play – went off (I think) quite well. There was a big crowd in the amphitheatre, 2,000 or so, and plenty of laughter at the clowning. I suppose it was worth the sweat and blood. Usual warm, insincere congratulations afterwards. Behind, during, panic after panic. Managing a cast of twenty Greek boys in the *Midsummer Night's Dream* is

---

[1] Sophocles Venizelos (1894–1964) was leader of the Liberal Party, which shared power with the National Progressive Centre Union Party. His father Eleutherios Venizelos (1864–1936), who had been prime minister in 1910–15, 1924, 1928–32 and 1933, was the most influential Greek statesman of the first half of the twentieth century.

[2] See note on page 180.

[3] In the *Colossus of Maroussi* (Penguin edition, p.56ff) Miller describes visiting the island with Katsimbalis and the poet Seferiades.

no drowsy summer afternoon. The strange team thrill of being backstage. A fight against failure, and knowing the truth.

Sharrocks and I drank late afterwards till 2.30 at George's, overlooking
the sea. S unbosomed himself a little – the revealing observation that
he didn't know how to be rude to people. A timid, shy person behind
the façade. He was drunkish at the end and when we got back to the
school tried to set alight the open-air theatre. But when the flames had
spread a few inches, he hastily beat them out. He did that twice, too
much himself to let himself go. I think that is all he will ever do – burn
small holes in the used décor of an empty theatre.

Now normality, and peace.

11 June

The futility of the school. Abdelides, the French master, an old, stut-
tering Rumanian Greek, self-centred, thin-skinned, a nervous and faintly
vicious old man. He asked Athanassiadis, a droll little clown of a twelve-
year-old boy with a weird broken voice, a question in Greek. A answered,
so plainly without thinking, without meaning to be rude, in English.
Something boiled up in Abdelides, and he started shouting and hitting
the boy till he burst into tears. A completely unbalanced burst of temper.
Abdelides went out past me. 'Mais pourquoi?' I said, 'Qu'est-ce qu'il a fait?'
'Je l'ai demandé' (the grammar mistake is typical) 'une question, il m'a
répondu en anglais. Voilà le type!' Poor little Athanassiadis sat sobbing and
protesting helplessly.

Abdelides gives farcical examinations. After he has given the questions, he goes round telling the boys what the answers are, so that his
own teaching results will be good. The Hippo, who had been invigilating
in one of his exams, came bubbling in this morning and asked me what
I thought he should do. Eager to foment trouble, I urged him to go to
the headmaster. Rather to my surprise – I think he wanted the kudos –
he went and asked the headmaster whether he was meant, as invigilator,
to prevent the examining master from helping the boys. The headmaster
said sharply that his business was to keep the boys quiet, and nothing
else, and implied that Abdelides was quite right to 'help' the boys.

Timaigenis, the theology master, told all the boys they would get an
extra mark if they wrote only one page in his examination.

Sometimes I get an attack of spleen – today I had five hours supervising study. The boys are shut in from four till nine, with only two small
breaks of ten and twenty minutes. Their day at the moment is: rise at
6, study 6–7.30, breakfast, exam 8–10.30, study 11–1, lunch, siesta 2–4,
study 4–9, supper, bed 10. An impossibly tough work routine – tonight
they sat there glassy-eyed, rattling their papers, yawning, restless, tired.
They are not even allowed to swim except on alternate days, in case
they get too exhausted to study.

All the petty intrigue, the hypocrisy, the shoddiness of the system choke me. The boys, generation after generation of them, are ruined by this atmosphere of the Jesuit college. Unnaturally strict morals, too much emphasis on work, constant dishonesty at all levels. Dishonesty in ideas, marks, aims, results. The boys should have the run of the island, be allowed more control over themselves, more time for hobbies, games, with a much stricter system of marking. Above all, a harsh system of punishment. Punishment is fresh air; without it the school will always remain stifled, a hothouse of compromises, intrigues, despised by the boys and hated by the masters.

Meanwhile the *cigales* begin to cry in chorus, the sun is ceaseless, burning hot, and the sea is blue, caressing and brilliant as ever. Thank God the breeze still holds.

Suetonius on Nero, the best villain in his gallery. He seems to have been absolutely evil by personal choice, logically, where the others were so by tradition or weakness. Nero, one feels, had it equally in him to become a very good man – at any rate, a very good artist and thinker, either a Nietzsche or a Camus. Most of his disaster was his position. As an individual he would have been a different person, but he saw the logical end of absolute power – absolute evil.

His remark: 'No prince has ever known what power he really has.' The whole of the page on his death is a masterly piece of historical writing, vivid, detailed. His remark: 'What an artist the world is losing' must be made with regard to the practice of absolute power. That was his art. His remark on the conclusion of the fabulously expensive Golden House:[1] 'At last I am beginning to be housed like a human being.'

One's relationship to the past. Nero attracts me by his complete savagery, his unique sardonic blackness. One cannot pity the age he tyrannized. It is too remote. Rather one welcomes the diversion, the colour and violence. To like history is to like the suffering of one's fellowmen. To like the being detached, vicariously enjoying. The historian is a sadist. If we say we pity the past, it is by convention. Logically there is no sense in pitying a *fait accompli* which cannot be mended. However barbaric it may have been, it is now truth, and truth is untouchable, irredeemable (unremediable).

Mrs Adossides, *la grande dame* of Spetsai. Sharrocks and I walked across to her estate on the other side of the island – an olive plantation, and a small but comfortable house surrounded by terraces, terraces alive with colour, sunlight and shadow on the many flowering shrubs. She is a stout old lady, with white hair and benevolent hooded eyes, with that

---

[1] The *domus aurea*, the name given to the colossal palace Nero had built for himself after the great fire which consumed half of Rome in AD 64.

long side-crease to them which seems always to indicate great humanity.
A tolerant profundity.

She is a great philanthropist, speaks five languages faultlessly, is widely
read, very alive, intelligent, outspoken. A faintly cantankerous, gruesome
old lady. She nursed all through the 1914–18 war and had a rough time
of it in the second one, and since then has been ceaselessly occupied
in the Red Cross tracing lost Greeks throughout Europe and in aiding
the stricken villages of Northern Greece. A great contempt for Unesco,
which issues pamphlets while people starve. She had many war stories,
dwelling in detail on nomads. Pain and suffering, for all her great efforts
to relieve them, seem to fascinate her.

We sat and watched the sun go down over the hills. An owl perched
on a nearby cypress and called weirdly. We had dinner, a very good
dinner, in the open air, by lamplight, with the stars brilliant in a velvet
sky. She talked about the Resistance, the Italians, her hatred of jazz. A
powerful, intellectual woman, the political matriarch-mother of thousands.

I admired her, and did not like her.

I caught a small octopus the other day. The underwater mask magni-
fies and it looked large. I stabbed at it with a stick but it crept under a
small rock, which after great effort I managed to overheave. A group of
small village boys gathered on shore near by and watched my titanic
struggles in a frightened, fascinated silence. They were obviously
expecting something quite unheard of. When I appeared with the
octopus writhing on the end of a stick and threw it to them to beat to
death their contempt was barely concealed. One of them, the smallest,
picked it up and said something which sounded like, 'Why didn't you
pull it out with your hand?'

It was only a foot long. I saw another the next day, even smaller, about
as small as an octopus can be. But still I could not bring myself to pick
it up. Something horrifying in the very appearance, the fluid sinuous
watching shape, even in its most miniature form.

21 June

Nearly the end. Term ends in three days. The small ones leave tomorrow.
A sense of change, plans, goodbyes, nostalgia and never again.

These last few weeks have been sun-drenched, nothing but sun. A
warm East wind all day, the racketing chorus of *tzitzikia*, Greek *cigales*,
inhabiting every pine-tree, every branch of every pine. Hours in the sea,
floating among fishes. Meals with Glaros, where the atmosphere between
us is almost that of an ideal (platonic) marriage. His eyes, a brilliant
dark liquid brown, with absolutely clear whites, occasionally cross mine.
I look under the lashes, we look into each other's minds. I suppose he

must sense something of what I feel, although I avoid all physical contact with him. I find now an increasing pleasure in entering the small boys' block, to move among them, be with them, laugh at and with them. Now they are all sun-tanned, Moorish, uninhibited, self-centred, ebullient; nothing pink-cheeked and butter-in-mouth about them. A running stream of small limbs, precocious, not yet tarnished by puberty. I do not see anything reprehensible in my pleasure, nor my indulging it. One can stand between vice and horror of vice, live on the fringe of commitment. The boys in the Eighth, who leave this year, fascinate me. Now they are full of touches, tender smiles for the more attractive small boys. A sudden realization of all the charms of sanctuary.

I am trying to blackmail the Committee into paying my fare back to England, not without wondering whether I am killing the goose that lays the golden eggs. After all, who can complain of existence here: eternal sunshine, an average of little more than two hours' work a day for £520 a year. No need for ideals, responsibility, with no sentiment of being ill-married to a second-best *métier*, since at Spetsai one can hardly think of oneself as a schoolmaster.

When I sit in the evening on the terrace over the sea at George's, watch the sun go down over the cypresses and white sea-houses, the sea grow calm as the wind drops, the mountains of Argolis go luminously blue and then velvet-black, with the stars above them. In the silence while I chew olives and listen to the fishermen gossip at the next table I know that I live, that the body lives.

What I have found at Spetsai is a bodily plenitude; to have bronzed arms, a good appetite, to feel strong, able to swim, dive, run, walk in the sun, live among rocks and pines and sunshine. To have all that is perhaps only a skin euphoria. But one must begin by elementals.

22 June
Today all the juniors left for Athens – a silence in the school, an emptiness in our affections. The buildings seem like ruins, no longer habited, monuments to the past. An incredible poignancy in empty schools – the absence of youth, cries, running feet, bells, laughter. These buildings especially revert so easily to silence: white barracks, stone corridors, the surrounding sea of cicada-voiced olives. The whole décor is sad and soulless, despite the brilliant heat and sun.

Stammatoyannis, the top boy in English in the Eighth, came in tonight and talked about the school. He described the scene on the jetty when the small boys left. All the Eighth class went down to see them off. There were tears everywhere. Ypsilanti, the school mascot and baby, was sobbing and did not want to leave. He kissed Adrianides, his 'boyfriend' in the Eighth. There were other emotional scenes of parting, with all the Eighth class crying for the sorrow of the last view of all their loved ones. Some of them had to leave the jetty, unable to stand the strain. All the small boys were in tears, especially the notorious group in the Third class – Glaros, Seduxis, Ypsilanti, Kyriacoulis, Rapas, Athanassiades – who are the *filles de joie* of the school. As S lovingly told all the details to me, it was humorous. But the poignant last days at school seemed to be symbolized by the small boy/big boy relationship. Even the soberest members of the Eighth seemed smitten.

S talked a good deal about homosexuality. He assured me that the love of the Eighth class for the small boys, was quite platonic and pure. Pure nonsense, but I believe they do see it like that. The Greeks have an immense capacity for deceiving themselves, but not for knowing it. He says there is a good deal of active homosexuality in the school, that Kesses the housemaster knows it, and shrugs his shoulders. I know there was a case a fortnight ago reported to the headmaster and completely hushed up by him. The two boys involved even continue to sleep in the same small dormitory. Some small boys have quite prostitutional reputations, and the name for the junior block among the senior boys is the 'brothel'.

An English master here last year, used to take his protégés to a room to do fencing and there caressed them. Bobes, headmaster two years ago, had a delicious habit of taking the pretty boys into his study and asking them whether they had washed their legs, making them take off their trousers under pretext of inspection, and then (this is where truth no doubt soars into myth) licking them all over. S was amusing about how the boys can smell a homosexual master a hundred miles off, and how they used their knowledge. We talked in the darkness – S to drown the pang of goodbye by describing it, and I because I dote on scandal, small school gossip.

The same night, the Hippo got drunk and gave us a disquisition on his love-life and his view of women. A kind of bestial clown, a mixture of brute stupidity, violent obscenity, and naïf to the point of our pure delight. The verb 'fuck' and its adjuncts must have been used never so often in so short a time. His complete contempt for women is almost comic in its violence. Copulation is the one object of life, and love ridiculous. In Greece he seems almost normal.

I was almost sad at leaving Spetsai. I had become attached to the small routine – the daily swims, the sun, the afternoon sleep. I was glad to think that I could come back. I talked over things about next year with the Vice-Head with pleasure, thinking of the future, the boys again, a year in peace.

I left with Sharrocks. We caught the dawn boat – a grey sea, cool air and thick heads, watched Spetsai go and then went down to a cabin to sleep all the way to the Piraeus. Athens seemed as busy, sham and dirty

as ever. All the women have completely bare brown arms, sexual, sinuous.
The streets seem full of naked warm embraces. I went to the Committee,
found that my blackmail (my fare or my resignation) had worked, and
that they had granted me a hundred pounds. I left the next day. A lonely
fortnight lies ahead. I feel vaguely that my planned holiday is a kind of
duty. Homage to the past.

1 July
The next morning I left for Mycenae. Bus journeys in Greece – or in
any country – effectively demonstrate the difference between nationalities. Here there are no rules, schedules, routines: people come late,
there are arguments, passengers missing, luggage to be loaded and
always greetings to be exchanged (one keeps on meeting the same
people in Greece – they all seem to know each other). No one is ever
left behind.

We struck west out of Athens along the coastal plain to Megara. Past
Eleusis with mountains to the north and an intensely blue sea to the
south, a dark blue, the only real colour in a landscape pale with heat.
Barren mountains, plains of olives, dry red earth. The island of Salamis
stood softly in the sea, heat-burned. Eleusis is ugly, a squalid little place;
and Megara the same. Nothing to equal the appalling makeshift ugliness
of these Greek provicial towns. Past Megara, the hills came down to the
sea and we swept along the red, broken cliffs where Theseus killed
Sciron.[1] Then down to the plain again, a plain traversed by dry river-
beds, profuse with pink and white rose-laurels. What are the characteristic colours of the Greek summer landscape? The parched dusty yellow
ochre of sere grass and straw, the red ochre of the dry earth, the drab
green of whatever plants still have sap. Only the pines and cypresses
retain their intensity amid the tired, sad green – silver-grey as the leaves
turn – of the olive. The grey-mauve, almost heat-annihilated mountains,
stained blue where the cloud-shadows fall; and the brilliant, living sea.

We stopped for an hour at Corinth, for the bus had a punctured tyre.
The town looked ramshackle, ugly, and I had neither the desire nor the
energy to visit it. A pretty young woman with three children got on
there: slim, very vivacious, in a bright frock and an elegant little straw
hat with a bright red ribbon. Her eyes were dark, flashing, her mouth
long and red, her teeth brilliantly white and gold. She laughed, talked,
settled her eldest children in their seats. Then she went to sit in the

---

[1] Sciron was a robber who attacked travellers and then threw them into the sea
after forcing them to wash his feet. On his way to Athens from Troezen, Theseus
encountered Sciron and meted out to him the same treatment. According to
Ovid, the sea refused to receive Sciron's bones, which were then transformed
into the 'broken cliffs' that JF mentions.

shade of a nearby café and suckled her youngest child. The suckling in public and her unusually smart travelling-dress seemed so incongruous that I could not help staring.

We left Corinth, headed out south past the huge grey-red hill of the Acrocorinth over undulating country towards the moorland hills.[1] We followed dry river-beds still choked with green vegetation, dense with bright pink rose-laurels. I watched the pretty young woman: her baby began to cry and she slipped a hand into her frock and pulled out her breast. Her husband laughed, made jokes. She flashed back answers and looked contented. The country became wilder, more hilly, and then we were running down into the Argive Plain, a kind of tiny Provence below the Lyonnais hills. Mountains all around us and the sea to the south, a plain of wide stubble-fields, barren stretches, studded with tobacco-fields, cypresses, olive-orchards and with long lines of Eucalyptus.

I was put off at a village on the main road. It seemed to consist of only a taverna and two or three cottages. *'Mykenes?'* I asked the tavern-keeper. He pointed towards the hills. I suddenly realized I would have to walk and regretted packing so much. *'Eine macrya?' 'Tessara kilometres,'* he said. I walked the four kilometres slowly, along a road shaded with eucalyptus that plumed in a bright, strong breeze.

At the village I found the small hotel, drank blessed beer, had lunch, slept, and went on my way to the ruins; at last excited now I was so near. Sharrocks had said that this was the most impressive thing that he had seen in Greece, and I didn't want to be disappointed. I was not.

There is something sphinx-like about Mycenae. You walk up a mounting road bordered with a profusion of white and pink laurel-roses. The mountains approach, begin to tower a little, but still there is no sign of Mycenae. There is a massive fragment of bridge at the valley-bottom made by giants. Then a savage gorge comes into sight and the left-height of it is Mycenae surrounded by its walls, impregnable, like a wild animal at the mouth of its lair, regal, grimly withdrawn from yet dominating all the plain and all the past. A man and a girl passed. I stood on the road, trying to find the Tomb of Atreus, looking back. The man came out from behind a bush, buttoning his flies. 'There!' he shouted, and pointed up a small track behind him. I retraced my steps and climbed a little way off up the road to the entrance.

Two huge walls leading to a vast stone door: through the door, impossible to describe what is through the door. Fear, the unknown, history, history suddenly alive, death, the womb, the past, the future. A pyramid-like grandeur and massivity. In this cutting, if one is alone, one cannot

---

[1] The Acrocorinth was the site of Corinth's Acropolis during ancient and medieval times. The fortified remains occupy the summit of a 500-metre-high pinnacle at the edge of the ancient city.

avoid the awe. The door and the darkness it frames are terrifying, fascinating. I walked down to the doorway, looked at the 113-ton lintel,
hesitated. It was broad sunlight; I went in. A vast cool beehive of stone.
There was enough light to see by, quite a lot of light after a few seconds.
A great silence. But if I stamped, a strange, clipped, reluctant echo. I
saw to the right another dark doorway; in there was absolute darkness,
the chapel of this antechapel. The room where the body was. I found
a box of matches and not too happily went on to the threshold – a wall
of blackness. I struck a match, then another – five or six, all of them
went out for some reason. I stood a moment, and went outside, without
having really entered the inner room. I felt oppressed, uneasy, as if
something was waiting for me to wait. Even in the cutting I felt still
hypnotized by that massive sphinx-like door.

An unforgettable moment, and terrifyingly ageless. Calling me back,
inside. It makes me morbid, strange to myself, necrophilous.

I reached the citadel. Rock nuthatches bobbed and cried from the
wall-tops. They seem to be everywhere at Mycenae, almost tame, brightly
crying, half enraged at the human intrusion.

The Gate of Lions is massive, majestic, almost medieval in its animal
and stone grandeur. I went in, looked at the so-called graves of
Agamemnon and his family, strolled and scrambled over the citadel. I
was alone. A hill of broken walls, foundations choked with sere grass
and dying flowers; shards everywhere, in all the trenches, sticking out
from the walls. I climbed to the top of the acropolis, where the palace
was, and looked out over the hazed Argolian Plain to the heat-grey
mountains opposite. Buzzards mewed in a gorge to the east. I walked
round the heavy walls, still alone, glad and awed to be alone. I found
the secret passage underground to the well, the passage that Henry
Miller described as so dark and terrifying.[1] I found a stump of candle
and lit it. Steps lead down for a way; then there is an abrupt turn and
a flight of steps going down into the darkness. I did not feel it very easy
to get down to the bottom – the silence, the darkness, the feeling that
someone is creeping on you from above and ignorance of what is below.
I felt a little afraid, but Miller is an incorrigible romantic. There was
nothing at the bottom except a dry stone-filled hole. But Miller turned
back before he reached the bottom. If he had not described it so?
Experiencing the opposite? Three of the nuthatches perched on the
wall and called in chorus. Heralds of the spirit-reign. Then a vixen

---

[1] In *The Colossus of Maroussi* Miller described making the descent with Lawrence
Durrell and Durrell's wife Nancy: 'I had two distinct fears – one, that the slender
buttress at the head of the stairs would give way and leave us to smother to
death in utter darkness, and two, that a mis-step would send me slithering down
into the pit amidst a spawn of snakes, lizards and bats.' (Penguin edition, p.218)

appeared and stood on a pile of stones some fifty yards away; I realized she must be the famous fox that has its earth under the tomb of Clytemnestra. But then I saw that she was Clytemnestra herself: a tall, thin, savage, beautiful creature, most unfoxlike. When I moved, she began to bark in a petulant, anxious way. At last she walked lightly off, bouncing her brush, flaunting her sins. It was not because of me that she left. Some sheep came past and after them the shepherd, a tall figure wrapped in a huge brown cloak. The sheep tunkled away past the citadel; a nightjar churred in the distance. First stars, and great silence. I started back, but some strange impulse made me turn off at the Tomb of Atreus. At first I just stood at the entrance to the cutting. The door, almost indistinguishable in the darkness, called me over-poweringly in.

I did go in, with a lighted candle into the inner tomb; I stood in its centre, daring the supernatural to manifest itself. Here if anywhere, at night, in the most ancient, most inner death-tomb, surely the dead would stir. I wanted to be profoundly amazed, paralysed with fear. But there was not the smallest sound. An all-possessing silent oblivion. I waited for perhaps five minutes. Death was as I had always believed it to be. Then I left, hurriedly, relieved and proud that the 'test' was over. I walked down the fragrant road. Fires burnt in the distant plain; a sliver of new moon shone out. Owls called at the Cyclopean bridge.[1] I could just make them out through field-glasses. Their screams redoubled; Clytemnestra slipped along the masonry, paused, sniffed, yapped once hungrily and sadly, and slid into darkness. I must have Agamemnon's blood.

Back to the village, by moonlight and flute sound. One of the shep-herds out in the fields was playing his pipe, and still playing after I had eaten a meal by lamplight and finally gone to bed.

The next morning I set off for the Heraeon,[2] the lonely temple where the Argives and their allies met. Where the Trojan war really began and Zeus married Hera. It involved walking south, along the foot of the mountains. I crossed the Argive steppes, long stretches of stubble dotted with turkeys, sheep, donkeys and ponies. This area has famous turkeys, and Homer's epithet 'horse-rearing' still describes the Argive plain. I felt happy, the sun was hot, there was a breeze, I was alone. I came to a small village, asked the way. They seemed to understand me. I walked on; on and on. Past the hill where I thought it was, down into a little

---

[1] 'Cyclopean' is the term for the characteristic Mycenaean building style of using limestone boulders without any binding matter.
[2] The Heraeon was the Sanctuary of Hera, the goddess who watched over the Argives. According to Greek myth, it was here that Agamemnon was chosen to be the leader of the Trojan expedition.

combe delightfully green and damp with cypresses and a lemon-grove.
There was even a trough of dirty water. Two farms, a Shangri-la. I climbed
up again and walked through an olive-orchard, an area rich with thyme
and bees' wings. The sun was very hot. A man appeared, riding a minute
donkey. He had a very official hat and much-patched trousers. We
exchanged good-days and suspicious glances. Nothing much is left of the
Heraeon. The foundations of various temples, a litter of stones, fragments
of Cyclopean wall. I sat on the small hill and watched a golden eagle being
attacked by two buzzards. A brilliantly black and white wheatear flashed
in the ruins. I hunted shards, and with overwhelming success. A cornelian
bead, a fragment of obsidian razor, many fine shards, a curious little metal
object in the crevice of a wall. I hunted and hunted and hunted, while
the sun scorched down from directly overhead. I resigned myself to miss
lunch. About two I suddenly realized I was parched with thirst. The walk
home was horrible, in blinding sunlight. In the lemon-grove combe I
looked vainly for fruit, but all I could find were two old lemons lying on
the ground. I picked them up and ate them out of sight of the two farms.
They were juiceless, slightly rotten, but kept me alive till I reached a small
village and could drink two lemonades in a startled village. So home.

In the evening, I walked up to see the other tombs, dark cuttings
among the stubble-backs and olive-orchards. On the hill behind the
village is the beautifully designed modern museum – strangely empty
and deserted. This is much the best way from the village to the citadel,
along the ridge, with the indigo sea of dark mountains at one's side.
Shard-hunting, I left it late to return and had a long stumble across
country back to the hotel. I passed a huge door, the entrance to a caved-
in beehive tomb – a druidical piece of architecture. Mycenae has more
than one tinge of Stonehenge.

There was a great deal of wind that night, rocking the shutters. I
wanted to go to the citadel, but I was too tired. I did not find Mycenae
dark and depressing, like many people. More a mystery, an enigmatic
majesty. It is more massive, more primitive than Knossos and Phaestos.[1]
But as there, one has the impression of an ideal society in a perfect
world – a cultural centre in a universe a man could easily contain and
travel. Air, openness, roads above the plain. Horsemen under the Gate
of Lions. Kings over the foothills on their way to the spacious Heraeon,
lying sunnily on its low spur. Argos, Tiryns, a ride away. All shards.

Ascent of Parnassus. It was partly the hothouse atmosphere of the luxury
hotel at Delphi – all comforts on the edge of civilization – partly the

---

[1] JF had visited the ruins of these Minoan towns during a visit to Crete the
previous Easter.

symbolism. I wanted to climb Mount Parnassus, the poets' mountain, to
have conquered it physically and thus symbolically.[1] The best base for
the attempt seemed the village of Arachova,[2] so I went there, by bus,
early next morning. At the bus-stop were other English people, laconic,
humorous, discussing bills. After the sybaritic, vulgar Americans of the
hotel, I found them unusually refreshing, endearing. A sudden small
wave of love for the English. I arrive at Arachova, found a minute 'hotel',
explained what I wanted. Like everyone else, they said a guide, a donkey
were necessary. There was a refuge, but it was very high and cold. The
son of the hotel proprietress came to help me. He spoke appalling
French, about as insufficient as my Greek. I said I wanted food. He was
a pale-faced, embarrassed boy of fifteen or sixteen, who considered
himself, I gathered, a cut above the villagers. He was worse than useless
as a help.

'I want chocolate,' I said. He found a shop with minute bars of chocolate. 'Big ones,' I said. 'There aren't any,' he answered, and looked
faintly disgusted. At the next shop we found large bars. The same with
eggs. I said I wanted hard-boiled eggs. *'Oeufs durs'* did not register. I did
not know the Greek for 'cooking', let alone 'boiled'. We went to two
tavernas – they seemed angry to see him and said they had no eggs.
The boy was profoundly discouraged.

'There are no eggs,' he said.

I was beginning to get angry. 'For Christ's sake, somebody must have
eggs.'

'No.'

'Look, all I need is three or four eggs, and somebody can cook them.'

'No. Nobody can cook them. *On ne peut pas. On ne peut pas.*'

He looked awkwardly down at the ground, embarrassed by my
persistence. He won. I made do with a small loaf, some cheese, and
chocolate.

Then we went for the key to the refuge, up a stony little sidestreet
to a house where a woman was working a loom in a dark room with a
barred window. She came out. Her father was away; he looked after the
key. 'When will he be back?' She shrugged her shoulders, suggested one
hour with plainly little hope. Her mother appeared above, demanded
all the relevant information. A woman with a child looking out of the
nearby window of a house covered in grape-vines. A girl carrying a bucket
stopped and listened. A Greek palaver ensued.

'It's no good,' said the boy, true to his part. 'You can't go up. *On ne*

---

[1] According to ancient Greek legend, the mountain was sacred to Apollo and
the Muses.

[2] This small town, which is in east central Greece, twenty-six kilometres to the
west of Levadia, sits at the foot of the southern side of Mount Parnassus.

peut pas.' I ignored him and talked in Greek. It seemed a letter was needed from the tourist office.

'It doesn't matter,' I said. More palaver. They suggested tomorrow.

'You need a guide. Do you know the way?'

'I know the way.' I mentioned the name of the summer village above Arachova. This was a mistake. It was not the way.

'Dexia,' said the woman. *'Ochi Kalyvia.'*[1]

'Ne, ne, xero – dexia.'[2]

That half-persuaded them. 'I must go this morning,' I said.

'He doesn't know the way,' said the younger woman – and then to the boy: 'You can show him.'

The boy backed visibly. 'No, no . . . not this morning . . . *then boro.'*[3] He has an impossibility fixation.

The old woman asked the crucial question. 'You must pay 10,000 for the key,'

'Of course,' I said, and put my hand in my pocket. The atmosphere visibly lightened. Plainly I was a sucker.

'That's all right,' said the old woman. 'Tomorrow. Get the key.' The younger woman came back with two keys and a door-handle. I began to visualize the refuge as a kind of Chapel Perilous, not only difficult to reach, but far from easy to enter.

But the preparing was done. I got rid of the boy, and set out, up through the vineyards above the deep wide Delphi valley, to the plateau of Livadi. These initial difficulties I regarded as those naturally attendant on the will to rise from the common ruck and an essential stage in the young artist's development.

It was hot, windless. Soon the road below began to look small. I mounted the diagonal wide track past a shrine and a dry spring. The spring made me think of water and that of my total ignorance of the way up. I had only a page from Baedeker with a few vague lines about the route. The woman had said it was difficult. I visualized all sorts of danger: thirst, falling, Communist bandits, even the supernatural. But above all I was happy to be going. I passed many people descending to Arachova from the summer village. *'Yassou,'*[4] they all said. *'Yassou,'* I answered.

One of them laughed. *'Na,*[5] there's an Englishman going to climb Parnassus.'

'Is it the right road?' I asked.

---

[1] 'Right ... No hut.'

[2] 'Yes, yes, I know – right.'

[3] 'I can't.'

[4] 'Hello.'

[5] 'There.'

They nodded, pointed to the cliffs above. I walked on, passing, though I did not know it then, the path to the refuge. I went on up the wide track, beginning to climb above the world. Opposite I could see another high plateau of bright red tilled earth and resplendent green fields. Below, far below, the sea of olives. At last the road curved round a small bluff to the top of the pass on to the plateau. The wind blew, a cooler wind. The plateau lay in a large depression before me: two or three miles of green fields and on the far side a compact little group of stone houses. To the west and north fir-covered hills, Nordic-looking hills, rose blackly up. To the east more fir-woods, great grey slopes up to a height where the trees thinned out, scattered and ended; and, above that, massive, curves and clouds, the arched back of the mountain proper. I walked along the stony path down to the level of the plateau, where small pinks and alpine parsley grew in the rocks. Wheatears flashed their tails. There seemed to be no one except at the village, and I had no idea where the path to the left was. A flock of hooded crows watched me suspiciously from a pile of stones, ominous vulturine birds. I came to the village and went up to two men standing outside their croft. Most of the cottages seemed desolate, ruined. They were helpful and inquisitive and two youths came up and showed me the path high up in the fir-woods. I set off again, began to climb up the bottom of a rocky valley towards the sound of goat-bells.

I came on a shepherd encamped with his family, a wife and three boys, under a large fir; a tanned, genial man. He told me the way, asked me to have lunch with him: tomatoes, cucumber, yoghurt, goat milk, cheese. He recited the list, pleased to be able to offer it, begging me almost. This was my first experience of the extraordinary hospitality of the shepherds of Parnassus. They all seem almost mythically kind. I saw specks of dirt floating on top of the milk, and asked for a glass of water. They watched me drink it, smiling. I looked at their shelter, made of fir-branches, stone and a bit of cloth for a roof – inside on the floor many dark pots and pans and a few carpets and blankets. Higher up, the shepherds' encampments are tiny houses made completely of stones, erected under bluffs, with small stone-walled sheepfolds near them, but they all seem furnished with this gypsy simplicity – makeshift carpets, sheepskin blankets, a few pans. And yet they live there for all the summer.

The path led up steeply and interminably through the fir-trees. There were many birds, tits, firecrests and butterflies. A kind of re-entry into the period of spring. A blackbird flew across a clearing. At last I came up on to a rocky, hilly plateau beneath the western summit. A cold wind blew out of the clouds, which kept on burying the mountain-tops above. The path meandered, forked twice. I hesitated, lost impetus and felt for the first time discouraged. Then, I did not realize that shepherds lived as high as this. It was cold, the clouds threatened, and the mountain-face above was glistening grey, a frozen, ominous grey. It was nothing like Greece. I went a little further down one of the paths, towards a valley. Suddenly a wisp of smoke curled out of the pines opposite. All my dismay disappeared; I walked quickly down the slope, and heard sheep-bells in the distance. The opposite side of the valley was steep, rock-strewn, a maze of fallen pines. I reached the fire, but there was no sign of life, only smouldering branches, a small carpet of creeping sparks. I looked round, half expecting to see myself surrounded by grim Red Indians – at least, bandits. But there was again the sound of sheep-bells faintly somewhere in the forest above me. I struggled up the hill, sweating and very thirsty. The sheep-bells became louder and sheep suddenly moved at the top of a clearing. In a minute I was at the shepherd's encampment. A severe-faced but kindly-spoken old patriarch of a man received me. He wanted to know all about me. He was joined by two youths and another man. Their hut was a mere wind-break; I could see how they slept, on the ground with a few rugs and skins and heavy over-coats. They gave me a fine bowl of water. I gave them cigarettes. All the shepherds seem to delight in cigarettes. The old man asked me to lie down and rest, to eat some food. But I asked the way to the *kataphygeion* – the refuge. One of the youths offered to guide me. He took his crook and overcoat and led the way uphill. He walked with a kind of long casual lilt, striding from rock to rock, balancing himself with his crook. It looked so easy, but I could not keep up with him. From time to time he stopped and asked me questions; picked up some cartridge cases – a relic of the Civil War – and talked about the Communists. I gathered he was against them although he seemed to have admired the number of troops and time it took to eradicate them on Parnassus. We rose out of the trees and walked along a series of little valleys below the looming summit. I asked him how far the central peak was. Two hours, he said, two and a half. It's a long way, and difficult to find. He tried to explain the route, but he used so many words I didn't know that it only confused me. We passed a deep small crevice. He said there was snow at the bottom, and threw a stone into the black opening. The stone hit the sides and then there was a strange silence, eternal, as if the chasm was bottomless. As far as I could see, it was.

A few minutes later we came to the refuge, tucked away in a small goyal. A minute squat building with a round roof and a small chimney, windowless, like the chapel of some very strict sect. The door was of rusty iron, with jagged bullet-holes in it. '*Communista*,' said the shep-herd, '*kaput*.' I tried to get the key to turn. Nothing happened. The shepherd kicked the door and it swung open; so much for the keys. Inside, bunks, mattresses, a stove, lamps, a saw, even a pair of skis. I was pleasantly surprised, even amazed, that the Greeks could organize a proper refuge. I talked with the shepherd for a while, eager to have some food, but disinclined to share it. In the end, after three cigarettes, he went away. I made an inventory and sat down to eat – a third of the cheese, a third of the loaf, a bar of chocolate. It was about three o'clock. I did not know what to do, whether to climb on or to wait till the next morning. In the end I compromised. I would reconnoitre, find the way, and go up it in the morning.

I put on my ski-jacket and set off; the wind was cold, cutting, surprisingly strong. I began to mount towards the clouds up a great rocky slope. It was steep and tiring, I had to rest every few minutes. Flowers came in increasing numbers – harebells, tiny mauve-blue gentians, delicate flowers of deep magenta-red. There were other flowers, stonecrop, campion, saxifrage in bloom, in the crannies of the turf. Suddenly, above me, incredibly it seemed, I heard sheep-bells. A figure appeared in the sky, almost in the clouds, crook in hand, overcoat wrapped around him. He climbed obliquely upwards, stopped every now and then to stare down at me far below. I saw his goats high above, where torn fragments of cloud hurtled past. I climbed on, feeling more tired at every step. I decided to traverse the slope, not to climb any more. It was much easier. I came to the ridge of the shoulder, and right into the full force of the wind – breathtaking, savagely cold, almost too much to stand in. But below to my surprise was a wide basin sloping upwards to two peaks and a col and, beyond the col, yet more peaks. To my right I could see patches of *névé* snow, brilliant white against the cliffs and scree-slopes to which they adhered. Below, in the basin, were stretches of green turf and, in one corner, a shepherd encampment. I had entered the paradise of the upper Parnassus.

It is a whole world by itself, a great basin surrounded by peaks, full of little valleys with lush green turf, studded with flowers, and several shepherd encampments. A mountain sanctuary. As I made my way across the scree-slopes to the col, the clouds began to clear, and the universe became superb. I felt free, fit, absolutely without tiredness. I moved over the rocks at shepherd speed, enjoying the constant need for judgement and agility. At the top of the col a whole series of peaks came in view. The problem was to find Lykeri, the highest summit.[1] They all looked about the same, although the furthest one, on the other side of a huge basin, seemed the tallest. I could see two shepherds a very long way off, too far to go and ask. I began to compromise; this surely was as good as the ascent of Parnassus. I could climb one of the near peaks, pretend it was the highest. The sun was beginning to decline. I climbed down and up to another col. Alpine crows sceeched overhead, there were

---

[1] Mount Parnassus has two summits, but with very little difference in height between them. Lykeri ('Wolf Mountain') is 8061ft high; and Gerontovrachos ('Old Man's Rock') is 7989 ft.

flowers everywhere, mountain asters, deep golden-yellow daisy-like flowers, and the countless deep pink stems of the geraniums. As I came to the top of this new col, the peak itself, hitherto hidden, unmistakably appeared. A regular-shaped, round-topped height, too remote to think of reaching in daylight – or so it seemed. I felt disappointed, began to lie to myself. I could tell some story about making a mistake unconvincingly over the highest peak, not being sure which it was. To the south I could see a nearby peak, and decided to head for that. Behind it was yet another valley-basin, rich in turf, with a huge flock of sheep and another encampment in it. The clouds had almost all gone and the view from the top of the peak was superb. But a mile away to the east there was still that round top rising above me, tantalizing, unconquered. I sat by the cairn and ate some chocolate. The setting sun accented all the contours, deep blue shadows and purple hills in the valleys and plains below. The sea was pale blue in the distance. I felt tired, content, but not absolutely content. I looked again at Lykeri, through field-glasses, unconsciously remembered all the symbolism I had attached to it.

And then, almost subconsciously, I set off for it, in spite of the late hour and being tired out. Preconceived determination, stronger than I had supposed, manifested itself in me, forced me on. I almost ran down the long slope to the foot of Lykeri and began to climb it at ridiculous speed. But it was too steep to be taken at a run. I slowed down, rested, saw the world at my feet. Near the top I came on beds of violets in bloom, big purple flowers, an extraordinary sight; and there was golden saxifrage as well. I 'started' two capercaillie, giant brown whirring partridges. The far side of Lykeri is precipitous, a huge chasm plunging down. With mounting exultation I zigzagged up to the little platform on the peak, with its stone cairn. I had an overpowering sense of victory, of self-satisfaction, a kind of atomic flash of inner pleasure. The sun was still just above the horizon. There were no clouds within twenty miles and the sky was of the purest, most serene blue, I felt immeasurably high, surrounded by air, remote from all towns, societies, troubles, beliefs, times, a central point in the universe; having entered, achieved it and now being rewarded. A natural monastery of the spirit.

There were other mountains, valleys, plains, seas in all directions, but I had no desire to know their names, only to be aware of their limitless presence below. Alpine swifts split the air down into the chasms and shadows to the east. The other peaks were gilded, striated with shadow.

Someone else had written, with a splendid classical Greek, the letters φως – light – in stones beside the cairn. Even I was fired to record. I wrote on a piece of paper, 'John Fowles, 4 July 1952, clear evening sky, superb visibility, violets in bloom on the southern slope – alone with the Alpine swifts and the Muses,' and put it in a tin which I placed in the centre of the cairn. The air was chilly, the sun began to sink. Still I was spellbound by the height, the absence of earth, mundanity, the majestic, divine solitude.

One of the moments one continues to live for. They repay all the months in the desert, the years in darkness. To rise out of time, to be absorbed into nature, to feel oneself completely existing among existence, as godlike as mortality can imagine.

Such adventures must be done alone. In company they lose their value. One has to pass through the dangers by oneself – the fatigue, the strange country, the silence. It is all part of the sense of victory won in the end. No guide, no maps. Alone.

I descended the steep slope. A flock of sheep appeared below, on the way back to the fold. As I reached the foot of the peak, a girl appeared and came towards me, a girl of fifteen or sixteen, with a nut-brown face and shrewd, shyly coquettish eyes. She wore an old brown coat and a brown headscarf, yet somehow contrived to appear beautiful. Her face was minxish, amused by me. We stood some twenty or thirty yards apart. She had a clear, clipped voice, had the authority, the presence of people who live on great solitudes, and used many words I could not understand. But I understood her faint contempt for me. Living under the shadow of Parnassus, the climb meant nothing to her – an hour's walk – and my pride was ridiculous. I was made to feel that I did not belong to this high upstairs world. It seemed to me extraordinary that a slip of a girl could exist in such a remote place. Her flock consisted of two hundred sheep, slowly grazing towards an encampment. We spoke of wolves. She seemed to admire me most when I said that I was going back to the refuge. 'It's a long way,' she said. 'It'll be dark.' I said that I knew the way, and pointed it out. She walked parallel but distant from me for a little way. I said goodbye, and watched her go back to her flock, singing softly.

I walked fast, in spite of aching feet. Dusk came fast, and with it an icy wind, frost in the air. But my day was not yet done. I jumped off a rock on to a small path. There was a vicious click, a sharp pain in my foot. I had trodden on a wolf-trap. I had a very unpleasant five minutes getting free. Fortunately it was not toothed and fortunately it gripped me by the heel. Even so, I gave my fingers a bad squeeze getting myself free. I went on, my fingers numb, then burning with pain. I passed under a high cliff with a gigantic glacial bowl at its foot. High up on the cliff-face were white streaks of *névé*, and the wind roared enormously above, like the wild sea. I made my way down to a shepherd encampment I had seen on my way up. But as soon as I came near, the dogs ran out at me, fierce, snarling, barking. There were three of them, big, black, grey and white. I lashed out at them with my stick and they rushed at me. One of them caught the stick in its teeth and another went behind me. I was just getting ready to be bitten when a shepherd-boy ran up and called them off. I was badly in need of water. He took me to their hut, outside which a large block of snow was thawing into a bowl. I took, a tin cup and drank avidly. The water was ice-cold, delicious. I told them about the trap. They laughed, the boy had just set it. Yes, there were wolves, two or three. A shepherd I met the next day said there were many.

I made my way on in darkness The moon and the afterlight gave me just enough light to see by. Even so I stumbled and fell many times – and looked round many times for a long grey shape. The wind was savage, strong and cold. At last I reached the refuge. There were bells all around it, an invisible flock and a barking dog. The shepherd came down to see me – a serious-faced, thick-voiced young man in a heavy overcoat. He helped me light the lamps, but they went out, so I lit a large fire and threw huge logs on it. It was cold enough for a blaze to be welcome. I sat on a bank and talked with the shepherd. He was suffering from conjunctivitis, no wonder in that wind. Every so often he went outside and called to his sheep with a high-pitched whistle. He asked me back to his shelter, but I felt too tired to move. He went off into the night and cold wind.

A strange, unreal, remote life in 1952. It is difficult to imagine what the mentality of a mountain shepherd can be like – a life of sun-hours, counting, milking, brittle stars, silences and cold winds, constant watchfulness against wolves, an existence of terrifying solitudes, on a different plane from ours below, uniquely independent.

I sat watching the fire, too tired to eat and very thirsty, but with no water. I bolted the door, got into my sleeping-bag, and slept. I had walked and climbed up some fifteen miles of very rough paths and scree-slopes, left summer in Arachova for spring on Parnassus. At some time in the night I heard a tearing, flapping noise outside the door – a wolf or fox or shepherd-dog by the sound of it, trying to kill something. But I was too tired even to look at that. When I woke properly, the sun was high; and I had slept for over twelve hours.

I cleaned the refuge, set off down past a shepherd *trypa*.[1] The shepherds, two bronzed men, were milking their sheep – one or two quick squirts from each animal. Twenty or thirty sheep gave only a bucketful. They gave me water and a slice of rich, sour cheese, which I ate with outward enjoyment and inward distaste; then a cup of still warm milk, which I swallowed with blatant haste, and said goodbye.

It took a long time to get down. My feet were swollen and sore, the sun was hot. In the pine-woods were many birds and butterflies – red-backed shrikes, cole tits, missel-thrushes, spotted woodpeckers, Dark Green and Queen of Spain fritillaries and a thousand Painted Ladies.

---

[1] *Trypa* is the Greek word for hole.

I skirted the northern edge of the plateau of Livadi, frequently resting, still without appetite. Over the brim of the plateau down into Arachova, my feet so sore I could not walk normally, though without limping.

But Parnassus was mine; and the other if I try enough.[1]

---

[1] 'By which I meant literary fame, success,' wrote JF in 1996. 'It is from this ascent that I date some real first belief in myself as a writer. Not, needless to say, from any evidence of writing skill, but sensing some quirk of age. It was also when I knew I loved Greece.'

Part Four

The Distant Princess

12 July 1952

Leigh. England dark, neutral-coloured, cloudy, cold. After Greece it seems like undergrowth after a clearing. The sober nonentity of the people, the meticulously detailed domestic routines; life not of essentials, but of superficials. Pleasures hedged in, restrained, half-enjoyed. The antlike busyness and occupation of all English people. No drones, no sun, no love. Here at home the short re-entry into all as it always has been – no warmth in the affection, the sentiment strictly banished, a two days' ripple of news and interest. I need a wife, a new centre of intimacy, if only to rediscover the heat in love and exercise unused affection.

F (my father) came up to my room this afternoon with a volume of short stories he has written, quite a thick bundle of typescript. Mutual embarrassment. He ran himself right down, dismissed them as self-amusement. I have read some of them. They are better than I thought, but not good enough to publish, although somebody might publish them. The worst ones are in a majority – semi-humorous accounts of village life with a store of antiquated *Punch* characters. Some of the short stories are quite good, but he has no feel for words, no literary artifice. He should go back to the war. [1]

23 July

Off again tomorrow, to Thouars, then Spain.[2] I feel I ought to be typewriting, saving money, hammering at the door of the BBC – instead I seem at the moment unable to do anything except keep abreast of travel arrangements, do the daily round. No creation, and all I have written seems green, raw, naïf. Too inturned. I must settle down to a month's typing when I get back. If I get back. If you travel enough, you must have a smash-up.

25 August

Spain. A strange month, burning hot, black, sad, poignant for me; an experience I would not have missed, for all its bitterness. Now I feel more remote, more isolated than ever. I was bewitched by Monique

---

[1] JF's father had on a previous occasion shown his son a novel he had written based on his experiences during the First World War.
[2] JF was going to join the same '*famille Thouarsaise*' group of young students with whom he had travelled to Switzerland, the Tyrol and Bavaria the previous year.

Baudouin; it was less a holiday in Spain than three weeks helplessly
watching around her. At the end, in Spain I could hardly conceal my
enchantment. At the real end, when we had parted, I had the most
profound attack of sorrow that I have experienced for many years, a
catastrophic realization of the utter impossibility of any love between
us, and of the ruthlessness of time, of the whole human predicament
in terms of my own person. The beauty of animal attachments, the
inevitability of death and separation. I feel myself still in a kind of trance,
unreal, disoriented; having met her was a glimpse of another world. A
chance of complete fulfilment, happiness on my dark earth. I loved not
so much what she was, as an ideal I could easily build from her reality.
I saw in her a shadow of the perfect woman, and in her youth an image
of all that tenderness and spontaneous gaiety my own youth has gone
without. Even now, already a fortnight since I last saw her, I think of
her a hundred times a day. I can recall all the moments we spent together,
her smiles, her moods, her positions, her absences, her movements, the
clothes she wore, the atmosphere, everything. Again and again I see
things to remind me of her; even the most tenuous associations, recalling
her vividly. Often I try to imagine her beside me, smiling at me, talking
to me. I fall into day-dreams. But it is not a thing of the flesh; I cannot
imagine myself even kissing her. A profound conviction that she is of
my spirit, *in* my spirit. Almost a romantic, platonic idealization, unlike
anything I have experienced before. Masochism perhaps. These were
and are moments when I enjoyed my sadness, the poignant freshness
of certain memories of her. Now I know that a life together would be
impossible, dispassionately I feel in her something cool, aloof, nunlike.
She has her provincial conventions, is Catholic, has an egoism, an accent,
the stereotyped tastes and expectations in love and marriage that I could
not satisfy. But in her essence, magic, she is my Gioconda.

To Paris by air. A dehydrated way of travelling; for all the joys of contact
with foreign places and foreign people one exchanges a joy in figures.
So many miles in so many hours. The modern trend – into the abstract.
But I find no glamour in speed, and I do not comprehend distance
expressed as a figure. But it was good to be in Paris again, more like a
return home than my real home. Almost the first person I met was one
of my girl students at Poitiers; all that life came back to me, faintly scented
with my own bad conscience. I tried to be affable, and left her as soon
as I could. I had to pay 525 francs for a miserable garret, a monstrous
price; but I felt extraordinarily happy to be returning to Thouars.
  Down by train, through well-remembered countryside to Thouars.
I was impatient, eager as a lover, to arrive. Opposite me was a middle-
aged Frenchman in a blue beret, who spoke to me in an incomprehensible accent from time to time. Scent of Gauloise, an old woman and her

granddaughter eating a picnic lunch; long bread, sausage, ham, apples, voices in the corridor. A surge of love for the French, their country, their way of life, their language. The French are sane egocentrics; their life is balanced; they admit their animality, but without denying spirituality. They live for themselves, but with discretion. They accept foreigners, judge them, do not flatter or damn them. A society of individuals, the golden mean, and the present heirs to ancient Greece. I felt all that in the train, and again and again during the days that followed. The more I travel and live abroad – and England now is a foreign country to me – the more I admire France, and feel that she is *my* country. Physically and spiritually I feel myself at home in France as nowhere else in the world.

The man opposite talked about Bressuire, his home town. We passed Saumur. I glimpsed a familiar face in the corridor, that of one of the most hideous and disapproving of my last year's pupils. A tall, Gorgon-faced girl. I could see she was determined to speak to me, and stared out of the window with a fixedness which disconcerted even the *homme de Bressuire*. I did meet her later, at Thouars, but in a crowd, and I was able to dismiss her with a few ungracious words, remaining true, I feel sure, to the character that now represents me at Poitiers.

Thouars. I walked through the ticket-barrier, and it was as if I had never left there. All the girls were there, André, faces I seemed to have seen only an hour before. Monique shy, Titi charming, André like a genial bear. If anything I was a little sad at the matter-of-factness of it all; I half expected songs, cheers, tears, the emotional town band. But then I liked it; it seemed simpler, more natural, to begin again as if one had never left off. I went off with André to his home, and again felt as if I had not been away. The same table, with fifteen or twenty people sitting down to an excellent meal and liberal wine. The same noisy laughter, business talk, shrewd gossip. The small sisters and the servant at one end. The nephews and brothers and wives and in-laws at the other. André opposite, more ursine than ever, asking me questions about birds and books and life in Greece.

After lunch he took me to see Ginette Poinot in her parents' furniture-shop. She was so changed that I was for a moment completely confused – more elegant and clipped than ever, perfectly made up, with brilliantly blonde hair done in a new style. I suppose she had dressed up for me, as she knew I was coming. But even so in a year she had blossomed; not last year's bud at all. She took us through a corridor of bourgeois furniture to a small backroom, and gave us Cointreau. With André there, I did not know what to say. We all felt stilted, embarrassed. There were silences, nervous moments. But I felt at ease, enjoying the moment, her elegance, the little awkwardnesses of our speech. I hoped André might leave us alone. In the end I stood up and said goodbye – all that either of us acknowledged of last year were one or two faint smiles of intelligence. Above all, it seemed to me, she saw that she had surprised me and that pleased her sense of irony.

Away. That first morning, at once, I felt that it was not going to be so memorable as the year before. There were a lot of new people, who instinctively I did not like at first sight. I felt old also, vastly old among the *jeunes*. Then, that I was there on false pretences, already much-travelled comparatively; that they felt I came only to add a new country to my list. I had lost my novelty, was no longer a toy that amused, but a plaything discarded, no longer *inconnu*. An impression that lasted more or less throughout the voyage.

We arrived at Bordeaux, had lunch. South from Bordeaux into the Landes, a desert of heath, sand and pine. In the middle of it, we had a puncture. I wandered about alone among the trees. No sign of life anywhere, not even birds. There was plenty of traffic on the road, an artery in a dead limb. The group sat about on the verges, talking. I felt foreign again, and depressed by the landscape. We got off again, behind schedule, and did the most interesting part of the day – the Biarritz coast – in darkness. I remember standing with Monique outside a grocer's, where we had bought fruit. Already we began to remember the old jokes, to tease; I because it was the only way to approach her and she because she was too kind to refuse to play. I don't think either of us was amused by it.

The next day, up at dawn and down the coast to Irun. A green coast of capes and bays like Brittany. Over the frontier, policemen wearing black coal-scuttle hats. One of the customs men going off duty absentmindedly took all our papers with him in his car, he had picked up the wrong attaché case. We had a long wait. Standing outside a church, Jouteau chasing Monique. Her eyes when she is being chased: black diamonds.

We moved on to San Sebastián, through green country disfigured by billboards. San Sebastián, a sprawling cosmopolitan *station balnéaire*, with a crowded beach and busy bay. We went swimming and were stared at by the crowd. Some of the others were sent back by the police for not having sufficiently extensive bathing-costumes. Spanish women in bathing-costumes with modesty skirts and the men in elongated trunks. Spanish middle-class townsmen reminded me continually of giraffes, ostriches. A mental conservatism stiffly upheld and continually outraged.

Lunch in a dark-timbered spacious room; each group around a table. My eyes met those of Monique several times. We had a way of smiling together, half-friendly, half-sarcastic, across rooms, other voices, other happenings. At the end I so wanted to be friendly that my smiles were painfully sour and sarcastic.

The rain stopped after lunch. We went through the deep gorge that is the true entry into Old Castile, on to that high, arid plateau which is an essential clue to Spanish character. I found it a dreadful landscape, without accent, charm or meaning. The whole of northern Spain, from Burgos to Madrid and beyond, is a cultivated desert. A real desert would have pleased me better. We came to Burgos at night and had dinner in a hotel like an English country inn. Begging children at the window. Monique's eyes again, from another table (a fortnight ago exactly, at this hour of writing, six in the evening, I was sitting beside her somewhere in central France, heading north, conscious only of her, her bent face, her small smile when she was serious).

I went out later with Paul Challet. We walked about a bit, it was cold. We sat at a café and drank cognac. Since André was with his fiancée most of the time, I was often with Paul. At times he irritated me, as all simple, enthusiastic people do. That night at Burgos I was thinking of Monique; the beginning of the torture, wondering where she was when not in sight. Paul has few topics of conversation: photography, speleology, travelling. Poor chap, I realized at the end that he loves Armèle. He was always near her, with a dog-like, apologetic, begging expression on his face. We went back to our *pension* to sleep. A Balzacian old man with a huge bunch of keys opened the street-door for us; the keyman for the whole street. A Balzacian occupation.

3rd. We started late since Michel Godichon had had his rucksack, with all his belongings in it, stolen. The first of many thefts; almost everywhere we lost things. Stealing seems to be the national sport of Spain; another by-product of Fascism. Rule by force above, and morals disappear below. We had lunch at a small village. I bought a loaf in the bakery with Monique, and shared it with her. The bare fact, but I remember her eyes, her standing behind me at the counter, counting out the money. The smallness of her hand.

After Valladolid the plain continued, but low mountains, blue and gentle, appeared. There were pine-groves with nesting storks, and a clear sunlight feel about the country which made it seem a little like Provence in spring.

We camped that night in a tiny upland village, where we were well-received. Everyone went to the village dance-hall. The whole population seemed to be there. The warmth and the wine excited everyone. Somebody began to play an antique barrel-organ and the villagers danced. Then there was a waltz and the group took the floor. They began normally, but under the eyes of several hundred solemn-faced villagers, the desire to clown was irresistible. They began to dance in an exaggerated fashion, to shout and sing, to jive and jitterbug. At each new tune it became more wild and more ridiculous. Because the villagers

did not seem to understand at all, they stared with open mouths, often
faintly disapproving. Occasionally a faint smile would cross their faces.
It was the traditional countryman's first visit to the capital. I drank a lot
of cognac and watched the surrounding faces. I stood for a time on a
window-ledge with Monique, and nearly asked her to dance. But I dance
so badly, and already I was certain that I did not want to dance badly
with *her*.

4th. We spent several hours visiting Avila. A cathedral, marred, like all
Spanish cathedrals, by the massive choir blanking the nave. Then down
to see a monastery on the outskirts of the town. Walking down that road,
I showed a newspaper joke to Monique. As she leant over to read it, I
think perhaps I began to realize what was happening. At any rate that
morning I was watching her all the time, walking beside her whenever
I could contrive it. Her slim, willowy walk, swaying, indolent in the heat,
always dragging behind, her hair, brushed back from her forehead and
tied in a ridiculously large chignon behind, the chignon itself with a
red and white scarf elegantly knotted over it, the ends floating behind
– a strangely poised head, from all angles. I prayed for her smiles, her
laughter, when the scarf danced and the chignon bobbed and her body
bent like a wand.

We saw the monastery cloisters, where Torquemada walked,[1] and the
tomb of Don Juan. '*The* Don Juan?' I asked the guide, but he seemed
never to have heard of Mozart and Molière. But in any case I touched
his tomb of white marble – and found it exceedingly cold.[2]

After Avila, mountains and thunderstorms. I slept. The Sierra de
Guadarrama are not great mountains, but after the monotony of Castile
they are pleasant. We came to the Escorial,[3] a vast barracks overlooking
the plain. I was reminded of Versailles, of the austere North. I liked the
animation of the great outside court, full of children playing ball,
gossiping mothers, tourists, strollers. At the ticket-window I met two
Englishmen, small, moustached, dapper and broke. I was happy to be
in the group. How I hate nearly all my compatriots! These two were
inoffensive enough. I spoke to Monique, in French, to make them feel
unhappy. A pretty girl and a foreign language; I had them both ways. I
hate guided visits also. Tapestries and royal apartments. The royal cata-
comb is in such bad taste – marble and gilt, the entrance like that to a

---

[1] The Convent of Santo Tomás. Tomás de Torquemada (1420–98), the arch-
inquisitor, is buried in the sacristy.

[2] This tomb belongs not to *the* Don Juan, but Prince Juan (1478–97), the only
son of Ferdinand and Isabella.

[3] The huge fortress, monastery and palace built by Philip II (1527–98) about
fifty kilometres north-west of Madrid.

restaurant of *première classe* – that it is at least amusing. A superb El Greco in the art gallery, daemonic and sulphurous, livid. Spain is a Byzantine country; El Greco must have been at home immediately.

5th. In the morning we washed at a well in the garden of a doctor's house near by. I liked to watch the girls washing and often arranged my time so as to coincide with theirs. I am not so hypocritical as to pretend it was not partly sexual curiosity. But mainly it was a sexless, aesthetic pleasure. They were like cats, feline, licking and dabbing at themselves with their flannels. They would unbutton their pyjama-jackets, uncover their shoulders, sometimes take off the jackets and stand in their brassières, pink silk on their white skin. One girl, especially, Geneviève Boinot, very small, delicately contrived, and a coquette, was especially delightful at her toilet – exactly like a serious kitten, and aware of her charms, since she was to take her time, which coincided usually with the maximum in the number of washing males. Neither she nor the others ever seemed to wash themselves briskly, with plenty of water and suds – always small pats and rubs, and dabs.

Monique, every morning, in pale blue pyjamas, with her initials on the pocket, her red scarf around her throat, walking seriously to wash.

To Madrid. An airy, modern city at first sight, full of rich buildings, flower-beds, fountains, tree-shadowed boulevards. Well-watered and Parisian. And without interest.

We passed into the Prado. A supermuseum, a museum cream-cake, too rich to be digested. I rushed from Velasquez to El Greco to Goya, then to the Flemish School, then to the Italian, then back to the Flamands, because they were so remarkable. Velasquez, I suspect, is a superb bore who discovered a pose and an expression. Goya astounded me by his technique – I had not realized his miraculous facility, his daring, his speed of stroke. A greater artist than either El Greco or Velasquez. A great spirit – daemonic and socialist. A defender of the poor. The intense indignation, the emotion, of the *Firing-Squad*, a *chef d'oeuvre*. The deliciously cruel satire of his academic portraits, brutes in finery. Then there is a superlative room of Flemish masterpieces, and the most extraordinary of all to me – Baldung Grien's two pictures – *The Three Graces* and *The Three Deaths*. The latter especially I find a profound and terrifyingly exact symbolization of the human predicament.[1] The expression in the girl's face is that of all deep loves of life,

---

[1] JF is thinking of *The Three Ages of Man* (1539): behind the naked figure of a young woman stands the old woman she will become, and then Death holding an hour glass. Hans Baldung (1484/5–1545) trained with Albrecht Dürer in Nuremberg. 'Grien' was a nickname probably indicating his preference for the colour green.

all sensualists and knowing death certainly. She has understood the problem, found the answer, but still cannot believe its inexorable cruelty. Time and Age – death are at her shoulders now and till the end. The brilliant light, the superficial realism and the underlying hallucinatory unreality give this picture unbelievable force. It burns, freezes, like a red-hot poker or bucket of icy water. It seems to me so little religious, so pessimistically materialist, that it might have been painted in the 1920s. An epochless picture. Black simplicity.

(A childish obsession with time. It is past midnight now, very early Monday morning, as I write. A fortnight ago she was sleeping in my arms, against me, as we ran through the night. I feel her still and the sorrow, acute as ever. I almost wish we had been killed together, at that moment when we were perhaps closest.)

André, Paul, Claudine and I went and had lunch in a snack-bar. I did not often enjoy being with them, a stolid trio, who avoided the *jeunes*. Claudine is a kind of universal mother, a Girl Guide-schoolmistress *née*, with sad spaniel-eyes and (one feels) a vast stock of unspoken prejudices. A strange wife for André. After lunch we walked towards the zoo, through a deserted park. It was hot and I felt profoundly sleepy. When we sat down to drink something, I dropped off to sleep almost at once, in the chair. We found the others – those who were not sleeping the night at Madrid – sitting on a grassy bank outside the Prado. I went and sat with the girls and they asked me about Greece. I spoke French badly, as I do sometimes. Not a question of will – one is in form, one is out. I heard my faults in pronunciation, my grammar faults, almost as if I was somebody else. Sometimes it is the opposite, and I admire my own fluency and accuracy.

We set off to find a camp near Madrid. I felt happy, since only half the group were there, and they the ones I liked best, the simpler, greener half. We bought food and a bottle of muscat in a small town, and camped on the way to Navalcamero, in a wide, dry river-bed, with a bridge alongside, that rumbled and swayed whenever a lorry or car crossed over. There was a pool fed by a little stream, deliciously cool at dusk. We swam. Nanni's demureness in a swimming-costume; a beautiful figure, a young Venus de Milo. I hunted frogs with André. Later the others played word-games. André and Claudine had gone off alone. I lay outside their circle, felt bitterly alone, unloved, out of the game. There was a forest of stars above. I listened to their voices, for *her* voice especially, and in the end went off alone to bed.

6th. Morning swim. Icy-cold and wonderful. Monique in a yellow woollen costume, a thin, lithe body, breasts like apples. We waited by the roadside for the others to come with the 'car' from Madrid. Monique sitting by a tree, writing in her notebook. It used to intrigue

me, to watch her writing – some of it was diary, but sometimes she
seemed to me to write in verse. I asked her once, and she laughed,
and seemed embarrassed. Everyone speaks of her as intelligent, the
young female genius of Thouars. She got her *bachot* at the earliest
possible age,[1] and is apparently a renowned worker. She has a serious
will, a maturity which contrasts perfectly with her lighter side, her
gaiety and exuberance.

To Toledo, an old, dense city on a hill, as Spanish as Madrid is un-
Spanish. Narrow streets, patios, grilles – not yet Andalusian, but halfway
there. The cathedral is magnificent, in spite of its ornaments. We
wandered about, visited the house of El Greco – which reminded me
for some reason of Shakespeare's house at Stratford – an Elizabethan
atmosphere.

We had lunch in a backstreet restaurant, a truly Spanish meal which
dragged on half the afternoon, interminably. Service in Spain is a miracle
of tardiness. Everything seems to have to be brought, cooked, allowed
to cool, before it can be served. Meanwhile we drink enormously, sadly
aware that it is too hot to make a scene, and that in any case one can
only sleep in the afternoon. That afternoon we did walk, when it was
still too hot to be out-of-doors. Burning cobbles, strips of shade. One
dreams of water, lime-juice, iced wine, beer, breezes, the sea. Only dust
and brilliant light. I felt anxious to be with the others, the *jeunes*. We
older ones have travelled too much, no longer feel the foreign glamour.
But with them, the *jeunes*, one felt again that lovely thrill of foreignness,
being abroad and seeing new things, the essence of travel.

They were all in the main square, I remember, drinking lemonades.
I found Monique, and felt relaxed again. If she was alone, in the
group, I was all right. But when she was not there, or away with somebody else, I was unhappy, anxious, dry – *un jaloux*. It was at Toledo
that I felt myself torn between Nanni and Monique. There is a kind
of coupling process in a group of young people. Young stags circling
young hinds; a psychological circling. I could see the others being
caught up in it – the girls with psychological downcast eyes and little
flashes of looks, laughter, the men strutting, associating, trumpeting.
The atmosphere is difficult. The couples in the group already in love
make love all the time; are always together, kiss in their seat, disappear together. The others, out in the cold, have, from this point of
view, a frozen look. For the *jeunes* the voyage is also a voyage in the
borderland of love. Mlle de Scudéry's *Carte du Tendre*, where one leaves
the village of *Nouvelle Amitié* and has all the sentiments between *Haine*

---

[1] The word *bachot* is colloquial for 'baccalauréat', the French school-leaving
examination leading to university entrance.

and *Amour* before one.[1] I was torn between two places. Nanni – on the foothills, pleasant enough, even beautiful – though her expression has something sulky, wilfully feminine, in it. A moody girl, a lover of dancing, gaiety, life; not self-sufficient, needing to be amused. Monique – in the mountains, remote, but far lovelier, with a profound smiling beauty and moments of austerity. Unattainable, but nearer heaven; and, except in moments of solitude, in the end I did not hesitate. I do not think Nanni would have been difficult at one point, whereas I knew Monique was never even distantly possible. Nanni represented a compromise, Monique an ideal. I shall forget the one, but never the other.

Monique's two extremes: an implike mischievousness, half her age, and an acrid silence, a complete inner withdrawal, twice her age. But nothing with her is fixed; all her moods are unstable. An iridescent temperament.

7th. We drove round the hills surrounding Toledo the next morning – the agglomeration of houses enchanted the others. More used to the white of Greece, I found it dirty, tarnished, sad. The gorge, with the muddy Tagus at the bottom, must have influenced El Greco. A city of the damned, a purgatorial landscape. Over an old bridge into the city again. I took two photos and managed to include Monique in both. In fact this time I only took photos that included her.

8th. A long day in the coach. In the morning I sat next to Monique, who was in the corner. She had another *soupirant*, a cousin of André's, a pleasant young simpleton, younger than she, who followed her everywhere, an image of my own libido. I stole his place from him to be next to her; after that he always suspected me. We came to the Sierra Morena, majestic country after the plains. The coach stopped several times, and the others got out. Normally I enjoyed the halts, but now I wanted to stay next to Monique. I found a praying mantis and frightened her with it. She pulled out her notebook and wrote something in it with an enigmatic smile. It looked like poetry. I asked her.

'*C'est pour moi. Personne d'autre ne le comprendra.*' And she put it away in her canvas bag. An old smoke-blue bag with a faintly Assyrian man's head and a girl's head embroidered on it in red and yellow silk thread,

---

[1] In her novel *Clélie* (1654) Madeleine de Scudéry (1608–1701) created an allegorical 'Map of Love', which described the route from 'Nouvelle Amitié' (New Friendship) to 'Love', which de Scudéry termed 'Le Tendre'. The traveller would pass through such hamlets as Tendresse or Constante Amitié, but, if he lost his way, would risk stumbling upon such dangers as the cliffs of Orgueil (Pride) or the Mer d'Inimitié (Sea of Enmity).

with her initials, MB. I remember we had just come to a village where we were going to eat. She saw me looking at it and suddenly said, *'C'est moi et mon Jules.'* It was like a sudden precipice. *'Tiens,'* she went on. *'Je vais vous montrer sa photo. Vous m'en direz quelque chose de gentil, hein?'* She delved in her *sac* and produced a minute photo of a dark-haired young man. At a loss, I said, *'Il a l'air très sérieux.'* And a little later, *'Qu'est-ce qu'il fait, comme métier?'*

'Il est dans la marine.'

Nanni said something I did not catch properly, something about him being very strong-willed, and Monique said yes.

That she should have an accepted boyfriend shocked me. She always seemed so withdrawn, remote. Now I saw a reason why. I felt sad, but relieved; at least there was no cause for jealousy in the group. But later I learned that she had a brother, and I wondered if it was him. By *'mon Jules'* I thought at first that she meant 'my boyfriend', the slang meaning of 'Jules'. But perhaps her brother's name was Jules. I could have asked, but preferred to remain uncertain. At the time I thought that it was a hint to me that she was not free. I still don't know, and often wonder. It was not like her to talk about herself. Discretion is one of her charms.

We had lunch in a small *bistro* in the village, the usual four of us together. I ate many green olives and grew intolerably melancholy. There was a drunkard at the next table and I felt like joining him. I could not shake off the impression that I had been warned off. We set off again in intense heat to find a place for the siesta. By the Guadalquivir – a brown, sluggishly rolling wide river. In the drenching heat we collapsed and undressed beneath a shady copse of aspens. The girls collected branches and lay on them. Nanni asleep, her full, graceful body like a sleeping Greek goddess. Perhaps it was because of the 'new' Monique, perhaps because of the green and white patterned bathing costume moulding the venereal lines of her body, but I decided to go for her.

Later we swam or waded in mud and *café au lait* till the middle of the stream where a strong current had scoured the mud away. When I was swimming somebody called out from the bank that I had had my photo in a Spanish newspaper. I laughed and swam further out and was swept away in the current down to the shallows where Jacotte was standing.

Jacotte, a strange girl. A tomboy, a nurse, a mother-cum-lover. A pretty face, an excellent figure, yet sexless. She gave herself a little way to everyone, sitting on their knees, her arms around them, *tutoyant* them; at first I thought she was a nymphomaniac. Perhaps she was, but an unvicious one. A strong, variable voice, a mimic, with a meridional accent. A commonsensical, shrewd, golden-hearted girl, adept with men; as if love was her favourite game but only a game. I carried her piggy-back over the mud ashore, pretending to drop her, laughing. But I find the sentimental condition of *camaraderie* difficult to maintain; French young people do it without difficulty. It is, in fact, physical closeness without sentiment; semi-naked play and no sex. From it one moves to sex without sentiment; and the death of love. A modern tendency; the abolition of the passions. But I, a renegade Puritan-Protestant, shall never feel at home in that brilliant world of sex and friendship without the shadows of love.

The photo was indistinct. I stood before the coach outside the Prado; the others were a little envious. I felt smugly proud, and went back into the water, to be with Nanni. She swam the breast-stroke, with her hair tied up and her head high out of the water. We rushed together down to the shallows and I took her hand to help her across the rapids ashore; and felt ten times more sexually excited at the touch of her hand than at the thighs of Jacotte around my neck. There were many peasant-women to watch us dress; in rags, with outstretched hands, and carrying rickety babies.

A sunset ride to Cordoba, grey in my memory, though there were no clouds. We camped by a little town, on the banks of the Guadalquivir still, at a place where there was a strangely isolated aqueduct or bridge, many arches leading nowhere. When we first arrived in the town there was a religious procession, endless acolytes and stooges. The Virgin was guarded by four soldiers carrying rifles; her smile above the barrels and black jackboots was ironic, I fancied. The *curé* followed, a tall, worldly-looking man, with a pompous little army officer beside him who kept on changing his white gloves from hand to hand. No longer *Trône et Autel*; *Mitrailleuse et Autel*.[1] Paul and I decided to have dinner in the village, and walked down a rough road. There were many stars, and I sang softly. I knew the others were behind us and suggested that we waited. I knew Monique and Nanni were with them. When they came close, I started to whine in Spanish, like a beggar. Walking beside them in darkness; Monique seemed more friendly than usual. Nanni sulky. And walking between them, I felt irresistibly drawn towards Monique, in spite of what I had learned that morning. We went to two restaurants, but they charged ridiculous prices. A frustrating hour searching for food. Paul and I bought wine and cheese and melon, and picnicked while the others ate their meal. Monique by Claude; I began to feel increasingly jealous of him. Thunder in May.

---

[1] 'No longer "Throne and Altar"; "Machine-gun and altar".' With the Concordat of Bologna in 1515, François I reached an agreement with the Pope – which would last until the French Revolution – giving the French crown almost complete control over the disposal of the higher positions in the French Catholic Church.

I went a little mad that night; perhaps the wine. The village was full, fiesta, and there was a small fair. I got Monique and Geneviève on the merry-go-round, a ramshackle thing that had to be pushed by hand. I suddenly felt happy and very excited, and started to poop-poop and dance and stand on the tiny horse's back like an *equestrienne*. Then I pushed the merry-go-round on and on while the proprietor tried to stop it. Then to the swings, where I swung with Nanni and then with Monique, wildly, poop-pooping and the others resting with open mouths by the rail. Then to a dwarf train-track. They wouldn't let me drive, but I collected all the tickets from the Spanish passengers and distributed them among the group, so then they could have two rides. Unfortunately the real collector came and the Spaniards started to shout, but they all saw the joke in the end. We set off through a tunnel where there was a ghost. I tried to snatch his broom the first time round, failed, and the second time jumped off on top of him. A terrified small boy. I jumped off and on the train, poop-pooped, every so often sat beside Monique, saw a kind of frightened admiration in her eyes, and did something else ridiculous – I suppose all I did was only an orchid I wanted to give her, something exotic, highly coloured. In the end I ran up a ladder and danced on the roof of the central kiosk. Came down, and was just about to jump through the door when I saw something terrible. Two naked children huddled together in a corner; thin, filthy, on a piece of sacking. Incredibly, in all that din around them, they were asleep. I saw the proprietor outside, a small, sallow, sad-eyed man in a stained suit. 'Yours?' I asked. He nodded. I gave him a cigarette, wished I had some money. I felt suddenly cold, frozen, old; the incident shocked, astounded me. I went up to Monique (Why? To show her my tender heart, my change of mood. But also because she was intelligent, was the only one there whom I felt might understand) and made her come and look at them. Her face slowly upturned to mine, one of her Madonna looks, a pure heart's pure compassion. She said something inaudible, and I followed her out. I remember walking home with Monique and a group, sad and sleepy, but faintly thrilled with my exploit.

9th. In the morning, a headache. I sat before my tent, and heard the others telling all those who had not been at the fair about what I had done. Laughter, as warm as the sun on my back. I went for a swim, and afterwards unsuccessfully hunted a tree-lizard with André.

We went to Cordoba. It was Sunday, very hot. We visited the Mosque, a classical garden of beautiful pillars and arches.[1] More than all the architectural beauty, I was impressed by a rough little cross scratched

---

[1] Cordoba Cathedral, known as La Mezquita ('The Mosque'), was originally the great mosque of the Ommayyad caliphs. It began to be built after the Moors entered Cordoba in the eighth century.

on the marble wall by the nails of an ancient Christian prisoner. The
Arabs kept him chained up there for ten years, and all he did was to
scratch this cross with his fingernails. It is difficult to imagine the
Kafkaesque horror of such a punishment.

An afternoon journey to Seville, in great heat. I sat opposite Nanni
and Monique, in the back holding the door open for air. Monique in the
briefest of geranium-red corduroy shorts, and an unbuttoned sleeveless
blouse; but something boyish, virginal in her. Nanni in brown shorts, fuller
legs, and a blue and white check shirt. We stopped to look at a large flock
of storks, a hundred or more, that flew up and wheeled all around us.
My own shorts, white legs, not masculine enough, not virile. City legs.

Seville after dark; Monique cold, beside me in the corner, wearing
her red jumper and my green and yellow square; holding her throat
and looking out. She had a bad throat, stirred up protective instincts.

We drove about Seville meaninglessly, hungry, with two or three
factions arguing about what we should do. In the end it was decided to
go and spend the night at a neighbouring village.

The village street was full, a crowd of strollers. They all gathered
round the coach, a sea of calling faces. When we got out, most of us in
shorts, the excitement was intense. We were surrounded, pressed against,
stared at like visitors from another planet. We bought some food in the
centre of the village, and went back to the coach to eat it. The crowd
grew and grew. We met Monique and Geneviève almost in tears. They
had been hustled and gaped into a state near hysteria. Titi had had her
off-the-shoulder blouse pulled up by the women. We had a meal at a
café table, almost unable to move. When we left, there were stares and
catcalls. It was like leaving a den of wild animals, and as near a riot as
I have experienced. An incredible savagery of curiosity, a *naiveté* and
hostility to foreigners. One side of Andalusia. The group were furious,
as excited as the Spaniards, everybody talking at once, the girls hysterical, the men (as always after the event) ready to *casser la gueule* of every
Spaniard in Spain. Paul and I looked at each other, and grinned quietly.

10th. Everybody washed at a fountain in the famous central courtyard.
Monique in blue pyjamas, small brown face, laughing, at her most Red
Indian. To Seville. I did not like Seville; it is not romantic, but a modern
city built around an old quarter; in an ugly plain and too touristic. We
split up in the main square; I hated that splitting into our own small
groups. It meant that I lost both Nanni and Monique. Nanni, I felt,
could see, was linking up with Jouteau. Also, in towns, the group was
absorbed, at its worst, in a way shown up as provincial; they seemed to
me unnatural, not themselves, straining to be modern, chasing a
chimera. I liked it best in the country, alone, on an island, as it were.
The city was the future; dispersal, separation, oblivion.

In the morning we saw the cathedral, which gives a colossal illusion of vastness. It seemed to me far and away the largest building I had ever entered. We mounted the Giralda tower, looked down on Seville.[1] It is not impressive – a large, sprawling, grey and white city in a tired plain. Later to the Alcazar.[2] A guide took us round the palace, stopping at every picture and telling us who it was – he must have been a monarchist. Art and history did not seem to interest him, for he told us nothing about the rooms and furniture – just royal names and relationships. In the Arab part he was more normal. I like the small grace, the gazelle-like quality in Moorish art, an immensity of slender detail. Something austere and reserved, inhuman in it. A décor for houris, in a vacuum, a creation that no one will ever look at. We went out in the great garden, tired, wandered among the fountains and the green lawns. André deliberately soaked himself under a gardener's hose. I was wearing my new trousers for the first time and split them trying to catch a frog in a lily-pond. We sat in the shade, let evening grow.

Some of us went to see some flamenco dancing. Monique in a blue, red, green tartan dress, and a white collar. I walked alone beside them, happy again to know her close. But the evening was sour; Monique felt ill and said she was going back to the hotel. Consternation in several hearts. But Michel took her arm and she went along. I bought two bunches of jasmine from one of the ubiquitous juvenile jasmine-sellers, and gave one each to Monique and Geneviève. In their hair, over the ears, ephemerals. We crossed the Guadalquivir, and came to an open-air nightclub – a commercial atmosphere, a dance-floor, surrounding tables.

Atmosphere apart, the dancing was magnificient. The most primitive dancing in Europe – with all the tenseness of an erection, the women titivating. The shadow of the penis everywhere. In the male dancing an anger, a fury, a defiance – a constant trampling and stamping, on the edge of savage excess. The women completely women, more sexual than if they were naked. The ballroom dancing that went on between the spasms of the professionals seemed insipid and ridiculous. The wonderful rhythms achieved by handclapping – there were three men and five girls – and the eight of them at the climaxes clapped in an intensely exciting series of cross-rhythms. I wandered round the dressing-rooms when they were off-stage – supple, vital women, and proud, arched men, like D. H. Lawrence ideal men and women. Strange and sad that

---

[1] Seville Cathedral is the largest Gothic structure in the world. It was built between 1402 and 1506 on the site of a twelfth-century mosque. The Giralda tower, nearly a hundred metres high, was originally the mosque's minaret.

[2] Incorporating fragments from earlier Moorish buildings, the Alcazar palace was built by Pedro I in the fourteenth century.

he never touched Spain. I stood on a bench at the back, beside Monique, when they danced, too conscious of her to watch them properly. We left early, all disappointed, tired. A walk back under the stars. Paul seemed to me bouncy, platitudinous, solid as rubber. I walked alone. Monique also seemed sad; but the Godichon brothers started to clown, and she started to giggle, a schoolgirl, at her least endearing for me. Claude took her arm, she was suddenly gay. I felt blue to the core, imagining that her Jules was there, his arm around her, almost wanting it, anything rather than this uncertainty. But then she was sad, withdrawn again. All beautiful women can change their moods in five seconds.

Another nuance of indigo over me was Nanni, that evening with Jouteau, dancing closely to him, and left behind at the nightclub with him; the *Carte du Tendre*; all roads blocked.

11th. A morning alone. I did not regret it. For a moment I was tired of the group, of the long grey vista between myself and Monique. I wandered about in the old quarter, which I found by chance, and which seemed doubly beautiful for being so unexpected. Here, in the narrow streets, the white walls and black grilles, the flashes of foliage, the clean grey shadows, I found the Seville of my anticipation. This is all one needs to see – architecturally – at Seville. One would do best to come, spend an hour in the old quarter, and leave. I was reminded of Oxford – still heart in the maelstrom. I bought some peaches and walked along eating them. It was midday, and I began to feel lonely again. I thought I would find someone in the gardens of the Alcazar. Sure enough, and my heart leapt, I found Paul with Monique and her group. I offered to lead them round the old quarter, and waited for them in a little garden by the cathedral, while they climbed the tower. I wrote a poem there about Monique, the first of a series. 'Bewitched by the world's most hopeless love'. A sonnet in fifteen minutes; I felt happy, and talked to a precocious little hotel tout, who spoke both English and French well.

We wandered back into the modern city, through streets under high awnings; bought fruit and sat at a café. I manoeuvered myself next to Monique, and felt happy again. Bought her an ice later in a confectioner's, and heard a little dryness in her thanks. *Tendresse se revèle.* Whenever that happens, I see myself distorted – a grotesque master fawning on a fairy princess. *La Belle et la Bête.* But in this case la Belle and the wicked witch are one and the same person.

The coach was late picking us up, and we sat for two hours on the steps of an open house, waiting. The only seat was right in front, a good seat and one saw well, but Nanni and Monique were at the back and I did not enjoy the ride to Rota. We passed through Jerez, where I learnt, from an English-speaking importer, that sweet sherry is an English bastard. The Spaniard takes it dry. I tasted a very fine dry Amontillado.

The main street pavements seemed lined with tables. I noticed that everybody drank coffee, in spite of it being *aperitif* hour. A prosperous place, to judge by the men's suits, and their sneers at my shorts. Monique was late when we left; running, panting, schoolgirl again in her exertion.

Over a desert to Rota, arriving at night. We went down the coast a little to an isolated bar among pine-covered sand-dunes. We walked a little way over the railway track to the edge of a low bluff, with sands and the sea below, the full moon on the water and the lights of Cadiz to the south. I was delighted to get back to the sea again. I never feel so free inland; on the edge of the sea one begins to escape.

We camped along the cliff-edge; I had a shock, seeing Monique and Claude standing together on a hillock, talking. Suddenly they came together, for a moment, just as if she had leant forward and kissed him. But it was moonlight and I could not be sure. I heard their low voices, and then they disappeared abruptly towards the trees. I had a violent attack of jealousy and, after a moment, followed them. But they had disappeared. I walked about aimlessly, hoping to see them with the others. Only they were missing. A few minutes later I saw Monique carrying a load of wood. I calmed down, but remembered the first shock.

12th. Morning swim, wide sands, wet, inciting one to leap, stand on one's hands, run. I ran, and crouched under the cliff to relieve myself. In the distance were some fishermen on the sand, hauling on lines. I felt fit, exuberant, and faintly excited at the thought of going to Africa. Strange how the moments one spends on a lavatory seat, or crouched somewhere, are often moments of slight anticipation, a kind of happy pause before action. Also one is obliged willy-nilly to consider one's animality. An excellent daily psychological discipline.

To Algeciras – a desert of saltings, guts, canals, mudbeds, wide horizons. Into the mountains, burnt dry, intensely hot.

Gibraltar, a surge of nationalism in me; jokes about *'la vieille Angleterre'*; Jouteau began to sing 'God Save the King', others joined in. A huge grey-white rock-whale, a stone ship, standing over Spain. But the isthmus, the umbilical cord; geography lasts longer than frontiers.

Algeciras, blinding heat. We had a bad meal in a tourist restaurant; the steak was tainted. An altercation with the 'patron'; I refused to pay, and felt ill and irritable. I hate terminus towns, endports. We were late for the Tangiers boat and had to run down the burning quays to get aboard in time. But aboard and away, with the sea blue and breezy, running away from the burning south, with Gibraltar crouched on our left and Africa's blue mountains ahead, I felt better. Most of the others felt ill, which pleased me. It was almost calm. We turned south-eastwards, went between mountains and tides and dancing wavelets, a little white-tipped.

M at the boat-deck after-rail corner, looking at the sea with intense seriousness, away from the others, I thought because it was the first time she had seen it, or possibly that she was simply sick. Forward, where the tide-races met, queer swirling currents and cross-seas, we saw many dolphins; at one time there were a dozen or more rushing and surging and leaping just ahead of the ship's bows. I could watch them endlessly, creatures without any personality, spirits of speed, springing up and gliding swiftly on just above the wavetops. Excited cries whenever they appeared.

Some of the group, led by Paul, wanted to go to Rabat, instead of resting at Tangiers. Monique was undecided, and I was jumping about internally, trying to discover what she would do. Paul wanted me to come. By this time I knew that I would do whatever M did. When we landed, she came to me and asked me if I was going. She had decided not to; I felt overjoyed as all the rest of her group were going; but short-lived joy, they found visas were necessary, and nobody went.

We came in closer to Spanish Morocco, a hint of wave-mountains, grey, blue, with white villages here and there. The Atlantic wind was cool, salt-laden. Tangiers took shape, a city of tall large blocks, an American-looking city, soft and luxurious in the setting sun. Landing, Arabs, a jumble of languages. A huge man in a red fez and a blue cloak. We were taken by a contact of someone to a camping-site outside the city. It was night, a city of limousines and neon lights. Where we camped, in the middle of a sand-dune, there was nothing, except for a few houses and shops on a nearby road. We bought some food from a shy, soft-spoken Arab shopkeeper, and ate it out on the dunes. It was cool after Spain, a night full of stars. M was not there, but N sat alone; I felt a new interest in her. Jouteau had stayed in Tangiers, in a hotel. We walked down towards the beach, but Paul was there to join us. We strolled a long way along the smooth sands, with all the multicoloured lights of the bay of Tangiers before us. I wanted to have her alone, and I ignored Paul. She walked between us and we exchanged platitudes. Before we went to bed, we did something that was to have unpleasant consequences – took Laffont's hat from his tent. A strange desire to hurt and annoy him. Later we slept together, the three of us, on the sand. So near and yet so far.

13th. We went on a tour of Tangiers, of the Arab quarter. Western Tangiers is full of luxury shops, chromium and plate-glass and office blocks and flat-blocks and rich hotels, the streets full of tarts of all nationalities and purposes. The poor and the rich, the donkey and the limousine. The Arab quarter is more interesting, involved, hidden, shuttered. Groups of women in white sitting along the steps, along the foot of shady walls. An animated, jostling market. Everywhere I was conscious of an independence, a faint

dry contempt for sightseers. Outside the quarter, in European surroundings, the Arab seems deferential. But here, or away from the city, he shows
no sign of inferiority. It is insufferable that one should expect them to
look inferior, but one does; the British Imperial heritage.

All through that morning intensely conscious of M – following her,
hanging back if she was behind, watching her secretly, not happy unless
I knew she was close, in my sight and hearing. From then on the holiday
was less a holiday in Spain as time with or without Monique.

We walked back to a hotel by the beach for lunch. I sat next to N, to
her faint – as I saw – regret. She kept on looking round at Jouteau, sitting
at another table. Afterwards with M and N and Geneviève and Jouteau
to have an ice-cream. An awkward little group, as if I had come too far
out in the open over M, shown too much preference. M was serious,
disinclined to laugh. I felt ill at ease, embarrassed. We joined the others
to go up Mont Tanger, a little outside the city. N decided not to go. As
Jouteau had just before said he was not going, I realized that N was definitely lost. I felt sad and bitter, a mood augmented by the fact that I went
to the Mont alone in a taxi. Each taxi held six people, and it so happened
that I was the odd one out. Pure chance, but it seemed to me symbolical of my position in the group, unattached, not very much liked, almost
unwanted. I have a disposition that is completely absorbed by personal
relationships if I am with friends or in a group. That is why I travel best
alone – with no group to obsess me. To leave the group was not enough
– once entered in it, I could leave it without regret. In this case I exaggerated my position ridiculously, out of an innate morbidity. But all the
time at Tangiers I felt that things were going wrong with regard to myself
and the others. I was jealous of Jouteau and N. With Monique I felt
grotesque, a Caliban to her Miranda. Yet every time she was with me, I
felt I had to clown, to tease, to do my tricks – a state I hated, and to
which only a Monique could have reconciled me.

A sad day; one gay passage in the morning when I walked beside
Monique on the way in to Tangiers. Then André, the chauffeur, tough
and usually oblivious to everyone else, remarked on her. '*Elle n'est pas
mal, la petite.*' From him, that meant a book of poems. He seemed a
little surprised; I understood; she grows on you; profound beauty, like
all other things profound, needs to be known. To myself I called her
chignonette. Her supple willowy walk, a classical movement, upright but
full of grace; her chignon floating behind her, balancing, giving her her
individual, unique outline. Monique.

But a sad day, thirteenth day; when the voyage seemed tasteless, and
my sorrows – as indeed they were – final.

14th. Up at dawn, along the sands into Tangiers, to catch our boat. I
felt happy to be going, that the group would have to spend the day

together. Alfred chased me over the sand, crying wildly, clutching at my orange sleeping-sack. We walked near Monique, chased around her. Perhaps I wanted to seem young, to dwarf that six or seven years between us.

Back to Algeciras. On the boat I wanted to sit near her; even man-oeuvered myself to be sitting opposite to where she was writing a letter. But she looked up, saw me, and moved away. Because of me? For that one moment, I imagined myself avoided, and drowned my regrets in a letter home. I think she was in one of her moods, restless, changeable. Everyone was subdued, the going north again, the beginning of the end.

Algeciras and blazing heat; southern Spain is a furnace in mid-August. We drove up the coast to Malaga, sweaty and uncomfortable, longing for a swim, but the puritan Richard insisted that we keep to the 'schedule'.

We camped for the night by the sea at Torremolinos. A sense of relief at having arrived. The sea was warm, the Mediterranean again, with a sandy steeply-shelving beach. Along the strand were erected bamboo beach-huts, which gave a strangely Polynesian air to the landscape.

Changing in the coach; Monique at her most playful; five minutes of teasing her, being teased back. Her nose crinkles and her eyes flash when she pretends to be angry and she punches with a quick bend and downward movement of her arm, comically ineffectual. Or again when she is amused in spite of herself, her reluctant smile contradicting her still complaining and teasing voice. *'Je ne vous parle plus. Vous êtes dégoutant.'* Her lips outraged, the *'plus'* accented and high-pitched as if her voice would break with indignation, and her eyes mischievously crow-footed with laughter. I accused her of standing outside the coach so that she could see the men undress and dress. Counter-accusations, punches, indiscreet comments. I call her *'la Bedouine'* to annoy her.

15th. Up early, for a swim. Up to the town for breakfast, a brandy and soda and a kilo of muscat grapes. The kilos of muscats I must have eaten – an incomparable hot weather fruit, the antithesis of dust.

To Malaga, a few miles away. It was Saturday, the beginning of the summer fiesta, the city crowded. Malaga left no distinct impression on me compared to Seville or Cordoba. A wide shady boulevard leading to the Plaza de Toros, an insignificant main square with a crowded, obscure quarter behind it. We wanted to see the bullfight, but the tickets were too dear for most of the *'jeunes'*, Monique, I saw to my sorrow, among them. It meant an afternoon, no doubt another evening, without her.

We waited about for the tickets, and *l'affaire* Laffont rose to an ugly little crux. At last he had realized that his hat had been stolen not by a Tangiers thief, but by one of us. He began to complain about the bad spirit, the lack of camaraderie, until someone produced the hat,

a crumpled shadow of its former self, and threw it at him. But that only
egged him on to further recriminations. Unfortunately there was an
element of truth in all he said, and the joke had been kept too long,
gone bad. He kept on saying, '*C'est hideux*.' '*Hideux*' became the 'parrot-
word' of the rest of the holiday. But when I told him he was making a
fuss about nothing, he shouted, 'Maybe you do things like that in
England, but in France we don't like it.' I felt a sudden simultaneous
spurt of guilt and anger. He had accused me of taking the hat – which
was more or less true – and dragged nationalities into it. I leant forward
and pulled down the hat (which he was now wearing) sharply over his
eyes, and said angrily, 'You be careful what you say. I didn't take your
hat. I know who did, but it wasn't me, so shut up.' This incident rankled
with me, because I felt that Laffont was right. And N knew perfectly
well that I had taken it. Although everyone said afterwards that he was
wrong, I think many of them secretly agreed with Laffont – rightly. And
they did not like the strong-arm much. I shook hands with him at once,
but Laffont will hate me to the end of his life. Although he is stupid
enough to discover hate, not for Christian reasons, but diplomatically,
by sheer pomposity. If I became famous, I am sure he would go around
saying that we were once great friends, and talk himself into believing
it.

At the garage where we left the coach, there was a Spaniard who
spoke English well, a perfume representative, very polite and gentle-
manly and hard to shake off. He took us to a restaurant. I walked with
him just behind Monique, talking in English. For a moment she looked
round at me – the only time I have ever felt that she admired me.
'Wonderful, isn't it?' I said dryly, 'I speak it just like a native.' She gave
one of her shy small-girl smiles, slightly puzzled. I tried to get him to
say something about the Franco regime, but he said everything was all
right. He did not sound so much scared to speak, as indifferent. He
took us to a little wineshop with some excellent Malaga, a brown wine,
sweet and fruity, with an exotic flavour of apricots. A meal in a little
backstreet restaurant – I was beside Monique, a position difficult to
maintain. I preferred to face her opposite, where I could watch her
every movement. Beside her, I felt I had to talk, and that was difficult.
I could never make my French clear enough for her to understand;
other people would understand, but not Monique. She would frown
wistfully, and say, '*Je ne comprends jamais ce que vous dîtes.*' This used to
make me seem more nervous every time I opened my mouth to her. She
had decided that I was incomprehensible, and never really tried to understand. At the end I talked more slowly with her, and she understood
better. During that meal, she seemed determined not to understand. I
felt that I was making a fool of myself. On the walls opposite, against
the ceiling there hung a mirror tilted so that one could see down on

to the table. Monique kept looking at this mirror and smiling. Sometimes it was at me, sometimes at other people. But I was too short-sighted to see which way her eyes were looking. I could only see that she was smiling, and so I smiled back. Once or twice I realized too late that the smile was for someone else. Once I saw Titi looking at me, a little drily, dispassionately, glimpsing something in my smile. Halfway through the meal, somebody came in late, and Monique jumped up to give him her seat. Half her generosity (she will help anyone at any time), half her moodiness, her need of change. In the coach she was always the first to offer her seat to anyone standing, the first to give help, the most dutiful, Madonna-like.

We took a fiacre to the Plaza de Toros. Crowds of people, animation, a converging on the high-walled colosseum. All one's Roman ancestry is stirred. We found our way up the stairs, feeling like actors backstage, making for an entrance. We surveyed on the second balcony, in blazing sunlight, dense, packed circles of animation. Although we had come an hour early, it seemed that there were no more free places. But we pushed along to a standing place at the rail, crowded together, stunned by the roar of voices. It reminded one of the ancient Elizabethan theatre, the Globe style. The Spaniards around us would have been more at home in a Tudor pit than Englishmen. Slowly the seats in the shade filled up; black and white mantillas, sun-glasses and rich dresses in the flower-and-flag-bedecked presidential box, a small segment of extreme luxury. We were parched in the hot sun and watched the lorry spraying the sand with water, turning it from pale to rich ochre. At last, the hour, a roar, and the slow strut of the personae across the sun into the shadow under the box.

Silence, the bull-door opens, an empty arena; a tense pause; a murmur, a shout, and the black bull trots angrily, pugnaciously into the eyes of all Malaga.

Bullfighting fires me every time that I see it – the spectacle, the beauty, the symbolism vastly outweigh the cruelty to the animal. It is less sadism that makes the audience so tense, so savage, at the climaxes, as the universal duel with death. Few people go in the hope of seeing a man killed or gored; it is the gamble, the risk, that one man accepts on behalf of all mankind – a fight against fate. When the bull dies, humanity has triumphed. In no sport is the issue so clear, the play so close to reality.

It is primitive, barbaric even; but I welcome it as a missing ingredient in the frozen modern man; the man who is all psychology, all mind, and not at all animal, the unbalanced twentieth-century ghostman. A dram of liquor on a Welsh Sunday. The last fight was superb, heightened by the comparative mediocrity of the others. Ordonez, a tall, slim young man, who had already won the best ovation for his first bull, apparently decided to try and win out the day. The bull was active, full of fight.

Ordonez began a wonderful series of *faenas*, every cape-pass perfectly executed, the bull dancing and lunging around his upright, swirling figure. There were one or two swift successions of passes when the bull seemed mystified by the cape, unable to best it. At each pass the crowd gasped louder, until Ordonez consummated one final masterpiece and, flowing his cape behind him, walked away in a thunder of applause. But the thunder went to his head, and at the height of his triumph he risked too much. The brilliance flashed into horror; one moment he was standing with the cape, the next moment in mid-air on the bull's tossing head, falling on the ground, the cape yards away, the bull with its head crushing down on him. The whole arena cried, was silent, everybody stood. A rush of the other matadors to aid him. The bull turned away.

Ordonez lies still, then moves. His head crouches on the sand. A helper tries to raise him. Ordonez sits up, pushes him away savagely, tries to stand up, falls on one knee. There is a great tear inside his thigh. Everybody helps him to his feet, he can hardly walk. They try and lead him to the barricade. He begins to swear, refuses to move and calls for his cape and killing-sword. They are reluctant to bring them to him. He is sobbing with pain and rage and disappointment, his face contorted. But he dominates the whole arena; the sword and the cape are brought. He arranges them, shakes off his supporters, and tries to walk towards the bull, almost falls. The other matadors come forward again, try to lead him away. Ordonez spits out something, gestures them all ways, stands there sweeping them away, leaving him alone once more with the bull. The bull moves in, lunges. Three perfect passes, stiff, with a little limp as he turns to meet the charging head each time. The bull stands, uncertain. Ordonez closes, shakes the cape. The bull stands still, almost amazed. Ordonez drops the cape, stands before the massive head, six feet from it. Suddenly throws the cape away, turns his back on the bull, and kneels, facing the presidential box, with his arms outstretched and his head thrown back.

An unforgettable moment; a shiver of silent admiration ran through me, ran through all the crowd – not so much in the loudness of the cry we gave, but in the quality of it. Twenty seconds later when he stood up, the bull stock-still, thunder-struck, there was a gargantuan storm of applause, a shower of hats, an enormous murmur all around.

Slowly Ordonez prepared for the moment of truth – aligned, painfully bent his knee, thrust – and the bull moved, so that the sword stuck for a moment, truth sprang out as the animal trotted away to another part of the arena. Ordonez limped quickly after it, cursing the other matadors who were trying to dissuade him once more. I was watching his face, twisted with agony, each time he made a step. Not once did he look at, or feel, his wound. He took up his stance again, aligned his sword, slowly, implacably, as if not even death could stop him from killing this bull. He plunged forward, almost deliberately on to the horns and struck right home. A few seconds later the bull was dead.

He got a tremendous ovation – a thousand hats, scarves, cigarettes, everything. And it is only now, a month later, that I can realize it was only a man killing an animal. At the time it seemed to me the greatest exhibition of human bravery I had ever seen. Yet only a man risking his life for mere entertainment – trapeze artists do the same. It seems it was the hottest day for many years. *'Que calor!' 'Que calor!'* Everyone said, *'Que calor!'* We walked slowly down dark narrow sidestreets, trying to find the restaurant where we had had lunch. At last we did, and the others, but I felt too hot to eat. Most of us sat in the ante-room, exhausted, wordless. I went out twice to drink beer. But however much we drank, ten minutes later one was thirsty again. Monique was there, with Claude, and wearily I noticed their new intimacy. The English-speaking Spaniard was there, but I had not the energy to talk with him. I gave Monique my parasol hat. *'Pas mal, hein, pour deux pesetes,'* I said, anxious to show that the gift was not serious. She laughed, tried it on, pulled a face, and five minutes after she had gone to eat, I found it crumpled behind a chair. I got tired of waiting for the meal to finish, and went with Paul and the English-speaking Spaniard to the fair. We passed a family sitting behind a garage – the owners apparently – in their best clothes, taking the air, and clapping two small girls in Andalusian dresses, who danced together exquisitely, their contrasts, their feet, their swirling red-spotted long white dresses all in symphony on the narrow pavement, under a streetlight. The fair was very large, a multitude of lights, an illuminated chandelier with hundreds of stalls and amusement booths, dance-floors, ghost-rides, valleys of love and all the rest. A cacophony of cheap music, tango, sambas, paso dobles; a vast throng, with jingling fiacres forcing a slow way through. The night and stars invisible. So different from the little fair near Cordoba. I looked for the others, but they were swallowed up in the vastness of the chandelier. Paul and the Spaniard and I fired at the shooting-booths, threw quoits. I won a cheap little statuette of the Virgin. There was a choice, but I chose Mary for Monique. At once I began to think of some teasing way of presenting it, rehearsing words, ridiculous phrases in my mouth. The Spaniard left us. Paul and I wandered back through the fair, I sad, remote, missing the others. We ran back to the main square for the rendezvous. Monique was there, alone; outside the coach. I made my speech and presentation. And I gave her the statuette. She was in a playful mood, laughed. She was sitting next to Claude. He had his arm around her shoulder. Happily Geneviève was on his knees. He spent all the time trying to make love to them both at the same time. Geneviève seemed to want it, Monique not, although she never seemed annoyed by his touches. He was always catching hands, pressing thighs and arms,

squeezing shoulders. No more than camaraderie, but irritating to me.
Debasing the coinage of love.

We camped some miles from Malaga. Halfway up into the sierra. I
laid out my sack under an olive-tree, close to the Monique group. I had
to spy on them, to see how the land lay. They always slept together,
touching, and I wanted to know the relative position of Claude and
Monique, especially when Geneviève moved away from them, and said
'Goodnight' in a piqued voice. There was a moon caught in the olive-
branches overhead. For a while I watched it, sat up to see if I could
distinguish how close they were, could not, lay back again, found an
indigo sadness in the sky, and almost at once slept.

16th. Up at dawn. Dawn in hill country, in mountains, is always a splendid hour. I climbed a little nearby hill and looked down at Malaga far
below. I remember that morning very well, the blue-green air, the coolness after the burning plain. Above all, because Monique sat beside me.
For a time she stood, then somebody said, 'There's a place beside John,'
and she came and sat there. I purred, between the magnificent landscape
and her presence, like a cream-fed cat. I tried to talk seriously with her,
but it was difficult. I was nervous, trying to be interesting, amusing. She
was sleepy, not bored, but uninterested. I asked her if she had left school.

'Oui.'

'Do you work at home?'

'No, I work in a laboratory.'

'In a laboratory!'

'Oui, je fais des analyses!' Her black eyes looked at me sideways, almost
with hostility. Of all the careers I might have imagined for her, that was
the last.

'What kind of analysis?'

'Everything . . . not always very nice things.' And her eyes smiled for
a moment.

'Vous chassez les baccilles, alors?'

'Oui, les baccilles.'

'C'est intéressant?'

'Oui. Ça m'intéresse.'

'The laboratory is big?'

'No. Not big.'

And so on.

She always has a short, precise way of answering questions, very seriously, intelligently, taking the question exactly at its own value, as if it
were written on paper, part of a form, ignoring all the irrelevant contexts.
I suddenly saw her in a new light, the working-girl scientist, in a white
smock, bent over a microscope handing in curt reports to a bespectacled
chief analyst: almost a nunlike existence, disinfected, hyper-strict.

'How long a holiday do you get?' I asked.

'Just these three weeks,' she answered.

I suddenly felt a fool, a drone, an insipid sentimental schoolmaster, an old doddering man beside this slim, young nineteen-year-old scientist. I ceased to talk with her, bitter that she asked me no questions, but stared impassively, drily out of the window. In her withdrawn moments, she was very remote. Was that her charm for me? Her complete sincerity with her own emotions. When she was gay, she was transparently gay, completely gay; when she was sad, serious. She made no concessions to the general mood, to what might have been expected of her. I have seen her coax out of her seriousness, her slow smiles, the awakening smiles of someone who has been genuinely asleep. None of the damned artificialities that clog the usual calculating feminine psychology.

We stopped at a point high above the valleys to look back over the Malaga plain; already a heat mist was draining the more distant colours. Monique got out before me and went to Claude, who took her by the shoulders and gently shook her. She shook herself free, but gently also, and began to laugh with Geneviève. It was not so much a love jealousy I felt with Claude – he loved Monique, but I could see that she did not love him in return. But together in their small group they were not bored. They laughed, danced a long time. I watched the three of them walk away to a better vantage point, felt bitterly bitter. I deliberately hung back when it was time to move off again, almost hoping that Claude would sit beside her, and give my resentment some real ground. But she was alone in the seat and Claude elsewhere. I sat down silently beside her. A little later she began to nod, to fall asleep, only to wake up every five seconds with the wheels' jolting. Lost again, no longer proud, I waited my chance. When she looked up after a particularly heavy jolt, I said gently, 'Sleep here . . . on my shoulder . . . if you'd like.' She had her small-girlish look, hesitant, faintly beseeching.

'Ça ne vous gênerait pas?'

I shrugged. 'Je n'ai pas sommeil. Allez-y.'

She tilted towards me, leant her head on my shoulder. A flash of intense, astoundingly intense happiness swept through me. She relaxed a little, more closely against me.

'Ça va?'

'Oui, c'est confortable.'

Then she was silent and myself very happy; I had never done anything but touch her hand before. Now to know her weight, the feel of her, her solidity – a new dimension. Her head, her hair brushing my cheek. Paul went past, looked at me strangely, almost with jealousy, I thought. And I looked back without smiling, perhaps a little vauntingly, bantam on the dungheap for this one small incident.

Michel behind me turned and laughed. *'Ah, ah, c'est comme ça que ça commence.'*

Titi also. *'Ah, oui.'*

I saw Claude out of the corner of my eye, a little silent.

But it did not last long, the coach stopped by a well so that we could wash and shave. Then when we were all there, with the usual clatter and scent of soap, I suddenly realized that Monique was not there; and a second later that Claude was also missing. I finished shaving, raced back to the coach: no sign of anyone. I looked around and saw no one and a thousand places to be concealed. I opened the coach door, sadly, entered, and there she was, fast asleep, stretched out on the wide back seat, her head on her arms, her shoulders high, her hip upstanding, small-waisted and the slim line of her long legs. She had some strange natural grace; lying down, she was a sleeping goddess, wonderfully moulded, relaxed, herself.

Again when we went on she came back to her old seat, and I sat beside her. For a time she was animated, talking with everybody except me, then sleepy again and my heart sang, as she looked without a smile, a little sideways at my shoulder. I patted again and she leant sideways.

'Ça ne vous gêne pas?'

'Pas du tout.'

But once again I was fated. The engine began to cough, to knock whenever we had to mount a hill. For a time we jogged spasmodically on, then there were a series of terrible knocks and the coach stopped. Although we did not know it then, it was really the end of the holiday.

The chauffeurs poked about while we stood around. About quarter of a mile away we could see a village. A landscape of scrubby stubble-fields, dry hills and valleys, and to the north the central range of the sierra, a high jagged line. André the chauffeur came out from under, serious-faced. *'C'est pour deux heures, au moins.'* Part of the universal gear was broken and would certainly be irreplaceable in the village, even if a garage existed. We trooped off towards the houses. The village was large, almost a small town, called Colmanar, an agglomeration of white sun-scorched houses. The village street was away downhill, framing a superb view of the blue and grey mountains ahead. The first houses turned out to be two cafés. We went into the second, out to the back where there were tables under the vine-covered trellis-roof. We ordered coffee; Paul bought a tin of peaches. Claude sat next to Monique, holding her hand, his arm on her shoulder. She was laughing, leaning towards him. Someone ran in and said that the Mass was just starting. They all jumped up, the Catholics. Claude took Monique's hand and led her out. Paul also went, and I was left alone.

Two of the blackshirt boys came in. There were two or three of them who always wore black shirts, nonentities. They wanted to go for a walk,

see '*le gibier du pays*'. We went on a little safari, myself leading, up a hill
out of the village, through sparse olive-orchards, down to a valley overgrown with prickly pears. I felt farouche, an immense desire to be alone.
They talked about nothing endlessly, two black parrots. At one they
started talking about lunch. I told them to go back, that I wanted no
food. As soon as they were out of sight I climbed up a little valley towards
some tree-tops. There was a trickle of water by the path and a cool fern-
surrounded well. Higher I came to a small copse, and then another, so
green and shady that one might have been in England. There were
many birds and no men. I sat by a little well, out of the sun, and felt
unutterably sad. I admitted to myself for the first time that I had fallen
in love with M; and fully admitted the other bitter realization that she
had no interest in me at all. Normally these two factors interact – one
realizes the impossibility at once, and accordingly a kind of self-pride
stops one from falling further. But M had slipped through in some mysterious way, taken my heart almost before I knew it, and now was walking
away with it – walking away for ever and not even knowing what she had
done. In that *bosquet*, I felt very remote from the group, from all life
and all commitments, and understood the psychology of the melancholy
anchorite. That hour in the copse was a kind of initiation. I saw that I
should get nothing but unhappiness by following M, that the rest of the
holiday would inevitably for me be of a sourness and bitterness that
would spoil all my past feelings about the group. It was not quite so;
but that morning I went back wide-eyed into my own small tragedy, puri-
fied as always by a stay in the wilderness.

When I got back, I ate some grapes and joined the others, who were
sleeping and lying under the trees by the roadside. M and her group
were not there, but I felt too hot and too tired, too immured to worry.
The villagers stood in the road above and stared at us. A crippled, trembling beggar came to each of us in turn. His thanks were so humble
and profuse that to give him money was not charity, but self-esteem
bought cheap.

That night was Nanni's night. After dinner she announced that she
was going to get drunk on Malaga. We were all sitting round a large
table and she sat there smiling like a virgin endlessly tired of her virginity;
and drank glass after glass of Malaga. I went and filled her glass at the
bar once or twice and put more than a dash of cognac to pep up the
process. Everyone began to tease her, make her see double, rock the
table, miscount the glasses she had had. Her eyes began to cloud, and
she talked in a loud voice unusual for her, but she held it admirably.
Jouteau watched with a little smile that held no amusement. He seemed
jealous of me because I led the teasing. She must have had ten or twelve
glasses, the best part of a bottle, when we decided to go down to the
village swing – five or six of us. The main street was crowded, and we

had the same effect as the Pied Piper of Hamelin. First of all children,
then youths, then everybody, laughing and shouting and jostling behind
us. I took Nanni on the swing – a sea of faces, tipping and tilting. She
began to croon with pleasure. The crowd got more and more excited,
and the swing-man with them, until I began to feel extremely scared,
as we threatened to go right round the top. The whole frame trembled
and lurched at each new plunge. Nanni screamed with excitement. I
made noises and tried not to imagine what would happen if we were
flung or crashed to the concrete ground below. We stopped in the end,
but Nanni wanted to go on and I had to experience the whole ordeal
again.

The crowd became uncontrollable. We walked back towards the café
singing arm in arm, dancing, with a mad crowd of villagers, several
hundred strong, behind us. They began to jostle and pinch and punch
us – all in good fun, but it began to get a little rough. There were little
groups running and shouting in all directions. All men except for the
children. I began to tire of the tumult and hubbub and went to the
back, where I could walk unnoticed. Suddenly, abruptly, there was
silence, and four policemen came up the centre of the road. Magically
the crowd melted away. A plump little man in a smart grey suit introduced himself: he was the local magistrate and apologized for the uproar.
Exchange of civilities – Jouteau began to talk law with him. I sat down
on a nearby wall, tired out. Nanni came and flopped beside me, took
my hand and leant against me, soft and yielding. I could have led her
away perhaps, felt very tempted to do so. But some inner pride stopped
me, the thought of her dancing with Jouteau. To have her, but not when
she was tipsy, so we sat there without talking. Jouteau kept on looking
round at us. He had that nervous half-smile, and I knew he was scared
of me, hated me. Or does one *hate* a rival? Rather the choice, all that
tends towards a rival in the loved woman.

Mostly out of spite I took Nanni away to have a drink. Jouteau came
soon afterwards, stood behind us with his half-smile. Paul seemed determined also to be spiteful and suggested we all sleep together. We climbed
up the hill opposite the restaurant to where Jouteau had pitched his
tent. I was very conscious of Nanni's softness and warmth, her laughter
and slow voice. A brilliant moon. We came on the tent under an olive-
tree, then the first lightning for tomorrow's thunder. The sides had been
slashed in several places by a razor-blade. We undressed, got into our
sleeping-sacks. Nanni slept right up against Jouteau's tent. When I turned
back from driving away the circle of spectators we had attracted, I saw
that she had slipped her hand under his tent flap inside. I knew a spasm
of jealousy and laid awake staring at the brilliant moon. My ears wide
open for the smallest sound of a whisper or movement. There was none.
Paul, with delightful obtuseness, was sleeping so close to Nanni that he

could have touched her. Poor Jouteau, he must have been furious, although from my point of view he had the last laugh, and I lay awake for a little time unable not to spy, as the night before.

17th. A sad lunch. News had come that the broken part could not be replaced for several days. M and Titi were ill with food-poisoning, someone else had a fever, short temper, fatigue, disintegration. The heat was appalling also.

A tired, dispiriting evening; general depression, not shared by myself. I drank a little. They sang, but without Monique and Titi it lacked vigour, was sad. Some sad madrigal by de Lassus. Everyone slept together, under a huge old walnut-tree, on a downhill slope out of sight of the road. I slept apart from the others a little, smugly congratulating myself on my position, calculated to avoid the early morning sun. Thirty sleep-sacks stretched out in the moonlight. Murmurs a while, then silence.

18th. The sun had woken up the others, as I had foretold. But I did not foretell that they would come all around me and chatter like magpies. Every so often, someone would say, *'Regardez John qui dort, c'est dégoutant,'* and I would groan, grunt, grumble. Drowsy, drowned in their voices. I liked it. We lay about under the tree, insulting each other, and feeling ill, till nearly ten. Every so often grunting herds of russet pigs would trot past, only kept away by heavy clods of earth.

Paul and I went to the fountain to wash. A sorry sight when we left it, the clear water cloudy with soap and the edges with suds. But it was delicious to wash in the little pool, in icy water, with the bare burnt hillsides all around me. I caught an enormous toad, which pissed prodigiously, and carried it back in my soapbag to the café, where it was viewed with general disgust.

Lunch under the walnut. I wanted to be at the café, near M. But a little later she came alone to sleep. Asleep, lying down, she always seemed so young and slim, nymphlike. She went away when Anique came, talking in her hard, shrill voice incessantly. I saw her lie down under an olive some way away. And could not resist going there myself some little while later, when another girl had already joined her. We lay there in silence. I can remember that hard earth, the heat and olive-branches, and her body in her tartan dress, her head on her right arm; on a cold dark September night. Oh for that sun, sunfever. Time and sun.

When she went back to the others I followed, saw jealously how Claude played with her, with his arm around her shoulder. But more than ever I felt sure she did not love him. An aloof indifference.

At six, an indignant meeting, led by Jouteau and myself. Richard and Laffont had gone off to Granada by bus. They were the leaders, and the group felt that they had not done their duty, arranged other transport, as they should. It was decided to re-elect André. Much the best thing, as he is respected, and a natural leader. We spent frustrating hours in the village trying to hire a lorry to take us to the nearest railway station. Everything seemed hopeless, but in the end a lorry-driver was found.

A scramble and midnight packing. We only had two or three hours' sleep. There was a little rain, and the others ran to the coach. But I slept on under the walnut.

19th. The driver woke me at three. Chaos in the road. The lorry, a very small one, was backed up to the broken-down coach – everybody apathetic, undecided. I suddenly felt a surge of energy, that bounce and drive I sometimes get when everyone else is exhausted – because, perhaps. I pushed them about, got them to hurry, loaded the lorry with all our gear, made them get in, and put up the tailboard.

A wonderful night voyage through the sierras to Loja. Brilliant starlight, large mountain shapes, velvet peaks. The lorry rushed on, drove uphill, swung round bends. I sat on the tailboard, wide-awake, strong, balanced, while the others slept on each other's shoulders, collapsed. Dawn came and the mountains grew grey, took shape, towered over us. M suddenly felt sick and came and sat beside me at the tailboard. Her knee pressed hard against mine, her head in her hands, melancholy, sweetness for me. I wanted to put my arm around her, comfort her. Too soon, with the sun just risen, we got to the station at Loja, the line running at the feet of some small hills. Coffee and cakes there. Our train came, with wide carriages, and long wood seats, no *parois*.[1] I felt very sleepy, the others suddenly alive and gay – they started to sing. The long carriage was full of Spanish peasants. Jouteau started to take a hat round, as a joke, talking like a flower-day champion to each passenger in turn. Without understanding a word of what he was saying, they began to laugh. Even more miraculous, and to our vast delight, most of them gave a little money. A wave of old spirit came over us; gaiety, absurdity, the group against the outside world.

At Granada we went to see about a camping-place. A busy, modern city, outside its monuments. In the end we found a cheap boarding-house in the ugly quarter near to the station, four to a room, but at least a roof. I had the city blues again, knew we would split into our little parties, and I not be with M.

I went off with Claudine to see the Alhambra. Far and away the holiest building I saw in Spain, and for me one of the supreme masterpieces of European architecture. To go with Chartres, and the Parthenon. There is in the Alhambra an atmosphere of serenity, of grace, of shade

---

[1] Partitions.

and discreet silences, which is overwhelmingly beautiful.[1] Each room,
each court, each pool, colonnade, fountain has a subtle air of mystery,
an aristocratic enigma. This is the oriental paradise, the Persian park
of wonders, the Old Man of the Mountain's hidden valley. Everywhere
one glimpses the Ionian spirit of ancient Greece, delicate, smiling, faintly
exotic and barbaric, feminine, above all graceful and profoundly enigmatic. The smile of the Caryatids of the great Erechtheion porch,[2] the
Da Vinci heads, the Gioconda strain in world art; one of the loveliest
and most mystical of all the attitudes to the universe. Something Chinese
also; silences and silent pools, peace and resignation, erotic sensations.
The fountains work feebly in the Alhambra now; a pity, since the fountain is an important part of the architecture, animating, focusing, the
environment. I felt very sad, very moved by the passed holiness of that
palace. Related it to my own life, and the absence of Monique, and then
suddenly realized that she was of the same nature as the palace, as the
Erechtheion girls, the Gioconda–St Anne strain.

We waited outside for the others. I had glimpsed Titi in the distance,
hoped M would be with her. But they must have left by some other
route. I sat with the others in the dark, a little away from them, feeling
very surly, melancholy and ripe for a poem. On the theme of:

> *She was not there, she was not there,*
> *Not there in the palace this evening*
> *But the palace was there, and she was*
> *The palace.*

I walked back with the others angrily, farouche. Jouteau had appeared
and gone off with Nanni. I do not believe I have ever suffered so acutely
for the absence of someone I loved. That, and a recurrent awareness
that I should never see her in the Alhambra, never go there again with
her, the old agonizing complex.

20th. A day at Granada, happy enough. It started well, when I woke,
and saw Monique in her blue pyjamas, standing at her window, sewing.

---

[1] Situated on a high plateau overlooking Granada, the Alhambra complex
contains a number of palaces built by a succession of Moorish rulers. Although
it was begun in the fourteenth century by Ibn el-Ahmar, the founder of the
Nasrite dynasty, most of what can be seen today was built by Yusuf I (1334–54)
and Mohammed V (1354–91). With its honeycomb cupolas, horseshoe arches
and delicate tracery, it brings to mind the sort of palace a Sultan might build
in an *Arabian Nights* tale.
[2] The Caryatids are the stone maidens who support the porch at the west end
of the Erectheion temple on the Acropolis.

I blew her a kiss with a faun's grin, saw her laugh, return it, both grin and kiss.[1]

But later she was gone, and I felt miserable again. I had a shower and breakfast, found myself alone with two nondescripts, hastily left them. Walked into town alone. Then all went well. I went into the Cathedral and there at once was Monique and her group. We went round the Cathedral together. I felt old in that young party. Noticed their ignorance, their bad taste (not hers; she rarely ventures an opinion, seems not to know art yet), their silliness. And always watching her, watching her. The three of them, Claude, Geneviève and Monique, always together, whispering, touching. He would be restless until he had them both in caressing range.

We had lunch together. I avoided Monique's eyes, tried to seem normal. She seemed specially aloof, to my joy, with Claude. He seemed worried by it, kept trying to make her laugh, warm her. I wonder now if it was because I was there, and she was being kind to me. But the more she withdrew, the more I admired her. All beautiful women, like all good mountains, are difficult to approach, and both when approached never wholly show themselves except in glimpses. The secret of charm of secrecy. To hold back, keep mysteries, not as an obvious mystification, but discreetly, with taste. In her case it is natural, subconscious, as it must be to have full charm. Full charm I shall never have.

Back with them, back to the *pension* for news of the coach. This evening perhaps, definitely tomorrow morning.

We went back into Granada, shopping; again I stayed with Monique,

---

[1] The glimpse of Monique occasioned this poem:

I blew her a kiss with a faun's grin
Saw her laugh, return both grin and kiss
Across the sunlit morning yard.

Her bent head at the window,
Sewing, and I in the shade not yet risen,
Full of sleep, still star-enchanted,
Watching her fingers pull their threads,
Arched in sunlight. She sat on the sill
In her blue pyjamas, and I in the patio
Not yet risen, caught in her sewing,
Her gaiety, grace and greenness,
Weighing that one second's lipsent kiss
Against the limitless whole of eternity.

En pension, Granada, 20 September 1952

unable to let her out of my sight. We came to a mantilla shop, and I
found a pretty one at a cheap price. She stood beside me, feeling it,
serious. She wanted one for her mother. I agreed to let her have it.
'Mais non, John, vous êtes le premier . . .' She turned over the pile wistfully; picked up that best one, and suddenly put it on.

Just for one second she attained a supreme beauty, a second which
flashed right through me. The shop was a little dark, the mantilla black
lace with small embroidered flowers. It framed her oval face, beautified
it, accented that strange Madonna quality in her. Her head was tilted a
little, she looked at me with a faint enigmatic smile, merely perhaps to
ask me if it suited her. But her expression was so soft, so sweet, so tender,
so mysterious that my own expression must have seemed strange, for
she turned away and quickly took it off. Again that St Anne strain, this
time unmistakably. The most wonderful expression a woman can achieve.

Back at the *pension*, a minor tragedy. Monique had lost her purse with
all her money. I was amused by the general concern among the men
and the indifference of the women. 'She's always losing things,' said
one of them. 'Not a chance of getting it back,' said another. But the
men – myself not least – were full of advice, hope, possibilities. As for
Monique, she wore that wistful little half-ashamed smile of the girl who
has suddenly collapsed from a woman back to a schoolgirl – that smile,
with a wry little touch of amusement at herself. When everyone else had
gone to her, I found her sitting on a bench, still wistful. I talked with
her for a moment, even suggested she came out on the patio. She said
she could not sleep, was wide-awake. I felt vastly tempted to sit beside
her, talk, comfort; and knew that if I did the game would be up. I could
control my speech, but not my eyes. The only way I could talk to her
was by averting my eyes, and over a long period that would seem strange.
So I left her. Five minutes later, returned; but the corridor was empty.
She had gone to bed, and I slept alone on the patio.

21st. We woke at dawn, waited outside a café for the coach to come.
Rather tired, forlorn, tense at the prospect – it had been decided to
drive non-stop to Thouars. A minimum of sleep, snatched meals, and
no tourism. The coach came, and the scattered group met.

We loaded our bags, and set off, singing for a while, exuberantly on
the move again. But those three days were unreal, lived in a feverish
dream, out of the dry passionate heart of Andalusia to the melancholy
of Thouars. For some reason I felt the transition through those three
days much more acutely than I had flying from Athens to London earlier,
but had time to appreciate it.

From Grenada north-east to Baza, with the snow-peaked Sierra Nevada
majestically massive on our right. Arid country, eroded soil. We passed
several termite villages, the houses hacked in the hillock-sides. Outer

ant-shaped hillocks, troglodytic openings. On and on all through the day, the country blurred in memory, sometimes singing, usually silent, a hot monotony. We stopped for a while to eat prickly pears; nothing very marvellous in them, a sweet insipidity, and pomegranate pips, and devilish hairs. I skinned myself badly and got the hairs in my lips. Monique was there and tried to pull them out. Her small cool finger-tips on my lips, like a nurse, deft, impersonal.

To Alicante at dusk. We stopped by a crowded beach, and changed into swimming-costumes in the coach; much stared at by the Spanish passers-by. The sea was unbelievably warm, like tepid tea. I swam out between two piers, and looked up at the rocky hill overlooking the town in the last faint touch of daylight. After dinner we set off again into the night and for me two or three hours of happiness. M was beside me in the back seat, between me and young Brosset, André's cousin. We rushed down the dark road, rows of black heads nodding together, only the high shoulders of the chauffeur alert and awake.

'*Je peux dormir sur ton épaule, John. Ça ne vous gêne pas?*'

I felt excellent. Claude was opposite, *jeune* Brosset sulky in his corner. Poor *jeune*, he was hopelessly in calf-love with her, following her every-where, standing by her seat for hours, pathetically eager to catch her smiles. She was briskly cool with him, never encouraging him, never cheaply dismaying, petulant. One of her mysteries – how she managed to be so sweet, so understanding, with everybody, and how she remained so aloof, secret, unattainable, if one tried to approach her. The perfect sister, mother, comrade, and all the lover in her locked away, but with hints of felicity quite out of the modern world.

The slumber was not too comfortable, so I patted my lap. She leant across and rested her head there, her body twisted sideways, an extra-ordinary position in which she always seemed able to go to sleep. I felt her head, her shoulder on my thighs, her small, compact body against mine. My left hand supported her head, my right rested on her hip. The darkness, the rushing onwards. Very gently the pressure of her body increased. She slept, relaxed, slumped on me. My hand shifted lightly, each new touch of her body an inspiration to me. It was as if I was trying to draw her into me, absorb her through my fingers. It was very hot, a sticky torrid heat which made the clothes cling, and the bodies were animal, in heat. I felt all the bitter-sweetness in the beautiful transient. Her small, hot body on my thighs, the hidden mistress in her, the dark-ness. Night lights flashed past occasionally, so that I saw her closed eyes, the long lashes on her cheek, the red scarf over her chignon, her little breasts obscurely outlined, her slim bare arms. Became excited out of myself, married her then, since never any time elsewhere, astonished, ashamed, and profoundly disturbed. She slept on unaware of all this, and I felt as if I was betrayed by my own body – the Greek horse,

enchanted, under some spell of her, had there made me blind to all
the dangers. I almost for a moment believed myself spelled. We stopped
for a moment, and I walked away in a kind of tumult. But when we
climbed back in, she leant sideways again, and I knew the same golden
ray, the same massed black storm clouds coming, and sat there in the
night, intensely aware, aware of each short second of her breathing,
of her.

We camped somewhere near Valencia. She got out of the coach and
disappeared with Claude into the darkness. But soon came back with
news of a place to sleep. She went with him, I believe, to set me upright,
not foster my illusions.

The others slept, but I went down over some small dunes to the sea
– a roaring line of waves, line after line of combers, a swish of shingle,
and the hissing backwash. I stood there, lost in the sea, then undressed
and waded in up to my waist. It was luke-warm and extraordinarily rough,
a passionate Spanish sea.

22nd. To Barcelona. To begin with, seat-squabbling. Everyone wants a
good seat, and tempers were under the surface. And several of us wanted
to be near Monique. For the first few miles we were at opposite ends
of the car, and I had an egg flip for breakfast out of spite. Got back
before the others, and chose the seat behind Monique. So passed the
day in comparative peace.

In the morning, I watched her combing out her long hair, down to
the middle of her back, almost black, luxuriant, silky. It framed her face,
gave her a Red Indian look; a beautiful wild deer-girl look, her eyes and
brown face under the frame of her hair. One of her exquisite secret
moments. She is coquettish, very careful with her hair, constantly touching
it, retying her red chignon-scarf. A characteristic pose, head half down,
her busy hands elegantly raised behind her head, her elbows like wings.

North, north, north. At Tortosa, near dark, to buy provisions. I had
no money left. M at the fountain. I splashed her, her mock anger. I
suddenly found my hat had gone, suspected M or possibly a village boy,
but because of what I had done to Laffont did not dare say anything.
The biter bit. It later appeared on my seat, and M confessed. That
morning, to my delight, she for some reason quarrelled with Claude.
She appeared hurt about something. He had probably gone too far; a
Breton, *gaillard*,[1] and unimaginative.

Tarragona. Grapes and cheese and the famous wine, which I thought
no better than that we had had elsewhere. M and Geneviève were at
the same restaurant, at another table, nibbling at ice-creams and talking

---

[1] Forward.

in animated low tones. I felt happy about Claude's disgrace, all the more
since he was leaving M the next day.

For the night voyage, M slept in the same seat as Geneviève. I was
not happy, nor unhappy. We went through Barcelona, a blaze of lights,
the great modern city. Stood for a moment at the harbour's edge, under
the black outline of the model of Christopher Columbus's ship,[1] stared
at the crowds for a moment, went on. We stopped to sleep about two,
on a deserted beach, with the sea in our ears, and many stars.

23rd and 24th. Up at dawn again. M coming up from the beach with
her blanket draped round her shoulders, her hair down, a squaw Venus,
advancing down the road towards me. A divinity, even at that hour.

Le Port Bou – frontier formalities, and an exhausted sadness. Spain
and sun all behind us – winter ahead. To Perpignan, happier since once
more she was beside me, by chance, and we said nothing important,
because I was too full of questions to speak.

She slept again, on my lap. I held her there, my face impassive,
knowing this would be the last time, the last chance. Her small, piquant
face with its pale brown skin, its sleeping eyes, the little mole above her
lip like a strangely placed beauty spot. Her hair brushed back so strongly,
straightly, into the red scarf and chignon. Her small, firm body, her
breathing. All too soon we came to Perpignan, and I prayed desperately
that time would stop, or we pass through. But I had to wake her, grip
her shoulder, shake her.

Perpignan, roads I have travelled before. An ugly town, but an old
friend. I recognized the familiar landmarks, the Castillet, a patisserie I
used to go to.[2] We had lunch, Paul and I and Monique's group in a
backstreet restaurant. Shaving at a washbasin, watching the others sitting
around the table, seeing if they were leaving me a place near her. I was
opposite. Spoke little, did not look at her unless I had to, saw Claude
trying to warm her. She was pleasant, but cool with him.

To Narbonne. *Etangs*, banal meridional plains. Claude said goodbye
to us all. M was asleep. The coach stopped at the station, we all got out.
M still asleep. 'Wake her,' said somebody. 'No, don't bother. It doesn't
matter,' said Claude, poor chap; though he will forget her long before
me. But she came out, rubbing her eyes, smiling shyly at him, shaking
his hand. Group photographs, last goodbyes. The holiday was over.

On inexorably towards Carcassonne. Monique on her own, with an

---

[1] A full-size replica of the *Santa Maria* is moored in the fourteenth-century Royal
Shipyards at Barcelona, now part of the Maritime Museum. It was from Barcelona
that Columbus set off on his famous trip when he discovered America.
[2] Perpignan is just a few kilometres to the north of Collioure, where JF stayed
in the summer of 1948. See introduction, page xiii.

empty place beside her. Brosset *jeune* eyed me. '*Il y a une place à côté de Monique, John, si tu n'es pas confortable là.*' He wanted it himself, I could see; was testing me. '*Je veux bien,*' I said, shrugging and inwardly dancing, and went and sat beside her. The most overt 'move' I had made. She must have realized the situation. It was a cloudy evening, sombre country on the way to Cahors. For a time we said nothing, she with her cold, dispassionate face looking out of the window, myself stealing glances sideways at her.

I asked her about work. '*Il faut que je travaille demain.*' We knew we would be travelling through the night, not at Thouars till eight in the morning. I marvelled at her toughness, felt brutally disillusioned by life taking this fairy and making her work to a laboratory routine, clock in at nine, come what may. I asked her more about her job, and got her to talk a little more warmly. Wished the group could come to England. This was the last year, though. I was silent and she spoke my thoughts. '*On ne se verra jamais, John.*' She meant by '*se*' – everyone – but it was for me only relevant to ourselves, and she said it so casually, dispassionately that it almost slapped me over the face. As if to say, 'You see, I don't care a damn really.' I hoped she might fall asleep, but she remained awake, sad.

We got a picnic supper at some small town at dusk. M was gayer, laughed when I made some joke. But I left her alone, too timid to advance at such a late hour.

We set off again. I had imagined spending that night beside her, having her sleep against me. But she sat now with Geneviève, opposite my seat, and I was with Alfred, least wanted at that moment. But he got up to go and sit with someone in the back, and the place was empty. I saw Monique nodding, her head back, and every few minutes looking up, wearily out of the window. I sat wide-awake, staring into the darkness, aware of the situation and the hopelessness. Suddenly her voice. 'John, John' – leaning across Geneviève to speak to me. My dry mouth. She smiled the smallest amount. '*Je ne peux pas dormir ici. Ça ne vous gêne pas?*' She was standing, I was standing to let her pass into the window seat. She slipped sideways at once into my arms, relaxed against me. I was drowned with happiness, a thousand times more happiness than embracing a naked G had ever given me.

I still cannot quite account for that sudden move of hers. For comfort? Or charity, since I cannot believe she had not guessed that I loved her. A moment of tenderness. Yet normally she never gave herself like that to anyone. I wondered if it was a sign to me, some hint.

Headlights flashed past us. I did not sleep, but nursed her body. She slept, heavily against me. At one place – Cahors – we got out for a minute, and when we went back I went in the window seat and let her rest in my arms, against my breast, holding all of her. I let my head bow, felt my head rest on hers. Our fingers touched, soon interlaced, but there was no pressure. For a time we changed, and I rested against her shoulder, but she seemed so slight, so fragile, that I was afraid to relax and let myself sleep. I tried sleeping with my head on her thighs, but that was no better. I was too alive to her, in any case, to think of sleep, and soon let her sleep in my arms again. She will never know – or will she, did she? – the fire she put into me, the happiness bestowed, by that one small whim, that coming across to me.

I knew then that I had for a moment known true love. I have never before felt myself capable of anything to keep a love. I would have done anything to prolong that night, given all my life to be petrified at that one point. Could have given all of myself without reserve or cynicism to her.

At Perigueux Françoise Brosset's young man left us. Françoise kissed him, and began to cry. Monique led her back inside and sat down with her, her arms around her. I could have cried myself. By a dreadful irony, the fat coarse Anique came and asked if the seat was free. '*Oui, oui,*' said Monique, behind. '*Allez-y. J'ai assez dormi. Vraiment.*' So the monster plumped down beside me. A little later, I looked round at Monique. She was sitting very upright, the sobbing Françoise on her shoulder, with remote eyes that looked at me almost without recognition; a woman comforting a woman's trouble, full of a noble compassion, the Madonna. I felt no longer jealous, now bitter, but sad. There is a wonderful nun in her, beyond analysis. The exalted, regal compassion of Notre Dame.

The rest, hell. I dozed, was cold. It rained continuously. Anique kept leaning against me, but I leant away from her. Through Poitiers, old memories, a grey wet dawn. I was suddenly gripped by stomach pains, a sharp attack of dysentery. The last hour or so was an agony for me, my mind and body fighting the grips that racked my intestines. The others sang. I saw Monique in the back, and an empty place beside her, but could not move. When we got to Thouars, I had to run for André's house, and even then all but arrived too late. A ridiculous, disgusting irony in things.

Fifteen minutes later, weak but relieved, I went back to the square to say goodbye. Catalpas and cold grey houses with light grey shutters. A few parents, a damp, cloudy sky and a pile of jetsam on the ground. I sorted out my belongings, and stood there sadly, shaking hands. When it came to Monique, her eyes met without teasing, with a smile – liking and friendship and sorrow at parting on her side, sweet and sincere and all I could expect. I nearly said something foolish – perhaps should have done. She climbed in the coach with some of the others, to go to her home on the other side of Thouars. I stood there with Paul, not watching anything else but her face through the window, looking back at us, sadly, gently. I blew her a kiss, she blew it back, waved and was gone.

I plunged into a sea of melancholy. Went back to André's, shaved and washed, packed up my things. I was anchorless, stagnant, all will, all hope gone in one breath; unable to get any way in again, wanting to fade out of the picture. I walked down to the station – a cold, grey day – and suddenly saw a notice on a door – Laboratoire Analytique – an ugly little house with a black brick wall, upright windows. Where she worked. On the way back from the station, I lingered, loitered there, in the faintest hope that she might be inside, see me, or be met by me as she came. Seeing that squat, grey building seemed too unbearably poignant. I walked back to André's drowned in misery.

Paul took me home with him to Cholet, some sixty miles away.[1] For once, his enthusiasm and earthiness soothed me, lulled me, and I was clinging to any link with Thouars, with her. Even now, I think of the comb I use as that which I bought at Thouars on the day I saw her last.

A quick lunch in Paul's flower-surrounded house, then to the train, a slow, springless, start-stopping French provincial train. It rained, grey clouds, small woods and poplars.

Ginette[2] was waiting for me at Paris – how I viewed the prospect of seeing her only with disgust. All of me went back to Thouars, was being wrenched away, my body torn in two. For an hour I was at grips with time, saw time's savagery as I have never seen it before. The impossibility of ever achieving Monique, the going-away, the constant departure. I sat there, unable to read, unable to sleep, only to cry silently.

This year it was not the group, but Monique. All that I liked best in them, all that I like best in France, was in her. This year she was a young woman, not last year's mischievous, wayward schoolgirl. Everything green and expectant in her, her swift moods, her laughter, gloom, gaiety, seriousness, April Monique – all that still sobs in the transient.

I have wallowed in the melancholy, idealized her, not talked of her faults, the practical things that would make me less romantic around her. But she touched the romantic spring in me, and that's well hidden. Right through the armour.

Fear of the transitory, ecstasy in it, is the oldest, truest suffering. A Roman road, forever straight. The landscapes change, but not the direction. What I felt in that little train to Angers, every lover has felt and every poet felt. Still a valid thing to express.

She made me a Romantic.

Made me examine my nationality till I see that France is my native country.

The sadness soon of sadness fading.

That tingling, ecstatic greenness when her voice leapt at the high-point of a song.

---

[1] Cholet is actually about fifty kilometres to the north-west of Thouars.
[2] i.e. Ginette Marcailloux.

2 September
Roy Christy, a friend of Denys Sharrocks, and a new candidate for Spetsai.
With a trim beard, wrinkled eyes, a wife and child. A lower middle-class
intellectual; but seriously a writer, it seems. Two works written. I had a
feeling of superiority – something about him molelike, industrious,
unimaginative. No holy fire.[1]

17 September
Leigh. Animal talk. How I hate the way my mother mothers the dog and
the bird and even the goldfish. Bright baby talk, as if they were human.
A gross lack of proportion. I would kill a thousand budgerigars to set
one wild sparrow free. This morning also, an indignant letter about the
cruelty of bullfighting in the *Daily Telegraph* – British sportsmanship and
all the rest of it. 'We hope Englishmen will refuse to support this barbaric
spectacle,' and so on. That puritanical tight-lipped urge to interfere. Of
course it is cruel. But so is life in Spain. No account taken of man's part,
the terrible risks, the savage poetry, the magnificence of wasted blood.
A luxury civilization can well afford. Only people who live out of the sun,
in the universal suburbia of modern England, could bleat so insipidly.

The intellectual Oxford accent – my own voice. I hate the colourless aristocracy of that voice, those sounds. Love more and more the provincial,
the strange, the sincere. A voice should have colour, not academic euphony.

A bitter little argument with Father about America. He shouted angrily
against the NS and N attitude to the USA.[2] We began to disagree

---

[1] Roy Christy, born in 1920, had been senior to Sharrocks at the King George
V Grammar School, Southport, and then attended Liverpool University, where
the two became friends. He graduated from Liverpool in architecture and joined
the staff of the Kingston College of Art and Architecture in 1948. At about the
same time he divorced his first wife, Marie Wright, a fellow student at Liverpool
whom he had married three years previously. In 1950 he married Elizabeth
Whitton, whom he had met in Kingston. They had a child, Anna, in the
November of that year but the added responsibility did not prevent him from
giving up his architectural practice with the aim of becoming a novelist. Of a
romantic, extrovert temperament, 'he lived under the illusion,' in the words of
JF, 'that he was D. H. Lawrence'. This being so, Sharrocks's stories of life on a
Greek island contained an obvious romantic appeal for Christy, who felt that
here was the place to provide him with literary inspiration. He applied for a
vacant teaching post and, with letters of support to the school's governors from
both Sharrocks and JF, got the job.
[2] The *New Statesman and Nation* was critical of both the USA's free market poli-
cies and her increasingly hostile attitude towards the Soviet Union, which the
magazine feared would provoke war.

violently. As a boy he used to crush me by his methods of argument –
red herrings, sophisms, a pugnacious, positive certainty in all he said.
Shades of a prosecuting counsel *manqué*. Now I can see all the non-
sequiturs and angry changes of subject when he is cornered. I try and
talk coldly, lucidly, objectively, on one point. He talks emotionally about
several.

'I think America's wonderful,' he said, 'wonderful, and do you know
why? Because she's top dog.'

'I don't see that that follows necessarily.'

'Of course it does. Everything that's top dog is wonderful. It must
be, to get top dog.'

'I suppose Hitler was wonderful in 1940–41. He was top dog then.'

'But he wasn't top dog then. We weren't beaten.'

'Then America's not top dog today. Russia isn't beaten.'

'Well, I'd damn well like to know who controls the Western world, if
America doesn't.'

So on and so on, hopping from one untenable position to another.
Ten minutes later he was denying that he had even said all that is top
dog is wonderful. I compared Greece and Rome, likened them to Europe
and N. America. But he hardly listened, and went on about America
and her money. 'If you've got the money, you've got everything. Nobody
else matters. Where would Europe be without America? Nowhere.
Europe's gutless, decadent, finished with.' He gets this from misinter-
preting Toynbee.[1] Nonsense about every new age being a better age
because it is new.

But the reference to Europe flicked me on the raw. The European
civilizations have been as great as anything the American or Asian eras
are likely to produce. A filthy intellectual treachery to his continent. It
made me so angry that I did not speak and listened to him racing off
on wilder and wilder tangents, with M putting in her appalling little
clichés – 'Of course, it's Russia against America now' – every few minutes.
He reads nothing but philosophy and logic and seems to have learnt
nothing from them. More pitiful I find the money complex: that all that
is gold must glitter. A personal worry, complex and repression, which
he allows to taint his universal views.

I heard a broadcast the other day by the best contemporary English
madrigalist. A flawless, heartless performance, as dry and hollow as an
old bone. I compared it with the green sincerity of the Thouarsaises.

---

[1] In his twelve-volume work *A Study of History* Arnold Toynbee (1889–1975), a
hugely influential figure of the time, had put forward the view that Western
civilization was in a process of decline, which only a re-awakening of spiritual
and religious values could reverse.

We are beginning to be dazzled by execution, rate technique above all other interpreters' virtues. I saw *Cosi Fan Tutti* in Paris, perfectly performed, on the highest level of competence, yet with not one moment of fire, real interpretive warmth. And a ballet performance here in Southend which was good enough, without any faults – and without any virtues. It is not only that the public want the big names with the big tricks, but the critics judge everything by the way the tricks are performed. Too much entertainment today is machine-crude, everywhere. More and more it is the warmth and the sincerity that engage *me.* I prefer amateurs, in the true sense, clumsily on fire to experts coldly perfect.

That is why I like jazz, New Orleans jazz, and all real folk music and folk art. Nowadays the experts seem to save their fire up for first nights and festivals; elsewhere they coast along. (A point for the film – only one effort needed, so burn in it.)

I have these days a sincerity complex. Trying to strip all the poses away, with myself and with others. It seems to me that I penetrate people, see through and into them, can analyse them exactly, know them better in the secret round than they know themselves. The appalling hypocrisy everywhere existent, rampant in the Anglo-Saxon psychology. I feel like a single upright figure in a multitude of fetish-worshipping carpet-creepers. Only the odd individuality impresses me.

Roy Christy impresses me a little. I spent a night with him at his mews flat at Hampton Court. A bearded, shrewd, jovial personality, very sincere and serious in his literary ambitions. He spoke vigorously, with a slight Lancashire accent; an intelligent, poor but happy man, whom I could not quite penetrate (and therefore liked). I read fragments of his novel, matter-of-fact and almost naïf. I was reminded of D. H. Lawrence, the Lawrence of *Sons and Lovers*, the industrial North. What I do not like in Northcountrymen is their quietness their lack of ostentation and fire – DHL is not typical with *his* fire – their drab mousiness and their tired domestic voices. Denys Sharrocks has it a little, and Christy as well, although they are both almost origin-free intellectuals.

I envied him his courage in changing careers in mid-stream; and his first horse, architecture, he rode very well; and now enters literature without a penny. And his wife, a matter-of-fact classless modern girl, tall, pretty and well-dressed, who had stuck by him and encouraged him to find himself.[1]

---

[1] Elizabeth Christy had been born in Walsall, near Birmingham, on 7 October 1925. Her father, Edgar Whitton, was an electrician, and her mother Doris (*née* Culm) was the daughter of a shaving brush manufacturer and had worked as a book-keeper. A sister, Joanne, would be born in 1940.

There was some embarrassment over money. God, how I wish one could treat money and love without feeling embarrassed. But I shall not be able to meet him again without remembering he owes me five shillings. While I was there, he showed me some of Denys Sharrocks' poems, written during the war. Unmusical, complex (and at one reading, almost meaningless) little bits of emotional experience. Denys will never come to anything. He has read too much; could be an erudite critic. Christy seems to read very little. 'Distracts me from writing,' he says. Time I read little also; knowing now all the major bones in the literary skeleton.

Parents on holiday in Suffolk; house to myself; a delicious sense of freedom, meals when I liked, bed when I liked, noisy jazz records at midnight. I revelled in it, and did nothing except revise a few old poems. I am getting more and more temperamental about being in the mood for writing. A matter not of willpower, but coaxing whatever one has of genius. Talent? Damn talent.

Part Five

Elizabeth

3 October 1952

To Greece again: at the last moment I packed this diary, unable to cut myself off from such bitter-sweet memories. Here the sun and strange existence is already burning the past away. Never so much difficulty in writing as here; a constant temptation to be idle in lotusland.

4 October

Arrival. Nothing changed; as if I had never been away. All the masters were there, sitting in a ring round a table. Exchange of platitudes. I tried to seem bright and happy.

Back at school I knew I had nowhere to sleep. My room was locked, and I could not get into the boys' block where there was a bed empty. Egyptiadis was with me, the good Samaritan, shouting for someone to open up. The Headmaster's window flung open, and he started to scream for silence. 'Tell the old bastard I've no bed,' I said. Egyptiadis did. 'That's his lookout for not coming earlier,' snapped the old fool, slamming his shutters to.

I passed a bitter uncomfortable night on the common-room couch, and got up at dawn stiff and tired.

A hot day full of trivialities. But the wonderful climate, wonderful island; brilliant light and warm blue sea. I swam for an hour, using feet-fins, felt what a fish must feel.

Tiny pale mauve and pink wild cyclamen in the garden, everywhere. On the arid olive-terraces tall asphodels: white candles, flames. Purple squills under the yellow-green newly needled pines. No autumn here.

Richly silent moonlit nights; moonlight over, in, everything, a still, barely lapping sea. Bats screaming, cricket-cries. Through the lunar peace, girls singing. Every night parties of girls, men, stroll along the coast road, singing. The semi-tropical night breeds a desire to sing.

But the natural perfection here is dangerous, dazzling. One feels tempted to plunge in it, run, sing, walk, botanize, birdwatch in it, be drowned in it, steeped in it, have all one's value as an individual stolen by it. A surfeit of air and light and wind.

The strange noonday silences at Spetsai, in the hills; sometimes when there is no wind, there is no movement at all, no thing living. The azure sky and brilliant sun, and sepulchre of a dead planet. So silent that one hears the rushing in one's ears.

6 October

Today the door opened and a long-bearded priest in his canonicals came in, holding a cross before him and a sprig of greenery in his hand. I stuttered and stood up. He flipped water on the floor, advanced the cross to my lips. I hesitated, could not think of anything to excuse myself, so kissed the cross. He sprinkled water over my head with the sprig, retreated, obeisances to my own bows and *enchantés*. A pleasant little ritual.

All part of the sanctification of the water ceremony. Blessing us for the new school year. The masters sat in the common-room, eating spicy little cakes covered in icing-sugar and drinking big glasses of cognac. The Greeks have to celebrate each festival. The compensation of the horror of being conventional.

Searching for a house for Roy Christy.[1] Interesting; for the first time I have been able to see some Spetsai interiors, and know more of the domestic economy of the island. A house here costs 2–300,000 drachma a month, furnished.[2] The furniture is simple enough. A padded long wall-seat, divans, bright cushions, indoor plants, appallingly coloured religious prints. Every house I have seen is as spotlessly clean inside as the new whitewash outside. Sanitation is poor, outside as a rule; cistern water; no taps. I went round these houses with Egyptiadis, an incongruous pair we must seem. He is incredibly willing and conscientious, so much so that it annoys me, as I suspect he knows. Also he will not translate exactly what I say. I know enough Greek to know that he does not speak as gently as I do. Much more shortly and sharply, without the frills and compliments. Seeing these houses makes me regret that I have no wife here myself. Even Ginette I could tolerate, for a lift out of prison, a home life.

A trip into the hills, the first since I came back. The usual solitude and silence – a desert of rocky slopes and pine-trees. The barrenness finally oppressed me, and I felt ill. I sat and thought of the future – nine months of island – never a chance of a wife and home. A feeling of doomed bachelordom. Eventually memories of Monique began to flood

---

[1] Roy Christy was due to arrive on Spetsai with his wife Elizabeth and their two-year-old daughter Anna. His living in a house in Spetsai town was an exception to the usual arrangement whereby teachers were lodged in school buildings. 'You *must* live out of school!' JF wrote to Roy in a letter explaining to him the conditions for his employment. 'I have tried to see their motive behind this, and came to the conclusion that they want to ensure you don't use the school kitchen. Also possibly second that Elizabeth may distract the boys (and masters!).'

[2] The exchange rate at this time was approximately 40,000 drachmas to a pound.

back to me; the pine-trees are recovering their caterpillar-ranged needles, are at the moment a brilliant yellow-green. Cyclamen grow everywhere, delicate, windblown, scentless creatures, Moniques. One of those spasms of intolerable nostalgia for her; increasingly rare; for that reason, none the less painful. I saw no one, could have been alone in the world; certainly felt it. How far is Thouars?

Guitar. I am now the intrigued owner of one – which Evangelos bought for me in Athens. I have a book on 'How to Play the Guitar', and realize the total ineptness of my fingers and the defects of my musical ear. I am not tone-deaf, but totally ignorant. Evangelos[1] has promised to teach me. A first lesson by lamplight in the dilapidated bedroom of his house was not a success. He has no idea how to teach me, although he can play so well himself. We listened to him playing. I shall have to learn from the book.

14 October
The Pedagocour, a kind of school court, where five masters judge the boys. A microcosm of Greece. Anyone can watch. The accused boy argues at great length and passionately, while the masters revel in their roles as prosecuting counsels. Justice is very Mediterranean – it is not the case in hand that is judged, so much as all the boy's past, his homosexual value, his father's influence, his character and work record, and all kinds of other irrelevant imponderables. I suppose that is true of all human justice. But never so transparently as here.

Egyptiadis. The latest 'joke' with him is to accuse him of having an illegimate son in the school. There's a small boy with a shaven head who certainly much resembles him. The other masters, especially the Hippo, and encouraged by the Headmaster, have pounced on this. Every time there is a gathering, it focuses automatically on Egyptiadis. He is the butt, the spittoon, the waste-sadism basket of the common-room – everyone vents their megalomania and their sniggers on him. They must have someone to tease, and make fun of, a fool to give themselves self-esteem.

I defend E a little, but he is such a cheek-turner that it is impossible.

He said the other day, 'One has to be a cynic in Greece.' A profoundly true remark. A true cynic would adore the hypocrisy and corruption here; a false cynic (*poseur*) can tolerate Greece but not without malice and a guilty conscience; a good man with no cynicism would hate Greece.

Again. 'You can say what you like in the USA but here it is best not

---

[1] Previously referred to by his diminutive name, Evangelakis.

to speak. If people don't understand what you say, they only laugh at you.' Also true. The Greeks sneer whenever their ignorance or philistinism seems in danger.

An unusual day here; windless, with the sun obscured by high vapour. Everything absolutely still, pearl-grey, smoke-grey, blue-grey, every colour in love with grey. I watched some fishermen hauling in their nets in the afternoon; as they hauled, with their trousers rolled over their brown thighs, in ragged shirts, they sang hymns, beautifully, slowly, mournfully, in tune with the day. A boat of an intense muted carmine came slowly over the water. The village priest, tall, black and grey, with his black orthodox hat and patriarchal beard, came down the jetty and looked benevolently on. A boy in green stood watching by the water.

Hummingbird hawkmoths. One of the commonest moths here. They sometimes fly into my room. Why should such sun-loving creatures fly into the shade? Watching one today, I guessed the reason. It flew round the room, hovering before each object, making an inventory. It came in search of flowers. At this time of year here, flowers grow mostly in what moisture rests in the sun-free hillsides and bottoms. How many ages to learn that? Both the moth and I. Myself as Darwin. The charm of field study is that, the effort to enter remote ways of existence. A kind of wanderlust. *Tout comprendre.* The other day I believe I noted a special cry that white wagtails use after fly-catching. Like learning a new word in a difficult language.

I believe that I became a poet by chance – being so pent up with creative force when I was twenty that it had to find an outlet – and poetry is the only act which someone completely without knowledge of techniques, without manual skill, can begin to practise. I think this was fortunate. I am not a narrow but perfect artist's artist – I feel myself fertile, sensitive, full of seeds, a catalyst, a watershed, an all-round intellect. At the moment, in poetry, being naïf in the attempt to be clear.

11 November

To Piraeus to meet Roy Christy and wife. Their boat came – formalities, greetings, two days, the Acropolis. They were like new toys to me; to watch their reactions, test them out, feel superior to them, their guide and interpreter. They seemed very British, British abroad, tasting the native dishes. Seemed more naïf than I had anticipated. We went, of course, to see the Parthenon. They wandered around rather coolly. Roy made some architectural comments, and seemed disappointed that there was so little to judge the architectural worth by. He did not seem to feel any of the romantic, symbolic side of it at all, the ruins, the ghosts, the wonderful situation. He said twice, 'You know, it was well worth coming up here.' Such a strange remark; as if he had supposed that it might have been a waste of time, and rather surprisingly wasn't.

The journey to Spetsai also, they took very calmly. Went to sleep where it became very interesting, sat in the saloon with their backs to the lovely islands. Makes a pleasant change from England, they seemed to imply. I cannot see Roy as much of a writer, if he takes things so prosaically. He seems to lack colour and sharpness of response – like Denys Sharrocks, almost completely oblivious to nature and his natural surroundings. He sees nothing astounding, nothing miraculous in his first glimpse of Poros, his first sight of a hibiscus. An atrophy of enthusiasm. Elizabeth is the same, tall, drooping, walking like a lanky dog, a rather distant person, happy-go-lucky, but self-willed and as unamazed as her husband by Greece. With him I feel it is obtuseness; with her a kind of feeling that it would be stupid to be amazed. The modern attitude of I-know-every-thing-so-nothing-can-shock-me – not an offensive, a defensive pose. Again and again and again I pity people who know nothing of nature; who will not let the world without man exalt them.

A white wagtail bobbing elegantly through a minute sparse forest of mauve autumn squills; I have watched it several times; an elegant little sight.

30 November

A pure, perfect day. The night before was vinous; we went to Giorgiou's,[1] drank, sang songs, joked; too much retsina. I had a head in the morning, a wonderful morning, zephyrs and dazzling sunshine. I got a lunch, and swung off into the hills, alone, inspired, full of the urge to walk. Up and up and up the goatpaths through the pines, through the air and the glades in sunshine. An emerald tree-lizard I gave chase to. Views back, white houses far below, small boats in the azure sea. Pines and sun and zephyrs and solitude. I took off my shirt and walked bare above. Up at last to the central ridge, with the sea shimmering and glittering on the other side between Spetsai and the Peloponnesus. Pale blue mountains and little spumelike wisps of white cloud splashing against them. I walked along the central ridge, plunged down through the pines again towards Anargyrios Bay.[2] I rattled down the scree between pines, in a hurry to reach the sea. Anargyrios Bay is a wonderfully peaceful, remote little settlement of four or five cottages. I stopped before one.

---

[1] A taverna on the road between Spetsai harbour and the school. Sometimes referred to by JF as George's.

[2] A bay on the west coast, i.e. on the far side of the island from the town of Spetsai.

An old man was doing something to an oil-drum. He had venerable eyebrows and a long white moustache. His wife came out also, toothless almost, wrinkled, freckled, bent, and very haglike, not at all the right Baucis to his Philemon.[1] But she was helpful enough. The bay is a wide, genial place, with a fine stone beach, backed by swordplants and glimpses of the cottages' white walls.

Up the hill along the coast and down to Holy Friday Bay (Agia Paraskevi).[2] It was not, to my surprise, deserted. Man Friday was bald but for a wisp, in shorts and a green shirt, brown-faced, freckled, with pleasant, amiable eyes; an old scout master, one would have said. He was the famous Mr Botasis, who owns the nearby Villa Jasmelia (jasmine).[3] He asked me up for coffee after my swim and, faunlike, disappeared.

I swam in the cold, brilliantly clear water, threw stones, and sunbathed. It is the most lovely and most lonely bay in the Mediterranean. A wide beach with a spacious pine-grove behind, a little chapel – and absolute peace. In its arms and beyond, the sea and the distant mountains of the Peloponnesus. I ate three eggs, some atrociously strong Roquefort and two apples. Felt good, pagan, animal, in perfect accord with nature.

Up to Jasmelia. He greeted me, took me into a comfortable salon, left me to stare at his pictures, his harmonium – he told me he had sung in opera professionally – to read his guest-book. An imposing list of celebrities have visited it. The elder great Venizelos laid the foundation stone,[4] and there are photos of him standing under an arcade there. Other photos, British admirals, royalty, writers, artists. Hundreds of graceful, arty little tributes. I wrote, 'Where the Mediterranean is most itself, and the host the most hospitable.' Rather like a visit to the dentist, the empty guest-book in front of one. He is a strange little man, childish, charming, full of vitality and enthusiasm; attractively vain, warm and hospitable. He took me all around the house, as thoroughly as if I were a prospective buyer. He planned and built it himself:

---

[1] According to Greek legend, Baucis and Philemon were an old couple who lived in poverty in a small cottage in Phrygia. One day Zeus and Hermes, who were travelling in disguise, came to the cottage and were received with such hospitality that Zeus changed the old couple's cottage into a temple. Here they lived together happily into extreme old age. So that the one should not have the sorrow of mourning the other, Zeus granted them their request that they should die at the same time, turning them into trees outside the temple.

[2] Going northwards up the west coast, this bay is the next one along from Anargyrios Bay.

[3] Botasis's ancestor had been a hero in the Greek war of independence. He and his villa would provide the inspiration for Maurice Conchis and Bourani in JF's novel *The Magus*.

[4] See note 1 on page 185.

not a beautiful house, but pleasant, with many round arches, and the most wonderful situation in the world, poised as it is on a bluff between two beautiful coves, with the pines plunging into the sea below, the whole Parnon range opposite and the sunny wooded hills of Spetsai behind.[1] One could not dream of a more perfect site – a sublime blend of wood, sea, sun, wind and mountain. Not a romantic, but a classical perfection.

We stood up on the roof terrace. Far away below a girl sang in a lonely valley, her voice wild, untrammelled, singing some Turkish song which drifted up to us in snatches, without reality. Then we saw a little boy running up a path to the house. 'A telegram,' Botasis said. As unexpected as Hermes. We went down a zig-zag road to his little private cove. He wore mountaineering boots, a sun-cap and huge dark glasses, talked incessantly about himself and Spetsai. We passed a tree. 'I never let anyone cut that tree except myself.' It grew right in the middle of the road, blocking the way. He talked about Anargyros: 'A very unhappy man, family trouble – that's why he left all his money to good works.' He showed me where he had grafted a pistachio on to a carob. He walked up the hill without pausing, panting terribly. It must be a great strain for a man of his age. He attacked the school, the headmaster, the Committee. Decidedly I liked him.

He walked halfway home with me, up two or three miles of his road, the apple of his eye. He kept on talking about it, the difficulties, the dynamite, stories from the years of its making: very good road, leading nowhere. We passed colonies of sprouting asphodel, green crowds of little men. The sunset and Parnon stood beautifully blue and clear-cut against a pale green sky, with the full moon sailing out of the east and the pine-woods. The inland stretch of the road was done by an Anatolian workman of his – several hundred yards of humbly engineered track running through the pines in the most solitary area of this island. He died, the workman, 'such a good workman', of famine during the Occupation. 'Poor fellow, his last words were, "Now my road will never be finished."' I told Botasis he ought to put up a stone to his memory.

I said goodbye at the end of his road and set off down the long winding Anargyrios road to the sea. A boy on a donkey, its bells rattling, cantered past. He sat with his knees drawn up high, leaning back, and the donkey's hooves drummed impressively on the beaten earth in the silent woods.

Back along the sea home. A wonderful moon, glittering paths of light, and brilliant enough to read by. Black pine-branches, shadows of cypress, and blisters on my feet.

---

[1] The Parnon range of mountains, in the south-east Peloponnesus, runs parallel to the coast of the Gulf of Argolis.

December

The Inquisition at Spetsai. Yesterday one of the waiters, a moronic-looking boy of eighteen or so, was caught stealing. He was put into prison by the police. He admitted stealing everything except some rain-coats. The police beat him up, but he refused to talk. He was then brought to the school, and interrogated there. He was starved, and beaten with sticks again. I came on him in the common-room. He was grovelling on a couch, crying, whining, red-faced. The dapper, hand-some, trim young police sergeant was standing over him holding a heavy rod. The boys could, and did, see what was going on through the door. That night they were full of rumours about what had been done to him. They said he had been pricked by needles, had been beaten and was being starved. Most of them seemed to think it was a joke. I got so angry that I had to go down to the Christys. A flash of lightning into the chaos of this benighted country.

I asked some of the masters about it today. They all agreed that he had been beaten up; and were all surprised when I criticized the police. He was a thief; the police were right to beat and torture him. This is Europe in 1952, after all the brutality of the War. Animals.

Roy Christy's novel. I don't go very much on his work. He has a flair for vivid landscape descriptions; but most of his books seem to be philo-sophical discussions; and the characters more viewpoints than anything else, mouthpieces, puppets. The atmosphere is so gloomy, and the psychology of the people so weird that the effect at times is almost comical. Very sincere. But he mixes up Catholicism, anti-anti-semitism, conscientious objection, theology, metaphysics and a dense, incompre-hensible theory of the Will (capital W) as history, or History in the Will. Very unpalatable.

Awkward to criticize it. I couldn't say I thought it was no good, that he ought to scrap it, and try again. He is such a down-to-earth, materi-alistic, jovial, careless, heavy-drinking hedonist in ordinary life that one can't help feeling the novel is phoney, purely contrived, and that he'd do much better to come down to earth, and be himself.

A new style in my poetry. Consciously Cavafy; unconsciously Robert Frost, some of Lawrence. The laconic, flat, colloquial style. It is a good medium to set off the gems. Another term passed here. I have been busy typing out *A Journey to Athens, 1952* to try on Roy Christy.[1] I am more certain of the idea, its weight and worth, than of anything else I have written.

---

[1] Written in the winter of 1952, *A Journey to Athens* was a fictionalized account of the journey JF had made down the Adriatic when he first arrived to teach at the school at the beginning of the year.

Though conscious still of the wrong, too self-conscious, too derivative style.

Otherwise keeping on an even keel; little involved in the school, enjoying the island though determined to leave it next year. I am drinking, smoking less, in a habit of mild abstinence. The Christys seem to me vaguely earthy, coarse, uncontrolled. Because they drink freely, smoke a lot, and fuss and trouble if they are deprived. He is a curious person, faintly obtuse and surprisingly perspicacious by turns; talented as an artist – a very small talent. And as a writer, very woolly and weird. No amount of good will can make him a genius that way. I do not like his free-and-easiness about borrowing things, his constant desire for 'booze' and 'cigarettes', his hearty short-lived enthusiasms for fishing, squash, tennis, films, everything.

I remember M and moments in Spain; but lie fixed in my one ambition.

Christmas Eve. The school is empty, haunted. My stomach is bad, the Christys have no money, the skies are grey, it rains. Nothing to be festive about. I went for a short walk into the hills; a grey, scudding, lowering evening sky. Everything damp, cold, lifeless. I came on a sheepfold with fifteen or twenty lambs, under the shelter of a large rock overhang. There was no shepherd. The lambs were snow-white, with precocious black faces. There was one almost wholly black. Down on the road below – it was the beginning of dusk – a woman and a man came by, riding donkeys. The woman had a green skirt and the white peasant scarf of happy occasions. The man was wearing an orange-red pullover under his coat, and I could hear him talking. He was talking loud, but there was also some acoustic trick which brought his voice close to me. It was a sudden touch of Nazareth, two peasants on donkeys, and myself on the lonely pine-covered hills above.

Christmas at Spetsai – not conspicuous by its festive spirit. That did not worry me much, but the Christys took it a little hard, as parties, food and drink play a not small part in their way of life. Roy must mention drink twenty times a day; a first-generation reaction, I suppose, to a teetotal past. We had Christmas dinner alone, in the school dining-room, a poor meal, with grey clouds and Roy outraged by Greek inhospitality – the boys were eating elsewhere, with the other masters.

A party in the evening at the Poseidonian;[1] the village notables at a Balzacian dance. It was more like France in the 1830s than one would have believed possible. Papas in suits and stiff collars, mamas fat and

---

[1] A hotel in Spetsai town.

forbidding, daughters demure and eyes cast down, a few gay cavaliers being monstrously immoral by dancing the tango. Everyone grouped round little tables, fourteen or fifteen at each table, very solemn, sipping the same glass of wine or liqueur all the evening. I thought it was quite amusing enough without joining in, but the Christys wanted to warm it up. Roy gets excited, extreme, very quickly. He danced a waltz alone with Elizabeth. Everyone watched them, in a complete silence. Elizabeth dances well, willowy, with faint Americanisms which I associated with WAAFs and WRNs. Roy rather stilted, comically, very bouncy and on tiptoe. There was a storm of applause when they finished, and it went to *their* heads and *my* distaste. I didn't like the exhibitionism. Roy kept on bouncing up, dancing. Elizabeth also was thirsty for what small lime-light the ovation offered. Roy went and asked the prettiest girl there to dance. A shocked silence while they tango'd round the floor, and some disapproving success. Elizabeth kept on asking me to dance. But I was determined not to; I hate that particular kind of trial. We became a little class-conscious; they, or she, thought I thought they were being flashy, vulgar, that Roy was drunk. I did, but I did not want to show it. Another party afterwards at Savanta's. More Greek music, Evangelakis miming and very exuberant, Roy the same, but drinking now, a model for young Silenus. Home later, singing by moonlight. I think they were a little shocked, disappointed in me. But on occasions like that, they are too boozy, too excited for me; drink for drink, I don't lose my head like Roy. He drinks more than me as a rule. He uses drink as a stimulant; if he comes to my room, and I have no drink, he seems lost, embarrassed.

Boxing Day was peerlessly blue, warm. I sat in my window all day, alone, stripped to the waist, and strumming my guitar. I enjoyed it much more than Christmas.

18 January 1953
I do not use this enough. I am slipping into oblivion here – full of projects never carried out. How much of creation is will to end. The will to begin; that is easy. But to carry on. I still have not agreed to compromise – and every project is so tested for height, stature, potential yield of significant glory, that the very time I take to survey them diminishes them, and makes them inadequate before I have seriously started the climb. Roy Christy apparently thought little of *A Journey to Athens*, but his likes and dislikes are so violent and personal that I am not worried by them. What worries me more is the style. Where is the style? It must begin to appear soon, or never. All the dross still, the inaccuracies, the inconsistencies, the imitations. Now, at the moment, it is the slick, modern, photographic, cinematic technique I hate. H. E. Bates, for instance; a wonderful craftsman, a realist with words, a literary

RA, and what do his impressions of life amount to? Nothing. Academy trash, beautifully done and totally without an inner spirit. Everywhere, everywhere now, that glossy magazine, polished, high-class reportage, stuffed with vivid phrases and wonderfully graphic adjectives. To hell with it.

Monique. Phoenix.

A heavy night with the Christys. A waste of time, I did not want to stay. With them one drinks, keeps sipping drinks. I wanted to be alone, using time. I hate the feeling that time is going, and I am not using it. A miserliness about time.

We had a ridiculous, heated argument about Nazi guilt. Roy arguing from some queer Catholic pacifist standpoint. He thinks the Nuremberg trials were wrong; violently wrong; that the Nazis should not have been punished; that the Allies were equally guilty when they raided the German cities. He seems to take no account of intentions, of the difference between the heat of battle and cold-blooded racial extermination.

I suggested that one might view the Nuremberg trials as the beginning of a new justice, and that a crime was a crime, for all there having been no law against it at the time of its perpetration. Because there was no law about gas-chambers, it does not mean that an Ohlendorf should be allowed to go free.[1] Roy argues in an abstract, Hyde Park meeting way.

Of course the Nazis are innocent insomuch as their aberrations were the result of economic and social conditions, past history. But then no animal is guilty in an absolute sense. Law and punishment are merely the temporary expedients of society; a kind of trellis for the tree to be trained against.

Well, shouted Roy, what about the charge that they were preparing for war? Of all the bloody hypocrisies. Look at the USA, us?

There's a difference between preparing for war, and preparing for war *and* declaring it. If America declares the next war, and loses it, then I should hope the world would try them as they tried the Nazis. You may make a law against murder, and then later, commit murder yourself, and be tried under your own law. That does not mean the law is wrong.

We shot off on another track, wildly. If he wasn't such an egocentric, I think he'd have started to think otherwise. But I got wild when he started talking about the mental conduct of the Allies towards the Nazi prisoners at Nuremberg.

---

[1] Otto Ohlendorf was the SS general in charge of Einsatzgruppe D, which murdered at least 90,000 people in Soviet Russia. A chief defendant at the Nuremberg trials, he was hanged in June 1951.

It was outrageous, said Roy. They were made to wear prison clothes. They were interrogated for hours without food. They were treated abominably.

I had had enough then, and started shouting myself about Belsen and the SS.

Then we got on to the Jews, the beginning and end of everything for Roy. The only homogeneous people, the core, the heart of the world, the only race with a mission, a sense of destiny, a 'historical sense', as Roy calls it. 'You're a Jew, John,' he said. 'You think like a Jew, and don't know it. You think you're French and ancient Greek, but you're a Jew.' We argued on and on, I not so much because I disagreed with him about the Jews, but because I was still feeling antagonistic. Of course, he takes an extreme view on the Jews, and on the future, which he won't admit exists; he lives in the present, being, never thinking of the future. Ideals are a chore, etc. The most naïf sort of illusion; the maddest of ideals, to deny all ideals. He got angry when I said that he was a hedonist, an existentialist – but in *la vie quotidienne* he really is. He drinks, thinks only of pleasures, convenience. He does literally concern himself with being, the here and the now. I called him a reactionary as well, a barbarian; and when I asked him why he wrote, he could not answer.

He has this strange erratic will. I know he imagines that he is strong-willed because he expresses himself violently, and follows his whims. He loves to shake you out of 'your lethargy'. But really that is an uncontrolled kind of will, therefore a weak one. His opinions, so extreme and untenable, are a symptom; and his automatic criticism of anything that transgresses his view of life.

25 January

A wet, grey January for Greece; but the sun at last. Today, a soft summer-ghost day. I walked in the hills, among the pines. No wind, no sound; when one sat still, there was nothing but the motionless trees in the slanting sunlight, a long-deserted temple. There was a sweet, honey, sap smell in the air. I found the first spider orchids. I sat on the wall of an old ruined cottage, felt the island charm, the heat, silence, the pines and the peace. There are moments when this place seems a wonderful remote paradise. On the way back the sea was shimmering lilac, pale blue, peacock blue, green amethyst. The islands to the east glowed blue and pink-purple against grey-black clouds behind them. And I met a party of three girls from the village, strolling arm in arm, and singing their hearts out, as they do in summer, in the heat of the night.

Archaic words – amid, amidst, should, dwell. I cannot think of them now. I am getting almost a complex about such words. Words I have been using for years suddenly seem to me tainted, treacherous, and I can't use them with pleasure or confidence any more. I must start writing them down, defining their infiltration. Clichés and anachronisms, a constant siege.

Spider orchids. I have two growing in a tin on my desk – fine, elegant little creatures, partly upstanding, the two flowers on each plant facing, Janus-like, two ways. Two broad green wings, two outflung arms, a green hood and a rich brown-velvet swollen lip, long and ursine.

I am also keeping a real spider – a lethargic blackish tarantula, a small one, in an empty cognac bottle. It has woven itself a poor kind of web, and eats a fair number of flies. It has massive bottle-green poison-fangs, and a certain morbid fascination for me. But I think the smell of cognac is affecting it. Today it ate nothing, and it is lying crouched, oblivious, unshakeable – on its way to nirvana, an eternity of fly-juice.

11 February
Apocryas.[1] The school dance. There was a very American young Greek there who came and sat at our table after dinner. He spoke, thought, danced, acted in so American a way that it was difficult to remember he was Greek. Dinner had been flat, the headmaster with us. There was plenty of wine. The Christys drank fast and fully, as usual, and the evening, for me, got progressively worse. First of all, there was the dancing. I cannot stand the publicity of dancing, the exhibition it invariably has to become here, when one is a foreigner in a crowd of natives. The others danced, I watched. Roy started to take on his quizzical, drug-eyed drunken look – a devil in him coming grinning and somnolent to the surface – and then the trouble began. There was still drink on the table when I suggested that we should go off to Savanta's, where another party was supposed to be taking place. 'I'm not going till all the booze is finished up.' That particular kind of alcoholism I can't stand. It is not dipsomania, but a worship of drink. It is the recurring subject in their conversation; what they would like to drink, how much they can drink, how much they would drink. Roy is always talking about the amount of drink he has had. If you do not drink as much as he does, there is a kind of implied contempt in his attitude which I find ridiculous and primitive. For him the prime social asset is a big drinking capacity. I drink about – in a usual drinking evening – three quarters of what he drinks. Then I am usually sober and he is quite drunk. I can see in his glazed eyes and faintly frenetic gestures that it is a drag for him. His voice gets loud, he sings at the top of his voice, and argues violently about nothing at all.

---

[1] See note 1 on page 173.

At last we started off down to Savanta's. The American put his arm
through Elizabeth's, and began to flirt with her. At Savanta's things were
flat. Evangelakis the guitarist was not there. Trouble blew up. Roy was
angry with Elizabeth for flirting. She was trying to be cool, dry and sophisticated, and not quite swimming the post. Evangelakis had been hired
to play somewhere, and I was right against going to get him, as Elizabeth
wanted. At last the nagging got so great that I took Roy out to find him.
We could hear him playing in a house in the hill quarter of the town.
The doors were locked. It was a private party. Roy still wanted to go in
and pull Evangelakis out. I told him he didn't know Greeks, had no idea
of manners. He lost his temper in his flap-armed way.

A complex situation at Savanta's: Roy angry with me, Elizabeth
taunting him. We shouted at each other, Elizabeth gesturing at me and
whispering about me to the American. 'Oh God, he's so . . .' Later on
we patched things up enough to decide to go and gatecrash the party.
Elizabeth took my arm outside, but I don't gell so easily.

We five of us, the Christys, the American and Papadakis[1] and I,
reached the house. Elizabeth started calling for Evangelakis. After a time
he came out of a side-door. We stood around him and after a while he
asked us in. It was a shop inside. The party had been in an adjoining
room, and we could see empty tables piled high with dirty plates. Five
people still sat there, tired and satiated, the way people do when all the
guests have left. Elizabeth got herself asked in, or walked in, and we
passed an uncomfortable half-hour. Elizabeth danced, mostly on her
own, her tall, well-dressed figure doing an improvised step, her arms
taut and her fingers snapping. It was not very brilliant. Roy's face was
aglow with pleasure, and the young American kept on saying,
'Wonderful! You're wonderful, Elizabeth!' I think she began to believe
it, but a wary, cynical smile on my face seemed to annoy her, as indeed
it was intended to. I could not understand how anyone could be so
insensitive to atmosphere. The four people whose party it had been had
ice in their eyes, and unconcealed hostility. Papadakis was there, and I
could talk to him in French, which was some consolation.

We got away in the end, and back to the Christys. The young American
and Elizabeth lagged behind most of the time, out of sight. Roy sang
in a loud, forced way, and Papadakis and I talked in French. At the
Christys, talk and more talk, and an uneasy balance between them and
myself.

They drive me into puritanism. I suppose it may be their working-
class complex which drives them into drink in society. They want to be
free, uninhibited. But to treat drink as the only road to gaiety, and to

---

[1] A new teacher at the school.

trample across other people's feelings in the desperate attempt to be gay; it is the modern egocentricity, the shallow, pale, Bohemianism of the emancipated working class. I shall put them into a book.

Part of the trouble here is undoubtedly Elizabeth. I made up my mind at the beginning to keep as distant from her as possible. One, the main reason, so as to keep the school and the island absolutely quiet. I would only have to be seen walking arm in arm with her for scandal to start making itself. Two, more important, I didn't, and don't want, to become in any way involved with her. The one place where an eternal triangle would be intolerable is on an island, however faintly the triangle might be traced. Here, the whole thing would be, as if on a stage, dramatically isolated. If I should develop too warm a friendship with her, I would have Roy against me. And I should be jealous of Roy. It is not a question of stark adultery, but only of those imperceptible day-to-day adumbrations of the concept of adultery. I am not aware of wanting to approach Elizabeth. But I was aware on Sunday that I was angry with the American for approaching her, which would seem to be jealousy.

It seems pompous, dry, naïf, foolish, to deny an affection for her, in that case. But I have searched everywhere in myself, consciously, and I still can't find it.

25 February

Another weary drinking-bout with the Christys. We had spent the day at Spetsopoula; a perfect blue-skied, blue sea'd brilliantly empty day. I took them up to the top of the island, which is one of the most beautiful viewpoints, sites, places, in the world. One of those places which seems to be the hub of a great wheel. Every region has its hub, but it is not always easy to find.

We had a a breezy trip back on a caique and when we got to town we went to Savanta's for a short *meze*. But it dragged on. Roy started to get drunk and excited. The Hippo joined us. We had ouzo, and then I sent out for some red wine. Roy and the Hippo started to sing. They must have sung – Roy without stop – for nearly four hours. We drank four or five bottles of red wine, myself most as I did not like the singing and thought that I might dull my awareness if I drank enough. All the songs; the Greek songs, opera, all the songs of the 1920s, dance songs. Roy sang them all at the top of his voice. He sings quite well, in tune, but there is something bright and hymnal which he introduces into all Greek songs, some timbre in his voice which turns the golden Mediterranean quality into gilt. He sang jazz and imitated Sinatra – very badly, embarrassingly inaccurate with his assumed American accent. Elizabeth sang best of all, in a soft, husky voice, the Hippo drumming away all the time.

Again I could feel a slight tension creeping in. I don't think I looked disapproving; but the very fact that I didn't sing and didn't much smile at some of Roy's impersonations seemed vaguely to annoy them. There was something defiant, jaunty about Roy. He was as good as saying, 'I'm having a good time, but I'm not tight, even though I look it.' There are two first stages of intoxication. One where one is drunk, and showing it, although one still knows one is drunk; and another where the drunkenness is known and concealed. Roy's knowledge that he is drunk is a kind of figleaf which he uses to cover his nakedness.

The other people in the restaurant looked disgusted, bored, hostile. Most of all old Lambrou, the owner, who had a frown like thunder all the evening.

The complete pointlessness of overdrinking. I was only aware of a growing disgust. I kept on drinking, outwardly indifferent. Roy has to drink, addicted as he is. He seems incapable of getting himself joyful, gay, without drink. When he drinks, he goes pagan, drugged animal, satyric. For him it is losing inhibitions; for me a nasty reversion to an irrational, crude, barbaric state. To me also it is a sign of a split personality. His psychology is not integrated with his artistic aims. He writes long, involved works full of strong-will philosophy and renunciation and misery and pessimism; and lives like a Rabelais. Or not like a Rabelais, because there is something fixed and neurotic about his drinking that is profoundly unhealthy.

Papadakis, oriental-looking, is always as polite, as diplomatic as a mandarin, as courteous as an abbé mandarin. He appears to have numerous influential connections, speaks continually of the reorganizing projects which he has in mind for the school. He is a person who seems undressed, incomplete, without a despatch case in his hand. In no time at all he has established an ascendancy over the other masters. He presents himself as an adjunct of the director, an outside adviser of the school. He is, in fact, much more cultured than the other so-called professors here. His French is fluent and his reading extensive. He knows Seferis well,[1] and Katsimbalis.[2] More interesting, he knew Cavafy in Alexandria and amused me a whole evening with his anecdotes of the life in the *cénacle* Cavafy, during his youth. Cavafy's rich, crowded salon, his quiet, slow speech, his tremendous erudition, and his 'poetic'

---

[1] Born in Smyrna, the poet George Seferis (1900–71) came with his family to live in Athens after the Greeks were driven out of Asia Minor. He worked in the Greek diplomatic corps and won the Nobel Prize for Literature in 1963 'for his eminent lyrical writing, inspired by a deep feeling for the Hellenic world of culture'.

[2] See note on page 180.

friends – wonderful *mezes*, a great man dressed in Egyptian clothes.[1] Papadakis once met a young Englishman there, who did not speak much. T. E. Lawrence. Papadakis is in many ways how I imagine Cavafy must have been.

Roy Christy describing Mediterranean culture and philosophy as a 'phoney, false hedonism'. His bias against classicism, Greece, France, is quite illogical, intuitional. He keeps on saying that one must live in the moment, not think of the future; and he lives more or less like that himself. But he will come out with wild statements about philosophy and art which make me wonder whether he is not joking. Like a blind D. H. Lawrence. He has a certain fire, a complexity, a quickness and violence which are not ordinary and which I envy him; but so much of him seems confused, lopsided, unempirical that the envy doesn't go far. Apocalyptics are a dime a dozen nowadays.

For me the classical side of the polarity which he is always talking about (Teutonic romanticism, Christianity, the North versus classicism – paganism – the South) is the only side a crusader, a progressive can adhere to. It is only a little clearing of light in a forest of darkness. But there is nothing to be gained by trying to reduce the light and impede the slow advance of reason.

He has shown me the rewritten first part of his novel. The style crude, violent, overemphatic, overviolent, with his *idées fixes* (Semitism, historical will and so on) dragged in in something of the naïve way a child will burst out with a secret it is intent to keep till later.

A thing that annoys me is the persistent, open way he talks of himself as a writer – my 'books', 'my agent', 'my work' – with all the confidence of a firmly established novelist. I never talk about my literary aims unless it is necessary for some reason – if somebody comes into my room and asks me what I am doing. It is not lack of confidence. I have plenty of ultimate confidence – too much perhaps – but I cannot tolerate that assumption of success which seems to me a kind of borrowing from next month's salary. Too much like talking oneself into an illusion. So I keep my ego quiet.

20 March

Another of my life-years nearly over. I still have that uncomfortable feeling that I should be breaking into a run, instead of plodding slowly

[1] The Greek poet Constantine Cavafy (1863–1933) was from Constantinople by descent, but was born in and spent most of his life in Alexandria, where he worked as a civil servant. His poems, which he privately printed himself, were circulated only among his friends during his lifetime, but he has since come to be regarded as one of the greatest Mediterranean poets of modern times.

on. I still disperse my effort among a multitude of projects. I still cannot bridge the vast distance that lies between the germ, the sudden rich expansion of an idea, and the flower, the slow execution and development of weeks and months. But I have not lost any confidence in myself. Each new defect I welcome. It is something to eliminate, another skin to peel off. I feel myself progressing inwards, constantly. And even if, from a literary point of view, my ultimate innermost self had no value, then I do not think I would regret the journey. At the moment, if I was to know now that all I might ever write must be completely valueless, or even almost valueless, I should feel bitterly disappointed. But I believe I could console myself. Nowadays I keep on catching myself being priggish. I can't detect any serious priggishness in my ordinary public conduct and conversation. But in writing, in my writing, there is so often so much serious self-analysis, young man's introspection, that the priggishness becomes really offensive. And I know it isn't enough that I know it and see it. I cannot help writing like that; it is a bad habit I have got into. And for the time being I cannot see how to write otherwise.

Journey to Crete, 1–14 April
Not a success, as holidays go. I spoilt it through charity. I left Spetsai a day later than the boys; a warm, blue day, dawn in Spetsai with the Christys. For weeks I have felt a kind of unconscious pressure on their part towards a loan. They had no money left for holidays. Every time I got a bit drunk with them, I kept on trickling my generosity under the table to keep it quiet. I safely got past countless dangerous moments, but at the end, the last moment, as they were sitting over coffee, I said to Roy, 'Would it help if I stake you your fares to Crete?' They didn't take long to decide. I don't know why I asked them. Their tastes are very different from mine. Now, afterwards, I regret it. They unsettled my holiday, and all I have gained is a little material about myself, and one or two moments of regret. I don't care very much about the money; I care a little more, but not much, about their lack of gratitude. I care more about another little incident. M[1] sent me a book for my birthday. Roy happened to pick it up a day or two before March 31st, and asked me if it was my birthday. Yes, I said, a Monday. But never a word from either of them on the Monday. Never a word about the sum of money I spent for them on tickets, either. Of course, they knew, and I knew, that Roy will never be able to pay it back. It's not much – £8 – nothing, and I would give it to them if asked. But I don't like their carelessness over money, their little egocentricity. They are good-timers, really, on

---

[1] i.e. JF's mother.

the grab, in an inoffensive way. Roy is physically a very sensitive person – rough cloth, strong sun, a minute's discomfort in a chair or a position, make him restless. He did not have that service toughening-up, khaki-serge, and heavy packs, and drill, and barrack-room life. In a group he always wants to lead the way – everybody to stop, to drink, to eat, to walk on, when he does. He is a latter-day D. H. Lawrence, but Lawrence without his charm, his knowledge of nature, of flowers, and birds, and earth. A tiny, blind, Lawrence-shadow.

I like Elizabeth better – laconic, with a style, unimpressed, untouched by anything except the present, and much more thoughtful and gracious than he is in the minute everyday affairs of life.

20 April
A school row. The English teachers were convened to a meeting with the headmaster and the deputy head, Anaspostopoules, and Papadakis. It seemed to be just a routine discussion, until A launched out on a criticism of English teaching, the low standards, the lack of interest, and the glorious *neiges d'antan*.[1] It took me rather by surprise, although I knew that he had been cultivating an animus against me for some time. But the astounding thing is that he does not know one word of English; yet he was quite definite that the standard of English had dropped. I have got to the stage now where I can hardly lose my temper at such a preposterous situation. His accusation was really based on the fact that I played tennis a lot last year, and I have played very little this. From that, he detects a lack of interest in the boys, thence in English. It is true that I have lost interest in the school, but I have been teaching English better than last year in all except one group, which is an irredeemable eighth-form squad of old sweats.

There was an exchange of tart comments, recriminations. No love lost between us. Roy got more angry than I did. I am now a soulless body within the school.

It is profoundly evil to be so dissociated from the organism in which one happens to be existing, both morally and emotionally. Even if I felt A's accusations to be correct, I could not feel any kind of guilt. The whole system of the school and the atmosphere it engenders oblige me to be irresponsible. I cannot in any case blinker myself, accept the rules of the game. A dangerous state. I intend to brass it, as soon as possible; not the inability to compromise, the cantankerous obstinate truthfulness, but the corrupt, complicated situations where such a quality is willy-nilly unnecessarily intensified.

---

[1] The phrase comes from a famous refrain in François Villon's 'Ballade des dames du temps jadis': *'Mais où sont les neiges d'antan?'* (Where are the snows of yesteryear?)

1 May

The Cs can sometimes exasperate me wildly with their egocentricity. It's all I can do to keep calm. And they drift carelessly on, thinking we make a good team, and never guessing the strain they put on my diplomacy and tolerance. With R it is money; he shows an excessive willingness to spend and to borrow. Often he says, 'Lend me a few thousand. I'll pay you back in a couple of days.' And then never does anything about it, so that I feel like a dun if I hint at repayment. He gives an impression that money is unimportant, to be spent, and his own attitude to it gay and Bohemian – but anyone as moneyless as he can act that part. He makes no attempt to save, to economize. They economize at home one day, and go into town the next to spend enough for three days. The question of the Cretan fares still rankles. It is more or less understood now that it was a gift on my part; but no thanks, no little gift, not even one of the many of his own paintings he has had framed. I am increasingly absorbed by the relationships that exist between small groups of people, increasingly sensitive to their *physical* egocentricity, their hedonism. Minute things like the way they always let me pay more than my fair share of the bill; the way I will order food, and they will take it when it comes, so that I have to wait for another portion (this has twice only happened, but it is symptomatic); their imperviousness to hints about small debts, inequalities in distribution. E has a petty little wilfulness about some things – I *must* have a cigarette, a coffee, a cake – which she exaggerates into a pose, a kind of feminine, childish cry for affection, building up a whim-myth about herself. R is the same. They clamour and squabble and whine about the slightest and most trivial wants, as if they are too Bohemian, too emancipated, 'too much themselves' to brook any restriction.

Tonight she started to read a paper I had just taken out of a packet from England, before I had seen it myself, and then borrowed it to read right through. On a desert island such trivial things assume magnitude. I have an almost pathological obsession about fair shares. How the Cs, always in front of me, grab every day a little more than their due. They are small people. They add a little colour, and a little danger, to society. They are people who are vehemently positive one day, and amiably or petulantly vague the next; they proceed by a series of unrelated enthusiasms. Nothing evil in them; only a vast thoughtlessness, a helpless irresponsibility. They would not jump headlong into hell, but slip down backwards, looking up to heaven. They are the corruption in society; people I must know, and surmount.

Maupassant. I am still reading him with undiminished pleasure. Why can you read de Maupassant longer than any other writer? First of all, the fertility and scope of his powers of fiction; then the absolute absence of comment; and then a quality difficult to describe – the power of

fluidly concentrating his colours, of extended thoroughness in the
painter, of one sequence and then the thinnest line of colour running
through to the next. A water-colour fluency of alternate elaborations
and barest suggestions. His peculiar genius (since all writing must skim
and elaborate) is that there is no change of rhythm, no switchback
feeling. Even in the shortest pieces, the blending and the tempo are
never strained, false.

3 May

Drinking all night with Cs; the fluctuation of the drachma means that
the salary here is doubled, so we celebrated. Elizabeth and I drank a
lot of ouzo in my room, and she was sick when Roy came to join us.
Then to George's, more ouzo, beer, a meeting with some Americans,
then whisky, R and E exuberant and exhibitionist (they treat new audiences like thirst-ravaged wanderers coming on a desert oasis), everybody
home to their house for coffee. A ruby dawn rose magnificently over
Hydra, Roy swam in the pink waves, and Anna was shown round.[1] As
we left, a boxer belonging to one of the Americans chased a white
chicken and left it for dead; its black jowl grotesquely smeared with
snowy feathers. It is the moment I remember best in a wasted night.

9 May

Another heavy night's drinking. Elizabeth and I had a rehearsal up in
the old amphitheatre, and came down in the right mood for a drink.
We drank a bottle of brandy between us, talked a lot in the darkness,
listened to the wireless. I can sense a growing tenderness between us.
I scrupulously avoid touching her, but our conversation is so open,
and other actions so unhidden, that lack of contact isn't a sufficient
check. R was angry when we got back to him, still sober – we both
have fine heads – but inclined to be amused by his anger. We went
off to town and he got drunk very fast on very little. Evangelakis was
on form, and there were a party of rich Greeks there. Roy began
'selling' himself in his special way, dominating things. I sat out at the
back, watching the expressions on people's faces. There was dancing,
Evangelakis singing, R singing. Finally we went home, about two. Roy
had got himself roaring drunk and was getting people to push him
around in a handcart. (The news was all round town the next day.)
We got him home, but then he wanted to go to bed, whereas we wanted
to stay up and sing. Which we did, till five in the morning, working

---

[1] This is the first mention in JF's diaries of Roy and Elizabeth's daughter, who
was then just two years old. Often she would be cared for by a local family called
Korkondilas, allowing Elizabeth and Roy to join JF in his exploration of the
island and further afield.

through a whole song-book and all the popular tunes we could remember. Roy slept, and we lay side by side on a bed in the living-room. Occasionally she would put her cool fingers on mine. But our eyes did not meet. We have got as near as one can to the danger-line; in the exciting area before. But I couldn't tolerate the faintest eternal triangle here.

17 May

The hot weather begins, and I can feel my resistance to her weakening. Even though I know it is only a result of the isolation, of the constant nearness, I can do nothing. Sometimes I see her watching me enigmatically, a little contemptuously, sometimes a little pityingly, as if the situation now amused her, then distressed her. We stayed drinking ouzo in my room till ten or so yesterday, and R was angry when we finally met him. He went off home to bed, and we went on to town, close, but a little embarrassed, and the evening went out to a cold finish. She asked me in for coffee, and I stayed with her till 2.30. But there was a restraint, a boredom in the air. All the time I know I want to explain the situation to her. It hangs over us, is implicit in her every gesture, is almost palpable at times. The very fact that I want to explain things to her – all the reasons why I (or we) cannot advance in affection – shows that I am looking for her sympathy, which is a thin disguise for love. Also I am in love – as I was with M[1] – with the whole procedure, the ritual of love, even though it is unhappy, and unsatisfiable. The inner mind enjoys the chance to desire and analyse the body.

21 May

A little rumour is going around that E and I are deceiving R. Inevitable on an island like this, sooner or later. I told E. She did not seem to worry much, and R laughed when we met to discuss things that night. I am seeing E too much alone, and for more reasons than gossip I should see her less. I find it increasingly difficult to cool down my pleasure at seeing her, to keep restrained when she is close, accidentally touching me.

I must get married next year, infallibly. I am determined to leave this island. There are a number of faint chances – a job in Peru, another at Winchester College, several in Greece. I want more and more – and more and more aware of mediocrity – to write. But I cannot settle down to work here, a strong daily routine of work, and I am beginning to wonder if I ever shall.

*

---

[1] i.e. Monique.

Absent-mindedness. The other night, in dinner, I reached out and picked
up a bottle of water and drank it down without thinking. It was only
when I put it down that I realized, by the boys' faces, what I had done.
Ypsilanti stared at my glass. I had an irresistible urge to laugh, and had
to rush out of the dining-room.

24 May
Evening out with E. We went to the cinema together – R tired, went
to bed early – drank ouzo at a taverna. But the situation is tense, subtle,
charged with electricity when we are alone – either that, or dull, silent,
hopeless. We went back a little tight, affectionate, but we walked apart,
shied at each small touch; yet did not want to go home. We went into
George's; down to the sea, sat on a rock, paddled our feet together
in the water, silent, touching. I could feel her perfectly ready to be
kissed, poised, ready to give. But the consequences were so evident
that I held against her. To kiss her here and there, in snatched
moments, and to live in a hell of jealousy. My abstention was purely
egocentric. I know how slippery that path is. We decided to go back
to school – it was 2 a.m. – and get cigarettes and sit somewhere. But
as we were slipping past their house, the light suddenly flashed on.
'That's torn it,' said E. We waited a while. The lights went out. 'I'll
have to go, John, he's waiting up for me.' We didn't look at each other.
My voice must have sounded bitter when I said, 'Goodnight.' I walked
home in a rage of disappointment. Ten minutes earlier or later, and
the light would have not been on. I was bitterly sorry that I hadn't
made a move earlier. The fever went off in the morning. I swam down
to their house, and felt a change in E. She was more reserved, indifferent. I imagined that R had had all the benefit of the titillating I
had done. Off and on all day, love-fever. I saw her alone again in the
evening. No mention of the evening before. If only one could explain
things. Today I felt a little contempt in her, as if I had missed my
chances. To hell with the flesh.

9 June
We – the three of us – spent the day on the other side of the island,
swimming and sunbathing. When we came back, Anna was ill, in a fever.
When we took her temperature, the thermometer showed 104°, and there
was something of a panic. The doctor sent for, a quarrel *va-et-vient*, advice,
searchings through books, unrest. Anna lay swaddled on a bed, still,
silent, mummified, only her blue eyes twitching about, fixing people in
a strange, other-worldly, hostile stare. I sat with her for a time, the first
time she has allowed me near her, stroking her hair, and Elizabeth
watching, in a small blue jacket and swimming-costume brassière, navy
blue jeans, lean, graceful, her face sun-browned, her headscarf red, a

little worried, motherly in her absent-minded way. She has a slow, drifting tempo in her life, dreamy, indifferent, having her own way by virtue of a sleepy, inarticulate refusal to be goaded. But she is not recalcitrant. She does, as a rule, exactly what you want, is never femininely – a trait in G[1] that I hate – capricious, pettily wilful. Her charm is in her individual matter-of-factness, her lack of passion, something not too stagnantly, sweetly comfortable, neutral in her. She would never make a great mistress, a historical lover; but an excellent partner for the day-to-day existence.

From a book on education by Papadakis: 'The next advance in humanity' – he means evolutionarily, what he calls a bio-psychic world society put in place of the present politico-economic structure – 'will be not more cynical, more sophisticated, intellectual, but simpler, more childlike, more sincere.'

What I continually feel nagging inside me. The need for a great clearing-away, a great simplification of the universe. More narrowly, in literature, a return to honest *naïveté*, to simple sincerity and simpler themes; a new classicism, a controlled simplification of the 1900–1950 complex labyrinth.

The sultry summer sun – the body-period – has set in. Days swimming, drinking, when this island enchants, haunts, entices one's soul and will and work away. One should get up and go.

Night fishing. How many nights ago I have already forgotten. A small boat, a lantern, silent water and the lit underwater world below. We have lately discovered a new taverna. Two whorish-looking daughters and a widowed mother own the place. We three, the two daughters and two fishermen, went out. A dull sport, as a sport. We sat and saw little. In the end lay, and dozed. I had E's hand on my arm; the stars above, the lap of the oars, the two girls crooning Greek songs softly . . .

And a strange dream about her. Erotic. But her weight on mine was real, as real as weight, and I thought, in the dream, Is this a dream, or has she slipped in here, come secretly to me? I have never had such a strange illusion before. My skin pressed down, giving before the ghostly body.

11 June
Sickness, sex is a sickness, a disease of the body. I am E-enchanted, so

---

[1] i.e. Ginette Marcailloux.

preoccupied by her that I find all daylight, all night-awake lives possessed by her. And all the time I know that it is not real love – not in the sense that I felt it for M – but a more physical lust, a loneliness that needs soothing. I spent all last night with her, sitting with her in their living-room – R had gone to bed – not touching, silent, awkward, but not unhappy. An empty, stale sort of evening. We were there till dawn, mostly leaning, shoulder to shoulder, out of the window over the sea.

R I can scarcely tolerate now. Clearly it must be jealousy, but also I find him such a tiring person to be with, so intensely egocentric. Every subject he treats as an aspect of his own personality. Always trying to impress, to win, gain, succeed, in even the most trivial points. A cockerel, always crowing out his virility. And so amoral about money and property that I now rate him in that respect as a child. E in comparison is cool, and sympathetic, silent. Sex apart, I find her an easier person to get on with.

I shall have to explain to her soon what the situation is. It will be interesting, as an experience, something to record.

Tonight they both came to drink. Drank, were a little affectionate together. I found some classical music on the radio. They were restless, and I contemptuous of them, who did not want to hear the music. So prickly a strain in the air, and their going, and the triangle distorted, myself left alone and feeling bitter. A situation which is bound to hurt sooner or later.

Weekend at Athens; and entry into a long-observed, long dreamed-of new world. This year has been a kind of slow moral crack-up; disgust with the school, spending too much money – God how money, even a little money, corrupts – falling for E. All that and the gathering heat, the summer solstice creeping up.

We went in to Piraeus at dawn, after sleeping on the sofas in the first-class lounge. E and I head to head on one of them, close. Dawn, pale blue and pink, amethyst and mauve, then greenish, yellowish, soft, very calm, with the shore lights gleaming like bright pearls against the black land.

Athens was hot, dusty; so many cheap things in the shops that we spent money madly, half the month's salary in two days. Roy completely abandoned, E the same, and I too weak and less obliged (being better off, though they need an adult to look after them economically) to resist them. It all ended up round about two o'clock on the second night with R not reeling, but very drunk in Zonar's.[1] Sympathy creeping up between E and me. We went home with R, put him into a hotel, and went out to have a coffee.

[1] A famous old café on Panepistimiou Street in central Athens. It closed in 2002.

I suggested a taxi to the Acropolis; a swift ride through empty
streets, so close, untouching. The Theseion[1] loomed for a second; we
climbed through the pine-woods, arrived at the foot of the steps to
the Propylaeon.[2] 'Let's walk back,' said E. I dismissed the taxi. We
walked hand in hand, pressing our arms together, up the steps. A
cigarette lighter glowed under a tree at the entrance, a night-
watchman. We had to turn back. A sea of lights stretching down to
Piraeus, stretching back north to Lycabettos.[3] Silence, the night,
spaces. The theatre of Herod Atticus,[4] a Colosseum bulk, loomed
blackly against the city. I suggested, not caring where we were as long
as it was solitary, the Areopagus.[5] There was a wire fence, trees, darkness under them, the rock-hewn steps that lead to the little bluff where
Saint Paul stood. And we stood, poised, between the first faint dawn
and the full moon. I suddenly felt angry with her, did not want to
touch her, to speak to her. And changed as swiftly when I touched
her hand to help her down the steps. We wandered down the side of
the Areopagus, and sat against a rock. She leant back against me, a
thin, grave body, silent, and I was silent. It was warm, 'pregnant with
silence' as she said afterwards, the light creeping greyly in against the
moonlight through the trees.

Then she whispered, 'Don't you think we should kiss or something?'
and I whispered something back. Her lips, warm, like velvet, and her
eyes, her rather cold grey-green eyes tender, misted, or my own emotion
misting, and everything, a thousand little incidents for months back,
suddenly falling into perspective, a hundred past miseries, hates, regrets,
illuminated, explained. She breathed, 'I've been wanting to do this for
so long.' And I said, 'So have I.' We moved to the other unfragmented
side of the rock and lay in the grass, kissing, caressing, whispering, drunk,
and astounded, exploring, discovering that we had both thought the
same, that the other was humouring, not really in love, with oneself.
Her face soft, transfigured, a new woman. We lay there till the first
sunlight came through the trees, and a white hen came and pecked

---

[1] Identified in the Middle Ages as the resting place of Theseus, the 'Theseion'
is now generally accepted to be the temple of Hephaestus, and as such more
usually known as the Hephaesteion.
[2] See note 2 on page 146.
[3] A high hill in north-east Athens.
[4] One of the last great public buildings to be built in Athens, the Odeion of
Herodes Atticus was a Roman theatre built in honour of Regilla, the wife of
Herodes, who died in AD 160. It sits at the south-west corner of the Acropolis.
[5] A rocky height to the west of the Acropolis, where meetings of the Council
took place in ancient Athens. St Paul gave his address to the Athenians here
(Acts xvii).

through the grass around us. She stood up and cried, 'because things are so sad', and I tried to comfort her. We had to leave. It was so light, and the place could be seen from the road. Hand in hand, arm against arm, down the road, in search of water to drink. We crossed a bridge to a restaurant, but all the waiters were asleep, on mattresses between the tables. So down again towards the town, passing the first people, strangely looked at, tall E with her mannequin figure and short hair, and I, rubbing arms, like adolescents. We went into a scrubby little taverna, sat at a blue table, and held hands, and then went back up the hill a little way and into the park around the theatre of Dionysius.[1] We found a shady, bushy corner up under the walls of the Acropolis, and kissed again, and again, and again. The way a dam breaks, a swift sweet catastrophe. In two hours we advanced so quickly, in touching our bodies, showing our minds. An old woman shuffled past and went into a shrine cut into the rock. Her thin, gentle body, her tiny breasts, her smooth, slim legs. In the end we had to go, in a taxi, our hands gripped tight, in silence until we were near the hotel and remembered R and the beginning of deception. We fixed a story, entered strangely into the morning foyer, pressed hands in the lift, knocked on the door, and he was in bed, and E went to sit by him and kiss him, while I peeped through the door at his upturned troubled face and lied.

We had to go off to the Committee, then. Afterwards, I was so tired I could hardly keep awake, and E not a great deal better. R was resentful, said we had got out of step. We arranged that E and I should go and sleep and meet R again at four. So at midday back to the hotel. We had adjacent rooms, and a connecting balcony. She lay on her back, in a blue, white and pink dress which she had loosened, her face flushed and staring. It was very hot, impossible to touch without sweating, and we lay clutched, fevered, fighting against sleep and lust and time. Undergoing a crisis of lust. I had to almost run out of the room, still burning with her. Then sleep.

We met Roy, and he had decided to go out to see some American friends. Once again the dice ran for us; E and I decided to go to a cinema, and arranged once more to meet R later. A hot cinema, hot hands, arms. A good film, but I could not take it in with her beside me. Intervals in a little alley outside, a kiss behind an opened door with someone playing a Mozart sonata in a room high above. Touches all the time, past things remembered, to explain to each other. I was so jubilant, so relieved that the tension had broken.

We spent the evening apart, with other people, brushed hands when we could. A kiss on the balcony with R in the room behind. In the

---

[1] Built by Lycurgus in 342–326 BC, this huge amphitheatre, with a seating capacity of 20,000, is situated on the south-eastern side of the Acropolis.

morning, when R went downstairs before me, another kiss, holding her in her blue nightgown for a hot moment.

We went to Spetsai at noon. We sat together, held hands, talked about each other, ourselves, dodging and trying not to dodge Roy. Both of us still hardly aware, hardly awake, in a dream. A meal in Spetsai, our feet touching under the table, our eyes meeting, conspiratorial. And a rushed first kiss on Spetsai, after a midnight swim, with her in her white costume, me in mine, in moonlight.

The next day she came to school with Anna, to swim; we sat on the beach, close, touching, forgetting Anna.

The days pass in a blur. Both Roy and I learnt when we got back from Athens that the school had fixed us.[1] It irked my pride to be kicked out of such a corrupt place, although dismissal is almost a certificate of moral integrity. I have no job, not much money in England.

But all that is irrelevant to the astounding natural warmth and harmony we have reached in three or four days. Today, kissing every moment when R was away, once only by a miracle avoiding being caught by him. He had gone into town (they are now living in the school, opposite my room) and E and I were kissing wildly only a moment before he appeared in the doorway. Kissing in the water, when R has his back turned. Kissing on the roof, when R is typing below. Kissing, touching, caressing. We both find so many corresponding qualities in each other, so much softness, harmony. She seems to me much younger, sweeter, almost a schoolgirl at moments, melting, abandoned.

The terrible part of the situation is R. We are all living on dynamite. He obviously realizes that he is estranged from E. But he does not seem to suspect us. And one day in the next three weeks I feel sure he will catch us kissing, and then God alone knows what will happen. Meanwhile, the danger adds spice to the love; adultery is a messy business. I feel no guilt about R. Love is a thing that has no moral laws. If he has lost E's love, and she has gained mine, the chemistry is done, and no amount of will, no amount of virtue, will undo it. But existence is doubly complicated – so difficult to work, so difficult to act before R, so difficult to hold back with E. At the moment, also, existence is wonderful.

A nightmare situation; E and I suddenly, violently, in love, and the three of us living in the school, almost in adjacent rooms. We spend all day

---

[1] They were dismissed. In a letter to JF, dated 24 June 1953, the President of the Committee wrote, 'the Headmaster of the School . . . proposes that you must not continue your teaching in our school for the next school year, as he judges you as unqualified in the fulfilment of your duties, not participating in the School life, as your contract clearly fixes'.

avoiding R, snatching kisses behind his back, touching feet beneath the table, exchanging swift looks, caught in all the corruption of adultery. We cannot escape the triangle. The strain on E is appalling. We both want to be lovers, get into bed, but that, here, would be complete madness. Love makes one so immoral, so anchorless, lost, bewildered. I cannot work, am profoundly disturbed by her presence or absence. I am still a little stunned by things, the swiftness, completeness, sweetness, bitterness. By all the strange, wayward charm of E, who gives and withdraws unpredictably, but never coquettishly.

The days are all the same; blue, hot, breeze at noon, sultry at night. We swim – E sylphlike in a white satin costume – we tan, we eat our meals together – at noon, in the building; at night, at George's bar or down in Spetsai. We are caught in the rigid society of three, inextricably entangled. I feel a monster to so blandly deceive R. He seems to trust me so absolutely. Both E and I are crossed with guilt. And at the moment, all but out of control. In one week we are already thinking in terms of sleeping together, divorce, on the problems of a major life change for both of us.

Coming in early one morning, with coffee, when I was still asleep. Fresh, smelling of soap water, like a girl of eighteen, in a pink-and-white striped summer dress. Lying beside me, and laughing; and a kiss, a long kiss, almost still in my sleep.

Wonderful days, gay, full of laughter, kisses, as if we were adolescents. And terrible days, guilt-ridden, neurotic, these, when the spark is imminent on the dynamite. Her sadness, tender eyes, tiredness. Her teasing, playfulness, smiles. Her hardness, indifference, callousness. She changes like the sea. R is more and more silent, bitter, estranged from us, and the bones of the situation more and more prominent. It is bound to burst out soon. Today was particularly terrible – R sending E into tears over some trivial matter when we were sitting in a café; E rushing away; R and I silent, and a terrible, strained day to follow. E and I had a talk when R was away. I felt her still in his power, since she pities him. If she left him, 'it would shatter his life'. I hinted at what could happen in England; but she did not bite, did not know. Life here, sun and sea and similar days, cannot look ahead. We live from hour to hour, from escape to escape, from pleasure to pleasure. A delightful, fatal onward glide. The plunge into reality will be appalling. If E wanted to, I think I would go through all the pain of a major break-up, divorce, finding a good job and all the rest of it. But I am not yet absolutely sure that I could have her completely. I want her body violently, her companionship profoundly, but I do not believe she has the stability and the respect (for me) that are necessary before one can make such a tremendous move. I feel she has an adolescent attraction for me, an Indian summer boy–girl pash, because I make her laugh, and tease her, and court her passionately. But not love. She keeps on saying, 'You're so nice', 'You're so sweet'. But love needs deeper qualities.

Love goes stale so fast. One ought to quit such affairs after the first week, without fail. Like a first cold plunge – sharp at first, but worth the shock for the following pleasure (of not growing stale). Love is corruption. I would not have believed myself (E says the same) so easily capable of deceiving Roy, so intensely, so frequently. Yesterday we were alone in the building, undressed, fell naked together on the bed, and only just avoided copulating. A sudden burst of lust that sears my conscience. And the child, running about, watching us. Sometimes I believe she knows.

The situation here becomes more theatrical every day. E and I can hardly conceal our desire to be alone. We spend our day dodging R, pretending to be concerned about him, and really treating him like a beggar. I never thought that love could turn one into such a rascal. Now he gives me an occasional haggard look full of suspicion. At first I felt a nasty flush of victory. To have taken E from him so easily and completely, to the point where she talks freely of him, tells me of things he has said about me. Now I feel only pity, distaste for my own role. But the growing liking, lust, sympathy, desire, affection that E and I feel between us are irresistible. We try and resist it, and always fail. R goes about alone, haunted, full of unspoken reproach. We sad and irrepressibly gay by turns. When the three of us are together, silences, banalities. E and I had a long talk today about England, what we should do there. Already we think in terms of a separation. Our love has come fast, intense, deep. A last feverish kiss at night at the foot of the stairs to the roof.

Love increasing every day; the situation has become extraordinary. E and I spend all our time together. We see Roy at mealtimes, then disappear. He is writing his book, seems not to notice the affaire going on under his nose. We kiss so often, and in such dangerous situations – when he leaves the room for a second, or in places where anyone might catch us – that sooner or later we are bound to be caught. I think R thinks that it is at the most a flirtation. He even gives me a kind of superior, jocular smile, as if to say, 'I know what's going on, my friend, with you and Elizabeth.' I don't know what would happen if he realized the full passion and tenderness we have awakened in each other, how profoundly he is deceived and betrayed. I realize now that he has never really understood Elizabeth, as he could never really, with his violently egocentric personality, understand anyone. He understands a certain Elizabeth, but not the Elizabeth the normal intelligent man would discover. I can feel in her a craving for normality, steadiness, the normal conversation of love. Also she has lost her own age, been dominated by his thirty-two. And I am, as she is, twenty-seven; and at times, a playful, youthful twenty-seven. R is so weird a personality, so bound up with philosophy and the Church, the problems of the flesh.[1] He married, the first time, a clever student, and lived a life of affaires, on both sides, modern and ambitious. That failed. The second marriage was a kind of mystical union; the amber light for marriages not consummated;[2] then, Elizabeth. A passionate affaire with a Finnish woman; but they never, apparently, touched with the body. Other affaires. To me, he is morally deranged, a violent, anti-social force with a talent for pastiche in art. A very petty image of D. H. Lawrence in some ways. I wonder – he isn't a fool, at any rate not insensitive – how much he really guesses about E and me. They live in a constant strain, unnaturally, in the sort of atmosphere-bubble that I would have to prick. I couldn't tolerate such a gap without trying to bridge it; but he lives with it.

E grows on me more every day; gay, mysterious, sad, frank, tender, sensitive, she is all one could want in a woman. Sometimes she is silent, inarticulate, unable to think or speak, and that is irksome to a quick-talking introvert like myself. But she has so many steady, earthy, common-sense qualities beneath the waywardness and the feminine will. She has the kind of looks that would keep for ever. Green eyes that can go cold and melt with softness, perfect shoulders, tiny breasts, and the slimmest of tall bodies. A gangling, elegant creature. There must be good blood in her somewhere.

The way a loved face changes; a new, inner face that appears when the eyes are close, and never, however great the love, when they are apart.

An afternoon lying together on the hill, under a pine-tree in sun-dappled shade; kissing, talking, over the blue sea, facing Argolis for hours.

She has asked me not to write about her in here. But I could not not write, loving her as I do. If it is a betrayal, then it is the modern variant of the eighteenth-century Rape of the Lock.[3] Sinning for love. And besides, what else I betrayed, I could not betray this diary.

---

[1] Shortly after meeting Elizabeth, Roy Christy, who had been brought up a Methodist, became a Catholic convert, having fallen under the influence of a Roman Catholic mystic and guru called Frederick Lohr.

[2] After he was divorced by his first wife, Marie, in 1948, Roy almost immediately got married again, as Denys Sharrocks recalled, to 'someone quite rich, possibly American, but she switched off on the very day of the honeymoon'.

[3] In Alexander Pope's mock-epic *The Rape of the Lock* (1714), an 'Adventurous Baron' enjoys a day out with a party of belles and beaux at Hampton Court Palace. When he cuts off a lock of hair from Belinda, one of the belles he is courting, she throws snuff in his face and attacks him with a hairpin.

Part Six

Return to England

28 July 1953
Back to England. Leigh, clouds, sick dreams. England in July a hell on earth.

The journey was terrible as well; from the moment we left Spetsai, there was no real freedom. During the day there was always Anna, during the night R to think of. The journey had no reality for me, nothing has any reality for me, except in connection with E. Everything revolves around her presence or absence and her mood. We kept on getting desperate, not out of temper with ourselves, but with the situation, the constant nervous strain.

The last days on Spetsai passed feverishly, in the brilliant heat, with E and I escaping away on our own for almost all of every day. How R, to the very end, seemed not to understand what was going on astounds me. We would mislead him, pass off absences of three or four hours as if they were nothing. He would wait for us, have meals without us, never see us except two or three times a day. And even when we were together, there was such a silent, tense atmosphere that he must have realized how desperately bored E and I were.

E and I spent all our time talking, talking about ourselves, our pasts, our lives. Making love, intimate, ignoring time. Ignoring time right until the very end, until the last hour, when it suddenly towered beside us, a shadow become giant.

We left Spetsai in a rush, leaving the packing until too late. The gardener, the photographer, anybody who came near us, like vultures, eager for all the remains from our packing feast. Bottles, old papers, clothes in rags, cardboard boxes, anything they took. A last meal at Savanta's, a few goodbyes. I felt indifferent, oblivious to all the usual parting sentiments. Love destroys landscapes; people are stronger than places. The long, last journey into Athens – E and I finding it impossible to be alone, impossible to be normal. Anna always around us, and R always watching us. Often, so often, I feel a bitchiness in her attitude to R and Anna. She gets petulant with them, snarls, sulks; no one could really be less a bitch than E. In any case, it makes me realize how terrible her position is for her to become like that.

She's loved a good deal, been loved; got into messes, had complicated affaires. R was a kind of frontier (into marriage, a brilliant man older and at first sight maturer than herself, someone on whom she could lean, find sanctuary, and forget the Bohemian past) she willingly crossed. She thought (she says) that she had finished with romance, sentiment about love. She was happy and unhappy with R. She soon found out that he was a lot less mature and easy to live with than she had at first imagined. They had quarrels and gay times; Anna, since Roy wanted a child. (Less through Catholicism, I should imagine, than a need to keep Elizabeth anchored.) Then we met; romance flooded in over the austerity of these years; all R's faults, his violent extremes of opinion, his drunkenness, his irresponsibility, avalanched down. I was tender, understanding, romantic with her, and it all came out, all the inside of her marriage. A terrible betrayal, between intelligent people; even if she was reconciled to R I should feel always that their marriage was false, hollow, a tree still standing, but once cut through . . .

She has been foul to Roy, I suppose, by any conventional standards. At the end, when we always sat together, always touching, never smiling except at each other, with R opposite or close, the situation was out of this century. I felt like an impudent young lover seducing the young wife before the old cuckold's very eyes. We had – all *three* of us – lost perspective: no doubt R still pretended to himself that our closeness was no more than a friendship; and we were so helplessly involved we could not stay apart.

Calais cold, a green, rough sea. E and I on deck together, in a corner, with spray flying past and the ship rolling. A stilted, bitter last moment of intimacy. I tried to say how much she meant to me, how much I wanted her. She was silent, inarticulate, unable to make any decision. Cried, and I could not comfort her, as R might come on us at any moment. The boat was full of English holiday-makers, rich and poor, *nouveaux riches* and blasé, Boy Scout and Chanel No. 5. But all the same, types, as easy to class as bits of mass-made machinery. We both felt a deep revulsion for everything English, all England. The greyness, drabness, raininess, uniformity of it all. Dover, a quick run through the Customs, R as gay as a lark. He loves England, and loved, plainly, the thought of our close separation.

E and I side by side again to London. R opposite, quizzical, throwing me minute triumphant glances (significantly, he made no suggestions about our meeting in the future); and a shrewd, very English, very cosmopolitan, very polite Englishman of middle age who sized up the situation at a glance. The dull greenness of everything, the cheap brick suburbs; London. Anna began to cry, and the journey ended in a terrible atmosphere of stress. She wouldn't stop crying, screamed every time her leg was touched; we had planned to have a last drink, but that was plainly impossible. We got a taxi to the nearest hospital, and there I last saw E, sitting in a bare waiting-room, clasping the sobbing Anna. She looked up at me, Elizabeth, her eyes infinitely sad and remote. I kissed her quickly and went. It was not a final parting. But it seemed then to constitute a frontier.

A cold, black journey to Leigh, and home. How I have slipped into the native in so short a time. It is as if I had never left. I say nothing about Greece, they tell me of all the minor things that have happened to a thousand people I have never heard of, and have no interest in.

I feel inhibited, hopeless, a boy again. No job, no money, no will. The weather cold, grey, raining. The same prison in the same prison-town. I suffocate, think of running away with E, spending all I have on one fine holiday. I must, first, get my two books to the agent;[1] then, live in London; there, handle the E affair. That is, find a job, find money, and take her.

Life here is fatal; I have described it a thousand times before, in the same words. My home is my hell.

Love, a wonderful aid to self-analysis; it makes one think. And love is the undressing of the soul. One has to explain oneself and explain the loved one. An intimate sincerity. E has a slowness, yet an intuition, which make her fascinating to know. Because she understands, and she chooses, the truth in what is said. She is weak, capricious, liable to fall, but only occasionally. She is the most balanced feminine woman I have met. Cool, elegant, collected in public; warm, passionate, playful in private. Sensitive, classless. I still cannot believe that she has fallen in love with me.

I told her one day that I thought she had a weakness. She had a great well of affection in her, which overflowed at intervals. She would always find new objects to love, and each would be better, more worthy of love, than the last. She was climbing the rungs of a ladder. I said I thought I might be able to make myself the last rung; at any rate, I should like to try to do that. I wonder if, after three years, she might not move on from me. Her moods change so; once she slips, she has no purchase. I should be eternally jealous of her absences, and distraught if she left me. But that could not stand in the way of the present intense love I feel. She has no faults, and I no qualms.

31 July

A day in London. Unending rain, and E. We met at the zoo, in the lion-house, spent all the day together. We got wet in the zoo, drank a lot in the evening, were deeply penetrated by one another. R knows the situ-

---

[1] *A Journey to Athens* (see note on page 260) and a second volume, called *An Island and Greece*, which was a fictionalized account of JF's first year teaching on Spetsai and travelling around Greece. A third volume, written in the winter of 1953, was devoted to the love-affair that ensued after the arrival on the island of Roy and Elizabeth Christy. *An Island and Greece* was then adopted as the title for all three volumes.

ation. Anna is ill in hospital, and he rang up E when she was visiting her. I was waiting outside. He demanded to see us. E stalled, and we spent an evening under the shadow of her home-going. I was afraid he might get violent.

I still haven't quite realized the mess we have got into. It has blown up so quickly, out of a clear sky, that I haven't properly taken stock.

E and R are completely estranged, no more want to live together. I and E are so swept away by romantic love that I mistrust what my heart says – that she is as near the ideal woman as I shall find. One month is not enough to recover from the initial glamour; we are both still spell-bound. True, from the beginning, I found her socially, as somebody else's wife, an ideal partner. Now, I hesitate, though less than with any other woman I have known. She hasn't the breeding, the culture, the articulateness I thought I must have. To compensate for that she has intuition, sincerity, looks and grace. I fear her weak will, or rather spas-modic will – the lack of endurance.

And none of us has any money; I have the most. R must resent that violently; almost as much as he resents the fact that it is me, of all people, his diametric temperamental and psychological opposite, who has taken E. There is Anna. Both E (who admits it) and R are totally unsuited to be parents. They are largely children themselves, morally. Adult in every-thing except that most important respect. And I am exactly opposite, morally adult and socially childish. If they separate, neither of them will want Anna. I would not take E with Anna. I don't like, don't want children of my own, let alone anybody else's. Children, they say, anchor a marriage. If a marriage needs an anchor, it is an imperfect one.

There's the whole paraphernalia of divorce, the whole battle I shall have to fight with convention. My parents will be shocked.

I have no job; no prospect of anything sound.

A situation to pass through; as always, or still, difficulties like these faintly exhilarate me. And the experiment of life with E is one I would not willingly forego.

The problem of marriage for the intelligently, darkly difficult; sensi-tive, quick, temperamental, they won't shut their eyes, sit still. They have to shift, change constantly, examine, question their relationships. The higher the intelligence and sensitivity, the deeper love, and the more perfect the mating must be.

7 August

More complications, more disintegration. Things are beginning to fall in on top of me. R has ordered E out. She cannot talk with him, cannot see Anna, cannot use the flat. She has gone to a friend, the friend whose husband she had an affaire with before she met R. This friend, who tolerated this affaire between her best friend and her husband (and before that E was her brother's mistress), is now at a crisis in her marriage, as her husband and she have decided to separate.[1] E and she are in the same state of disintegration. E now has no money, is dependent on me. She came down here – a terrible mistake on my part – alone, and now my parents have become embroiled in the whole thing. That is, I have admitted the separation, but not my own love involvement. I have made out that I am the friend go-between. My mother normally conventional but, extraordinarily, understanding, and my father, for all his reading, violent and conventional.

E came down strictly only for the day, but we deliberately missed the last train, came back home, and spent all the next day, the bank holiday, down in Old Leigh and on the marshes, talking, making love, rather enjoying ourselves among the masses. We went down to Benfleet, had a split and reconciliation in the heart of a thicket on the hill above Benfleet. 'You're so scared,' she said, 'so bound up in your parents.' She was right. This is a climax. I must break away from the parent complex, and subconsciously that is probably why I brought her down here, to precipitate a crisis. My parents treated her as a gold-digger: 'no stability', 'out for what she can get'.

But this conception of love and life are so inadequate for highly self-conscious, complex beings like R and E and myself. It is like fuelling resentment for recruits who cannot drill like old soldiers.

27 September

Oxford. Six strange weeks with E, how does one synthesize six weeks? It can't be done. We must have spent well over half of it in bed. Never up before midday; never anything but out of time.

I must try and remember from the beginning. The beginning was one evening at Fenchurch Street Station. She was late, distraught, and we went into a pub outside. She cried. R had gone round to her friend's flat, where she was staying, and created a scene. It was the baby, Anna, that was the trouble. Where was she to go when she came out of hospital? R, at first telling E to get out, had changed his mind. Now he wanted a compromise. E to take Anna, and to live on her own, away from him, and away from me. I could only try and clarify the situation a little. E was torn, but determined that she must look after Anna, if nothing else could be found. To make things worse, R had telephoned her parents and told them everything. The only possibility seemed to be that she should go home with Anna for a fortnight, leaving R time to make other arrangements. I was against this; not so much because of a fortnight without her, but because I knew that

---

[1] The 'friend' was Betty Pace, Elizabeth's best friend when she was growing up in Birmingham.

R would make no attempt to free her. The impasse would be prolonged indefinitely.

We eventually went off in a taxi to Paddington. And driving through a nearby street, we saw an illuminated sign: 'Acropolis Hotel'. It seemed too good to be true. We stopped the taxi, and I heard the sound of Greek music. We went in and got a room, spoke Greek to the proprietors. We felt as happy as two foreigners finding their fellow-countrymen. It was a sordid little back room looking down the rears of a dozen bleak tenements. We didn't mind, of course. We were too preoccupied – eager and afraid – with sleeping together. A telephone call to Roy reduced E to tears; then we went back to bed, and managed to find some sanctuary.

The next day I saw Roy, at his request; he was controlled, quiet, familiar, less reserved than I, though I felt no guilt – at any rate, no more guilty than him. We met outside Kensington High Street tube station and walked down to Edwardes Square, to a pub with tables outside, the Scarsdale Arms. I remember that we even talked about the architecture, with unnatural naturalness. R seemed able to forget that I had, only the night before, possessed his wife. I could not; and I despised him for being able to do it.

He did most of the talking – about himself, his guilt, his nature; how he had gone through life hectoring people, indulging his own ego, wrecking every happy situation he had found himself in. In spite of the fact that he talked mainly in Catholic terms, I was reminded of a Communist self-criticism. The criticisms were severe, but there was an unbearable complacency about them. Both Communists and Catholics are the same – they think that confession absolves them of all their sins. R wallowed – it is the *mot juste* – in self-examination. He talked a lot about E, too. Of her will, of their psychical antipathy; but would go back to the Catholic conception of a marriage in eternity. We drank beer; Roy pints to my half-pints. I offered him some food, but he said he couldn't eat; implied, somehow, that I was of coarse metal in being able to do so. He told me all about his nausea, his sleeplessness, a naïf request for sympathy that I found both odious and pathetic. I suppose my contempt for him, which grew, was irrational and unjustified; he was really being very civilized and decent. But I should have liked a little more primitive pride. He said that he was going to reform, would never drink heavily again. This was at his third pint; he was quite sober, of course, but talking more and more. Even began to praise me rather mildly; said that after John Liddell,[1] I was his best friend; how much, under other circumstances, he could have liked me. I suggested that he put Anna into a convent, and he agreed that it would be the best idea. He would go that

---

[1] John Liddell was an aspiring writer who, like Roy, had fallen under the influence of Frederick Lohr.

same afternoon. We parted in the tenderest of atmospheres. I was glad
to get back to E and to be able to blow my top a little. And glad, I
suppose, to be able to run Roy down. R and I, as if the situation we are
in is not enough, are such fundamentally opposed characters that I should
feel eternally bound to fight against him and his influence, however we
might be placed. E is a kind of ordinary human, a figure in the street,
torn between the two of us, the light and the darkness, the black and
the white. She is that, I suppose, in the profoundest sense; R and I are
both, in widely differing ways – Catholic and Puritan – religious people.
I am morally religious; he is metaphysically so. We are both priests struggling for her soul – or really, in the end, for our own.

We met John Liddell, E and I, later that day. Curiosity on both our
parts, I think. He appeared neat, a small head and shrewd eyes, reserved.
We only talked banalities. I had a feeling that he was rather like me in
some ways; wondered if he found R scientifically fascinating as I do, and
whether R realized that even here, with his best friend, he might be
half a guinea-pig.

I rang up R late that night; he was almost hysterical because the
Catholics he had seen had not been able to help him. Or rather they
had asked him what seemed to me normal enough questions, but he
found that any questions were out of place; charity should be quite
blind. He raved on about the Catholic Church – the Mother Superior
had referred to Anna as 'the little one' and this for some reason had
infuriated him. 'The little one,' he kept on spitting out, 'the little one'
– and seemed to forget everything else. As if I was some friend he could
pour all his woes out to.

The next day, I rang him up again, and he had completely changed.
He was very calm, practical, though still overdramatizing himself,
describing his sleeplessness, lack of appetite, incompetence over Anna's
clothes.

'Do you know what happened this morning?' he said. 'I washed her
little trousers and socks and put the socks on top of the trousers and
all the dye came out. Oh, you've no idea, John, how difficult it all is.
There's no way of drying anything.'

'Isn't there an electric fire?' I asked.

'Oh, I suppose so,' he said rather petulantly.

He had arranged for Anna to go into an Anglican home. He wanted
E to buy some clothes for Anna. We were free to leave London. We went
round to see E's friend Betty, I out of curiosity again, wanting to know
all the protagonists. A quiet, shy little woman whom I felt faintly hostile
to me. We bought the clothes, I took them round and left them for Roy.

It was good to get away to Oxford; a little strange to be free, absolutely
on our own. We had tea in the restaurant car, opposite a general in mufti
and an upper-class tart. The one stiff, the other grotesquely affected.

Oxford again. I saw it with affection; a place I know, a place I could live in. We stayed a night at the King's Arms, then moved out to a room in a suburban house up the Banbury Road. Thence, a week later, to a flat in Warnborough Road.

I went at once to see the Porters, and found them changed. I suppose I had rather deified them abroad, forgotten their faults. They were very kind in the way of hospitality, and so on. But I could not for a time climb (or fall) back into their North Oxford world. It rather shocked Elizabeth, silenced her; offended me. Eileen seemed to have lost her naturalness, to have become malicious, coldly intellectual, a cat. Podge something of a clever bore, with his ridiculous views on certain things – Americans, for instance – and his party attitudes. We met a young composer, John Veale;[1] an amusing, iconoclastic, anecdotal conversationalist, dominating the talk, and, finally, boring. A vital, very intelligent person, for all that. A bright, calm, metallic wife who reminded me of a wooden ship's figurehead. They both swore, talked a little more obscenely and frankly than was necessary to show that they were fully emancipated from the conventions. We had a punting-party with them, and other meetings, met a don at Jesus, Jewish, plump and faintly Johnsonian, fond of pronouncements, and his mistress, a shallow, pretty creature indistinguishable from the type North Oxford had made her.

A rather unpleasant world when one plunges into it; cold, and only exhilarating when it is left. Only good by contrast; not good intrinsically. The first impression is of shallowness, glitter, an eighteenth-century love of amusement as an end in itself. Very quick-thinking conversation, full of subtleties, implications. Upmanship all the time; everybody thinks of himself, thinks how to denigrate the good things that other people say. One never bluntly disagrees in North Oxford; one is catty. Everybody is catty, prepared to sacrifice a good deal for a witty remark or an outrageous maliciousness. Conversation here takes the place of bridge elsewhere; it has become as much a game as cards, and people tot up their conversational scores at the end of each evening.

Both E and I were a bit lost in this world. I felt myself both below and above it, both provincial and celestial. E was very silent, reserved. I admired her silence. So many women would have tried to join in on their level, to ape them. I watched anxiously to see if she would resist the temptation, and when she once or twice hesitated, spoke, tried to be clever, I was afraid, partly because I knew the others would sneer, and partly because nothing destroys love – as I found with G^2 – so quickly as embarrassment. Although none of these people were snobs, I could

---

[1] John Veale (1922–) wrote scores for British feature films during the 1950s and 1960s and also composed a dozen or so concert works.
[2] Ginette Marcailloux.

also sense that E knew herself not of their class. She hadn't quite the right accent or quite the slickness – and nowhere near the quickness – of expression. And it seemed to anger her when I sometimes did reply in their key and style.

But other people did not impinge much on our isolation. We were together always, all the time, had frequent, and for me, insanely ridiculous quarrels which we resolved immediately in delightful hours of remorseful self-analysis. Our life was Bohemian in the extreme; we had no clock, lived by desires; slept, ate, made love when we wanted. Took no exercise, went to parks, cinemas, read papers, argued, kissed, wrote letters. I applied for various jobs, without any interest in getting them, since I had enough money to last another month or two without working. I am quite feckless about the future; so certain that I shall never want to do anything but write, that whatever work I take up other than that will be purgatory. Neither E nor I have any time-sense, any morality about routines and conventions. On the whole, for me, a very happy time; a complex happiness; sex, of course; she never tires me that way, never ceases, by simply being present, to seduce me; companionship, being totally absorbed and absorbing somebody else; intention, being two against the world; domesticity – there was little of that, but I would never like much of it – having meals, washing up, seeing her clean things – not often, she's no housewife; an eventual fault, probably; and feeling that I was re-educating her, gradually pulling her out of the quagmire of religiose immorality and metaphysical nonsense R had dragged her into. Trying to make her control herself, control her moods, her black angers, her sulkiness, a little; very exciting, seeing her rebel against new views of things, yet feeling the seed settle in her. A slow, cautious, mental digestion; the only peasant thing about her. Most rare virtue in her case; she would be intolerable if she was quick-witted.

We were both weary of conversation about the future; she not being able to decide about R and Anna, treasuring a little, I thought, her dilemma, pleased to have something I could not touch. I did no writing, and that upset me. She was restless on her own, distracted me too much. And we had quarrels. Never about our real selves, or our predicament, or our past actions with regard to one another; always about literary, artistic things. She would get so bitter and involved that I was at first amused and later, usually, as irritated as she was. There was a violent argument on Australia – whether it would ever produce a significant corpus of art or realism in the theatre. Then, when I asked her a sarcastic question ('Have you ever heard of Strindberg?'), she lost her temper and hit me hard across the ear, a quite extraordinary thing. Once involved in a literary argument, she loses all sense of proportion. At times she seemed to hate me so violently that I felt as if she didn't live in my world at all. The difficulty is that she is so inarticulate, and really, for all her intuition and innate taste, and all her belated attempts to educate herself, ignorant. She would get furious with me when I started to give names and talk -isms; but the fury was really with herself and her lack of articulation. Very often what she was saying was right – at any rate, a perfectly legitimate point of view. But she would hold it so exclusively against me, so vehemently, that I would deliberately mis-understand (than which nothing was more liable to make things worse) and mislead her. I must seem to her no more than a dry prig at such times. But I suppose only a literature graduate would maintain that his views on literature should carry more weight than a mere layman's – or lay woman's.

So it was that, partly; her resistance to that gap in learning between us, that educational abyss which irks her. And when she argued, like a woman, she would always become personal. And she had a whole host of adjectives – 'ridiculous', 'stupid', 'suburban', 'middle-class', 'public-school', 'slick' – which were all 'I hate you' expressions, aimed to hurt, especially the latter four. She talked of being classless, and annoyed me by her presumption; I had not the heart – or the courage – to tell her that at times she did seem to me still classed, inasmuch as she was inhib-ited by her working-class origins with the 'classless' middle class like the Veales and the Porters. How I tried to explain to her another time that in being so violently 'classless', she was still, in fact, influenced by the working class, since hate is a connection as much as love. It irritates her that I still adhere to certain things in the middle class, certain con-ventions. But I could not persuade her that that is a stage only reached after the complete 'classless' revolt.

Our quarrels, too, came partly from our love of quarrel. Do moderns have to quarrel, struggle, to be happy? Is the battle of the sexes the spice of original life? Certainly, I could predict our quarrels. Several days of happiness, and then we would clash, fiercely, over some absurd artistic point. There would be words, hurt silences, reconciliations always initi-ated by me (since I was never really involved in the things we were arguing about, and regarded the whole business as a psychological sick-ness which had to be cured as quickly as possible), the tears, tender embracings, which I am sure we both loved. E had her catharsis, I had my superiority complex.

We were so much in love, so much of the time, that these quarrels seemed quite normal to me. At other times I got angry with her for being indecisive about the future – what she would do in it; her feel-ings about R and Anna. And there were other strains; mere physical things, changes of mood, irritations. But love was dominant, and when we were gay and happy, we were often enough perfectly so.

*

F arguing, hectoring, talking above everyone else. Strange views, Victorian views, Huxleyan, a kind of out-dated Protestant free-thinker.[1] Reform the creed, modernize the Church, and so on. Talkers should beware; they never hear other people's views, give themselves no chance to develop, alienate everybody around them. The art of talking well is listening well. My father says things like 'now we're descending to personalities' – as if any argument between people was not a question of personalities. Increasingly I find quarrels difficult to accept at face value. With F I see an inferiority complex having its say. I see a different truth from the one under discussion, the argument in perspective.

What a distance separates me from 1946. I found an old diary today. The entries are so naïf and puerile that they frighten me. For instance: 'Dec 27th – Go to Uncle S[2] at Rochford all day. Pretty shambolic. Dec 28th – Go shooting – no luck. Dec 29th – Travel to Pompey for demob. Dec 30th – Meet Dobby. Get demobbed. Rotten journey back.' As inarticulate as a dummy.

The glorious life. 'Jan 9. March across Dartmoor – bloody awful wind and rain. Wet up to waist. Get in and try and light fires in rain. Jan 10. Chokka. Compass march at night – come back to Thurlestone at 3. Get torn off a strip in inspection – extra parade.' My insufficiency as an officer cadet was my only redeeming feature.[3]

'Jan 15. Milling at night.[4] I get a bit knocked about.' Diabolic practice. 'Jan 16. Officers' piss-up at Grizzle Club. I keep sober, but most others tight.'

Art. 'Jan 21. *Keys of the Kingdom* – good flick.'

'May 25th. Go to Abbotsbury with Bob P (Paine) – get a chewing-off from a swanherd.'

Shall I ever overcome my past? That, and at twenty.

---

[1] JF is thinking of Thomas Henry Huxley here (1825–95), grandfather of Aldous and Julian. Professor of natural history at the Royal School of Mines, he was a supporter of Darwin's theories and wrote several influential books on evolution, religion and philosophy.

[2] i.e. Uncle Stanley. See introduction, page x.

[3] JF joined the Royal Marines in late 1944 and, after six weeks' basic training, at Deal, completed his officer training at Thurlestone in Devon. He recalled displaying an inability to 'think on your feet' during an exercise and the officer in charge expressing the opinion that he would make a very bad marine officer. However, he passed out successfully into the regular Marines in July 1945. See introduction, page xii.

[4] Milling involved boxing all out for three minutes.

27 October
We met again in London, at Paddington, and had a taut little reunion, full of the difficulties of getting to know someone all over again. Strange how one can think constantly of a person, yet find them changed in even a week. We went to a hotel in Bayswater, rediscovered the bodily past, the excitement of love. There was never a less boring woman physically; the change from ugly into beautiful is always done with a magical swiftness. A stroke of a hair-brush, a minute change in position, in dress. She has that constant concern about her own appearance which is foul in a plain woman and delicious in a beauty; an unending coquetry.

We had a terrible time in London; first of all, trying to find a flat. An endless search, agencies, shop-windows, telephone calls, tubes, snatched meals, tired evenings, a gathering hopelessness. London – always covered in mist, dirty, foul-aired, so gigantic and heartless – appalled me. The isolation of the individual in it terrifies me. We went to two agencies who gave us lists of flats in return for a deposit. But none of them suited us; E got worn out, neurotic, and quarrelled, rightly I see now, with my lack of discrimination. But in me, a countryman, an addict of light, of open space, London excites a claustrophobia, a sense of not being able to see, which made me prepared to accept any room as a sanctuary. Money also was running short. I had no job. And over us was hanging Roy. Roy, uneasy conscience dogging our footsteps, the accuser, Roy, somebody we might bump into in any street. We moved out to Belsize Park, hated that area, and Hampstead. In the end we moved back to Notting Hill Gate, to a little room we had looked at the first day, and then rejected. At least it was central, reasonably snug, and in London snugness is essential to keep out the grey, cold, milling exterior, and quiet. Nor was it suburban. Oh the horror of the London suburbs. I hate London; hate being poor in London. One can be poor in Paris, Edinburgh, other cities; but not in London.

We had happier moments, but not many. A Sunday afternoon on Hampstead Heath, grass and an impression of country, strolling bourgeois by the ponds, a copper and blue tinge in the distance. Some good films.

But all the time we felt that we were being dogged by fate. We could not settle down, regard anything as permanent. Lived rather desperately from day to day. Roy got on to us – ringing up a flat agency where we had left our address. Anna, it seemed, was very ill; she had become a baby again, receded psychologically back to the beginning. E must go back to look after her. Days of being torn. I saw R once; he didn't like it, was pugnacious, wilful, emanated – for me – evil. I argued with E. At times not certain whether it was not all a release for me; at any rate from the present unease and London, if not definitively from E. I made up my mind several times to go, yet quailed whenever the possibility neared reality. Argued, as I felt, violently against Roy and his dark,

Victorian way of life. E told me much of his view of her, what he willed her to be – matronly, a home-former, a mother. And he hated her lightness ('frivolity'), her youth. He is a thoroughly Victorian non-conformist character in many ways. Old-fashioned about sex and morals; yet as lax as an old rope about money and drink. A hatred of frivolity; yet a capacity for neurotic excitement. A dark, stern sense of duty; yet no personal responsibility. And an egocentric of staggering dimensions. E was wrong, perhaps, to leave her child at that point, when it was still in hospital. But it was Roy who forced her into the decision (that is, put his own problem before the child's – which he has done throughout), Roy who refused to compromise, refused to let her take Anna north. Roy who put Anna into a home, did not see her enough, and finally came back to E demanding that she should take Anna and accusing her of cruelty. Really what E did was to walk out on two sick children.

E saw Roy two or three times, hesitated. He issued an ultimatum – either she should take Anna, or he would get a divorce. He said at the same time that he wasn't using Anna as a lever. Yet he had kept her in the house for weeks just in order to be able to present E with her. Elizabeth was torn between the two extremes – all for me one time, all for Anna the next. We had a terrible few days. And then she seemed, a little despairingly under her air of gaiety, to have finally chosen me. R was going to take Anna north to his sister's the next day. Early the next morning the phone rang. Her friend Betty, full of Anna, how ill she was, how changed. 'It's like the child herself speaking,' said E. She rang up R, who was on the point of leaving for Euston Station. Went to see him, agreed to take Anna to her home that afternoon.

It all happened so swiftly, terribly, as if on a stage. If that phone call had not come – and I felt it was timed, a part of the plan. If Roy had not been so unscrupulous, so determined to get E back at any cost.

We met for a last lunch, had a fuss with the landlady. Drank two gins and walked out in the park, to the round pond. Fallen leaves, smouldering bonfires, winter coats, a pale sun. We were too grey and shocked to become emotional, had not had time to readjust ourselves. I suddenly realized that I did not want to part with her, that it would be a disaster. A taxi, tears – there had been tears for days, though – a last touch, and I got out at Baker Street, while she went on to Euston. A long, empty journey home to despair.

I had little time to wallow in it. The next morning I was off to Ashridge for an interview.[1] A post as tutor was vacant there. I was lucky in a way.

---

[1] The Ashridge College of Citizenship was situated in a large manor house near Berkhamstead, Hertfordshire. It had been founded by the Conservative Party as an adult training college in 1929. An associated girls' finishing school, the Ashridge House of Citizenship for Girls, was established in 1950.

At least it kept my mind off Elizabeth a little. A preliminary interview
with a business potentate in London. A tall, suave commanding tycoon
with a grey silk tie, a large cigar and a red carnation in his black coat.
He was bluff and awkward with me, I was independent back. As I didn't
care much about a post in a Tory institution, I said I was a socialist and
a non-Christian. He didn't seem to like me much; I disliked him also.

Down to Ashridge with another candidate. A mock Gothic monster
in a lovely park. The décor like something out of *Citizen Kane* – vast
baronial halls, Venetian ceilings, battlements. I hated it. But the gardens
and parks were superb, stirred all the countryman in me. The inter-
viewing was informal; a tall, clever, dumb, uncertain young man, Peter
Sutcliffe, who is going; an earnest, Scoutmastery Senior Tutor, John
Cross; an old, bluff economist with dark, judging eyes, L. H. Sutton.
And the Admiral, Sir Roger Boyd.[1] I liked him. A small, wiry, charming
but steely man. There were girls running about, from the finishing
school. Small flocks of industrialists. Everyone with labels in their lapels.
I didn't like that. But there were the grounds.

The Admiral offered me the job with a story about how the Chairman
of the Far East Committee in the House of Commons was also a director
of the most crooked trading firm in China.

I don't know what to do now. I must have a job and this, apart from
Ashridge being a remote island, and the whole situation (my being disas-
sociated from the organization I work in) similar to that at Spetsai, is
not badly paid and gives me free time. But it means that I cannot have
E any more.

I didn't want the job; probably that's why I got it, I looked sincere.
Marines, cricket (the Lady B is a Marine daughter, the Admiral a keen
cricketer), a Public Schoolboy, gentleman, and so on, all that helped
me.

In London again, I worked all the afternoon in the Nat. Hist. Museum,
lost myself there – and couldn't deny a glow of pleasure at the thought
of the job I'd landed. Any fish being a catch if one is starving.

2 November
A frenetic daily correspondance between E and me; longer letters, and
on a high sincere level for the most part. She is the woman who has an
inner bitch to contend with; she commits sacrifices as if they were crimes,
and indulges her desires in exactly the same way. Her guilty conscience
extends over a vast field; and she cannot plunge one way or the other
without some kind of agony. She is, in fact, someone who needs leading,

---

[1] His correct name was Admiral Sir Denis Boyd (1891–1965). He had been 5th
Sea Lord during the Second World War, retired from the Royal Navy in 1949,
and was principal of Ashridge College from 1950 to 1957.

forcing, as she half realizes herself, but subtly; Roy forced her and slowly she rose up against him. I could, no doubt, if I had any money to launch the project, carry her off. She is unhappy at Birmingham and R has done nothing to help; he sent her no money, and no advice, and arranged no alternative accommodation.

But money is the root of all evil; and all good. I have none left now. As it is, I shall go to Ashridge penniless. In other words, I must go to Ashridge. I was never so careless about a post. For me it is yet another step in the widening gap between what I want to do and what I have to do. A place to exist in, no more.

It is a single post; there would be no hope of E and I being together there; even if there was, she hasn't the sense of humour, the resilience, the ability to compromise, to be amused by the place and the institution. So, short of a *deus ex machina*, we are condemned. She by her guilt, I by my poverty; our love, if it survives, will have as much self-confidence as love should ever have. Or will it be exhausted by the battle?

Tomorrow I know the agony; we meet for a day at Birmingham.

5 November

Return from Birmingham. Another sad, anxious, desperate meeting. A dull, vast city, teeming with uniform bustle. I hated it. The ugliest of cities, and the people not one thing or the other; more northern than southern, but most of all a middle mediocrity, a Brummy limbo.

E looked old, hag-ridden, exhausted nervously. For the first time I fully realized what the home background was. Her father an irrational man of violent words and tempers; a drunkard; a man with a sense of failure; with some sparks of a better man extinguished in him (but not forgotten) by drudgery. Her mother a tired, will-less mouse of a woman, with no courage, no fibre, no backbone left in her. Both of them obsessed by the financial aspect – E being a burden on them. (R has been able to send her only £2.) Having to live, the parents, E, the sister, Anna in one single living-room. There was enormous difficulty for E in leaving Anna for the day to be with me; the child's grandmother said she didn't want to look after her, couldn't. E had to fight to get her to do it. She spent the night with me, sordidly, feverishly, in a hotel. Left early and came back at noon, to say that they had said nothing, had received her at breakfast in a terrible silence, and that she knew she would have to go through a terrible scene when she finally went back. The day was passed in the shadow of that; we went to the matinée at a theatre, saw a competent production of *Pygmalion*, then wandered hopelessly about the dark streets of central Birmingham for an hour, and drank a little until eight, when I caught a train to Oxford.

The situation has paralysed her; I try and force her to make a clean break with the past, but she is haunted by Anna, her duty. She hates

R increasingly, yet cannot send Anna back to him when she knows that
he will not look after her.

9 November

To Ashridge today. I feel exhilarated by the idea of it; not one tenth as
nervous as new jobs normally make me. Why? Processes of age. But I
feel much more assured now than I used to – dangerous, Ashridge may
teach me. Partly E – to have got her, such an affaire, inevitably flatters
the self-esteem in me. Pumps out the male. And to have all but finished
the Greek book, that also. And a new philosophy – existentialist – which
has been forming in me since I went to Greece – and which I can only
now begin to sense as clearly active in me. One carries concepts about
for years sometimes before they finally take effect – as friends may one
day fall in love. This formulation has been helped by a book –
Existentialism from Within, by E. L. Allen.[1] Lucid, though Christian viewpoint. Reading it, so much of what I have been thinking recently became
coherent; especially the de Beauvoir/Camus view of man conquering
the absurdity of his condition. All their conclusions I had already arrived
at independently.[2]

16 November

Already a week at Ashridge; four days doing nothing, then a course for
three days. I have fluctuated between boredom, distaste and excitement.
The great mock-Gothic pile, the lawns, shrubberies, the pre-fab where
I live, the isolation from towns. I feel myself changing outwardly,
reverting to type. Being the public schoolboy and officer; I hate it, but
have to be it.

I have also forgotten what it was like to be thrown before the crowd,
to have to speak to large audiences, act, behave, think before them. All
the time here one is playing a part, being something one is not, like a
liberal in a Communist country. Here I am more like a Communist in
a Tory county. Or to be precise, an existentialist in a faintly conservative community. I see that they have little idea of what I am really like.

John Cross is my largest companion. An exact fit for the job here –
sexless, full of *bonhomie* and sense of duty, earnest in some things, cynical
in others. Naïf, yet knowledgeable. Bespectacled, shy, yet full, when
needed, of a cheery Butlin-camper's *joie de vivre*. Leading the dance,
making people laugh, cheering them up and on. A man who has found
his place and career. I don't think much of him, yet I like him. A certain

---

[1] Published by Routledge & Kegan Paul in 1953.
[2] In face of an apparently meaningless universe, the existentialist can give his
own life individual meaning by making active choices about who he is and what
he believes. JF displays this existentialist consciousness in the pages that follow.

oldgirlishness which never becomes obtrusive, a conventional sort of naughtiness (swearing and getting excited on two ciders and a gin and orange), which is only the reverse of oldgirlishness.

Laurence Sutton, the Director of Education, a large, saturnine man of sixty or so; one of the numerous drags on progress.

The Admiral, small, alert, like a small, bright bird, but with a deep voice, very assured, commanding, a penetrating, examining sort of presence; too much authority, which makes me unable to stand up to him, to be any other than my old self to him. A junior officer. With E behind me, I can now meet men on superior terms. I don't feel in any sense sexually their inferior, and not – in many cases – merely their equals; their betters. I now have to find an equivalent to E in life – a series of books, successes of some kind. I can't bank my way through with no credit in the celebrity bank.

Admiral's wife, a vast Britannia woman, brick-faced, eighteen stone and six feet tall, looming and lurching about like an ocean-going liner about to dock. The dinosaur, I call her; a huge body and a tiny brain. Quite incredibly stupid; the daughter of several generations of Marines, which might easily explain that.

Capt Gordon, one-armed, bluff, old-boy-ing all the time, like a squirrel, timid but anxious to please, assertive but hastily withdrawing.

Hazel, one of the girls' tutors. Very English, pretty, lissom, well-built, exuding sex vitality although she ignores it – God, how sexless Englishwomen try to be – and quick, excitable, gurgly in her conversation. A touch of the Girl Guide and the hockey forward mixed with the sophistication of an Oxford graduate. A sort of problem I should like to solve; I think that it is the Englishwoman's great charm; she has the basic physical beauty, and she has to be thawed, released, emancipated. This girl represents a sort of splendid physical machine one wants to set in motion.

Many of the girls here are like that – so pretty, and so frozen; so dulled by the stiflingly narrow conventions in which they are brought up. They are easy-speaking now, in 1953, about sex; but the basic denial is still there.

23 November
The E situation seems at last somewhere near resolution. A few days ago she wrote a sharp letter to R, who had previously written her a stupid loving-Victorian-husband sort of letter, about her returning to the path of duty and her old self. Now he says that he has been 'humiliated' enough and wishes for a divorce immediately. He wants custody of Anna.

He said he would come at once (to Birmingham) to take her. But then, in a later telegram, that his sister won't have the child, so nothing can be done. A typical violent decision, withdrawn almost as soon as it

is made. He accuses me of 'spinelessness', because I have not 'offered'
to take Anna. But all along he has been quite categorical that Anna
must remain with him; that he would never let Elizabeth have the child
if she was living with me. He is so wild, confused, incomprehensible.

I went up to Oxford, stayed with the Porters. Then E, in black,
beautiful to me, silent, balanced; happier, I thought. We had only a few
hours together, a tense, excited embrace under a little bridge on the
canal by the station – very close, how close we stand at times. Can love
have any other test of worth? The closeness and despair one feels, the
sexual twinship in suffering. I wished we could have spent the night
together. E belongs, touches, in my inner self. She has reality there;
does not pretend to respect the outer, convention-tyrannized self that
dogs me. I am quite sure I want to live with her, quite sure we belong
to each other, and that I must let nothing stand in our way. Certainly
nothing like my job in this insipid institution.

From a review (*Sunday Times*, 22 Nov 53) by Raymond Mortimer: 'Belief
in sin is more advantageous to the novelist, I think, than belief merely
in right and wrong . . . Catholicism makes a particular appeal to the
imaginative writer, because it renders every act potentially momentous,
and fraught with consequences that may be eternal.'

Existentialism.

The girls here. I am beginning to get to know some of them. Rather
like the boys at Spetsai, charming, spoilt, and as often as not the children of broken marriages. Some of them are quite exceptionally pretty
– Nordic blondes; an exuberant, noisy Greek; a very rich, dark and
voluptuous little Persian. All types of conventional English beauty. But
how much better the foreign girls dress; how much more girls, how
much more allied to love, they are. They wear sex, gallantly, with so
much ease.

28 November
The mess gets daily messier. R has now decided that E must keep Anna.
That he has no more responsibility towards her. The divorce letter,
though, seems to have been no more than a violent bluff. Both E and
R are at complete loggerheads, and plainly neither of them want the
responsibility of the child. I cannot afford to take it on. E cannot both
look after the child and earn her own living. The impasse seems absolute.
I have got to the stage where I wonder whether the whole thing is worth
going on with. It needs an act of courage on somebody's part. E to
renounce Anna altogether, or I to leave this job, find a better-paid one,
and take on E and Anna (but that needs more than courage – a great
deal of good fortune). R to take Anna, but his spite and egocentricity

are more than a match for his paternity and his Catholicism. The key to the whole situation is money. If any one of us had it, then all our troubles would be solved. Money, root of so many goods and evils.

Also here, I am constantly tested sexually – aware of the damnable masculine promiscuity that makes man ashamed of himself every time a new pretty woman passes. That Marcel thought has such relevance here – marriage as an act, the creation of fidelity.[1]

20 December

Leigh. First period at Ashridge finished. The engine was beginning to wobble; end of term cannot have come too soon. One so easily slips, when one welcomes experience. It was a South African girl, very smooth, snobbish, sharp; pert, quick, intelligent – comparatively, at Ashridge. Smart, compact, small and with a full, tempting body. Carrying herself well, always well-dressed: aloof, not enthusiastic about Ashridge. With dark, very dark, indigo-washed grey eyes, alive, penetrating, expressive, in a sophisticated, plump little very pretty face. And the most perfect complexion I have ever wanted to touch. Very much an untouchable; a rich man's daughter, knowing all the social and sexual answers. Very tempting; and I let myself be tempted, as she did, in return. Nothing was declared; but eyes said a lot, and we seemed always to meet, so often to be together. To be sitting together; untangled; and not bored. She quite supplanted E. All thoughts, dreams around her; letters to E a duty. All the joy-miseries of young love – inability to concentrate, to work, loss of appetite, consciousness of foolishness; in a closed community like Ashridge, a liaison is bound to be noticed, almost before it is aware of itself.

We, and two other girls, went one evening to Little Gaddesden to hear a young guitarist, Julian Bream, play exquisitely in the Elizabethan manor house.[2] An old carved mantelpiece, panelling, the soft lute and guitar, a handful of musical people. Then a walk home; I held one girl by the arm and Sally by the hand. A small, cold, unmoving hand; unmoving, but it made no attempt at withdrawal. Only in the last few days were things too tense – we lost control. Became unnatural. I don't know how we shall get through the next few months. She goes back in April.

Two moral problems. One, I have definitely resolved, in myself, not

---

[1] JF is thinking of the French Christian existentialist Gabriel Marcel (1889–1973), who emphasized in his philosophy the importance of concrete experience over the abstract formulation of systems. In *Le Mystère de l'être* (1951) he argued that while being could be recognized as a fact, its nature eluded objective analysis. Human fufilment required a personal engagement with the mystery of being which accorded full importance to values such as faith and love that the scientific thinking of an impersonal mechanistic world tended to dismiss.

[2] Little Gaddesden was the nearest village to the college.

to have E if it means taking Anna. That quite apart from the economic difficulties; something physical, animal, in me revolts against that. But I know that I am wrong. The only virtue is in deciding now; to have made any other decision would have been as honest as a bankrupt's cheque. Two, the spectre of promiscuity, coming to haunt the nice rationalist erections of fidelity; I love E, I will be faithful to her. But I am parted from E, and Sally appears. And all's in chaos. I know myself promiscuous, incapable of a separated fidelity; even living conjugally, I doubt, now. How much of this is existentialist will?

Ashridge, place, life, I like. The country-house life, maids, visitors; the seventy girls, rich and happy, an integral part of the architecture, like fountains in Spain; the staff cynicism and the student enthusiasm; the absence of haste, city things. The routine, the formalities. A weird out-of-date organism, a stranded whale, gracious and amusing to live in. A healthy amount of absurdity and eccentricity.

I enjoy it.

A day and night in London with E. She's now living with Anna in a fine Regency house in Edwardes Square. A madhouse, run by a beautiful, fey Irishwoman with grey hair and an exquisitely noble, almost supremely beautiful face; who's a congenital liar, and has a weakness for living in a charitable mess, surrounded by mothers, children, poets and unpaid bills. A little mad Irish world in the middle of London. So dirty, carnal, friendly, neurotic; no one quite sure where tomorrow will come from; enjoying and rueing.

E goes out to work each day, nine till six, behind the perfumery counter of a store. The child is looked after in the mad Irish house. Poor E. She has all the trouble of Anna, the expense – Roy is broke again; there is a lectureship at Swansea which he is hoping to obtain. But E did not think that he would finally take it, even though it is worth £1,000 a year.

She accused me of being bored by the whole situation. It is true; I am tired of it. At the same time, I am conscious of being altogether self-centred in my actions. I ought to be paying E something. She has barely enough for the necessities of life. Seems not to eat. But she is tough, resilient, resourceful in the miserable circumstances of London.

Worse than that, I am guilty about Anna. I watched her today, and she stared back in a strange hostile way; yet I could not find the least pity for the child. She was a fact, an abstract something, within the normal bounds of human obligations, to be pushed aside. I cannot disregard her; yet I cannot consider her.

I want a free relationship with E, where we could travel, live together, in fidelity – matrimony I care not one damn about. I am so conscious of a deep central instability, not in any particular bad sense – an inner fluidity, thirst for liberty, especially in movement. I have no wish for money, but enough to live simply, and to travel humbly; not the intolerable burden of a ménage, an economic vampire of a situation where all power of movement was lost. All of which is against the logical ethical course of action.

29 December
Thankful that Christmas is past. A depressing season. In material terms, plenty to drink and eat at Leigh; but I feel so much a fish out of water in the suburban world of little girls, uncles, aunts and Christmas trees that I become coldly ascetic. Eat little, and control the intoxicating process. Feel mean to my parents; ungrateful, remote, a sulky enigma.

To London on Boxing Day, and E. Two delicious nights in a room overlooking Edwardes Square. Then trouble, poverty-ridden days; apart we can be thrifty, together we are lost. Spend what little we have wildly. She has no job, no money; I have two pounds in the bank, and no pay till the end of January. I need new clothes, and must pay for the Greek book to be typed out. She's absolutely bound by Anna; the prospect, if one dares to lift one's eyes from the present, is grey, bleak, midwinter in all ways. We day-dream about the South, voyages, journeys, sojourns in the sun.

On Christmas Eve E went out on a nightclub crawl with her old lover, Betty's brother, Alan. She ended up, as she put it, in his bed. He tried to make love to her; she said she didn't even allow him to kiss her. I was disgusted, furious, jealous, unable to trust her at all to begin with; though I later sensed her love for me. But she has that fundamental instability, that lack of control at the moment of crisis (rather than a continual fecklessness), which makes me wonder whether I should not drop her and have done.

The child haunts me, too. I detest it. It is an 'it', not a 'she'. It moans, cries, whines, loses its temper; is thoroughly spoilt by its parents and its past. It needs a year under a strict nanny, an old-fashioned regularity of routine, cleanliness, order. Not the present chaos of a mad rooming-house. But I cannot accept responsibility for it. It has the ugly egocentric face of R already; will be wild, spoilt, a mess all its life. We exchange hostile stares when we meet. I make no move to put it at ease.

And E – at times she is beautiful to me, poised, warm, so easy to be with; sensual, casual, undemanding yet affectionate. But at others, ugly, vulgar, her past self. A kind of cheap shopgirl that rises in her, and clashes with me. Her face becomes lined, a shade prostitutional; lived too much, too hard. Though she can seem young, with her fine figure, so very young, at other times. And there is the fact, the practical facts, of what she has done. Worked miserably in a shop, supported the child, carved out a niche in London for herself and the child. And London is like granite for the poor and provincial. She is half heroine, purely contemporary heroine; and that queer core of truth in her, her rarest possession. That drives her on, would drive her on endlessly; and would always make me regret her.

6 January 1954

A miserable day; darkness flooded the interior. Doubt about my writing; a deep, all-pervading doubt. The agonizingly slow progress I make towards coherence and grace; the constant misuse, semantic and euphonic, of words. The effort to achieve something more than platitudes seems wasted, in vain. I am fatally chained to my past, and to this Leigh environment which formed me, directly and indirectly. I have no ease, no aptitude for writing. It is almost always an act of will. I know the Greek book is not good enough. And E, who has read a little of it, agrees; it needs rewriting. I can't bear to think what that involves. Meanwhile E is living through hell in London, jobless and moneyless. Yesterday she went and sold her only overcoat and her wedding-ring – had £3 for them. She is living on the fringe of existence, and I feel totally guilty because I do not help her. I have my grandfather's ring which I could sell; I know it is ridiculous to feel sentimental about such baubles; indeed I don't. But I am afraid of hurting my father's feelings if I sell it. In short, it is still my feelings that count above her misery.

21 January

Back at Ashridge. E and I had a night in a hotel near Euston, twelve hours' peace before we plunged back into the turmoil, the tense, grey life to which we seem eternally condemned. She lives so near the fringe of breakdown, so constantly without money, food, hope, that I can only marvel at her resilience. The shortage of money is really acute now. She never has enough to pay her rent on time; and lives on bare necessities. Yet, together, we don't economize; we seem incapable of it. A pound on lunch and a cinema, when by a cheaper choice we could have had them for half the price. We are in harmony now at any rate; live in and for each other; a completely satisfying relationship, and closer to love than anything else I have experienced – a mature, desperate love, a love that seems the only sane, healthy, comforting thing in an absurd, sick and desolate environment. All we can do is cling, and hope. Hope.

Ashridge is the same, the time away four days, not weeks. Already, in less than twenty-four hours, I never left. Sally is back, still forward, watching for me, and I for her, more certain than ever though I am of E – and how slim, mature, sincere she seems beside the over-glamorized remembrance, now plump reality, of Sally. Sally is back, and I have the same flirtatious feel towards her. Badminton. She played with the Admiral, and Diana opposite me. Coffee afterwards; and then she sat waiting for me to join her. Which I did not; but the effort it needed to come away was considerable. True morality is the most arduous of virtues. The struggle of 'free' will against all that is determined; something that is creative, but as hard to create, continuously, as poetry.

29 January

Another desperate night and a day with E in London. A bitterly cold spell, which intensifies the misery. Her situation is now wholly absurd; she has been told by Sybil that she must leave 35 Edwardes Square as she does not pay her rent. She has been dismissed from the social survey job. She has no money. R will take Anna and find a nurse – he has a fairly good job again at the moment – and E has to fend for herself. But she has promised to find R a flat. So spends her days flat-hunting when she knows she will be out on the pavement from Saturday onwards. As usual, the strain of living on the brink of a precipice made us love fully, happily, warmly. But the despair increases externally. She is still controlled by R in many ways; lost by his accusations and Christian terminology. She says she is not, but I feel it.

We went to see a Dufy exhibition at the Tate; and the first person we saw there was Sally. It was embarrassing, a risk I ought not to have taken. I said something quickly to Sally and passed the other way. E seemed suddenly mature; she thought Sally was ugly. I for a time did not tell her like it was, but the deception made me shiver, a strange, intense cold penetrated me; so I told her. The exhibition was gay; Dufy walks on a high thin ridge; only fractional differences cause his falling – his fine balancing aloft. His failures are abysmal, and his successes clever and pleasing.

Sally now haunts me, seems to waylay me wherever I go at Ashridge. She half-seriously proposes to spend her twenty-first birthday inheritance on a drive from Tangiers to Johannesburg; and asks me to come. It flatters me to have her at my feet; bores also, of course, and at times, in this strict palace of the proprieties, frustrates and embarrasses. Not that she now appears as anything but a moment's *faute de mieux* diversion in the absence of the reality of E.

3 February

A difficult time; here I divagate, distract myself with trivialities, avoid issues, deceive myself that I develop in silence. The Greek book has lost impetus. I love E, but only when I am with her. I am tempted by Sally, and enjoy refusing, at each new opportunity, the temptation. Such abstraction has an ominous parallel with the teasing foreplay of copulation; I am not gulled by it. E is now living fully apart from R and Anna. A divorce will presumably follow, and my situation here will be dubious. The only consolation is that I do not feel quite so dissociated from Ashridge. I can see more virtues in it, a slight *raison* for its *être*, and I

can better control my criticism of it. The problem of fidelity continues
to absorb me. It is not only Sally – she excites me by her now quite
obvious desire to be kissed – but other girls. One especially, another
South African, the grave, enigmatic, moody Sanchia. A statuesque face,
and a self-dramatizing power which is remarkable; a silent girl, shy, but
deep. Able to entertain; a mime, a dry wit, very cool, sane, balanced,
yet able to be her age as well as strangely mature. She wears always a
strange South African scent, sweet yet elusive, some exotic flower. Is not
easily tangible, understandable. Sally and I sat in front of the fire last
night while she told us ghost stories which she invented on the spur of
the moment. Telling them in her rich young voice, acting the parts,
staring into the fire. I suddenly felt an incommunicable sense of love
and respect for her. A beautiful, and so obviously an intelligent and
cultured young woman; an enigma-woman, the da Vinci breed, the *kore*
smile. But above all, what E lacks, a virgin freshness, a something not
yet moulded. The beauty of a snow-white page waiting to be written on.

9 February

A strange time; I feel suspended. A sharp exchange of letters between
E and me. I sent her cruel letters of advice; she angry woman's answers.
A growing tenderness between Sally and me, an inability to remain apart.
Now we touch hands, touch, have looks, overt subterfuges. We have
been for two gay, shy, absurdly youthful walks; I feel much younger. E
is older than me, in some ways so much older. And Sally is like spring,
a soft, smooth, plump spring with dark eyes and a firm young body. At
times she is very pretty, vital, so warm; and we move very close, tense
with the delicious danger of contact. It is the best period of love, the
constant walking in danger, the not-quite-certainty of everything, the
looks that plumb and lose their nerve, the touches that taper with
awkward silences. It is not the childish awkwardness of calf-loving adolescents, it is an eighteenth-century love of the nuances of galantine. We
both enjoy the indecision, the flirtation. Sooner or later, an explosion
will take place. We shall kiss; but I want that to happen not soon, perhaps
not till the very end.

Poor E, in misery in London, lost, broke, homeless; I can do nothing
about her. I still feel the deep, almost indestructible relationship that
binds us; Sally does not seem so much hostile to it as complementary.
She is the immediate superficial woman, E the remote real one; and
distance is all. It is ignoble, hedonist; but I find Sally quite irresistible,
and E, at the moment, dispensable.

12 February

To London to see E for the first time in ten days; ten terrible days for
her; when she most needed me, and I stayed at Ashridge; wrote hard prig

letters; dallied with Sally. Now she lives in a sort of brothel-cum-rooming house in a once respectable easy Victorian street in old-fashioned Bayswater;[1] she wasn't there when I arrived, and there was no message. I waited for an hour, full of longing for her; and eventually discovered that she was working in the City. When I met her, at 5.30, she was cold, distant at first; but in her room, by firelight, we went to bed, and spent the night in a complete harmony. A curious unworldly passion that invades us; anyone outside us must think me a callous prig and her an immoral neurotic. That is what we are, in society, socially; but to each other, we are perfect sanctuary. There is nothing logical in our love; it ought to have died long ago, been defiled, but it burns on with a clear brilliance and purity.

Yet Sally is in my veins now; when I came back to Ashridge, I found her not an anticlimax, but as tempting as before. She is a little strange, doubtful after my absence; but the arrow still sticks. E has been chased by Tex (Betty's husband), whom at one time she loved – has kissed him, got drunk with him. He wants her to go and live with him, another of the moths round the candle of her. I felt – perhaps because of Sally, but oddly – no jealousy.

I am getting into trouble here; or perhaps it is a guilty conscience. Sally has been warned she is 'putting me in an awkward position'. The high-ups seem to watch me with a muted suspicion. The Admiral seems almost afraid to speak to me, a situation which I find as intolerable as he does. It has only just occurred to me that he might be not frightened of me but of his inability to understand me. That is the trouble with cultivating a mask; it only works on stage; mingling with the audience, day in, day out, it must be seen for what it is. And with the Admiral especially, I use the mask; but very often, when I am not talking directly to him, even though he may be present, I drop it.

Partly it is that this job is so ridiculously undemanding; an office-boy could do it. I have no teaching; no responsibility; no duties other than the most trivial. But no work does not make Jack a bright boy. He vegetates, rusticates, ruins himself.

22 February

The next stop on the road to hell; another lump of plaster off the façade; another failure; I have succumbed to the temptations of Sally. I have not yet by a long chalk drunk; and all the time I am falling, falling; and occasionally I strike a rock on the way down, in case I should forget I was falling. Not that I feel myself in love with her, as I was and am with

---

[1] A few days later, Elizabeth would find a flat at 8 Holly Hill, Hampstead.

E. This is a more animal attraction, a desire to feel her firm fine breasts, to kiss and caress her. In a sense, since she is one of the prettiest girls here, to conquer her. A mere Casanova affaire. Already I know that she cannot kiss one fraction as well as E. That she is on the brink of plumpness; at the moment she is superb, the best figure among all those shapely young things, but in the moment lies the ghost, the too substantial likelihood of the future. And her mind, though South African, not cliché- and convention-ridden, is far from mature; mostly superficial. And her pale face, without cosmetics, falls from grace into plain plumpness. Her eyes are dark blue, Antwerp blue, very alive, her finest feature.

We walked out to the end of the Golden Valley gateway,[1] a dank, grey Sunday and sat and kissed in the middle of a tangle of undergrowth. And again today, in the badminton court. But the war is on; our moves are watched, the world is against us.

I am guilty, very guilty, towards E. But I know Sally is returning to South Africa in six weeks' time. I suppose I now believe in suffering; call it experience, and enjoy it. There are so many parallels between love and religion; the religious world is a parody of the sex world. And if I ever became religious, then it would be, I believe, a kind of complex sexual sublimation. Now, in sex, I am the sinning Catholic; for I believe in love, *la création de la fidélité*, as I believe in nothing else. And I believe in E as the personification of that belief. Yet I sin, and I still believe. I still love E, yet I amuse myself with Sally, and it is not altogether amusement. She, like me, like everybody, has her mask, and the lifting of that mask is one of the transient experiences in existence, moments which redeem the mass of time, the monotony of isolation. Just to rest closely against another person, to kiss them softly, to see them soften, is worth all the risk of offending society.

I suppose one is only half capable of loving two women at the same time. Yet at the moment I feel no sense of torment, no violent necessity to choose between them. I feel guilt, of course; but guilt, in this age, has become almost a pleasure and a normality.

26 February

Two nights in London with E. In a way I had feared them, and my own powers of deceit. But I did not foresee the obvious result. How greatly the contact with Sally would enhance E; I have never found her so mature, natural, and lovable. She represents the almost perfect woman, so warm and so complete, so complex after the shallow twenty-year-old sophistication of Sally that within ten minutes of seeing E again I did not know how I could have been so ridiculous as to have fallen for

---

[1] A valley on the Ashridge estate, which had been landscaped at the end of the eighteenth century after the inspiration of Capability Brown.

Sally. Sooner or later I shall have to tell E. Till then, till Sally goes
home to South Africa, I must play the bigamist. Sally, when I came
back, was so happy to see me, and so pretty, that I found the transference of interest and affection from the one to the other surprisingly,
dismayingly, easy. They are so entirely different, and what I feel for
them is so entirely different, that I do not feel anything incompatible
in the situation.

Perhaps it is that I'm hunting the woman archetype, and have found
it in E, yet have to make sure that it is really there. I suppose I might
one day lose E because of this, or some similar escapade. Yet she is the
one woman I have known whom I cannot imagine losing. She is more
woman than any other woman; and her sexuality, her warmth, her beauty,
are of the sort that do not stale. While about with Sally I am tired of
her tight little mouth, her plump body, and her small bright voice that
cannot drop its public tone and accent. E is a fulfilled personality,
comparatively; 'individuated', in Jungian terms. While Sally is a type, a
product of her past and her environment.

Also Sally has the few qualities that E lacks; a certain foreignness, and
a youth and freshness. A simplicity and an upper-classness. Physically,
superb breasts, skin, smallness. But such things are only tiny defects in
the greatness of E.

I am reading a lot of psychology at the moment; Jung mainly. Vitally
important knowledge.

1 March

Life fluctuates on its descending way; a series of misses, failed attempts
at perfection; a growing awareness of the gap between imagination and
reality. Life is based on so many unrealities at the moment. It is like
standing on moving stones; none of them give a firm foothold. Life
here is an appalling waste of time, a long day in a vacuum. I grow
increasingly dissociated from the institution; have even a hunger for
responsibility, labour, which is not natural to me. I have not even now
the sense of faith with E. I love her as much, perhaps more, but she
seems to me to recede each time I betray her. It is not a very serious
betrayal; already I look forward to the time when Sally will have disappeared. Now we go for walks, and embrace in the undergrowth, like
country lovers. Her prettiness, her softness, are mildly exciting, enough
to distract me from any more serious work. In a way I feel women, or
perhaps promiscuity, are a sickness I have to work out of my system;
and then at last I shall be able to approach E and love her as I should.
I have guilt, a need of guilt, a need of expiation. I almost wish, sometimes, that I could be caught out here, and dismissed with ignominy.
That Ashridge was past.

6 March

Another night in London with E. The pretence this time was less easy; rather, the enjoyment less acute. I hate to have to betray her. Several times she accused me of kissing someone else, Sally; it must have been some strange intuition that made her do it. But the laughing denial – its very insincerity so plausibly teasing – wiped out the suspicion with frightening ease. It is not difficult to deceive, even when the protagonists are as close as we two are. What we could not conceal is an insincerity in our love for each other; but an insincerity in our life is so easy to hide. There is something so free and tender and companionable in E; something deeply understandable and understanding, in the field of personal relationships. An intuitive genius for truth, for what rings true. To a far lesser extent, it is in Sally. But here she seems a seeker after truth; she hates the humbug of Ashridge. Like me, she overcondemns, slashes too wide. Our cynicism is cheaply produced; but at least we have flashes of vision, a feeling of truth, some kind of sincerity, in all this surrounding hypocrisy. I find in her a dilute version of what exists powerfully in E – integrity, sincerity, hate of the persona.

Meanwhile I go on, dissociated, playing two games, and tired of both.

20 March

Five days in London. With E. Happy ones mainly, in spite of our extreme poverty. One dreadful evening, when we had to drag across London to Kensington to fetch a coat from Betty at 35 Edwardes Square. She needed it to appear presentable at some interview. Betty did not want to lend the coat, and I did not want to traipse across London. Whereupon E suddenly broke down, and I as suddenly realized the narrow division between the stability and the despair. Life is very tough for her, very much a struggle, especially financially. At times I feel that I have been outrageously callous towards her; yet I still feel that the distinction of our love is partly due to the fact that I have always made it clear to her that I am not able to support her – and more important still, that that inability doesn't worry me. So our love has remained less complex, purer in motive, since there is no guilt, and no gratitude, to confuse the true relationship between us.

I came back to Ashridge and Sally. Once again the transition from the deep reality of E to the amusing pastime of Sally came with an ease almost disgusting. I think it is easy because in my own terms I am not betraying either; they are totally different, extremes in almost every way, and the relationships I have with them is totally different. I want to go on with E; and I shall be glad when Sally goes yet I'm not bored with Sally in any way. It is an affaire that has its own special poetry. Yet I fear an atrophy of my powers of moral judgement. And I get a smug young man's kick out of having two women both so interested in me. But the experience is bound to have a bad taste. One day I shall have to spit it out and tell E. The difficulty would be to ever make her see the innocence of the betrayal. All it has done, in fact, is to make me more than ever certain that I love her, and need her. Whereas a thousand Sally's could not add up to the smallest necessity.

I went to see Paul Scott of Pearn, Pollinger & Higham's about my books.[1] His opinion encouraged me. He seemed to think that I would one day be published. A tired, smooth, vague, judging man. I must polish off the Greek book now.

Ashridge has helped me to understand one of my defects. More and more I realize that my memory is my weakest fault. I can remember, at will, so little. Memory is an indispensable tool in many jobs – lecturing, for instance. But it is the salvation for the poet-writer. Therefore I no longer try and pretend that I have a memory.

23 March
Sanchia Humphries. I spent a whole evening alone with her today, talking in that intimate, understanding way which is the surest sign of growing affection. Such a strange creature, so young-old, a *kore*, a moody, mysterious yet firmly moral creature. A girl one could never approach lightly, nor lightly leave. A deep lake after Sally's rippling shallow stream. Sally bores me now, increasingly. The whole relationship with her is artificial, physically conventional, finally futile. Sanchia told me more about herself in one evening than Sally in all our intimate moments. Conversation with Sally is never more than a conventional groan about the present, about Ashridge, about the subterfuges we have to employ. We have been so successful that the spirit of danger no longer tickles our palates much. Sanchia has a confused but profound stock of imaginative ideas. She has no cultural pretensions; yet has a quick and completely female intuition. Is shy; yet an accomplished actress. Above all, is straight, straight as a wild young shoot. Her home life in Johannesburg is unsatisfactory; an indulgent father, a mother Irish, neurotic and absorbed in dog-breeding – an unhappy marriage. A violent, gifted older sister, an adopted brother. A house with a long, dark corridor and rooms on either side. The mother and sister squabble, to the point of attempted murder. Sanchia was often beaten, and finally was ordered away to England to regain some stability. How much of all this is truth, strangely, I cannot tell. She lies, jokingly, so immaculately well that – 'Wolf!' – one never quite knows how much to believe her. But even that ambiguity I find attractive.

*

---

[1] Paul Scott (1920–78) would later become famous as the author of the novels known as the 'Raj Quartet'.

A growing discontent with my position here. There is a continual subconscious battle of the personalities between myself and the dreadful Boyds. He has lost his charm for me; I see him now as a spoilt old man, sharp as a fox on his own behalf. His marriage with the vulgar monstrosity of Lady B has caused him, one, to have, as a Catholic, to discipline himself to bear the cross of a bad marriage – whence comes his fierce insistence on the established order, though he likes to break it in little ways himself. Two, he has a kind of thirst for missed happiness which leads him to indulge himself now, and resent any kind of competition. Between them they exert a fearsome power of boredom. They cut short arguments with personal and irrelevant anecdotes. They are almost brutally snobbish. And the only consolation is that I have a small, happy feeling that they begin to perceive my contempt for them.

The real trouble, though, is deeper than the Boyds, infuriating though they are. I am incapable of working *under* anybody at all. I was born a hopeless insubordinate. I can't really see any hope (chance) of happiness until I write purely for myself. God, how I hate the tyranny of hierarchies; of being a component, and never a whole.

29 March

I have to a certain extent been caught in my own trap here. The persona has been so elaborate yet so artificial that subconsciously people must realize that it is a mask, even if they cannot analyse it. After all, why should I still hide what I truly am? Instead of trying to conceal my real self completely, I ought to reveal it as much as is compatible with this environment. Deceiving the world is too much a luxury, too objective. I suppose in me it is caused by my long-standing shyness about literary ambition – further back than that, a fear of the parent-figure. The Victorian virtues were instilled in me, despite the decadent, disintegrating environment of the '30s and '40s. I have my father's subconscious respect for authority – it is deeply ingrained in me, that subservience, and deeply hated. I am a matrist self in a patrist pattern. It was easy to escape, in the physical sense, all the complex personal and social aspects of the parent-figure past; but far more difficult to treat that past naturally. I suffered too much both in it and escaping from it. I hate it disproportionately. I cannot really forgive my parents for stamping me so violently in *their* pattern; and I cannot forgive myself for having allowed my unforgiveness to turn sour in ingratitude and mockery of them. They no longer frighten me; I suppress, consciously, my guilt towards them. But it is them and the fear of disobeying their way of life that have made me so overuse the mask, and hesitate, always, to drop it.

31 March

Another life-year. I got through the day without being wished one single happy return. I no longer make resolutions on this day, no longer think of it as a milestone. Time goes faster now, and I am sure of nothing; but more able to be content with little.

But this evening I was sad that E had not telephoned. She was out when I rang through, and I felt hurt, lonely. But I had only the moment before been in the crypt with Sally. A betrayer has no rights. Sally and I meet now always in the morning, when all the world's in chapel. Walk a little way; spring – green, juvenile, sappy – is here; grey and powder-yellow catkins against a bright blue sky; daffodils, the first chiffchaffs, cawing of rooks, warmth of sunshine, dew, sparkle and the murmur of lawn-mowers. The year's turned. We went up out on the heath the other afternoon, found a glade in the gorse and lay there, yet the mood is autumnal; dry-eyed, affectionate, controlled. We part so soon, and Africa is far, so far. This morning she wore her slate-grey suit, with a slit skirt and a plunging bosom; her white, clear, smooth skin. She was so poised, graceful, perfectly proportioned that I suddenly felt proud to have known her.

In the evenings, after dinner, we go in the crypt, and kiss and walk up and down, and talk. We walk in a certain way, very close, arms entwined, and kiss in the shadows of the old columns. A strange place to sport with Amaryllis, yet not unpiquant. I feel sorry she is going, as if I were losing a pet dog. And she has had an immense value for me, because Ashridge has in many ways crushed me, tried to dwarf me, ignored me. Infuriated and tyrannized me, and she has been the secret consolation, the card up my sleeve. Through her I have satisfied many inclinations to revenge.

The latest teacup typhoon is over lesson-reading. The Admiral is constantly criticizing both my reading and my choice. So I have refused to read any more. This morning he told John Cross that everyone must read from the Passion from now on. John is furious at being dictated to, Harry Gordon angry at the Admiral's interference. General *brouhaha*. How we waste our emotions in England.

6 April
A last night with Sally. We went up to the Bridgewater Arms, drank a little, and planned a midnight sortie. It was dangerous, unnecessary, but I have got tired of the conventions, the hideous, blind obeying that smothers life at Ashridge. The rules, one must break the rules once in a while; we both planned and approached the whole thing with a pleas-urable excitement. At midnight she slipped out of a ground-floor window and we went over to a back room of the Lime Walk, delighted, bubbling over with it. Children, shameful, cocksure, crowing against the adult

universe. We undressed and went to bed, caressed, kissed, lay a long time, murmured, slept, and did not make love. It reminded me of some scene from Casanova or Defoe; certainly there is a special pleasure in sailing so close to the wind. Being naked, having all liberties but the last. She has such a firm, full, splendid little body. It was the experience for a last encounter. In retrospect it will appear shameful; but now it is still warm, exciting, a rose in the night. Grey crowing of rooks in the first light; a pallid, sleepless day; and I now *en route* for E.

20 April

Ashridge without the girls is existence without thought – possible, but unpleasant. A faint poignant absence of Sally. A determined effort to finish the Greek book; an anxiety about the future. I have said I shall leave in September, but where I will go then, I have no idea. I want time to write, and money to support E. Irreconcilables. I have just given my first lecture here, a considerable improvement on my Poitiers experiences. A test to mark progress by; I convinced rather than bored, surprised rather than disgusted.

Now three weeks' holiday in Hampstead.

10 May

Past. How short three weeks are, how unrewarding time can be. Full weeks once, now already empty husks, forgotten spaces.

At Hampstead, the quiet life, alone in the flat. Mostly a period of deep, satisfying love; quarrels, nags, bitterness, but a deep firm undercurrent of natural love. It is certainly not that I feel certain of E; but that I feel certain that we love each other as simply and as absolutely as our natures are capable. The physical base is solid, the spiritual structure is much more firm than we consciously feel. At times we hate each other; but the swiftness and eagerness of our reconciliations – the very absorption we show in our quarrels, our inability to grow bored with each other's faults – are proof of our closeness. We are hypersensitive to each other's words; we know what are tests, what are truths, what are tricks, what are sins.

I came back to Ashridge today drugged, still in E's world, her close, warm, intensely real, sincere world of individual pleasures, constant probing experiences, constant sincerity in personal relationships. The intimate, soft world of love – from that into the conventional, public, old-fashioned standard of society here, a society day, lifeless, soulless, formalized away from nature, as lonely as the skinny white body of a monk, unreal, a blasphemy against real life. How they live in society, the English; even in private, they live publicly, like good little social units, not like themselves, individual human beings. One second of E's world is worth a thousand years of Ashridge. In her world one is sincere and at rest with oneself; in this, one

lies continually to one's beliefs and inclinations. I find it agony to humour
the platitudes, nauseating to condone the errors. I am useless here.

Yet a gay blue flood of myosotis flooding down a bank; birdsong; the
country has charms.

12 May

Warm days, the sky like blue wool, stifling the earth; at night, remote,
faint airs from the south; perfumes, ghosts; a great white cloud of waxen
magnolia flames in moonlight, so oriental, so romantically beautiful,
yet smelling of horse-piss. I had just rung E and felt lonely. She is seeing
R every day, and I am jealous. I daily expect the end of the affaire. She
said one day, 'Why do you worry? You're getting the best of me.' I
suppose it is true. Before she must have been too meretriciously sulky,
too young, to have pleased me; and she will soon be too old, too worn
to have even initially attracted me. Though she has infinite resources
of attraction; but never more so than at her present point of maturity.

14 May

Twenty-four hours with E; at times I feel our liaison is a tragedy; our love
grows, and inexorably a sense of hopelessness, primarily financial. I feel
so completely uncertain about the future. At least I know I want to remain,
at any cost, with E. But I cannot reconcile myself to a career, to the futile
effort of work that a career demands. I have a bitter hatred now of organ-
izations; I cannot obey, no longer tolerate any but my own discipline. I
want, in spite of a growing self-dissatisfaction, to write. I never seem to
have any time here to write; it is impossible to concentrate. The Greek
book, finally with the agents, bores me. It is not the book I wanted it to
be, and what work remains to be done with it disgusts me. But how
intensely now I love E, and miss her when I am away. She is the one sane
person in a hostile world. Once I could take jobs blithely, as evil necessities. Reality, the world of my own will and desires, has made former
compromises increasingly difficult to stomach. It is E's fever; the terrible
search for truth that drives one out of all static situations, that makes
one a kind of psychological wandering Jew, eternally restless, dissatisfied.

But the affection between us, the deep warmth, the heat, love, passion
– that is the truth, and all the rest is lies and irrelevance.

R has again found a good job; lives with a French household. I can
hardly believe that E will not go back to him soon, that our present love
is not so intense because she senses – probably subconsciously – the
inevitable parting. Is it guilt in her? I feel stupidly jealous of R. It is the
fault of our own intimacy; when two people go so far into each other
as we have done, the rest of the outside world is ash-grey and cold,
hideously grey and cold. Separation is a kind of fate worse than death.

*

E is all sympathy, and no control. She feels everything, ignores nothing. Yet there is a vast silent gap between her vision and her expression. She has a fear of the world that is almost childish.

Women are the missing half of male intelligence. They are like spectacles, they improve our inevitably – because we are sexed – short-sighted vision. And the reverse is true. A woman is the ideal companion, merely from this point of view of comprehension of the universe. But the company of males is redundant; it either presents an inferior version of one's own view; or improves upon it. In both cases it is insufferable.

15 May

Report from Pearn, P & H on the Greek book – unfavourable. A shock, one hopes too much against hope. I still cannot accept the essential fact about my literary ambitions – that I did not exist, in the literary sense, until I was twenty-one, and even then I had several years of errors and pitfalls to experience. One tends to compare onself with coevals. But I must learn to forgo that pleasure; for many years it will be too bitter. Debit side – 'a series of chapters, rather than a book, with a sprinkling of pleasant but not very original comments'.

'Only narrowly avoids making all the obvious remarks.'

'A procession of places, irrelevant meals and chance encounters.'

Of my prose – 'it lacks the power of compelling unresisting attention . . . usually fluent and quite clear in meaning, but he goes no further than that in matters which require a much more sensitive instrument of description to make them valuable.'

Finally – 'too messy a book to find a publisher'. Credit – on the school – 'his book immediately improves in flavour, individuality and confidence' . . . because I became 'more than an intelligent tourist . . . part of the landscape'.

'I am very worried about being unfair to him because he is so close to writing a good book; but I am sure he lacks that touch of magic which would have brought real life and sparkle to his fervent admiration for beauty, his feeling for the past, his sense of the drama in strange places. All these things are obvious and admirable in him, but they do not cohere into a pattern of recreation sufficiently fresh and stimulating to offer serious pleasure.'

I need to 'force a design on, discipline material that might well be saleable'.

A fair report; it hits all my premonitions on their heads. And I am less despairing than I could have expected. I don't know why I harboured the little delusion that I might deceive experts with my inadequacies.

*

Sanchia Humphries. She hits a right phrase occasionally. Why she likes Africa: 'Because of the air – it's air nobody else has ever breathed.' That's what's wrong with English air. Too much exhaled.

3 June

Ten days with E in Hampstead. Coming back to Ashridge was like returning from a long voyage. We seemed in a way to have run, in that short time, the whole length of an affaire. From Monday to Saturday it was love and lust and adolescence all the time; a perfectly happy period, in complete harmony. But on Saturday we spent the whole night in one of our dreadful hopeless quarrels – she sunk into a kind of vicious despair from which she cannot be moved. Any normal attempts at comfort infuriate her; everything reasonable becomes a cliché – as it no doubt is, absolutely. This time she was racked by the total hopelessness of all relationships; the lack of faith, the lack of hope in our own especially. She went to sleep at dawn, which infuriated me; and slept till one o'clock. We achieved a partial reconciliation at teatime. But for the next four days we were out of touch, tired, exhausted with each other, still in love, but seeing love as a tyranny, not as a consolation.

Partly it all came because she started work again – after a month's absence – on the Monday. And for her, with her total inability to economize, the emotional impact of work drives out all other feelings. It makes her very nearly impossible to live with. But I felt myself, for all the crises of nerves, the hate, the deliberate, sadistic way in which she attacks me, unmistakably in love with her. She has the pure, essence of woman in her, and for that I am prepared to tolerate her lack of social grace, her lack of diplomacy, her harsh criticisms of me and my work (I wrote a short story about the quarrel which she tore to shreds), her inarticulateness, her childish hate of feeling intellectually inferior, her laziness, her lethargy. She is one of those rare people with whom life could never be quite ordinary. She is hypercritical of every single thing, thought and being that crosses her path. Which needs a courage and an effort I often do not possess. She was out late one night, seeing Roy, who now is working in London. I got in a temper with her because I was afraid she might not come back. Drunk too much ouzo. All fears, until the bell rang and I became all resentment. How love loves to hate. The pleasure of having a good reason for feeling hurt.

She often accuses me, in what I write, of using a *Woman's Own* style. By which she means sentimentality, triviality, banality, the cheap poignancy and hackneyed language of the women's magazine stories. I know that by the standards and tastes of the age that is true. This is an austere, severe, black age in serious art, as a reaction against the ubiquitous insincerity and conventionality of commercial art. Unless a thing is tragic, wry, perverted, bizarre, it is not contemporary. Optimism, happy endings, even ambiguous endings, are out of date.

One might make it one's task to resuscitate happiness, normality, sentiment in the best sense, the poignancy of noble emotions fighting ignoble drives, but to avoid the Rubenesque. A happiness of the sun, not of artificial lamps.

I want to tell the story like a kind of tragic strip. To try and write well without the glossy brilliance of technique that the literary magazines demand. *Simplicitas*.

9 June

I have, this last week, been writing poems again, the first for some months. I do not know what mechanism triggers the poetic state of mind. Why it happens that the mind starts thinking again rhythmically, in images, metaphors, why certain aspects, truths, words should present themselves in the form of potential poems.

I find it difficult to write 'modern' poetry; the poetry of violently contradictory elements. Such poetry was perhaps necessary at first to express the bewildering complexity of the New Knowledge. But it soon becomes a mere concentration of extremes, a futile shaking of the kaleidoscope, in which the occurrence of patterns of merit is partly fortuitous. Where the poet is insincere, using his obscure images to cover up his own poverty of true invention.

It seems to me that these are the two great legacies of what we call 'modern poetry' – poetry written between 1908, say, and 1954 – one, the power of the violent metaphor or simile to express a universal; two, the use of pastiche, of which T. S. Eliot is the great genius. Pastiche raised to a virtue, an honourable poetic metaphor. To be fully conscious of all the adumbrations.

I personally am swinging away from a poetry of mood, of atmosphere, descriptive poetry. I am looking for a poetry of truths, of emotions. And expressed in a simpler, less violent language. Leaning more towards *naïveté* and archaism than complexity and contemporaneity.

I write love poems sometimes. But it only occurred to me the other day that they are not presentable. It is not that I am technically in the least ashamed of them. But it is impossible to publicize highly charged emotion now. I could not do it, even with E.

13 June

I am once again getting entangled in a maze of projects. When I should drop everything and rewrite the Greek book.

*

A difficult time with E. I am in a way jealous of R, whom she now sees frequently. He is being very successful architecturally; earning plenty of money, and doing competition designs. He has just won a big one. I feel increasingly dependent on her love. And she needs me less and less; and admits that Anna haunts her, that she is as much in love with Anna as anything else at the moment.

14 June
Two splended letters from her. Sometimes she writes near genius. So full of sane, warm, classical love. There can never be another like her.

Chesterfield's clever joke about copulation – effort considerable, position ridiculous and the expense damnable.[1] I hate it, hate it altogether, Lawrentian hate. The urbane mind about sex. A petty compensating of the worst order.

21 June
Five days with E. Affection, passion, love. And hopelessness. But impossibility of separation; and on the whole, happiness in the moment. I hardly belong to Ashridge. Most of me with E and a lot of me concerned about the uncertain future.

I must find work in London. I must write. I must get published. Nothing but musts, such work ahead. I live too much in the present.

23 June
Watching a display of dancing given by children at the Little Gaddesden village primary school. They did English folk dances. It was a bright blue day, fleecy clouds, green grass. The dances sprightly, pastoral, a sad lonely ghost. I had a sudden whiff of sorrow for the past. England my England, England's mysterious deep ghost, sprightly, green; I see it in the shade of the great beeches. Very rarely. One day I must catch it in Robin Hood, the remotest and perhaps profoundest of my projects.[2]

---

[1] 'Chesterfield' is the statesman and writer Philip Dormer Stanhope, 4th earl of Chesterfield (1694–1773). The correct quotation, attributed to him, is: 'The pleasure is momentary, the position ridiculous, and the expense damnable.'
[2] In his essay 'On being English but not British', 1964 (reprinted in *Wormholes*, Jonathan Cape, 1998, page 96), JF explained the deep appeal to him of the Robin Hood myth. It represented 'the survival in the English mind of that very primitive yet potent archetypal concept, the Just Outlaw. . . He is the man who always, when faced with either taking to the forest or accepting injustice, runs for the trees.' Although JF would repeatedly return to the theme in his writing, the only published work to draw on it is the story 'Poor Koko', in *The Ebony Tower*.

27 June

An odd day; odd days. I suddenly find myself indifferent to E. For months now I have been oblivious to other women – ever since Sally left in fact. But now, bang, I find myself suddenly tormented by other women, by a mushrooming polygamous urge to love. Two possibilities – the charming, subtle, enigmatic Sanchia and a rather stupid but exceedingly pretty girl called May McNeil. This latter has conquered an American, which irritates me. She has a sylph figure and a traditionally exciting past. I feel some response from her. I made my interest in her quite clear. And was then horrified to find her so stupid, and myself being duped by the body again. But she has a body difficult to ignore or forget.

Sanchia I walked with all the afternoon and evening. A white face under black hair, a red bud of a mouth under her ridiculously *retroussé* nose. A sky-blue mackintosh with brass bobbles. A fairy-like, fantasizing, childish, sage, charming, infinitely charming person. She lacks passion, it is true (or appears to lack it), and she still has a schoolgirlishness which exacts discords still. But such a wife; and there exists (or rather the potentialities exist) between us an accord of unusual natures, a harmony.

A fierce wind all day, absurd for June. Blue skies and white towers, pluming branches. We wandered through the woods, had a pleasant tea at LG. 'The sky's a jewel,' she said, 'and the clouds are claws and the afternoon's lovely because everything else is so pewtery.' How apt 'pewtery' was – how, at first incongruous, it seemed accurate; the incongruous charm of midsummer England. Pleasant, English, only superficially banal.

1 July

A little enchanted by Sanchia. Some of it is deliberate on her part; a kind of revenge for her sex. She thinks me, I suppose, dangerous; and if I don't see her nowadays, I miss her. I walk about in a permanent state of electricity; pent-up till she appears, and then a current goes coursing out and around her. I am quite sure that sentiment must have its own microwaves. And she is one of those rare people whom I suspect of having a receiving set. Also what I feel for her is marital; I haven't felt it for anyone else. It may be something in my own age; now is perhaps the time when I would in any case be looking for marital attachments. But I feel that it is perhaps something more subtle; what I look for in a woman is mystery. G had none, which is why I fell so swiftly out of love with her. E has, but no fantasy. Sanchia looks as if she might have an enduring mystery. The wish to marry is in proportion to the belief in the depth of mystery in the woman married. Some such formula.

2 July

'Curio'; she used it of herself, the bad angle on her rarity. Accusing me of treating her as one. And I suppose it was an opportunity, which I only rather ambiguously took, of protesting what I really feel for her. I had asked her to go for a walk, and she came; a cool, grey night with high swathes of vapour veiling the stars. We walked down a long deserted ride in the afterglow, talked, talked all the time. That tender self-revealing talk of the uncertainty in love, hints, ambiguities, laughter, seriousness; I am beginning to feel seriously appalled at the thought of losing her presence. I can't suppose that she has anything more than interest or liking for me. Physically she is very unapproachable, virginal, armoured. One might almost suspect frigidity, a physical failing, if her voice didn't have moments of warmth; and little movements of her body. I think perhaps it is sheer inexperience; though she would never be the animal-woman. A charm which attracts me as I grow older. And she has, as she says, great self-pride, a great need for sanctuary in herself; she has to withdraw constantly. And that also, recognizing, I find charming. If only I could be loved by her – act out the part, and start a new life. Absurd, but that also is her charm; she is what I no longer deserve to know. Innocent intelligence, virginity, a whole unadulterated bud. As if in my cult of love I needed something fresh and gleaming to worship; an infantile drive? Something untarnished.

We didn't once touch, not even fingertips. And she'll pass me today in the corridor as if we were almost strangers, as if it was two other people who walked so slowly, closely down the beech-rides, in the night, and stared at Mars, and between the branches to the south. I pointed out Cygnus, flying gigantically south-west. She couldn't see it. 'I can see shapes everywhere,' she said. 'But you mustn't cheat,' I answered. 'You must only use the agreed constellations.' And I suddenly saw the sky as a kaleidoscope for her, infinitely deep and changing, as it really was, incoherent beautiful chaos and, for me, a man's set of arbitrary patterns; man and woman views. That is her – all woman.

5 July

Four days with E. I was as near as can be to leaving her. For I felt, when I first saw her, for the first time, no love; only a prospect of boredom. She is much too sensitive for me to be able to hide such a change. And she seemed so lonely, so hopeless that in the end I was resigned to her again. Pity has broken into our love; it will fester, I think. I wrote her a letter on Sunday – when she went to meet R and A – to say that I wanted to leave her; but it became increasingly hedged in with reservations. She came back late and a little drunk, attempting pathetically to be cynical; finally crying, terribly, in great loneliness. But she had already realized that I was touched by someone at Ashridge – even that it was Sanchia.

And Roy asked her abruptly whether she wanted a divorce, and then told her he was in love with someone else, a model. So that she was forsaken everywhere; and it was impossible to give her such a letter, leave her in distress at such a moment.

It wasn't a very good letter; nothing short of a long novel would suffice, so complicated are motives in our sort of world. I could justify myself on conventional moral grounds (leaving her), but that would be too intolerably sanctimonious. The main reasons are simple – S (perhaps because she, not being touched, remains idealized) represents not so much a counter-attraction to E as a proof of my own instability; my own longings for a more formal, more fantastic relationship than the 'total' love which E and I pursue – it is not enough that we can behave naturally as naked animals, and naked souls, in each other's presence. I remember having a talk about this with Sanchia. I said it was the only possible relationship between two intelligent people. But she disliked the idea. 'I must have something hidden,' she said, one must allow the other certain secrets. Which is precisely what E and I cannot do – such a sincerity and transparency is unusual in its way. But exhausting; and all of life without one's love gets squeezed out in the process. There's no time for anything but the relationship.

I want to write. I never have time to write these days; I need solitude, celibacy, in order to indulge the process of self-love that writing is. I would love a year free of all female contact.

And there is guilt; the guilt between E and me for what we have done to R and A. It haunts our lives, it is waiting around each corner, at the end of each day, and it irritates me now like the carrying of an unnecessary weight during a mountain climb, like a tweed coat on a hot day.

There is all that; and still my very considerable love for E. For there's no one like her, no woman I could imagine more complex in her moods, more purely and widely woman.

10 July
Another nocturnal walk with S. She was in a different mood, buoyant, light, girlish, and I was tense, tired, depressed. It was very dark, the sky full of drizzle; heavy, low clouds and dark masses of trees. We walked and talked, and occasionally I touched her, to steady her, or to show her an easier path. It was very dark, and I had a hundred opportunities to kiss her. But she, of all women (and supposing I was thinking of her in hunter/prey terms), needs careful stalking, delicate playing. She would be so easy to shock. Indeed, I felt like shocking her, just to see what she would do; and also out of a more noble impulse, to check the disease, to so shock her that the affaire would end. But then again, I decided that I didn't want to shock her; not only for the sake of the chase, but because she has put so much trust in me.

We didn't get back to Ashridge till one o'clock, and the front door was locked. And as we were standing there, a car suddenly swept round the bend and we were caught like escaping prisoners in its glare. I flinched back against the wall, but the car drove straight towards us and stopped outside the front door. I walked away hastily, guiltily, in the full glare of the headlights, furious, frightened, caught with my trousers down. By the grace of Venus, they were three of the American girls late back from London. I heard them talking about me and giggling. 'He sure is an immoral character, that John,' said one of them. It seems amusing now, but terrifying at the time. Absurd, how the social taboos, so artificial, so primitive, can at such movements catch one off balance and assume a sudden looming reality.

I held her hand for odd seconds; a very warm hand.

What Sanchia has and E has not – poetic fantasy.

12 July

Another mad, absurd walk with Sanchia till one in the morning; and this time I felt quite surely that she wanted to be held – not so much kissed, she's too shy, altogether too virginal. A schoolgirl in love, though so oddly mature in many other ways.

I feel sad when I'm with her; sad about E, sad about myself, least sad for Sanchia. I feel free of E in a sense, lightened, released into the liberty of my own world again. That love was too intense to live with. I am still light and tender with E, but it is a kind of tapering off of love, a thinning out, a rarifaction into nothing. What I now find attractive is the thought of two years' solitude – or a year's – with Sanchia as a remote Beatrice to prevent the desert from being absolute. Nine years between us, it's too much for any serious marriage.

But I held her hand a little last night and when we parted, kissed the side of her head; and tweaked her hair once. I have a different sentiment for her, something more conventional than what I feel for E or G. E is an equal striving to be a superior, too close, too like for life together to be possible. One can't exist all one's life in a tension. S is distant, junior, not an equal because she does not combat ideas; perhaps it is because there is no class bond between E and me – no will to lubricate our relationship. We have to clash because we have no common bonds, no common system of conventions.

As for Sally, I wish I might never hear from her again.

14 July

Night with E. I forget what a strange, beautiful creature she is. We made love very well; no simulation of passion needed. And I know all the pleasures Sanchia could never give me. She would never have what E has, a trained, passionate body. Making love requires a certain animal lack of humour – Sanchia has too much fantasy, feyness, whimsicality. But I also thought often of her, of the special rare pleasures one might gain from her presence. And she also is infinitely educable; and very true, like E. They both have a weak stomach for deception – perhaps that is why I attract them.

E and I now sense the end of the affaire – a little sad and desperate, ominous silences. A hopelessness.

But the distinction of beauty; E is unique in her looks; the perfect modern well-formed beauty; a fierce, proud face. But ageing . . .

16 July
Back from London, and E. And at last the question of parting is broached; and everything is in a flux again. I missed her at a cinema, and we were tense against each other all the way home; then made love, well and warmly. And afterwards I started to talk about separation; we talked all night. Indefinite decisions; a clinging on her part; I was dry and cool and remote, classically sad, frozen. But on the way back to Ashridge despair began to thaw out; I left her standing in the middle of the room, weeping. Intolerable, the thought of never seeing her again; moment of loss, moment of truth. Back at Ashridge a glimpse of Sanchia during lunch, excitement. But she went away for the weekend afterwards. I wrote a letter to E telling her of Sanchia and all the complexities of the affaire. Taut because Sanchia is away till Sunday, taut because E is so beautiful, lovable – she even attained nobility last night – and I love her, taut because Sanchia leaves England in a fortnight, taut because I have half-rejected E from my life, sick of women, sex, my religious conception of love, and oh so tired.

The night before I was out with Sanchia again in brilliant moonlight and a clear sky. It was cold, a heavy dew. We walked and something seemed lost; we walked too far apart, talked too trivially; and I touched her outwardly. A week ago I could have said 'I love you' easily; now it seems impossible. We sat on a gate and a badger came right below us, a very bizarre incident, ambling round our feet and suddenly lumbering off. I want to kiss her because she is so unkissable; no physical desire, she doesn't excite, except by her feyness.

And I'm a little afraid of her; some of the girls caught her slipping out one night, and asked her where she was going; and she just said, 'Walking with John.' No subterfuge.

J. Cross said she talked with him till 12.15 last night; I was jealous to hear it. Then consoled; she may have been waiting for me.

24 July
Bitter-sweet days with S. Our walks become more tense and awkward; not only the effort of suppression; she was teased by all the others. So two nights ago she said she wouldn't come out again, because it was getting

too difficult. I kissed her, on the mouth, once. And went away the next night to E, and loved her very much. So tall, so warm, so experienced, a pebble smoothed by the sea. But the two places, the two women, don't live in the same world. I came back, and Sanchia gave me a poem, immature, faulty, but peculiarly personal. A serious poem, ambiguous.

E wrote a very good letter about discipline the other day – about the capacity for two loves and its control. But what I feel for them both is so absurd/unrelated; and equally irresistible. Though I am so dishonest now that even the superego must be contaminated. A hedonist, a satyr of the emotions.

25 July
A talking all night with Sanchia; till four in the morning. We talked about ourselves clinically, sitting in armchairs on opposite sides of the room; it was an empty, resonant room and we could not clearly hear what each other was saying; a dreamlike, desultory effect. She talked of loyalty; there is a boy in Africa, an unofficial engagement. And I talked of my love for her, flippant and serious by patches. I am possessed by her now. She is an enchantress, in the vast sense; more than a touch of the sea about her. Can't bear to lose her, see her go, leave my life. Perhaps it is this imminent and apparently eternal disappearance that makes her so precious so suddenly; for the last few days, I am lost in her. It is one way one touches the human condition, the essence of it; with G and Sally I was loved more than I loved, and when we parted, I could adopt a kind of gay attitude of relief; but Sanchia, like Monique, touches the unattainable. With them both I sense all kinds of worlds I can never achieve; they love me less than I love them.

And there is E – when I woke up this morning, I wanted to do nothing except phone her. Urgently, just to hear her voice; reality; not dreams, idealizations, classical myths. An equal love.

Darkness in the future, all kinds of unresolved problems; letters to and from Sanchia; whether to see her in London; no work; no writing; no money; but a sense of living.

Beginning of a novel – 'I committed suicide today.'

26 July
More talking with Sanchia; her face is a kaleidoscope, a procession of women, a constantly changing series of expressions. Most people seem, by their faces, to live in an almost dead calm; Sanchia in a teasing, gay, sad continual breeze. April's child.

All her family history; her fears, her feelings; a great platonic affection between us. She said, of her young man in Jo'burg, yesterday, 'I've got to go back to him, and I've given my mind to somebody else.'

27 July
Victims at last; we sat half the night in a sofa in one of the lounges, closer and warmer. Until in the end I kissed her, and she cried; then laughed, and told me I was only the second man she had ever kissed. Something of the nightmare in it; the late hours and the sleeplessness, the sleepiness, the near separation. She was suddenly small and dependent, so very small, and I felt old and paternal; a flow of warmth, of relief from tension.

And so free from guilt; innocent.

Today she walks about in a magenta dress; laughs at me, looks coy, acts; talks of other things and brings in inconsequential remarks in her typical way. Produces the play, the person most in demand here.

I've drafted yet another letter of farewell to E and this time I must send it.

I day-dream this: a separation from E, a growing sureness of love between S and me until I can get her to marry me. She goes to Denmark, then home to SA. Somewhere I earn money and go and get her.

I've never wanted to marry anyone so much before.

28 July
Fin de jeu. The building like a furniture depository, a morgue, a closed museum; echoing voices in a great silence. That is the disadvantage of great buildings – they need great length of tenure, a constancy of inmates. People who know each other and each other's past and future, not a constantly shifting population; soil for flowers to grow in, not sand blown over desert rock. Always autumn in a house like this, a school, a cottage – a scurry of leaves, an October road.

And Sanchia; the last few days have been such a neurotic time – the play, sleeplessness, my guilt, her guilt, our love, the way we have deceived everyone. We went out again last night after the play, which was a flop – except for her brief entrances – in a sea-green dress, very blue jade, a deep harmonious colour for her black hair and her white face and her red mouth. Elegant, very abrupt, elusive.

Caught her afterwards; she walked down to the beech-ride and swung on the see-saw tree – a tree with a low springy bough. And after a while I kissed her again, and we walked back, sad, gay, very tired, and kissed. A small mouth, but warm. And she sat on my lap in the badminton court and kissed very passionately – heat inside, as I knew there must be; so small, so dependent. Then suddenly stood up and walked away. She came and sat with me for a while this morning in our sitting-room, 34. Cool, aloof, white; non-committal. But I believe that love is a communication; what one feels is there in the other person to be awakened. She hides much; and I have had enough of open love.

And love her now. The future's grey, grey; the chances of our ever having a life together are infinitesimal. But that small distant light seems better than all the open dazzle of E. Poor E; she is disintegrating again, or rather life disintegrates around her. She let the flat before making certain of a place to move to; the problem of Anna again is alive. R wants to send her away to his sister's; E wants to take her and look after her. Broken phone calls from me to her; the great separation is coming. It's in the air like thunder; I long for rain; solitude to grow green in.

S left a rose on my desk today. I didn't find it till she'd gone. A dead rosebud slashed in half, as if by scissors. And a piece of paper underneath, with the one 'John!' scrawled on it. Typical of her; ambiguous, mystifying, delightful.

Nipped in the bud? That would be her sense of humour.

Two long talks with E on the phone. I must see her once more; then no more. A long letter to Sanchia, also. Duplicity; but the letter to S was sincere, and the phone calls duty. Not that I still don't have love, and anguish at the thought of its ending, for E. But what I feel for S goes so deep; perhaps because it is straight, and what I have felt for E has had, in the nature of circumstances, to be crooked. Or does it go deep because I wish to be gone deep into? How much of a love is self-centred? Not an external influence, but a void inside that demands to be, a yearning for even further interpenetration? A female thing; a man in me loves E, and a complete bisexuality (psychological) in me loves S.

How much of my writing here this last year has concerned women and my relations to them; too long a desert, too lush an oasis.

How poor a picture of the age this diary would give a historian of the future; I put down none of the public anxieties – the H-bomb, the Indo-Chinese trouble, the Egyptian trouble, all the rest.[1] None even of my own troubles, outside the field of love. Existentialism misapplied.

---

[1] The US had exploded a hydrogen bomb in 1952, the Soviet Union a year later. On 26 July the Soviet Union proposed a conference on collective European security, emphasizing the destructiveness of the new weapons and the consequent importance of controlling them.

In Indo-China France and her allies had been fighting the Viet Minh for eight years. In July 1954 an international conference was held to negotiate a ceasefire. On 21 July it was agreed that Vietnam would be divided into two parts, the communist-led Viet Minh taking control of the area north of the 17th parallel. Elections were to be held within two years to determine the eventual future of the country.

On 28 July, Britain and Egypt reached an agreement that British troops would leave the Suez Canal Zone within twenty months.

2 August

Absurd, human situation; I go and see E; and on all trivial levels – what I now feel are trivial; familiarity breeds triviality – it was so easy, so happy. To be affectionate, to have a meal, to drink wine, to make love, to talk.

But S always in the background; and when I returned to Ashridge, a letter from her; an odd, young, atrociously spelt 'desultory' letter. But it bit deep in me; and I lived through the weekend expecting another on Monday. There was none, and I've lived through the day as miserably as I was expectantly happy yesterday. Itching to ring her up, to go and see her, anything to see her. A fever; I can't prevent it, only reduce it. Already I have written four letters to her one. Ridiculous; but the beginning of all difficult enterprises are ridiculous.

Tormented by her.

Too much torment even for guilt. *Phèdre.*

Yesterday, my lecture on existentialism; plenty of bouquets for it. Except from the Admiral, who has kept a stony silence. So eager, so effusive people are, starved of philosophy – so that if one talks of their souls, their morals, their beings, they are happy. I gave a grossly over-simplified view of the subject; but at least it may make some of them think for a few seconds.

9 August

Clarification of situation; perhaps I was right to hang on, not to make any violent decisions. On Friday I met E for lunch, and then on to the zoo to meet Sanchia. A miserable time on the whole; dissonances, the worst in each of us. The zoo was crowded, the weather wet, our nerves frayed. She wanted it to be a gay last evening together; I was to take her to a 'low dive', to 'amuse' her. And I revolted; I didn't want to do anything but talk. I had a horror of meeting E. We sat and drank in a little pub off Piccadilly for a while – there was a storm, sheets of rain, lightning. She in blue, in her light blue mackintosh with its absurd hat. What has she? Not E's easy animal beauty. No good looks; if I analyse her face, she is plain. But unforgettable; because I have never seen any one even remotely like her?

In the end we went to a cinema, and after a while I took her hand, and it was feverishly warm and responsive. So odd, how she keeps so aloof for almost all the time, and then the heat seeps out like steam through a leaking pipe. Coffee and sandwiches in a café, a walking-round, hand in hand, of Leicester Square. Then I said, 'Shall we meet again?' And she said, 'No, I don't think so.' And I was sad and relieved. A last sight of her on a departing tube, shot into darkness as if out of time, a white face and black hair and a splash of pale blue into oblivion.

Home to Leigh. It was two in the morning when I arrived; the exhausted sky arched clear, star-wracked; curlew feeding out on the mud-flats. Cold air, not a light anywhere, the whole town dead. And I was intolerably sad.

It is a kind of raw nerve which certain women flick – a more sentimental susceptibility? – but it seems to me to flood light over existence. Sanchia, the unobtainable; all the links that bound me to the South, E; the mundane mess. Time passing, youth gone, clutching hands out of the maelstrom. A great sad sore view of life, a sorrow, a sob; there is all that, the romanticization of the impossible. A convenient symbol to hang frustrations around; a lancing of all the pustulous boil of the imagined but unrealizable.

All that – at Aix, and with Monique – but this time love also for the object. If I had had the money, I would have married her; tried. Did, in fact, during the thunderstorm, nearly propose.

And E. I saw her next day, spent it in Hampstead with her; and the next. The same tired routine of cinema and pubs; with its comforts, of course. Absolute ease of companionship, no physical inhibitions, a kind of twinness about us. And her body remains infinitely attractive. But in public she is so – not smart, not elegant, not chic. A little tired, dragging, Bohemian; gamin. Urchin charm; which at times becomes embarassing. I sense now why R wanted to make a 'matron' of her – not only his Victorianism. I, too, want desperately to spruce her up; her slow individual tempo saps all one's energy. And her face is drawn, old at times; lacking, for all its beauty, the qualities of S. Gravity, aloofness, those candid eyes, that unpredictability of expression which captivates me. And a certain prolixity, vulgarity in E; in Sanchia, a reserve, a careful choice. It may be merely the difference between a primary school and Roedean – education and the lack of it. E says that I am a snob. But there is something in accent, in carriage, in habits; an economy, an order, where E is all confusion and exasperation.

But she has courage, E. And she persists in loving me, even though I don't deserve her respect, let alone her love. Calls herself, so accurately, a 'faithful mistress'.

Curious how now I have become a woman-charmer, who never thought of myself as handsome at all, or attractive. E says it is because I have vitality, a 'strong' character. I can see that I have more intelligence, much more sensitivity with regard to women than most Englishmen – but 'strength of character'? I look for the truth, but I don't act by it. I have deceived both S and E abominably about each other. I lie to my parents. I am too lazy – or too much in love with ruin, the experience of ruin? – to look after my future. And yet I feel, for all that, a slow thickening, maturing, always at work; nothing to be smug about.

Of course, to be – in the best sense – English: objective, unemotional, sane, balanced and physically vital. I have a little of both qualities – Mediterranean being and an Oxford head; that would account for some of it.

I wrote a letter to S today, about how I loved her; humbling myself in a way. I have never made the first declaration before; and I think Sanchia is the first woman I have seduced rather more than been seduced by. Always the drugger, never the drugged.

12 August
No letter from S; and I feel cooled, relieved. In London yesterday I was afraid, not anxious, that I might meet her. And the acute pain, poignancy, of leaving, separation, has already ludicrously diminished.

13 August
I've never been able to read Virginia Woolf – something precious, feminine in her writing; not a great defect, except to me. But the other day, the one following the day I left Sanchia, and I was feeling battered, mentally exhausted, I picked up *Mrs Dalloway* and suddenly found myself completely absorbed.

One has to be relaxed, washed out, completely open to appreciate the stream-of-consciousness school. I don't know whether one could will oneself into that state – whether it wouldn't always have to be fortuitous, externally produced.

Southend, where before I've always been irritated. A cool stream, not a confused ornamental backwater, a lily pond.

And then there was Mrs Dalloway, reminding me so much of S. And Peter Walsh, me.[1]

31 August
A pure blue day, clear and exuberant; not a cloud. The first this summer. I spent ten days with E. Now she is living in a little cottage at the end of a large garden of a house in Fitzjohn's Avenue.[2] The usual life – despair alternating with periods of happiness, love and hate and remorse.

We seemed to end on a happy note; I had to come back to Ashridge for a last time, a Saturday. She rode on the bus as far as Watford; there seemed to be a great sure depth of warmth between us. Then suddenly three days later, a letter. She has had an unpleasant affair with some man she asked in for a coffee; that infuriates me. Her tartishness; the other night I made her walk ahead of me in the street, and no less than three lots of men spoke to her in one minute. Something meretricious, promiscuous in her. She has cut her hair short, which makes her as attractive as she has been for a long time, and I get pride out of her attraction for other men; but fury at her stupidity. On top of this she

---

[1] Described as 'charming, clever, and with ideas about everything', Peter Walsh was the old friend that Clarissa Dalloway passed over to marry her MP husband instead.

[2] Mount Grove Cottage, Prince Arthur Road, Hampstead.

has been sacked once again from her job. A hopeless misfit; no hope of her ever settling down at work. I despair at such times; she has the *nostalgie de la boue*, she plunges into messes as if they were magnets to her. Sanchia seems almost forgotten, past. Only here, of course, are there continual twinges, cuts of pain.

The intense femininity of E – her absolute lack of self-control. It makes her, in the present, difficult to have; and in the future, terrifying to undertake.

4 September

Storms with E. A broken phone call; all to pieces. A wrecked personality; torn; self-lacerating. Now because R won't allow her to see Anna; and she is furiously jealous that he is having an affaire with some other woman. I try and retain her soul; but she is destined to tragedy, will always plunge into the agony. Something Greek about her; Phaedra, a Woman of Troy; a terrifying and fascinating quality. I don't know what it is, what in other women I should call neurosis, lack of control, and dismiss; but grand in her.

Some lovely weather; blue, serene days. Rooks caw and pigeons purr as if it was spring; somnolent September; hunter's moon and evening mist. I leave Ashridge in two days; an autumnal regret for this lovely heart of England. Incomparably green and gracious. Because nothing dangerous inhabits it; because it is fertile, contained, aged, cultivated, familiar, at peace; and, above all, because it is so very lovely. Not like Greece, flashing out its supreme beauty every day of the year; but only perhaps once or twice a season, like all true feminine beauty. One could have a love affaire with Greece, but marry no one else but England.

Kicking myself out of comfort again; I don't know how long I can go on doing it. Only a madman would throw up this job, objectively.[1] With all its amenities, and England so green about it. One could vegetate quite serenely, cultivate one's garden. If I wasn't always reaching for a higher rung on my own peculiar ladder.

5 September

How relative things are; I read what I wrote in July, and it is written by a total stranger. I wanted absolutely to marry S then; and now I am amused by the idea. We have an absurd notion of the continuity of our emotions and desires; most appear quite incapable of learning how temporary, of the present, they are. I think it is an inability to analyse;

---

[1] To be with Elizabeth, JF had successfully applied for a position at St Godric's, a secretarial college and language school in Hampstead.

they cannot detect the reality from its mark. A desire is like a rotting apple – the skin rots last. It goes bad from the core, the heart outwards. I think this awareness of the instability of desire and emotion accounts for my power of independence; also for my cynicism; and what some have been kind enough to call my integrity, or maturity. Because at the moment I desire an emotion, I realize them far more than those who do not see them as transient, fugitive things; I love more intensely. And because I do not pretend that they continue very long.

This means that to will their continuance – the existentialist decision against nature, chaos – is doubly hard.

This explains the violent conflicts in my relationship with E – a kind of rhythmic magnetic attraction and repulsion. It is not that at the beginning of a period of repulsion I have to will against an endless desert; I merely have to wait for the pendulum, the rhythm, to operate. I can be sure of the recurrent periods of deep attraction. And that is the kind of certainty (as in writing poetry) that sustains in the drought.

14 September
Torn, lacerating days; it might be a childbirth, and it seems almost certain to be a death agony. E has just left to see R in Bayswater; I sit in the cottage flat and know that I was never nearer to losing her. I left Ashridge in a calm whimper and came here. I have, I suppose, become so used to E that the possibility of her leaving me was hardly credible. But it has happened, as the result of the S affaire in no small part. And the damming-up of all her will to expiate; her feeling of loss with regard to Anna; and the fact also that Roy is now well off, with a good job, and she has been living for too long on the fringe of poverty. The whole change was triggered by this affaire of R's with another woman; she had no certainty of me, and to see her child and R also detach themselves from her was too much.

I wasn't fully aware of what was going on; and took it all lightly on the whole. Until one evening she went to see R and returned in tears, saying she'd promised to go back. That was on Thursday. All that night and the next day was tears, tears, tears; an agony of remorse. She didn't know what had happened, as if she had gone mad.

I suddenly felt the bottom of the world falling out, and made her stay on for at least the weekend. She rang up Roy on Friday; he wanted to go to Abingdon for the weekend, and so two farewell weekends were agreed upon. We argued and argued all that weekend; I felt I was fighting for her soul; in a losing battle, since the odds were so heavy. Every time I thought of living without her, of going to the cinema, of walking down streets, of having meals without her, I felt so sick and frightened that I used any, any argument to try and persuade her to stay. And I have at last realized how profound my love for her had and has gone. And, for all her faults – and perhaps because of them – I can love her as I have never been able to love before. There are doubts; there is the eternal other mistress, freedom and time to write; there is the financial situation – I can hardly afford to keep myself till the next job starts, let alone her; there is the sense of guilt – doubt that anything could ever compensate her for the loss of Anna or even Roy; there is the obscure adolescent worry that she is not idealizable, not the wife-image; there is a doubt of my own (far more than of her) power of fidelity; there is even the feeling that if she returns to R, the situation will be cleared, not only now, but also to make way for a total return; there is a feeling that the real crux is almost religious – between R and me – and therefore false. There's all that; and the passionate physical love; and the fear of solitude, the need for a companion; and the knowledge that all her truths, her needs, her whims are so like mine – the brother-and-sisterliness in us; all personal, self-centred things, insufficient reasons, in such an issue, to give me any right to keep her.

(One hour since she left; she must be with him now. I feel relieved that the hour has gone. If she is coming back, she comes back sooner now; but that 'if', that 'if'. A great fear of her not coming back this one last time.)

There are those doubts. I could not not have them, but a new certainty overrides them that I want E for life. And I wrote a letter to R saying that I was now fully prepared to marry E and he need have no worries on that score. And I asked her to marry me as well, a dozen times.

Above all, she is in my and I in her veins. We both recognize the extraordinary vitality of our love, which has kept her waiting for me (the irony, that now I've come, it's too late; and to have come, of all places, to Hampstead) through thick and so much thin; the quite intolerable longing we have for each other at all such moments of parting; the profound depths we have touched in each other; and the complete harmony of our everyday relationship. It is a kind of Tristan and Iseult love; incorruptible, but condemned.[1] I do not think we could not love

---

[1] Although over the centuries there have been many forms of this medieval romance, based on a Celtic legend, the central story is as follows. King Mark of Cornwall wishes to marry Princess Iseult. He sends his nephew Tristan to Ireland with his petition. It is accepted, but on the journey back to Cornwall Tristan and Iseult by accident drink the love potion that Iseult's mother had prepared for her and King Mark. They fall fatally in love. After many attempts by Mark to trap and punish them, Tristan eventually agrees that he must give up Iseult and go into exile in Britanny. Here he marries a duke's daughter, Iseult of the White Hands, for her name only and does not consummate the marriage. But wounded by a poisoned arrow, he sends for the Iseult he loves, the only person who can heal him. If she agrees to come, the ship bearing her message is to have a white sail; if not, a black one. But Tristan's jealous wife, seeing the ship approach with its white sail and Iseult aboard, tells him that it carries a black sail. Tristan dies and Iseult, arriving too late, dies herself from grief.

each other, ever. We might forget, betray, on many superficial levels, but not the deep-running current between us; we could never interrupt that. And now, to cut that off in midstream, at its height, is to court disaster. One cannot extinguish such a fire; you can damp it for a while, but the flames will flash up at the first small chance.

R has a power over E that bewilders me. She constantly remarks on his ugliness, his selfishness, his brutality; yet they fascinate her. Tonight, just before she went, she said, 'Roy's got a curse on me. He humiliates me, and I let him do it. I can lie awake all night hating him, and it's no good. All I do is destroy something in myself.' I tell her certain views are false, that she believes them only because R has told her that they are true; and she agrees, but I can see them still there in her eyes. It is true; she is under his curse, and I believe in the end that he will destroy her.

Or another way of seeing it; two English intellectuals, would-be writers, an island. One runs off with wife of another. They live together, more or less together, for a year; then part. As if in a literary history; a newspaper report. Other people, not us. Never us.

17 September

A decision at last, the truth of the situation; that she and Roy are incompatible, and no amount of moralizing about marriage, no amount of remorse about Anna, could have led to any success. They are both dominated in a sense by concepts, which blind them to facts. E has only recently been able to accept the truth that Anna is perfectly happy without her; and that her sense of 'guilt' about Anna is largely a reluctance to lose her – natural enough, but an impossibly slender basis for a reconciliation with Roy.

I'd arrived, waiting for her, at a state of nervous exhaustion and apprehension which revealed the truth of the matter to me. That it might be difficult to keep her, but it was intolerable to lose her. By the time she got back from Bayswater, on the last tube, I had decided that the worst had happened. Great flood of relief when she finally came, sense of release.

Afterwards, of course, trepidations, financial and temporary; not for any aspect of our relationship, our love. She doesn't fit in anywhere socially, but that is precisely her charm, outside society. She has no sense of time, but nor have I when I can afford to ignore it. She is as variable as April, but uniformity bores. No fault without a compensation, and I am not being Panglossian. Our life has to be integrated somehow into society now. That won't be easy. But I have confidence – too much – in my powers of persuasion; I think I can make her, not what I like, but more in my mould. There are several important reconstructions to be carried out in her character; in mine also, of course.

I have to make the existentialist decision now. To choose, and to fight for the choice. Above all, to concentrate; to write; to tame the flesh and force the mind. One has to discover one's true natural self; and then one has to work out an appropriate approach for it to society; the best way to fit it in. Which I have not yet – this latter – dared to undertake.

22 September
Now it is poverty; no time to be poor, when winter looms close ahead. I have the grasshopper complex: the indolent, futile, good-time, time-frittering grasshopper in the land of arts; worst of all, a thinking grasshopper, knowing the condition to which it is condemned. Normality, for E and I, seems a mirage; it is always just outside our grasp. I have to carry on a sort of semi-criminal existence in this one-person flat; we daren't let it be known that two people live here. That would be the final disaster, to be out in the streets at this juncture. There is difficulty in finding E a job, partly because of her sensitivity, partly because of her lack of drive; we sap each other's energy in some strange way, with regard to the exterior world. I have such a desire to write at the moment, also; yet she is too unsettled to allow me to withdraw. We had a violent quarrel one night which was precisely to do with this; because I had been 'preoccupied' all day, which was true. She felt relegated to the 'whore-housekeeper' role. Our old fault of living much too close together; but she needs a man, of course, far more than most women, knows her dependence and hates it.

She has also this odd inability to deal with time; she looks at a clock-face always as if she hates it. Unfortunately it contaminates me, largely because it is sane and civilized. E calls it 'being too anxious to get on to the next minute to enjoy the present one'; which is perfect, in any other situation but this.

25 September
Going home, really to borrow money. Except that I couldn't bring myself to do it. A great gulf now separates us, since I will not talk of E to them, though they seem to have guessed of the nature of things. I don't know if it is honest to say that it is for them that I keep so sensitive; not wanting them to worry or to suspect all sorts of wrong motives and emotions. Or whether it is not that I don't want to confess my departure from their straight and narrow path, don't want to be bothered by their advice or their reproach. Pride. And also the difficulty of explaining the fact to them, since they could not comprehend the subtleties of modern morality.

E called it the worst kind of pride when I said that I refused money – F actually offered to give me a cheque if I needed it. It is pride in part. But also I know their capacity for worry, to say nothing of all in the past that I shall never repay them for; not being anything like what they wished me to be.

*

There was another quarrel when I got back to Hampstead, since E had read all that's here in my absence; I read a lot out the other day, but she accused me of having 'edited' it. Which was a little, but not so much as she made out, true. The usual hostility, despair, cynicisms, sarcasms, analyses; her disillusionment, disenchantment, 'hollow' of love for me. I was angry at leaving this about; a knife in a nursery. But confident that my love could carry her anger at all the deceptions and her corresponding doubt; quite sure of her, too, that what she was saying was irrelevant to what she felt. I think a truce with personal relationships here; leave them alone for a while; a matter of necessity.

27 September
Blue; lovely blue imperial omphalos; London today; the river keeping its heart clean, running, changing, cleaning, and the buildings like lines of jetsam along the banks; as exciting, as full of possibilities, as tidelines after a storm; healthy, though so many dead things are washed up; beautiful old thriving London, sea salt, hearts of salt, not oak, and the soot and the seagulls. It was the last day of freedom, freedom from work; the new job tomorrow. I met E at Charing Cross, auspiciously in sunlight; she had just got a job. In her sober black dress, and white-black checkerboard shirt. We caught a riverboat from Westminster pier to Greenwich. A revelatory view of London, an apple cut in half; a new foreign wonderland, a trip up the Amazon, quite unexpected; and shaming, that I had not done it before.

13 October
Life in Hampstead. The secretarial college is a seedy, mediocre institution. Two or three Victorian houses; at least with no pretentions; the mere cramming of 16–18-year-old girls who are not intelligent enough to aim higher than a secretarial career. The staff are female, loquacious, a mixture of failures and mice. The atmosphere perfectly uneducational; a pale ghost of a 'common-room' (staff-room, it is called). Factory, office atmosphere; all the teaching is strictly practical. The director is a pale, plump young man who is a town councillor and who goes to Tory conferences.[1] The virtual power is in the hands of the secretary, a somewhat blowsy, powerful kind of woman who is easy to play. I teach small classes of foreign girls – temperamental Greeks, noisy, lively French, silent, aloof

---

[1] John Loveridge, whose family owned St Godric's, was a year older than JF. Deeply involved in Conservative politics, he had stood unsuccessfully as a Member of Parliament for the constituency of Aberavon (1951) and Brixton (1952). He would eventually become a Member for first Hornchurch (1970–74) and then Upminster (1974–83). He was knighted in 1988.

Icelanders, and a mixture of all the other nations, never the English girls. Hate the job; *mais il faut vivre.*

E goes out to work at Gamage's, selling little lead Knights of the Round Table. The MGM film is the centre motif of their Christmas toy department. Long hours, little money.

A day-to-day life, the major unit a week; one cannot think beyond a week. Friday is the climax, payday; we live from paypacket to paypacket. There are various urgent needs; an overcoat for E, a new coat for me; and to satisfy them is as much as we are capable of at the moment.

An additional trouble is that this little cottage flat is for one person, and I have to live a semi-criminal existence in it; fugitive from justice. I have to try and pretend that I am not here when E is out; not go outside, not even stand at the window. A dog's life.

Though Hampstead has its consolations; and when E and I are happy, we usually contrive to be very simply and purely happy; and we know, or I know, that what lies between us is infinitely worth suffering for.

20 October

Time in a swift, dangerous flow; too urgent for writing, here or anywhere else; urgent, but not exciting; urgent and monotonous the life of the city-dweller; and if that was not enough, the effort of 'living in sin'. I feel perfectly settled in E – though even as I write, she is missing and I presume with R – settled in myself, at peace as regards love. My only anxieties are whether she will stay with me and whether she will last out the long, difficult road that must mean; the sheer physical – to say nothing of the psychological – hardship of being a shop assistant at Gamage's. No doubts now that we represent for each other, as regards attraction, the almost perfect partner. We have that, and a multitude of obstacles – both in jobs we hate, poor even then; and she is tormented by guilt still. We are trying to find a better flat, something more spacious than one small room and a single bed. Meanwhile I continue to live here like an escaped prisoner. Cheap flats, in Hampstead, are as rare as swallows in winter.

18 November

There are two kinds of writer: those who have genius for some genre, Molière, Racine, Dostoevsky, Mansfield; and others who have merely a universal mind and find the written word their best means of expression, Gide, Goethe, D. H. Lawrence; mind-writers and genre-writers. And I'm a mind-writer; all the genres interest me. I feel master of none, yet at home in all. And why not present all one's work – if one is a mind-writer (much more occupied with ideas than with words) – as it comes out; in years, or periods of time; short stories, fragments of plays,

poems, essays, notes, criticisms, journals; the aim being a portrait of
the total living artist, not a classified museum. Let the neurologists do
the sorting.

Katherine Mansfield (Alpers).[1] One of E's idols; and a little one of mine.
So much of the Mansfield–Murry story, especially the first three years,
like the life that E and I have lived and lead; the mattresses on the floor,
the continual camping-out, the hunt for the 'perfect' (i.e. cheap, airy,
light, snug, spacious – non-existent) flat. The stress and strain between
the sensitive female and the cerebral male. KM was articulate, of course,
but one can't live near to E and dismiss her silence; the mind bubbles,
ferments; but it's a long way below ground.[2]

22 November
Denys S has decided to go to Indonesia, plus wife, plus child. Foolish,
the current picaresque, the restlessness, the need for change; all part
of the great post-war emancipation of the individual; energy-washing.

23 November
Femininity of Mansfield; descriptions, reactions, moods, relationships –
a world without social or moral values and didacticism; the woman
describing the man's world – clinically, really, if 'clinical' hadn't such
antiseptic, scientific, cold connotations. More of the future than the
man's view; Woolf is the same. Joyce, James, must have had large anima.
It is the man who must have a team; and the female who watches the
match. Personal moral? Feminization of my literary sensibility.

25 November
Why does Plato's account of the death of Socrates always, always, make
me cry? All the four gospels leave me cold and indifferent. It is an
outrage that Jesus of Nazareth gets so much devotion, still; a monument
of human stupidity, a symptom of their psychological imbalance.

---

[1] Antony Alpers, Jonathan Cape, 1954.
[2] Katherine Mansfield met John Middleton Murry in December 1911 when she
contributed a story to *Rhythm*, the literary magazine that he edited. Mansfield,
who was separated from her first husband, invited Murry to become her lodger.
They fell in love and, over the next three years – living in considerable poverty
on the meagre earnings from their literary careers – were constantly on the
move in their search for a place where they felt comfortable and which they
could afford. Strains began to appear in the relationship as Katherine Mansfield
found herself increasingly tired of what Alpers described as Murry's 'oppressive
cerebrality' and longing for a more prosperous and carefree life.

Three plays. *The Death of Socrates*; *The Death of Christ*; *The Life of Robin Hood.*

E. Xanthippe![1]

29 November
Weekend at Oxford, with the Porters. I felt far removed from Oxford, a little disturbed by its muddled grace and its brilliance. But it is a hollow town. The University seems young, offensively callous. On Sunday morning, little groups of earnest young men in dark suits and college scarves – the scarf seems sadly ubiquitous now, though the uniform can surely never be a symbol of freedom of thought – hymn books in hand. An oppressive air of religiosity everywhere, everywhere; and an absurd sign in a shop – 'Buy Dad an Xmas present here' – which tells sufficient about the change in character these last few years.

Dichotomy with the donnish North Oxford world – all cerebrality, scepticism or intellectual Catholicism. The Tolkiens, Faith and Christopher, came around for coffee and discussion; clouds of perfumed talk; style and amusement value; poses, dialectics. A French form of conversation, continental, elegant, though always leaping off into typically British elaborate absurdities. A deliberate misuse of the discoveries of logical positivism; they play on the treachery of words.

They make me feel lumpish, clumsy, an ox in a rococo salon. And the oxen feel them despicable, frivolous, sad. For they have the tragedy of clowns, harlequins, in a way; impotent, hollow men, who have to clown, to parade their post, their style, to quiet their starring egos. Neither the Tolkiens nor the Porters have a happy relationship; they lack something at the centre, some certainty, some warmth, some peasant depth and simplicity which E and I possess. She sat there silent throughout, half dazzled, half disgusted; which I no longer mind, knowing her stillness does run so deep; and amused by the puzzled looks. She has an apprehension of essentials; they a mastery of superficials – danger of the brain. Plato's harmony; but their brains are their tyrants, the heart and the loins oppressed.

Parenthood. The Porters do not punish Catherine; everything is carefully explained. A fundamentally Socratic view of intelligence equalling goodness. But I did not like Podge urinating in front of her; and when she clambered on the banisters, with a twelve foot drop below, I found his nonchalant 'Terribly dangerous, but one has to let them do it' appalling. One does not endanger or shock one's child to impress

---

[1] Xanthippe was Socrates' wife and renowned for her bad temper.

strangers in this house of one's enlightened views on education. A pervasive egocentricity.

The stagnation of being civilized. The need for action; civilization has almost a pejorative sense, that some main artery has become severed.

The writer wants to include the whole world; all the whole world expects of a writer is some new flavour. Greatness is confused with individuality, 'vision' with word-ingenuity. E criticizes a series of short stories I have written recently – contrived, and so on. But the accusation of 'no distinction of style' worries me. I don't like glossy writing – intellectual writing, where everything not pristinely new is a cliché. It's too easy to think up clever similes and metaphors, much too easy. Partly it's the new complexity, the fear of committing oneself to truths of any kind, the pathological contemporary fear of seeming naïf. Which means that the ambiguity pays off – or at worst it's a fair insurance.

But it's an end to a means – when I've time, I'll dress those stories up. And of course that is the function of the new artist – Picasso-like, to *use* all the techniques. Master of all, slave of none.

12 December
Nuit blanche, during which we examined everything, said most of the unforgivable things, and decided nothing. As usual it came at the end of a happy day. E's reiterant theme now is the problem of guidance, purpose – she constantly accuses me of not telling her 'where I'm going, what's the point of all this, of what the hell there is to live by.' Of course, the conditions in which we live are nerve-wracking; this tiny one-room flat, this perpetual lack of money, her work. She accuses me now also of having blighted the relationship (Sally and Sanchia). I can't do anything there – if she chooses to treat all that as blight, then blight it must be.

But the desire for guidance – that is out of her deepest nature. It is what has driven her from man to man, the belief that somewhere is a perfect state of love, somewhere a perfect husband and lover – a Roy with his authority and his noble concepts of love and marriage and a John with his pagan love and his pleasure – both of us in one. But sooner or later she ends any relationship – either she leaves, or she drives her man mad with the nagging. It's hopeless to try and explain or argue with her in such moods – whatever one says is twisted. This mothlike predilection for truth, a glowing, pure truth is terrifying – because it can only end in death and suffering. If I thought it would help I would send her back to R. But Roy's conceptions of human nature are so idealistic, so Catholic, so much dogma and so little actual psychological fact, that a return seems to me to be a sentence of penal servitude – deserved, possibly, but whose only effect would be to add hate to her resentment. Like a hardened criminal, she 'has it in' for life.

Her craving for order: I tell her that there is no order, that one can only get it at the expense of reality, that happiness, in an absurd world, is only possible by self-deception or by what consolation can be drawn from seeing more or less in perspective – i.e. that reality is chaos, and our own value a combination of our recognition of that fact and of our attempts to remedy it. But she, of course, wants a faith, an explanation, a panacea.

17 December

Waiting for her; she has gone to Roy's end-of-term celebrations. I have no right to feel resentful; but I do. It seems to me to be an appalling error, this prolongation, endless, indefinite, between Roy and her. I feel so certain not that their marriage would break a second time but that it would be basically unhappy. And for Roy to wish, and E to consent, that she should pretend she is his wife seems to me to be a masquerade in bad cause. An experiment, she called it. All that is of the twenties. Of course, I am as guilty; but I kept my guilt at a distance. I can excuse her seeing Anna – but to see Roy for a gay evening. How can one lack pride as much as Roy? I find it perverted, suspect illicit pleasure in such a doubtful situation.

I constantly have to accept the possibility of her going; it couldn't be anything less than terrible. But she threatens me with it so often now that I have prepared a sort of emergency set of emotions. I don't know how one would get over the temporary violent pain, except by telling oneself that it would not last for ever. The damage would be to my faith in love, in women; if I ever become permanently objective about them, as I so easily might, then love is not possible.

It's love against society; all the weight of money, convention, peace, order. I am mad to go on struggling.

23 December

Finished the first very rough draft of *The Passenger*. A whole range of plays. Several short stories also, this last month. But time, time, I never have time to revise them.

24 December

Another Christmas apart for E and me. We go to our homes; after that, all flux and uncertainty. She goes for a fortnight to Harrogate; after that, the effort of finding another job. She understandably dreads it. As time goes on, it appears increasingly improbable that we can go on living together; and as improbable that we shall ever be out of love. What an improvident person I am; my complete lack of earning power; of any real desire to earn. No wonder E longs after R's £1,000 a year. But perhaps, in some subterranean way, that is a charm, in this financial world, to be feckless.

I have no pay till Jan 8th – and we have about £10 to last us till then – quite impossible.

2 January 1955

Christmas and the old year gone; a dull, sad Christmas at home, stuffing and drinking; all the hypocrisy of a festival without a true heart; at least, the heart concealed; the old pagan midwinter miracle – that is beautiful, the green heart in the black world. But all the Christian farrago, the hideous Christian resurgence. I sat and vegetated, hurt my liver; missed E terribly, and read Shakespeare – an intense pleasure. Especially *Measure for Measure*, a comedy like a groan, a key work.

5 January

Ten days' adieu to E – she goes to Harrogate for the Toy Fair. I took her down to Swiss Cottage to meet the car taking her there; eight o'clock on a raw, grey day; black coat and geranium cap, unthawed snow. The man who employs her seems pure at heart; but to see her climb into his luxury car and whisked away up the Finchley Road – my inability to try and earn is a pimp. We have never been more in love than during these few days between Christmas and this departure. Heat in the snow, long drowsy hours in bed, passion in sex, like gloves to each other – and then this, sending her away; any sending away of such love is a prostitution.

Walking back up Fitzjohn's Avenue, alone; all grey, cold, thawing, slush and dirty snow; massive, dull oblivious houses, hurrying, oblivious passers-by. An endless ascent, straight, lined by black, bare trees, the houses – as the future, without her, must be.

Empty, hollow without E; can't settle down until I hear from her. The acid test, absence, of the value of love.

A phrase from Hemingway's *To Have and to Have Not*. After Harry dies, Marie says: 'You just go dead inside and everything is easy. You just get dead like most people are most of the time.' And, 'Nobody knows the way you feel, because they don't know what it's all about that way.'

It's true; deep love is like a current; has the two values of the word; both sweeps away, isolates – and lights. And that's how I feel – a broken bulb; fused.

12 January

Sudden telegram from Liz – that she returns tonight, three days before expected. Inrush of anxieties; with her, one is always in the avalanche area. A row with Gee, her employer? A dozen possibilities.

Long letters from her. Very good, many of her letters, and things have seemed to be fairly all right, but how typical of her not to indicate at all what is wrong – or not wrong.

And I was feeling so in love with her. But the trouble always comes, with us, out of the blue skies.

13 January

E came back, and nothing was strange; merely that Gee had decided that there was no more point in her staying in Harrogate. A feeling of warmth, quiet happiness. Two good omens – the day E was due back, a letter offering her a possible job arrived. And now we have found a flat to move into, in the Vale of Health, where Lawrence once lived.[1] Two top floor rooms in a Victorian row, solid and clean, and fine views. We both feel excited. It was snowing when we went down to see it; branches all white with it, and the world muffled. A drink in a pub near the pond, and a jazz band improbably practising next door.

25 January

Moved, to the top floor of a Victorian house in the Vale of Health. It has views, over the pond at the back; over a little square to the front and up the hill to Jack Straw's Castle. At night, a deep-sea world up there – eel-buses, unknown fish, winking of orange crossing-beacons. Tracery of black branches against grey skies; the sun hasn't shone, in any sense, since we arrived. Gulls on the frozen pond; it's an old, clean but frosty house; two old country-spinster landladies; hopelessly ugly furniture, wallpaper, carpets, lino, which all drown E in misery, quite apart from the – for us – new situation of she having to do the pretending – I not the lover in secret. Many doubts about the future, Anna; the move could not have been more miserable. It was quite devoid of any of the excitement of new rooms to inhabit. At the best E is unadaptable; and this was too much. So we are still half camping out, with only the essentials unpacked, as if this is only a temporary waiting-room. Gypsies.

Of course, I like it – the space, the green, the height over the ground. I don't think I'd mind even an *oubliette*, if it had a view.

Cocteau season at the Everyman; a very rococo personage. He has the ambivalent talent of the eighteenth century; touches everything with grace, and infects it with superficiality. Not sincere; a lively brain without a centre. But *L'Eternel retour* is a very good film; inimitable, and very moving.[2] But perhaps it is *Tristan and Iseult*, the love story; in art, a *retour* can eternally be made to it. And having lived with, living with Iseult in the forest . . .

---

[1] During 1915 Lawrence lived at 1 Byron Villas.
[2] Made by Jean Cocteau in 1943 in collaboration with the director Jean Delannoy, *L'Eternel retour* was a modern reworking of the Tristan and Iseult story. See note on page 337.

27 January

E; her paucity of vocabulary; she doesn't talk about seagulls, but about 'white things'. She says, 'A brown pheasant sits in the tree and looks at me.' And a dream of hers, that she was trying to put shillings, at Mount Grove Cottage, into a gas-meter. How I came to help her, looked at the meter, then at the shillings, and said: 'It's not them, Elizabeth. It's you.' Comic, or significant?

There were ducks wheeling round the pond this morning; and tufted duck diving; ghost flocks of gulls. And quacking of mallard drakes in the night; owl-cries. This must be the strangest little oasis within the whole of London proper; right that D. H. Lawrence should have lived here.

1 February

Another of the violent stormy periods. We argued all of Friday night. Thursday had been all love, but on Friday morning E came on the letters from Sanchia, turned up forty minutes late for lunch with me, and then everything deteriorated; arguments and tension. She wouldn't get up the next morning, so I went to ring up Roy and met him for lunch. Six pints of beer for him. We both agreed on all E's faults; both said we were profoundly in love with her. But whereas I went to meet him prepared to make the great sacrifice, I came away more than ever resolved not to make it. There is something in R so ineffably self-centred that one cannot not oppose him. E says he is a gigantic person, in faults as in virtues; but I cannot believe that any person so muddled and limited in his views will ever be gigantic. Of course, he has a Svengalic fascination for her; and he is in black and white, where the rest are in grey. What he believes and disbelieves, he does absolutely. That in art is permissible – since everything in art is permissible – but in morality, and in personal relationships, one cannot be piebald without being a social and personal menace. All my being revolts against that dichotomy in Roy – that supreme aura of certainty, of his own rightness and everyone else's wrongness, which is the great psychological spine of Catholicism; and that Nordic impulsiveness, supposed violence, great dark twisted mass of unexamined ego. Men like Roy will not act on self-analysis; they will not relate themselves to the outer world; they will not admit, since to admit is to humble the ego, that there are values outside their philosophy.

R and I argued about physical love – animal lust, as he calls it. He refuses to give it any importance in a personal relationship; and there we parted at complete loggerheads. I came back to Hampstead desperately afraid that E might have gone; but we found ourselves flung together as violently as ever before.

*

DHL, *The White Peacock*; the writing is at times as naïf as a schoolboy's; patches of brilliance, of course. But the miracle – even when the writing is most naïf, the characters seem real. One doesn't think of the charcters as unreally naïf; they are real characters described naïvely.

Gide, *Thesée*. A great novel; Gide is the only Theseus – the bluff, iconoclastic, free-thinking.[1] The unknown, a ritualistic world. The Individual destroying a religious society. Destroyer of religious society. Destroyer of civilization, therefore the most civilized.

7 February
Contact with Gide; I've never made it before. Yet feel a great twinness with him, a sympathy, now.

12 February
Miss Skinner, the landlady here; a master of the kind. Anus-dominated; she has a pathological hate of dirt. She has already doubted – justly, of course – whether we were married; called us Bo'emians; and this morning came up and expressed her horror at the mess we lived in. Nine milk-bottles, she said it was one day last week, and the bed unmade all day. It's true, we live Irish; but not dirty. I felt I ought to get angry; but she was such a perfect specimen of prejudiced ignorance that it almost pleased me to hear her 'carry on'. 'You've no right to put pictures on the walls,' she said. 'I don't like it. That' – pointing to a Greek vase-painting copy, with the Minotaur showing a neat penis – 'filthy I call it.'

'You'd never find any place like this,' she said. One could as well explain French irregular verbs to a toad as attempt to justify oneself with such monolithic guardians of public morality.

13 February
Another upheaval, spasm in our life; we decided to leave here. E had an evening with R, with the usual positive-negative effect. All that such meetings achieve is an awareness that she is on a tightrope, a frontier between two hostile countries. We went to see a new flat on Saturday; took it. It's expensive, but pleasant, and the landpeople are civilized after the ogress above whom we live now. On Sunday, great debate; E said she could never divorce R. But the day ended by our taking tea with the new landpeople and giving notice here. Monday was all loss

---

[1] In *Thesée*, Gide's last novel, Theseus defeats the minotaur, falls in love with Ariadne, the daughter of King Minos, only to abandon her at Naxos. He then founds Athens, where he settles to look forward to a contented old age. He is depicted as the ultimate 'free man', an individual who has managed to free himself from the shackles of the past, guilt and regret.

and disaster; E's new job, in a basement, depresses her violently; futility, centrelessness, and our poverty, our desperate economy of leaping from payday to payday, with a sense of raging torrent below. Her old questions: Where are we going? What does it all mean? And when I give no answer: You're hopeless. You're negative. You don't *help* me. Guidance, she craves guidance. Sometimes I feel that any charlatan philosophy, any diversion, as long as it sounded convincing, would satisfy her. But I am clear on the main outlines of this situation: I shall write; that is the essential. I love her, and she loves me. I don't believe she will ever be happy with R. Therefore she has to accompany me on my destiny. She can't hesitate much longer; and I can't go on climbing my mountain with her on my back; by my side, with me, yes, always; but not both her *and* the mountain. It's not possible.

22 February
So many ideas for plays in my head – I could write for ten years. And no time, never any time.

Sacrifice: I sometimes feel I could sacrifice E to writing. But I don't believe that would *ever* be a simple case of writing seeming more important than the woman; but merely that to sacrifice the woman would consecrate the writing. Which is not morally admissible; any more than I would take aphrodisiacs the better to love.

The new flat (55 Frognal) suits us better. More comforts, privacy, a much pleasanter atmosphere. But things between us still uneasy, unsettled; I can sense in E a boredom, a lack of interest. She is not getting enough out of us; 'a wider life', 'stimulation', 'hollow relationship' – they always come up when we quarrel. Of course, it is basically her own inner emptiness; lack of self-confidence, creativity, a rich imaginitive life. There was never a woman less self-sufficient psychologically. And she is so pathetically ill at ease in any company, because of her lack of education, of *savoir faire*. She can't pass off anything, can't stand up on her own with strangers of our own class and type. She is classless, but without the ability or the audacity of classlessness. She sat in Roy's shade, which finally drove her out in the sun; but now she hankers to go back. The terms change; his shade was sunshine, and the sun she's in is cold, is shade.

25 February
I'm typing out a play: *The Passenger*. The five pages of which E read and hated violently; worthless, cheap, nauseating, she used all her adjectives. I was as shocked as she was; and lived in a sort of unhappy tension all the evening, Denys S being here. I think she may be right – not in the

violence of her reaction, but about the cheapness of the writing. Am tormented by doubts – style, any kind of style, eludes me. Am I floundering after the unattainable? And is literature perhaps only a means, not an end, worse still, a cul-de-sac for me? I feel so inarticulate sometimes; as if all this writing, painting, suffering were only a blind groping on my part, where others, so many others, can see. There is all hell for me in such doubts; I can perceive the urge to self-fulfilment, self-discovery, suddenly, not as a *raison d'être*, but a cancer.

(Later): But a feeling of catharsis; of being pruned; sap rushing out into better shoots. Of the important thing; not the badness, ugliness, of the present foliage, but the force, the blood-pressure of the sap.

17 April
Age; an ominous one, the twenty-ninth birthday. The sands of my twenties slipping out, and still nothing done, nothing solved, no hope of relaxation. I am rewriting the Greek book, and I at last believe that some of it is worth printing. But it lacks polish, it divagates, repeats itself; the mind resists specialization, yet to make oneself heard one must be special. There's no glory left in mere generality of temperament.

The Turkish job has fallen through. Not that I greatly mind. It is another door closed; I am forced to continue the struggle with myself. And I am certain that that is what matters: self-conquest, self-discovery.

Also E decided, on April 2nd, to go back to R at the end of this month – at the end because he didn't want to interrupt a holiday in Scotland, and because he said he couldn't, with his £1,000 a year pittance, afford to take her till next month. So I am reduced to the role of hotel-keeper; I find it all disgusting in a way – on the other hand, E requires that I should not complain. There are occasional outbursts, but I know at heart she is not unhappy. She is living again on the brink of tragedy, and I am, at her going, in love with her. I don't doubt that she will go to R. She doesn't love him, but she doesn't know what love is. I try and dissuade her, of course; but there is too much what she wants. To break up my life, send me raving sad. I believe now that there is, comparatively, a bond between us of the more deep and indestructible kind – a duality, a twinness which makes me dread the thought of any other relationship. That, after this, could only be formal, the shadow of our closeness, our living in and through each other.

6 May
Unhappy times; Denys has been here for several days, prior to his departure to Indonesia; a sense of his going – not particularly any loss, but a dissociation of physical presence; his going and E threatening to go. Blindly, desperately determined that she must go. It saddens me, this

falling apart, this air of separation between us; as if it is necessary to destroy our love in order to forget we ever possessed it. E is moody, temperamental, looking for any chink in our relationship, trying with a fixed and blind wilfulness to find some escape from love. Goading me also to try and retain her – that I should show her how high I value her.

She is a morbid, spiteful creature at times nowadays; quite unable to reconcile herself to any decision, an involvement of loss. And so critical – so pathologically critical of any attempts I make to be objective. 'Roy's so objective,' she said, 'he's in love with me, but he remains objective.' I try to explain that love and objectivity are incompatibles. But she is so hoplessly blind still where R is concerned – and of course, that braggadocio, that easy air of self-confidence, that dogmatism, are all winning to a woman; they are qualities which require full abandonment. E wants to be able to forget herself – but only at times; and that she should suppose she can do it through R is her own pathetic fallacy.

I have moments of struggle – anxious to control, to fight for her, as R is fighting. For a conviction of inner rightness – Denys agrees that R's basic drive is domination. Any other man but he would in the normal circumstances – for E is as cold as ice to him – refuse to humble himself so far. E believes it is a disinterested love of her that makes him so persistent. But he desperately needs to recover her for his own peace of mind.

I find horrible in E, too, the evidences of her two-year cycle – a fascination for the new man, the new lover. I feel ashamed that I can't conquer that; alarmed that there's not enough pride in her to make her fear its recurrence.

But I'm convinced that it is love not to force her to stay, since one cannot force love. E loves force and respects it; but I've felt at times she was growing out of that primitive sense of mind. Now I feel I was wrong. I hide many things from her; ambitions which are certainties. I have stopped any attempts at publishing anything. As if I wanted her to decide for me at my worst, to take me at the lowest valuation, and not because, as she so desperately wants, I am worth marrying, marriageable. I may lose my resolution, and call her bluff; I suppose I'd get some moral satisfaction in being the dynamiter and not the dynamited.

The other aspect of this is literary; that reduction of all emotion to the rank of experience; that almost joyous love of experiment, suffering, because it all tempers, forges the blade. Even E – writing (increasingly I think of it more as thinking; so much of writing is no more than the description of superficials, authoricism instead of ethicism) is my first mistress. Even all this; with E, when she accuses me, rightly, of not caring, I can only shrug. I can't tell her it's all literature, literature all the time, that I analyse, savour, store. Even her going is valuable, to be welcomed. I think she often feels that I am not, by her notions, literary enough;

and I don't disillusion her. Is it compensation? To lack the energy, the will to enter into communion, and so to overvalue the externality of one's attitude. Buddhism – I find many useful definitions there, names. Though even names disinterest me now – the great generalizing element in me is growing, growing, and all the details, the humans, the things, the faces, the names, go to the wall.

19 May

E has told R to go ahead with a divorce; but I shall not believe in it till the commissioner pronounces it. With her, a decision is only taken when it has a loophole; and I am sure she now thinks that she will, in any case, be able to stop any proceedings which may be in progress.

20 June

Once I used to try and prevent myself from writing here; now it's the opposite. I excuse my laziness, and call it literary economy – an old, familiar process. But life isn't stimulating at this point – inward, not outward. The details are unimportant. The Greek book is finally publishable now; E seems mine now, for better or for worse; we are very poor; live from week to week, with no prospects of clothes, holidays, a home. But I feel confident. I *will* be a writer; and the best of my age, when I'm done.

More violence with E, and all is in the balance again. It is mainly over Anna, guilt and shame and confusion and that typical profound and perverse will to continue the condition. She is hopelessly stagnant in such situations, and I have got to the state where I despair of ever getting to happiness with her. It is as if she has some cancer of the mind that flares up at fixed intervals, and which has to destroy before it is satiated. She makes no effort to find out how Anna is, because it is 'against the core of her being' to ring up Mollie Lohr.[1] When I call that pride, she screams. But she is consumed with self-pride; self-shame especially, which she refuses to see as an inverted pride. She calls herself sensitive, but she is it only to her feelings; no external sensitivity. Only a madman would keep on with her in these states – in them, she seems to plunge out of control, into a chaos of clouds and darkness and all one can do is follow her through all the maze till time brings her level again.

An odd, affected girl who works at Heal's with E – so affected that it was like a caricature. She said of Rhodesia, 'Of course, the lions and snakes there aren't quite the same as in the Union.' As if, dreadful creatures, they had not been educated at quite the right schools.

---

[1] Mollie Lohr, was the wife of Roy's religious mentor, Frederick Lohr. Roy had given Anna to her to look after.

Recorder; the pleasant hours I waste with it. I transcribe pieces from the Fitwilliam Virginal Book.[1] Farnaby, Byrd, Dowland, those are the great discoveries for me – Farnaby for his quaintness, Dowland for his sadness, Byrd for his greatness. Piquant Farnaby, bitter Dowland and everything Byrd.[2]

25 June

I've now created a life-current for myself – a philosophical stream in which I can live; a frame, a system of measurement; a base. The self. It's what I've always been striving after; for in England, being English, public schoolboy, ex-officer, Christian, Oxford, the barriers one has to tear down to achieve a belief in self! Everything here is against it. I think that's why I love E. There are a thousand things she is not, which other women are, but she is *unique*, pure perfect self, unparalleled.

Midsummer's night. I believe it has more significance for me than all the other holidays of the year – a deep power of making aware. The four great festivals of the year should be midwinter day, for death; spring, for life in death; midsummer's day, for life; autumn, death in life.

6 July

Dull, life; the old midsummer blues. Spectre of poverty. E and I struggle through each week, earning just enough between us to live from Friday to Friday. We make about £13 between us; £5 for rent and the other £8 evaporates like dew on a hot day. Endless prospect of no holidays, no luxuries; no divorce, no release; no freedom. Love – that's strong. We're certain of that. And she looks more beautiful than ever, and I need her more than ever, and she is as distracting as ever. I can only work on my own, in my own silence; not hers, other people's. I seethe with irritation over the time wasted on domestic things – cooking, cleaning, washing-up, bed-making. At the work I have to do at the college – the futile teaching, lecturing, fiddling; correcting the grammar of pseudomorons, future shopgirls, typists, female riff-raff; typing away at the Greek book at the fag-ends of

---

[1] The largest manuscript collection of English keyboard music surviving from the sixteenth and seventeenth centuries, transcribed by Francis Tregian (c.1574–1619) while he was in the Fleet prison for recusancy. Among the chief composers are William Byrd, John Bull and Giles Farnaby.

[2] Giles Farnaby (1563–1640) composed madrigals, settings for psalms and many keyboard pieces. William Byrd (1540–1623) was both a composer and a music publisher. Although he was prosecuted several times as a Catholic recusant, he wrote music for both the Anglican and Catholic services, as well as madrigals and songs for strings. A lutenist and composer, John Dowland (1563–1626) is regarded as perhaps the greatest composer of lute music and lute songs.

days. But worst of all is the stupidity. I work surrounded with it, in it, of it
finally; have to tolerate it. Sometimes I think I only want to have a book
published in order to be rude, to cut this present into little shreds and
ribbons and scatter it into oblivion. Above all, of course, to justify it. That
is always why one goes to the top; to pay for the ascent already made.

1 August

Nuit blanche after a warm weekend; it is now as predictable as the swing
of a pendulum. About bedtime she read Hemingway's story 'Hills like
Elephants', applied it to our own relationship, and then spent the whole
night in a string of neurotic accusations and self-accusations – the most
purely neurotic I have ever seen with E.[1] Her behaviour is becoming
alarmingly schizophrenic – her sweetness and warmth (what she called
later 'living without thinking') in the morning are at a vast extreme
from the mulishness and bitterness of the evening.

The main problem is her sense of guilt over Anna – this turns all
pleasure in our relationship very swiftly sour. We don't make love. We
fiddle while Rome burns. It rattles about inside the hull of her mind,
this guilt, like a piece of heavy machinery. Of course it must be lashed
down, or it will sink her. This lashing-down – what I call accepting one's
guilt, incorporating one's past evil in one's present self – she terms 'moral
aerobics'. The only real attitude for her is to have the guilt ever-fresh,
to suffer it and resuffer it. I can't get her to see it clinically; that one has
to disinfect and allow a wound to heal. She says that because of what we
have done, our relationship is doomed; its centre will always be rotten.
I find it difficult to treat such primitive Catholic mumbo-jumbo seriously;
but I have to realize that she believes profoundly that we cannot control
the effects of past actions. When she moans and moans about the rotten
centre, I hate her for her great, stupid deadweight of repressed humanity;
who won't fight the good fight, but surrenders to circumstance. It's not
a religious position; religious people (and doctrines) allow that a sin can
be expiated – present good actions can conquer past evil ones. It is a
psychological one – Puritan, only bogusly religious.

E is incapable of seeing life in humanist terms of expediencies,
compromises, golden means; she has to have violent disciplines and
indisciplines. She is always saying now that she has no authority to
guide her; that R was the only authority she ever had and I have failed
her by not replacing him. My usual defence (it is all as familiar as two
old friends playing chess) is that until she comes to me (that is, stops

---

[1] In 'Hills like Elephants' a man tries to persuade his girfriend to have an abortion. The conversation marks a breakdown in trust and communication between
the couple. The girl knows that their relationship can never be the same again,
in spite of the man's repeated assurances to the contrary.

threatening to return to Roy), until she is as dependent emotionally on me as I am on her, I have no hold on her. A secondary defence is the psychiatric one; that since I am part of her neurosis, it is impossible for me to cure it.

5 September
Waiting to hear about the Greek book; it's dreadful, this gap between the final private creation and the outer public response. I fear the worst. Which would *not* be that they had lost the manuscript.

7 September
I waste too much time recorder-playing; Serbian dances, Couperin, the Elizabethans. I can play quite fast now, and can manage more of the trills, mordents and other arabesques. But music eludes me; I know more and more what it sounds like, but its inner structure is a mystery to me. Scales, intervals, harmonies, all Greek. At the moment, I can't write; I divagate, get lost two ways wherever I start. Grim periods; akin to constipation.

Once again E and I are on the thinnest ice financially. We have had to get through this week on thirty shillings – she was not paid for her week's holiday – and that's nothing these days. St Godric's, the dull, easy routine, has me in its grip; faint perfume of many nationalities, continual self-disgust.

I'm getting fat; everyone's worried. E and M are worried. I have a paunch. I feel fat. A fat Roman senator. Can't imagine myself as a fat man.

Sunday. Violent squall with E; one of her intolerable plunges into depression, when she pulls all the world down with her. It started because she wanted to see Anna, but refused to ring up R to see if that was possible. One of her attacks on poverty – which she calls Bohemianism – and our manner of life. Nothing so violently bourgeois as her longing for good clothes, a nice home. Very ugly. She becomes more and more perverse and spiteful in such moods; disintegrating; self-recriminatory, self-immolating.

I learn all about love–hate; the nature of emotion; the conflict of love and knowledge – the better I know this periodic plunge of E's, the more difficult I find it to forgive or love her. She teaches me humanity.

But later, in a pub, she said in her loose, spiteful way, 'We may as well part.' And I walked out, saying, 'Carry on.' Pointless words, pointless actions. I am torn and disturbed now. Wait in the dark room for her footsteps. The violence of love. All violence.

She came back half drunk and half sham-drunk; more violence, vileness; a terrible hollow flippancy, wild insults. She tries to destroy the whole male principle in me. I become purely clinical. Then in the end we came to the heart of the matter. 'You don't know,' she said, 'what it's like to wake up hating yourself and not knowing how to get through the day with that hate. You're noble and perfect, you prig! you . . .' etc. Very true. I have never woken like that. I've never been able to *loathe* myself.

There's more in my superego than mere conscience. I disapprove of myself, but I never cease to interest myself. I examine myself closely, but I never blame myself. Perhaps it is because all my sins have been willed, and rarely or never impulsive. They have been passed by the board of censors, so to speak, before becoming public. My superego is an admiring, indulgent censor. E's is harsh and tyrannical.

Or perhaps it is that the voice of my censor is muffled in a cloud. Love is intestinal; it needs a purge. We get constipated with loving; hating flushes out the insults, the rancour, the waste.

9 September

Feuillère. It puzzles me, all to do with her role in *La Dame aux Camélias*. The next day E and I went and saw a film with Caron and Astaire. A patently trivial film. Yet it raised far more emotion in me than all Feuillère's great art.[1]

Why does the cinema move easily? Size of figures on screen. Looking up, not down. Inescapability of screen. Also the sudden power to change subject or the angle; so that one's attention can't stray. Also the absence of the actor from the role; the vast importance of present eye – present actor, present eye – past actor. The past performance hamstrings criticism by its pastness. One plunges, in a film, into a past dream-scream. In a play, it is always a present participation. One is never completely *on* the stage as one is *in* the screen. One's emotions are, in this age, both suppressed and repressed. Therefore the 'past dream-scream' quality of the cinema is more conducive to the outcropping of emotion.

Other points – the cinema close-up. Far more moving and far more revealing. On stage, guess at tears; on screen, see tears. Also, on stage, gestures will away the curtain; but on screen, the actor has got to do much more realistically. The camera-eye means that the cinema actor must be realistic, since a film cannot be anything but uneasily fantastic. All great actors have managed to convey personality. This corrupts our requirements of what a stage actor must be like. We demand cinematic reality and personality. The kind of gesture which was once needed to 'carry' to the back of the theatre, the cinema has now made too

---

[1] Edwige Feuillère (1907–98) was a leading actress of French stage and screen. After her successful appearance as Marguerite Gautier in *La Dame aux Camélias* at the Edinburgh Festival, the play was transferred to the Duke of York's Theatre in London, where JF and Elizabeth would have seen it. The Astaire and Caron film that they saw the next day was *Daddy Long Legs*.

'theatrical'. Many of our film actors overact to a disconcerting degree.

Not simply realism, but a *real* style for the play. In the realistic play not real enough. Emotion must be real.

24 September

Another violent quarrel with E; an old one. I saying I won't make any attempt to get a better job till she finally decides to stay with me; she saying that she will not decide until I have a good job. She was hysterically angry because I hadn't applied for a job in Brussels. The final date for application was yesterday. So I typed it off this morning, and took it down to Belgrave Square by hand. Although she chose many of the wrong reasons for getting angry she was right. The misery of this poverty-conditioned existence can't go on.

Scarron. I bought a little 1668 edition of his plays for five pence at Norman's. Odd the mixture of seventeenth-century nicety and sixteenth coarseness. Vigour of *Jodelet.* Some good lines.[1] Odd the pleasure of old books, old things. I have a craving for it nowadays. The shoddy instability of the present? Or the importance of time?

6 October

This diary has suffered these last two years. It no longer – it seems to me – adequately reflects either my physical or my mental life. It does all – this period – seem something of a desert, in any case. I lack no confidence that the desert will end. I can think, I can write; I know that. But waiting-rooms are always dull.

Writing: the Greek book has been criticized by the agent's reader – he calls it 'shapeless, discursive'; but Paul Scott thinks it worth a trial with the publishers. I have just finished an opuscule – 'For a Casebook' – which I intend to try on the *London Magazine* and *Encounter.*[2]

Meanwhile, this:; I've decided to keep, for a month, a ritual day-to-day account of events; what's interesting me; what we do.

7 October

E's thirtieth birthday. I had no money to buy her a present for the

---

[1] Paul Scarron (1610–60), a poet, satirist and dramatist, whose comedies anticipated the style of Molière. Most well known of these was *Jodelet, ou le maître valet* (1645).

[2] Although it was rejected by *Encounter* and the *London Magazine,* 'For a Casebook' was one of JF's few short stories from this period to be preserved. It tells the story of a man who spies on a struggling young writer and his lover, composing letters to the writer which he never sends. His sense of inadequacy eventually drives him to suicide.

morning; but it was understood that I was to buy her some shoes when I had my Friday pay packet. I met her after work; she was wearing a new pale blue crochet-work dress, very elegant. She was excited, too excited; the evening was an anti-climax. We went to Schmidt's in Soho and had Jager schnitzel, then to the Festival Hall to hear a concert – trite except for Shostakovich's fifth.

On Fridays I always have lunch with Fletcher, a fellow-teacher, in the Guinness pub in Hampstead. A small concession to normality. His hair is very sparse. What there is of it springs lightly up off his pate.

8 October

Saturday. In the morning I typed out the 'Casebook', did a little shopping. E came back at two; we had lunch. But I discovered that she had arranged to see R and Anna at four. Some tension; I don't mind her seeing Anna. But evenings with R I find messy. However, she came back and met me in the G pub at 7.30. She had just seen an address on a tobacconist's board (we want a cheaper, warmer flat, and tobacconists' boards are the unofficial estate agencies for London furnished rooms) and I went off to telephone about it. We went to see it. But it was no good. Too small, and the woman who owned the house – a daytime nursery school – too unhappy. Back home, we had a bath together, a little domestic pleasure, faint sexuality, we both enjoy.

9 October

Lie in bed, of course. Sunday lunch. E recently bought a beautiful oblong casserole of blue stoneware, and in it we make rich stews of meat, red peppers, tomatoes, onions, bay, garlic, black peppercorns; hot, complex and satisfying. Love in the afternoon; still as fresh as when we began; sleep. I woke up in a warm grey dusk; the first faint ray of light from the streetlamp slanting the ceiling. E's naked body hot against mine; heat, nakedness, contentedness; love has a simple syndrome. Then we listen to *Journey into Space*, an absurd but absorbing radio serial of war between Mars and Earth; rockets and risks every thirty seconds. Now E irons, and I write this.

10 October

Monday always melancholy. I work from 9.15–10. From 10 to 11, I shop, every day. I don't dislike shopping, but hate the routine of having to choose what to buy. There are certain shops I always go to. I always buy my papers here, and my cigarettes there; all fruit and vegetables from a little shop in Perrins Walk; bread from the baker's opposite Church Row. Exotic cheeses and garlic sausage from a little delicatessen opposite Perrins Walk. As small and familiar a shopping area as a village. Then 11–1 teaching again. From 9.15 to 10 I teach the English girls the rudiments of their own language

– all the stupid, pretty ones (the two adjectives seem to go together). From 11–12 it is a class of good (advanced) beginners – a French girl, a Czech, a Swede, a Cypriot, a Norwegian, a Turk, a Greek, an Italian. They fit in well, all eager, moderately intelligent. Oh, at 11 the tea-break: Miss Robinson with her long mane of red hair over her haggard face, Fletcher always pressing services on one – cups of tea, cigarettes. I always accept now. It used to annoy me. But now I find it kinder to us both to accept. His hobby is giving; with him, I make mine accepting.

Today I had a free afternoon. I typed away at the play; some of it goes, some doesn't. I have to pace up and down citing it. There's too much machinery; mere plot structure. But it is becoming something. Though I have prose, it slips away as soon as it's down. Really with prose one needs long and elaborate stage directions before any phrase; in poetry, the directions are in the verse, the enjambments, the stress.

In the evening – nothing. We listened to *The Great Gatsby* on the wireless. As strangely perfect as ever. Then lay in bed, warm; small children; slept heavily.

11 October
Tuesday. The same. Tell one, tell all.

In the afternoon I ran additionally a Greek translation class. The night is *Goon Show* night. An absurd radio comic programme; it's mad, quick, inconsequential. It feels contemporary. This is modern humour. Other radio shows an old-fashioned humour. We laugh at them, but out of habit. This is our humour.

12 October
Wednesday: same programme; French instead of Greek translation.

At four I was to meet E down by the Playhouse cinema. We had tea in one of the countless new espresso bars. China tea. A strangely 1890 serving-girl – red-haired, white face, free-figured, kohled eyes.

A good film – *East of Eden*; rather, a fairish film, brilliantly acted. Julie Harris and James Dean. How far above all English film-acting! Partly the old class trouble; all acting in England is hampered by the public archetype – the middle-class accent and code – which is the audience's standard for home judgement. How to break him down?

The film also annoyed us because it ended in a welter of sentiment; curiously it was quite logical and lifelike. Strange, how unsatisfying a happy ending is; how we crave eternal bitterness and destruction. E called it simply 'inartistic'; I'm afraid the reasons are much deeper, much more self-revealing.

13 October
To the dentist in the afternoon. He is on his best dentistical behaviour with me. Books from the library – Tallis keyboard pieces, Tudor England history, Spender's poems.

14 October
Friday. I teach all day, on psychology, the cinema; drink with Fletcher at lunchtime; a heavy, fuddled afternoon. E and I – I always meet her on a Friday – me in a bad mood, failed to agree on what to do. We had to drink to smooth things over. Beer and wine boredom. I need her and I need time, time, time, to read and write. I loathe wasted time.

15 October
Saturday. One in four E gets as a holiday – so we lay in bed and loved; our love-making is, for me and I think for her, now as wholesome and continuously, enigmatically fresh as bread. I don't feel bored with her, ever. I wonder if it isn't that one begins to realize that sex is so fundamentally egocentric a process. It only needs two things; sensual pleasure, of course, and love-pleasure – the sensation of being loved (i.e. causing pleasure). It is something which is easy to obtain; it doesn't require constant titillation, novelty. It merely requires to be considered as a natural function; and only secondarily a psychological one. I find E easily melts, in bed, into Woman, the female principle, and I equally into Man. I still like looking at pretty women; but I feel *absolutely* no desire to get to know their bodies. I can love on an archetypal level with E; other personal temptations are all included in it.

We shopped in the morning; went to the launderette. I still have to steel myself to go in it – so much snobbishness I still have – and fear to be seen by my pupils. Went to the Library – Martial[1] – in the evening. Listened to a play on the BBC, *The Watch on the Rhine*.[2] And then we had a row. E furious about the lack of commitment (i.e. mine and hers) compared to the political theories. I argued that what mattered then was the attitude of the individual to society, and now it is the attitude of the individual to himself. Bitterness and hate; I ride these storms now, admit wrongness in me, try and shame her into peace and proportion. Her main accusation last night was concerning my lack of seriousness

---

[1] The Roman poet Marcus Valerius Martialis (c.40–c.104), who in twelve books of epigrams offered a witty, candid and often biting social commentary on contemporary Roman life.

[2] A radio version of Lillian Hellman's 1941 play about an American family who wake up to the dangers of neutrality when their daughter returns from Europe married to a German opponent of the Nazi regime.

with her. It is true; I don't talk seriously with her about moral problems. Only *my* morality and *my* philosophy.

16 October

Sunday. Somewhat weary day – she is cross, nagging, dour. We had a carne con chilli stew, (read the *S Times* and *Observer*), having walked up to J. Staw's Castle and back by way of *apéritif* – a cold blue day, bright and cutting. I had writing neurosis – desire to write, but inability to settle down to it.

In the evening a good film of Huston's – *The Red Badge of Courage*[1] – and Raimu in *César*.[2] A dear old sweet film. The former gave a powerful impression of the atmosphere of a mid-nineteenth-century battlefield. The problem of fear: more and more I feel certain I shall not fight if there is another war. The punishing cruelty of it. I am sure I am a total coward. I could take a risk on my own, but fall at the spin of a wheel or a distant general's command . . . I feel certain also than I can best serve mankind by living, not dying. Martyrdom, yes; but not an atom of massacre.

The dreadful heresy of the nobility of battle – war as the great testing-ground of manhood. Bravery, gambling with death; after he has gambled with death, the boy is a man. When will it all be seen for what it is? As primitive as the most primitive initiation ceremony?

E's demand, too, of last night – that one must be committed – that's the soul of war in each person. That it's good to be committed, that it's good to be 'tempered' in risk – humanity is despair.

17 October

Monday always blue; cold, icy blue. It rained, which is always miserable. The rain seeps up through my one pair of shoes and I huddle along in my torn plastic mackintosh. I am immersed in Martial at the moment, as fresh and real and full-flavoured as Villon;[3] an intensely human character. His eye, bitter and denigratory, is of this age. He is alive today.

In the evening we rearranged the kitchen furniture; in cold weather, the big room is uninhabitable.

---

[1] Adapted from Stephen Crane's novel about a young recruit's first experience of battle during the American Civil War.

[2] Directed by Marcel Pagnol in 1936 and starring Raimu as César, the patron of the Bar de la Marine at the Vieux Port, Marseilles, this was the third film in Marcel Pagnol's *Marius* trilogy.

[3] See note on page 32.

18 October
Reading *The Rock Pool*.[1] Curious that such an exceptional arbiter as Connolly doesn't write immaculately well; no one could doubt his sincerity. But the result is overcrowded, Byzantine, when the aim is obviously classical Greek. Also it isn't quite a true story; a brilliant picture of a might-have-been; everything is a world where all is for the worse.

19 October
E. out in the evening; so I reread the first act of the *Y Man*. It begins to be something.

20 October
Rain all day; I have only one pair of rain-proof shoes, old, good ones I bought at Poitiers. And no raincoat.

Martial again in the evening; under his spell. The subtlety of the seventeenth century, the cynicism of the twentieth century, but the excoriating hate and bitterness are always fresh. Every city needs the lash of Martial. Love at night; as fresh as an orchard. I'm not sure – isn't it really the basic harmony?

21 October
The spell of words. I can interest them, but the girl of eighteen is the most introverted creature in nature.

To the cinema with E; a windy, wet night. When it is doubly good to be in bed.

22 October
Saturday; the play. The second attack goes slowly. I have to act it all; get lost in dreams, side-lanes. Shopping, and a late lunch; the usual routine when E works on Saturday. Then in the evening we had Sheila Lea and the Ardaghs in; a tense, rather unhappy couple. She seems to suffer: fastidious and ill-matched. He works on *The Times*. Loud-voiced and opinionated. They goggled a little at Sheila; she told her funny story about E. Raymond – who lives in the flat below – how he came up one evening and asked her to stop her cat from walking over the floor – one-inch carpet – as the noise hindered his concentration.

---

[1] *The Rock Pool* (1936) was the only novel of Cyril Connolly, the founding editor with Steven Spender of the literary magazine *Horizon*. It tells the adventures of a literary young man from Oxford who spends the summer in an artistic colony of expatriates on the French Riviera. He has come to study the community dispassionately as though he were a naturalist observing the life of a rock pool, but he soon finds himself pulled down into their world.

I felt a bit tired by it all. Mulled cider and dull conversation; but then I find almost all conversation dull.

23 October

Sunday. Work a little at play; read Sunday papers; see another film. *The Deep Blue Sea.* We thought Vivien Leigh best and all the rest miscast. But everyone else thinks exactly the opposite.

24 October

Monday. In the evening, we papered a screen, listened to *Passage to India.* It's like waiting at an execution; hardly literature; history. Apple-green wall-paper with little motifs. Like Matisse. For the rest, Martial and the play.

25 October

Meeting with Roy; he started jaunty, ended collapsed; the usual violent self-pity, discrimination to prove the validity of his despair. It was all this: 'Why should I suffer, why should I still love E, and let her love you, and you her, and be happy?' That happiness of ours infuriates him; he is really a disguised case of jealousy now. Talking with him is a clinical occupation. He has to be humoured, indulged, checked. His mind went on with a shocking inconsequence; denying himself, hardly listening to what I say, seizing isolated words and running after them. He keeps on repeating the phrase, 'I don't see why I should be the one left out.'

And I say, 'But you see, it's a stone wall.'

Then he says, 'Well, you don't recognize my position. It's time you thought of me.'

'We do.'

And on it goes.

He claimed last night to have created E; she should therefore never have left him. The Mephistopheles complex. I accused him of leaving E precisely because of that – his own reflection in her mirror. Because he knew he was so malleable.

26 October

Having said – last night – that he never wanted to see E again, R is now out with her. I seriously believe he is going mad.

Nothing happened; talk, talk.

27 October

–

28 October

Half-term. Fletcher and I drank too much Guinness at lunchtime. I was fuddled, sick with it. Pointless drinking; in the evening with E to *Waiting for Godot*; everyone goes, so we must. But no seats for three weeks. So we went to see a film instead.[1]

29 October

Now near end of Act 2 of Part 2 of *The Young Man*. Sleep all afternoon; and a nice evening indoors. E at her best; loving, housewifely; ended in a hot naked tumble on the carpet and cushions in front of the fire.

30 October

E all in pieces; temper tantrums all day; shouting, violence; a day completely naked; we drank in the evening, re-achieved a lull.

31 October

My half-term. I prepared for an interview – publicity officer with UIPN[2] in Brussels – learning all the names of birds in French. E came back exhausted and then once more in a foul temper – ironing a suit, teri shirt, etc. *Prater Violet* on the wireless,[3] and the announcement that Margaret has renounced Townsend.[4] The world so stupid; that we too should have to drag on through these stupid men infuriated me. Finally, at last, we both fell to sleep.

1 November

Interview at Belgrave Square, for the UIPN job. A pompous board, an hour of futile questions, a realization on both sides that it was all a waste of time; my qualifications not being at all what was required. Some of their questions were so silly that I felt like Alice in court. I can't imagine

---

[1] After opening at the Arts Theatre Club on 3 August 1955, Peter Hall's production of Samuel Beckett's play transferred on 12 September to the Criterion Theatre in the West End, where it enjoyed an extremely successful run.

[2] Union Internationale pour la Protection de la Nature, an organization created in 1948 under the auspices of Unesco and the French government.

[3] A radio adaptation of Christopher Isherwood's satirical novel about the film industry which was set in 1930s Vienna.

[4] i.e. Group Captain Peter Townsend (1914–1995), the World War II hero and royal equerry with whom Princess Margaret had been in a very public romance since 1953. It was particularly controversial because Townsend was a divorcée. On the evening of 31 October 1955, a personal message was issued by Princess Margaret from Clarence House: 'I would like it to be known that I have decided not to marry Group Captain Peter Townsend. I have been aware that, subject to my renouncing my rights of succession, it might have been possible for me to contract a civil marriage. But, mindful of the Church's teaching that Christian marriage is indissoluble, and conscious of my duty to the Commonwealth, I have resolved to put these considerations before any others.'

why I was shortlisted – lunch with E; very depressed. A futile journey to Earl's Court for flat address from an agency; read a serialized fragment of a naval novel – *HMS Ulysses* – sheer rubbish for which the writer was paid £60,000 before publication.[1] It makes me feel ill.

2 November

Almost a relief to go back to work. Terrible; revealing the oases that routines can become.

3 November

We went to a party with the young couple the female half of which G. Mansell, our neighbour, is having a namby-pamby flirtation with. A dull party; people who talk about themselves, their jobs; *enfin*, their nothingness. GM is a rather ambivalent young man; BBC producer, Anglo-French – super-French in England and (I'm sure) super-English in France. Very diplomatic – so much so that he is careful not to appear so. The usual smooth yes-boy; he'll go far; you have to be intelligent to be smooth; but it's a horizontal, never vertical farness.[2]

The young couple. Sue and David Harley; an odd, sad modern couple. Sue is small, pretty and eager; he is spineless, pleasant, drifting. Small people. She and GM are psychologically intertwined; sometimes physically, even in front of the husband. She rings GM up every morning; I hear them arranging to meet for lunch. She frequently visits him alone here. I don't know how many admirably sophisticated understandings have been arrived at in this triangle; but I find it vaguely obscene. When people live without love, for me they are always sinners.

4 November

Friday. Another bad evening with E. She is as useless emotionally as a pre-migration bird. A rather mournful supper of baked potatoes; our staple diet.

5 November

Saturday. *YM* play in the morning; cold and heavy and pedantic in the third act. Too plebeian. Plod, plod, plod. Shop, clean house, cook lunch.

---

[1] *HMS Ulysses* was the first novel of the bestselling adventure writer Alistair MacLean (1922–87). He had been invited to write it by the publishers William Collins after winning a short story competition in the *Glasgow Herald* the previous year.
[2] Gerard Mansell (b.1921) was at this time working for the BBC European Service. As JF predicted, he did go far, becoming Director of Programmes for BBC Radio (1970) and Deputy Director General of the BBC (1977–81).

Rest of day in. Peaceful, pleasant. Bartok's children's pieces; E reading Koestler. I roughed out something for the *Observer* competition – a stupid short story. Can't afford to ignore the chance – though it's a vile prostitution.

7 November
Monday. Winter is here; and all the attendant doubts.

8 November
Tuesday. Reading *L'Immoraliste* – a masterwork. Gide tells great subtleties very simply. The third act of the *YM* is bogged down hopelessly. E has been to the doctor's; he has told her she needs psychiatric treatment. I suppose she would seem abnormal to a normal person. But I pity the psychiatrist who has to treat her. He couldn't discover anything R or I haven't told her – or that she doesn't know herself; and she would be immutable.

Afternoon (it is Sunday) with R. We drank coffee in coffee bars off Baker Street. Act the parts of *Huis Clos*; we both see the situation precisely now, and agree on it. But R has fallen a long way; even subtracting the self-pity and the self-heroification, he has sincerely crumpled; and I feel, perhaps for the first time, genuinely and continually sorry for him. We are morally imprisoned in a cast-iron situation; he can't take E back, I can't let her go, since the love-mystery is between E and me. R has only two people to talk to. J. Liddell is in India. There is me. I suppose it is something that we can meet on a deep and sympathetic level; that he can explain all his emptiness, of which I am the main cause, to me. As if we know we are victims of life, of emotions, situations, personal characteristics. A sort of sad nobility about it all – the twentieth-century equivalent of the eighteenth-century *mariage mondain*. They managed to live in peace *with* the eternal triangle; we manage to think in peace *about* it.

To some, all this would, and will, if it is ever known, seem incredible. To suburban morality – but adding and subtracting; this is in the realm of the higher mathematics.

12 November
Suddenly seeing my reflection in a bus window. It was night. Lines of worry between my eyebrows. I tried to alter my expression so as to smooth them away. But they wouldn't go. They wouldn't go.

The *YM* (second draft) completed. This third act is still a mess. The difficulty in playwriting for me is spoken style. To make the characters something more than epigrammatists' or mere stock intellectual-play

characters. To endear them to the spectator. That's so difficult when
they are dealing with ideas and abstractions. I can feel myself doing it
at times; and at others everything slips, is impossible.

A friend of E's is giving a big party, to which we are invited. The whole
idea literally nauseates me. It upsets my stomach. I don't know why I
can't just ignore it till it comes. But a hundred foolish anxieties nag at
me – my clothes, E's clothes, our illegal situation. The kind of party it
might be – whether I shall be made to perform; and so on; and so on.
Hopelessly lacking in egocentricity. I am an excentric. Absorbed by the
effect I shall have on the world.

A dreadful party. Such shallow, primitive people, looking uglier than
the fauna of rich suburbia. A monstrous piece of stockbroker's Tudor;
two neurotic parents, two neurotic children and some fifty vulgar, noisy,
dull people. The ugliest gilt. Dancing to bad jazz; on my part, a somewhat desperate searching for some kind of intellectual response.
Nauseating, at such parties, is the sad animal scramble for the
smooching-partner – the final public kissing in the darkened room. E
and I sat in a room which had been converted into a bar, talked aimlessly
with a Russian dancer and waited for someone to take us home. The
pretty girl who invited us had a kind of sad-clown inconsequence – a
flitting, frivolous charm. Ruined by the bad marriage of her parents and
the money which had doubtless prevented them from separating. I found
her grey eyes pathetically vacant. All these parties reveal the hideous
average of urban humanity. Empty, empty, empty.

25 November
Another party – at the Ardaghs. He is a young climber on *The Times*
staff. A conversation party – all people who are on the climb. All conversation built round the question of 'What do you do?' – with implications. Are you any use to me? Are you worth impressing? Is your job
better than mine?
  I present mine as a kind of absurd joke.

11 December
Flu. Liz has had it, I am about to. She is at her bitchiest; gaunt and
obtuse and despairing. I feel too feverish to care. Last night it was a
long attack on the *Explorer* – how, in short, it wasn't worth going on with.
People unreal, style bad, Boots' library, women's magazine, all that. She
is right and wrong about the book, but hopelessly alienating in her
manner. It's fatal having a woman like her about when one is writing.
Criticisms could help, but not her wholesale annihilation.
  Altogether, the situation seems to be tightening on us, inexorably,

like some medieval torture machine. A growing pressure, and one day there will be a scream, or a jet of blood, and we shall reveal the truth to ourselves.

The money side is as bad as any – it is like driving a nitro-glycerine truck, living on week-to-week wages. If one of us slips, then there is chaos. I read in the local *Southend Standard* about Mike Turner – a 'fine' young PSB[1] caught in a sordid, stupid court case over money loaned to a prostitute. Pitied him with all the pity of fellow-feeling. Knowing that sort of condition, and fearing it. What happens when the divorce comes?

But I go on hoping. Something will happen. We cannot stop fighting; it is a difficult operation. Existence is a downhill slope.

15 December

Flu; a vile illness. It corrupts the whole body. Impossible to read seriously, impossible to sleep at nights, impossible to write. Nightmare illness; everything foetid, miasmic, gangrenous. E away at work each day; I listen to the wireless, but that would drive a person mad with the artificiality and banality. Unimaginably banal and artificial voices. And the horrible, coarse popular music, the moronic crooners singing their moronic lyrics. Everyone on the BBC talks as if they are a little bit older and cleverer than anybody else, but they're doing their damnedest to conceal it; it must be the Corporation theory of broadcasting 'approach'. And the implication that all sorts of really unimportant things are serious. When I was ill, at night, absurd tussles with logical problems – quite futile problems of moral values that seemed life and death. One night they all came out well. The more absurd the problem, the more rapidly I solved it. I slept that night.

Flu has left me feeling like an old carpet – but it doesn't end old wishes. I try to write, but it is hopeless. I write threadbare rubbish. I can't think coherently, and I am unusually depressed. The feeling of changelessness about everything – and my apparently overall prospect of poverty. I read *Aaron's Rod* and that distressed me – that Lawrence could write with ease, without revising. One feels it all poured out in a steady (from his point of view) spate. The harder, the more carefully I write or strive to write, the more typical and commonplace mine seems to become.

L had his *idée fixe* and a descriptive trick (repeating), but the real distinctiveness is the warmth of the writing – the feeling that it has all gushed out altogether – that is what gives it its sharp feeling of life, too – an immediate birth into the world, not a complicated surgery-aided labour.

---

[1] Public School Boy.

19 December
The weird effects of the flu continue – a feeling of dissociation from all past and future. A total inability to hope – dreadful, that disappearance of the faculty of hope. Despair rampant; all offset by the hateful festive season. I feel lost about writing – totally unable to write or think of writing and green with spite at other people's success. How we lack money! And how impossible the earning of money has become. I cannot imagine ever earning more than £550 a year. Yet I would do anything to earn it. Midwinters are always depressing, but this the most for many years.

27 December
Another Christmas at home – food and drink, feed and drink. Long periods of sitting, saying nothing. Each time I go home I see them smaller and sharper, monstrously clear. And a numbing, terrible incapacity to pretend that I don't see them so. As solid as a block of ice, this barrier between us; nothing can pierce it. I went intending to tell them about E – but also aware that I was making a test of it, and that it might well be a purely self-concerned confession. But they are so incapable of understanding the complications of the affaire. And there is Hazel; she is a touch gawky, pale, sad, old-before-she-is-young. It would only need my bad example to make any sexual happiness on her side twice as difficult to attain. I'm scared dumb that they will try and bring her up in an even more inhibited way, with even more fatal results. Also fear they might not understand at all, or misunderstand; fear even that they would try and help. It would always be a hostile meeting.

   In a sense I felt will-less. I feel sick about the badness of that relationship. Sick of the badness of my writing, of the bad ease with which I conceive and imagine and the dull mess it all is when I try and put it into words. Sick of writing and having to write – sick of the poverty I have condemned myself to. Sick also of the badness E insists on putting into our relationship – a relationship which won't break but which she won't allow to stick. She refuses to make the great step – will go on seeing R when she's tired of me.

   Sick of the whole lot, at this time.

   To say nothing of a universal metaphysical sickness I feel; the meaninglessness of life; of matter, of mind.

5 January 1956
Working at the *Explorer*. Half-written. Damp and dry. One invents it all. Pushes it out. And it begins to live it's own strange life. Takes charge here, loses strength there. It's like continually reviving a corpse. What I know is right is the skeleton. The flesh – that is what obstructs me. The flesh and skin.

10 January
Ukase on the Greek book; three publishers have turned it down. Collins
with an interest in my future work; Secker and Warburg, prepared to
see it again if it's altered. I suppose it could be worse. I've passed the
frontier; between what one very much wants to do and what one must
do. The one leads to the other.

But it's a grim prospect. Not the mere time it takes to get into print.
That's a matter of patience. But the seemingly constant gap between
self-criticism and reality; I'm never satisfied. Never feel, except in
moments, that I have disarmed my upper self.

Yet I must go this way. I cannot just be, and do. Must make.

An evening with the two Denisons, our landlords. All the tenants, two
female medical students, a television writer, G. Mansell, ourselves; in a
comic nightmare of a social evening. D is a bore of considerable magnitude – a Continental bore (his origins and English are piebald) with a
skin like elephant hide and a monumental banality of expression and
thought. A kind of human Albert Memorial. He talks and talks, with
terrible slowness, thoroughness, obviousness. Continentals never realize
that the art of English conversation is the art of the unsaid. A fat little
man, he was persuaded, against a richly unreal reluctance, to play the
piano. Which he played, Brahms and Chopin, at half-speed and fortis-
simo. Thump, thump, thump; gradually the music-stool edged away from
his bulging rump. I and E could hardly hold our laughter in. But the
rest, rubbish about nationalities and influence of climate on character,
hours and hours of it, was deep in hell. GM is as almost as big a bore;
he laughs at Denison, but in another twenty-five years he will be Denison.

28 January
I am at my old game again of changing horses in mid-stream; halfway
through the Farnaby novel. I've just written a longish story. Now I want
to write a play. I feel very strongly this play-writing urge; more and more
I believe that ideas can only be 'put over' dramatically. That characters
can only be 'put over' in words.

I want to write a play about world population – an old man in a house
during a flight of refugees. His hate of people. The stupidity of breeding
like flies.

And a comedy. The princess-clown theme. Lawrence and the world.
In the frame of the existing theatre. The Theseus play is too big and
complex a theme to start with.

Graves, *The Greek Myths*. I nibble at it as at some delicious cake. Intensely
evocative, poetic. Each myth and its explanation like a poem. If only I had
learnt them young; the impossibility of remembering all the spiced details.

I get pleasure too from reading the OED – the pure charm of words.
I read slowly through the whole dictionary, missing nothing. Only halfway
through C. But life is long.

8 February

I'm stuck on the Farnaby novel. It needs to go in the third person –
one has to be analytic now. Can't be introspective – the whole nature
of the twentieth century is against it. Or else a very cold first person,
which would destroy what little sympathy the characters can create. And
it needs time. I can't write in the dribs and drabs of time away from the
college; and in the evening it's difficult with E. Now things at last seem
to be settled down in the right place. I saw R last week about a divorce;
he is definitely (he says) going to start proceedings. But he needs £60
to set the ball rolling – which I must find. I suspect he is trying to avoid
paying anything at all. We men great friends, as usual; he has a humanity,
full of power and warmth that I can appreciate now the battle's over.
But so much self-pity and so much self-preoccupation and nothing
creative to exonerate it – it's stagnant and rather sickening; very quickly
so. I'm always glad to meet him; and glad to get away.

Jane Austen. Curious way in which men never really enter her world;
they swim on the other side of the glass from the women. All the women
in a glass bell, and the men outside it. Purity of Elinor in *S and S*; pure
reason. As cold as ice; yet the priggishness extraordinarily absent,
banned. She doesn't merely try to seem to be right; *is* right. Once a
character is built up like that, everything she says which reveals emotion
(or sensibility) has tremendous sympathetic force. The old pleasure of
seeing injustice end in justice. Justice isn't enough. We have to be sated
on the injustice before it has any appeal. Nothing really attracts us until
we have too much of its contrary. It's a principle that can be extended
to any art.

10 February

Bitterly cold weather; grey skies and a continual scurf of falling snow. I
dream every night of green islands and South.

A literary magazine – *Stand*. Awful poetry – all cerebral rubbish.[1] Poetry
is an attitude, not an ability of mind. Nothing to do with word-juggling,
complexity, ambiguity. Poetry is a tone of voice. They haven't got a tone
of voice, these poets. What voice they have is dreamlike, a bloodless,

---

[1] Containing poetry, fiction and criticism, the quarterly magazine *Stand* was
founded in 1952 by the poet Jon Silkin (1930–97) as 'an attempt to remedy the
intellectual situation of reader and poet'.

swooning – swooning, their language swims, uses semi-archaic words like swoon.

Poetry must be sincere, must be felt with the *whole* being. And until the whole being has some value, then the poetry can be worth nothing.

Two things about my poetry – I more and more admire it. It is worrying, how good it sometimes seems to me. Because I cannot believe that it is *truly* good; and therefore I have to suppose that it is the egomania of age beginning.

Also, when I write a reasonable poem, I can't be in the mood for it for more than an hour or so. No poetic stamina. Now it is curious that that is precisely how I am generally. Good for one go, very good, according to E, but then I've had enough. I can't imagine a happy night of love, only a happy hour of love.

14 March

Plus c'est la même chose. Another three weeks and I shall be thirty. 'What a landmark,' says my mother. It is difficult to disbelieve the illusion. But the dates in sun-time are not the landmarks; my landmark, the one I go for across this interminable desert, is literary success. I divagate still; I play the flute, I dream, drift, float on air. I wait for the poems to loom or slip out of the mist; catch them, set them or reject them. Very like entomology, poetry. Scoring-boards, public images; the breeding of caterpillars. Poem-caterpillars require time; insatiable for time.

My *commedia dell'arte* play is stuck in the mist; too frivolous, banal. Novel remote and abandoned.

E and I spring loves and neurotic hates – mainly because of poverty, this dirty, barren flat, the prospect of endless work.

But I still feel far from the bottom – an ambivalent feeling now. I don't know if it means I have a long way to sink down before I drown, or plenty more time to rise.

31 March

Thirtieth birthday. 'Nothing to say,' as the criminals reply.

I went home – E to hers – for Easter. Impossibility of telling them the truth. I am a coward. But they are hopeless to approach. If there are much younger children than the elder, the family relationship is broken. I can't begin to see how to bring the two worlds together – my real world and the make-believe one they suppose I inhabit. Not that I lie to them, except by omission.

8 May

Today a private detective called. A grizzled, very gentle, nice man, very methodical and undetective-like. He laboriously wrote down adultery statements for us to sign. We fed him with facts which he chewed and regurgitated in a series of constabular one-clause statements. An ex-policeman probably. I felt rather stimulated by it; E looked shocked, but he was as soft as oil. Absurd, of course; that love and personal relationships have to be so mishandled by society; the profoundest things in life treated so naïf-mechanically. His description for the Greek phase was 'We became friendly and fell in love'. I felt we should have defended ourselves a little; but it is hardly worth worrying about in view of the nature of the case. The photograph we gave the detective was so foolish and licentious – it was the one taken at Heal's dance, excessively bad and unreal – that the judge is bound to think the worse of us. But the detective says that the courts get through 125 cases a morning, so not to worry. Except about paying for it.

14 May
Storm with E. Finally of value, like all storms, because it enabled me to see, in one of those moments in ménage-wars when one can think of nothing more to say, a perfectly obvious truth about myself; a Freudian truth. I have always been aware of it, but I have never seen it objectively before. For some months now I have been in a chronically will-less state; I haven't felt any less interested in life – I've written a fair number of poems – but I have felt unable to fight, or move. A kind of paralysis in which only in the (in terms of energy) value of poetry have I regained any liberty. The play, the novel, have been untouched. I have a number of small things I could be trying to publish. But I have felt completely incapable of leaving the shore of this enchanted island. I think that is why – in a recent bad film about Ulysses – I found the Circe sequence oddly powerful.[1]

For the root of all this I didn't search very far. But I had a vaguely generalized feeling that it was self-punishment, a sort of sinner's remorse, a *nostalgie de la boue*, a need to fall again, to be a failure, even to drive E away and be completely alone again; a sort of purge – one of the ridiculous but irreversible mental processes which are based on the interstices, the need to excrete bad material. The very kind of puritanical masochism I never have, abhor for its non-Greekness.

But now I see that the rest of it all lies in my adolescence, when I was so lonely that I had to masturbate so much, which finally made me self-sufficient, as encased as a caddis-fly, as Crusoe-like as could be. I don't need to make contact with the outer world, because my inner world conquered me before I could begin to think independently. I

---

[1] The 'bad film' was a 1954 Italian production, *Ulysses*, starring Kirk Douglas as Ulysses and Silvana Mangano as Circe/Penelope.

have got to break out of that fortress, to realize that the sort of metaphors by which I picture my progress – climbing the mountain by the difficult route, or ignoring the idiots who have climbed the foothills and who crow off them at those like myself (who are still lower than they because they are aiming finally much higher) – are only egocentric pictures.

I don't know why I've never seen this great Freudian truth about myself before. Except that there is an inexplicable gap between the consciousness of and seeing a truth.

This diary, of course, is a kind of masturbation *agent provocateur*. But to think of the whole development as the good extrovert public acting-deciding-publishing me fighting the bad inner enchanted-island me is a valueless simplification. I have to leave the island. But I could only escape on a raft of island materials; it is the island which must help me to escape from it. One cannot escape from Circe without Circe's help.

27 May
The Ardaghs to supper; we like her; he is a naïf, clumsy, self-confident young man whom she evidently mothers. We had a metaphysical discussion in which I – as E put it – 'lorded' it. It is bad to feel so superior to people who are really so much more of a success in life. Finally G. Mansell came in and talked with his usual heavy, horrendous importance about Algeria. It sickens me that one is *The Times*'s Paris correspondent and the other a BBC producer and I am nothing.

Not that they are much comparison – they are career men. Scum.

15 June
I'm going through (mad!) a period of separation from all I admire, all I hope for, want to be. It's as if I'm exiled from myself. I can't write, because I don't want to write. I can never say what I want to say in the way I want to say it. Something saps me all the time. A feeling of helplessness, that if this is the process, this is the process. But I don't know where this fatalism comes from in me; rather, where it lives. I know where it comes from; from the lazy, timid onanistic ego, which likes whining and suffering, enduring. But I know all that; it shouldn't so dominate me. I never try and get anything published because of it. If I was never to be published, its dream would be shattered; if I was, the same. I almost never try to improve our worldly position because of it. It's like being blindfolded in a room of cruel Eumenides; each time one takes a step forward to do something, one is tripped, pushed back, sapped. Always sapped.

14 July
Meeting Ronnie Payne after an interval of several years – successful,

steady, greatly set in the world.[1] He hadn't changed – charmed E (his rather silent, soulful second wife charmed me too; in fact all charmed all, which I suspect) and amused me. I always feel that he is shallow; I don't know if it isn't a preconception that makes it impossible for me to see him objectively. But I still felt it; that he was much older than me in worldly things, and much younger at the core.

But I didn't feel envious in any deep way; I expected I would. But I didn't; I begin to be what I am.

They were also the first people E and I have met and liked for years.

Winning technique. I have none of the science; one has to work at it; learn words; deceive – deceive all the time. In literature one can only represent the truth of illusions. It is not sincerity (which I have) that is required, but the illusion of sincerity. Just as certain silences in music give the feeling of mystery, exaltation, tragedy better than any music. I'm going to start a purely technical notebook, and leave this for the purely personal record.

Everything I do which is not what I feel I ought to be doing is inertia.

21 July
A party at the Loveridges', in one of the late Victorian palacettes in West Heath Road – all the staff, a sort of slightly ashamed and unnatural look in their faces. E all dressed up; I too. General air of genteel dissipation. Old Loveridge has a face grotesquely like the girl in *La Strada*, with comic eyebrows, inarticulateness, and a bright, lunatically innocent little smile; like a solemn little bird; always about to babble into song and laughter at unexpected moments; I talked about the ambassadress in Italy, Mrs Claire Luce, and the poisoning she had got from green arsenical paint in her bedroom.[2]

'Perhaps it was her razor,' said the old man, very solemnly.

'Razor?'

'That often gives your ars-e-nic.'

'Arsenic?'

'Arsenic.'

'Razor?'

---

[1] Ronnie Payne had by this time become the Paris correspondent of the *Daily Telegraph*.
[2] Mrs Claire Luce (1903–1987), who had been appointed US ambassador to Italy in 1953, had been intermittently ill ever since she took up her post. Eventually it was discovered that paint dust from her bedroom ceiling contained high quantities of arsenate of lead. The story was made public on 16 July in that week's issue of *Time*. Mrs Luce's husband, Henry R. Luce, was the proprietor of the magazine.

'It often gives your arsenic.'

'Your arsenic?'

His bland little face bubbled. 'Arse a nick,' he whispered, and hopped up and down just like an overjoyed child, while I tried to cover my slowness.

The L's are an odd lot; stuffed full of neo-Victorian prejudices, yet good in almost a Quaker sense. The college gardener was there, and all the chars, as should be. I knew the gardener very well, yet I several times wondered who the man with the limp was. My own prejudice blinded me; I only realized who he was at the very end. I was sorry I hadn't spoken to him, then. The seigneur complex – the gracious descent to one's inferiors.

We drank enormously, for those days – twelve or fifteen gin-and-Frenches each. Later we went on to the flat of the de la Mahotières[1] – and E was sick. She fell over in the lavatory and knocked over some planks and was crawling about among them when someone came in – she hadn't locked the door. I found her lying on their bed. It was all a joke, really. We reeled back home – I've never seen her so drunk – and I undressed her. But she got off to work this morning; Dionysius brings out the best in her character.

Garbo, *Camille*. What a face! It is almost the Platonic face – the ideal female face. Of course, she can act – she learnt to cinema-act before any other woman – and her voice is unique. But it's just the pure mysterious beauty, a delicious freak, a fifty-years-of-world-population to one chance.

28 July
Etker, my Turkish pupil – a slim girl with a plump, incongruous pink face and extraordinarily brilliant eyes, luminous, shimmering, swimming in intelligence. She is ugly, but her eyes are very remarkable; also her odd 'feel' for English. She can't write it grammatically, but she has done some translations of Orhan Veli which really do not need touching.[2] I would say she had great possibilities as a writer. I've encouraged her to write, given her Mansfield's name; Mansfield seems obviously her natural affinity. There must surely be a place for her in a country like Turkey. She has given me a *tribouki*, a cloth, a record of Turkish folk music, as parting presents; I dimly sense that she feels I have done something in her life; perhaps determined her to write. Feel touched and embarrassed; she is one of the few worthwhile human beings I have met; and for being at St Godric's, the more unexpected.

---

[1] One of the de la Mahotières was a teacher at St Godric's.
[2] Born in Istanbul in 1914, Orhan Veli was a leading Turkish poet and editor of the literary journal *Yaprak*. An alcoholic, he died from a brain haemorrhage in 1950.

5 August
Day in the country; a frustration that had needed lancing. Country is one of the many necessary valves in my life; I suspect it bores me really; but I can't exist without the occasional trial of it.

It rained all the way out to Great Missenden; damp veils of rain on the dull pocks of subtopia. But the sun came out as we went into the Chilterns. Delicious, that first re-entry into the boyhood world of the country, where nothing is forgotten; names, but not scenes, sights, sounds. Some little corners of fields, of woods, are as familiar, as inexhaustibly delicious as Mozart or Marivaux, as Joyce or Donne. Also it is living away from the country; one becomes unimaginably acute when one goes back; the banal recovers for a moment the magical; even the simplest flowers and birds.

Suez Canal scare;[1] hideous bellicosity of the Tories; pachydermatous lumberings of the great powers. It is like the antediluvian manoeuvrings of two great extinct monsters, too stupid to contain more than one idea at a time in their pin-brains; fight. We are fleas on the master's back; one is as helpless as a flea. Britain is in a hopelessly immoral position; one can only fight; ruins at least would clothe the British nakedness. I shall be a conscientious objector, if it comes to it.

18 August
John Osborne, *Look Back in Anger*. A much better play than I expected; and surely the best of the Lucky Jim movement. It was the goodness of the dialogue that captured me – good, bitter, black dialogue and a death to all the old verbal and mental clichés of the London stage. The critics have gone wrong over it; it's the present production, not the characterization or the plot that's at fault.[2] Of course, all that Jimmy Porter

---

[1] On 26 July 1956, after the British refused to finance the Aswan High Dam, President Nasser of Egypt nationalized the Suez Canal, which had been owned by the Franco-British Suez Canal Company. The British government, announcing that it was not prepared to see the canal in the unfettered control of Egypt, despatched Royal Navy ships to the Middle East and called up the Army Reserve.
[2] The enormous success of Kingsley Amis's 1954 novel about a lecturer in a provincial university had created a vogue for anti-establishment literature that anticipated the arrival of the 'Angry Young Men' with Osborne's play. When *Look Back in Anger* opened in May 1956, the consensus of the critics was that Osborne had produced a rant rather than a well-crafted play. 'Its total gesture is altogether inadequate,' declared *The Times*. 'The piece consists largely of angry tirades.' The two notable exceptions were Harold Hobson in the *Sunday Times* and Kenneth Tynan in the *Observer*, who both gave the play rave notices. JF would have seen the original Tony Richardson production for the English Stage Company which opened at the Royal Court Theatre on 8 May 1956 and ran there in repertory until 27 October 1956.

sees is the futility and mess of life. But if you have fine eyesight and a love of light and open air *and* are walled in by shoddy brick buildings, it is not construction which comes to mind.

It's a warning notice, this play: demolitions about to begin. It moved me, too; and I haven't been sincerely moved for a long time.

25 August

Halfway revising *The Joker* – now *The Magus*. The construction is all right. But constant slipping-down in technique; invasion of clichés. I have to treat each sentence drill-fashion. Is it necessary? Is it succinct? Is it clear? Is it elegant? Has it clichés? It usually has.

7 October

Personal style: I'm writing the second draft of *The Magus*. So much has been debunked, deflated, proved void, pretensions in these last fifty years that all styles have been contaminated; they need purifying, especially in the expression of meaning. This means a much more frank, colloquial, lively, sharp style. A dash of Rousseau; Pepys; Hemingway; the Lucky Jim school; clean, bare, unacademic; above all unacademic and unobscure. There is never *any* excuse for obscurity *in prose*.

9 October

After all these months of working on *The Magus*, I suddenly realized today the parallels with *The Tempest*; Prospero, Miranda, Antonio, Caliban.

30 October

The vertiginous stupidity of the world. First Hungary, now Egypt. We weep tears of rage over Russia's brutality in the one and in the same week start a concerted attack against Egypt under conditions which plainly call for international intervention.[1] All the Tory party has ensured is that the Arabs will hate Britain and France for the next hundred years. And the worst thing of all is that both the Russian and the British stupidity were caused by the vanity of a handful of men – the Khrushchevs and Edens who control history. It is not the great men who do harm; but the little men trying to be great.

---

[1] On 25 October Russia ordered Soviet forces to put down an anti-Communist uprising in Hungary. On 29 October, Israeli forces invaded Egypt and advanced towards the Suez Canal. The next day the British Prime Minster Sir Anthony Eden announced to Parliament that the French and British governments had issued an ultimatum to both Egypt and Israel that a Franco-British force would intervene unless both Egyptian and Israeli forces drew back from the canal zone.

9 November

Fletcher was talking Tory nonsense to a circle of the foolish women in the common-room at St Godric's and I wanted to contradict, argue, but what's the use?

I comprehend the '30s now; I could jettison many things now. I thought I had managed to rise above the political world. Even Egypt I could feel impartial about; the emotionalism of woolly-minded liberals soon ensured that.

But Hungary sticks in the gut.

We'll never wash that blood away.

Braque exhibition – we got in at the last hour, literally. Crowded with people who did not seem to understand what it was all about, all prickling with an undirected kind of sensitivity.

But beautiful pictures; Braque is the best of them all, in the end. Partly because his is a pure peasant style; no cerebral experiments, no mind-teasing. Simply, his version of the objects, craftsmanship to the point of genius. All his colours are perfect, harmonious, all his shapes are deep, round, warm, full, from the earth, like Maillol women. A kind of inspired village painter.

It is one great purpose in art, the discovery of peace; all the attraction of Braque is inward, in the painting. You have to see Braque and be indrawn into his peace. Or put in another way – his paintings do not mind if they are seen, they do not cry out to be seen, they do not call attention; they are, and you can see them if you need them, but they exist as only masterpieces (very few Picassos, for instance) exist, in themselves – beyond spectatorhood, so to speak. I think I would rather own a Braque than *any* work by *any* other modern painter.

28 November

Cold, winter cold, and the old spectre of personal poverty, personal failure – one and the same, of course. Comfortable heating, money to buy clothes even though one has clothes – those are not necessities of life, but they seem it. I have only the old duffel-coat, threadbare now, so shabby that in spite of all the ways I have changed, I am ashamed to wear it. E wants a new coat, too. I gave her the rent money today to buy shoes. Next door the spectacle of the cosy, conventional Ms – always happy, in the best possible world – that is sickening. And the whole world sickening. The ghastly slowness with which I work; a pile of correcting; Hungary, Egypt; E's unhappiness. Frost on everything, the black frost.

30 November

John Wyllie, *Riot.* That clean, objective, brutally cut, cinematic style. I feel it is wrong now. The cinema does that; the novel should be doing something else, something the cinema (actually or potentially) cannot do better. To express the states, words, thoughts, motives, the cinema cannot.

The Ms invited us next door to play a new game – Scrabble. The poverty of minds that can spend such evenings playing such rubbish – every move took three or four minutes, the element of chance was enormous. The Ms are *wonderfully* slow, really; like human snails, hardly credible.

8 December

A new magazine – the *New Scientist.* As I grow older, that takes the place of the older nostalgias – to have been a scientist. But I don't know – there's a pleasure in being able to have only to know the principles, the skeletons. The bird's eye view which only a layman can have – and I still think it is better to be an indifferent polymath than a brilliant scientist.

I like, in sound science writing, the current vertiginous drops – the holes in the floor of the battlements, through which oil was poured, the sudden realization that the battlements jutted beyond the walls. I get that in the *New Scientist*, sudden extraordinary problems and possibilities.

12 December

Meeting with Roy – I feared the worst, but it was almost the best. After talking round the mulberry bush for an hour, in an odd little box – like a confessional, as he said – in an old nicotine-coloured pub off Baker Street, he plunged in.

The divorce action took place a week ago. But the shock is in the judge's ruling – costs to be shared. It seems to have hit Roy surprisingly hard, perhaps where it hurts most; in the judgement of authority. I was amazed that the divorce court laws could produce such an enlightened judge and judgement, and Roy shocked that society, so to speak, hadn't declared positively for him. Then the reason for the meeting came out. He had decided that as I was morally guilty, I had to pay all the costs; a little later, he explained, with some loss of his usual self-conviction, that if I didn't pay, he could hold up the decree absolute for another eighteen months, and also exact maintenance for the upkeep of Anna from Elizabeth.

More and more it seemed that this question of costs was a symbol for him. If I would pay, then he would be innocent. So then we got back to the original guilt – whose was it? From then on, I attacked all the time, and flattered him to prevent a scene. Finally it came to us sitting in an espresso bar and discussing his life, and the fact that he was a genius, and

yet must do without love relationships. He said he couldn't blackmail me
and would go and see the lawyers again. We parted good friends again.

He hasn't lost all his old magnetism, his intense interest in everything
– even the most devastating criticism – about himself. I felt sorry for
him, because he is really unpredictable and in his struggle with everything external to him he is quite capable of absurdly vindictive cruelty,
though he isn't a conventionally cruel person.

Still, it's a relief. My first impulse was to write a letter home, telling
them everything – but the thought of having to discuss it all over
Christmas, that nightmare season, chills me to the marrow. The lament-
able thing, as I only fully realized when the letter was ready to be posted,
is that I have not the least idea what their reaction will be – it may be
quite understanding, it may be blind shock and hurt rage. So now I
have decided to wait, to tell them perhaps at Christmas, but I doubt
that. I am sick to death of the whole relationship with them. I can pity
them, I don't mind their being what they are, but I can't stand that rage
and reproach when I do not fulfil the image of Fillebrooke Avenue.

The blackest part of it all is the money. Every week we get through,
every ten pounds I find to hand downstairs for the rent – a miracle.
Then one has no reserves, one lives on one's nerves. I hate Christmas
most of all because it is the time when one needs, always, more money
than normally, and we always seem to have less than normally.

Hateful season of hypocrisy.

Dickens – those awful hyperbolic parenthetic clauses. That is the worst
thing in his writing. Like an irregular teat, a constant stopping and
starting.

And the unreality of his world (in *Barnaby Rudge*) – the dreadful
conventional beauty, jollity, cosiness, whatever of his characters. They
exist in his mind, not in the world. It would be interesting to have a
theory on that – the origins of his characterization. Where does it come
from, the too artistic, too real, too graphic, too vivid, too tragic, too
comic Dickensian world?

But his richness. It is like roast goose, reading him once again.

20 December
E and R in a piece of Scottfitzgeraldry. R rang me up and announced
that he'd decided, after all, that he would like to see E and take her
out to dinner. Everyone very kind; R wishing me the best of
Christmases. However, it all ended with E ringing me up in a peculiarly distraught state at eight the next morning, having spent the night
with R in his flat. She said she had been wandering about Leicester
Square. Copious tears. It seemed he had made her very drunk on an

empty stomach and they had then, in their old way, moved about, until by the small hours things had got thoroughly nasty, and he even tried to seduce her. And fallen asleep finally on a settee, which E left when she woke up at dawn.

I didn't sleep much. I guessed R would take her to his new Cheyne Walk flat and try a little cuckolding of the cuckolder – and that (quite apart from it being E's 'time') he wouldn't get far. But I was afraid she might have got killed. Such things don't make me angry any more. R is a child, and E has all the old maenad incapacity for staying out of the occasional orgy. She is wallowing now in guilt and self-disgust (a Zola-esque fatalism – R tells her that her father is 'mean, obstinate and stupid' and that she is the same) and talks about this as the lesson at last learnt. But E has a mind quite incapable of ever learning by experience – her memory has no moral powers. All her evenings with R end like this one – in disgust, all the futile stupidity in illogical humanity; yet she never remembers.

I cannot even feel angry about R's dreadful ugliness and cruelty – a nice nasty touch was the exhibition of all Anna's pictures in his flat, apparently – because he is a person devoid of good will. When one is as empty as he is, the worst is all one can expect.

But I had hoped E had got a little more self-control now. Deathwishes; once it would have made me furious; now I can only smile. When you realize that nothing will do any good, it is best to smile. That's the deepest, simplest classical lesson.

Stew. We have a stew every weekend. We could afford joints (rather joints would not be any more extravagant than many other of our foods), but we prefer stews. I make them, and they are the best stews I have ever eaten. The recipe varies, but it is roughly this. Fry meat and onions together in butter. Boil water in the same pan when it is emptied and make a purée of tomato-sauce, black pepper, saffron. Put a sage-leaf and a chilli at the bottom of a casserole. Then parsnips, onions, carrots, swedes, chestnuts (essential), haricot-beans or split-peas, a garlic-clove. Peppers and mushrooms, if in season. Cook for at least four, preferably six or seven hours at low heat in the oven.

A little poetry book of 1844–1845, with the works of three poetesses, in a binding of the period. It cost sixpence in Norman's. Norman is a bluff, awkward, friendly second-hand bookseller with a mind like a jackdaw's nest and a shop which must rank as one of the dirtiest, most disorganized and lovable in North London.[1] I would like to go there more often.

---

[1] Norman's bookshop was at 2 Heath Street, on the corner of Perrins Lane, Hampstead.

Prices vary according to Norman's mood. He sold me a gorgeous, huge child's history of the French Revolution for 2/6.

The poetesses are Felicia Hemans, a terribly insipid, sentimental, superficial, cerebral bore. But she had a quick enough life.[1] Ann Radcliffe – not much ear, but some pleasant fragments of 1800 delight in batsy gloom and soft despair.[2] But the best is the one I can't trace – Frances Anne Butler (Fanny Kemble).[3] One or two surprisingly passionate poems – they reminded me of Louise Labé[4] – a lot of rubbish, too, but the Sapphic touch, here and there.

Books as documents. More and more it is psychological, sociological, anthropological, historical values that I seek in books. This means that bad books are often more 'valuable' and amusing than good books. A bad novel of 1857 tells one much more about 1857 than a good one.

That is the problem. When there is a writer, his relation with his age's historical characteristics. Radcliffe – is she a romantic or did she 'cash in' – as we say now – psychologically? Or was she a victim of romanticism? (One uses a mode, a *Weltanschauung*, and one becomes it.) How much deliberate, how much unconscious, how much in her by nature, how much put in by the age? That is the only way to analyse a writer – anthropologically.

First of all his nature.

Then how much it is in harmony, or not, with the existing Zeitgeist.

How much it uses the Zeitgeist and for what ends.

How much it is moulded by the Zeitgeist.

---

[1] Born Felicia Dorothea Browne in 1793, she published the first of many volumes of poems when she was fifteen. With their historical, patriotic themes, they were hugely popular and included, most famously, 'Casabianca', with its opening line, 'The boy stood on the burning deck...' She married Captain Hemans in 1812, had five sons then separated from him in 1818. She died in 1835.

[2] Ann Radcliffe (1764–1823) was better known as a writer of such Gothic romances as *The Mysteries of Udolpho* (1794) and *The Italian* (1797).

[3] Fanny Kemble (1809–93) was the daughter of the actor Charles Kemble, and became herself an extremely successful albeit unwilling actress of her day, commenting of her stage career, 'I never presented myself before an audience without a shrinking feeling of reluctance.' In 1834 she married the American plantation owner Pearce Butler but, shocked by the treatment of the slaves on his estate, divorced him in 1849 and made a reputation for herself as a leading abolitionist with the publication of *Journal of a Residence on a Georgian Plantation* in 1863. Besides this and the single book of poems published in 1844, she wrote several volumes of memoirs, plays and translations of Dumas and Schiller.

[4] Born in Lyons, the poetess Louise Labé (c.1525–65) wrote a number of love elegies and sonnets.

How much, in the cases of genius, it modifies the Zeitgeist.

Presumably, it is clear; one should not easily sacrifice one's nature. It doesn't do to sell out too quickly. This does not mean that one should reject one's time. Because it is the latest, it must, potentially, be the best time, with the most material for artistic creation, philosophical analysis, scientific discovery.

This is not what the anthropologist wants. It wants people to be typical of their period.

A good human being must fox the anthropologist.

Christmas home. Now at least there is the television to fill in the boring hours. It sweeps down on people like this, television, and gains them as Circe gained the sailors. One has to be a Ulysses, if only for that. It shows what people are – idle machines. They crave entertainment, amusement. Partly it is laziness, the television. And partly it is a better sense of their own inadequacy, their own emptiness. My father justifies it: 'I've got nothing better to do.' It is the only justification, and at the end of one's life, one knows the futility of idealistic talk about self-entertainment and the value of creativity.

Ominous is the peculiar respect the television has for the tele-personality. The so-far-yet-so-near quality of each face explains that – and the sense of the others, the vast fellow-audience.

Reassuring, the size of the screen. When everyone is reduced to puppet-size, grandeur is impossible. Greatness cannot be communicated in under twenty-five square feet. Twenty-one square feet are still lacking.

I had the usual multiple nausea; the meal I enjoyed most was with E, when we met again on Boxing Day evening, and had some meat I had brought back and half a bottle of bad Spanish wine. A day apart brings all our doubts to heel.

Two new old books – an edition of the first fifty numbers of the *Tatler*. That cost me 6d. I think the bookseller mad to let such a book leave him so cheap. As if he sold London, 1709, for 6d.

And a *Collection des Mémoires relatife à la Révolution Française. Memoires sur les Journées de Septembre, 1792* – a fiercely, gorily, anti-revolutionary blast of 1823. Eyewitness accounts; deeply imbued with the *Daily Telegraph* mentality. I like this book not least for being riddled with bookworms – and nothing could be cleaner than the holes they make. Like leaf-cutter bees; such neat destroyers cannot be vermin.

E and I have a certain telepathic power; a month or two ago we lay in our single bed and had several quite remarkable proofs. Guessing one of a class of objects – Greenland, of all the countries in the world; melon, of all the fruits. And several other near misses. There can only be one explanation of this. The creation of a thought in the brain must emit some kind of characteristic wave. Very often it is general characterstics that come, and one is inclined to guess from there – a certain shape, colour, size, or initial capital letter.

One has to be very passive if one is receiving; anonymous and receptive, till a certain characteristic is repeated, surges up out of the unconscious. That is plainly where the receiving goes on.

I should like to make a lot more experiments. But E is too spasmodic in concentration to be any good as a guinea-pig.

10 February 1957
Hard Times. I'm doing this pious and intolerably right book – no wonder the Communists like Dickens; he has just their universal righteousness – with the girls. It bores them stiff. It would bore any decent young person stiff. But there are compensations. The astounding chapter on the terrace over the lake, with the two young men; Tom Gradgrind biting pink rosebuds in half and Harthouse the grand master at seduction.[1] The thing that makes one smile is the genius of it; all the rest of the book is journalism, dull (and first quality) lead to set this one beautiful glimpse of the forbidden world on the other side of the great Victorian wall.

15 February
A sad book find. *The Poetical Remains of Lucretia Davidson* (pub. 1843) – who died, aged sixteen, on Aug 27th, 1825.

She was an American child-genius; that is, she could write bad fashionable poetry with some ease – romantic and insipid poetry. Very pious, precious poetry.

There is a 'Life' of her, though, which is oddly sad. One can see there, beneath all the piety and the odious sanctimoniousness of the age, that a remarkable creature existed. She has symptoms of hypomanic depression. That is clear. But the 'Life' gives all sorts of strange little details about her that make her live again, pathetically. She sits in her room, writing, writing; in a fever about words; knowing she was going to die young (they all knew that, in those days, but she *did* die young);

---

[1] JF is thinking of book 2, chapter 7 ('Gunpowder'). Unprincipled politician James Harthouse conceives of the idea of seducing pretty Louisa Bounderby, who is in a loveless marriage with the very rich and much older Josiah Bounderby. The heavy debts of Louisa's beloved brother, Tom Gradgrind, present him with an opportunity to work his way into her affections. By a lake on Bounderby's estate Harthouse discusses with Tom the 'horrible mess' he has got himself into. Tom picks to pieces some rosebuds, making his anxiety plain: 'He took to biting the rosebuds now, and tearing them away from his teeth with a hand that trembled like an old man's.'

she was beautiful, hectically beautiful; hung an Aeolian harp in her window. An harp-muse.

Two fine last poems, when she knew she was going to die: 'My Last Farewell to My Harp' – this is fine in the context of her life; one goes through the means of expression to the external condition. 'The Fear of Madness' – this is a remarkable poem.

It ends:

> . . . *this hot brain* . . .
> . . . *Be cold, and motionless, and still,*
> *A tenant of its lowly bed,*
> *But let not dark delirium steal –*

Why was this not finished? The obvious rhyme is 'dead'. Why, why, why? There it ends, unfinished. A magnificent penultimate line, and the even finer magnificence of an absent last line.

She was a whimsical girl, too; fond of involved jokes, self-absorbed. Reminding me strongly of S.

Such books have a vividness for me which I know must be strange; because until recently I did not have this power of plunging back into the past; but not in the usual sense – this is a stepping out of one line into another parallel line. It is only an illusion, the pastness – it's all parallel.

27 February

I went home yesterday and told my parents about us. They were as mild and pleased as kittens. My first reaction was that I had been silly to hesitate so long; and then that after all it had perhaps made them understand; and be so mild.

2 March

Today we moved to a new flat – the flat next door. The M's are moving to Belsize Park. More where they belong.

It has a nice large room facing west – a sunny room. We've been without the sun too long.

And a little bedroom with a double bed. A separate bedroom is the dreamt-of luxury. And the doubleness of the bed.

We can call this a flat and not lie; much.

But the upheaval. That's a nightmare; it ought to be fun, but I feel ill. I've just had two days in bed with something vague, an odd, seedy vague sort of fever. But E's a good woman nowadays.

19 March

Beowulf. A fresh experience. Simple, quick, violent, complete; the whole society distilled. It is what all such poetry should be; a substitute for the age. So that subsequent archaelogical discussions illustrate the poem; not the age.

And very modern, that frank despair at the human condition; a clean, deep black background to all the blood and bronze and Viking clutter.

E has done all the decorating; I stained the floor. The walls, white, very pale grey and a muted, ducal frost green. Last month we bought an old chair; have framed pictures. A heliograph of a Meryon etching.[1] A Modigliani reproduction. We went home last Sunday; food, satiety, small talk. They seemed glad. E preternaturally well-behaved, F nervous, M talking, talking. I don't think it had ever seemed so vegetal; meals, meals, meals, TV, small talk, armchairs, cigarettes, meals again. Smothering.

Now we are to get married: 10 o'clock on All Fool's Day. But I'll have to change it. We might get publicity; couldn't stand that.

22 March
I have a Greek pupil, a rich, coarse Thessalian girl. She tries not to be, but can't suppress a natural camel, codfish commonness. I had a dream about her. She was standing naked in a room with myself and several other people and urinating. She said, 'It doesn't matter.' This ugly Greek incident – there's a treachery in dreams. It works like this – one gains certain vague conceptions about a person. They become symbolized in dreams. The crude, extreme symbolization then, in its turn, secretly fortifies the previous conceptions. I am sure this explains many unreasoning dislikes – if one only knew, there have been terrible scenes in the fantasy world of the unconscious. The foundations of one's rational attitude are destroyed; we are all leaning towers of Pisa.

The reverse? Are some likings explained by dream pleasure-associations?

This girl is vulgar; but not so ineffably vulgar as I now imagine.

The conscious mind makes plaster figures; the dream world of the unconscious casts them in bronze.

E and I went down to Kentish and Camden Town to scout round for old furniture; exciting how infinitely remote that world is from Hampstead. Peeling, pitted, endlessly dirty houses; children playing in the streets. The people all poor, or flashy; junk-shops, cheap grocers. E remarked that when she asked for half a pound of cheese they cut it and cut it again till it weighed exactly what she wanted; not as here, where nobody minds paying for a two-ounce miscalculation. It was a

---

[1] i.e. the French artist Charles Meryon (1821–68), best known for his architectural images of Paris.

blue-pink hazy day; Camden Town Market, as alive as only markets can be; jostling, laughing, seething, eyeing over, swindling, bartering, an aesthetic pleasure. Hampstead like Paris, afterwards.

31 March

Home; just. R made one desperate attempt to break us. This time he tried to persuade E that she should go and see his psychoanalyst. He is undergoing therapy and plainly wanted to introduce her into the circle. I was furious. We had a night-long row about it, E and I. Finally came out of it an hour before we were due to catch the train to Leigh. It was my birthday. A slow journey through Essex; the country vernal, primrose and spring grass. The parents very kind; excited, planful, inexhaustibly planful; it gave me a kind of retrospective guilt. They want us there all the time; try and swallow E whole, like greedy children. I hope there won't be trouble later. They gave us £50 as a wedding present; I should pay D. Sharrocks back. But money has been so rare these last years that I doubt if I shall.

2 April

We got married today; a grey day, a grey day, but mist-grey; and the mist cleared when we went off; E in a pale yellowy-green suit, olive shoes, an egg-custard-yellow hat. We met the Kemps, whom we haven't seen for months, but they do not change; if we saw them after a thousand years it would be like a week – we met them at Belsize Park, had a drink. I felt nervous; didn't want to be seen, as no one at the college knows. I'm going back tomorrow; and couldn't stand the odd looks such unromantic behaviour would bring me. But no one saw us; we slipped in. A sort of boardroom with canvas and steel tube pile-chairs; a large gilt basket of faded flowers; two men, one rather bored and beery, the other suave. The silly little ritual, so short, so empty. Outside a tired little garden, and the chimney of the hospital furnace gently smoking in the pale blue sky. I paid the 11/3, we slipped out, up the road to the nearest pub. Then home to our nice new flat, and a nice good lunch, and Asti Spumante, and the sun in the room, and a feeling that it is good to be married, because it was fundamentally unnecessary – marriage won't alter our relationship which is outside anthropology; because none the less we are now what the others think, or expect, or hope, we are – legal; and as a sort of symbol, a crowned, sealed look-we-have-come-throughness.

The Kemps gave us a pepper-mill; and a friend of E's, a Canadian architect, brash, glossy, like a sober American car, bought a nice Persian vase.

So we're married.

Part Seven

Married Life in London

2 April 1957

Adler:[1] I find him more convincing than Freud; Freud is convincing in relating to childhood and adolescence; and inasmuch as adults are the children of their own young selves, valid. But of all that changes an adult, the sexual portion, Adler takes over. E has got herself into a position vis-à-vis her work and the women she works with which is classically Adlerian. Insecurity and inferiority. A violent fit of hysteria because I inadvertently told them our phone number. It is terrifying, the neurotic plunge: dizzying, alienating to watch. When I saw her red, convulsed, screaming face, I felt I was looking at a totally strange being; not only not E, but not human. Exactly the appearance of a young child in a tantrum. It might seem very worrying; but I think, in E's – a rare case – it is healthy – a self-purging response to her feeling of inferiority, without the usual ulterior motions of hysteria. And much better than melancholia, or the other tricks of the bloody psyche. On the other hand, she has a long way to go in facing, admitting, accepting her basic nature and all its defects: if only she could read text books!

She makes me feel dangerously, unnaturally stable, self-solved. And convinced that neurosis is essential in a good woman, just as the reverse is true of a man.

The new general human neurosis is partly hers, a dissatisfaction neurosis; the gap between readiness to enjoy and opportunity to enjoy. Or perhaps it should be called the Tantalus complex.

It has arisen like this: vast diffusion of mass communication, increase in general education, general knowledge, general culture; cheap reproductions, cheap editions, radio, gramophone, film – everywhere images of what life can be – altering every level from the peasant to the poor intellectual; and a frustrated yet growing ability to enjoy an ever-widening variety of pleasures both vulgar, physical and refined, intellectual.

Opposed to this, a world ever more overpopulated, with general poverty more and more inevitable. Even the conception of poverty

---

[1] Alfred Adler (1870–1937) developed a system of 'individual psychology' which maintained that the key motivation in human behaviour is self-realization. When this drive is frustrated, it leads to feelings of inadequacy and attempts to compensate, which may develop into an inferiority complex that comes to dominate behaviour.

changes; each year comparative poverty becomes comparatively more; the chances of enjoying all one wants to enjoy become progressively less – it is bad enough being confined to an adult enjoyment span of a mere sixty years. This is aggravation and inflammation; there is going to be more and more dissatisfaction.

To say nothing of the diluted phenomenon of the decline in all the great movements of moral authority – till now it has always been Christian, Buddhist, to conquer dissatisfaction, to be contented with one's lot, etc – this wasn't the moment to burn *that* medicine cupboard, even if its drugs had been misused.

29 April
For Easter to Leigh. I was suffering from atrocious piles. An ignoble complaint.

We walked every day; came back and ate large meals; watched the telly.

The thing that is wrong with it is its size; however good the programmes were they would be toy programmes. You could play Beethoven on a toy piano, but it would never rise out of the frame of the toy performance.

It is toy-vision television.

The drama has to be on the human scale.

Good walks.

The Adulterer. I began it happily, and it flowed – like a straight road; now it's all turns, twists, wrong routes, road blocks, and I can't even take up anything else. Yet it reads so badly. I have no interest in describing people physically and socially; it is only the implications of their actions which interest me. The usual view – of *all* writers and critics – is that unless the source is absolutely clear, objective, three-dimensional, etc – convincingly unstereotyped – the actions have no value, the exceptions all belonging to the category of symbolical novel, i.e., anything from Kafka to a fairy story, in the largest sense. But I am trying to obtain a reality seen only in the actions and the psychology and theories of the actions. None of the usual photographer's paraphernalia.

A feeling exactly akin to constipation with this book; must do it and can't do it.

Two spectacles.

The Diary of Anne Frank.[1] It didn't move me terribly. It is moving in

---

[1] The diary was dramatized for the stage by Frances Goodrich and Albert Hackett. Originally performed on Broadway the previous year (and winning a Tony award for Best Play of the Year), it opened in London on 29 November 1956 at the Phoenix Theatre.

itself, but there is a pastness about it, a finality that the realism of the production accentuated. It needs an absolutely stylized *mise en scène* to destroy its fixed location in time.

It suffers, too, from a lack of generalizations (perhaps the book doesn't) – the stage needs spacious language to conquer its real spatial limitations.

The Birth of a Nation – ten times as moving.[1] In all ways it is the cinema that excels in expressing the sense of time past. In a play, however well the past is represented, one is always aware that the action is also present. In a film, the seen and represented action is also past. One can almost make an equation of it – $a \times \frac{1}{b} = c$ – where a is the actual date of the action represented, b the date when the film is made, c the beauty of time-awareness. When a and b are very close, then the more movingly time can be used. I wonder really whether it wouldn't be better, for instance, to make a film of a certain action at a certain date as much as possible in the style of that date – *Birth of a Nation* is, of course, a work of genius. But it also gains enormously from its technical deficiencies, its antique appearance *as* film; all the differences between now and 1913 make the 1860s and '70s more plausible. No film today, however skilfully done, could make a street in a Southern town look as genuinely old as it does in any of the flickering, jerky sequences of Griffith's creation. This would be true even if it were not the masterpiece it is.

June

Curzon, *Monasteries*; one of the best six travel books in the English language; the most charming of all. This obeys the essential rule of the good travel book; it must be about the traveller, not the travels. But not all about the traveller, nothing about the travels; but simply, that as the traveller travels, we progressively travel into the traveller.[2]

Curzon has something springlike, candid, open-eyed, urbane yet fresh – naturally urbane. And the sense of humour, the indispensable sense of humour.

*

---

[1] Released in 1915, D. W. Griffith's epic of the American civil war was based on the play *The Clansman* by Thomas Dixon Jr. The film was infamous for glorifying the Ku Klux Klan, but was a landmark in the early history of Hollywood cinema for its artistic innovation, pioneering so many of the techniques that would become staples of film-making, from the use of parallel action to the close-up.

[2] Robert Curzon (1810–72) was the 14th Baron Zouche. *A Visit to the Monasteries of the Levant* (1849) was a record of his journey through Greece, Palestine and Egypt in search of ancient manuscripts.

Home for Whitsun. We hate the boredom of it – that minute bird cage
of a house. One can only go out or watch the TV. F has a sort of second
youth; he enjoys being gallant to E. Anecdotal. I find a curious shift in
my attitude to them. I like, tolerate, pity him; M annoys me, irritates
me to the point where I cannot be civil and won't chat to her, won't
look at her. She talks even more than she ever did; but I don't think I
have ever seen it so clearly – her fault is not endless chipping-in, it is
her inability to listen. *She never hears a thought*; all she hears are certain
words, which she reacts to by interrupting. H seems a refreshing noncon-
formity. But it is a dreadful, monstrous cul-de-sac, Fillebrooke Avenue.

27 July

We went to the studio of Hilda, a German refugee who teaches E pottery,
to fetch some bowls E has made. The door, a bilious yellow, was opened
by Paul, her husband, a sculptor. A tall, dusty, converted stable with
the accumulated bric-à-brac of years of unsuccessful creation. All his
sculpture is of the female body, school of Maillol; Hilda's pottery is
clumsy, both in shape and decoration. There is, in both of them, a
terrible creative clumsiness. So the studio is a huge litter of clumsi-
nesses – dusty heads and torsos, crude sketches on yellowing paper, old
postcards, newspaper cuttings, bad pottery; the only proper furniture
is an ancient armchair and a stained table. There was a tray on which
all his tools were laid, as in an operating theatre. On a ledge some
twelve feet up the wall were a row of yellowing plaster heads, all covered
in dust. Hilda's part of the studio is up a little spiral staircase, iron and
egg-blue; her wheel and a large array of bottles and potters' junk. The
kiln is below.

Hilda wasn't there, so he talked to us a little; a stout, bulbous-nosed
German Bohemian dressed in a sort of thigh-length smock, with an old
curved pipe. As he talked, he waved a double-ended spatula. We
discussed the studio; what it had been, its advantages and disadvantages.
One part was curtained off, because he sleeps there, against the law.

He seems quite happy bumbling about with his plaster. The whole
feeling ought to be tragic. Two whole lives devoted to Art (they are both
in their sixties), and the contribution to Art, objectively, none. But it is
like under-stone life, life under the sea – in itself, it exudes a feeling of
balance and satisfaction, even harmony. It is the feeling one has with
children, before they are educated, when they have no external aesthetic
values. As long as they create, they are happy. This is what (objective)
artistic failure must do – drive one back to the child's level. With Paul,
one felt, it was no longer very serious; creating was so serious that it
became essential – outside the category of seriousness. But what one
created no longer much mattered. In a sense, then, he had discovered
something essential – or rather, that was what I felt in him.

I come increasingly to feel that the creative psychic mechanism is as important as the sexual – and that it works in a similar way. The need to create, the demiurge, is as basic as the libido. If it is frustrated, it manifests itself in other ways – in collecting, in business, in a thousand activities which are not strictly creative in the artistic sense. The fundamental demiurge is the urge to create beauty. All creations can be judged aesthetically; but true demiurgic creations can only be judged aesthetically. All moral judgements are, in fact, disguised aesthetic judgements; works of art with a specific main moral purpose can and should be judged aesthetically; the relative beauty of the attempted good. The demiurge can be abused, as can the libido, by excessive indulgence. It can cause revolutions if its demands are not satisfied. More of the troubles of the modern world are caused by demiurgic frustration than by sexual. Another important part of the mechanism – intake, output (digestion). If the organism takes in more beauty (experience of beauty) than it puts out (childbirth or excrement, good art or bad art; aesthetic *value* doesn't matter here), then a psychological unbalance analogous to constipation takes place. Modern society aggravates this condition by providing far more opportunities for enjoying (taking in) than for creating (getting rid of) – all normal people are now demiurgically constipated.

That is why people like Paul, who ought to be neurotic failures, are not. His bowels work.

And that is why one must create.

August

Can't write at the moment. I could persist all day. I have it in my head that I must write a comedy – certainly a play of some kind. Yet none of the ideas I have please me. So I feel empty, castrated, impotent – yet it is an airy, floating sort of feeling. A fallow feeling; the days drift pleasantly by; E and I continue to live like lovers. We had two days at Leigh; two fine days out – we walked along the hills to Hadleigh Castle;[1] I botanized – the huge absorbing pleasure of being among flowers again. We climbed up past a sloping hill of clover to the hill that faces the castle hill. I found an old shard there – medieval, or older. Then we went down through the scrub to the railway. Green plover among a herd of Friesian bullocks; honeysuckle. Up again to the old castle, the ash-grey stone towers, down the long ridge back to Leigh. And the next day out on the mud, with newly arrived dunlin as tame as sparrows; turnstone, terns, goosander. The empty, far mud, the creeks, the sharp shells on my bare

---

[1] About a mile inland from Leigh-on-Sea, the ruins of the thirteenth-century Hadleigh Castle, which were the subject of a Constable painting, overlook the Essex marshes and the Thames estuary.

feet. And wandering back over the marshes. At home they fed us and bored us. Mother is a terror now; endless prattle. The wretched TV, reducing everything to the status of toy, peepshow. But enjoyable.

Rotifers, under the microscope; ceaseless energy.

11 September
Term has started, is a week old. I haven't written for six or seven weeks now. It feels strange, as if I really was what I appear. As if the people who think they know me did know me.

1 October
Graves and Frost: Frost is a minor major poet, Graves a major minor poet. What I don't like about Graves is the mythification of all experience; even though he stopped using the symbols of folk myth and Celtic whimsy, the myth is the common factor of his verse. The events of his life are presented in a mythlike way; Robert Graves the poet writes a folk tale about Robert Graves the experiencer, the man. This is fatal in major poetry; modern poetry must be a discreet expression of the I of the poet; there must be the voice – as Yeats, Lawrence had it, and Frost has – speaking straight out of the poem. There are times when Graves nearly manages it – especially in some of his love poems. But too much mythification, generalization.

But these highest reservations apart, he is a fine, neat poet; there are one or two perfect things – 'An English Wood', 'Full Moon', 'Ulysses' – of their kind.

Graves does not create a world; only a view of the world.

When Graves does speak unmythically, it doesn't work. It is obvious, if one thinks. No one mythifies if they can speak directly. But if the poet's personality is weak (especially literary, scholastic, book-stuffed, as G's is), then it is only by the mythification (or elaboration, or obscuring) of the simple, weak personality that any writing is possible. The only fear, then, is how well, how amusingly, or elegantly or cunningly, the poet or writer conceals the fact that he has nothing to say.

Nemo – is not this fear of inner nothingness a much more accurate definition of the psychic urge than Freud's libido or Adler's superiority-drive?[1] Especially where writers are concerned. All writing is a reaction against nemo; most intellectuals behave in relation to certain ideals of life – to certain ideal plans of life – which are themselves related to the essential valuelessness of life. This is an inevitable result of death; if life was endless, there would always be a potential value in it. One day, the

---

[1] JF would devote a chapter to this concept of the 'nemo' in his philosophical manifesto, *The Aristos* (1965).

ideal might come. But so little time, and certain extinction, make the possession, and evaluation, of mortality the preoccupation of us all.

Sublimation, here, takes the form of activity which is harmful, or neutral, to our attempts at building a valuable, durable self. Pastime occupations, such as work, play – there is no name for the true anti-nemo activity. Creativity-time, total-being time, poiesis-time. Nemo and poiesis, our two poles.

20 November

I neglect this. But life is smooth now, rutted, placid, domestic. No sin, and not much guilt; guilt for Anna, but one that is comfortably suppressed. Mostly it is enjoying peace; we are grafted, indispensable to one another. I am rewriting *The Magus*. I feel stiller, less torn, by the problems of writing. That is, I shall write, as always; but it must be massive, positive, worked. The only worry is money; we never have any. I can do admirably with very little, but E has broody periods; non-making, domestic, vegetative, planter-culture moods. I see myself strongly in (*Joseph Andrews*) Wilson; and it appeals to me more and more, that Age of Reason resignation, self-sufficiency.[1] It is an attitude which requires one physical support – a good, active imagination. Not the visionary, fantastic function of imagination so much as its practical fire-warming, hypothesizing one. I cannot stop thinking about death; it has become so much a part of my daily life – this might happen, that might happen – and not only to myself, to E also. And I can apply external catastrophes so easily in my imagination; everything bad, so to speak, 'happens' to me (so does everything good, but that is universal). This would make me a coward, probably, in a war. And it means that the dark is peppered over all the light. But that is surely how the garden-cultivating philosopher functions; he can stick his garden and his poverty because he is constantly aware that there are so many potentially worse situations.

Emma. What a mystery it is – I can't remember the last novel that gave me so much pleasure. It is years away.

A number of isolated observations –

1. Part of her charm is, from a literary point of view, stage magic. How is this object suspended without support in mid-air? How is it that her charm is not analysable? The answer is, of course, that her charm is that she is extremely difficult to analyse. The apparatus, the

---

[1] In Henry Fielding's novel *The Adventures of Joseph Andrews and His Friend, Mr Abraham Adams* (1742), Mr Wilson is a country gentleman whom Andrews encounters on his travels. In a long account of his life, he tells Andrews how, after many misadventures in London, he found love, married and retired from the emptiness of the city to live a contented life in the country.

technique, the covered traces. Other writers exhibit them – in the pre-self-conscious days, bluntly, like Fielding, openly in the course of the story; in the post-self-conscious days, externally, like Flaubert – voluminous correspondence; autobiography, and so on. Jane was an anal type; all dirt removed – not only in the absence of 'physical' scenes and descriptions, but in this technical cleansing of her work. She has the prime skill of the great conjuror. It *is* a trick, but she forbids the thought.

2. Dialogue. Anybody can build up a fine realistic character by outward description. It is when the character begins to show himself inwardly, through the windows of inverted commas, that the trouble starts. With Jane, absolute authenticity of dialogue. (Characteristic of all 'great' novelists – British empiricism dictating taste.)

3. Careful incorporation of faults; imperfection is reality. Her *tours de force* are the characters who are impossible to like to begin with – Emma, Eleanor, for instance – and when she persuades and teaches us to like against our will; that is, the world being base, priggishness is often the carapace, and first-seen façade, of true virtue. This is deeply, not obviously, true.

4. Suspense. Talking about characters chapters before they appear; never hurrying events, so that one accepts her tempo. As soon as a writer throws in short cuts, speedy action, we know he is trying to please us. Therefore, is afraid of us. Jane pleases us in her way; other writers please us in our way.

5. She is a tremendous snob in the only manner about which snobbishness is justified – social (*not* society) behaviour. Her good people are those who put the feelings of others before their own; her bad, the reverse kind. Her good characters are sometimes led (like Emma) to try and conduct, govern, the feelings of others in an effort to make them happy – and the result may be unhappiness (Harriet is finally happy). And the bad ones may, out of *amour propre*, put on the mask of sympathy and charity (Mrs Elton). But the distinction is always clear. Emma is right, and Mrs Elton is a cad.

6. Her often-noted smallness of scope in scene and social milieu. This insularity, this two-inch bit of irony, has this special effect – it also limits the perceiving field of the viewer. Other novels are battlefields; we stand on a hill and all is before us; or spectacles in arenas, performances before stadiums. But her work is seen through a keyhole, through a door ajar on a private garden. She engenders a feeling of private entry – the reader, not a reader. There is no background; it is private. It is also mysterious. That is why one mysteriously participates in her novels (as also in Henry James, Woolf, etc).

7. Her often-praised sub-satire. This is the prime source of her realism. Characters like Emma and Eleanor would seem unreal (have seemed

unreal in thousands of unsatirically coloured novels) without the Miss Bates's and Mrs Jennings's.

8. How brilliantly she does garrulity. And uses it to move on the action.

30 November
Heraclitus; the power of his philosophy stuns me. It is precisely what I have tried to give *The Magus* – though, of course, 'Magus' becomes precisely the wrong word. Henceforth, it must be *The Aristos*. I shall add Conchis's commentary on Heraclitus to the book.[1]

The power of the riddle, the epigram, the ambiguous presentation; but one must have a truth first. The process is: find a truth, then conceal it almost. Never that of so much modern art: conceal, then hope to reveal a truth.

30 December
Christmas past. We spent it alone, here, and enjoyed it tolerably; as much as it can be enjoyed by the poor. More and more it becomes the rich man's festival – the proving ordeal – how much one can spend, and how fast.

Denys S is back, *en route* for Indonesia again. He has given me an aboriginal-sounding bamboo flute. I sat and played with it for several hours, and now I can sound it, after a fashion. The intervals appear to be oriental; at its best it has a kind of melancholy inconsequence that is very soothing. The lowest notes are very deep and far.

And also he gave us a fine little primitive softwood carving, black; a pregnant woman with a bird's head rising out of the mouth of a fish, skywards; it is roughly done, but with great force. One could not imagine a more powerfully symbolic figure, for the size.

Persuasion. The great pleasures of this book are the nautical characters and the fine exhibition of Jane Austen's scheme of morality. Sir Walter

---

[1] The pre-Socratic philosopher Heraclitus of Ephesus (c.540 BC – 480 BC) conceived the universe as a continuous conflict of opposites governed by Logos (reason). In human affairs, the chief divide lay between *hoi aristoi*, the good ones, and *hoi polloi*, the many. While the *aristoi* provided the intellectual élite that enabled society to advance, *hoi polloi* without reflection followed the path that had been set out for them. The supreme good is the *aristos*, 'of a person or thing, the best or most excellent of its kind'. JF drew on Heraclitus for both his novel *The Magus* and his philosophical treatise *The Aristos*. In the second half of the 1950s, the two projects overlapped and developed in parallel, so that for a while JF took to referring to the novel as 'The Magaristos'. Conchis's commentary on Heraclitus that JF here considers adding to *The Magus* was in effect the work that would be published separately as *The Aristos*.

Elliot and Elizabeth are the absolute wrong end of the scale (so much so that they are hardly credible as Anne's father and sister – though the three sisters make a very nicely typical Adlerian range) and Anne at the absolute right end – that is to say she is both perceptive and sympathetic. In between come the sailors, Croft, Harville, Wentworth, who represent a kind of middle stage towards goodness; at least they are not pretentious; there are the Musgroves, who are good-hearted, but more or less fortuitously. All Jane's novels have those four moral states: the absolutely bad (i.e. the pretentious or the positively evil) – Willoughly, Mr Elliot; the easily swayed, who deserve some sympathy in their badness; the good, though less through inner perception than by circumstance; the fortuitously good, the absolute good – Anne Elliot, Elinor, Emma (most interesting, since she changes categories during the novel). I was arguing with D yesterday about Jane. He said her novels lacked 'nothingness', the sense of absolute despair or horror which one finds in, say, Dickens, and all twentieth-century novels. I don't think this criticism (a serious one to D, though even if it were proved, I could still defend J) is meaningful. The 'nothingness', when analysed, presumably means descriptions of the terrible conditions in which some humans live; descriptions of states of mind when life seems meaningless: Miss Haversham, the Gradgrinds, the *Hard Times* side of Dickens.

But just as the range of character in JA is so narrow compared to Dickens, so is the range on the scale absoluteness–nothingness. One must take the relativist view: Marianne's despair, Emma's self-discovery, Captain Wentworth's unhappiness – out of context, compared to Dickens' unhappy characters, it is easy to denigrate their real value. But in her world, their unhappiness is the nothingness.

Besides, hers is an abstraction of reality, a philosophy on a pin's head. But the qualities she most admires have an equal value, into whatever 'larger', 'more real' they may be transposed. Perception and sympathy – Greek and Christian – that is why her heroines, in spite of their occasional snobbishness, priggishness, are great. Dickens was fine at the bad 'uns; but Jane for virtue.

11 January 1958
In bed with the Asian flu.

One becomes very sensitive to words, writers. Someone has always to be dominating me. Now it is Coleridge – or rather his intelligence. He is an aristos; he must have read Heraclitus, or the neo-Heracliteans, to get his concept of polarity.

A curious thing. I went to sleep (in bed) directly after lunch and E had gone to work. About ten to three, I woke up with a distinct impression that a piece of crockery had just broken; a cup rolled off the draining-board into the sink. But I didn't get up and went to sleep again.

When E came back, we discover at that time she and her 'ladies' at the Research Univ[1] were discussing poltergeists; in particular one (in Church Row) that broke crockery.

And of course we found nothing broken.

K. Amis. *Lucky Jim*. How much funnier and less significant this is than I thought – silly story, silly characters, real farce (comedy without reality). An achievement. And yet how amoral, disengaged, trivial, insular. Not this way to Parnassus.

Coleridge – what a freak. A great mind and a good-for-nothing will. So much of his writing is flatulent, page-filling; and then there are rifts of divine sense and clarity. And so disingenuous about himself as a writer. I find his verse – once its historical significance is forgotten – often rather dull, and sometimes nauseatingly dull.

He hadn't got an ear for verse. An eye, but not an ear.

25 January
Today, in thawing, dark slush, on my way to post a letter, I heard church bells strike the three-quarter; then a sudden jangle of memory-images, all to do with lawns and summer, towers, Bedford, Oxford – nothing precise. Yet its imprecision is of a conscious kind, very central, statistically typical. It is as if all the precise stored memories, in the stampede for consciousness, are hastily impressed, one over the other, to get a common memory-figure.

Vague, but holding inherently all that past.

It is something I would like to be able to do in poetry, where I fly too often after the fresh, unique image; since that seems cleverer.

But somewhere there is this memory-figure (or image). I cannot isolate it from the banal, unimaginative image, yet I feel it can be done; or at least, it is a factor to consider in the choice of 'clever' image.

Back at St G's; the staff were solicitous – how did I feel? There is a kind of simple goodheartedness there, a delicate, elusive aroma arising from so many dull, ordinary people.

The classes, too, have a corporate spirit that is odd.

It is something to do with intelligence. Where the combined IQs of a class show an average below a certain mark, the class is doomed –

---

[1] JF means the Medical Research Council, Mount Vernon, Hampstead, where Elizabeth had recently begun to work.

even the intelligent ones are doomed. A sort of unconscious telepathic herd awareness of their intellectual status, enough or not enough.

E's father is ill; she went up to B'ham to see him. Emaciated, feeble, dying. The doctors have been slack, or honest; one can't tell. A Zolaesque kind of situation; the unaided victim of destiny, the historical situation, the uncomprehendingness of the protagonists. E's mother seems incapable of really looking after him. Her father, a bundle of prejudices. We wrote a letter to the doctor, formal and technical, and rather pompous, but it seemed to have the desired effect. He has been taken to hospital – suspected malignant growth.

Thuring. An insipid, intelligent grannyish creature. Very attentive. Always knows answers, and answers – at first this is annoying, but then rather admirable. Has the courage of her knowledge. A prig. A Jane Austen heroine, Swiss-Belgian. My best pupil, but I dislike her. It would be wrong to deny her a certain freshness and honesty of mind. Emma.

Bina. Persian-French, but she looks like a pretty Scotch girl. Winsome, sleepy, self-mocking. Temperamental. She reads in a hurry, well. Can't spell. Although she smiles all the time, gently, harmlessly, she never goes out of control, like all the others at times. Can always read. Within her nature, deeper, more serious than the others. The Persian smiling resistance to life and the serious French – a Protestant French – sense of the seriousness of life. Like all such hybrids, much more interesting than the pure Europeans.

Alp. An odd, small creature. A great quiff of coarse blonde-brown hair. A pudgy, frequently flushing face. Pig's eyes – but the eyes themselves are delicate and sensitive, a clear grey-blue, not cold, but very timid. She writes well, a sense of words. She *sees*, as Turks sometimes seem to; especially physical things. They can put physical moments in beautifully clear, fresh sentences – childlike, but not childish. She is shy with everyone, Alp. But absorbs, stores, almost visibly.

Drieux. A heavy, bespectacled, strict-faced dumpling of a girl. Flemish-French. Very shy. A prim mouth in a heavy face, a boyish haircut. Heavy accent. Earnestness, effort. A carthorse girl, plodding, plodding.

Romano. Exactly the opposite. A very pretty Bulgarian-Portuguese. Delicate and indolent, but with a quick, easily absorbed mind. Very pale, a head of black falling curls, very elegant, with great dark eyes – staring, rather disconcerting eyes. A touch of the Jew. That is most likely. She does no work, is not good at English, seems often not to understand. Stares, day-dreams. A small white fish in her movements.

Bourla. Greek. Freckled, fiercely down-to-ground. Also Scottish – thrifty, sceptical. Always sits on my right hand. Sometimes giggles, but generally gets angry if others do so. A stocky girl, with a great sack of good sense. I like her in a man-to-man sort of way.

Androusto, her friend, wife in a sense. A dark, pleasant Greek. Prettier, more erratic. Heavy-voiced, slow, dreams a little. Has a sort of modernity, an acceptance of things. Diligent, moral. Happy, one feels; her life will be happy, in every ordinary sense.

Lavik. Norwegian. A tall, slim, fine Nordic, with clear, dark eyes and a pinchedness of face that makes her seem a little cold, stern, bored. But she laughs, reads very well, is English – like a nice girl from the very North of England. Clothes rather shabby, hair rather severe. Has that Ibsenian paradox – *naïveté* and a mysterious, deep emptiness in her. Seems to understand only on most superficial level, yet no, she cannot be superficial. They are strange, Norwegians – like tall, simple flowers among chattering birds. A different phylum almost.

Rapazoglou. An unattractive, shifty, lazy girl, a gaunt grey mare of a girl. Lies, evades, mutters jokes. She is intelligent. A typical Adlerian case, against all authority, all constraint, all emotion. I dislike her the most. We are at poles, at war. A camel, giraffe.

Zeidor. A delicious, plump, gurgling Greek pippin, as loquacious and gay as a swallow in summer. Can't keep quiet, can't concentrate. Laughs, always laughs. Dashes off her work. A clear olive skin and clear black eyebrows, hair smoothed back into a bun. A child, but so sunny, like the smell of warm olive oil in the sun. I can't keep a straight face when she laughs – as she always does when I complain about the work she does or does not do. Has pleasant stretches of childlike absorption. I like her, in a perfectly non-sexual way, as much as I dislike Rapaz.

1 February

Kyrinkida. A Cypriot, small with a delicate Anatolian face. Her family are fighters for freedom. She is a pathological whisperer, giggler, disturber and yet a rare specimen – intelligent. Close to me, she is always serious, nervous, quick. But bubbles out, as soon as I look somewhere else. A delicate smallness, incessant restlessness.

Cuek. A Czech, quite impenetrable. She always looks cross, or hurt, or hopelessly puzzled. She knows less than the others and has no confidence. A beetroot shyness; the anger may be a symptom of it. But it is a kind of swan-anger, cross-browed, implacable in a minor way, inherent.

Stephanian. An Armenian Persian. A very small, perfectly developed, very pretty girl. She walks with a kind of harem sway, is all sensuality, self-concern, under an innocent, dutiful, prudish manner. Politer than any. Her English is not good. Sometimes, rarely, she laughs, a deep, sensual surprising laugh of pure humour. She excites me sexually, as none of the others do. It may be her long hair, female hair. She is without any coquettishness. And final sad fact, an all-pervading body odour. I can smell it before I go in the room. She tries to drown it with cheap scent, which is almost worse. Sometimes she doesn't smell. It is what the others always say: the Siamese and Persians never wash.

Arcadia. An admirably quick worker. Humorous, impatient, mistrustful. I don't really like her. She is the Odysseus side of Greek character – nimble-witted, unenchantable, quick as a knife on what is false. If I make a mistake, she is always the first to spot it. Everything but facts bores her. She says she does not understand, meaning that it is not worth her understanding. Anti-poetic. Hard for profit. A small, compact white-faced girl – stocky and Northern. She is Macedonian – dour, almost. But her eyes are very bright and brilliantly alert. Sometimes when she tries to read, which she does faster than any English person could, she starts laughing uncontrollably, and says, surprised, 'I can't read,' then everyone laughs, and sets her off again.

I see these girls twice a day. Grammar for an hour, 'set' books for an hour, *Joseph Andrews, The Doctor's Dilemma* . . . Always a little struggle for control. I always win, but at the expense of being too stern, too cold, aloof. They respect this, but dislike me. Yet I have a sort of knowledge of them which is as psychologically intimate as it is physically the opposite.

7 February
E's father died today; a day of sleety snow. I have been living on my own for two or three days. I had never seen him. I can't feel any loss, or sadness, except through E. She says, 'He was riddled with cancer.' 'He looks from one to another with such a sad long look each time.' 'He said it was nice to wake' – when they were with him at the hospital he kept on dozing off – 'and see us there.' 'His face is unable to move or express anything, but his eyes are sometimes clear and he looks so pitiful.' 'It is a pathetic and terribly sad thing. Not ugly as I imagined, but infinitely sad – a man waiting for death.'

And now he is dead.

9 February
Sunday. To Birmingham, to see E, who has been up there since last Tuesday. A dull journey, warm, balmy in London, but cold up there; flooded fields, powder and desolation of thin snow. The meadows a heartless, clouded mud-green, a terrible colour.

E looking tired and chirpy at New Street; our meeting as good as new bread. We went to a pub and had two Worthingtons each. She has organized everything, in a way enjoys being able to cope so well. To her home, through dull streets, nineteenth-century brick, and then along a more rural road, through a barrier of slag-heaps, crowded with sere, dripping spikes of rosebay. An estate of little brick boxes, like the little models we used in the war on the sandtable; here, a town. A little box of a house, hard-pressed on either side. No escape from *les autres*.

We stayed there till the train went to go back; E and I alone in the front parlour, courting, so to speak. Meal in a little kitchen. Photographs, mainly of E; her life has been a riot of hair-styles. Her sister[1] is a great tall white giraffe, very Methodist, correct, adult, twenty times more adult than I shall ever be; the adultest girl of fifteen I have ever seen. So serious, premeditated.

E's mother spoke of Edgar, the departed, in the present tense. Death destroys the sequential aspect of life. Instead, it becomes transversal; that consoles. E's father in several photographs. I'd never seen him before. To me he looked gaunt, severe, embittered, an unhappy, hating man, very tall, lean as a pole, like a professional cricketer, a fast bowler. But he lives on in his daughters.

They didn't want me to come to the funeral on Thursday; vague promptings – officer and gentleman – inside me. But of course they are right. It is a formality; no necrophilia with them. No religious conventions; all the blinds were drawn, though. The neighbours, always (says E) when there is a death, make a collection. Her mother asked them not to. 'My father despised them all, anyway,' said E. But it is a strange old pagan, pre-pagan, habit. Honouring the dead.

E rather shy all the time; bossy and daughterly by turns; ugly and beautiful, as usual. Kissing her seemed strange. We live so close normally, touching close, that any separation seems a rift. But there's always the mysterious sureness at the bottom of it. The is-this-it, this-is-it question and answer.

Then back. And Hampstead as beautiful as a Cretan hilltop.

3 March

At home for a weekend. I was morose. I can't help it, it makes me morose. The sacrifice of everything to the meal; it's always the next meal. She slaves, really. E has to tell me she is remarkable for a near-sixty. To me she remains the great enemy of my adult self – the great vegetable mother, ignorer of arts, thoughts, realities, trampler-down of all my father's best qualities. E and I like him more and more.

My analysis is this. I was cosseted by M into late adolescence. It was she probably who engineered my term away from Bedford.[2] Why did she cosset me? Death of next child, the still-born. Also, a totally untalented woman, unintelligent in all external ways (i.e. not domestically, but everywhere else). F probably gave her a feeling of inferiority very early on. She may have thus tried to dominate me; I was F's surrogate. Or it may be a result of some sexual disparity between them? At a time when he

---

[1] Joanne.

[2] See introduction, page x.

needed affection, she gave it to me. To see F as a tyrannical, austere paterfamilias is absurd; but M is younger than him, and has always obeyed him implicitly in major things. Her own father was more the Victorian father; she mothered her younger brother, and elder-sistered me.[1] That is the Adlerian situation, clearly.[2] She is cast as tyrant, but with none of the tyrant's powers. She is not malicious, nitty, evil, inconsiderate, catty, steely – she has the morals of a convent sister. That is her conflict. That is why she overrides all conversation, won't listen to anyone, misquotes, mispronounces, misremembers (although she delights in reminding me of trivial incidents from my childhood – she knows I hate this, because now she does it obliquely) to a degree where only a psychological explanation makes sense. And yet does it all with an air of utter innocence. One can't be angry – actively remonstrate; one can only be morose.

I, of course, felt betrayed. Possibly the arrival of H affected me traumatically more than I know. In any case, I began to grow out of that particular need – sisterly affection. The next need is intellectual. There she fails completely. I am retarded by her intellectually (just as she never gave F any chance to be himself – at least as he might have been) then, as well as sentimentally. First, she stood between me and girls, then she stood between me and ideas. All this, really, even though she isn't Celtic in other ways, is Cornish. Black, involved, incoiled obstinacy. One can't call it maliciousness, because it is all unconscious. She couldn't bear it a moment to know she was such a peasant-female monster.

But as E points out when I tell her her own mother must not be blamed for her deficiencies – sloth, vacuity, fecklessness (the typical syndrome of town-peasant civilizations, the disease which gave rise to Methodism) – I behave as if M can be and is blamed.

I still feel resentment against her. To show sentiment or softness to her still presents itself as a throwing in of the towel – yes, tradition is best, like mother, like son, *plus ça change*, collapse all along the line. If I was kind to her, it would be to deny evolution. That sounds an empty generalization, a poor excuse for unkindness. But evolution makes it impossible for me even to pretend the kindness she perhaps craves.

We travelled back on a beautiful blue, bright day. Woke up in the morning – windows luminous blue squares. Like Greece. And Old Leigh, like Greece, sparkling tide, silver, blue, diamonds – and the trawling-caiques. We drank beer on a sunny deserted terrace of a pub. Caught the next

---

[1] JF's maternal grandfather John Richards (1864–1930), who had come to London from his native Cornwall soon after his marriage to Elizabeth Pascoe Whear, was chief buyer of lace for the John Lewis department store. Gladys May, the eldest of his two children, was born in 1899 and Stanley in 1905.

[2] See note on page 393.

train. London in an amber mist – decadent, Turneresque; giant kilns pouring white smoke into the honey-dusty air. I can't ever remember such a change – between the clear, warm brilliance of Leigh and the great smoke-dream of London. Two other worlds.

Working now at the *Phil H M* – constantly afraid that it will be anticipated. The ideas in it are latent everywhere – examples everywhere. Yet I can't work consistently – spurt and lag, drift, row. It doesn't make me neurotic any more. I can only create in this way, in a succession of 'right' moods. Perhaps it is because I lack no confidence, ultimately; I lack confidence technically. I have to wait for the ideas to carry the style. I don't think I shall ever have a style to carry the ideas. But in a scientific world it is the ideas that count.

'a sure symptom of love is general incivility' – P & P.[1] E and I rate high here. In the last three months we have had precisely three visits – we could really sustain a desert island perfectly well. It was our first wedding anniversary on the 2nd – absurd to worship such dates, but they are convenient as stock-taking pauses. We still go on with the same one-in-twoness – with a curious equality, considering we are so unlike in countless ways. She has acquired this last year, also, a firm balance I never thought possible – an ability to accept, to shift the ballast, take the blows. There is still Anna; Roy seems to have disappeared. We haven't seen him since the hectic last days of D. Sharrocks' leave.

The difference between Jane Austen and other novelists. They would consider Mr Bennet sufficient; but she goes the step further – to Elizabeth. There is, in all her heroines, an absolute moral perfection – charming prigs, practical saints, their hate of pretence, their love of justice, the admittal of the powers of the ego, the libido. Their natural goodness. She does this better than anyone else in English (in world?) literature – that is why, beyond all her great gifts of selection, dialogue, psychological shrewdness, she is great.

J. Austen, *Northanger Abbey*. A deliciously swashbuckling piece of malice; but off-centre; too full of the joy of pinning; of cutting style; this is *haute couture* – horticulture. E.

Pride and Prejudice. The most tensely sexual of all. It is the secret of her novels – that sheen of sexuality upon everything. The minute detailing of the foreplay.

That, and the exquisite calculation of chances – who will be paired off together?

---

[1] *Pride and Prejudice*.

Sex and hazard.

Also the intense concern she creates for her characters – such a concern – for Emma and Knightley, Elizabeth and Darcy – that they move like no other characters in literature. Live, so that it is a living concern.

R and Juliet. I'm doing it with the girls. It bores them terribly, especially the conceits. The scientific age has brought a two-edged literalness. They are like snails, won't be coaxed from their shells. S does it, of course, in the end. They laugh at Romeo grovelling on the ground, but when Friar Laurence starts his tirade of reproach, all silence.[1] Strange, the boomerangs of S's genius – just as you think him done for, he has them. I think it is a danger – they live in exile from the fantastic, the baroque, metaphorical way of thinking. It is not that that is how S's age thought, and that this is how they think; they live in exile from poetry. It is really far more terrible than the defeat of religion by science – a pseudo-science. It is not faith that it matters to have lost these last three hundred years, but poetic feeling.

I mean, of course, a common poetic feeling; actual poets and poetry are only symptomatic of the richness or poverty of the common poetic feeling of the age.

12 April

E's mother has been here for a week – a strain, though not for the stock reasons; as a mother-in-law she could not be bettered. But she is of a hopeless shallowness, childishness, vacancy; it is as if she was arrested at the age of twelve. Perfectly childlike, she does exactly what she is told. E bullies her up hill and down dale in a gentle sort of way. Her mother has really no clear image of her – and E is all her father, physically and mentally.

She eats sweets, nibbles, selects, connoisseurs like a child. And reads what she calls 'books' – 'I'll look at my book' – magazines. Reads them laboriously, carefully, from cover to cover. Everything new bewilders and fascinates her. If she wasn't in the shape of an elderly woman, it would be rather charming. As it is, it is superficially grotesque, quickly irritating (one makes a joke, she carries it on, like a child, too long) – and profoundly, of course, pathetic. There is still a will to learn there, a kind of unbroken expectation; almost a sweetness, at moments.

---

[1] After Friar Laurence tells Romeo that he has been banished from Verona, Romeo falls to the ground and threatens to kill himself. The friar rebukes him: 'Hold thy desperate hand. Art thou a man? Thy form cries out thou art. Thy tears are womanish, thy wild acts denote the unreasonable fury of a beast. Unseemly woman in a seeming man, or ill-beseeming beast in seeming both! Thou hast amazed me. By my holy order, I thought thy disposition better tempered . . .'

And almost a terrible tiredness, a prenatal, absolutely inescapable tiredness – a hopelessness. One hears it in the voice – the flat, beaten, whining Birmingham accent with its hideous dipthongs and depressive sentence stress. The eternal wet day in the endless working-class suburb.

What depths of will-lessness there must be in those who don't escape from it – even the poorest and humblest. It isn't a matter of taste, Birmingham; it's a fundamental attack on life.

Jane, *Sanditon*. I think this promised best of all – a delicious gallery of grotesques – Alice in Wonderland. Charlotte is Alice – Dodgson must have read this – the Mad Hatter's Tea-party of Chap 10. Chaps 7, 8 and 10 are about the funniest in English literature. The delicious ambiguity of Charlotte's attitude – both malicious and innocent – and always right, so effortlessly central.

28 April

What a diary must preserve – the attitudes and nature of the diarist. Therefore, all excision, amendment, clarification, cleaning; one must think. The language can be cleaned, perhaps; but every change from the written word is a lie. In my case, if I ever revised, I should want to hide the self-excusing, the priggishness.

30 April

Visit to Catherine Ginsberg, Roy's psychiatrist. R has moved, we cannot get in touch with him. E cannot see Anna without his permission.

A horrid brick block off the Edgware Road; seedy, 1930s gloom. The waiting-room was heavy, hot; icons, wood carvings, a gilt crucifix; like a town priest's study. She was like an elderly modiste. Sharp and dominating, immediately hostile to me; or perhaps her sharp probing was natural in the circumstances. But she took Roy's side in a manner that seemed a little strange. You're lying, she seemed to say, in a careful Germanic voice. The facts are otherwise, stop being slippery. Why hadn't E been to see her before? Why hadn't we got custody of Anna? Didn't we want Anna as a tool, to cement our marriage? Were we happy (surely not)? She would say nothing. It was not my concern. She must see E. Neither of us was to see Roy.

I found it hopelessly unsatisfactory. Her influence over Roy I find easy to imagine. A *Mutter*-will.

Other questions. Would we take Anna? Yes.

She kept on calling me the obstacle. She evidently meant as regards R's reluctance to part with Anna; but no doubt it is in other ways too. The great Catholic womb. What always has been, always must be.

Perhaps the oddest thing was first. When I arrived, a girl who opened the door said it was a mistake. Tuesday, not today (Monday) at six. But

I had written it down as she spoke, and repeated it. And she seems too methodical to make mistakes of that kind.

4 May
We went to Kew today; a pure blue Sunday. E with a cold, in her best grey coat. Trees and sky and the beautifully plump and elegant toy of glass. E didn't like it. Walked slowly, frowning, very adult; then sucking an orange ice-lolly on the station platform, incongruously childlike. I liked it, the moving groups over the grass, the singing birds, absurd profusion of flowers. Very impressionist, such scenes. For fine Sundays, nothing can beat impressionism.

Rent increase; already they take five guineas a week. Now it's to be six. We shall have to leave. It's too much to lose each week, even with E working, as she now is, full-time at the MRC.[1] Poverty is now part of me; but I sense a kind of revolution coming. There is still very little I would (indeed could) do for money; but sometimes the strain rises above the surface of my acceptance. The great black back of this wall-to-wall poverty that we have had for the last four or five years; we swing from Friday to Friday. Like squirrels on the run; it doesn't do to think of a branch or Friday giving way.

10 May
Creation by effort; it is despised. What is admired is the 'natural' genius of the 'born' artist. An artist 'creates' in 'mystery'. All these views of art are semi-religious – art as symbol of the mysterious. It seems to me that it is a phase that is disappearing; has already disappeared in poetry; the 'natural', 'born' poet is in these days a museum figure. People like Dylan Thomas may seem 'born' poets; but he laboured as hard as Mallarmé over his poems.[2] The more self-conscious art becomes, the more artificial, the more self-made, the artist must be. It is, increasingly, a matter of will and effort – the part played by innate gifts diminishes proportionately.

It is something no critic takes into account. But in a properly humanist critical theory, the artist's struggle to express himself would count in the final evaluation.

I say this partly for myself. I seem to have endless obstacles to over-come – laziness, doubt, slowness, the cliché – so that if I finally achieve

[1] Medical Research Council.
[2] Stéphane Mallarmé (1842–1898) believed that the poet's chief purpose was to express the ideal of things – to describe, for example, not an individual flower but the essence of all flowers. In the pursuit of this ideal, he engaged in a life-long struggle to create a more intensely concentrated language capable of expressing such essences.

anything, at least it will be in spite of myself; self-taught, self-made. And no aid from the bloody muses.

Frances Mary Peard, *One Year* (1869).[1] An interesting bit of Victoriana, mainly because of the influence of Jane; still something of her clear vision and moral centrality. Also the pious, priggish tone of Mrs Hofland.[2] But it has its charms, that rural mid-Victorian world; vicarage piety, smothered undercurrents, tortured conscience. What I would like to know is how they behaved sexually. How actual is the impression given? Did sexual enjoyment, naked dilly-dallying, exist, and was not spoken of? Or was it not spoken of because it did not exist? Or was the little that did exist so forbidden, so secret, so deliciously un-Victorian, that it was enough? Delicate little orgies of lust and conscience that could only keep the age going by being unrecorded?

E. M. Hull, *The Sheik*.[3] Books like these – their extraordinary popularity – are ten times more valuable to a historian than the literary masterpieces. The undercurrent of sadism in this book, for instance; the inherent fascism.

1 June
The Moscow Arts Theatre, *Uncle Vanya*. This is precisely why I don't go to the theatre, because no one acts like this – with absolute lack of effort. These Russian actors, like their best musicians, have no technique – by which I mean, of course, that their technique is so perfect, so assured (and must therefore also be so instinctive) that it disappears.[4] Even the

---

[1] Frances Mary Peard (1835–1922) was a prolific writer of historical novels and romances, chiefly for young girls. *One Year* chronicles the twelve-month journey from sorrow to happiness of Ursule, orphaned daughter of a French artist.

[2] Mrs Hofland (1770–1844) was a popular writer of children's books and rather pompous moral tales. She was married to the landscape painter Thomas Christopher Hofland.

[3] Published in 1919, *The Sheik* was the first novel of Edith Maude Hull, the wife of a Derbyshire pig farmer. It told the story of English aristocrat Diana Mayo, who is captured by an Arab sheikh during her travels in the desert. After at first putting up spirited resistance, she is ravished again and again, but eventually falls in love with her captor who turns out to be the long-lost son of an English nobleman. Critics dismissed the novel as pornographic trash, but it was a best-seller and turned into a Rudolph Valentino film in 1921.

[4] Over a period of a week in mid-May, the Moscow Arts Theatre put on three Chekhov plays at the Sadler's Wells Theatre – *The Cherry Orchard*, *The Three Sisters* and *Uncle Vanya*. In the latter, *The Times* reviewer wrote of the cast's performance: 'It is the demonstration that actors working together as a permanent company can emerge from months of rigorous rehearsing with the instancy and freshness of their night-to-night attack unimpaired (*Times*, 19 May 1958).'

best English actors and actresses are too consciously in command of their technique – they show off. These Russians never show off – they are beyond that. There is consequently none of that conflict of stage personalities always implicit in English casts. The Russians are a team – there is a level at which they must acknowledge superiority or inferiority, but it is beyond the level of technique.

I think – though none of the critics I've read mention this – it can only come from one thing – a deep and profound discipline; all the conceit, the love of limelight, the egocentricity is drilled, produced out of them. They do not set themselves on the stage; they are *mise en scène*. I have an idea that they would fall a little short at the very highest level in drama – at *Hamlet, Oedipus Rex,* or any great poetic tragedy. They would not have quite the same soaring freedom; the element of the mechanical in their methods would show up. But for all realism, comedy, tragi-comedy, prose tragedy (how well they must do Ibsen!), they are on a quite different, and higher, level than anything in the West; and this must be precisely because they come from a Socialist society. Such self-abnegation could not exist in a capitalist world.

The only thing I disliked was the Marxist interpretion of *Uncle Vanya* – making Astra the play's central character, and Uncle Vanya a vaguely effete number two. To justify this, the play has to be turned into more of a comedy than it is; but it is fundamentally a tragedy. Whatever Chekov said about farces, he meant metaphysically, not literally. His plays show that certain lives are a farce; but the central characters themselves are not farcical. Sympathetical similes, perhaps, but not guffaws.

We went to the Moscow Arts with Podge – who seems more eagerly and enthusiastically different than ever. He told an amusing story about Allen Ginsberg, one of the new American literary clique – the Beat Generation – who came to Oxford to lecture to the Jesus College Literary Society. Ginsberg started his lecture by saying that he had landed in Ireland before coming on to England. 'Soon as I landed, I felt a kind of weight pressing on the top of my head. And I knew what it was. I knew what it was. It was the Church. And you know what I did? I went straight into the first church, and I went straight up the aisle of that church, and I stood before the altar. I stood right there in front of the altar. And you know what I did? I masturbated, right there. And that was good. That was *real.*'

The Literary Society, said Podge, rose to a man and hurled him gently out of the room.

8 July
Dream. A lecture-hall or large refectory; a long table. An atmosphere vaguely religious, serious. I am at the bottom of the table; at the top is

a slightly raised transverse table. A kind of brains trust; I despise them. They appeal with great respect to an old woman – she is to help them answer. But she seems disconcerted and tongue-tied. I leave the room. Outside, in the darkness, I see from an open doorway that it is raining hard. I shall have to wait to go. I am isolated, apart from all the people in the room; yet I feel quite sure of myself, untroubled.

(This somewhat puzzles me; the night before I was reading Martin's *The Experiment in Depth*,[1] a Jungian attempt at a new philosophy. A rather naïf one, in many ways – far-fetched, I thought, in its clinical examples of dreams and their Jungian interpretation. The 'old woman' is plainly the Magna Mater[2] not coming up to scratch. My scepticism asserting itself?)

Mark Twain, *A Tramp Abroad*. Funnier than my two previous favourite funny authors – Jerome K. Jerome and Thurber; and I see why. They are both no more than plagiarizers of Clemens. Jerome even uses the same name – Harris. And Thurber's drawings, his famous simple style – pure Twain. Twain's the great source.[3]

11 July

Dream. In a church or chapel. I am sitting, a scattered congregation. There is a disturbance at the front. It is G. Mansell. He is being ejected. But then I am suddenly aware that everyone is watching me. They are standing. I am sitting. A vague determination to go on sitting.

(This has an obvious dramatic explanation – envy of G. Mansell's success as a BBC producer, etc. Contempt for him, then shame at my own situation.)

12 July

Dream. I am sitting in a class with one of my girls (the ugliest, Drieux) on my knee. It is not erotic; appears normal. Later, as I want to go on with a lesson, some of them start shouting and throwing their books. I

---

[1] In *Experiment in Depth* (Routledge & Kegan Paul, 1955) P. W. Martin considered how the psychologist Carl Jung, the poet T. S. Eliot and the historian A. J. Toynbee had, from their different perspectives, made use of a 'mythical method' – an exploration of the symbols, vision and ideas which, acting on the unconscious, enable communities to find new values and aims. Believing that this method had been mostly misused by totalitarian ideologues, Martin set out to establish how it could be put to better purpose.

[2] Carl Jung's archetype of the primordial mother image.

[3] *A Tramp Abroad* is a comic account of clergyman Joseph Twichell's journey on foot through Germany, Switzerland and Italy in 1878. His travelling companion is Mr Harris, whom he hires 'in the capacity of agent'.

do not insist, end the lesson, thinking, 'They have given me a present, I mustn't be strict.' But I was hurt that they wanted the lesson to end.

(This is also from a type of dream I have had before – what I will call the 'school' dream. Drieux was the one who chose and bought the two records they gave me as a present recently.

These are fragments of dream. On both mornings I remembered to remember within thirty seconds of waking – but it was too late. The second dream was definitely a 'school' dream; the one on the 11th had completely gone – but for the chapel scene.)

13 July

Dream. Completely disappeared.

14 July

Dream. I had two distinct major themes; and dimly recalled them when half awake. But what the themes were, I do not know. (These last two days the dreams have been difficult to remember. Therefore significant; the unconscious guards its secrets? As mysteries?)

16 July

Dream. General theme – a staff-room. Also a theme I have dreamt before.

(I woke and remembered many details. But went to sleep again, and now they are all gone.

I went to bed in a worried state, and woke up worried. But the dream seemed restful.)

17 July

Dream. Nothing recalled.

19 July

Dream. Three incidents. One at Ipplepen. I am walking along a road with M and F and E? I see a path to the right. I know that if I go up it a little way, I shall have a view down a hedge where there are often rabbits. But when I go up the path, it opens out into a wide valley of fields – no rabbits, and unlike Devon. But I see old Major, the farmer, approaching from the road. I feel vaguely guilty.

Two (earlier or later?). At a school – oddly enough it has features that are reminiscent of Bedford, Spetsai and Ashridge. Stone floors. I seem to be running away from something, though without any great sense of fear. I mounted stairs and got into a large attic, apparently over a domed roof. Eventually I got into difficulties as I explored this roof. There were beams half-hidden in plaster. Footing was difficult. I was afraid of falling through, but once again no urgent sense of fear. I got back to the door of the attic.

Three. Very obscure. I am with a group of people, standing near railway lines; there is a high pole fence on either side. Everyone seems worried a horse cannot jump the fence, because there is another fence too close to it. (I soon aftwards saw newsreels of the International Horse Show.) A train passes. A black square satchel falls; it has a lamp and flags inside. It evidently belongs to the guard. The guard appears. He has jumped off the train. We walk away? (Only very vaguely remembered.)

(One. I remember there was such a corner, when I used to see – and poach – Major's rabbits. But I can't remember it in detail consciously – whence the illogical change of scenery?

Two. The attic loft with the dome recalls two incidents long, long ago. A visit to Canterbury Cathedral, when I was taken round the vault-spaces in the roof. And a similar place at Ashridge.

Three. The guard. A driver did recently leap from a train just as it was about to crash.)

1 August
Drunk. End of term, so Fletcher and I drank too much. When I was drunk I noticed that to me he was an '*égout*'. Fletcher-*égout*. Also I talk to the future. That is, I imagine that in some future age time is conquered; they come back and watch us; so I speak to them.

Another observation – alcohol makes everything more upward. You fix a point and everything flows upward. Perhaps alcohol is no more than an upward-motion-inducing drug.

Ashridge. We went back there with F. The whole huge monster deserted. We walked through the house, and not a soul; I mean not a soul doubly. A terrible soullessness in everything. The gardens still smooth, well-kept, peaceful. *Sic transit* . . . but for me, it was the personal past. A strange sort of affection, quite unexpected. The place seems to be almost certainly doomed. It ceases to function as a college in another two months.[1] For me it is haunted by those girls – Sally and Sanchia, and the rest of them; all the noise of a big evening there, two or three hundred people – and the gardens. The gardens and the girls; a sort of lost labyrinth; a labyrinth like the Minoan caves, like the maze dances – it is impossible to say what their real significance was. So at Ashridge I found something I couldn't analyse, beyond the mere conventional sorrow at time past, both personal and architectural; a kind of deep myth that is still there, still living. Only one would never find it out. But

---

[1] The girls' finishing school was moved to new premises in Aylesbury, and a year later the Ashridge estate would become host to a new educational establishment, the Ashridge Management College, which still exists today.

I felt it acutely once or twice, as if it had happened only yesterday, as if
it was still to come. Immutability of some events.

2 August
I accidentally dropped my new spectacles – in their case. I immediately
remembered that in a dream recently I did actually break them.

5 September
Term has started again. Flocks of Greeks, the usual strange hybrids –
Persian-Germans, French-Chinese. Bawdiness, provincialism. And I see
quicker how they will develop. But I shall not have a class to compare with
last year's. None of them interest me much. A Persian-German has psychological (and ornithological) possibilities; will repay watching. And there is
a fine Cretan, fine in her Turkish-Greek amiability of countenance and
nobility of temperament, pride and indolence. Not a literal indolence, she
works and notes down very conscientiously, but the racial one.

Stephanian came back today, presented me with a cigarette but full
of various exotic Persian smokeables. So pretty that I felt quite dizzy
afterwards; a milky blue suit and a deep tan and an elegance that would
not disgrace the rue de la Paix. Afterwards in the public library I stood
and admired the magnificent perfume of the woman next to me; it
seemed to follow me wherever I went. It was on the box.

Stephanian is an oddly provoking mixture of prettiness, elegance,
simplicity, gaiety, and sweat; *faisandée.*

15 September
Dr Zhivago, Pasternak. This is a great novel. That is, in spite of a pedes-
trian translation and innate faults (or deliberate lacks, like pauses in
music) it is of great size. The characters have greatness, and that in the
face of their transience – which means, of course, that he has touched
their essence. When the essence is arrived at, then his method is
successful – or any method (Joyce, Woolf, Kafka, etc).

Very close parallels with impressionist art – Debussy above all.
Coincidence piled on coincidence – why has no one thought of this
before? What is the functioning of any machine but an extraordinary
series of coincidences?

The best thing is the tragic love affaire, arrived at by the most skilful
understatement; and infinitely more real than other literary tragic love
affaires of this century. *For Whom The Bell Tolls?* – sentimental in comparison. Perhaps that of *The Great Gatsby* was near it. But that was a particular civilization condemned by implication, whereas Pasternak's lovers
are the hub of the book. Lara is an anima-figure, of course; if for no
other reason, she and Zhivago must separate – to preserve her as anima,
as well as soul of Russia and the other obvious symbolizations.

24 October
Stendhal, *Chartreuse de Parme.* I enjoyed this; read it at great gulps. Here and there one stops, and wonders why it is a great novel; but then it always takes you by surprise. Like Puccini.

Voltaire and Racine are Stendhal's effective parents; the irony and bitter egoism of the one, the grandeur and formality of the other. At even his most romantic, Stendhal describes, observes.

In Stendhal, too, that priggishness I like in Jane A; his is a more snobbish, aristocratic priggishness; but profoundly right. JA's centrality is moral; Stendhal's is political, social. Contempt for the morally weak; contempt for the politically corrupt.

And then, his excellent plainness of style. The more romantic one's material, the plainer one's rendition. And vice versa.

9 November
Jackson Pollock. Exhibition at Whitechapel Gallery. Great wad-sized canvases dribbled, splashed, slashed with colour. Dozens of eminently serious people staring at them. Pollock's artistic qualities seem fairly clear – now and then a nice sense of colour (and often, not) and a way with sloppy, casual arabesques ('squiggles'). Why he has turned the art world upside-down seems no less clear. One, he is sailing a point nearer non-art, or nature, or hazard, or chaos; two, absolute rejection of all inhibition; three, enormous scope for criticism. This last point is the most important. Increasingly, in all the arts, the adjective 'great' means 'interesting' or 'giving scope for discussion and display of sensitivity and abuse'. Words like 'seminal', 'significant', 'central' – they mean simply that the art so described is so ambiguous that the spectator can find in it what he wants to find. Of course there may be a certain skill in achieving such ambiguity, or meaninglessness. True, too, that if the age finds an artist great, he must be, in at least one sense, great, and of value.

I felt, in the gallery, there is something intolerably decadent in this art. Not decadent in the mere breakdown of the rules – nor as the fuddy-duddies of the Royal Academy use 'decadent' – and not even decadent in its personal intention, but decadent in the way it is abused by the age. This is a spectator age; we are like the eighteenth-century crowds who would gape at any novelty. Our novelties are then extreme art forms. There is something for everyone in them; and fundamentally, they touch nowhere. I'm sure Pollock was deeply serious; but all he turned out is divertissements.

Also, his art is easy to imitate. It requires no discipline and no genius (now that he has discovered the technique), but only a flair of a kind thousands of people with an 'eye' for colour possess. But all great art has this in common; it is inimitable. It transcends, it stands apart, it is isolated. We lose ourselves in what we could never create.

Some of his paintings are agreeable. *One*, a vast pattern of splashes, greens, faded purples, zinc whites, dull browns. *Summertime*. These two would make a nice background to real art. *Scent* – a fuzz of Dufy colours, pinks, whites, yellows, geraniums. He touched an essence there.

And one remarkable picture, called *Deep*. Clouds of white parting to reveal a rift, sepia, indigo, flecked red. Here he did arrive at something profound, and valid. Psychoanalytically and poetically, and in a purely technical sense. An abstraction of the mystery. But it seemed the only picture no one looked twice at.

A beautiful experience. An exhibition of classical Indian dancing by Indrani.[1] An endless fluency of pose, the rippling hands, the jingling feet; dance of the eyes, dance of the smile – the whole gamut of the smiles, hands, arms, legs, hips, feet. European dancing is monochrome in comparison; dull, affected.

Indrani is very beautiful, too; girlish and mature at the same time. The music full of sinuosities, recapitulations, syncopations. What we search for in Spanish and Balkan folk music is in India; what we glimpse in them in the remote distance is what is present in Indian music. I was so absorbed that I sat stiffly; lost. Had the almost lost feeling of enthusiasm, of alienation. So charmed that the eternal twentieth-century power to criticize was lost. Such dancing steals the mind away.

11 January 1959
Graham Greene, *The Quiet American*. A kind of conjuring trick, that economy in story-telling, it ruins one's taste for other styles; or rather for any other style of story-telling. The only kind of writing it doesn't shabbify is the poetic, the evocative of mood. Woolf, say, a James – the prose poets. But when they try and have one foot in both camps (one in the Greene-land, the other in poetry), the result is always a little . . . blurred, irritating. Greene is like Holbein; so true, in many ways, that all other techniques of portraiture seem tedious. The dangers are obvious; if Holbein painted a man with a straight nose as a man with a crooked nose, we should believe in the crooked nose. Surrounded by reality, the lie is easy. And Greene slips in all sorts of psychological and even physical inaccuracies; that is, he is normally so *vraisemblable* that he can be *invraisemblable* with impunity.

Defoe – Wilkie Collins – Greene.

---

[1] Daughter of the well-known dancer and teacher Ragini Devi, in a succession of international tours Indrani Bajpai Rahman (1930–1999) introduced Indian classical dance to audiences around the world. On this particular tour she adopted the south Indian dance style of *bharata natyam*.

12 February
E being ill. Fainting, being sick, groaning, diarrhoea, all at the same time (about 5 a.m.). A vile rebellion of the intestines. The doctor said it was gastro-enteritis.

We seem at last likely to move – to a flat in Church Row, No. 28. The corner-house. Derelict. It is owned by the Western Investment Company – a Mr Shinder, a shifty, swindling sort of name. I don't trust them an inch; and it will cost us more to live there than here, and here is already more than enough. But the place excites. To live in a 1720 house and up in the sky, surrounded by roofs, gardens, vistas. Anyone sensible would turn it down, for economic reasons (given our income – as it is we owe rent here. E is overdrawn), and so ought we. But I hope violently that we get in.

The Aristos. I get no further with it. Laziness, partly; and lack of time. I need stretches of several hours free to concentrate on it. The ideas I see everywhere, in every book, in every paper. And I feel resigned to seeing the ideas stated elsewhere. Perhaps better. More cautiously than I ever could or would.

The Greek poems seem nearly ready. I do nothing. It may be my general constipatedness. But every time I look at them after a period of not looking, there are alterations. And I feel instinctively that they are *not* ready. Some need destroying, and there are gaps. I get stuck with lines. The current one is 'From the salt orchards of the sea' – a poem will coalesce round it, but lines like these rattle down the slope, won't be fixed, embedded.

14 February
The cry of the rag and bone man. Sad, remote – the last of the street-cries. It was a terrible patina of goneness, remoteness. A last cry of the old life, the terrible, beautiful old world of the unprotected individual; of the individual, in short.

19 February
John Braine, *Room at the Top.* Cheap stuff, really; Arnold Bennett all over again. *The Card.*[1] But it has a certain power. At least it avoids the deathly

[1] Braine's novel (1957) follows the fortunes of the opportunistic Joe Lampton, who schemes and sleeps his way to the top in a provincial town. Denry Machin, the hero of Arnold Bennett's 'Five Towns' novel *The Card* (1911), shows a similar appetite for material success, through a series of adventures quickly rising from solicitor's clerk to become mayor of the Potteries town of Bursley.

pallor of most of our literature – the damned civilization in all its manifestations. Something living, unscrupulous, Elizabethan in this book. But terrible faults – is the hero worshipped or satirized? A fatal case of the first person singular. No objectivity of the kind needed in this book is possible.

A worshipping, in any case, of the least pleasant aspects.

DHL. Look! We have come through! For the first time L's poetry bored me. The constant lack of any real rhythm, the lines clotted with too many repetitions, the thickness of the colours; there is, too, an incipient *mièvrerie*, an affected sentimentality that misses by miles. A matter of balance – the more intimate the subject, the more classical the treatment. At least, a bit more of that. Everything is flooded and gushed away. Here and there, splendid poems. But the sequence is indigestible. I've been reading a lot of Yeats recently. That splendid always unexpected limpid rhythmic voice; the clean, mysterious images, bright as songs. The truth is, Lawrence is not much of a *poet* beside Yeats. Y married music and meaning; Lawrence got his emotions out. Lawrence despised, or talented, the medium; Yeats venerated it. Lawrence isn't really a poet at all, but an emotion; a wordy emotion. A hit-or-miss man with words; and Yeats was an oracle; that is, was both inspired and cautious. An interloper, Lawrence; a defiler of the poetic tradition.

10 March
A smell of gas while I was giving a private lesson to Villitsueth, my Siamese. I didn't think much of it. When Villitsueth had gone I went outside the door to see if I could trace the source. The little woman in the next-door flat appeared – weeping, face distraught. Her young husband had tried to kill himself. She didn't tell us this, we learnt it by listening to the phone calls she made.

I'd seen him come in only half an hour before; and he must have known we were in, for the door was open – I was standing in the bathroom looking out for Villitsueth. I suppose he expected us to rescue him sooner than we did. For the gas to come through into our flat he must have left a cupboard door open (one they always keep shut normally); and he must have left the door on the latch, since his wife got in without difficulty.

A very quiet couple; too quiet, when one looks back. They never quarrel, one never sees them. She said over the phone, 'He's done it again.' He walks heavily, on his heels, and says the time of day in a loud voice.

I don't find the fact of it puzzling; but the reality is strange – the coming in and turning on the gas, the step into death amid the petty trivia of the evening. As if one looked up and the old man himself was there, in the door; the skull with the sockets.

*

Scott Fitzgerald, *The Beautiful and the Damned.* SF seems to me to get better and better. This is a tragedy, not just a trial run for *The Great Gatsby.* But a genuinely tragic vision, and one of the saddest, and most beautiful, of the century.[1] The trouble is that it has to be seen through the tinsel (the best-quality tinsel) of his clever-cleverness with words. I don't know if it is even a fault – because the truth, the true tragedy, can be felt again and again through the too clever, too bright language, and that is the age, after all. I mean this is not what SF intended, but it is what happened – that is, the division between his own intuitive sense of tragedy and waste and his determination to describe brilliantly is also typical of the age. A writer with cancer writing about cancer; and not really knowing he has cancer.

18 March
We signed the lease for the flat at 28 Church Row today. We have borrowed £90 from E's mother to finance us. But already I foresee terrible financial complications. At first we thought we could do it all ourselves; now we are calling in an electrician, a plasterer-plumber, and I can see nothing but bills ahead. I spent two hours this afternoon stripping paper off the walls of the back room. There are five coats of paint beneath, the bottom-most an old soft blue, I like to think a Georgian blue. The walls swell out in badly patched boils and carbuncles. It's like getting to know a woman – all the hidden bad points, the weaknesses; it will make the little place better to live in. With decorators, one does not know the real house. It is hidden away from one.

A man from the electricity board came while I was there, a little buck-rabbit of a man who would have nothing to do with the meter-box. 'Fifty years of old equipment there,' he said, 'all those wires. How do I know what they are?' As he had come to test the electricity, I thought he should know. But it seems he only looks at the finished job. Before he could operate, our electrician would have to label the wires, and another 'official' (*jadis* workman) called a meter-fixer would fix the meter. The mad provincialism of the twentieth century. He was not a bad man. He put it all down to the atom-bomb – the indifference of our landlord, the shoddiness of even his own fellow-officials' work. 'Nobody cares – we're all going up in a year or two. Why worry? I ask you.' I said yes, I agree. 'There's no stability in the world.' I agreed with that, too. E alternates between enthusiasm and depression. She is suddenly horsy – I don't know why it is so, but horsy, equine she is. Bossy, noisy, hooves on

---

[1] In F. Scott Fitzgerald's second novel (1922), Anthony Patch marries famous socialite Gloria Gilbert and squanders away the promise of a huge inheritance. Together the couple are, in Fitzgerald's words, 'wrecked on the shoals of dissipation'.

cobbles, horse-piss, brash; weird sallies into characters that don't suit
her. The business-woman, the woman-who-knows-her-mind, the *House
and Garden* woman, the everybody-says-so woman.

On verra.

13 April

28 Church Row. We moved in here a fortnight ago, and the place is still
a sty, but gradually it begins to have the appearance of the well-decorated
and enviable flat. All these days are screwing, unscrewing, chipping,
planing, plastering, sweeping, washing, sawing; and E paints. My hands are
grimed beyond redemption. I'll have to wait for fresh skin to grow. On
the whole I have enjoyed it. A flat in a state of virgin dereliction is like a
bad hedge; it's a pleasure to plash, even though one's vaguely haunted by
the futility of it all. It will go dirty again, and derelict; and we have only
the seven-year lease. It is silly to do things for eternity. Nevertheless one is
caught up in the perfection mania; always the last touch.

55 Frognal was being converted in our last week there; walls down,
the two flats turned into four. A young second-hand and antique dealer
from Kentish Town helped us to move. We carried everything down the
two floors at 55 and up the three here. At the end of that day, I felt
more exhausted than I have for years. Since farming days. The strange
way muscles won't obey the will; the fingers unable to grip.

For several days, all draughts and dirt. I spent a lot of time on a
chimney-piece; pointing it and levelling it up. It had been boarded in
and was all crumbling. Now it looks good. Tearing out shelves, simplifying things. There was an overlay, everywhere, of unnecessary paper,
hooks, screens, pipes, wires. Making doors and windows fit.

But the sunlight and the roofs, chimneys, views, the immediate acces-
sibility of old Hampstead, that is delightful. E went off the rails once or
twice; 'marish. She loses her head over details, sets ideals and cries at
their impossibility. We spend too much money, and in typical fashion
spend pounds on expensive food. We need some luxury.

We bought a marble-topped washstand for the kitchen. Painted white,
it will do well. 30/-.

I have done a lot of plastering; a most enjoyable occupation. We know
all about the various chemicals and materials needed for dozens of jobs,
filler- and cleaner-wise.

There's not much of the original structure – the window embrasures,
the uphill-downhill floors, one or two beams. But we can't complain; it
feels like an old house, is very soundproof, individual, high over traffic,
and ours; so we have to like it.

Strange, the experience of the first ten days, cut off from the world.
We lived the place, really, quite separated, isolated, buried. Going back
to work, normality was unreal.

1 May

Poem-making is arranging words as one wants to express meanings one wants to express. The usual argument against this kind of definition is that it leads to the Ivory Tower – to isolationism, anarchy, etc. But there is a natural insurance against such possibilities – that is, the *total* meaning one wants to express is always affected by, and therefore includes, a public reaction. Only a minute proportion of poets have ever really *meant*, 'This is my poem, this is what I say, and I do not care whether it is ever read by anyone or not.' Order in poetry grows like order in society, out of the nature of things. There is a natural fulcrum between what a poet wants to say and between the esteem he wishes to attract. With one, it is almost all self-expression and to hell with the esteem; with another it is public respect and *sauve-qui-peut* for his deepest personal aims. And the test is empirical – is the poet balanced and happy as a poet making the poems he makes? If he is, he is at his fulcrum; if he isn't, something wrong. And all great poets have a fulcrum near the centre (ignoring some so-called great poets of recent times, whose 'greatness' is only a symptom of the age they live in).

'A symptom of the age' – well, the age is a sickness. 'What's wrong with him?' 'He's got the age.'

5 May

Brontë, *Wuthering Heights*. Rereading this, and falling again under its spell. Why is it one of the five or six great English novels? Firstly, because it is entirely true of the imaginative world; that is, the unconscious world and the day-dream world. And where it outrages ordinary reality, it gains. (When did I read it last? In New College Gardens in 1949, I think.)[1] I marked the romantically 'precious' passages only to see this time how little their preciosity matters. It has more imaginative reality, if anything. Second, Heathcliff; he is *sui generis*, an archetype in every man – something from Othello? Third, timelessness, though rooted in time. This polarity, the feeling of period, and the impression of eternal psychological truth (Heathcliff is man, Catherine his ideal), of the other domaine, so close, so far. Lastly, the polarity of the whole, the fierce extremes so boldly married.

Sitting on our roof, a strange cry. A frantic ki-ki-ki, endlessly repeated. A crow flew over, chased by a hawk. The hawk kept on attacking, twisting, falling. I hadn't the glasses, but the facts could be deduced. The crow

---

[1] See page 36.

didn't cry, therefore it could not open its beak. The only thing a crow
could take that would make a hawk so angry is the hawk's young or one
of its eggs. It must have been this. Besides, the cry was distressing. A
great calamity.

June
Look Back in Anger. The film. Very impressive, in this age and time. It
has all sorts of implausibilities and psychological *non sequiturs*, but the
tone is exactly right – the sourness of the anger, the wilful bitterness,
the hatred of the heart. And the refusal to do anything, to act positively, to *pretend* – that is this age, exactly. The death of pretence is the
death of the old society. But as yet, no new birth, no pregnancy
apparent.

6 July
First draft of a new work, *Tesserae*, almost finished.[1]

A medicine for entero-colitis. It has exactly the flavour of the pollen of
wild orchids. These curious parallels between flavours and smells and
moods often present themselves to me.

I had one the other morning walking down Arkwright Road. It was
a grey day, with a warm dry wind blowing up the hill. In those banal,
so known surroundings, I had a delicious remote evocation of a place,
a mood – almost another being, a racial memory. There is often something wild and natural in such moments, not of this age, not my conscious
self. The smells of winds particularly cause these moments. Suddenly,
for no reason, evocations, re-evocations. I cannot say what the moment
in AR evoked – a wooded landscape, a pleasing feeling of dominating,
then descending, glades . . . A curious element was the grey sky. It made
the mood more mysterious.

I am ill with entero-colitis. It is also very hot, blind blue skies. I sweat
all the time, have stomach gripe. The doctor came and looked at me;
was curt, then, when I spoke rather sharply, ungraciously polite. A
humourless civil-servant doctor. Chisholm, the usual doctor (this was his
partner), is universally despised in Hampstead. He won't diagnose, he
smiles, he is vaguely silly, he is interested in things around one's room.
But this doctor was worse, hideously sure of himself; I had hardly begun
the symptoms before he was diagnosing. And when I said, 'But I've got

---

[1] Conceived as a mosaic of narrative fragments, this unpublished manuscript,
which would be revised many times over the years, began as an account of a
friend's destructive love affair and developed into a novel of JF's early married
life.

a sore throat . . .' he said, 'The infection's moved down to the stomach.' If I had said I was also seeing the Holy Trinity on top of the wardrobe every evening, he would have shown no surprise. I think he was socially ill at ease – a grammar-schoolboy doctor. Dangerous, men who protect themselves with their profession. He asked me what my age was, as he was filling in a prescription form. 'Thirty-three,' I said. Later, I saw that it said on the form, 'Prescriptions may not be given to children under fourteen.'

Roman pantomime – skill of Americans with musical comedy. Imperial security – debased and vulgar art forms.

Art sprang naturally out of Greek life, and out of English life (to a lesser degree). But the Romans had no natural source; they copied from Greece. The Americans either copy from England (Europe) (like the great Roman writers from Greece) or try and be American and sink into the debased art form. When Americans and Romans are great, it is in spite of that fact that they are Americans and Romans. When Greeks and Englishmen are great, it is because they are Greek and English. At this level, of great art, the otherwise invidious comparison does not hold. It is only the causes of greatness which are different.

1 August
Taking oneself seriously – this is the problem in poetry, and where a lot of clever people fail. It needs a certain simplicity, a naïvety.

The world (our knowledge of it) becomes increasingly complex. Therefore we need increasing recourse to a shorthand for it – to symbolize and synthesize it.

The usual objection to this is that of the scientist-philosopher; that all statements introducing factors not describing the physical facts are non-scientific; therefore bad. But they are simply non-scientific. In fact synthetic words are like the aeroplane; they are essential if one man is to know all the world. To know the world may mean (to have scientific sense) to know every detail of the world. But the obvious impossibility of that proves the validity of the other sort of synthetic knowledge.

Also, the educative point of view. How else *teach* the world to the world?

3 August
I begin to feel better now, after whatever obscure illness it was I had. I have now more or less finished *Tesserae*. The temptation is to add and add to it, but it must be short. Whatever else, to hell with verbosity.

I have now to get published: *Tesserae*, *The Aristos*, the play about the young officer (which needs rehandling), and the Spetsai novel, the *Magaristes*, or *Magus*. Then dimly, it will be Robin Hood.

I have many poems ready, too.

I become lazy over this; I need another stationary month. Though *Tesserae* is an extension of this, really.

E may have conceived. That is to say, we haven't worried, once or twice, about contraceptives. This is not the novelists' view of the business. In the world you decide to have a child and go headlong into it. Perhaps headlong is not the right word – also with calculation, financial and physical. But we have left it in hazard. E wants a child, so do I – for her, and also, I realize, for F. I feel this so strongly – that he wants us to have a child – that I think the feeling must be real in him. Though, of course, they never mention it. The other novelists' theory is that you have it at a moment of intense passion or harmony, as a kind of glove thrown in the face of mortality; whereas we treated the whole matter dubiously and semi-comically. The truth is that intense passion is impossible in the kind of non-tensional relationship I have tried to achieve with E; and that we have a stable harmony now. The mysterium, so to speak, is beyond the seedling stage, needs no special case or comment. In any case, there's something right about begetting in hazard, half by accident, perhapsing a child. By 'right' here I mean conforming to the deepest reality.

I've been reading, with the aid of a crib, Horace recently. I *must* master Latin. The thing I like about the Roman poets – above all, Martial, Juvenal, Horace – their anti-Roman qualities. It's true we think of them as the 'fine flower' – to use the old cliché – of the Roman civilization. But in fact they are all against it; their standards are Greek, Socratic, rather than Roman. It's a kind of malicious historical irony that they should be assimilated to the ages they attacked. Take away the fifteen or twenty great poets and historians of Rome and what is one left? A civilization that stinks.

The same, as usual, in America.

Dictum: the great Roman and American writers are great in spite of being Roman and American.

The greatness of the Greek civilization is that just as it planted colonies all round the then known world, it has planted a colony in every mind that has come into contact with it.

We may be Roman in our exteriors, but it is a Greek in the citadel of the mind.

1 September

ELR[1] is leaving St G's. So I find myself in her job. Head, as they call it, of the English Department, as they call it. This morning, first day of term, I sit in a marquee with the other heads facing two hundred girls. Bla from John, bla from the Air Commodore,[2] flowerbanks of pretty faces, pretty for someone. Rather banal, most of their prettiness. But how rare the dowdy ones are!

I get £100 a year more; not much more than a pound a week when tax is deducted. And much more than an hour a week extra. So there is nothing to feel better about. However, on examination, I do. Being frank, I do. Pretention lurks in me. The hideous mutating love of the uniform. The extra pip.

28 September

Saying goodbye to ELR. Fletcher and I went to her room, in Buckland Crescent, off Swiss Cottage. A horrid square room with ochre peeling wallpaper and decomposing stucco; an enormous litter of papers, envelopes, filthy cooking utensils, discarded clothes, boxes, papers, papers, all the scum of her life there. She was anxious about everything, wrought up, emotionally resolved not to be emotional. We stood around drinking whisky while she finished her packing; then to Victoria, more whisky. We got her aboard the night ferry, and walked away, waving to her and saying to each other what hell she was going into.[3] And so on. Really one doesn't feel much pity for her because she's happier walking into hell than being in limbo, determinedly, Canadian-Scottishly, anti-Methodistically. Still, she is one of those distinct personalities one doesn't like moving out of one's life; something clear, predictable, to which one can orientate oneself, gone. A lot of pious head-shaking has accompanied her going, but she couldn't have provoked it if she hadn't been the sort of person who would always have gone. Also, she has turned the contingent into the inevitable; so few have the courage, or the strength of perversity, to do that that a lot of the insiders' pity is sheer sour grapes. I mean, she has a certain small, yet tragic stature.

Her going means I am loaded down with petty details – list-making, timetable-twisting, report-writing. Futile activities that make me waste time. The dreadful organizing, everything-must-function-smoothly tic I thought I kicked off after Bedford.

---

[1] Lorraine Robinson.

[2] A cousin of John Loveridge, the Air Commodore was responsible for the general administration of the college.

[3] Lorraine Robinson had left her job at St Godric's in order to join her lover in France.

*

Great Expectations. Chap 29. This is one of those remarkable seminal chapters in Dickens which really touch something very deep and vast.[1] Archetypal chapters.

Emily Bronte conceived *Wuthering Heights* when she read this chapter. I regard this as quite certain, in spite of the fact that WH was written in 1846 and GE in 1861. Somewhere the continuum lies. Estella–Miss Havisham represent a kind of Heathcliff–Catherine pole; Pip is Edgar Linton; Joe is Nelly Dean.

Our two new tutors. A Mrs Curry; pretty, nervous, on a curious balance between being intellectual and being sharp and being frightened. But agreeably green, fresh; a gull's wing, rowan-tree sort of girl. A Miss Brameld, thirty, lady-like, one-eyed, painted, plausible, betrayed, one suspects, by some PSB cad, very elocution-voiced. She seemed cultured. But then, when we were looking through the book cupboard for some books for a class, and I showed her *The Great Gatsby*, and said, 'This might do,' she looked vague. I thought she meant that she didn't think it would do. But then, the bitch, she said, 'Who was Gatsby? Ought one to have heard of him?'

30 September
Apples in a basin of water with the tap running hard; they have a strange way of queueing up to go under the jet of water from the tap. As if eager for the force. Some profound secret in the movement – life itself, some innermost mechanical secret.

E   A dirty joke from one of her women.
A girl was raped. She went to the police.
'Can you describe the man?'
'No,' she said.
'Is there nothing?'
'Well, I think he was a conservative.'
'A conservative?'
'I think so.'

---

[1] Pip, having become a gentleman in London, returns after many years to the house of Miss Haversham. His love for the beautiful Estella, Miss Haversham's ward, is rekindled. Estella warns him that she has no heart, but Miss Haversham – whose own lover deserted her on her wedding night – urges him to love Estella however cruel she might be. 'If she favours you, love her. If she wounds you, love her. If she tears your heart to pieces – and as it gets older and stronger, it will tear deeper – love her, love her, love her!'

'But how could you tell?'
'Because I've never had it so good.'[1]

The General Election. I felt excited about it, and furious when the results were announced.[2] Nothing could better illustrate the alienation of the individual from society. If you were able to go up to any individual Englishman and say, 'Yours is the casting vote. Will you or will you not condone Cyprus, Suez, Aden?' He would vote against. But in fact he knows his vote counts for nothing. That democracy is a sham when the democrat becomes a cipher instead of a voice. It's nonsense to talk of apathy. A man in a condemned cell may look apathetic, but he's simply condemned, he's hopeless, he knows he's an atom on a beach. So he votes for his stomach, or not at all. For the status quo.

1 November
A wood near South Mimms. We went for one of our country days. Caught the wrong bus, found ourselves at Potter's Bar, walked towards what we hoped would be the country. But it wasn't. Miles of the Great Wen, suburbs, buses, garages, shop rows, concrete, asphalt. E began to cry. But then we came to more open country, and a bypass. Eight lapwing in a meadow, and on the far side of the bypass a great stubble field. We moved up it into a wood. Had lunch looking down across the field to the distant bypass; the cars tearing, zipping, streaming along it. The similarity with ants very striking; terrifying. And the wood strangely withdrawn from it; very mysterious, autumn-mysterious with wren song and robin song, a great peace, a great harvest-in. The wren and dunnock song is especially mysterious – remote, guarding; even rather frightening. The happiness I get when I enter the country again, after months away from it, is so intense that it always surprises me.

---

[1] The phrase 'You never had it so good' was popularly identified with the Conservative election campaign, which was taking place at this time. Originally a slogan for the Democratic Party during the 1952 US election campaign, the British prime minister Harold Macmillan first borrowed it for a speech he made in July 1957: 'Let us be frank about it: most of our people have never had it so good.'
[2] The General Election was held on 8 October 1959. The Conservatives were re-elected with an increased majority of 100 in spite of a number of foreign policy débâcles. In November 1956 the British had had to withdraw their forces from the Suez Canal zone after a UN-imposed armistice. In Cyprus, a campaign of violence against British rule and growing intercommunal strife between the Greek and Turkish communities had led to an abortive British plan for partition of the island. In the British protectorate of Aden, Arab nationalists were agitating for independence after a state of emergency had been declared in 1958.

Particularly so this day, which started so badly; and this pocket of real country seemed almost magically there. The wood was very pretty, an open brackeny wood, full of woodpigeons. We collected acorns, we came on a fine view to the north. Pheasants belled. We came on a crabapple tree, picked up half a basket of apples. The night dew rising, dank, very English. Always the roar of the bypass traffic. We walked along it and up a side-road to South Mimms, feeling people from another world, the old world. It gets more and more striking. The business of the roads, and the peace of the country, only a few hundred yards away. Man is totally urban now.

25 December
Christmas alone with E. We had a duck for dinner; she gave me Johnson's *Lives of the Poets*; we listened to a reading of *Beppo*.[1] Rain and wind.

January 1960
The 'language' of music and language proper (words) – the main difference is in the function of the individual note and the individual word. A note has no meaning by itself; it gains meaning by being put in a series. A word has meaning by itself; it may be ambiguous until it is placed in a context, but its meaning, or meanings, are fixed. A musical note is totally unfixed in meaning of any kind – linguistic, reminiscent, literary, emotional, psychological; even *in* a harmonic (simultaneous) group or a melodic series its meanings are manifold; depending on the temperament, race, musical experience, etc, of the listener. I think this is of importance in poetry. First of all, as regards poetry *as* music; there cannot really be 'musical' poetry, because the ultimate aims of the two arts are incompatible. Music uses a 'language' whose direct beauty and necessary effect is to multiply meaning, and even then non-linguistic meanings; poetry uses a language which must have meaning (whether the poet wishes it or not). Most of the so-called 'musical' devices in poetry – alliteration, resonance, rhyme, etc – are in fact rhythmic devices, adjuncts of music. The true sister of poetry is dancing; definitely not music in its melodic and harmonic aspects.

Secondly, the multiple imagery and ambiguities of post-symbolist verse – are these not precisely the results one would expect of an attempt to effect a shotgun marriage between music and poetry? It is impossible to get the same.

29 January
Translating Martial – the problem of the aphorism, the aphoristic line.

---

[1] Lord Byron's *Beppo: A Venetian Story* (1818), which was broadcast in the evening on the BBC Third Programme.

One cannot make it sound modern. Not the language problem – but the way of thinking. An aphorism is a generalization, therefore not modern. So much of Martial – the cynical, bitter, ironic, sarcastic, scourging side of him – goes straight into modern language. But the Roman side, the classical side, the memorably summarizing side – that's the obstacle.

Another thing – the difference between the translating with and without crib; the much greater pleasure (despite effort, despite risk of mistranslation at my level of Latin) in the translating without. The one is like the journey and the visit to the place itself; the other, a film or photograph. Beautiful when the meaning dawns through one's misty ignorance.

25 February
The Fall. This myth comes from man's jealousy of animals. From his envy of those who cannot compare and imagine; who need not.

I read Virgil, the *Eclogues*; so beautiful so far it's enough to make one weep. The extraordinary way he loads a single line.

Brotherhood – a SPCK[1] novel of the 1880s – undated and anonymous. Written in a wonderfully sober clerical grey. *Sans* light, *sans* colour, *sans* blood; yet the characters have a kind of life. And I suspect (it's easy to despise such salvationist tracts) requiring more skill than one likes to grant. The characters have a sort of moral force; a *caricature* of piety and do-goodiness. The solemnity! The earnestness! The incorruptibility of the good! The total irredeemability of the evil! A most perfectly *Victorian* book.

Hierarchy: women *must* look up to men. Workers respect employers. All things have a place. Being good, for a Victorian, was putting things in their place, and being in one's right place. A moral attempt to simplify in an age of artistic and intellectual diversification. Think of the cluttered, fussy Victorian room of the 1880s; and of those weird do-good creatures, with their moral simplicity, their one-truth will.

Virgil – the great mystery of the fourth eclogue (*Sicelides Musae* . . .). All the attempts to make it a prophecy of Christ.[2] Why not simply that the apostles, Jesus himself, knew the eclogue; incorporated it in their own deliberately constructed myth? Says Luke to Matthew (or vice versa), 'Here's this Roman poet the Romans are always talking about, with his

---

[1] The Society for Promoting Christian Knowledge.
[2] Eclogue 4, written in 40 BC, prophesies the coming of a child under whose rule peace and the Golden Age will be restored.

ideas of '*ultima aetas*', '*iam redit et virgo*', '*nova progenies caelo demittitur alto*', '*genus aurea*' – why don't we use this stuff?' Of course the 'stuff' is common cultural property. But Virgil did not foresee; the Apostles may have looked back.

29 February
Montrachet. A beautiful wine. When it is drunk, something gone for ever. Wine a living animal. It isn't often like this; an object of folk art, folk craft.

The Scholar Gipsy. The greatest poem between the Romantics and the *Waste Land*.
In his preface to the 1853 poems, Arnold keeps on hinting at what I kick out at in modern poets. His words: 'We have poems which seem to exist merely for the sake of the single lines and passages; not for the sake of producing any total-impression.' And 'he who seeks to arrive at poetry merely by mechanism, in which he can acquire an artisan's readiness, and is without soul and matter'. Precisely: technicomania.

20 March
An *Alarme for Sinners* (Robert Foulkes), 1679. An interesting pamphlet Norman has lent me. I bought it later. Foulkes was vicar of Stanton-Lacy in Shropshire; seduced a girl and killed the child she got by him; executed Jan 31st 1678. A terrified fear of eternal fire.

Two more of E's ladies' jokes.
A man went to a chiropodist, a girl. But as soon as he sat down he opened his trousers.
'That's not a foot!'
'Oh, well, if you're going to *quibble over* half an inch,' he replies.
The god Thor took human shape and spent the night with a woman he had seen. In the morning he decided to reveal himself.
'I'm Thor,' he said.
'So'm I,' said his bedfellow, 'but it was worth it.'

30 March
Vanity Fair. I am reading this for the first time.
What is unimaginable today – the method of presentation. The constant use of well-I-must-get-on-with-my-story; appeals to the self ('in my experience . . .'), cunning self-deprecation ('this is not a great novel' – *scilicet* this is a great novel); self-conscious flourishes of style, exuberance of examples and images. Thackeray is a dandy for all his anti-dandyism; and his literary technique is stuffed full of what he attacked socially and morally – pretence and pretentiousness. I'm not

complaining about this, it's very agreeable. But it means that his attack on false values, by using false values in presentation, a sort of Vauxhall fairground bravura legerdemain – barker, mesmerist, magician all in one – fails miserably beside a writer who uses no false values in making the same attack – that is, Jane.

Flash monkeys and macaronis beside her, all the Dickens's and Thackerays.

Smoking, or rather, not smoking. Having reached the thirty a day mark, and having wanted to stop for weeks, last Monday – today is Saturday – I stopped; and haven't smoked a cigarette since. The easiest way to do it – this didn't occur to me till Friday – is to personify, diabolify the craving. When I feel I must smoke, I say, 'It is Satan calling.' This *does* help. His favourite arguments are 'What does it matter? Why waste the effort? You'll smoke again one day' and 'One doesn't matter. Just one.' His principal ally, *beyond any doubt at all*, is boredom. The craving is strongest when (and sometimes it has to be discovered) one is bored. Correcting or doing college work (sitting in my little office), at end of lessons (treadmill), with people who bore me, walking along familiar pavements, doing anything that is daily bread and duty as opposed to free will. Even after meals, it's a sort of prospective boredom – waiting for appetite to build up again. I also smoke when writing, but this is a frustration and boredom symptom. I reach for the cigarette when momentarily stuck.

I have smoked a few cigars; it seems to me they are not pernicious because one smokes them for themselves, and not for one's nerves.

My allies against Satan: Satan himself (awareness of him); pride (a false value, but still!); cancer of the throat; self-experimentation; and money. Five shillings a day, thirty-five shillings a week, seven pounds a month, eighty-four a year – ridiculous. One's nerves aren't worth it.

8 April

I don't look much in the mirror here nowadays; not that the face bores. But it frightens. All I have got over these years is a bit of mastery over words – but it is an unproved mastery. A philosophy that seems to work; but I don't know that it's not really simply a rationalization of my natural fatalism, or phlegm. I continue to live in the illusion of greatness, in contemporary terms. That I do and/or will write better than the contemporary mob, the fashionably famous. But sometimes everything crumbles. My new poetic style. The broken, ritual rhetoric – typographical rhetoric – it collapses, it doesn't bite, have any edge. I think of my poems in these groups – the Robin Hood sequence, the latest, which is still shadowy or clumsy, in rough state mostly, incomplete, the Greek poems and the rest, all lumped together, good and bad, in two green folders.

The Greek poems cause me trouble because they are disparate. The Mycenae sequence is whole, there are island and 'site' poems that are whole, and then others written in an older style. They all clash together. I have two prose works – *The Aristos*, which needs cleaning up, but is otherwise complete. *Tesserae* also clashes – it won't run smoothly. What I must do soon is make a determined attempt to publish poems; to publish the poems in the later style, even though they'll get thrown back again and again. But I have the old numb reluctance: I want and do not want to emerge. *Odi et amo* . . . and the thing that might solve all, E conceiving, won't come about. She hates her job, the dullness of it and the women under her. I don't hate my job because it's dull; it's not dull. But I hate it because it takes time. Silence and time are the two things we are poor in. When I do have a day or evening free, I am so stunned that I can hardly use it. I feel a child would be good. Good for E for usual reasons; good for me as a push off the plank, the necessity to swim. Because to live, with E earning nothing, would not be easy. It would be very nearly impossible. And I feel starved of the impossible. Life is too safe.

30 April

Denys and M. Sharrocks have been staying here from Indonesia. Though I like him – and her – the strain and effort of present living make all personal relationships difficult for me. We are glad to see Denys, yet there is a sort of stress present at once. It took the form of teasing, badinage. Not being serious about anything. Of course they're a bit nervous, M especially, of being enthusiastic; there are contretemps. They sneer in the wrong places, they seem to me not to have any fixed points, landmarks to navigate by. M is irritating, too. Uncultured and uncertain, and making up for it by being capricious, wilful, suddenly violent, suddenly veering. 'She's an actress,' says E, but that makes it worse. I don't like people who behave like the stereotype of their profession. Denys hasn't changed; he is pro-American, under the influence of the New Criticism,[1] and the 'adjusted' Americans he has met in Indonesia. Futile to argue about it. I suppose one might have wanted to become Roman after meeting Horace (there must have been a lot of Horaces); one could shrug off the mob and the arena and the Subura[2] and the rest of it. But America brings out the Martial in me. It's the wrong road, it's the blundering through, the lack of finesse, of economy. One of those civilizations that buys its passage through history – a Jos

---

[1] An influential mid-twentieth-century movement in American literary criticism which held that poems should be considered as self-sufficient objects in themselves, without reference to the extrinsic circumstances of their creation.

[2] A district in ancient Rome notorious for its licence and squalor.

Sedley civilization,[1] pays any money for its horses – I mean, it has no inner motion, grace, charm of civilization. It doesn't walk or sail, like a good civilization. It gets there Pullman.

We make an awkward rhomboid sort of quartet – D and E and I balance, and M doesn't. Then D and E have their many similarities; that is D plays them up, presents himself as the drifting, time-careless, faintly clownish, drinking-smoking, lost, castrated intellectual; the sort of thing E rather likes. But really he's got a good hard head in a way. I never felt this pose in him so clearly. His world of ideas is utterly disconnected with reality. He doesn't feel, I am sure, as, say, Podge and I feel about ideas. For him they are things you have because they particularize you, they distinguish you; but they have nothing to do with what you actually effect in life. This seems to me peculiarly provincial – that is, characteristic of non-Oxford education – but it doesn't seem obviously provincial because D's ideas are good and modern and fashionable. Just as provincials hide their provinciality by wearing smart clothes; yet remaining essentially provincial. This is in no way hypocritical in D – it's probably a case of insecurity, a source of inadequacy. Above all, I find it sad. All the caddis-case of the latest ideas and critical views he erects around himself; one senses the inner defencelessness. The imbalance comes out, too, in his lack of contact with now. He doesn't enjoy contact with now: with food, art, any concrete actual source of pleasure. He thinks he does; but compared to other people, both E and I feel he doesn't. He enjoys for the sake of seeming to enjoy. Or one might say, he really enjoys only two things – smoking cigarettes and drinking. And they are in his case compulsional and alienating (from reality) activities. They help him to lose touch; to re-enter his idea world. Whereas Podge and I keep only a few fixed ideas culled from the French, and don't at all keep up with the latest critical trends and labelling articles, with *Encounter* and *Time* and the rest – but live like peasants, in this, compared to D. He is a displaced person. But meanwhile, he makes a good living; perhaps it is better to dissociate the two worlds, from this point of view.

2 May
The only thing I really want, that I could pray for, is an extra hour a day to read and write. The impossible shortness of each day.

---

[1] Jos Sedley is the fat and gluttonous do-nothing brother of Becky Sharp's school-friend Amelia in Thackeray's *Vanity Fair*, whom Becky schemes unsuccessfully to marry for his fortune.

26 June
With JSF[1] in Kent. A clear day, but with a stiff wind; the sky blue, but the sea strangely green. Jade-green flecked white. We walked along the cliffs to Kingsdown,[2] between the sloping cornfields and the great white drop to the shingle and the green sea. Chalkland flowers.

We drove out into the countryside, to a fragment of road that is Roman, a heavy sun-drenched hedge, the straight lane, a field of ripening barley. I caught a large slow-worm, warm smooth silk, winding, anxiety.

Our last stop was in rather lost country between Selstead and Lydden.[3] We pushed over a rotten gate and walked through tall grass and nettles to the small dilapidated tower of a Crusaders' chapel. Dusk, dense shrubs, dankness. Old vaulting. Ivy-covered windows, glimpses of deserted rooms, passages. Eventually we found, behind a canopy of ivy and herbage, an open doorway. A warren of damp, dark rooms, vague clatterings, an over-powering impression of death; not philosophical or everyday or medical death, but mouldering, haunting, undying death. It hung through the place almost palpably. The chapel had been converted, apparently in the seventeenth, and again in the mid-nineteenth, into a farmhouse. Everywhere the old chapel windows, medieval stone; trite Victorian wall-paper, dingy chocolate paint. Thud of footsteps, even our voices sound dead. The atmosphere is fascinating, evil and oppressive beyond words. An upstairs room where the only light is from the narrow arched top of a chapel window, reaching from the floor to above waist-high, the window choked with ivy, the last sun trying to get through, yellow and green underwater light, almost phosphorescent. The strangest feeling in that room – of death and mystery, that reality is sinister. Everything in this place conjoined perfectly to create the atmosphere of active, still powerful decay – evil to all that is light and reason. An old privy in the under-growth outside. Envelopes to the last owner on the cellar stairs. Wind in the rafters and through the broken tiles of the roof. Emptiness, empti-ness, emptiness. After a day of sunshine and sea, of smiling countryside, carfuls of families, tritenesses – this forgotten place!

Finally the ride back to St Margaret's.[4] The lighthouse to the east, a rose-pink tower rising unnaturally, glowing in an unearthly way, over a great slow back of dark red earth; behind the tower the sea-sky, pearl-grey, faintly nacreous, greyly opulscent.

I enjoyed this day. I felt ill, but I lived it.

---

[1] John Fletcher, JF's fellow-teacher at St Godric's College.
[2] Kingsdown is a village on the Kent coast about two miles south of Deal.
[3] Two villages about three miles apart and five miles inland from the Dover–Folkestone stretch of the Kentish coast.
[4] St Margaret's at Cliffe is a small town on St Margaret's Bay, about three miles up the coast from Dover.

28 June
The chapel of St John: I can't stop thinking about it. It had one of the most powerful atmospheres I have ever sensed. A kind of Manichaean aura – nature, of the dark side, triumphing over civilization, decay superseding growth. It symbolized some obscure and universal turning of the tide, a moment when all progress ceases, and the backswing starts. If the house-chapel had been more ruined, it would have been different. As it was, it was *perfectly* sinister, a shadowed island, a secret dark nucleus, in the sea or desert of banality and ordinary growth.

Norman's. Richard Corbet's *Poems*, 1807. 7/6. An excellent buy. A fine jolly fellow, Corbet; and a good middling-minor poet.[1] Though the question is, could one, in his age, with that common vocabulary and metaphor-mania, write bad poetry?

3 July
Mary Shelley, *Frankenstein*. A classic in spite of itself; an incredibly botched story, clumsy rhetorical dialogue, total inability to create atmosphere – yet it comes off. I think it is because it has a symbolical truth and power that is outstanding – a wonderful archetypal idea, while even the smallest characters have symbolical power.

Frankenstein and his monster – the I – the natural self and the persona. The monster is pitiful, misunderstood, in no way guilty (Mary S herself never worked this out); that is, the persona society forces us to assume is pitiful . . . etc. Good touches – the monster's amazement that summer ends. The saving of the drowning girl.

The symbolism of the final arctic voyage.

The strangest thing in this – as in other 'gothic' novels – is the total inability to create atmosphere in narrative; to see the difference between Romantic descriptions of landscapes and psychological states and descriptions of the actual *feeling* of events. Sensibility was in fact (as of course Jane realized, and explained in *S and S*) a sort of blinkering of the mind – sensitivity craved the set-piece about the wild and grandiose, the lonely, the alpine (literally and metaphorically – I mean both in landscape and in mood descriptions) – it saw things in a purely static way. Events are not susceptible of this treatment. Writers like M. Shelley are schizophrenic – they yearn to the Romantic set-piece, they are forced to narrative. This sort of writing, based on a love of the idea of a thing and an indifference to, a boredom with, facts (as we see in the childish machinery of *Frankenstein*) is fatal to the novel. Perhaps this is why there is no great

---

[1] Famed for his conviviality and appointed royal chaplain to James I on account of his 'fine fancy and preaching', Richard Corbet (1582–1635) wrote poems of a mostly satirical nature. He became bishop of Oxford and then Norwich.

Romantic novel; in fact the greatest R novel is Emily Brontë's – and that
was written after the discovery of 'atmosphere' writing by Dickens and
the rest. In short, a technique had been evolved for the feeling.

13 July
L'Education Sentimentale. One of the very greatest novels: of course, Frédéric
is something more than a mere weak, hollow hero; perhaps F only makes
him seem so to bring out his saving virtue – his undying idealism, his
belief, which none of the others have, in love, transcendental love.[1]

The most brilliant of all the brilliant passages in the book is the farewell
of Madame Arnoux and Frédéric (Chap VI, Part III) – no, brilliant's too
cheap a word to use of it. The most profound, most instinct with genius,
the nonpareil – because here all the massive contempt (indifference?) for
Frédéric we have stored up is suddenly turned upside down; and becomes
pity, and the subtlest sort of pity – not just pity at their unfulfilled love
(though F asks for that, too, with supreme simplicity), but pity at their
hopeless inadequacy, their sense of their own *inefficiency* as lovers. So we
pity them not for what they have failed to enjoy, but for what they are; she
not only virtuous but a coward, he not only will-less but a coward – that
turning to make a cigarette, that silence, that mother's kiss, that *'Et ce fut
tout.'* How cheap Dickens and Thackeray seem beside work of this order!

Eliot, *Middlemarch.* A splendid Victorian book. If Eliot is a greater writer
than Jane, which I can't concede, it is in the greater complexity of her
irony – not in all the other greater complexities (of type, scene, use)
that she possesses. What I find wrong is the wordiness of her intellectual passages – the columns of the nave too thick for their function.
The roof, excellent – that is, dialogue, characterization. And the
construction of the whole, excellent.

Mr Casaubon – thinking of his wings and never flying.[2]

*

---

[1] In Gustave Flaubert's *L'Education sentimentale* law student Frédéric Moreau falls
in love with Madame Arnoux, but does not have the courage to declare his feelings. Madame Arnoux leaves Paris with her husband while Frédéric travels
aimlessly for many years, then returns to Paris, still in love with Madame Arnoux.
After many years go by, he meets her again. They talk of what might have been,
for she had guessed his love and returned it. She then leaves, leaving him a
lock of her hair, now white.

[2] Edward Casaubon is the pedantic clergyman and scholar in *Middlemarch* who
marries the much younger Dorothea Brooke in the hope of dispelling the loneliness of his studies. He dies before he can make her promise to compile and
publish the notes to *A Key to All Mythologies*, the text he has been researching
for years.

D. Sharrocks. His curious illusion about the 'human contact'; complains that he can't find it in England. What does he mean exactly by it? (D turns me Socratic; and though I ask the right Socratic questions, I find that they do not affect him – so wonder if Socrates knew a secret despair; convincing the little logical mind and failing with all the rest.) He says he wants to meet people, in a pub, in a market, and have 'human contact' with them. The mysterious phrase. When I told him how we had talked with a publican about an infra-red toaster and that I called that 'human contact', he obviously thought I was joking. Of course, by 'human contact' he means talk about books, poetry, ideas, the beautiful experience. He knows it is so absurd to expect this in ordinary life that he can't even bring himself to define 'human contact'; if it is defined, his ghost is proved pointless.

He wants to go abroad again. And angry about this, I said that I felt I had to stay in England. Reasons: one, going abroad means change, means glutting of the senses with new superficial impressions, means therefore loss of time and I have no time to spare (though I live as if I had). Two, language. I hate the mist of never fully understanding the foreign – and by understanding I mean more than meaning, I mean every nuance of intonation. Three, I stay here till I publish work, I stay at St G's till I publish work. This is a kind of wilderness situation; one wills the wilderness. The danger is that one goes up with it, one gets Casaubonitis. In the end, one never returns from it.

31 August

Middlemarch. A great book that would be even greater if it were cut by a quarter; but especially the last chapter, that traditional summary resumé of what came after: Lydgate killed off in a paragraph, Dorothea married and mother, Frank and Mary white-haired. Jane never made such errors – a few years ahead, perhaps, but never a lifetime. The trouble with G. Eliot is that she condescends, gently, often enough, and self-deprecatingly, but still *de haut en bas*, or rather from the universal to the limited; something of the Victorian mama in her, something reginal; and she has the craving of the age for authority, to be authority. She swamps one in heavy silks, while Jane is all sprigged muslin, altogether lighter and sparser. Jane doesn't condescend, she simply fabricates a world; she does not rule over it, she does not condescend out of it, even only to offer herself (as G sometimes pretends) as a guide to it. In a way J is remoter (irrespective of chronology), aloofer, but her world is more whole and in the highest sense more real.

4 September

Oppenheim. Something of a phenomenon; she is irritating me again, as she does every few months. Sometimes I feel I would go to any ends to get her sacked; sacking would be justified, as she dissatisfies more students than all the rest of us together. She is like some dish that looks appealing, or at least eatable; and yet it brings on nausea at the first mouthful. She has in her a terrible cupidity, a determination to have her rights, or more; a kind of obliqueness of attention that makes whatever one says to her ricochet off. And then one is at the mercy of her ego and her mouth. She is *faisandée,* too; an air of lesbianism, of refugeeism, of endless unpopularity, putting people's backs up, revolting them obscurely. At the same time getting their pity – partly a deliberate seeking-out to get pity, partly a reaction to the ugliness of her. She made me angry today and I bit her hard, several times, behind her back. I should feel guilty, but I don't.

11 September
Picasso Exhibition.[1] A revelation – of his weakness. Why has Picasso never gone back to a realist or impressionist phase? A neurotic going outward, running away from his own shadow; so much of his work is doodling, dead-end experiment. Somewhere in him, a bottomless complex of insecurity and inferiority; compensations, ceaseless 'outgoing of creative energy' (i.e. inability to meditate) and constant 'changes of style and technique' (i.e. never concentrates enough to penetrate).

He innovated very little – certainly not the first cubist, or the first distortionist; but quick as a flash on to new ideas. A vulgarizer of the really original; a propagator of fashions.

I kept on thinking of the Braque exhibition as we went round;[2] how much greater a painter Braque is.

The two vastly overrated artists of our century: Picasso, Matisse.

13 September
The Little Ballet Troupe, Bombay. A very talented and delightful Indian company – a dozen dances, a handful of musicians.[3] This Indian dancing and Indian music I find ten times more beautiful (in the simplest and best sense) than the best Europe can offer. It seems to me to have precisely what is indigenous to the very essence of music and ballet – that is a certain spontaneity and *lack of cerebrality.* I mean

---

[1] Presented by the Arts Council, this exhibition was held at the Tate Gallery from 6 July to 18 September 1960, and drew a record crowd of 450,000.
[2] See page 380.
[3] After appearing at the Edinburgh Festival, the troupe performed for a week at London's Scala Theatre. Of the two ballet-dramas they staged in the course of the week JF saw *Panchatantra* ('The Art of Making Friends'), which consisted of a series of Aesop-like tales.

music and dancing on all of the senses, and the deepest senses, pre-visual. Cerebral imitation and voguish mannerisms are fatal to this *simplicitas musicae* – like overgrilling a good steak. As I write I am listening to the Goldberg Variations. A critic might say that they exhibit cerebral imitation and voguish mannerisms (the French overture, etc), but the heart of the music – that is, the pure emotion it arouses, as opposed to the delight at the technical skill in composition – is as simple as daisies in a meadow. The same is true of Stravinsky; even the most cerebral, Webern.

8 October

I have bronchitis; a not very agreeable new experience. Sat in the kitchen and read Martial all day. Feel him very close. I rely much more on the 'line' guess now in my Latin. That is, I have a guess at the meaning of a line or lines, and then I try to establish that meaning grammatically, word by word. This is a much better way than the cautious word-by-word technique.

Post-coitum epitheton. (E) Sunsetty.

Three party conferences. The Liberals – children playing at kings and queens; the Socialists, passionate, sincere, adult, but sadly unfascinated; the Tories, hollow platitudes, the village hall. Even the *Telegraph* admits that there is no Tory enthusiasm – 'rows of empty seats'. The only party that seems real, contemporary, adult and alive, is the Socialist. To me, that is; the reality of contemporary Britain is the woolly-minded bourgeois mediocrity of the Conservatives.

24 October

Being ill. I am so grateful to have a day to myself that I always think of myself as a malingerer. Even when I am ill as now (with bronchitis). Terrible, to so welcome illness.

I have reread and am revising *A Journey to Athens*. Hopelessly naïf, a lot of it, but it still pleases me as very little I write pleases me. It *says* something; clumsily, but solidly.

25 October

To Chisholm about my bronchitis. He said, after the purely medical examination, that I didn't look happy, 'as if you were a refugee from a better milieu'. I hadn't slept the night before, was unshaven, felt ill, so perhaps the haunted look was explicable. However, he was right. I've been writing poems about exile for several years now. The first I recall off-hand is the one about the shadows of swordplants – must be at least four years old. I took it as primarily a literary attitude, but of course it is really (deeply) emotional (as I had realized, but perhaps have never analysed – I mean, that it was also emotional). I miss Greece most violently (it made me cry yesterday, reading the description of that first morning in *A Journey to Athens*) and it makes me cry now just writing the first few words of this sentence. (I almost inserted 'nearly', because there is no word to express this feeling – tears don't pour down my face, but I feel cut to the very core of my being, my eyes brim.) I am going to analyse myself now, in interlocutory form, imagining C as the analyst.

C. You look worried. What worries you most?

I. Time – the lack of it.

C. Why?

I. I think the main reason is that the only 'work' I want to do is write. Even though I know I wouldn't be much good at writing regularly.

C. Why couldn't you write regularly?

I. Because I can only write well in certain moods. If I force myself to write willy-nilly, the writing deteriorates rapidly. Because I'm easily distracted; I have an insatiable greed for new experience, literary or direct.

C. Which most?

I. Literary. Artistic, anyway.

C. So you want to lead a life of leisure, writing only when the mood takes you.

I. Yes. Except I object to 'leisure'. A life of freedom from the need to earn bread.

C. What other worries have you?

I. Financial – we earn enough to live quite well, but little gets saved. We rather live from hand to mouth, though we're never short of money to spend. We make about £1500 net between us; that may sound a lot, but we feel deprived of many things.

C. What?

I. I would like to buy a house, a car, a country cottage; old books and objets d'art and records. Perhaps I can't explain it simply by this – I feel guilty if I buy anything for my personal pleasure which costs more than about ten shillings. And holidays. I can never go on a holiday without a sense of financial strain. But overall I don't feel very worried by the money business.

C. You're nearly thirty-five. Do you secretly resent the fact that your wife still has to work?

I. Yes, I'd like E to have a baby. She can't conceive. That is an additional worry.

C. Do you want a baby?

I. I suspect I do. I'm afraid of all the problems – financial and domestic. I mainly want a baby for E's sake – also for my father's.

C. Not your mother?

I. Mostly my father.

C. Other worries?

I. Writing and not being published.

C. You've tried to get work published?

I. I've tried one book. No luck.

C. A bad report?

I. Some reports were bad, others more or less encouraging.

C. Were the criticisms justified?

I. Many of them. I am revising part of the book now, and a lot has to be changed. Ineptitudes of expression mainly.

C. Why have you not tried to get other work published? Have you written more?

I. I've written some other books. But I produce very slowly, and time seems to help. I mean I write down very quickly; but I always feel the need to revise and revise. Sometimes it takes me years to see what's wrong with a poem – even the most obvious things. So I tend to let whatever I write mature, or lie fallow, for long periods.

C. Have you written nothing of which you can say, 'I can revise no more'?

I. Some poems.

C. Have you tried to publish them?

I. No.

C. Why not?

I. A combination of factors. First of all, there is a sort of consti-pation of mind which affects all my activities. I don't mean my mind's sluggish – it's probably overactive. But I tend to seethe inwardly when others shout; to be much more reasonable when I speak than I feel; not to 'give' to people; to avoid new things – whatever they may be, from a new shirt to a change in a rela-tionship. I think I admire the eighteenth-century because of this – no Romantic tearing-up of the rules.

C. The other factors?

I. Too much ambition. I want only the very best, and I know by experience that what seems the very best one day, or month, or year, is often plainly not, the next. Mallarmé is a figure that haunts me.[1] I overenjoy this sort of difficulty, this necessary

---

[1] In pursuit of an ideal poetic language, Mallarmé strove endlessly for a never-to-be-achieved perfection. Like JF was doing at this stage, he supported himself by teaching English. See note 2 on page 412.

patience of the fastidious writer. The reverse of all this, of course, is that I fear publication and criticism.

C. Is that perhaps not the crux of the matter? The constipating agent?

I. It's certainly important. For instance, I often imagine I am a famous writer, I have Mitty day-dreams, and I enjoy that state. I think I enjoy anonymity, too. It's the climb to Parnassus I can't face. I'm all right at the beginning, I should be in ecstasy at the top; it's the in-between.

C. Isn't that a childish attitude? Is there any other way to the top?

I. Yes. Writing a book which is immediately recognized as worthwhile – I mean, not just technically skilful, but expressing the whole man. So I'd be flung from the bottom to the top of Parnassus. I have climbed Parnassus literally when I lived in Greece. It was hard-going. But I can't apply the obvious moral to my metaphorical Parnassus. I can't accept the humble slog.

C. If you published a book and it was badly reviewed, what do you imagine would happen?

I. I'd be disappointed, of course.

C. Your wife?

I. I trust her. She wouldn't hold it against me in any sense.

C. Other people?

I. My parents and friends – I should feel ashamed with them, perhaps. But much more, with colleagues and students. That's why I dream of anonymity.

C. So you rate their judgements?

I. Not their judgements; their attitudes to me. All my books involve a laying-bare of myself. If the laying-bare was a success, I wouldn't mind. But if not, it would be a sort of double shame.

C. Why are all your books a laying-bare of yourself?

I. Because I feel that my self is the only thing I really know. I think of my self almost as an 'it' – something separate from me. When I write poems about myself, I sometimes put the verb following I into the third person. 'I likes or dislikes' . . . that sort of thing.

C. Is this a real split in your personality, or simply a poetic choice?

I. A split. I often think of my self as an 'other'. I know it's bad, it drives one to observation and contemplation – an inaction, constipation again.

C. How about your ordinary work at St G's?

I. I don't like St G's and I don't like working there. But it has advantages.

C. Tell me.

I. I am my own master, I can teach as I like. I have no interference at all on the academic side. I don't like any work imposed on me by financial circumstances – but as I have to do such work, I accept teaching, and quite enjoy it.

C. And the disadvantages?

I. I don't like working in a school that has no academic standing at all; it's really a sausage machine for exam results. I would like to teach better than I do; I could teach better, but I begrudge any wasted minute out of work hours. I mean, I don't read enough technical books, and so on. I'm not inefficient; but I'm not as good as I could be.

C. Are you ashamed to tell people – friends you haven't seen for a long time, and so on – where you work? Of the work itself?

I. I'm not ashamed of the work itself at all. Of where I work, yes. But I'm also ashamed to be ashamed. I mean I believe myself to be above such things, and it disgusts me to blush when I say, 'At a secretarial college for girls.' I don't always feel too happy about the work, because teaching English is regarded as work anyone can do – but I know it isn't.

C. Why don't you get a job of which you are in all ways unashamed?

I. I can't think of any work except writing which would not make me in some sense ashamed.

C. A better teaching job?

I. I could find a better-paid one, perhaps. But the academic conditions I teach under are as good as I would find. The governing reason here is that I dread the idea of the loss of time in adapting myself to a new environment, a new job, perhaps a new language. You see, time, the shortage of it, dominates all my thoughts. I know the minimum of time I can devote to my present job without letting down the students or my employer.

C. This doesn't give you a guilty conscience?

I. Pricks – no more. I am underpaid. My employer and I have achieved a *modus vivendi* – he underpays me, but he doesn't drive me at all. He underfeeds his horses, but he doesn't ride them hard.

C. Would it be accurate to say that the circumstances of your present job facilitate this splitting of your personality?

I. Very. In one world I think of myself as a treadmill donkey; in the other, the real one, I am my own master. That is why I don't want what many would call a 'better' job – it would almost certainly demand more integration of my two selves. In a sense I force myself to do this job in order to force myself to hate it; I am very scared of jobs that dominate one's life, that turn from means into ends. I usually manage to shut my work out when I shut the front door coming home. I feel everything conspires against the person I want to be; I have to fight tooth and nail to preserve the image. This isn't altogether an illusion. My parents have never believed in me except as a gifted treadmill donkey; nor have my few friends. I don't even trust E; like all women, she has an innate respect for the treadmill donkey. For instance, I have more than once suggested that she should stop work; we would have to make great economies – give up smoking, secondhand shopping, have only the cheapest holiday, buy few clothes, and so on. Yet she refuses. That is incomprehensible to me. I would make any sacrifice (short of giving her up) to escape the treadmill 'work'. You can call it mild schizophrenia, if you like. But to me it is a mark of defending the besieged city of my real self. My two separated selves are my walls, so to speak.

C. The weak spot in your defences seems to me to be in your fear of being published. I can see that you have arguments to defend the status quo of your life. But surely the easiest way to raise the siege is to publish. If you are universally condemned as a writer, you are defending a worthless city. If you are lionized, the siege will end; if – surely this is the most likely – you are neither condemned nor lionized, you may have to go on with the siege, but there is at least something to defend. Do you not agree?

(Collapse of schizophrenic party.)

Part Eight

Childlessness

19 November 1960

Saying goodbye to D and M. They are off to Laos. E is envious of them, of their money, their sailing off, their new world. I sat in the King of Bohemia at lunch today and discussed it with D. That is, got out of him the normal times involved in his sort of work. He confirmed all my instincts against going to Asia – or anywhere where one is required to teach according to the new linguistics. It means forty hours of work a week; one has to receive students; and in the time one has off one is eager to go out and see and meet – whether it's a long holiday or a weekend or an evening. Such a job eats up time – it is all work and recovering or relaxing or being a dutiful European, fraternizing, sight-seeing. In any case I have to 'aim off', even with Denys. For he's not a creative person, and when I talked to him about my obsession with time, I could see he didn't really feel what it meant to me. 'One *could* write,' he says; but I'd be like him, and wouldn't. And then he's not a natural historian; I know the excitement of a new flora and fauna would swamp me. Be death to me.

The four of us don't get on together. E has been snappy and catty, M looks from one to the other of us as if we're all mad, and D and I get torn among various allegiances. Yet he and I passed a quiet and tranquil three or four hours together today. He remains the one male person who never bores or irritates me, and with whom I actually like being.

24 November

Poetry is controlled schizophrenia.

Most modern poets write *to* their poem; not out of it. Many write a poem and have no contact with it – even though it is above themselves. It is an artefact; they make it and leave it. But real poets are in their poems; they inhabit their poems after they have made them. For ever.

2 December

Macaulay (of the letters of Dorothy Osborne, Sir W Temple's wife) – that you can get more history out of such a series of love letters, more life, more knowledge of a society, than out of bales of diplomatic despatches.[1] Good for Macaulay!

*

---

[1] Dorothy Osborne (1627–1695) met Sir William Temple (1628–1699), diplomat and essayist, in 1648 on the Isle of Wight and, after considerable family

The Collector. I started this a week ago. Refreshing, not to write of oneself. The collector himself is to symbolize the mediocrity of our present society; the caught one, its hope and true vitality, pointlessly, maliciously crushed.

Ingratiation – the key craft in this age. In England it is the Age of Ingratiation. Particularly striking on the BBC – everything trying to be liked, liked, liked.

C'est ou l'art ou l'amour – a line that occurred to me when E was washing my hair.

17 December

E going out happy, coming back distraught. Roy had refused to let her see Anna before Christmas. From what she said, he sounded drunk, at his diabolic worst, a sort of cosmic meanmindedness.

23 December

Recording more poems. Curiously sad, that voice. I feel sad, sadness is my blood, but my voice doesn't sound sad to me as I speak normally. Reading poems is good, because it confirms the inner ear. Not that I think of the inner ear much when writing – it's more the arrangement on the page. But these poems seem rhythmical enough. They please me ominously well, some of them. I distrust the narcissistic euphony a tape-recorder gives. Even my guitar-playing sounds interesting to me on it – and I know that is thoroughly bad.

The Romans, obsessed by the Orpheus in Hades motif – the suffering ended, the peace and mercy brought there by his music. The therapeutic power of art. Of course we pity the intelligent ancients for not knowing all we know; yet to know what we know in ancient Rome would have been a worse Hades than any they could image. And we forget there is an ignorance both ways – not the petty detailed ignorance that historians are always moaning about (if only I could spend one hour in ancient Athens), but the sort of deep ignorance that even ten years in ancient Athens could never dissipate. I mean the ignorance of ancient *being*, which nothing short of being in an ancient mind would end.

We often fall into the trap of thinking highly sensitive people are a sort of modern invention. But people like Catullus and Horace and

---

opposition, married him in 1654. The 'love letters' were written in the two years leading up to this marriage. They first appeared in an appendix to a biography of Temple by T. P. Courtenay, and were then published in their own edition in 1888.

Martial are as sensitive as any modern intellectual; it is simply the imagery and the threshold of their imagery which have (by constant intervening from us) become worn – no longer the imagery of sensitivity at all. So that Catullus seems at times a bit simple, Horace a bit academic, Martial a bit sour. I mean, their poems are like faded prints – no, worn statuary. Of course, there is the age – the patina-beauty – but the pristine impact is for ever lost. And a great part of that impact would have been in fields (or images) which seem to us naïf – like Orpheus in Hades. The great mysterious unexplained world, still (even to the most intelligent) magic, unprincipled, wild, novel; no street lights in ancient Rome. And ordered things like certain scales, certain Greek architectural harmonies, must have seemed so deeply divine that we cannot begin to feel them as a man like Horace, for all his comparative sophistication, must have felt them. *'Amatilis insania'* for us has a sort of fuddy-duddy sound – 'a pleasing frenzy' my crib says, but the phrase is untranslatable because the whole mystery of inspiration is despised in the modern world. This whole ode (III.iv) is a good example of the un-get-at-ability of the ancient mind.[1] It is hopeless to try to get at it through English, through the Elizabethan and later translators. It is like occidental music on oriental instruments.

(I am reading a lot of Latin verse at the moment. If only someone would explain to me how it is thought they read and recited! Useless, the text books!)

2 January 1961

We spent Christmas at Leigh. I feared the prospect so much that it turned out less tediously dreadful than I expected (perhaps we deliberately over-fear all the time?). M's cooking as good and the food as overplentiful as usual. But I enjoyed a 1920 port and a 1933 cigar; I seem to remember reading somewhere that a cigar's age is immaterial – after eighteen months they deteriorate, but this was still very fragrant. A width of aroma. M still the tyrant of any conversation; I go mute under it, but E keeps a sort of sweet, dutiful reasonableness. We both feel an affection for F; a curiously stock figure in some ways, yet with his own romantic depths. Talking about apples with him, remembering forgotten names and looking them up in his books; a magical world, that of apples, whose varieties can be traced back to definite places and men, even sometimes to one special tree. A super day-dream of mine (and it seems, of F's) is to own a huge orchard which is a living museum of apple varieties – a new garden of the Hesperides. The apple is a magical fruit – eating one of F's prize Coxes and a late-kept James Grieve, like a cross between an excellent melon and

---

[1] In Ode 3.4 Horace calls upon the Muses to provide him with inspiration and wisdom.

a ripe peach, I could only think of the other magical product, wine. I
mean, something harmonious in the best apples and wines.

6 January
Ashcroft in *The Duchess of Malfi* – perhaps not a perfect casting, but she
makes it perfect.[1] At 53 is 33 at the most, at moments 23; and again
demonstrates that she has that extraordinary cathartic power which she
alone possesses of living English actresses. Every time I see her I feel
sure she is a great actress, in the sense that Siddons, Kemble and Duse
were great. She is not conceded their greatness, because greatness in
acting can only be assessed by the whole emotion of the whole being;
and in this age we do not (it is not 'done' to) respond in that way –
the more fools us. Well, I say 'us'; the only thing that prevented me
from sobbing out loud or breaking into tears when she gave the great
death speech ('geometric hinges') was a fear of breaking the absolute
silence (I shut my eyes on one occasion and I might have been sitting
alone, with only her voice, in an empty theatre). I remember once
lecturing on the theatre and reading out Byron's description of Kean
in *Macbeth* – his convulsions, the voices of the actors drowned in the
sobbing and emotional upset of the audience around him. But of course
great acting should do that – if it doesn't, then it (or its audience) kills
something. Ashcroft is a very accomplished actress technically, with a
beautifully pure voice; and at the great moments it becomes *the* human
voice; she universalizes the particular emotion of a particular situation
– even so far-fetched a one as Webster's.

Not to criticize Webster – this play is as great as Shakespeare's – and
to Webster's credit that S could not have written it; plot or lines. Webster's
imagery is thinner, blacker, tauter than Shakespeare's. E said she couldn't
follow it 'because she didn't know it'; sometimes one wishes S hadn't
existed.

Dickens, *Our Mutual Friend*. Why is this so little considered? A *wonderful*
exhibition of polyphony, the first fifteen chapters or so; one forgets the
sheer wonder in Dickens. How could any one man do it all? Only
Shakespeare to compare. His instinct for the archetypal situation
(Chapter 1) – fishing up the dead;[2] the fantastic contrasts, between the

---

[1] On 15 December 1960 the Shakespeare Memorial Company, which was shortly
afterwards renamed the Royal Shakespeare Company, moved into its new
London home, the Aldwych. Peggy Ashcroft took the title role in this opening
production.
[2] In chapter 1, 'On the Look-Out', father and daughter Gaffer and Lizzie
Hexham, out in a boat on the Thames, discover a corpse while trawling the
river for valuables.

Veneering world and the river and the dust-heap world. Gets the richness of London, absolutely.

Then the way he varies his style – the deadly and mercilessly exuberant sabrework in the shallow Veneerings, the massive sarcasm against the solid Victorian Podsnaps.[1] No wonder the Communists idolize him – his hatred is profound, but his expression of it is revolutionary. He doesn't merely satirize the Veneerings and Podsnaps, he hangs them off the lamp-posts of his brilliance with words.

Jenny Wren:[2] 'Come back and be dead!'

15 January

All day reading *Our Mutual Friend*. In a sort of coma. It is still one of the most delicious aesthetic experiences – the utter plunge into a great novel. The giving of oneself, so that one lives only in the characters and the age and the writer's mind. *OMF* has its faults – too much of the *vox humana*, though it is done so openly, with so fantastic a determination to kick an inhuman age into humanity, that to complain is to be aesthetic at the expense of morality. Wrayburn might well have been killed off, to kill the cloying Bk IV.[3]

21 January

Joke. What happened to the Eskimo engaged couple? One night she broke it off.

From an Icelandic student's comp on *Emma*: 'Mr Elton made a pass at Emma and she had to fight him off.'

A nice kid, this one. A Greek seduced her last term, got her with child, and then said his mother wouldn't want him to be marrying an immoral girl. She tried to get an abortion, made a mess of it, and went into hospital, where they did the job properly. Now she is as right as rain.

*

---

[1] Dickens satirizes the Veneerings and the Podsnaps as representatives of a new breed of middle-class businessmen who have made their fortunes through speculation and are largely blind to the social problems of their time.

[2] A crippled young dressmaker whose real name is Fanny Cleaver. She looks after her drunken father and rents a room to Lizzie Hexham, to whom she shows devotion and loyalty.

[3] Eugene Wrayburn is the indolent upper-class barrister who falls in love with and eventually marries Lizzie Hexam. He nearly is 'killed off' when he is thrown into the river by Bradley Headstone, his rival for Lizzie's affections, but Lizzie rescues him, and the novel draws to a close with conventionally happy endings for its heroes.

Elmer Gantry. A travesty of the novel. The usual horrible commercial compromise – all issues blurred.[1] This Hollywood habit of vulgarizing noble (the *Iliad*) or honest (like Sinclair Lewis's novel) books is one of the most detestable aspects of the USA. It suggests that all art is venal. Babbitt appears in the film and is well-satirized – but one suspects that Babbitt really made the film. It's no good attacking hypocrisy when the whole film is based on a hypocritical view of the sanctity of the word and the artist. The trouble is, of course, that the *égalité* part of the American character is a boomerang – everyone is to be allowed to speak their mind, free speech is all. In the end there's so much free speech that nobody knows what true speech is any more. Adjectives like 'frank', 'outspoken', 'hard-hitting', are taken to be synonymous with 'true'.

In the cinema, a girl. With red hair and a curious flat snub-nosed face. Slim, tall, very upright, *soignée*. Sitting alone. I sat between her and E. Intensely *poetic* and exciting, sitting between them; two opposites (with their secret complementarities, of course). I was annoyed with E over some trivial thing. Mysterious current between this unknown girl and my mind. I only half-glimpsed her; but there was something in her flat face, something both virginal and wildly sexual, elegant and hermetic, fragile. They are strangely beautiful, these semi-sexual, semi-mythological ('priestess in the dark grove') encounters. Afterwards I saw her sitting alone in an empty restaurant, waiting for a thousand things, staring down at the white cloth in front of her. A red-haired girl with almost a negroid face. Not aware of her power, of course. But it's as real as the clothes around her.

1 March
A period of no time – too little sleep, too much doing one thing for half an hour, another for another, and so on. Existing.

Reading Montaigne again – peace and light in all the triviality of the day.[2] A fine European, Montaigne, a fine individual, who destroys time

---

[1] Richard Brooks's 1960 film starred Burt Lancaster in the title role as the salesman with a shady past who becomes a revivalist preacher. He joins the ministry of Sister Sharon Falconer (Jean Simmons), and with his electrifying sermons helps her to achieve her dream of building a tabernacle. Only the first half of Sinclair Lewis's 1927 novel was used for the film adaptation. The script also imported the character of George Babbitt, the Midwestern businessman who yearns to lead a more exciting life, from Sinclair Lewis's 1922 novel *Babbitt*.

[2] After studying law, Michel Eyquem Montaigne (1533–1592) became a counsellor to the *Parlement* of Bordeaux, but in 1571 retired to his lands at Montaigne in Périgord, where he composed his *Essais*.The word is Montaigne's invention: an essay was an *assay*, a trial of an idea or thought. In an attempt at gaining wisdom, the *Essais* amount to an examination of his own habits, thoughts and

so easily that reading him is like a peculiarly untarnished miracle. He comes across the first hundred years as fresh as yesterday. Not that his being of yesterday would be much to recommend him. But he is of the no-time. His extraordinary reality, humanity. The complete man.

His *coq-à-l'âne* technique.[1] Thoroughly human. His extraordinary passage on his own inability to urinate in public (chapter 3).

If only one book could be saved from the holocaust – Shakespeare, I suppose. But after that, Montaigne.

Poems. A sudden feeling of disgust with them – at their rhetoric, their tares, their failure to be in my voice. So I have been rearranging them. A fat file of them I shall keep to add to this one day – that far-off day in which I see myself dictating this to some secretary, and having it all shipshape, as it should be. And a thin file of those that disgust me least. Strange, such times. I ride them out well enough because there is bad art everywhere in the world today – bad art and stupidity. And if one needs to comfort the bruised heart with comparisons – then it's easy enough.

E. She has been to the fertility clinic. They say that the fault is (anatomically) with her. If children are impossible, it won't worry me very much. It is all one with the greater exile; and a love that has to be nourished by children is not my sort. Possibly E's; she undergoes all the strains. Work, childlessness, thwarted personal ambition. Sometimes she can't see the love for all the horrors in the way. I live too much in my world – and she has no noospheric world to live in. I get crotchety, irritated, when she sits and sighs and does nothing. My days are always too short (she is in bed now and will resent my not coming); hers lack the centralizing coherence of success and conformity to the sufficient norm. She is always accusing me of hating her, wishing she were not here; but I need her nagging. Peace is an illusion I still have, but a true illusion – a false belief known to be false. The sun may seem to circle the earth but I know it doesn't. And in any case, the kind of exacerbating tension that exists sometimes between us is love; only not called it.

*

emotions, as well as those of the society about him, but lead increasingly to the conclusion that such knowledge is beyond attainment. *'Que sais-je?'* became the motto he adopted from 1576. Montaigne's uncompromising quest after the truth was an inspiration for JF in writing his own diaries.

[1] JF means that Montaigne jumps from one subject to another (*sauter de coq à l'âne*).

Thoreau, *Walden*.[1] A very fine fantasy. Since I don't find Thoreau to be trusted very far. Too quirky, too Shavian in his reasonings; his determination to be different. I mean, it is a work of the order of *Utopia* or *Candide*. Once one has brushed aside the air of rather greasy reality, yankee hard-headedness, it is full of poetry, shrewdness and a delightful humanity.

Another thing is that Thoreau represents perfectly a common archetypal myth – not the silly Golden Age myth, which no one has ever taken seriously (except as a jolly conceit), but the oh so poetical theory that it's easy to quit the city and cultivate the cabbagepatch, the nice bean-rows. Live on Irish stew and lake water.

It attracts me profoundly.

His 'having no genius for charity'; as with Montaigne, one feels sometimes that it is almost oneself writing. The saying of the forbidden things.

His rage to live time to the full. 'Killing time is wasting eternity.'

31 March

E gave me a quarter-bottle of whisky, a half-bottle of Madeira, eau-de-Cologne, cigars, a beautiful dark olive-green tie, and a record of the summer-voiced Peggy Lee. And yesterday, with part of a cheque from E, I bought Isaac d'Israeli's *Flim-Flams* (1806), a charming three-volume attack on late eighteenth-century notions and intellectual quirks. Sternesque, but still genuinely funny, which one can't really say for Sterne. I paid Norman 25/- for it. I want to buy Comenius' *Janua Linguarum Trilinguis*,[2] but he almost snatched it away from me, saying it was 'a very old friend' and was going to be rebound. Childishly jealous; shocked that I should think of buying it.

E has recently read *The Collector* and resented it – she has taken the attack on the uneducated to her heart.[3] Whereas it has seemed

---

[1] In 1845 the American author Henry David Thoreau (1817–1862) removed himself from society and built himself a wooden hut on the edge of Walden Pond, near Concord, Massachusetts. *Walden, or Life in the Woods* (1854) describes this attempt at self-sufficiency.

[2] Comenius was the Latinized name of the Czech educationalist and writer John Amos Komensky (1592–1670), who believed that a knowledge of Latin was the key to understanding European culture. Seeking to teach the language by 'nature's way' rather than the old pedantic methods, he wrote the *Janua Linguarum*, which with parallel texts described facts about the world in both Czech and Latin. The work was subsequently translated into sixteen European languages.

[3] In *The Collector* an uneducated clerk and butterfly collector Frederick Clegg kidnaps and imprisons art student Miranda Grey.

throughout (and still) to me an exterior work, with nothing of us in it, except in a few superficial details. I can't get her to realize how symbolical it is intended to be. Platonic. Gold against lead. Of course, like everyone else today, all her sympathies are for the leaden-souled. Metaphysically, they deserve pity. They did not choose to be leaden-souled. But civilization is an attempt to referee this match – 'the injustice of things (gold and lead souls) requires absolute quality of individual fortune' versus 'progress depends on the golden souls'. In my terms, the Aristos is in Miranda, the Polloi in Clegg; and the Polloi are swamping, stifling, murdering by not officiously striving to keep alive, the Aristoi.

1–3 April
At Leigh. Alone with them. Angel in France. It rained most of the time. It bores me terribly, being with them. The absolute empty dryness of such an existence. We seize on the little felicities – M's cooking, F's sporadic culture and old man's endearingness. But the deadness at the heart of things. They shuffle through life now, subsisting mainly on television and gossip; gossip gone over and over again, miserlily. Perhaps if we had children it would give them more life. They don't ask about it, but it crops up in all M's talk. A car and a child, that's all they want for themselves in us. Perhaps it's just my own sense of guilt that makes them irritate me. Their remoteness. It is partly Leigh, too, which seems deepsunk in the '20s and '30s – not only architecturally (what a blessing a Baedeker raid would have been!) but in every other way. So that even the conversation about contemporary events seems peculiarly old-fashioned. This feeling of time past, of people absolutely based in the manners, attitudes, orders of thirty and forty years ago – peeping their horns out at today, like snails. But happier back in the shell. Snail-towns, these like Leigh.

9 May
Eliz forced me to apply for a job in Greece (Athens, the British Institute) a month ago. I felt in a way that I would like it – that it should be attempted, so 'forced' is the wrong word, inasmuch as it wasn't totally against my will. Instinctively I was against it. For financial reasons – the cost of uprooting oneself here and getting there and making some sort of niche in Athens. The anxiety of the new job. The affection I feel for this flat and whatever belongings we have collected. A feeling that I'm on top of the job at St Godric's – though that's really a despicable reason, I know. All these reasons.

But the main one is that my feelings towards Greece ('towards' is sympathetic) are emotional. Greece is something pure, refined, golden, uncontaminated in my mind; all the dross and impurities I know it has (that I saw perfectly well when I was there) have sunk away in these years in exile. A realist would say, 'Shatter the dream!' But my Greece seems to me something valuable. I don't want to destroy it. And I know a month in Athens would tarnish it beyond hope. The way all this symbolizes itself for me is in the Greek poems. I don't want to go back to Greece until they are published. Until I feel they are finished (perfected). They, so to speak, *prove* the years in exile. I shall go back to Greece, but only when the last visit is digested. And the idea of going back there again has been like being faced with a heavy meal too soon after the previous one.

It's clear now I haven't got the job. I suppose the trouble in 1953 put it out of the question from the beginning.[1] I've felt much happier since I have known this.

This feeling that I must face out my destiny *here* is overpoweringly strong.

These last months have also been bedevilled by the question of E's fertility. The insufflation and X-ray processes have been negative (we've looked it all up in a gruesome book – *Diseases of Women* from the MRC library), and the next dilemma is a salpingostomy, with only a 1 in 4 or 1 in 6 chance at the end of it. The childlessness doesn't worry me much in daylight. I think about it at night sometimes, I have pasha and Sultan of Zanzibar thoughts. It just makes life a little barer and sadder than it already is. One becomes a little more (outwardly) the man of reason, cynically Panglossian ('there must be some reason for it'). Hard-cased, perhaps. But I'd swap the paternity of all the children of the world for five years' freedom from earning bread and butter.

At St G's things change a little. A new salary scale. We begin to get something like a decent wage for the job. I get £1,445 a year. It's created a lot of ill feeling; everyone's for more money, but some get more money than others. So jealousy, all the money snobbisms and hysteria of this 1961 world. The secretarial staff-room represents a good cross-section of lower to middle middle-class society; noticeable that class problems hardly ever raise or rise their heads. But this money business happens all the time. Discreet showing off, vulgar showing off, inverted forms ('money doesn't worry me'). It's rampant.

Our (the Eng. Dep.) little room is a haven of niceness in comparison. We all get on well – or would, were it not for Oppenheim. I've written a memo saying I want her sacked. Feelings of guilt – she's fifty-four, etc. But she exploits the college, me, the others, the students.

---

[1] See note on page 280.

Never such an abuser of relationships. There will be terrible unpleasantness, if JWL can ever be brought to dislodge her. But something must be done.

23 May

Old Bailey. Jury duty. I tried to get out of it. Then succumbed to the drama. It's plain the jurors like their work. Quite apart from the unusualness, the normal thank-God-for-an-end-to-peace reasons, and the deference, the judge bowing to them and so on, there's the joy of sitting in judgement. It's a nice cosy experience of megalomania. Yesterday we all assembled in Court 1, and were called. I was detailed for this morning. But was drawn as a reserve juror. So spent the day in the back of the court listening. Most of the jurors are lower middle-class at best – New People. Rankers risen in the war, shopkeepers and so on. Very few PSBs and Oxbridgers. Why?

This morning we had a run of 'guilty' pleas. First, Jones, the puellicide, a stout, strong, balding man in a shiny royal blue suit. A boozer-red face, a meaty man. It was legal nitter-natter about his trial. Then a man who had tried to kill his wife. The prosecuting counsel rattled off the facts quickly, ten minutes. A policeman said, 'Yes, sir . . . Yes, sir,' and it was over. Three years. It seemed a very little time to decide to imprison for such a long time. Three summers, in twenty minutes. The man's wife and her father sat in front of me. She was twisting up a handkerchief, as they do in the films (the whole business of the courtroom is more theatrical and cinematical than real). When the defending counsel said, 'This man still loves his wife,' she bowed her head and shivered. When the sentence was delivered, the father said, cheerfully, 'There you are, three years.' And the man went down as if he hadn't understood; that an evening's despair and rage and jealousy could end so.

The prisoners rise from below – out of hell and back to hell. They suddenly emerge in the room full of watching faces, the hieratic assembly. The whole thing is a barbaric sacrifice. Ritually. Again and again today I saw how travestied. These men (and the woman) were sick, mad. They should have been coming to a panel of doctors. Not to the high priest in a red robe with the terrible sacrificial knife of society-must-be-revenged in his hand.

The next case was a young man who lived alone – very alone – with his widowed mother. He had gone out one evening in his car and shot a woman. He'd never seen her before. 'He just felt he wanted to shoot somebody.' He told the police, 'It was nothing. I don't care.' He wouldn't talk to his defence counsel. A tall, jaunty, truculent young man, Mr Justice Sachs didn't like him and gave him ten years. A psychopath a mile off.

Then came a Cypriot woman who had bungled an abortion. The Greek boy and a tarty little trollop with beehive blonde hair sat at the back. The boy didn't look at the girl, who gave him a hard thoughtful stare. The Cypriot woman had to have everything interpreted to her. Bewildered. The boy and his trollop needed the eighteen months she got.

Then a terrible case. A little doddering fellow, in a loose white shirt and bundled tie, pathetic old clothes, glasses, fumbling, groping, inarticulate. When he came in the dock he sat in a strange position, his head right down, below the level of the dock. Then sat weeping. He had five children, all mentally deficient, like himself. His elder daughter had had two illegitimate daughters, both (he said) stillborn. He had put both bodies on the fire and burnt them all night. One wondered about incest. A kind of abysm, quite bottomless, of human suffering. The only clear thing about the man was that he suffered. He filled the court with it, sitting bowed almost flat to his knees on the chair. The judge showed mercy and deferred sentence pending medical examination. The little man did not even understand that, and his stupid, clumsy body had to be pushed back down to hell by the warders. It wasn't he who was judged, though; it was our society. Beyond that – life, the whole merciless system of evolution.

The last case was a murder trial. An Irish labourer had come home drunk and killed his brother with a knife, in a fit of temper. Another little man, untidy, in an old grey suit, with spectacles. Witnesses go over the facts again and again. It is clear what happened. He was goaded beyond endurance. Strange little facts. They had only one knife to eat with. They slept in a double bed together.

Very mythical, this morning. Abel and Cain. Tereus and Itys.[1] Terrible archetypal situations. Perhaps it is simply that evil is primitive, and good is highly artificial and modern.

The posies the judges carry – very symbolic. Like the ritual purification flowers of ancient myth.

Curious loophole – no attempt is made to establish a juror's identity. It is assumed that you are who you say you are. So why not change places?

26 May
Still at the Old Bailey. The Irish labourer got his murder charge reduced to manslaughter – four years. Then I was impanelled on a jury – it is an arson case. A Geordie lodger who (it is alleged) had a row with his

---

[1] In Greek myth Tereus, the King of Phrace, ate his young son Itys, after his wife Procne had killed Itys and served him up for dinner.

landlady (and mistress?), smashed the window of her glass flat-door (all
in a Canning Town council block) at midnight, and came back at 4.30
a.m. to burn down the curtain she had put in its place. At the magistrate's court she and her daughter said it *was* him; now they deny it.
They visit him in prison. A general dealer has a perfect alibi for him;
pros. counsel asks him if he has not twelve previous convictions for
dishonesty. 'I never told a lie. I stole and owned up.' Everyone, one feels
– the witnesses on both sides, the 'victims' and the accused – are all
against the court and the police. They wish it had never come to this.
One witness seems honest; a hard blonde neighbour, who swears she
heard him shout, and saw his back, on the night of the crime. The case
is open. I know he is guilty, but doubts are there. He's a Geordie, it
could be true (as he claims) that he was in a drunken stupor at the
time. Ours is an 'educated' jury – at least five PSBs. They seem equally
divided. Canvassing has started. It's all over two feet of charred wood,
one can't take it seriously.

The boredom of the court – endless chipping away at stone.

The judge (Sachs) is the best thing. He minces sedately on, like an
elderly transvestite, holding his posy. Then sits like a champion mouser,
lazy and sleepy, but quick as a flash with the legal paw. Baby-faced, with
a pursed mouth, a blue jowl, a rare boyish grin. Pince-nez, which he
changes for glasses. An absurd little man, really; yet his essential justice
is felt. He personifies common sense; he'd never transgress it. And
everyone else in the court would; or could. And he could not.

Old Bailey. We have listened to our Scot's case. He got another old hag
to lie for him. But Sachs summed up heavily for the prosecution. And
we all duly raised our hands in the jury-room, at once, when the foreman
asked for the 'guiltys'. I should have pressed the bell (to go back in
court) at once. But the others wanted to discuss it. Curiously aggressive.
First the educated ones and then the uneducated ones, who took the
obvious and heavily underlined it. And we each had to say something,
as if it was a round of dirty jokes. I didn't say anything – there was
nothing to say. Some of the others put on weighty member-of-the-jury
voices. 'You've got to look at it like this . . .'

At the sentencing, it turned out then the little Scotsman had been
in prison off and on for years. I watched him as the foreman said 'guilty';
he shut his eyes. That was genuine. He suffered. He got three years.

My inadequacy with other men. The average man doesn't listen to himself,
doesn't think of anything but making his stand, declaring his territory.
My fellow-jurors did it by a bit of dirty-joking, stag-party behaviour; by
swapping notes on their cars, their homes, their businesses. The clearest
case was an ex-police-sergeant, risen in the war; a massive self-salesman.

Being nice to us all, running things in the jury-room, always letting us know he had got on in the world, he was one of us (the educated ones). And they all have a weighty, heavy determination to get respect for themselves that I can only achieve by saying things I don't mean, in ways I don't mean, in a voice I don't mean. I enjoy watching and listening to them, but communicating is hell.

While we were waiting to be released we heard a fragment of another case. A little red-haired Irish biddy who had been raped in a lavatory by a West Indian. The fantastic details which had to be elicited. Exactly what clothes he had torn off her, how, where they lay. He had thrown her to the ground, lay on her with his trouser buttons undone.

'And then?' asked the prosecution counsel, in the jolly this-is-all-quite-normal voice young barristers seem to have.

Silence.

'Did you see something?'

Silence.

'Just call it by the name you generally call it by.'

Silence.

Mr Justice Sachs intervenes. 'Was there something projecting from the opened buttons?'

'Yes, sir.'

'That object is called the person in this court. The accused's person was projecting from his trousers.'

'Thank you, me lud.'

'And then what happened?'

'I felt a pain, sir.'

'Where was this pain?'

And so on. If it weren't so tragically sordid, it would be comic. It has its magnificence, in a way. The manner in which such matters are examined is a triumph of the puritan tradition – a refusal to avoid the truth joined with a hatred of it so intense that it cauterizes the snigger or the leer. The antiseptic court.

Millidge and Locket, *British Spiders*. I bought this standard work with the three pounds I got for my jury duty. A sudden feeling that my acquisitiveness (for knowledge) needed a jolt. And then no one knows about spiders. I went out on the roof and almost immediately found a fat house-spider, but couldn't pick it up. Spiders and crustaceans terrify something in my subconscious. And octopi. They are charming creatures, of course – or some of them. Tonight I have had *sittaeus pubescens*, a dusky little jumping spider, under the glass. He (it was a male) has a fine square carapace with two huge goggle eyes flanked by two little ones, red-black, and two more behind, then two more miles away at the back of his head. A little town-tit of a spider. I 'drowned' him to keep him quiet, then gave him artificial respiration with the point of a needle. He suddenly jerked, turned a somersault and was as fit as ever. A fine coat of brown, white and black hairs, with a russet fleck or two – like a high-quality tweed. Great charm, the salticids.[1]

23 June

Dog days. My hayfever began two or three weeks ago, and now it always brings on asthma. I feel weak, I can't breathe. Or think. Or do. Days burnt like five-pound notes in a fire. Like the five-pound notes, they don't seem to buy much at the best of times now. I grow tired of myself and my words and my poems. Time shrivels them up into husks, like spiders in alcohol.

27 June

Oppenheim. At last she has the sack. I have forced the issue, Gilbert rooting for me from the touchlines (some sort of Christian conscience holding her from properly joining in – or so it seems). The Air Commodore treating it as a statistical juggle – drop one, pick up another. So I feel it is all my own work. A little aghast and taut, yet not unproud of my handiwork. Visions of the wretched woman out of work – endlessly humiliated. She is like a burr – must be shaken off, must be shaken off, irritates – and yet it is her mode of survival. To cling. There's proof enough of her badness as a teacher. It's the shotgun at the old dog's head. Kindness – but always the doubt that it's too easy a way out – for killed and killer.

Today she was very quiet. A show of normality. Hurt. A determination to do her duty to the end. Quietly sitting in a corner – not her at all. We (Gilbert and I) thought she would fight, blow up, run away (I presumed a cheque would go with the letter of dismissal, but it would be like JWL's canniness to keep it back to the month's end). Anything but this great hurt quietness; this nothing-became-her-like-the-leaving-of-it. All a bit put on. We shall see.

Oppenheim. Two hours with her. Why had I done this to her? Lengthy defences. Gradually I let things out to her. 'It's the students. We cannot ignore their grievances.' I expect her to pull out a pistol, burst into tears, anything. But she is quiet, very reasonable. 'What am I to do? What am I expected to do?' The others think I am a cad and traitor to get her sacked so. But they can easily be talked round.

---

[1] i.e. jumping spiders.

7 July

She has gone. No recriminations. The others have swallowed it. I have twinges of guilt. I should have warned her more frequently, helped her more, tried more. But the innocent lamb she has been this last week doesn't make me forget the old vixen she has been so often before. Why was she such a hatable person? She was cultured, had all the right political views, and so on. But she wasn't English. No sense of humour over culture; something bullying and condescending about her liberalism. A sort of mistaken idea (common with all these German and Middle European refugees) that being English is being permanently one up – this belief that it is English to praise and publicize one's views and tastes is doubled by their instinctive belief that they are better, anywhere, than the English. The English were put into the world to be outwitted and despised and imitated in order to be made fools of by the superior Middle European. Oppenheim was a wonderful proof of the *difficulty* of being English: it's not enough to speak the language perfectly, to have spent most of one's life here, to count oneself fully English. Being English is a way of behaving, an attitude to others (of which the essentials are humorous tolerance and an enormous public respect for others). Of course foreigners soon twig that the respect is only public – and so denounce our hypocrisy. But it's a hypocrisy they can't copy. Oppenheim never got it off – one could always tell when she was lying, when she was speaking with an ulterior motive. So that she was transparent. She despised the others in a heavily humorous way for their lack of culture and *savoir vivre*, but the fact is that foreigners (however superior their knowledge) are like children with postmasters when they try to live as English people among the English. Their command of English may be perfect, but their command of the art of hypocrisy will always give them away. They will learn the English thing to say, but not the quintessential English secret, the thing you do not say. That's why I hated Oppenheim. She *demanded* to be taken as English; and yet she never learnt what we do not say.

14 July

A meeting with Roy and his *en troisième noces*, Judy.[1] Last time E went to Putney, Anna asked her to her school concert. General consternation. So we were to meet, to get together 'like adults' (ominous words), talk it out together. So we met and went to a Baker Street pub. Judy is a thin brown-gingery-haired girl with a silly toothy mouth and nice (with all that insipid word conveys) eyes – behind spectacles. Amiable platitudes were exchanged about Anna. Then I brought up the business of

---

[1] In July 1959 Roy Christy married Judy Boydell. The couple would have two children, Adam in 1962 and Rachel in 1965.

her coming to stay with us. And all the 'like adults' masks dropped off, and they were the Russians and we were the Americans. White-faced 'niet' on one side and indignation on the other. Roy full of Roy, Judy with 'little woman' ideas: 'We must recognize that we all feel possessive' (= I feel possessive and you shan't have Anna). *Our* having Anna to stay, in short, was out of the question. It's a waste of time arguing with them – they are mean-minded, both of them. Frightened. Provincial. Hallmark of a provincial – he takes his emotions seriously. Second hallmark – he takes everything he possesses too seriously.

Judy's a bit of wax for Roy to put his Victorian seal on. He's scared stiff of losing Anna's respect and love. It must be near the root of his neurosis – his whole attitude can be explained by this fear. And Eliz, of course, is the fear incarnate. And all I did this evening was to floodlight her existence.

21 July
Letter from the British Council. Odd. They half-apologize for not having invited me to interview, assure me that any future application will be considered, and sent a list of other jobs. It makes my self-esteem feel better. And I never wanted to go in any case.

2 August
I have the time. But can't work. Dog days. Nothing I write interests me. Waste time on the guitar, on spiders, fiddling with plants. We are having our August holiday late, perhaps that's it. A general revulsion from any duty. I do some work. But through the year I think of free days as paradise – to write all day. And then when they come – nothing. I seem to be at the bottom of a pit. Mind won't concentrate.

7 August
Bank Holiday. We went up to Wendover to do our usual walk. Over the fields up to Dunsmore and on to Wheathamstead wood. Spiders dominate my days in the country now. The pursuit of them opens a new world. The very small world of the small insect – under bushes, deep in the undergrowth, beneath the mat, the green outer skin of plants. Where beauty is rarely more than five millimetres long. The nicest spiders I caught were a male and female *Evarcha falcata*. A very smart male – cream, coffee, burnt umber and russet. A beautiful bit of evolution. 'Handsome,' say the worthy Locket and Millidge, but aesthetics is not their forte. Spiders are, in fact, beautiful, and the business of identifying them very tedious; I am constantly defeated. I can't yet (as I can with flowers) know, or guess pretty well, what family they belong to. And insects seem to intoxicate the taxonomists and classifiers. If they can spot a stray trichobothrium, a one-millimetre shift of one of the eyes, a

nothing that's new, then they flag up a species. Martin Lister claimed he knew all the British species in 1678 – 38 of them, he thought.[1] Today there are 560. The 560 is more scientific, the 38 wiser.

17 August
These last ten days little done. I've read, discovered, fallen for Catullus. *Venit, vincit.* The incredible misunderstandings of the professors – not only modern English, probably, but of all the academes since – their priggishness. The text plus translation I read him in (the Loeb) is farcical; and all the other translations (Landor, Flecker, etc) just as bad. The whole key to the master is that of sex and obscenity; if you are frightened of sex and blush at obscenity you have no right to approach Catullus. In fact, it's obvious he has a deadly fascination for the academics. They tiptoe to the door, peep in, blanch and twist their tongues in knots to avoid telling anyone what they have seen. I have tried translating some of the obscenest poems into English. They go perfectly well, as long as you use the normal middle-class obscenities. Fuck, bugger, bastard, and so on. So long as you avoid *all* euphemism. That's what makes Catullus obscene – the whole business of trying to stifle such a violent, sad, wild, green genius. He didn't write in blood and tears and vitriol to be translated into water.[2]

Each day – it's been coldish, unAugustan August – I do the same things. Go the round of my spiders on the roof; feed them a fly or two, tickle the webs, wash up, make the bed, do a little shopping, fiddle-fuddle. And the rest is supposed to be on *The Aristos*. But its apophthegmic nature is exhausting. It changes shape – new ideas, new shores, new stresses, it exhausts me with its size. Like trying to handle a big sail in a high wind. Flags loose, wraps round me, I see nothing. But there are times when I have it set, and we *move*. The idea (in July) was to enter it for the competition. But it's too vast, too unformed. Every ridge shows a lying valley and yet another upward slope.

---

[1] A physician and natural historian, Sir Martin Lister (1639–1712) wrote *English Spiders*, the first serious attempt at a comprehensive classification.

[2] Born in Verona, Catullus (c.84–c.54 BC) as a young man went to Rome, where he was a leading figure in a literary circle known as 'the neoterics', 'the young ones'. Of his poems, most well known are the twenty-five which concern his love affair with a married woman whom he calls 'Lesbia'. Highly crafted but spontaneous, they capture with an extraordinary frankness and intensity all the emotions of love from ecstasy to disillusionment and despair. The response of many Victorian and early twentieth-century scholars was to shy away from their openness. Even as recently as 1961, C.J. Fordyce's OUP commentary would omit several poems on the grounds of their perceived obscenity.

20 August
Theridion ovatum. I've been keeping a female, pale yellow, carmine stripes, and her blue-green egg-cocoon in a cage for about six weeks. Today the minute spiders hatched out – a seething mass. Each small spider an opaque pale-butter abdomen with a transparent sea-green carapace.

A way of women to keep beautiful – to retain the power of being temperamentally adolescent. To cry easily, to be irrational, to storm. So that the behaviour remains girl's, even though the body does not. Eliz does this.

Voice analysis – how people give themselves away on the wireless. There ought to be some scientific way of correlating character and voice. I am thinking of something purely phonetic – no concern with accent, pronunciation or meaning or choice of words. That is, the things we usually go by. But a purely statistical measurement of duration, pitch, speed, all of which could be plotted on a graph or indexed by some formula. One would have to begin by correlating voice to something less vague than character – perhaps to IQ, or some special feature, like aggressiveness, shyness.

7 September
Reading Montluc[1] and Montaigne.[2] Montluc is a fine minor eccentric of literature. Whenever he goes into action in his autobiography, he is splendid, as fine an action writer as one could wish. Patches of dullness (peace, or 'not in action') – the military mind doesn't change; soldiers are never human beings. Montaigne makes me ashamed of what I have used this diary for these last years – a lack of frankness, a lack of the self-truth, of giving in the Montaigne sense (*on se prête aux autrui*, etc). Partly it's because I can't regard this as truly private any more; Eliz may look at it at any time. From now on, though, I shall re-enthrone Montaigne.

23 September
Evening with Jean Bromley, one of the English teachers at St G's. A roomful of young people, a little wine, polite chit-chat, silences. Terrible, the provincials. Spiritual, of course, not geographical; provinciality is a matter of mind, now – in London. They won't say anything shocking, won't start any worthwhile talking-point; partly it's a sort of shyness, a belief that being unprovincial is not being enthusiastic about anything,

---

[1] Blaise de Lasseran-Massencôme Montluc (1502–1577) was a soldier who took part in nearly all France's wars between 1521 and his death. He became *maréchal de France* in 1574 and wrote his memoirs, *Commentaires*, with the intention that they should serve as a manual for young officers.
[2] See note 2 on page 456.

never asking anything of anyone (names, job, beliefs – all taboo). Art is taboo ('Have you seen . . .' passes). So one's in a room full of little inhibitions; everyone frightened of showing off – both of being urbane and of being provincial. Awful no man's land of trivialities.

Cobban's *History of Modern France*. Disastrous, the post-Revolution history of France. Does the wonderful selfism in the arts balance the atrocious selfishness of the race? All the bitter blood; it makes me hate France. And then here's Montaigne, smiling at me.

Montluc would have loved the nineteenth century; right up his wretched street.

27 September
K. Amis – *Take a Girl With You*. A sick, nasty book; redeemed by its readability and its occasional cleverness. Amis's skill lies in the creation of caricatures – a Dickensian skill, really. The trouble is that some future age will take the picture as realistic, as we have done with too many of Dickens's. It deserves a name, this confusion – the Dickens illusion.

The smallness of Amis is seen when we get back to the life he is trying to caricature, the ideas he is trying to illustrate, which seem to be these: One, sex is a beastly imposition. Des Grieux[1] said 'Deliver us from love', Amis's characters seem to imply (not say), 'Deliver us from sex'. Two, everybody is immoral and treacherous in personal relationships; if they are not, they are 'stooges' or 'prigs'. Three, love is a myth, it doesn't exist (no two contemporary intelligent people could ever remain sexually faithful to each other).

He is a puritan, of course; on top of that, a born sneerer; against the capital, the urbane, the 'nobler' emotions, the heart, the good. Very often he is on target; merciless against pretentiousness. But it's like the hosing technique with a machine-gun. Every associated idea in sight gets mown down.

I don't like his clotted impasto style. Sometimes it hits; but it never touches. Flays. Snatches one has to read three times because of bad construction. Misplaced 'only's' on every page.

Remain his great saving graces: his contemporaneity (people like this don't exist, but the broken-down details of them do) and his sarcastic wit.

6 October
St G's. Farce. We had the termly evening party for the new foreign students last night. Coffee and polite chat, followed by lantern slides

---

[1] The chief protagonist of the romance *Manon Lescaut* written by the Abbé Prévost (1697–1763). Led by his helpless passion for Manon Lescaut, the chevalier des Grieux passes through a series of unhappy adventures.

and a short homily from me – being kind to one another. All a puffed-up attempt at selling St G's and England and London. Horrible slides of famous buildings in sunlight, dear old Beefeaters, dear old Chelsea Pensioners, dear old flowersellers, dear old London, the dear old in fact. And then Gilbert said: 'The police rang this afternoon to say that there is a rapist loose in Hampstead, the girls mustn't go out at night alone, and if a car stops beside them they must run.'

Delicious; it was worth the wasted hour to hear it.

I have a larger department now; secretarials as well. The English teachers haven't got over the Oppenheim business, something vaguely hurt and betrayed-child in their eyes; failure to communicate. They don't like my cynicism and my using swear-words and sex-words; I think they suspect I don't do enough teaching. They all got a rise recently, and there's nothing like a rise for making people dissatisfied. Odd, but it's so. One sees it in the nation as a whole. It's an addiction. One can live without it, but once it starts, it's hell when it stops. I like the secretarial tutors rather better than the English; something irremediably provincial and mousy about my lot. Curry with all her inhibitions, Brockwell with her man-in-the-streetish-ness, a sweet, nice woman, but like all such, insipid. Bromley an Oxford woman-graduate mouse; Oxford and English literature and everything else have left her quite untouched. Brameld is just ignorant and stupid, really; a sort of eternal schoolmarm. The new one from Dublin is odd, two-faced. I don't know what she thinks. They have small jokes among themselves, little advanced opinions that they retract like a snail its horns at the first touch. And one feels they don't really care a bugger for anything real in life, like the banning of the bomb, or poetry, or great art, or truth to oneself; but only for their little pseudo-bourgeois homes and lives. Their interests in art and so on are voguish; they nibble at life. Provincials.

Some of the secretarials are good: Mrs Barret, an old Scotswoman who knows Durrell and Miller; a nice tart brisk left-winger. I hear her making fun of the black girls and they all like her – sure sign of a good heart, and there's a Jewess, a Mrs Singer, who doesn't know one tenth of the 'culture' stuff the others do, but who manages to be more contemporary than all of them. A sort of brisk-and-lazy acceptance of things and people as they are. Not giving oneself any airs, just getting on with the job. Smoking and acting, not never-smoking and talking about acting. None of the English teachers smoke; something sexless in non-smoking women. Perhaps that's their trouble; they haven't got a scrap of sex. Old Mrs Barret had, one can feel it; and Mrs Singer has, in a contemporary way. She never uses it, as they (the E teachers) do sometimes, in a feeble sort of way. But she has it. I've decided these two, and Fletcher, are the human beings there. The rest are dummies.

I have times of worry when I feel they don't like me. I feel I'm mean,

I never make the ritual offer of the box of biscuits and so on. I feel I don't help them enough over their teaching. Not much communication in short; but then it seems general these days. No one communicates any more in England. I can do it ten times better with the students; they know what I mean, they'll come halfway to meet me.

13 October
Looking at old photographs at Leigh last weekend. Of grandfathers, grandmothers, fathers of people I hardly remember. Groups of people all dead. The worst one (the Victorian photos are too remote to worry) was a faded little snap of the Fillebrooke tennis club – Mr Avila, Mr Turle, Mr Murley, Mr Norman, Mr Mumford, all those father-figures of my first decade – and all dead. My father survives them all. I felt it unbearable looking at all those figures of the dead, with my father there. We walked in Chalkwell Back the Sunday morning and I wanted to turn to him and say, 'I don't want you to die.' But you can't say simple things like that. Or we, the English, can't.

Daphne Turner. A new English teacher we have, from Dublin. A first in English from Trinity. I don't think she likes the work, or us, much. I don't blame her. Hell for a lively, sensitive Irish girl, the stale potatoes of that staff-room. Today she said, à propos of a radio programme, 'I expect it was the Dublin accent in all its glory.' I said, 'You sound sarcastic.' And suddenly she bellowed, 'A tanner the praties, a tanner the praties' in an extraordinary voice. Angry – or fed up with us. I don't know. It was against me. But I liked her for it.

Women's magazine story. That English could be so used! As if one receptacle served as both communion cup and chamber-pot.

22 October
I have applied for a post in the BBC – producer/programme assistant in a new recorded broadcasts scheme.

I'm reading a good book on Byron, by L. E. Vulliamy. It's his aristocracy that gets one in the end – using aristocracy in the modern sense. His snobbism, his stupid, vulgar belief in blood – and then his tremendous style. It seems that in the smaller things of life he had no style (at least in the Italian years). But there's a kind of brilliant dandy elegance in all he says. In fact Byron had no taste in any direct contact with life; his taste was all in the delivery of his opinion of life. Whence his infuriating flippancy; and the triumphs of *Don Juan*.

Vulliamy, in Chapter 1, makes a brilliant distinction between cant and hypocrisy. Cant is the maintenance of opinions and views that one knows no one really believes in; it is a step beyond hypocrisy. Hypocrisy is a matter of plain straightforward deception. The hypocrite pretends to believe in something he does not. The canter maintains something he does not believe in out of sheer laziness; or even envy. Foreigners never understand this about England – we are not a nation of hypocrites, but one of canters. We not only lie about our beliefs, we don't care whether people know we lie or not. I think this explains the English reticence. We are great ones for going on instinct. We know on one level that we don't believe what we say. But we think that our view could ultimately be defended. It could somewhere be proved that the English way of life is the best. But it would be unEnglish to articulate this. So besides the true canting, there's a lot of spurious canting. We are liars who don't mind being taken for liars and who secretly think we are not liars.

30 October

Portugese student tried to commit suicide the other day. Broken home, broken love affaire, tragedy, the lot. Grotesque detail: after the forty aspirins she took six mothballs.

Antonioni, *Le Amiche*.[1] At first sight (for the first two or three reels) this seems rather a banal film and one can easily imagine a not very intelligent (or sensitive) person calling it a dull (or futile) film. And another sort of viewer, looking for for the satirical punches on the nose and the *parti pris* of the average left-wing film, would find it irritatingly ambiguous. In fact what Antonioni seems to me to be doing is something analogous to the Wittgenstein purification of philosophy; or to the standard scientific approach today.[2] That is, presenting the facts with

---

[1] Directed by Antonioni in 1955 from a script by Suso Cecchi d'Amico, the film told the story of Clelia who leaves Rome to found a fashion house in her native Turin. When Rosetta, the girl staying in the hotel room next to her, attempts suicide, Clelia finds herself entangled in Rosetta's circle of rich young women. She also begins to fall in love with Carlo, the assistant of the architect who is supervising the decoration of her premises. When Rosetta, who has an unrequited love for a painter called Lorenzo, makes a second successful attempt at suicide, Clelia accuses one of Rosetta's friends, the heartless and superficial Momina, of being morally responsible for her death, and returns to Rome, abandoning her relationship with Carlo.

[2] Ludwig Wittgenstein (1889–1951) maintained that there was no philosophical proposition or philosophical knowledge on which everyone could agree. The task of philosophy was not to assert a final truth, which does not exist, but to unravel the ambiguities of language from which all philosophical confusions result. His work, set out in the *Tractatus Logico-Philosophicus* (1921) and the posthumous *Philosophical Investigations* (1953), provided the foundation for the analytical, linguistic approach to philosophy that has dominated the second half of the twentieth century.

complete dispassion. We are not to be prompted in our reactions at all. Not to be made to feel pity or anger, above all. If we feel those things, we have to make them ourselves. The film won't help. It just gives data. It doesn't assemble, or sum up, or judge. Not this is what ought to be, but simply this is.

In technical terms, he 'unloads' the script and resists all sentimentality of angle. But this objectivity, this pure light on the events, is mainly camerawork – to be precise, distance of lens from actor. Hardly any real close-ups. Plenty of retreating from the camera, or the camera retreating. Long shots. He has learnt how to use the camera as alienator and observer at the same time. Look at these objects; but don't identify yourself with them. A very cool lens.

The facts he presents in Le Amiche, and which he himself does not judge, can be judged. He says middle-class society is spiritually bankrupt. There is the bitchy, sexy grass-widow; the rich little trollop; the career girl with her denial of her sex; the self-centred bad artist; the good-time architect; even the girl who kills herself is futile, untragic. The life-symbol is the artist's wife – the mother-earth figure, eternally forgiving. Self-sacrificing. Trying to arrange something decent. The film ends on her. But the fact that the Americans are buying her pottery has its obvious sinister symbolism, too.

1 November
Worlds I would not like to live in: when the best poetry came from the machines.

Antonioni, *L'Avventura*.[1] This is another remarkable film – with a much more obvious remarkableness than *Le Amiche*. The same alienation effect is achieved, through camerawork again and through the general unreality of the story and the ambiance. I suppose his claim would be that the film means nothing. It's a deliberate attempt to act symbols free of meaning (therefore analogous to abstract art). The film could mean a dozen things. The vanished girl could be faith, the architect modern man. Claudia some vague idea like love, forgiveness; and so on. What seem clear to me are these two things: one, the intention of the film is to create a very pure sense of mystery, to distil pure mystery, in fact; two, it is also to distil the essence of romantic love. All the way through there is a Tristan

---

[1] Directed and written by Antonioni in 1960 and starring Monica Vitti, Lea Massari and Gabriele Ferzetti. Anna disappears on a deserted island during a yacht cruise. Her lover, an architect called Sandro, and her friend Claudia search for her first on the island and then on the Italian mainland. As Anna's two friends eventually give up the search for her, an unstable romantic relationship develops between them.

and Isolde atmosphere of guilt and irresistible passion, of loss and betrayal – a thoroughly Celtic atmosphere, in fact.[1] The only essential thing, the film says, is romantic love. All the other loves in the film are corrupt; of necessity, since only romantic love can last and any other love is a descent, a corruption. Yet the architect betrays Claudia almost as soon as they have come together in their forest of Morois[2] – the Sicilian villages – and this could mean that modern man cannot ever be Tristan again. Certainly Antonioni seems to despise his Tristan. Sandro has already made Anna (the girl who vanishes) unhappy – and he is corrupt careerwise. The island is the modern condition, obviously; barren love, because no more than sex. The disappearance is a kind of loophole through which Claudia and the architect might have found salvation – and do not.

The protagonists are all rich, semi-noble; the traditional class for the tragic character. Of course, Antonioni isn't going for tragedy; the new necessity is the complex character. And complexity, like tragedy, requires the unusual person. Ordinary poor people weren't complex. Perhaps, too, A's characters symbolize the materialistic modern world; rich in everything except spiritual values.

The oddest thing about this film was that it made both E and I feel ugly and depressed. Of course, in a sense we have lived it (strangely, that didn't occur to me till now, a day later). Passion, guilt, Mediterranean landscape, plenty of money. All that intensity. And so the dullness of life as it is hit us savagely in the face. The total lack of *avventura*. Of course we both know that to seek the old intensity of the prime experience is a myth. It can't be ever again. But then we have in our life together disproved the message of the film (that modern man and woman can't live out the Tristan and Isolde situation); in fact, the message of the film may be less sad than it seems. It may be this, that romantic love is so intense that it will overcome any betrayal; and that it is in the nature of romantic lovers to try to escape their love, either by seeking a man or woman that reminds them of their partner as he or she was *at the time of the prime experience* or by trying to neutralize the romantic love by indulging in something much more banal – sex, infidelity, cynicism and so on. The latter is alien to blasphemy; of course no one believes more intensely in the *existence* of a god than the blasphemer.

21 November
La Dolce Vita. Fascinatingly scandalous, of course. But a bit meretricious, too. Like *Daily Express* journalism – as one admires the technical skill, one despises it. Falling in love with what one loves, there's the rub. And

---

[1] See the note on the Tristan and Iseult legend on page 337.
[2] The forest where Tristan lay with Iseult.

then he spoils it by the last shot, the little Botticelli girl's gay smile into the camera; like a lump of sugar at the bottom of a dry martini.[1] *L'Avventura* is a ten times better film.

22 November

E's doomsday. We went down to the hospital at 9.30; it's near the Angel, in Liverpool Road. The aura of the institution: everything practical, old-fashioned, stern; chipped, the paint room; only cleanliness to save the whole place from being a rubbish-dump. But her ward was – is – rather restful, stagelike, a great tall rectangular barn, painted a cool blue, always warm, a sort of *flottant* tropical sea atmosphere, the two lines of women like creatures at the sea-bottom, all pink and blue and pale. Black-mussel visitors, like crabs, vile things. Quite out of place. Very much a fish-tank, or aviary, the ward.

I went again the same evening. E 'sucked' into the atmosphere; nothing exists outside the fish-tank. Most of the other women are hysterectomies, fibroid cases. An old woman of ninety-one, who keeps moaning that she wants to die. 'Please, God, let me die.'

23 November

The operation is tomorrow. Righting of the uterus; and the salpingostomy. The surgeon is a Miss Moore. She came round, apparently rudely, with her train of students. E has 'a fine healthy body, as you see . . . I expect I shall have to amputate here.' The wretched Fallopian tube? 'Well, we'll see the whole picture tomorrow.' One is strung up by the legs, it seems. The incision may be frontal, lateral . . .

E was laughing, excited. 'So interesting, the ritual of it all.' It seems to shock me more than her. The machine haunts the hospital, the body as machine. And I loathe the machine-talk of doctors.

The sister let me come in this evening (strictly, no visitors). So we sat with the curtains around us, filled in a football pool. Hopeless, hospital visiting. One has to play at being someone, at being people one isn't, we aren't. A pale young nurse came and said things I couldn't

---

[1] Released in 1960, Federico Fellini's film follows the vain search for fulfilment of journalist Marcello Rubini (Marcello Mastroianni), who, seduced by the celebrity life he reports on, lacks the moral courage to fulfil his dreams of becoming a serious writer. In an attempt to write a novel, he abandons the 'dolce vita' of Rome for the seaside, where he meets the teenage Paola, whose innocence contrasts with the jaded models, starlets and society figures of the city, but he soon drifts back into this shallow world. In the final scene, he collapses on the beach after a drunken orgy. In the distance he sees Paola, a symbol of purity, calling to him but cannot hear her over the roar of the sea. He waves, but then turns away and wanders back to the party.

14. Anna, Roy and Elizabeth Christy and John Fowles, 1952

15. Elizabeth, Anna, Roy Christy and John with students of the Anargyrios School

16 Elizabeth and John, 1953

17. John and Elizabeth in Greece

18. John outside St Godric's, Hampstead, *c.* 1956

19. At 63 Fillebrook Avenue, Leigh-on-Sea, 31 March 1957, two days before Elizabeth Christy married John Fowles. *Left to right*: Hazel, Gladys May, Elizabeth, Robert

20. Elizabeth and John, 28 Church Row, Hampstead

21. John at Church Row

22. John and Elizabeth

23. Elizabeth, John and 'Podge' Porter, en route to Northern France

24. John in Rome

25. Cheltenham Literary Festival, October 1963, John Fowles's first public literary appearance. *Left to right*: John Bayley, John Fowles, Iris Murdoch, J.B. Priestley, Anne Scott, Frederic Raphael, Gabriel Fielding

26. John and Elizabeth, Underhill Farm, Lyme Regis, Dorset

hear between the curtain. I had to go, it seemed, because she came back. So three kisses (these days become spiny with superstition) and there's nothing one can say; one can't doubt tomorrow. 'It'll be all right.'

The recovery period will be at least two weeks (in hospital). All this means our life will change. A tack. The opponent makes a move; the repercussions remain to be seen. That doesn't matter, of course. It's even a pleasure, especially for E. To smash the routine.

I don't like death so close when I have no control. I have counting obsessions: if I can get to that step before the minuterie clicks out, it will be all right. In my usual way, I imagine all the avenues out of the situation; all back, the worst. I imagine getting struck down myself, some diabolical joke on the part of fate.

In one way, imagining the worst seems an exorcism, and in another an invitation to the three grim sisters.

I live in the kitchen, keep a sort of routine, can't be bothered to put cooking knowledge into practice. The flat seems too big for one; one room would do, really.

24 November

Feeling sick all day, sympathetic pains. E rang me up at 10.30 (I had to ask Sewell to leave my office, and then we talked as if a third person was present). Hopeless, such situations, pre-operation. Lunch with Fletcher, and not really hearing what he said. I went down to the library, killing time really, to the Polish junk-shop and bought some old records, and then I couldn't stand it any longer and telephoned the hospital, the sister sounding almost surprised that I should bother to ring. 'Yes, quite all right. Satisfactory. She's left the theatre.' Then I went up to the little delicatessen in West End Lane, home, postcards to Birmingham and Leigh. Read the Greene *A Burnt-Out Case* at a sitting. Out of sheer relief, the awkward corner passed.

JWL. I went to see him today, when E was in the theatre. I told him he was withdrawing too much. Ridiculous when one has to be avuncular with one's boss. Of course, he's petrified with timidity. And desperate to be liked. In every little rich man there is a Macmillan crying to get out. *A Burnt-Out Case.* Very readable, of course, like all Greene. One can imagine critics of 2061 puzzling over that readability. Some writers dry out rapidly after death (Bulwer-Lytton). The whole book seems too short to me, too cursory. Some of the dialogue has a stilted rapidity that is amateurish in its effect. Developments take place too fast to be credible. As if Greene isn't very interested in how his ideas get said, or in whether it's the moment to say them.

Some unlikely characters, too. This is ten times better than most
contemporary books, of course; it is by the standards of *Heart of
Darkness* that it fails.

A general fault in Greene: excessive neatness. A mania for the
minimum. The times when he is a little sloppy stick out like dirty rugs
or dust in an anal-type suburban housewife's sitting-room. *A Burnt-Out
Case* is a sketch, not a novel.

28 November

I have visited Eliz twice. Yesterday (Saturday) I thought she would be
on her back, pale. But she really looked as if she had been having a
rest cure. Overslept. Unable to breath, sighing and puffing and looking
round the ward as if it was a bad film and *she* wasn't going to sit through
it another minute. A feeling of relief there, and then bitter sadness,
because the operation was apparently not successful – the Fallopian
tubes are too heavily encysted to be made patent. The house-doctor has
told her there is a chance – 'such things happen'; but that may be no
more than the sugar coating on the truth. One can't tell. I hadn't been
able to do anything all day. The workmen were here doing things to
the roof, and others fitting in a stove. Everything like that seems unreal
– the business of living, or writing, or doing anything except catching
the Bank tube to the Angel. I am reading a lot, as a drug. I went out
to buy a present and couldn't see anything I liked or Eliz would like;
only a Battersea box, an inch long – the Gift is Small but Love is All –
ten guineas. I half-bought it, didn't, did; then didn't. Money, and indecision hangs over these days, even though the sword of Damocles has
fallen.

I came back to Hampstead and went to the Parish Church to hear
Britten's St Nicholas cantata – with Peter Pears. Le tout-Hampstead there;
very liberal and intellectual, in their pretty white, gold, pink and blue
church. I enjoyed the Britten; Pears in the pulpit; the three blood-red
little choristers pacing down the aisle and singing their lovely melismatic
alleluias.

Then came back here and drank too much whisky and tried to write
letters to people: unEnglish letters, too revealing – the prison of being
English! – which I tore up this morning.

Today she cried when I came in, because I was a few minutes late.
But then was better. Still can't breathe. She had bread and honey for
tea and I ate a small pink cake. There was a service in the morning, it
seemed a person telling them they were all wicked, all sinners. One can
only laugh. Old women in to die, hysterectomies, salpingostomies and
the everlasting C of E.

This evening I pulled myself together, boy-scouted the kitchen and long room into shape. I can write here in the long room; perhaps, like Haydn, I need the freshly laundered cuffs.

JWL came at ten to one, to ask me to lunch. Everything in a mess. He sort of peeped round, hopped about trying to think of something to say. Could he help in any way? Kind, gauche little man. I kept on saying, 'It is sweet of you, it is very sweet of you, but . . .' Not kind; sweet. The word one uses to women. He didn't seem to notice.

31 November
On the surgeon's report it said: 'Virtually hopeless.'

Reading poems. I have totally forgotten some of them, even a good one written only this last October. A shock, seeing them again. Why should it be a shock?

My mind is useless these days. Can't think inwards, as if I've been cut off from my own inner world.

2 December
Modern poets – a sort of mock modesty. 'We know our place, we will not raise our eyes.' So they write excessively neat little poems about little incidents. Craftsman poems. As if poetry was akin to furniture-making or pottery. Their only similarity is that all give pleasure.

4 December
Eliz much better. Even looks absurdly well. She had her last set of stitches out today. A strange interlude this has been. I seem to have existed through it, no more, had no time. I woke up very tired, and now it's 12.30 again. Every day there are a dozen 'important' things to do, and only half get done. I felt angry against fate for a few days, but you can't be angry against hazard, especially when you believe in the principle of chance. I suppose I don't really care about children. The idea – the house in the country, the nursery, the voices in the orchard, all that sunlit vision of children – that attracts. But the reality. Perhaps it's even a sigh of relief. And an odd feeling that this is something to store up, a sort of deep-freeze *casus belli*, if one is ever needed, against the human condition. A reason to be pitied. A distinction, even. My philosophy works, sometimes ominously well.

My hatred of crowds, the obviousness of crowds, anything *en masse*. Is this why I like little-known books? A general desire to escape the main world.

8 December
Eliz came back today from hospital.

Reading my 'seconds'; not good enough, two files – of good, and not-so-good poems. I'm going to divide them up differently. It's a sort of occupational disease – poem-sorting. A meanness. There is only one poem – the good.

14 December
Days of beautiful cold. Dusk sky, a smoky amberish pink, all earth objects against it a dense luminous black – no, the darkest grey next to black. (This is at Leigh.) The church and the cedars and the crowds in the Broadway and a voluptuously smooth Salvation Army brass band. Very beautiful. The neon lights at this time of this sort of day are splendidly pure; as characteristically mid-twentieth century as gaslights of the mid-nineteenth. I suppose the mid-twenty-first will have perpetual daylight in every inhabited street. Poor fools!

20 December
Murder of Mrs Weare, 1824. A splendid fragment of local colour. The fine old Trafalgar England turning a bit sour. Nothing takes me back quite so intensely as these old verbatim trial reports. The characters don't normally appear in the room as one reads, but they're at the door. The judge's autograph is in this copy; a fine judge, whose every sentence, every gravity, every smile reminded me of Mr Justice Sachs. Beautifully English, that massive and almost vain determination to be fair ('*nobody* shall make *me* sully the purity of justice; justice, the palladium of our nation'); and superbly English, the unchanging goodness of the judges (nicely offset by the equally unchanging silliness of the barristers). If there was a God, he would use the language of a Mr Justice Sachs; something divine in this tradition.

I've gulped this book down in two evenings – like a journey into space. Price: 15/–.

Letter from Eliz:

Tuesday, December 18th.

Dear Boy

Rest my writing pad on one of your books. *Birds of the night.* Which is by the self same authors *Birds of the Day* I notice.

Lying beneath eiderdown – an hour's respite.

Yesterday morning, crisp, clear cold, sunlight. Walk with F. Hand in hand to make his shop calls we went. Gay-dog chitchat in each. Very important in wineshop. Placed his order for Christmas. I sat. A tweedy gent of 45ish came in and smiled at me. Nice walk.

Woke this morning to sounds of frightful row downstairs. Wine order delivered, *all wrong*. Made his day. He darted out to 'blow them up'. All set to go. But Maggie came. Washing machine pounding away, dog barking, your M screaming welcome. I am in bed eating your pears calmly. What a start to a day. F appears on stage more in control and cheerfully offers to walk back with Maggie. As his rage over wine is subsided, your mother has the reins again. 'Rob,' she yells, 'this floor is to be tidied before you go out.' He is a child again, he obeys. Maggie goes alone. Perhaps, an hour later, I am out. I meet him – he's perky and bright. He greets me. 'Just been to the wineshop and I've given them a good blowing up. Marvellous day again.' I say I'll be all right on my own. But I wasn't really. Got madly tired. Did no more than previous days. But it hit me suddenly without warning. God, I was annoyed with myself. Afraid and lonely. Great stretches of road I had to traverse. Wanted to get down and crawl like a beaten, sick animal.

Had got presents for B'ham, hated them in B'ham.

It was their fault, not mine.

Speechless and faint I came in like a dying thing. 'Still, you'll be glad you've got their presents,' your M remarked.

The afternoons are incredible. Lunch over, coffee is taken in front of dining-room fire. We three sit on those clublike armchairs. Six legs jostle for a place around the hearth. M proceeds to talk without pause. F listens and will, but rarely, make an observation. It is Family History – hers, or anyone's. She weaves herself into a kind of spell. Words which express nothing. Subject covered – no less than birth, marriage and death and remarriage. The whole complex pattern of generation upon generation. It has as much meaning as a recipe. Is this the cake mixture – life? I feel brain-washed.

Same performance again this afternoon. I had to come back to bed after an hour. I felt myself sinking into this terrible void she weaves.

I seem to release the hinge which holds back her floodgate of talk. I notice she is really *quite* silent with your F and comparatively silent with Hazel.

It is quite different here without you – an atmosphere I cannot quite express yet. Perhaps it is just me. I feel absurd.

I have chosen a bad time to write to you. Are you warm? Well-fed and sleeping nicely? Doing nice things. Why and where? I seem to have got involved today on all the things I shouldn't. All concerned with other people. Long, long talk on what Tots said about me,[1] more about my working or not working. I am disinterested, it touched me as much and as little as the rest of the talk. Words, words. Endless words. Yet I feel physically sick and battered with them, bruised by them. No telly this evening. Only the rustle and bustle of parcel wrapping – silly gifts for silly people. Your F staying with us helpless and silent, not reading, not taking part, not going away to watch the telly and be damned. Pathetic, it bothered me. Last night he and I watched the telly. Big world stuff, all of it (your M busy in kitchen throughout), journalistic stuff – good, like a good read of the paper, but less effort. Telly on its best level, in fact. Felt very charitable towards it.

Haven't read anything. There is honestly *no time* – no possible chance either.

I suppose it's one o'clock now. Came to bed twelve-ish, must go to sleep. Another day. Please come and make me sane some day soon. Am I an alien burdensome thing?

Wednesday. Trotted out, sitting in the café you noted as VAST. It isn't. It has smell, like grease-fog. I'll post this for what it's worth.

Think I'll survive until you return. I'm all right really.

Love and Love
from me

29 December
Eliz has been down in Leigh since the 16th, so she sent me this letter which gets the life at 63 and the effect it has on us (and would have on any other normal person) pretty well. The monster there is my mother, whose endless hatred of every world beyond her own infinitesimally small one grows bitterer and bitterer. Poor F keeps up a sort of façade

---

[1] 'Tots' was Aunt Dorothy, a sister of JF's father.

of *respectez-la-mère* ('She won't like it if we don't do it her way.' But said without any emphasis on 'she' and 'her' – with an awesome respect, in fact a grim shaking of the head). But Eliz says they snap at each other when not on their best behaviour. M is a weird case. Her cooking seems to me to get better, she works harder than ever, and sometimes I see her as pursued by an avenging cloud of minor worries and solicitudes. That is, she is genuinely worried that one isn't having enough to eat; this or that trivial point *must* be discussed for the nth time. But too often the timing of her solicitudes is malicious. She wants to break every contact with the outside world.

She has her stock 'funny' subjects. Drink, especially my father and drink. Art – she sends a card to her art teacher (evening classes) and signs it Mrs Picasso. My father – she makes fun of him at every opportunity.

His words are absurd, of course. The world of high finance, jeremiads against Labour and anything that is likely to bring his shares down in price. The old officer-mess world – Nigel Dennis's Co-warden of the Badgeries.[1] A terrible thirst at Leigh for regalia and pomp and circumstance. Who can blame them? Cooped up in the foul little town, with its grey streets of grey houses and grey people, all dying – even the young people without any real sign of youth. Young Conservatism rife. Hazel is one. Mindless, really. Kind and quite jolly, but mindless. Cultureless.

I bought some nice bits of pot this time. Another of my mother's joke subjects. I sometimes think she wishes I took after (physically) F; but the convention is that I am 'a Richards', so she can't make fun of me as much as she sometimes seems secretly to wish.

The pots are the only things that make Leigh tolerable. There are three or four shops with odd bits of pre-Victorian pottery still to be had cheap (by London standards) – and the coming on something pretty in those shops is like a flower in a desert. I had this feeling most of all when I saw a broken and bracketed eighteenth-century mug, blue underglaze and enamelled flowers and figures above – probably oriental-export, but there's just a chance it might be Plymouth or Bristol – in a glass case. Something someone had worked over and loved. Beautiful. Human. It's the *second-handness of life* that's so loathsome at Leigh, the debased standards that govern every home, the hostility to everything unLeighlike.

---

[1] A reference to the 1955 satirical novel *Cards of Identity* by Nigel Dennis (1912–1989), which in 1956 was also adapted for the stage at the Royal Court Theatre. During a conference held in a country manor by a secret society called the Identity Club, one of the members presents a paper, 'The Case of the Co-Warden of the Badgeries', on badger worship.

The pots and the seascapes. Eliz and I left the busy Christmas Broadway in Leigh to go into the churchyard, the pearl-grey, amber, pink, through the stark black elm-branches, Kent a bitter grey-blue seven miles away across the evening estuary. It was iron-cold. We stood there with the old church between us and the crowds with the river before us, a winter variant of *L'Embarcation pour Cythère*, as other-worldly (though of this world) it seemed, at Leigh, as Watteau's picture.

And on the day after Boxing Day we went down Southend High Street to the sea, very calm and cold, shifting the shingle gently. A few wisps of gold-fire cloud, translucent against all the blue and grey of the dusk river. A flight of brent geese flew over the pier. And a wader I couldn't identify kept on coming in to land at our feet, then swept off sandpiper-like and back again, silent. It has its beauties, this filthy wen; but one has to be absolutely foreign to it. Eliz and I manage this as soon as we leave Fillebrooke Avenue. But at 63, it's inescapable. The whole town of hollow lives presses down on one.

Lying in bed together, naked, and being afraid of every squeak of the wretched floor and bed.

Basil Glover[1] – his firm was 'hammered' last week on the Stock Exchange. F's Old Testament glee. Uncle S[2] had invested £750 through them not long before. 'He'll be lucky if he ever sees that again.' I said I thought the Stock Exchange had a contingency fund and never let the investors down. '*If* their losses are really what they declared,' says F, 'you mark my words, the banks are in this.' He loves financial improvidence, as I love bad English or false reasoning. Poor Basil G came in for a drink and got hammered again, by words, from F. 'You'll have to be patient. People are not going to forget this.'

'I've had two offers of jobs already,' says B.

'People are not going to forget it,' says F.

BG is a typical Leighite – minorest of public schools, rose to captain in war, a 'John, old boy' type, all the queer voice-swagger of a class-riddled mind. Terrible hollow man, like a glove puppet. Cultureless again, thoughtless. A pathetic silly pawn in the City rat race. The sort of man who died by the million in World War I at the behest of some idiot general, himself no more than a red-tabbed and brass-hatted version of the Basil Glovers he was sending to their deaths. BG's father did in fact die in that war, so perhaps some destiny is still being played out. A pawn-wish akin to the deathwish.

There it is. I tried once again to analyse my feelings. One third guilt, consisting of one sixth shame that I am not the son they want (rich, car-owning, famous, child-begetting), one sixth that they are not the

---

[1] A neighbour of the Fowles's, who was slightly older than JF.
[2] i.e. Uncle Stanley.

parents I want. The two are related: if I was the son they wanted, they might let me make them the parents they should be (that is, they would let me treat them for the comic old children they are). One third sheer irritation, at my mother's logorrhoea and F's ghastly Lord Mayor's Show brand of conservatism. And one third love.

Juvenal. Another time-breaker.[1] A tall, bitter man, a true (as opposed to the false ones he slashes at) Stoic; whereas Martial is small and foxy. Two sorts of satirists. The Voiture/Voltaire kind, small, sharp men – the greatest of type, Voltaire, Martial, have hearts, but buried deep. The Juvenal/Johnson type are more senatorial, graver, less mobile, less spiteful, hit harder, because seemingly less partial.

A feature I like in Juvenal ('like'? Perhaps 'pity') – his sticking to the city he hated. The 'odi et amo' complex. I feel it for contemporary England. A loathing for so much of it; and yet a deep feeling that permanently to leave England, in any circumstances, is impossible.

30 December

Why are all great satirists conservatives? Not mere red-faced Bullingdon Club reactionaries,[2] of course, but longers after the ancient virtues – Juvenal and Martial looking back to the Republic. Why not forward, to some better age? It's a father-figure art-form, perhaps: the satirist takes on himself the communal guilt, he hates the present, and the hate isolates him; too many for the present.

Penelope Mortimer, *Saturday Lunch with the Brownings*. A perfect example of the mid-century smart style. Absolute cleanliness; strict functionalism. Short sentences, carefully chosen non-function words (nouns, adjectives, verbs). And the camera-eye, the total withdrawal of the artist from the canvas. No heart, no persona even; the creator absconditus.

Eliz's version of her ordeal:

When I wake I am surprised that I am not stiff and immovable with fear. The previous day I had spent wound taut, hysteria controlled, but tight and ready to snap. It is possible, I had reminded myself, that I shall not go tomorrow but will be carried off, be carried away nevertheless

---

[1] Decimus Iunius Iuvenalis (c.60–136) was a contemporary and friend of Martial. His sixteen satires, written from an angry Stoic's viewpoint, expose the vices, misery and poverty of a decadent Rome.

[2] The Bullingdon Club was an undergraduate club at Oxford University known for its mostly upper-class membership and rowdy dinners. It was satirized by Evelyn Waugh in *Decline and Fall* as the Bollinger Club.

somewhere as a case. But it is all right. Sometime, during the night the switch has been thrown, as usual in situations. The essential part of myself is cut out and from henceforth everything will be registered on a dial and all I, the important *I*, is 'watch the readings'. So I tick on through the tube journey, the taxi-ride, even the interest of the new bits of London. Nothing touches me. Into the gates, into the right place, hand over the papers. Into the ward. And suddenly a breakdown in current, but it is very brief. Go through all the motions of being received as a patient, take it all strong and clear, J leaves me, readings still very good. Sit and wait. Note that at any moment they will pounce with their machinery. That terrible poking and scraping at the very centre of the mystery of my sex. I feel I could and would laugh in D. H. Lawrence's face at his puny squeamishness when he faced his so-called ordeal at the army call-up medical. Hastily withdraw this line of thinking, it is sabotage, the current will be well and truly off if such notional ideas take hold.

Aware that another woman is sitting beside me, we are both waiting for a bed. At least an hour has passed, we have been given coffee. I do my knitting, have returned the dozens of smiles the nurses have given me as they bounce back and forth involved with the others in the beds. Those ghastly other patients in beds. I am not one of them. I do what I make a point of never doing, I open the conversation with a stranger. I say, 'Do you think we shall get a bed before night falls?' From that moment on it is all changed; we pitch ourselves into normally worldly conversation, we feel ourselves alien in this world of sickness. We go over all the subjects as far removed as possible. We have all sorts of points of contact. We have lunch together sitting at table, giving a cold eye to the poor figures in the bed. We are impatient when we are disturbed by the various preliminaries to this in-patient existence. The long questioning by the doctors, the medical students, the blood testing. Then we are given our beds, but we are quickly out of them and continue sitting in chairs chatting away as if our life depended on it.

So the first day passed. The second similarly, except she cursed them for already setting up the brain-softening process. We stayed in our beds longer. We had to anyway. Things were noticeably moving.

This day I begin to make contact. I am absorbed in the life of the ward, there is something of the Waaf hut spirit in me still.[1] I talk to dozens of people. I seem to become a member. For part of the day I leave my great chum of yesterday, she has gathered an enormous collection of detective fiction from somewhere and devours one book after another. I think she vaguely despises my capacity for 'joining'. Her name

---

[1] Elizabeth had served in the Women's Auxiliary Air Force during the Second World War.

is Purcell, I envy her name. I dislike her accent and think it is high time
she lost it. It is Geordie and she has been in London for years, there is
nothing particularly provincial about her anyway. All the others are
stoutly earthy people, in this ward. Incredibly stupid and ignorant about
what is happening to them or what has already happened. But they are
so very well-meaning and cheerful for the most part that I gravitate
towards them for comfort. The post-op ones are a mine of information
about what to expect and how to behave and when it is nasty and when
the nastiness stops. They make it all sound all right really and we are
all in it together anyway. I adopt their spirit, it is quite definitely my
long-buried Waaf spirit I recognize – but never mind, it does. I make
myself helpful with the nurses. I am accepted by them as OK. I manage
to give them the impression that hospital routine is almost second nature
to me – I think. I feel the crack in my façade now and then. The round-
faced black girl, who will cry and moan a lot, and the old ancient Miss
Lorimer, the governess of ninety-one, who has had all her cancerous
inside removed, bother me. I am too close to Miss Lorimer for comfort.
Her prayers came as an enormous shock. We had settled down at 9.30,
I looking forward to a good night as I had gratefully taken the dose
they had offered. 'God, help me to die,' she repeated over and over.
Not the senile moan of an ignorant old lady. Her voice is a cultured
voice, it betrayed her – she still had too much awareness to support her
dreadful body. Why? Why? Who is allowing this monstrous thing? The
horror of living, of being forced to go on living. The whole horror of
life for all of us is gathered in that one ancient body.

Awake on THE day. The post-op hearties yell at us to eat all the breakfast, as we shan't get another meal that day. It is very menacing somehow.
I refrain from telling them that I would not eat bacon and eggs at five
o'clock in the morning even if it was my last meal. The six of us for the
theatre must bathe after breakfast. We go two by two. Two bathe in the
same room, for modesty a curtain between. I suggest gaily to my chum
we should bathe together. We don't seem to get in at the right time. I
am the last and join the old lady of seventy-five. I feel nice and safe with
her suddenly. A placid, simple, nice old soul, and after our bath I sit
on her bed and talk. She is very quiet and rather lost and unfamiliar
with hospital routine. On the other side of her is an old lady of eighty-
six, newly arrived. I give her some of my orange to eat and listen to her
talk. A good old Cockney sparrow, office cleaner. Between these two I
spend an hour or more, feeling myself quite lost in their world of hard
work, in fact really totally unware of myself, I lose myself in them. I feel
only pity and affection for them. When I move away from their beds, it
is a bad move. What interests me now is the rota. Who is first on the
list. The nurses are still uncertain. They come now to check hearts and

lungs. I am singled out as an X-ray case. I feel this will be my reprieve.
They'll decide my lungs aren't clear enough. I am rushed into the operation gown for this. They don't seem to make sense of the first film so
another is taken. Ah, yes, as I thought, I think. But no, the second is
clear. I return and still feel jumpy about the list. I notice Sister and a
nurse checking names over on a bit of paper, so calmly go to the desk
and look at it when they move away. Wave my fingers at the others and
call out their numbers and names, as if they are the winning tickets in
a raffle. I am number three. Madame Purcell is still buried in her detective fiction. The time moves on, she doesn't seem at all concerned. I
am. I feel the need to get in touch with reality suddenly and nervously
ring J. I feel he'll be irritated. I watch the time for a half-hour so that
I know I shall speak to him in his office. I don't know how to behave
when I speak to him, so make use of my cheerful Waafishness – we are
all in it together in here, you know. Feel mean when I put the phone
down, as if I should have given him a last message, said something for
once which had sense and meaning. I sit and knit and watch the clock.
They come to prepare the beds now. They are to be made in a special
way, so that senseless bodies can be hauled on to them rather than in
them. I help the nurse to do mine. She is grateful and it is nice to have
her appreciate it. They get out six sets of operation garb, lay them neatly
on the table, lunch is brought round to the others while we are being
prepared. I get a glimpse of the meal, it looks simply superb, feel very
resentful that I am not getting any. I get cross with Madame Purcell,
ask her why she is so unconcerned sitting there with her damned detective fiction. 'Don't you realize number one and two are already being
got up in that awful uniform, and I am number three,' I tell her. She
looks quite bewildered at my sharpness, and apologizes, and as she looks
up, the nurses point to her and the rest of us to get behind our bed
curtains. And so we are all picked off now, I think, and that is that. It
is very silent in the ward. The others plough through their meal. Then
in bustles a nurse for the preparation, swooping swiftly round the blue
curtains. She is not satisfied with the previous day's shaving, so attends
to that again. Attempts to help me into long stockings and insists that
I must have another clean gown, even if the other one has been on only
a couple of hours. I will not have her dress me, it seemed so ridiculous,
put the whole lot on myself, wrapping the cloth on my head. I take off
my wedding ring. This shocks her. It is only diamonds they insist are
removed. This will not do taking off wedding rings and she insists on
getting it out of my bag and I have it on again wrapped round in the
correct fashion with adhesive tape. I get well and truly swabbed with
ether, minute dots of grime scratched from my navel. I feel finally deliciously inhumanly clean. I feel a nice job, a good machine now. Almost
completely without emotion. I lie on the bed. Because as a child I have

been told that it is not for getting into, I am covered with blankets. Underneath me is the bed which will receive the other unconscious me. I feel suspended. I cannot see the clock, I see nothing but the blue bed curtains. I wait. She comes with the jab. Into my bottom it goes, and immediately into my spinal column the stuff takes action. I feel a slow paralysis. She says kindly, 'You will feel a bit drowsy in a while.' I hear the trolley coming for number one. And I am taken by surprise when they come for me. Two chaps in white hats and masks wait beside the high, long trolley. I feel their effort as they lift me. Sister smiles and helps them wrap innumerable red blankets around me. I try to speak and smile. We all move off. I look at the clock: it is almost three o'clock. I feel pleased to be able to do that much. Sharp cold air as we leave the ward, along stretches of open ground we go, they talk above me as I am bounded along, and hold on to my chart and file as it lies on my chest and make sure that the blanket is well around my chin.

The air is icy cold on my face, I feel in great danger of bouncing off the thing as we trundle on.

Then through swing doors. I lift my head up quickly to see what sort of place I am in; one of the men sharply pops it down again and says don't be nosy. It seems a scruffy sort of place, all noice and activity, like a kitchen of a large hotel. I feel rather fed up with being conscious and yet paralysed. We wait a moment and then other people alongside me, Sister introduces them, tells them my name, tells me they will be with me. Chap looks terribly nice, huge round greenish eyes over his mask, girls dark-eyed. They stand and they talk to Sister. The chap is rubbing my shoulder in a most friendly and pleasant way meanwhile. Combination of the drug and this humane introduction business make me suddenly feel that the whole thing is rather a grand experience and these people are the best friends in the world. He stops rubbing my shoulder and is suddenly very interested in my arm, this he takes very gently and rubs too, I feel the most amazing affection for this man and I feel he obviously feels the same for me. Then the sharp injection into the vein in my arm. The needle goes in; but I didn't feel it come out.

I am aware I have been dropped on to something soft. All over I hear, You are back in your own bed. It is nice and warm. For a moment I feel a child again. Then suddenly I ask myself, Is it over? Have I actually done it? The great aching numbness where my stomach once was tells me yes. Feeling of blessed relief, and a few words to myself on the theme, You have gone through with it, you finally did it, and how I cannot believe it. So I sleep – an endless sea of sleep. I feel myself stretched out rigid in the bed on my back, my arms folded carefully high on my chest. I am a stone effigy, I shall never move again.

Part Nine

Climbing Parnassus

7 January 1962
My two aims in poetry.

1. To find a way through to the heart.
2. To put pressure on words.

As regards the first: the direct appeal is no go. The approach is by some other, more devious route. Analogy with climbing. The direct routes to Mont Blanc have all been climbed endless times; so the glory now (it is said) is in the indirect routes, the routes in themselves, not the peak. This feeling (that all the peaks are conquered) is common in all the modern arts; whence the preoccupation with technique, with the manner in which a poetic problem is climbed, not the problem itself. That is, the subject is now a field for exercise and exhibition. Analogy between the natural gymnastic powers of primitive man, Tarzan-man, and the life and aims of the gymnasium gymnast.

By 'heart', I mean all that is not such work – pitch and gymnasium work. I mean all in which the subject is at least as important as treatment. That is, the meaning is as important as the words in which it is expressed. *La pensée vaut le style.*

The devious route must lead to the peak, not only to itself.

As regards the second: a technical device. To break up metre by suppressing function words. A kind of jumping-two-instead-of-one effect. Or shunting trucks. Words jolting other words violently forward.

We went to a party in Hampstead Garden Suburb last night. Richard and Jean Taylor. A roomful of bright and fairly successful young people. I didn't want to go, as the Taylors are close friends of the Hendrys, who, sure enough, were there.

Stilted conversation – I could think of nothing to say. I don't want to know such people (as the Hendrys) because of the waste of time the knowing them requires. Eliz thinks I am unsocial in this, but it was she who insisted that we should break off relationships before. As for the (to me) soft impeachment of being unsocial, I couldn't deny it. Such parties, and the prospects of evenings with couples like the Hendrys (the latest films, plays, books – the deadly servile dullness of such talk), they bore me stiff. I pump people in such circumstances, if there's anything to pump out; with people one knows very well there's nothing left to pump. So there's no more than a void. Once every six months is enough to see most people. And a very few, more often.

10 January
Ronnie Payne. We haven't seen them for years. Quieter. Lonely people, like ourselves; only they seem fiercer, unhappier about it.

He had some good stories, as usual. One about *The Times* correspondent in Paris, a Giles. Very snobbishly proud that his wife was Lady Kitty. Some Frenchman asked him to a reception. 'And bring Mrs Giles.'

'Well, actually she isn't *Mrs* Giles . . .'

'Never mind, never mind, bring her along anyhow!'

24 January
Will in wordcraft gets one nowhere.

30 January
Waking up in the middle of the night. The very thin old moon supporting the bright ashen grey dead moon. A sort of voyeur impression. Seeing the moon naked for the first time.

8 February
Kamin. A Tanganyika Gujerati. She failed a shorthand test (by two words – nothing) this morning. During the lunch-hour she slashed the back of her hand repeatedly with a razor-blade. Why? 'It gives me relief,' she said, 'I've often done it before.' Sure enough, I saw scars on her inner arm when she turned her wrists round for me to look. Hysteria? Masochism? She sat quietly smiling, politely deprecating all the fuss. I felt it was something very Oriental. Not for Europeans to understand.

The Common Market. The peculiar assumption (on both sides) that the matter can be decided only on economic grounds. As if to adduce historical, cultural, emotional, or internationalist arguments is mere sentimentality. It seems to me that the economic is the least important aspect; and that the politicians' failure to see this justifies the contempt one feels for them. I want to be European, not Commonwealth-British.[1]

*

---

[1] Although Britain had initially refused to join the European Economic Community, by 1962 the economic benefits of membership had become increasingly apparent and the British government decided to begin negotiations to join. Its application was vetoed the following year by the French president de Gaulle on the grounds that Britain was too closely tied to the US.

Antonioni, *La Notte*.[1] Another very good film, misunderstood by the critics, it seems. This one is pure Racine: stylized 'noble' characters exhibiting a kind of geometric psychology, all predestined in true Jansenist style, and acting out their fates mathematically. The décor is contemporary, but I can't see any real application. Antonioni makes certain general statements about the human condition and human relationships, just as Racine does. I can't imagine that one is meant to be moved; catharsis is impossible. The right reaction is one of keen intellectual pleasure – 'pure' intellectual pleasure, 'pure' in the sense that we talk of 'pure' mathematics.

We have lately reknotted our relationship with Jennifer Ardagh. She has separated from the egregious John. A nicely ice-cool woman, with a sort of impatience with the cliché expression and the cliché thought, and indeed with her own cliché blue-stocking oversensitivity and shyness. We had coffee with her the other day – dull and stilted, but the evening produced a fine monster, a Mrs Bolton-Smith, an earnest muscular Christian of forty or so. Dressed in a black dress, vicar's dowdy wife style, her hair done the *hausfrau* way, no make-up, hard grey eyes glinting behind spectacles. Full of girlishry, spinning her necklace round, gurgling and giggling at her own jokes. One of the new Christians, eager to mildly shock, to be 'young'. Throwing words like 'egghead' and 'beatnik' around; then dragging one back to her faith, always rubbing one's nose in it (I said the public schools killed Christianity and she rose, naïve trout, with a great splash). Rugby, she said, gave the boys a simply splendid Christian spirit, the real thing – good works, good works, good works. When Jennifer told a story about her little boy – they were in a Catholic church and he said 'I don't think God lives here' – the B-S crowed, crowed, and cried, 'Sucks to the Pope!'

Of Gainsborough's masterpiece at Kenwood: 'I simply adore her. She's such a minx! A real minx! Every fold of her dress is erotic! Such a minx.'

But her best expression was 'You either have Lord, or you don't.'

17 February
Being in exile from the now. I've been in bed with a cold. Reading Swift and Fielding. So every conformation of shadow and sunlight (especially) becomes eighteenth century. I mean I hear things and see things and I seem to see and hear them through eighteenth-century eyes and ears. The effort is to live in the now, not in the then.

TV adverts. A phrase I noticed: coffee-pot fresh.

[1] Made in 1960, the film stars Marcello Mastroianni and Jeanne Moreau as a married couple who discover over the course of an afternoon and an all-night party that their love for each other has died.

26 February
It was pronounced – 'coffeepotfresh'. This is the new use in English,
bound to spread and spread. The packaging and concentrating of the
key words in a statement (the phrase was advertising powdered coffee,
fitly enough). I suppose it comes from Joyce and the experiments of
the 1920s, via *Time* magazine, although of course the tendency to
agglutinate is as old as the language. I foresee a dim future for a lot
of the old structure words (pressure of time, pressure of space).

'Today the weather is as cold as can be' = today's coldscanbe weather.

Coolorchardrecalling reckless love

Poetry hasn't exploited it yet.

The cut-throat cleverness of young intellectuals today; *terrified* of not
seeming clever. The public isn't with them, except inasmuch (perhaps
a pretty heavy exception) as the critics lead the unthinking. But since
it is young intellectuals (and intellectuals of all ages always want to seem
young) that command the field in the newspaper and magazine offices,
the intellectual cleverness gets as much space as it wants. I think it is a
phenomenon, a compensation, of non-creativeness. So we let deaf men
choose our music.

28 February
Two poems. One about Devon – Ipplepen. Going to the Charlesmouths'
one day, and walking with Hazel Charlesmouth – with a girl – to see
some cyclamen blooming. I think the first I had ever seen growing 'wild'.
This memory came up when we were talking about Ipplepen down at
Leigh. A recurrence of forgotten things; the box-bush outside Mr Petrie's
door; the date carved over the door at Dornafield farm; and the cyclamen
incident. I can't remember what Hazel C looked like (I had no sex
feeling for her); or what the house looked like. Only a very dim memory
of walking with a faceless, nameless girl to see these wild cyclamen and
being delighted with them.

The other poem, about will-lessness. A characteristic (of me) refusal
to do at the right time what must be done. The symbolism I've used is
of lying in bed. But in fact I rarely lie in bed awake. I get up. My usual
will-lessness is attached to things like marking; also to my writing and
the revising of it. I won't do it when I should; I do a dozen trivial things
rather than do it. I often explain this so: 'I am not in the mood for
writing. The muse (or the mythical future perfect novel) demands that
I don't write.' I get a sort of perverse satisfaction out of not doing what
I myself want to do; saving it up, perhaps – and all the Freudian anal
connotations. It also seems to me to be a device to prove myself free. All

that is determined (that must be done, like marking) is against freedom; and that all-determined includes the things one determines for oneself (that one wants to do), so that even the most noble and moral of these latter personal determinations (i.e. not just the sensual and selfish desires) are tyrants of the 'free self'. Thus I often experience a wanting-to-do-yet-not-doing state that I relate to constipation, but in fact it is not analogous, since there is no physical obstacle to not doing. Constipation is wanting-to-do-but-unable-to-do. Of course a cynic would sneer at all this explanation of sheer idleness. I think I would like to be free of the state; on the other hand, it is the I I live with. If I get pressure into poems and words sometimes, it is because of this state. It seems to me an unpleasant state, often quite incomprehensible in the way it can prevent me from doing anything serious for days on end; but my poems would probably defend it, if they had a spokesman, as a state of latency, a very necessary winter.

2 March

A certain kind of car horn: even on a cold winter's morning it suggests hot summer evenings.

9 March

I've half got Eliz into a job at St G's. As appointments secretary, for two and a half months in the summer. While I was discussing it with JWL, he had a call from his estate agent. They were discussing some property deal. 'I'll make a direct approach,' says JWL, 'by a roundabout political way.' Not meant to be funny. He meant he'd get an MP friend to speak to the Ministry concerned.

Naghari, a Persian student. She has an interesting idea about the staleness of all literary imagery, all imagery, and how the space age has come to refresh the symbol-starved mind.

The new axis will be out-space/earth. The man-besieged situation. Taking the place of the heaven/hell one – the man torn. We are all isolates, attacked or in danger of attack from things unknown, beyond all control.

So there is threat, and danger; and a flow of fresh feelings and images. Linguistically, I liked the American hour-by-hour commentary on the Glenn flight. The new words: 'I am go, the capsule is go.' 'Countdown.' 'Retros.'[1]

---

[1] On 20 February 1962 Lieutenant-Colonel John Glenn became the second American to go into space – and the first to orbit the earth – when his Mercury spacecraft, 'Friendship VII', took off from Cape Canaveral, Florida, and orbited the earth three times. Glenn's communication with Mission Control during the five-hour flight was broadcast around the world.

10 March
Adverbs I use in talking far too often: absolutely, completely, utterly, absurdly, fantastically, incredibly. Also their adjectives. They are fairly common among exasperated (with the human condition) intellectuals today. We have to express our judgements in satirical terms. We even cartoon our opinions. Perhaps it's the central will-lessness, the inability to act (either we don't, though we could, or we don't because we know we can't, however hard we act, affect), which makes this use of 'violent', extreme adverbs and adjectives so ubiquitous. And self-irritating.

Volcano. A fascinating film or subject that makes any film of it fascinating. Pieces of lava being ejected like human cannonballs; a peculiarly graceful deceleration, rallentando, pause and acceleration down to earth again. The torn fragments like great cherry-red rags against the smoke and the pale blue sky. Like fire-dolphins leaping. Magma the molten mass that becomes lava. Lapithae – the rain of small stones.

16 March
Pat Brown. A secretarial 'tutor' at St G's. Last year she cut herself slightly on a Gestetner. Her hand got worse and worse. She began to wear her arm in a sling. She bravely pooh-poohed any idea of suing the college. The finger would have to be amputated, then the hand. She waited and waited, one specialist said it would get better, another feared the worst. Everyone was very sympathetic. She was in pain. There was no hope. The arm would have to come off. She could no longer work (she had bravely carried on doing little jobs).

And now she's in a mental home. There was never anything wrong with her at all. But she could never type as well as a typing teacher should.

21 March
Ayout. An Egyptian girl. She came into my office this afternoon, having been absent all day. In a black headscarf. She stood by the wall and just said, '*Mon père est mort.*' Apparently he had died this same morning, at dawn, driving between Alexandria and Cairo. Smacked into another car. I made her sit down at the other desk and we talked about her family and her father. I like her, dangerous to like pretty nubile girls, but she has intelligence, a certain uprightness. I had her in earlier this term to warn her not to let herself be picked up by strange men in the Finchley Road clubs; and I liked then the way she shrugged the whole business off – as petty and absurd. She's the sort of Egyptian that one finds in Orwell's books; very highly civilized. She's begun to write well, with a fair eye and a certain agreeable bitterness of tone. The situation was explained this afternoon. Nasser has it in for her family; her father is

the last adult male of his line (though there's a ten-year-old brother in
Beirut); her mother is a Turk, very retiring, easy prey for the Egyptians;
they are Christians, were once very rich, still have money abroad; her
fiancé is a young millionaire, in prison for life; she has written begging
for his freedom, to Nasser, who's told her he will never be released; her
mother can't leave Egypt, because then all her family will suffer. It's a
'poor little rich girl' situation, of course. But watching her talk in her
rapid Alexandrian French, one did sense tragedy – the day's real, intense
and terrible Greek tragedy superimposed on a deeper, rich tragedy. *Je
savais qu'il allait mourir.'* The accident might have been staged, a political murder. But beyond that, a deeper fatality. The death of a caste.

I asked silly questions. Impossible to communicate sympathy in such
circumstances. One says the tritest things. There were silences and she
didn't go away, she sat twitching her scarf round her white, shocked
face. I think she despises other women, she wanted to be with a man a
while. In the end, when she left, she kept on saying, *'Vous êtes charmant,
vous êtes très gentil.'* A sexuality comes from death, a rapprochement; a
feeling of nakedness, of isolation, of cold. Gilbert and Sewell were
cynical; they both said it was probably a hoax, and if I didn't despise
them both, I'd have to be angry. Eliz, too, saw only the unpleasant side,
the coarsest end-product – the sexiness. It needs an ugly word.

For me it was one of the 'loaded', pregnant incidents that can't be
explained. I mean, essentially poetic, or metaphysical. The beauty of
death and death in time, an incident at dawn in Egypt stabbing through
an afternoon in Hampstead. The remoteness of this girl's life and her
tragic face (she is normally gay, a deliberate clown). Death is beautiful,
time is beautiful, and the girl was for an hour beautiful. A sudden intensity. Like a flow of words. A syncopation. Death has nothing to do with
it, nor has whatever 'sex' was implicit. But her standing there saying,
'Mon père est mort.'

24 March

Reading back through old diaries. Fantastic outbursts of priggishness,
of vanity, of expectations. The temptation is to suppress such blemishes.
But that defeats the diary. This is, and always will be, what one was. I'm
glad I've kept it for so long. Since 1948. I'm sorry I spent so much time
on recording thoughts and ideas and views of ideas, and so little on
people and events.

The *nostalgie de soi* – the impossible desire to go back in oneself, and
to re-experience the past. I don't mean so that one can act differently.
That is not a nostalgia, but a physical impossibility. But to recreate the
past – by an effort of will, of concentrated recall, by going back to the
places again, to see what lost memories surge up. The winter dead
branches, and the miracle of buds.

'La grande definite, en tout, c'est d'oublier.' Céline, *Voyage au bout de la nuit.*

The Ayout business. Such experiences are to me intensely *aesthetic.* Only very secondarily emotionally or sexually affective.

Leavis/Snow. I am all for Leavis. I thought his attack on Snow one of the justest and most massive slams at a plaster-of-paris genius since the last century.[1] Perhaps Snow himself is not to blame. But his reputation is absurd. He can't begin to write dialogue, or create scenes, or convincing intelligent people. Between Leavis's passionate contempt for the second-rate and Snow's cardboard eminence it is absurd to hesitate. Significant that all the second-raters in the literary world, the 'distinguished' critics and telepundits, have come twinklefoot and duck-arsed to screech their horror at Leavis.[2] These are the real two cultures – the true, and the second-rate.

I broke a mirror in my office at St Godric's (to be exact, it 'broke all of itself', suddenly electing to slip off a filing cabinet). Seven years' bad luck. The bad luck started very genially, as the backing of the mirror turned out to be a charming Baxter print of a mid-Victorian pin-up girl.

30 March
With Podge. He took away the first fifty pages of *The Collector* to read in Oxford recently. He thinks it 'up to standard', 'publishable', but wouldn't say any more. It annoys me a little, as he was the one who insisted that he should take it away and read it. Plainly his silence means, 'It is bad, but I'm not going to say so.' I feel he doesn't like to think of me as doing something well. To think differently than him.

Yesterday was one of his impenetrable days – what Eliz calls his 'hedge'

---

[1] In 1959 the novelist C. P. Snow gave a lecture at Cambridge called 'The Two Cultures and the Scientific Revolution', in which he held that English cultural life was split between science and the arts, and that more importance should be attached to the former. Three years later the distinguished literary critic F. R. Leavis took him to task in a Cambridge lecture of his own. In 'The Significance of C. P. Snow', which was reprinted in the *Spectator* of 8 March 1962, he made a savage attack both on Snow's materialistic vision of the future and on his standing as a novelist. 'It is ridiculous to credit him with any capacity for serious thinking about the problems on which he offers to advise the world.' Leavis further added: 'Snow not only hasn't in him the beginnings of a novelist; he is utterly without a glimmer of what creative literature is, or why it matters.'
[2] The week after Leavis's article appeared, the *Spectator* carried seventeen letters, all defending Snow and expressing their anger at Leavis's comments.

high around him. He is on the Snow side of the Leavis/Snow battle; said he couldn't finish Waugh's *Unconditional Surrender*; found *L'Avventura* very ordinary. It is almost (with someone so intelligent) as if he is being obtuse to test me out. A sort of *perverse* hatred of sentimentality in him – a hatred of success, from the highest and most actual and distant (from his own life) to the not even actual and highly improbable (my own venture with *The Collector*). So there is a sourness in him sometimes that at other times is astringency, logical positivism, etc. He won't take the work of anyone he knows (John Veale,[1] Elizabeth Mavor)[2] seriously; he *insists* that one takes it for granted that their only motive is to make money. 'There's money in it,' he says, as if no one around *him* is ever going to get away with talk about art, or love of life, or philosophical feeling.

For several years now I have felt, in this way, older to him, a feeling that he is only half a human being. An admirable half, but with his further side forever in darkness. It must be linked with his marriage – a premature killing-off of all tenderness, all sex, all sentiment (in the eighteenth-century and good sense of the word).

The Collector is being typed out. The confidence I feel in it is inexplicable. Eliz doesn't like it, Podge apparently doesn't, I can't imagine any publishers, readers or, if it gets so far, contemporary critics, liking it. And yet I feel it is complete, it says what I want to say. Details are wrong, could be improved, no doubt, but it's like a poem. I *know* the backbone is right.

The Giant Snakes, Pope. An interesting book. Snakes copulate for hours, sometimes a day at a time. They sense by heat.

A nice story about what to do when attacked by a python. You lie flat, with your arms and legs together, so that you are swallowable. Do not allow snake to get head under you (for the hug). In the end he will give up and begin to swallow you, starting at the feet. Keep absolutely still, otherwise he still may start constricting. When he has reached your knees, sit up, take your knife out, and quietly slit his distended jaw.

And spend the rest of your life in an asylum.

6 April

The impossibility of writing poetry except when I am alone. It is the aimlessness of other people that is so irritating, the feeling that they

---

[1] See note 1 on page 294.
[2] Elizabeth Mavor (1927–   ) wrote several novels and biographies, including *Summer in the Greenhouse* (1959), *The Temple of Flora* (1961), *The Virgin Mistress: A Biography of the Duchess of Kingston* (1964), *The Ladies of Llangollen: A Study in Romantic Friendship* (1971) and the Booker-nominated *The Green Equinox* (1973).

have to kill that same time one is making love to. Waiting for it to be time to go to bed, or something. And in the poem there is no time; and at the making of it, no time. I need a vacuum of no-time around me. I don't care if Eliz is here, in another room. I don't care how much noise there is outside. As long as it's not music, I can't stand music and poetry.

The idea that the poetic world (Parnassus) is remote from the ordinary, quite wrong. It is simply a step sideways, a second away. Because one goes weeks without a poem, one forgets it. I deduce this mainly from the speed with which one leaves the poetic world – in the time it takes to look up from a poem and say something trite or silly. Coming to, and leaving Parnassus are instantaneous actions.

8 April
Watts, *The Way of Zen*. An intelligent man, a good book.[1] I think I have, and Europe has, laughed at Zen too long. Again and again in this book I read statements and prescriptions I arrived at in *The Aristos* years ago; the need to get to the 'now', and so on. In fact, I am, inasmuch as I have any religion, far more Zen than Christian. My indifference to good and evil, my feeling that it is impossible to say that evil always breeds evil, and good, good – all that is Zen. Sometimes the similarity of ideas has been so great that it is as if I opened another man's book and read the same poem by him that I had written. *Déjà vu*, in fact.

Zen is unbeatable as a recipe for *living*. The point is whether we are here for living, or not. Zen has nothing to say about the being-dead, our duty to make ourselves into useful post-mortals (or the rare few, immortals). That is, in European terms, our 'duty' to the world in and to which we shall be totally dead. (I say 'totally dead' – pleonasm. But of course I'm not talking about life-after-death or any rubbish like that.)

Practically everyone we know is actively in conversation against the H-bomb.[2] I am totally indifferent to the whole problem. First of all (at a simple realpolitik level) Britain's foregoing of the bomb and sending

---

[1] Born in England in 1915, Alan Watts (1915–1973) went to the United States in 1938, where he built up a reputation as the foremost interpreter of Eastern philosophy to the West. Published in 1957, his two-part *The Way of Zen* became the classic introduction to Zen Buddhism. The first part explained its history and background, and the second its principles, which – in short – involve the importance of living in the moment, accepting the transience of nature and understanding the interconnectedness of all things.

[2] The issue was topical because at the beginning of the previous month Britain had carried out its first underground nuclear test in Nevada.

the Americans away will not alter the probabilities of survival of Britain in a world nuclear war. It is even arguable that it lessens those probabilities – by simplifying the issues, setting the USA and USSR even more starkly against each other, and offering (even more invitingly than at present) a battleground that will save the two great protagonists from having to see their own homelands laid waste.

I am indifferent, socially, because so many people *enjoy* opposing the H-bomb. In my terms, they counter-oppose it. That is, opposing it exercises their *personal desire* of opposition; and one doesn't wish the end of what one desires. In ordinary terms, it is an OK attitude among *soi-disant* liberals.

I am indifferent, metaphysically or philosophically, because the consequences of evil are often good. In Zen terms, because the evil is the good.

I am indifferent, on a personal level, because even if I did oppose it, I should not agree that the present is the best method of opposing *for myself.*

9 April
The film on volcanoes. Only today did I see why I liked it so much, and the word 'magma'. Every good poem is a volcanic eruption, a bursting-out of the magma in the mind. I don't mean the 'white-hot inspiration' non-poets like to imagine; but that overcoming, that piercing, of the hard crust of normality, banal outwardness, incohate and chaotic words. The breaking through of any poem.

Verse is an act of will, a boring down to get magma; a poem is the magma bursting or flowing or oozing or seeping from below. You can say, perhaps, where the volcano is likely to come; the area in which new volcanoes are likely to come. But to time them is impossible. And the distribution area is probably a false analogy; the poem-volcano may come anywhere in the globe.

13–15 April
Terrible weekend at Leigh. Very cold, in spite of the date. Inane talk, wasted hours. Pure *maya*;[1] an endless meaningless cascade of grey little facts.

Oliver Twist – a nasty book. It shows up Dickens for what he is, a brilliant and magnificent second-rater. The gilt wears off, just as it wears off Victorian plates, far more quickly than off the genuine article (i.e. Jane

---

[1] A Zen word (of Hindu origin) for the state of experiencing an illusion.

Austen). I see that the *Quarterly Review* for 1837, after fearing the worst for *Pickwick Papers*, thinks *Oliver Twist* will raise Dickens's stock; just as one would expect. It's a book for the age – Rose, Harry Maylie, Mrs Maylie and Oliver are artistically vile creatures. The only good characters are 'bad' ones. Then there is the bourgeois snobbism and the anti-semitism.

Great writers create lovable good characters – good 'good' characters.

22 April

E went out today, Easter Sunday, with her mother and sister. They are here for the holiday. They drive us mad. Mother can't be hated; she 'means well', with all the good and all the irritated impotence the phrase contains.

When they went out I watched a girl on a roof opposite, across the back gardens of Church Row. It was the first good day this year, peerless English blue sky, cloudless, light warm airs, green buds, pink sparks of almond blossom, buoyant birds. The girl was on a roof with a man who kept on photographing her, endlessly. I couldn't make out if he was her father or not; incestuous thoughts, if he was. I watched them through a telescope, and I could see she was a very pretty girl, Irish-looking, red-gold hair and green eyes, mischievous, quick, teasing, sulky, all a bit put on, as if she knew she was being watched by more than one man. A sort of amateur film starlet – or perhaps a real one. There was a hard-faced duenna, a bright blonde of forty or so, who didn't give them a look as they waltzed round the roof, the girl taking up a hundred poses a minute. She was wearing a very pretty bright green and blue Italian sun-dress and a carmine straw hat. Ravishingly pretty, on the dirty roof, and the man like an ox with his light-meter and Rolliflex. She broke into an Indian dance at one point – quite expertly, she must have lived in India – and then it became the twist. Then she coquettishly turned and took her bra off from underneath her dress and draped herself round chimney pots. It is curious, watching people through a telescope. Like watching birds. It is as if one has never seen the wild (unrestrained, I don't mean wild = excited) face before. She was utterly absorbed in her own prettiness, this girl; kept on holding out her bare arms and hands to look at them, posing, even when the ox-man was not watching. Later she took off her dress and lay in a bikini; stood up for a moment, her long hair round her shoulders, for all the world like a Botticelli Venus or Primavera. She had just that small-breasted wide-hipped slim-round beauty; and then some pregnant shyness. That impression they give of being poised, in swiftest passage, between the angelic and the sexual. To begin with, my motives were perhaps bad – just a mere idle curiosity, the pleasure I always have in looking at things (and people are in this context simply the most interesting things, and pretty girls visually the most interesting people), but slowly I realized it was an intensely *beautiful* experience, just as the one with Ayout (21st

March). One has such a load of conventions, of guilt objects and actions, in one that it takes time to disentangle the motives. The English gentleman says, 'This is caddish, watching a girl in the sun through a telescope'; the psychologist says, 'This is voyeurism, this shows maladjustment'. But (the truth of this is again and again in the Zen book I have been reading) the beauty of the event is quite separate from the motives of the observer. The aesthetic justification is in practice not so immoral as it seems. To be a voyeur *all the time* (granting the premise) could never be justified aesthetically. The Zen argument is simply that: never try to categorize events, never search any one category. Giving is remaining sensitive to events.

In European terms this was a Primavera experience. It is grey and cold again today – Easter Monday – and to look on that roof, so dull, so banal, under the cotton-grey sky! Of course the event was miraculous, intensely poetic, seedlike, with the vividness of those rare occasions when ordinary life and time modulate into art – into forms that the greatest art strives for. That is the event. What observers of me would say (and we judge all the actions of such third persons) is irrelevant.

This experience made me brilliantly, feverishly happy. It made me still happy when the others came back. Deeply happy to have E; because such experiences cannot help being suspect if one is lonely. The experiences of a solitary are always tainted with onanism. One can only own (in both senses of the word) them out of an emotionally still centre – that is, certainly of love. Of course I don't deny the sexuality of such experiences; but the thing I see now is that because such visions are sexual in form they need not be hidden away. There is nothing shameful in them. To maintain that there is is to say that it is shameful to find certain aspects (i.e. the ritual, or the architecture) of religion beautiful because one does not believe in the dogma.

Céline, *Voyage au bout de la nuit*. A remarkable book. I put it with Malraux's *La Condition humaine* and Camus's *La Peste*. Hundreds of sons, this book. A whole American tradition – the Lost Generation through to the Beat writers. Sartre's novels. The sharp, sour impotence – it reminds me of *Candide*. And La Rochefoucauld.[1]

4 May
The Collector has been typed out. Eliz has taken it to an agent. James Kinross, of Anthony Sheil Ltd.

It cost £21, the typing.

Now I work on *A Journey to Athens*.

*

---

[1] See note on page 89.

Swifts.

At Bath.[1] Everyone seemed to be having a holiday this year; it's part of the New Rich World. One deserves two holidays a year.

Bath is a shock after London – a great soft slow city, rich-seeming and civilized. One accepts the fallacy that outside London there is only the desert. The truth is, of course, that some provincial styles are as good living styles as the capital's. Only the capital is contemporary. I kept on feeling at Bath that the people were smug, insular, but that is a by-product of the good provincial style. Everything is a little old-fashioned; hostile to the capital; self-consciously Bathian, or whatever.

We went by train – into sunshine. I have never travelled from Paddington without this happening. I expect it to happen. Somewhere beyond Reading the sun always comes out.

We came back to London by bus. Rather a long journey, hideous after Reading. London begins at Slough. And London seems twisted, blackened, too crowded after Bath. Too dense.

I kept on saying I would like to live at Bath when I was there, but it seems to me enervating in two ways. Climatewise: we wanted to sleep all the time. And culturewise: one lives in the past there. Too much softness and wetness; not enough cold, dry, black.

Like Aix-en-Provence: a perfect place, to live out of life.

14 May
Eliz working at St G's.

15 May
A letter from Mr Kinross.

Dear Mr Fowles,

THE COLLECTOR

Thank you very much for giving us the opportunity of reading this novel.

I find it extraordinarily promising, in a spine-chilling sort of way, and I should like to congratulate you on an extremely well accomplished feat of characterization throughout the first half.

I am not entirely satisfied that the construction is quite right, since the book is so sharply divided into two related but totally

---

[1] JF and Elizabeth were there from 24 to 29 April.

different points of view. I have a feeling that this sharp division rather tends to detract from the overall building up into a sustained climax, but even so, this is a highly promising effort, which deserves much praise.

Is there any chance of your coming to see me, because I would much appreciate having a word with you before deciding whether to send it out?

If you were a full-time novelist, I would probably make a series of suggestions which might result in a sort of inter-cutting of experiences, or even possibly a transference of the second half of the book into a new first part. On the other hand, I can well appreciate that such heavy work would probably appal you, and in any case, one never knows whether changes like this may not have disastrous results, once an author starts tinkering about with the structure of a book.

Do come and see me, in any case, I should very much like to meet you.

Yours sincerely,

James Kinross
Director and Literary Manager[1]

18 May
I went to see Mr Kinross, a large man in a very light-windowed opulent attic office in Grafton Street. It was like a bit of psychotherapy; so many compliments that I couldn't help smiling with pleasure – and at the absurdity of it. Kinross is liberal with intensifiers, a sort of amiable old Etonian elephant, sea-lion. Impossible to tell what lies under all the talk, the praise, the vagueness – whether shrewdness or unplumbed depths of blah. I honestly don't know. Probably the first. I quite liked him. I liked it when he said, 'Stephen Spender, I loathe the bastard.' For his smugness, it seems.

Bulwer-Lytton,[2] *Pelham* (1828). A terribly bad picaresque novel, full of improbabilities and slick generalizations and French flu and everything else in the literary dustbin. Yet it keeps one reading. It has life, a sort of rapid springing narrative rhythm. Like a not very good American

---

[1] James Kinross was a literary agent at Anthony Sheil Ltd. He had been recommended by JF's typist, Mrs Shirley.
[2] Edward Bulwer-Lytton (1803–1873), an extremely popular Victorian writer, whose prolific output included historical novels, science fiction and tales of the occult.

film; its pace saves it. Like an Amis novel. Kingsley Amis is the Bulwer-Lytton of our age.

21 May

Dear Mr Fowles,

THE COLLECTOR

Many thanks for your letter of the 20th May.

You can rest assured that your book (which is going to Cape today) is travelling under your new pseudonym.[1]

I was certainly delighted to meet you, and very much look forward to seeing the other work we discussed. By all means let us have a second copy of THE COLLECTOR. There might be film possibilities.

Yours sincerely,

James Kinross
Director and Literary Manager

24 May

Denys Sharrocks is back from Laos. Unchanged, even a little younger. I am glad to see him, but you forget old friends' faults in their absence. His acting a part always, or almost always; one can't ever get to the centre of him. He tells funny stories about Laos and Karachi, all the accents carefully and well mimicked. Flees into his stock self very swiftly – the northerner, the suspector-of-the-south; and the worsted-by-life. And there's a sort of not very credible virility he puts on – the drinker, womanizer, the untameable-eternal-man sort of thing. You can't get him to be serious about himself; or about anything except books. Both he and Monica have this vile and dreadful post-war habit (it started with *ITMA*,[2] though no doubt it could be heard in the very first green room) of killing the serious or the sincere by striking into funny accents. It's the convenient modern way of covering up, one, stupidity, two, shallowness of heart. If you get intellectually or emotionally out of your depth, start putting on a funny voice, drag everything back to the silliest level.

These are only very minor blemishes in Denys, who remains, we still

---

[1] Richard Whitton. The name was a combination of the maiden names of JF's mother and his wife, respectively 'Richards' and 'Whitton'.

[2] A hugely successful BBC radio comedy show broadcast during the 1940s, *ITMA* was short for *It's That Man Again*.

feel, a charming and essentially gentle drifter through life. He remains sensitive; and in the small things of life, a brilliant diplomat. With him, I admit that; it seems a virtue worth having. Even his funny-voice stuff is perhaps tact: not alienating Monica.

We've decided we can't really stand Monica. Eliz calls her hatchet-faced. With Denys she becomes irritatingly girlish. Keeps on squawking, sounding spoilt, heavily kittenish. She resents us, and the sort of talk we have. Her culture is thin, so she hates culture. One feels vinegar in her, determination to suffer, to make herself and her vinegar heeded. A kind of pig, really. Deeply selfish.

Britten, *Requiem*. This is the greatest thing in British art since 1922. (*The Waste Land* and *Ulysses*.)

All that *is* has *survived*. (What doesn't survive never speaks. I mean that the world we live in is largely a survived world and all our arts are created by survivors.)

3 June

I've been rereading *An Island and Greece* for the first time since 1955.[1] Terrible, a great deal of it. The priggishness, the belletrist style, the wild improbabilities in the fiction part and the dialogue. It failed, one, because it is neither fish nor fowl (nor Fowles) – the lapses from travelogue into fiction are ridiculous; two, it was an attempt to stuff everything into one small bag. In many ways I've been living on those two years ever since (and I don't mean this in the living on one's success sense) – it was an incredibly rich meal. I haven't digested it yet. To have tried to do it so fast was ridiculous.

11 June

Francis Bacon at the Tate. A curious case of vision, of world-view, triumphing over everything. He's plainly not a good painterly painter by any standard. Nothing neat about him. You feel he scuffs and smears and stabs and sabres until something is hit off; and that he destroys a lot is very credible. The misfires must be many. What he has, brilliantly, is the ability to leave out and the ability to site the centre (fulcrum) of the picture. His 'vision' is the horror of humanity and the horror of the flesh. The emptiness of man; the bestiality of man; the beastliness of flesh. Two naked men wrestling on a bed; and the carcass-crucifixion. I think (unless he changes style) his reputation will sink. There's too much expressionistic (Germany of the thirties) decadence in his attitude. The

---

[1] See note on page 289.

gratuitous seeking of the perverse; the split-open stomach. I mean, he is a witness, not a maker. A Goya who never did anything but the etchings.

19 June
Michael Sharrocks. The little boys in his primary school (Christchurch Hill) have split into two rival gangs. They spend all their free time fighting.
'Don't you play games?'
'We fight. Only girls play games.'
Any boy who doesn't join a gang is repeatedly beaten up and bullied. Michael doesn't like either gang, but thinks he might join one 'for a few days'. Talk of microcosms!

Stan Barstow, *A Kind of Loving*. 'Like Zola' says the blurb. But all these provincial novels are the very antithesis of Zola in all but the attention to realistic detail. Zola is dispassionate, his characters are seen, not felt. Barstow is a sentimentalist; that is, like Sillitoe and Braine, he creates a hero who can be liked through all his faults. I don't much like this typically contemporary business of the love affaire between the writer and his hero – something narcissistic, but the last person to approve would be Zola.

3 July
We've spent a weekend in Oxford with Podge. Eileen's away in France, with the Tolkiens. Taking us when we arrived for a ridiculously expensive and bad meal in a chi-chi Italian restaurant. Going to the Ashmolean. The beautifully haunting Palmers. Then (Saturday afternoon) punting up to the Victoria.[1] With a friend of Podge, a pretty, shade too eager woman in her thirties. Like all the Oxford people, too brittle. If one takes them at their own valuation they make one feel bovine, dull; at one's own valuation, they are paper butterflies, the fragile cases of sea-urchins. Beautiful, but dead. We went out to Garsington later to meet Elizabeth[2] and Haro Hodson, the *Observer* vignettist. In a cottage, once the annexe of Lady Ottoline Morrell's house, across the lane. And as the eager E. Mavor talked about Lady Ottie, I couldn't help thinking of Lawrence and his loathing of Oxbridge. Later she said, of a book, 'But if it's amusing – that's all one can ask, isn't it?' And that sums them up. Their test is amusingness. And they have a sharp small hatred of seriousness; though they like to make it clear that they 'feel'. A miserable and pitiable lot, really. Podge eggs them on, seems to agree with them, and yet manages to remain separate; or at least to keep his Oxford

---

[1] The Victoria Arms, a popular riverside pub on the Cherwell.
[2] i.e. Elizabeth Mavor, who was married to Haro Hodson.

eccentricities and his humanity apart. Haro Hodson is a namby-pamby little man; feline, purring and clawed in turn. His wife has that breathy enthusiasm, that earnest bending forward, that determination to express herself, to be equal to men, and a woman: not sexually attractive at all, these graduate and graduated women. They impose. Even, as with E. Mavor, the ideas seem all right in most ways.

An evening at Jean Simpson's house. Podge playing the piano, tunes of the twenties. A down-under physicist, not amused; shy, hating it. The silliness; and being silly himself, in calf love with J. Simpson.

Driving to Studholme Priory, a mournful hotel. Four aimless elderly guests wandering over the lawns, weird lonely drifters. We sat on the back lawn having tea, laughing; served by a crucified (at having to do it) ex-colonel. Disapprobation from guests, proprietors, lawn, house, trees, the lot. This hotel had the very special flavour of fallen old houses. We laughed, but the air is tragic; the sulphur of the fall. Then on to a small stately home to see the garden. A lovely view east across England, the green, blue hills, yellow charlock fields, single elms, delicate slices of English colour under the evening June sky. The owner (John Thomson, Woodperry House) took some kind of liking to us, showed us round. A pretty house of the 1720s, still very baroque, with modillioned cornices; fine porcelain in every room. 'I'm thinking of restoring the arcade. What d'you think?' Curiously like Michael Farrer – that Mitford touch. I'm reading Jessica Mitford's *Hons and Rebels*. Her remark that her parents would have been amazed if anyone had called them snobbish. For them snobbishness was a distinctively middle-class index, a bourgeois thing. 'They never looked down on people; they simply looked straight ahead.' This man had that; charming to us, to his cowman, to everyone; and somehow, as it always was with Michael Farrer, the gulf is more *there* than if he was the most outrageous snob. You can't despise such people, as you can snobs. They are cased in their unassailable rightness. Their own-ness.

4 July

Dear Mr Fowles,

THE COLLECTOR

I am sure you will be delighted to hear the long period of waiting has been worthwhile.

Tom Maschler tells me that Cape would like to take THE COLLECTOR. The actual terms are: an advance of £150 against Royalties of 10% to 3500, 12½ from 3500 to 7000, and 15% from 7000 to 15,000. Since Cape is worried about the libraries taking this book, I have had to allow them a 10% interest in any possible stage or film rights, but under the circumstances, this is fair enough, since in return, they guarantee to give the book extensive publicity. Normally, we don't encourage publishers to take this stand, but the circumstances are rather exceptional with fiction taking such a beating these days.

I have accepted these terms, because I think it very much to your advantage to become a Cape author. They have an exceptional list, and it is quite a distinction to score right away with a first-class publisher.

Would you telephone me tomorrow, when I can tell you a little more? Tom Maschler would like to meet you, and discuss the book. I think you will like him.

Congratulations! I am sure this news will come as a literary shot in the arm.

Yours sincerely,

James Kinross
Director and Literary Manager

One doesn't quite believe it when it comes. Not that I haven't kept a belief in the book. But I've had no belief in the agency and publishing world.

6 July
I've been to see Tom Maschler, of Cape. An intelligent, frank, tall Jew – all frankness, where Kinross isn't. Less charm, but more truth, one feels. He seems to think Kinross a bit stupid ('He obviously hasn't understood the book'), but as he says, one can't ask more of an agent than to 'place' a first novel first go. Maschler seems fairly optimistic – it should get published in America, he thinks it stands a chance of getting filmed, and even staged. But he was grim about the fiction situation in general. Apparently 1,500 copies is a very good sale for a first novel nowadays. Malcolm Lowry's book, recently rave-reviewed by Toynbee, has sold only 1,800 copies in a month.[1] Murdoch's novels, which sell about 10,000 copies, are the bestsellers today, and then only because she is the OK suburban woman's novelist – not too hard to understand, and looks good on the coffee-table.

As with all these publishing people, I felt both stupid and wise with Maschler. A feeling that all he really wants is a tough, hard, glossy end-product – something that will sell, that will be in vogue. A good shrewd

---

[1] Jonathan Cape had just published Lowry's collection of short stories, *Hear Us O Lord from Heaven Thy Dwelling Place*, reviewed by Philip Toynbee (1916–81) in the *Observer*.

judge of what will sell today; but I wouldn't back him to pick what will be read in 2062.

8 July

Dear Mr Maschler,

THE COLLECTOR

Revision. Here is the altered version. I have cut the girl's diary into the monster's narrative at p. 163, when she is just clearly beginning to be very ill. I have rewritten pages 397–401, which were formerly in the present tense; so all his narration is now in the past, though I have added 'today' to the last sentence, to make it clear that the coda brings us up to 'now'. I have also cut about a page out of the first thirteen, as you suggested, and the flow-in certainly seems smoother.

Pseudonym. I've thought this over, and decided definitely to use my own name. Come what may.

Commas. You mentioned that the book would be vetted for wrong punctuation and so on. This worries me a little, as I have calculated all the deliberate errors in sections 1, 3 and 4 fairly carefully, and the sub-standard punctuation goes along with the sub-standard everything else. In the girl's section, 2, I have deliberately avoided using semi-colons.

Film Possibilities. I don't know how serious you were about showing the manuscript to Karel Reisz.[1] But I do have a couple of pages of ideas for turning it into a film jotted down, and I'd willingly let you have them if they might help. They would probably do the opposite!

Why I wrote it. I think I gave you the wrong impression – that all this came from a newspaper incident of some years ago[2] (there was a similar case in the North of England last year, by the way). But the whole idea of the-woman-in-the-dungeon has interested me since I saw Bartok's *Bluebeard's Castle*,[3] which was before the

---

[1] The film director Karel Reisz (1926–2002) had just achieved a notable success with his version of Alan Sillitoe's novel *Saturday Night and Sunday Morning*.

[2] This concerned a man who had kidnapped a girl and imprisoned her for several weeks in an air-raid shelter at the bottom of his garden.

[3] In *Bluebeard's Castle* (1911), Duke Bluebeard warns his new bride Judith not to open any of the seven doors in his castle, but impelled by curiosity one by one she opens them to discover first his torture chamber, then other dark details of his past, until eventually she opens the last door to discover the ghosts of Bluebeard's previous wives.

air-raid shelter case. In any case I had the wine before the bottle
– I don't get this Bluebeard bottle and then think up things to put
into it.

What I'm trying to say is that for me this side of the novel is
unimportant. For some time I'd been looking for a theme that
would allow me to do these things:

1. present a character who was inarticulate and nasty, as opposed
to the 'good' inarticulate hero, who seems to be top dog in post-
war fiction and whose inarticulateness is presented as a kind of
crowning glory.

2. present a character who is articulate and intelligent – the
kind of young person I try to make Miranda Grey – and who is
quite clearly a better person because she has had a better education.

3. attack the money-minus-morality society (the affluent, the
acquisitive) we have lived in since 1951.

Finally, I know French literature rather better than English, and
almost all the novelists, historical and modern, I admire most are
French (though Jane Austen would top my list). I *feel* more influenced by writers like Gide and Camus, and even Laclos, than by
any English writers.

11 July

Dear John Fowles,

Many thanks for your letter of 8th July and for making the changes
so quickly. At a glance, it looks as though you have done the
trick.

I am glad you have decided to use your own name for, as you
know, I am very optimistic regarding the chances of THE
COLLECTOR and also your future work. I think you might have
regretted a pseudonym.

Regarding the editorial work, I really do not think you have
anything to worry about. In the first place, our Editor is highly
sensitive and, in the second place, it is your book and I can promise
you that we will not make any changes of which you do not approve.
It is obvious to me that you work in a very careful and intentional
way but it may, nevertheless, be possible to make an odd improvement. That is all we are concerned with.

Of course, I am serious about showing the manuscript to Karel
Reisz, so please let me have your couple of pages.

May I take this opportunity of saying, again, that I am
extremely pleased that we shall be publishing THE COLLECTOR

and very much look forward to working with you in the future.

Yours sincerely,

Tom Maschler

Dear Mr Fowles

THE COLLECTOR

Thank you so much for your letter of the 13th July. I think it is
excellent that Maschler should show the manuscript to Karel Reisz.
Should he arouse interest, so much the better. Meantime, we have
a copy out with 20th Century Fox.

I thought you would like to know that Capes are now drawing
up the contract. They offered half the advance on signature, and
half on publication, but I have chiselled them down to £100 on
signature, and £50 on publication.

Of course, this is more or less the usual thing, but I have the
strongest feeling that you could probably use a large drink to celebrate the occasion, so I pushed hard as a result!

With all best wishes,

Yours sincerely,

James Kinross
Director and Literary Manager

14 July
Down at Leigh. The usual nightmare – no communication. They will
not let me grow up. And their world shrivels – terrible how it grows
smaller and smaller, and deader and deader; like a museum no one ever
visits. When I told F about *The Collector*, he seemed to feel nothing but
worry and gloom. I must 'get a good lawyer'; would it affect my job?
Was it wise? Terrible again – all his petit bourgeois fears came tumbling
out – not one word of congratulation or pleasure of any sort. I said I
didn't want M to know yet. She'd only blab the news all round Leigh,
and get it garbled in the process. He seemed delighted to be able to
change the subject, and made no further reference to it through the
weekend.

How much nearer I feel to the Roman poets (I was reading Tibullus
at Leigh) than to the people around me. It frightens me, the
small-mindedness of this present world (that is, my feeling of remote-

ness from it). My parents, the creatures I work with; even D and M.
We went with them last night to Wapping and the Grapes. Monica at
her awful provincial-actress worst, when almost everything she says
grates shrilly on our tiredness. She will use accents, silly accents, badly
done; wrongly timed, everything. A sort of clawing-down of every situation, as if she's trying to stop a sheet bellying up and blowing away.

I think it's all symptomatic of a general overwhelmedness; people
can't face the world any more on their own two feet. There are too
many experts, too many brains trusts, panels, personalities, artists; a
whole host of interpreters and 'successful' people who want to be listened
to and looked up to. So the ordinary man and woman can't see the
world any more for the terrible smog of interpretations and opinions
foisted on them by their society. All small people now are frightened to
advance any opinion about anything outside the superficialities of their
daily lives. They get resentful if other small people (such as myself) try
to be serious or offer opinions. Only people who have appeared on the
TV may offer opinions. And the rest of us must live in the silliest part
of our silly nows, and hate each non-conformer.

21 July

We hope to go to Rome for five weeks – through a friend of Jean Bromley
at St G's. We've let D and M in on it, partly because of their car, partly
because Denys is Denys. We've seen him twice since the Wapping fiasco;
and liked him so much both times. His quietness and unpretentiousness; he's always his age, by himself. We think he's failed to 'teach'
(educate) M. He talked about 'making something of his life' the other
evening; an aura of failure that irritates me sometimes – it makes me
want to shake him by the shoulders – but sometimes it has a genuine
sadness. A kind of elegiacity about him.

The Italian holiday seems fixed up. Denys and Monica; even the Porters.
Everybody anxious of us. It's been a jumpy, neurotic July. I can't sleep,
can't concentrate. I signed the *The Collector* contract today. But I can't
write.

31 July (written in Rome)

To Italy, with D and M, in their car. All this holiday was arranged in a
rush, in these last two weeks. Seemed always doubtful whether the flat
in Rome would finally be available, whether D could come, whether
Podge would come. Constant fiddle-faddle of letters and telegrams that
lasted until we left. A faint rather silly need to get in touch with Roy in
order to let him know we were all going to Rome together. Not that
Roy and Judy don't invite such skewering and needling.

D and M are anti-French and pro-Italian. For charm and general willingness, the Italians have the French licked. And the bourgeois French are vile, only a very short head behind the bourgeois Belgians and the bourgeois Germans, and a good length from the bourgeois English. The *Paris Match* world is essentially a bourgeois one. For all that, I prefer the French to the Italians, as people, and I think, am almost sure, that I prefer the Spaniards and the Greeks to both (this is, as people). What the Italians seem to me to lack is any stiffness or hardness – backbone. There is a general *mollitia*; I see the dictionary gives softness-tenderness-flexibility-pliancy-mildness-gentleness-sensibility for it. Plenty of that, at every corner in Italy; and evidence of true backbone not only in the obvious art and history things, but still in the country, in peasant faces. Yet the general feel is *mollitia*. Great flexibility in handling things like road-building, plumbing gadgetry, anything to do with engineering or design. Great helpfulness to foreigners. No race feeling. A sort of universal urbanity.

It's not that Italian males don't look virile and strong – they are as much that as the women are pretty, much more so than the French. But you feel it's a kind of formal masculinity – if you put masculinity and backbone into them it has to be a sort of platonic operation. You have to read it into them. It doesn't come out of them, as it does in Spain and Greece, and impress itself.

Pathetic, too, is the way the males isolate themselves from the females in public. This sitting and standing around of the men while the women pass, in pairs or groups, during the passegiata every evening. It seems stagy, contrived, beside the freedom of the sexes in Anglo-Saxonia and Scandinavia, and beside the clawing village women of Andalusia or the absolute suppression of the woman in Greece.

Italy's a sort of open-arms country – too soft, too easy, for me. This is not to wish that it didn't exist – it's an essential part of the European stew. The oil, the fat. But it lacks the sharp taste of the vegetables and the meat.

Into Italy, through Sestrières. Italian words. Horrid, having to visit a country where one speaks less than a little. It reduces the experience to a lark. One's eyes enter too far ahead of one's mind. So a lot of giggles in the car.

We stopped at Pinerolo, a dull town. Slept in a hotel with a balcony overlooking a market. Incomprehensible Piedmontese voices at six in the morning. A meal, not understanding half the menu. *Alla milanese* means schnitzel – rather disappointing comedowns like that.

Italian food is much better than French, at a simple level. Almost everything seems reasonably well cooked and presented. But there is a considerable monotony. All the way down to Rome the restaurants had the same dishes.

12 August

In one way a lot of Rome disappoints; I don't know why, but for me this is Jamesville. The Pincio disappointed because it isn't the great sloping high terrace I imagined from James; and the Colosseum isn't the place where Hudson met the Princess Casamassima.[1] The Colosseum is vile, a gigantic public lavatory by the night smell of it, a central for the young spivs and layabouts of Rome. It is all that is vile in ancient Rome: over-bearing, a bully building, a vast baroque torture-chamber. One *cannot* not think of the human beings and animals that suffered endlessly here – the folly of a civilization devoted to entertainment at all costs, not culture. Killing and pain as amusers. And the hideous vulgarity; the eternal world of the TV spectacular, the detergent-sponsored trash-play, the garish, ostentatious, cheap, shoddy . . .

St Peter's, too, is ugly, lying there like a monstrous lobster with its colonnade claws waiting to clutch one into the black maw of the Great Catholic Lie. A feeling of cheat about it; if our headquarters building is as big as this, we must be right. It brings out Dissent like a rash; a strawberry allergy.

13 August

To Tivoli. Very pleasant, the way the mountains rise as soon as one leaves Rome eastwards. Immediately one is past Tivoli, on the Avezzano road, the country becomes beautiful – wild, as it always was, the people peasant-like and poor. Abrupt hills covered in scrub; long pink and pale brown hill-villages on the crests. Both green and barren, this landscape. At Vicovaro we forked left and went up towards Licenza,[2] a fine wild valley, green with oaks and olives and vines and vegetables, a delicate thin balance between the wild and cultivated. Almost English hedges; hazels and brambles and bryony. Up a winding path of stone, with the spectacular little town of Licenza opposite and stranded on its crest – they seem (as Highet says)[3] to draw back from the valleys, these Sabine towns. Like spinsters caught by a mouse. An absolute reluctance to descend.

Horace's Sabine farm – *o rus, quando ego te aspiciam*[4] – well, no wonder he wanted to see it so much. As it is now, it sits in a little orchard clearing

---

[1] JF is thinking of Henry James's first novel *Roderick Hudson*, about an American artist who travels to Rome with his rich patron. There he falls in love with the extremely beautiful Christine Light, who at the bidding of her family marries the Prince Casamassima.

[2] A medieval hill town about fifty kilometres inland from Rome. The remains of Horace's villa are just outside the town.

[3] i.e. Gilbert Highet (1906–1978), whose book *Poets in a Landscape* (1957) related his pilgrimage to places associated with seven Roman poets.

[4] 'O, countryside, when will I see you?' Horace, *Satires*, 2.6.85.

in a momentarily flat place in the hills, cool, green, silent, a sort of gigantic bower, after the August sledgehammer of Rome. An exquisite bottom-of-the-garden place. Not much to see, building-wise. 'His' bedroom, 'his' *triclinium*, the usual optimistic attributions. A charming *nymphaeum* (in the imagination) – four fountains, flowers, a pillared patio; a fishpond, a *piscina*. A nice old guide – but precisely what one does not want in such places – showed us round. I could have lingered there all day, just being where Horace was being. And Maecenas and Virgil. One feels Horace very close, in the herbage, and in the situation; in the cicadas and the great tawny and red hornets going into a cloven olive-stem; up the stony path to the fons Bandusiae: a spout of cold water, *potabile ma fredissima*, the guide said. *Saxis cavis* makes sense, the water springs from the lip of a tiny moss-covered cirque, some ten feet high, into a little basin of criss-crossed channels, choked with waterplants.[1] Huge water-thistles, eight feet high. It simply hasn't changed.

Coming back, a huge soft butter-yellow moon over the luminous dusk-blue mountains; and at Tivoli, and past Tivoli into Rome, an ugly descent into 1962.

The gap between Horace and his servants. Their total inability to understand his verse; they would still have been in the quantity-stress world of Plautus and Ennius and all folk poetry. The weird little master from Rome speaking his strange broken flow of words. The quantity-quality cross-chop must have seemed to them like Webern to a Balham bus-conductor; a madness. So if Horace went to Rome and Tivoli, it must have been to be heard; the same with Martial and Juvenal. Their use of words forced them to frequent the city they loathed.

Roman skies during the last hour of day. All peachskin colours, ambers, lemons, pinkishnesses; with blues, smoke-greys, they sink liquescently through one another. You can forgive the city everything. The scudding bats; and the merciful ponentino.[2] What Rome would be like without it I can't imagine. Impossible. So we owe the city to the wind.

16 August

D and M set off today to go back to England. Not too soon, really. One can't help feeling affection and a pity for Denys, but it's difficult to keep patience with Monica. We have more or less done so for Denys's sake, but at times it was touch-and-go.

The basic pattern in Monica is a furious compensation for an inferiority

---

[1] In Ode 3.13, Horace celebrates a 'Bandusian spring', which may have been on his Sabine farm, and makes mention of its *saxis cavis*, hollow rocks.

[2] A west wind that rises from the Tyrrhenian sea in the afternoon and cools the city.

complex; an always ugly determination to state her own point of view and to play down anyone else's. Her contrariness is almost a conditioned reflex; one is surprised when it doesn't appear, and she agrees with something that has been said.

Denys, because of all his gentleness that is also weakness, hasn't done his duty; taught her to be less cantankerous. He sometimes sided with us against her, but always self-excusingly, self-deprecatingly – as if it was a show of independence for our benefit.

Sometimes she would talk and talk, silly clichés, pointlessnesses, and neither E nor I would answer; but Denys always attentive: yes, yes. Yes, love. Feeding her voracious appetite for attention and agreement.

One of her most odious personae is that of the little-girl wife. A peculiar little spoilt whine – I'm hunnngry, I'm ti-ered, I'm hot. It would go on for hours sometimes, interspersed with girlish singing; and – Denys, are you happy; are you happy, Denys? Hallo, Denys (Lancashire accent).

She must have known it was irritating; even Denys began to take corners too fast at times. But just as, when he did corner too fast, her whining and backseat-driving increased, so did her irritating manner increase when we were plainly irritated and unamused. She has a nasty, almost spiteful, determination not to let other people's disapproval change her ways.

Sudden showy solicitudes for Denys – poor Denys; Denys never thinks of himself. Denys is so kind, he's absurd.

Her walk – always too quick, as if she knows where she's going and nothing's going to stop her. Her wide hips rigid, and with peculiar cutting movements of her arms that make her shoulders pivot and swing. Rather like the way the Wrens used to march in the war. The very antithesis of the way the Italian women walk, or the sort of easy English way E walks. A stagy walk; she doesn't realize it looks masculine.

One day she method-acted carsickness – all because once before Asti Spumante made her feel sick. We all said you couldn't judge a wine by one occasion; but she wanted to be right and sick.

Disagreements with me: she always takes me too seriously and I make her click into her mantis position as soon as I speak. I said life was too short to study small cultures – 'small cultures are as important as big ones'. I said the skaters on a stream reminded me of the human condition – 'I don't feel like a skater at all. I know what I'm doing and where I'm going.' I said ordinary people in the advanced civilizations were more and more stereotyped (moulded by society) – 'I think ordinary people are good, and they're all different.'

She loathes, too, 'being told what to like'. But it isn't the quite natural distaste of being led in aesthetic matters; it's a total rejection of any pointing out of what has pleased one. As if all the pleasure in the thing is in having seen it or spotted it first – not in the thing itself. Denys, too, is a bit like this. A prickly provincial fear of being condescended to; but alas, they take the most innocent enthusiasms or wishes to share enjoyment as condescension. Because I said a bottle of Valpólicella (both E and Denys agreeing) was good, she said it was bad, 'the worst red wine we've had'. Both she and Denys fly at food-talk and wine-talk. 'Thank God I've got vulgar tastes,' said Denys about another wine. 'All I want is a wine you can drink a lot of.' This absurd provincial view of all drink as alcohol.

And then the accents: whenever M feels herself getting out of her depth, the dreadful accents. And Denys feeds her there, too.

Denys's trouble is his really fantastic gentleness – his hopeless respect for life, his inability to kill anything, even a wasp. Driving wildly along a road below Horace's farm, just because a thin dog followed us a few yards, looking for food. Distraught when a frog I had caught leapt out of my hand into the bowels of the hot engine of the car. It hopped out, unhurt, but he was really distressed by the incident.

The same nervous distress when E was in a temper, and walked off; far more upset than I was. A funny little white frightened-boy look, a snuffling giggle. 'She's like a caged lioness,' he said. 'You can see her tail lashing.' Snuffle, snuffle.

This is how Monica has got her iron grip on him; she just puts on her small-hurt-animal face and voice and she has him on his knees, at her mercy. So he is pulled down to her wretched narrow world, with all its provincial inhibitions and pettinesses. He is so weak that he sinks with her.

A terrible octopus-and-swimmer marriage, or so it seems to us; the merciless exploitation of a fault.

I wanted to show them both what I had written about this trip (not this lambasting of them, of course), because the written word forces one to think. I thought it might jerk Denys into writing. And prick her conscience a bit. But I let E talk me out of it – she thought M would 'just laugh and put on an accent'. I wouldn't have cared if she had. One can't be hurt by people for whom one hasn't the least respect. I would have liked, too, to have shown D the translations of Catullus I'm doing; but we don't talk about my writing, or about me. I sensed this very strongly these last days; and at times I felt angry – why do we always have to talk about Denys and his past and his view of his past and why he is guilty about this and about that – that sort of childishly egocentric sulkiness. Why does everyone let Denys be bound up in himself in public – why not me?

But then I remember to be 'sporting'. I've won this first set, so to speak, and it's been a shock – yet another – for Denys and his poor dreams. I know my typing, my early rising and not siesta-ing (he sleeps all the time) were irritating to him. And his talking about himself is his last sanctuary, in a way.

Curious, all that set he comes from – the Southport intellectuals, all so bound up in themselves and their aspirations (their chief enjoyment being to talk about what they want to do and why they haven't done it; or never did it), and all mother-worshippers as well. Terribly unmale, in any real sense. Like D. H. Lawrence, in that way: virility-conscious (car-driving, drinking a lot), but putting up with a crowd of women who all want stunning slaps across their domineering faces. A deep sexlessness in them, really.

This preoccupation with self comes out in their approach to the outside world – as tourists, they are like people with one-glass heads. A very little, and the nausea of having to look at other people's cleverness (i.e. great art) attacks them. They have to sink back round the café table and analyse what they feel. Anything to avoid having to look at and enjoy other people, other things.

The provincial: one who fears others and otherness. Who can enjoy external objects only to the extent that they serve as mirrors. That is why Denys liked Donatello, and seemed offput by Michelangelo. All a good look at a Michelangelo does is to show a very very small observer (if one's using the work as a mirror); a provincial to scale.

Totally non-Zen, such an attitude. Hearing the others describe tea-leaves in a cup-bottom as Zen. Their dreadful provincial-European misunderstanding of the word. And I couldn't say anything because it would be clever old John showing off again. And Denys always has to show he too is cultured – if I say something about Latin poetry he has to say something, too; a compulsive evening up.

He's always helping ladies over the stile; giving them information about things, cliché views; bits of things he's read. It's all wrong. The things themselves matter more. I mean, if you have knowledge about things, you appreciate things-plus-your-knowledge; but that doesn't mean there's less pleasure to be got from things-minus-knowledge. It's exactly the stile: by helping ladies over them, you get them to believe they can't cross the stile by themselves. A double-edged chivalry, in fact. Turning realities, women, into myths, ladies.

All this is hard on Denys. Because there are many many times when his gentleness, his caution, his hatred of cruelty and violence of any kind, public or private, are fine rare qualities. And of all the people I know, he would be least out of place in a Fra Angelico of the Apostles: he'd loathe to be told it; but he has the makings of a saint. And his tragedy is that he is so, and his situation is one where to be saintlike can only seem a futile waste of an intelligent life.

Sitting next to two young Italians – very handsome young men in uniform – possible officer cadets. Beyond them, four English girls: silly milky faces, primped hair, mouthing words too much – they were suburban Londoners trying to be genteel. One of the Italians got talking with them. Absurd, this contrast between the lithe brown man and the fussy, giggling English typists-on-holiday.

It was a shock to see such white, insipid creatures, afters these sexual, brown, vigorously feminine Italian women. Like sour milk and coffee cream.

A day through ancient Rome. The awful white horror of the Vittorio Emmanuele monument – perhaps the greatest proof existent of the futility of nationalist art?[1] Behind it, the splendid and serene Piazza di Campidoglio; Michelangelo again, massive yet muscled, perfectly stately and perfectly human.

The view of the Forum and the Palatine and Aventine from the Capitol.

Then the Forum and the Palatine. Rather terrifying, this huge civilization reduced to this park of ruins; the bones of a giant. Here one feels none of the Etruscan nostalgia, no sadness, simply a kind of melancholy awe; it is much more beautiful than I had expected, especially on the Palatine, yet one knows that this is the heart of Rome, and the heart is dead. The past is more real than the present; and though it is a past one may respect, a huge segment of the European psyche, one can't love it. A conviction that the whole ancient city was a huge folly, a historical mistake that we are still paying for.

Physically, and especially towards evening, there is a melting luminous light on everything, on the brick and marble ruins, the huge umbrella pines, the cypresses, the sere grass; sky of an ageless softness, an antique blue.

The picturesqueness of Roman ruins, using that word in its true sense. Pictures at every step. Shapes, vistas, volumes, arches, cubes, the whole pierced by blue sky, by shadow, earth, sunlight. The whole alphabet of the abstract architectural shape.

The only flower, this hot season, is the mauve-blue and white hypericum that grows lushly out of the dryest walls.

We've been also down the Via Appia Antica, which has the same air of massive fallen folly, ruins in noble landscapes. One isn't touched; the experience is cool.

We're amazed, when we look back, at how little D and M saw when they were here; a week of endlessly hanging around, Monica always washing. They're victims of the car; the wheel has them right beneath it.

---

[1] The huge temple-like structure on the lower slopes of the Capitoline Hill, known as the *Altare della Patria*, was opened in 1911 to celebrate the unification of Italy, but is commonly regarded as one of the ugliest monuments in the city.

Domitian. All the marble in his huge palace had to be polished like glass; so that he could always see behind him.

20 August
Podge and Cathy have arrived. We looked forward to them coming, and now we're disappointed. Something of the old woman about Podge, endless worrying about things that don't need worry or even a second's thought; a kind of *horror silentiae*, a ceaseless weaving of little things to do, to prepare, to plan, to discuss, to talk about, so that one ends by re-entering silence, when one's free of him for a minute, as one drinks water when one's hot.

Like all non-creators he makes an elaborate art of his life, creates it all the time and tries to place us all around him, to enmesh us, like a gear-wheel.

This is the great abysm I feel between me and the non-creator. It has very little to do with being published. I've always had it. But I have no need to create each hour of each day, in the sense that both Podge and Denys seem to have. The ordinary day is something to live through, to lie doggo in; it's creating that's real – not living.

Cathy is not, but looks, a young teenage beat, strongly, primly herself, with her pink-red face and green eyes and obliquely quick mind, a sort of tyro-mermaid hairstyle.

We went with them this morning to see the Pantheon, another work of the Roman engineer. To be admired; it doesn't touch.

The Piazza Navona; a square with a strong character, a thin long rectangle with Bernini fountains. A good garden-statuary man, Bernini – he improves when one doesn't have to take him seriously and examine the details. And a rotten baroque church by Borromini: all ostentation.

Hadrian's villa.[1] Whenever you feel jaded with Rome, it brings out some new surprise. The villa is rather like the Palatine; it gives one a puritan shock, that it should have been so big, the slaves involved, the Goering-like rape of statues from other countries, and so on; and then parts of it are so delicious that it seems not to matter. Because if we could we would all live like the better Roman emperors; if not the worse. The part E and I liked best was the Canopus, the long lake with its arcades of statues, its two swans, its curious classical stillness. Like all the best sacred groves, it excludes the outside world, exacts its own serenity.

Hadrian's villa, like the Domus Aurea,[2] has the fallen-meteor feeling.

---

[1] This vast complex of about thirty buildings situated on a hillside just outside Tivoli, twenty-eight kilometres to the east of Rome, was the Emperor Hadrian's preferred imperial residence.
[2] See note on page 187.

Of a terrible plunge down through time. Again and again in these
Imperial Roman and Renaissance palaces (as in the best English country-
houses) I have the feeling that this is what we (man) are one day to be.
We shall have invented a substitute for slaves. We shall have severely
reduced the population of the world. But we shall all have our Canopi
and our Serapeia,[1] our golden houses, our water-gardens, in which we
shall live (*sans* guilt) as emperors.

Of course the imperial way of life is indefensible; but because it is a
glimpse of the – or a – perfect way of life, it also seems indispensable.

Podge: his extraordinary feverish restlessness. Although it irritates us
(and Cathy), it's really much more a matter for pity than irritation. It's
as if he can't tolerate any inward turning on himself, any silence, any
pause. He is constantly organizing, washing up, jumping up and emptying
ashtrays, throwing away minute pieces of paper, reading extracts from
whatever he is looking at, starting new topics, dropping old ones in
midstream. One wouldn't mind if he speeded things; but he spends so
much time discussing, proposing new plans, saying he'll do one thing,
and then changing his mind at the last moment, in a perpetual zigzag,
like the pond-skaters, that he hinders rather than advances the day. Even
his solicitudes, about doing the shopping, or washing up, come to seem
no more than an excuse to fiddle-faddle, to look busy.

It's plainly some inner compulsion; it seems to me it's partly put on
for Cathy's benefit. E thinks it is sexual sublimation, which is very
possible.

I think it is also something even sadder, simply an attempt to convince
both Cathy and Eileen that without him they would be lost. One mani-
festation of his fussing is over Cathy: a constant telling her what and
what not to do. Even the arch-crime of telling her what she likes and
does not like. Podge plays down all the museums – 'let's give it half an
hour', 'nothing here for me' (standing at the postcard-table outside the
Capitoline Pinacoteca). The poor child is frightened to seem interested,
and at the same time evidently is interested. For her age, she is alarmingly shrewd and penetrating, though she (typically enough) covers her
weapons. A charming but untouchable creature, really: sensitive and
tender, and yet with those warning green eyes. *Noli me tangere.*

This energy comes out in P also in the additional details he now puts
in his stories – to prolong them, to make them longer fields of exercise. And he has almost ceased to listen to anyone else – one tells him
things half a dozen times and he forgets, and asks again, and as he asks,
one can hear that he isn't interested, the question is only to destroy the
usurping silence.

---

[1] A reference to another feature of Hadrian's villa – the Temple of Serapis situated at the end of the Canopus lake and colonnade.

St Peter's. We went round the interior today; and it is no better than the outside. A huge baroque show-off, with literally not one good work of art (the Michelangelo *Pietà* was not on view) to redeem it. It seems to me a totally dead building; a tomb, not a church. And ten thousand St Peter's could not tip the balance against a Chartres, or even a Wells.

Aïda in the Caracalla Baths.[1] A very grandiose spectacle, thoroughly Roman in all its parts. As a production, absurd. The Grand March scene had entire regiments of extras marching on to an already crowded stage – there must have been two or three hundred aboard at the end, and four horses. Bravo, bravo, shouted the Italians, when the horses appeared; when a real camel was seen outside the temple in the moonlight; when the bass gave Aïda a spectacular thrust to her knees. It's the *grands coups de théâtre* that get, not the music.

The big gesture dominates the Italians, in all their arts. The baroque, the superb, the colossal. They have no idea of Greek form, or the French genius for texture, or the English for understatement. (Thus Shakespeare, Dickens, Emily Brontë are 'Italian'.)

They're supposed to feel life more strongly; but I think they gesture because they don't feel – it's a feeling-substitute, an alienator from the true feeling. Perhaps that's why they're such a 'sunny', un-neurotic lot. They never have feeling-constipation, never have feelings to work off; but only the next gesture to think about.

Subiaco. A very pretty town in the mountains. We walked out to the two Benedictine monasteries. The others turned back after the first one, but I went on to the Sacro Speco.[2] Fine wall-paints, the monks singing Vespers first in the lower church, then in the upper. Weird paintings of Death, riding his horse and pricking a young falconer on the neck with his long sword. The opposite wall shows a girl fresh in her coffin, with the bones beginning to stick through her flesh; and then as a skeleton. As powerful a memento mori as I can remember. In a courtyard, hooded crows and ravens. The holy rose-bush; the saint threw himself on a bramble to mortify the flesh, but at once it put forth roses. Two monks, an old one and a young one, coming together laughing after Vespers; the old one scolding the younger, the younger turning, pointing to something in one of the murals that had distracted him during the singing of the office. I got my usual sharp whiff of envy for the monastic life, the simplicity and discipline and above all the solitude.

---

[1] A vast semi-ruined complex of baths built by the Emperor Caracalla (AD 188–217), which could accommodate 1,500 bathers.

[2] The 'holy cave' where St Benedict lived as a hermit before establishing several monasteries in and around Subiaco. He then went to Monte Cassino near Naples where he wrote the famous Rule for monasteries.

A very lovely solitude in this swallow's nest monastery. A path leads to it through groves of ilex, up the side of a green mountain valley with a stream far below; the path tapers to a narrow flight of steps that twist up round a wall of rock; then a little Gothic corridor-loggia looking out over the valley below. Some fine Peruginoesque frescoes, on the inner wall.

The evening ride back to Rome: long green valleys, hilltop villages, aspens, the sky turning through the softest blues to the veining amber-pink.

6 September

The journey home. The others were sad to leave, but I was glad to go. Not that I didn't like Rome and the Italian experience, but five weeks without seriously writing or thinking, but seeing, travelling, conversing – I was glad to get away from all that. Out of Rome, E crying in the corridor, and past Tarquinia on its hill, out of hot, golden Italy into green, April-morning France; two hours in Paris, sharp and brisk and complex, so nice after the Romans and Rome; then the boat at Boulogne and across into the grey of England. We got home about ten.

There's no pleasure in travelling any more; the bad meals on the trains, the expense of porters, of everything; the international trains are nets to catch money; tourists and travellers a vein to be mercilessly exploited.

The grey shock of England and the English. I haven't had the extent of my exile from land and people so clear for a long time. They are foreign to me, and so the land seems foreign. It is impossible to communicate with the British, to say what one thinks in the language that one thinks in; always this rapid translation into 'British' from the English words in one's head, into what-is-accepted and what-is-expected. So there is no communication, no love; one can only observe and hate or mock at Britain as it is.

All the Western European countries are deep in selfishness at the moment, all rich, all bent on getting pleasure out of life. It is irrational to hate this country for being so stodgily selfish, so mousily booming. It's perhaps a sign of health, a feeling among even the stupidest masses that things aren't quite as rosy as they seem. But coming back to England from Italy – it seems most like a colossal lack of style, an almost total inability to design life, to express life through the way one lives one's daily life. The British sit like a fat pasty-faced bespectacled girl at the European party.

This terrible scuttle back to England: as if they are so glad to be back.

The 1962 British seem really to still believe Britain is best. Cleaner, nicer, honester, more civilized. I said earlier that the Italians were no more than the oil or the fat in the great stew; then the British are the water.

An extraordinary book we read in Rome – the banned-in-England *My Life with Princess Margaret,* by a former footman.[1] Written, or ghosted, in a nauseatingly cloying, inverted style: the man sounds like a voyeur and a fetishist. He constantly uses turns of phrase (and the sort of euphemism, in particular) that I gave the monster in *The Collector.* Again and again he praises, or smirks at, behaviour by the filthy little prig-princess that any decent person would despise; and the horror is not that he does this, but that one knows millions of silly men and women in America and here will or would agree with him. A whole society wrote this miserable book, not one man.

A putti. We bought him in the Via Nomentana as our memento of the holiday. Seventeenth- or eighteenth-century, carved-wood and painted, with grey-black eyes, pink cheeks, a minute penis, and a charming wide-awake yet serene small smile.

11 September
The meaning of 'real' in 'real self'. The way Podge exteriorizes his whims and moods and tries to present them as his 'reality'; so he denies all his inconsistencies, changes of mind. He tries to pass off the gay, bright, busy Podge as the real Podge – the 'fun' criterion and so on is 'real' – not frippery or a persona. Whereas I'm both too lazy (and too afraid) to reveal my real self and too misanthropic to keep up a convincing persona of some other self. This keeping-up of a convincing persona, this creation of one's own public face, makes the face become the real face. The only way to keep the real inner self alive is to keep the persona a blank, a shield, a thing the real self doesn't respect or value – make it a painted prop, a cursory screen. Not an elaborate baroque structure. With so many people so much creative energy, so much labour and energy, and dishonesty, goes into the persona; and the real self is told it is not the real self, and becomes a prisoner in a castle. Terrible experiments are practised on it. Things get to the point where the owner would rather die than admit the real self is not the great plaster façade his mischannelled psyche has created.

The real self is the self most valued by the owner: the 'inner' self or the 'public' self.

It is this preservation at all costs (or, to be precise, at the cost of an engaging and fully fabricated 'read' public self) of the 'real' inner self that makes the poet. *Not* the skill with words; but the skill at preserving one's own reality.

---

[1] The name of the footman was David John Payne and the book was published that year in America by Gold Medal Books.

17 September
Home. A brisk mediocrity.

Existentialist notions of solitude; I feel myself closer and closer to the composite Sartre-Beauvoir-Camus character. This feeling closer comes from within, comes from circumstances (my nature, upbringing, history, etc) that existed and dominated me long before I had even heard the names 'Sartre' or 'existentialism'. But if I write down this feeling closer (as I am in *Tesserae* and in some recent poems) it seems or could seem a pose-feeling – a Roquentin[1] – mask I assume. It isn't. But it is unfortunate to be naturally what so many others have stated artificially.

25 September
Cape have turned down *A Journey to Athens*. 'It reads too much like a young man's book.' Maschler thinks it would spoil the effect of *The Collector. Tant pis*: it'll have to go back into cold storage.

Feverish night (I've got a cold) – series of waking dreams about the psychology of personality. They seemed to be full of a brilliant penetration of the nature of self. Mostly in the form of forced puns; some in French. Later, when I was properly awake, I couldn't remember any of them, but I had all that feeling of authentic loss revelatory dreams leave behind them. That one has slipped far deeper into the hinterland, the hinterland one has been trying to penetrate by conscious means. A weird glitter of profound paradoxes; left with a handful of ashes.

I couldn't sleep afterwards, and it seemed the paradoxes were centred round a Bardot-like personage. (Last week there was a so-called 'frank' interview with her in *Paris Match*. I read it on Sunday.) It seemed part of the lost dreamscape was situated in an exchange of questions between an interviewer and a Monroe-Bardot figure. Nothing sexual at all: but a series of statements and definitions of self in the context of having great publicity and wanting private peace.

I think I'm going to write about it. It suddenly seemed a loaded theme. I see it in the form of a dialogue. Not a novel. Or a peculiar throwaway sort of novel, if it is one. Perhaps only a long short story.

This all came the night before I heard from Cape.

30 September
E and I have been revising *A Journey to Athens*. I was stupid to let Kinross

---

[1] The chief protagonist of Jean-Paul Sartre's novel *La Nausée*, Antoine Roquentin, regards objects and people about him as just a façade that masks the purposelessness of existence.

have it straight from Mrs Shirley. I never saw her typescript. We've changed a number of things, cut a lot. But the damage is done, as regards Cape's. I told Kinross not to send it to them before I had revised it. I feel angry with him, too.

3 October
Eliz is in hospital (the Florence Nightingale in Lisson Grove). A new surgeon – Miss Moore-White – has seen her X-rays. The previous operation was wrongly done – all might have been well if *she*'d done it in the first place. The usual maddening medical vagueness and contradiction. The implication is that we were ridiculous to try and have the operation performed 'on the State'. 'You go to the NHS for colds, not for operations,' said a shocked woman in the next bed at the FN – the very idea of expecting the State to provide successful operations!

It makes me furious. I suppose one is expected to be violently against the Health Service, now. But the thing that is wrong is the medical mind, the hate pent up in each doctor against the system they work under. It is the doctors who are rotten, not the idea. A great deadweight of doctors who hope the system will crumble.

The decision to have the operation has been Eliz's. It's been a sort of existentialist situation. That is, I have felt that it must be her decision. This is the situation where it is monstrous to decide for another person; the other, the self, Eliz, decides and her decision becomes part of her life, and by making her brave decision she makes something as real and almost as valuable as a child. We know the chance of success is minute; and we both know that if there is success there are a thousand troubles – a child one has paid so much for, *un tant attendu,* will breed anxiety, will seem intolerably fragile; but the thing we must be is certain, that a child is for ever impossible, and this really is why she has had the operation. One has to force an answer out of destiny sometimes – a yes or a no; and if one stakes enough, the answer comes. We shall know now.

4 October
Terrible, the day before the operation. I saw her in. It's a tatty little place, a Hospital for Gentlewomen – so we felt a sort of pitying affection for it. Eliz in her Chanel suit and red glass beads, looking so fit. It's the voluntary giving-up of health and being normal that is so painful. One doesn't have to do it; and yet one is doing it. Sitting beside her in bed, a curious futility in the air; as always, not knowing what to say. Going away for three hours, killing time until the next visiting hour, at seven. London and Baker Street strange, very strange because it was the day of the great rail strike. Hardly any people or any traffic – like Victorian photographs of streets, all bare and peaceful under a grey-white light. I

went to the Wallace Collection, looked at the pictures without really seeing them; went to the Classic and saw bits of *A Streetcar Named Desire*, a cartoon, a newsreel; and back to the hospital, and the awful last conversation – so unreal, these last minutes together. And the last kiss and the last word and the last touch and the last sight.

I couldn't do anything all day today. 4.15, the theatre hour, and I went and had a cup of tea in the staff-room, fiddled in the office. Then went home and fiddled about with the guitar. Telephoned at six, but 'she would still be in the theatre another half-hour'. An incoherent Irish nurse, who sounded as if it was not my wife or me that worried her, but this weird invention, the telephone. Finally, at seven, a sane English voice. 'She (Miss Moore-White) has done what she can. Mrs Fowles has come round. She's all right.'

7 October

Podge in London, visiting Eliz. He and I went afterwards to his mother's house in Bayswater and had supper in a curious large dim ground-floor room. The room a sort of battleship-grey, lit by a mournful bulb dustily embedded in a sad Victorian chandelier. Canaries flew through the twilight. His brother Geoffrey was there, an absolute hollow man; his voice seems to be a conditioned reflex. He answers because you ask; an aura about him of death and solitude and failure, and the old woman, his mother, hovering in the background. He's living there only temporarily, but I felt it was his true home. His wife, Wendy, has hereditary syphilis, now in its tertiary stage. They are divorced. But Wendy rings up Podge every week in Oxford, and his mother has coffee with her from time to time. Geoffrey talks all the time of her, though he's engaged to a weird Spanish refugee. One ought to feel sad, but it's high Chekhov; and played as such by Podge.

He told me a good deal, at last, about himself and Eileen: her flight from reason, her hatred of all he stands for, the terrible tension in Oxford, which Cathy now feels. E has long wanted P to go to a psychiatrist, so now, 'to get peace', he goes. 'I want advice, I want to know just how three people like us live in a small house like that.' We hold no brief for Eileen, with her sharp tongue and Irish obliqueness of mind; her jumping to extremes and general intellectual quirkishness. But of course P has this beaver-mindedness, this busy amassing of twigs to build the great rational dam – except that he isn't really rational, so often, and merely picks up twigs to look busy. And there is his absolute lack of contact with things in themselves – so that all his physical contacts, food, conversation, drink, art, are a series of quick dippings-in, sips, and a dashing-on. I made this general criticism of his Oxford circle – that their language made stability impossible. I quoted to him Eliz Mavor's remark 'If a book is fun, what more can one ask?' And of course Podge said that all she meant by that was that 'we have all suffered and we've all lost ideals and now we get what hedonistic pleasure we can out of life' – which I had supposed she meant. But these brittle masks of insincerity that little group put on when they meet together – Podge most of all – seem to me dangerous toys. One doesn't drive a fast car with a windscreen of ordinary household glass; and their real faces will one day all be slashed.

I liked Podge very much again this time. He remains, beneath all the clowning and the inconsistencies, a fierce radical. I share his horror of this beastly society and world we live in, and like him, I recognize only two possibilities of decency in this world – one is either a Sartrean or a Marxist. He said that this morning, and I thought, yes. Yes, yes, yes.

Short of money. Touching bottom again. Soon we're going to be truly stuck. I shall have to get an overdraft. We have saved a little this year, in a deposit account; but to save, in any real sense, seems as ridiculously impossible now as it did ten years ago.

10 October

Martin Cameron. The poor old Scotsman who was teaching shorthand with us in the spring and went back to Glasgow for the summer, and returned here this term. A miserable, feckless creature, too soft and gentle to please anyone – one of the sugary, weak tea Scots. He died on Tuesday in New End, at one o'clock in the morning. It's been a greater shock to everyone than I expected. A lot of the students weeping, the Greeks especially. He died alone, he died alone, they kept on saying. You always die alone, I said. But they wanted a great keening, moaning family death for the poor man. Since he's been ill, the women in the staff-room have helped him – old Mrs Barret and the golden-hearted Marion Singer; and there's been a searching of consciences since he died. His loneliness stands out like a sore thumb among the comfortable small worlds we inhabit; and none of us did anything to help until it was too late.

He had a quiff and a great plump pink face, like a sausage; a portly stance; a boyish Scottish whisht way of intoning sentences very high when you'd said something that shocked him. But the great thing about him was his extraordinary mildness – the women called him womanish, but it wasn't that, it was a sort of innocence. He'd never had any sex, a glass of sherry made him tipsy and maudlin, he always thought so well of people. A failure, an absolute failure, he always seemed; but now I look back on him and find a kind of Christlike meekness and mildness in him. Very faint, but there: *il voulait bien.*

He was the very antithesis of the twentieth-century man: no hardness, no independence (though he had to be solitary most of his life), no tough fatalism. A man like a glass of milk. That's what people have realized – that a man like a glass of milk is more than something to be despised.

The wretched dying old women in Eliz's ward: they don't die quietly at all. Middle-class dying old women (as these are) seem to me rather worse than working-class d.o.w. The ones with Eliz spill out all their middle-class neuroses: 'I can't bear it, I can't bear it.' (They're not in pain; it's a childlike whimper to get attention.) 'I shall get a doctor to tell you how to do this properly.' (To the nurses.) 'Call the car. I'm going out for a drive.' An absurd jumble of illusions, the horrid bare bones of the effete bourgeoisie. Avoid all suffering, keep inferiors down, enjoy the good things of life, whimper and bully. Eliz doesn't seem to notice it, but I think this hospital, so much better than the other in nursing skills and food, lacks humanity, and horribly. The hideous ghost of the lady, as opposed to the woman, stalks each ward along with the ghost of the great arch lady nurse, Florence Nightingale herself.

11 October
I went to Golders Green Crematorium this morning for poor Martin Cameron's funeral. A morning of Scotch mist, appropriately grey and mild. There were about twelve of us there, from the various departments. The crematorium is a complex of brick buildings with asphalted yards; a doorway leads to an arcade, and there's a shrubberied green lawn. We went and stood there, and made weak jokes, and a far black figure scattered ash, watched by a little knot of people, then stood still, as if he'd forgotten something. Praying, one supposes. It's rather like a swagger golf-club, the crematorium, one half expects figures with bags to appear at any moment, or someone to cry 'Fore!'

We then went and waited in the waiting-room. Awkward silences. Mournful autumnal water-colours. Notices: 'As all sects use our chapels, incense may *not* be used,' and 'Light refreshments may be had in the forecourt.' Finally we were ushered into a little chapel, Byzantine-Romanesque brick walls, oak pews, Turkey carpets on stone-paved floor. The ceiling was a bright sky-blue, floodlit by concealed lights. Instead of an altar there was a sort of puppet-theatre opening, framed in Corinthian columns with a broken pediment, through which one could see the coffin on a stainless-steel runway.

A dour-voiced Presbyterian minister read the service for the dead. Another character droned away on the harmonium, while the undertaker remained seated throughout in the little hall a few feet behind us. Absurd rubbish, the service for the dead, in magnificent language – so silly that I felt a sudden sense of shock sitting there. That we could all be listening to it and call ourselves adults.

'Ashes to ashes and dust to dust . . .' – that I can accept – and the purple watered-silk curtain was slowly unwound down over the little puppet-theatre hole (I'd already heard shufflings and noises behind the scenes) and the coffin disappeared.

It was all over in fifteen minutes – a joke. It came as a shock that the poor man's sister was weeping.

16 October
An hour and a half with Tom Maschler. I like him more now. He's a totally different species to me; extrovert, *débrouillard*, pushing, shrewdly and aggressively with-it. I put on a wise-old-country-bird act with him, ask his advice on what I should do next. His advice coincided with my feeling: get on with *The Magus*. He's spoken to Karel Reisz about *The Collector*. Chopping, the Fleming cover man,[1] is doing the cover – he's a super-realist, I don't like the facile luridity of his work. I've seen the blurb – horrible, like being stripped naked before a crowd. They're printing 5,000, instead of the usual 3,000. 'Next July'll do fine,' said Maschler, when I asked him when he would like a new manuscript. A relief in a way – nine months' grace. And a bore, the wait.

A work of art can only be persuasive; never provative. Science proves; art persuades.

24 October
Cuba crisis.[2] It is extraordinary, the little effect this is having on people. They do nothing but joke about it. Endless jokes, in class, in the common-room. 'There's one thing – we've eaten our last English breakfast,' said one of the Greeks. I explained how this part of Hampstead was tilted to receive the maximum blast – huge laughter. And the staff-room full of sick humour. I suggested a notice to be put up: 'Owing to the end of the world today, there will be no classes tomorrow.' Very funny. But for a moment this morning my Proficiency class went out of control: all shouting at the same time, a glimpse of the hysterical anxiety that underlies everything these hours. I had it walking along Fitzjohn's this afternoon – the feeling that at any moment the huge heat-blast would come, all the houses fall. I don't know why, it was the thought of the leaves being blown off the trees that seemed worst – the first gale will

---

[1] Beginning with *From Russia With Love* (1957), Richard Chopping provided the hardback dust-jacket artwork for all but four of Ian Fleming's Bond novels.
[2] The US blockade of Cuba that followed the discovery of Soviet nuclear missiles on the island began on 24 October. The world feared a possible nuclear conflict as Soviet cargo ships continued to head towards the quarantine zone, which the Soviet government had declared illegal.

blow them off, anyway. The end of the world has seemed close these last few hours. The relief if we survive will be ludicrous. I think we will, because the Russians are only playing chess – Cuba is a trap sacrifice. But the vileness of this world, the things this vileness proves – the rottenness of all present political theories and philosophies and religions, for a start.

There's a no-holds-barred at the moment between Maschler and James Kinross. Kinross says, 'He's a bagman, he ought to be flogging cigarettes round the Brandenburger Tor.' 'He's so damned vague,' says Maschler. 'Sometimes I think he doesn't know who the hell you are.' Maschler wants to sell *The Collector* to Simon and Schuster. He says he'll do it himself for nothing because he likes the book, and because 'I would like to do them a favour.' But he also told Little, Brown's about the book, and now Kinross has sent it to them. Or he thinks it will have gone to them. As usual, he's vague. It's in New York, that's all we know. Maschler's latest news is that the book is being brought back from the printers, so that a big man from British Lion can look at it. 'It's all rather chi-chi,' says M, 'but it may work.' I can see what Kinross hates in him; but my guess is that he sells a pound to a Kinross penny.

31 October

Dear Fowles,

BETWEEN[1]

I have now had a chance to read this manuscript very carefully, and I am afraid that I thoroughly agree with Maschler's opinion.

Although this shows considerable literary promise, and some extremely good characterization, I don't think for one moment that its publication would in any way enhance the reputation which I am sure you are going to acquire as a result of *The Collector*. Honestly, I think it would be disastrous to consider publishing this work. Firstly, because the central theme is far too slender to support a book, and secondly because there is a slightly disconcerting *naïveté* about the narrator, which, whatever one's politics, is going to grate a bit on the susceptibilities of English readers.

I do hope that you will forgive me if I am entirely frank, and say that the narrator's outlook here strikes me as being a sort of

---

[1] This manuscript was the revised and renamed version of *A Journey to Athens*. See page 529 and note on page 260.

political Uriah Heep. Don't be furious. I should be a very bad agent, were I not to anticipate the unfriendly reaction this sort of viewpoint is liable to create.

Why don't you give me a ring, when we can discuss this in more detail? Meantime, I am taking the liberty of returning your manuscript under separate cover. I think you should put this aside for a bit, because basically there is material here for something much stronger. But *don't* consider publishing it, even under another name.

With every best wish,

Yours sincerely,

James Kinross
Literary Manager

4 November
I am hard at work on *The Magus*. Maschler the other day was talking about the 'stylelessness' of Grahame Greene. But I take it Greene is trying to suppress style as an expression of self – in other words, a style as clear as glass. It seems to me that this is not at all as easy as Maschler was implying. For highly literate (in other words, almost all) writers, the temptation to use rare or rarish words, to start metaphor-making, to construct elaborate sentences, to 'Jamesify' is almost irresistible. To overload words with one's own literateness. On the other hand, one can be too simple, and the effect is the same – one is seeing the story, the events, the world of the book, through glass that is not clear. I am *not* saying that the engraved glass (say Woolf, James), stained glass (say Faulkner, Joyce, Lawrence), frosted glass (the working-class-narrator school) styles are wrong. Fred in *The Collector* is frosted glass. But I feel drawn to the clear-glass (Greene, Waugh, Forster) tradition. Defoe–Fielding, not Sterne.

5 November
Two telegrams today – of congratulations. One from Kinross, the other from Maschler. Little, Brown's, in America have offered 3,500 dollars for *The Collector*. This is apparently well above average – 1,500 dollars, according to Maschler. We're going to offer it to Simon and Schuster, just to see if they'll bid more.

All this is curiously unexciting – unreal, perhaps. I think when it is published, the reality will come. At the moment I feel anxious about *The Magus* – it is terrible how a work-in-progress's worth can fluctuate. One day I feel it is splendid, the next wretched. In general, I feel happy.

As if I am *clear* of the field – not *ahead* of the field. The image of the right map-reading exercise, the cross-country run, keeps with me these days. The mass start, the enormous relief when at last one is alone. In space.

Cover of *The Collector* – by Tom Adams. I misunderstood Maschler. He said 'like Chopping'. Apparently Adams doesn't like Chopping and wanted to do a *trompe-l'oeil* cover to show that he can deceive-eye even better than Chopping. Which he does. A pale clouded yellow, an old key, a hank of fair hair (each hair painted separately) on a background of cork. Cape seem very excited by it. And I was, too.

12 November

Leigh. All death and money down there now – all the talk is of the dead, the dying and the money they will leave. Pure Ionesco conversations. M has an extraordinary genius for picking on totally irrelevant things – dates, details of meals. If the world ended, for her it would be the day after she had a letter from Hazel. She told E of Hazel's 'tragedy': some young man she hoped Hazel might hook. But he wanted to go to bed with her; and she refused, poor nit. It is hopelessly unemancipated; she wrote to M for advice, which seems incredible in this day and age. The poor kid has never got free of the insipid cling of the Leigh mind: cold fish and respectability.

J. Loveridge. I told him about *The Collector* today. He received the news fairly well. Then revealed, to my amazement, that he was a poet. He's written a long series on Elizabeth I, in sonnet form. 'I read one to a friend and he burst into tears.' I shuffled about, muttered things; it was difficult not to laugh. And pathetic: the ambitious little man with his secret poems.

If I like J. Joveridge, I loathe his damned cousin, the Air Commodore, who tries to introduce the language of the station commandant, the petty martinet, into all his work. Absurd pomposities and officialese: he 'issues directives'. 'Examiners should note' (he means us when we're marking college scholarship papers) this and that. He has a mania for graphs, systems, timetables, figures, facts; a born thrower-out of the baby with the 'inefficient' bath water. I suppose such men are really modern variants of the *miles gloriosus*, and should be treated as the figures of fun they really are. Easy for the audience, but not such fun on the stage. All his hectoring and bullying are on paper; and I'll have my revenge on him one day – on paper.

20 November
Proof copies of *The Collector*. It becomes real, reads much better than
before. Also the first publicity; an advertisement in the *Bookseller*.

A dinner with Jennifer Ardagh. Rather stiff and stilted; she has a genius
for getting unnatural people around her. Her boss, John Rosenberg,
head of MGM in London, a ridiculous man; he speaks with that odd
Establishment voice, always very loud and nasal, very penetrating, with
a sort of fossilized and faintly cynical elegance, or would-be elegance.
Much use of 'one'. The same voice as Jennifer's ex-husband, curiously
enough. Another young man from the *TLS*, Alan Davies; small, one-
eyed, also trenchant, or would-be trenchant, and fossilized. Remote,
such men, from living words, from creating. The eunuchs of literature,
stuck at the harem doors. If they do write, at best they achieve a Firbank,
a Chesterfield. The MGM man went on about how he wanted to live in
some country house in Dorset. And then when we left, J told us the
astounding truth – he was American. He's also a Jew. Ashamed of both,
so he puts on this astounding voice-mask.

We stayed on at the end, and J poured out her marital woes to us
again (she did it a month ago). I tried this time to sidetrack on to
us, our past: but she wants to talk and talk about herself. So odd, when
we know her so little. Some sort of elective affinity, I suppose. I like her
because she is capable of behaving existentially – as she did with the
half-baked John Ardagh. That is, overcoming all her past and choosing
to chuck him out. But she does still collect sickening middle-class
zombies round her, and I can't stand that.

22 November
Impossibility of sustained work. I just have no time.

Night like that of Sep 25th. I was very tired, slept badly. A night full of
half-waking dreams about anguish. Once again I could remember
nothing when I woke up – only a general certainty of having 'seen'
something remarkable. On this occasion it was the complex subtlety of
existence as a producer of anguish; the necessity of anguish. All use of
words, all conceiving of ideas, all consciousness is anguish. The effect
was very dry. Like seeing the beautiful efficiency of one's enemy's plans.

There are three levels of understanding of existentialism. The silly and
fallacious idea prevalent in the late forties – existentialism as the latest
style of Bohemianism; what beatnikism is today. The second, an intellectual notion, a knowledge of the theories, and no more. The third, a
being existentialist, a feeling oneself irretrievably this: existentialist. The
two most important existential feelings seem to me to be one, anguish,

two, sense of isolation of self. Two can of course be a form of one. But it need not be. It is pleasurably dry. It gives one a sanctuary. No one and nothing can reach into the heart of that isolation; I exist there purely; I am uncontaminable.

8/9 December
Podge here for the weekend. Ronnie and Betsa Payne came to tea. Podge and I dislike Ronnie Payne's world: Fleet Street and its tinsel glamour. We all said we hate the new television man: the telepundit, the TV 'expert', the man sucked dry by his public image. But it's the old 'disclaim' business. The insurance in vogue. RP, in particular, wants to be such a person – has always wanted to be so. And Podge in his cynical way will admire any kind of false brilliance. There's a sort of moral new music; he is adept at hitting between the old notes of the scale. They both made fun of me and *The Collector* – men-of-the-world with a born Candide.

Not that I don't admire Podge for his political commitment. He wrote to thank Russell for his action over Cuba – and had a letter back;[1] went to the House of Commons to lobby that sinister and ambitious man Woodhouse.[2] He is constantly *acting*; is concerned.

13 December
Kinross. I'm reading his Irish novel.[3] Absurdly bad – cliché-ridden, ungrammatical and badly punctuated, and full of 'sham' drinking and 'sham' sex. And how can he possibly judge me?

14 December
Ogden (Kinross's partner) rang today – some by-blow of Columbia have made an offer for *The Collector*. £1,000 for the option, £6,000 if taken up in nine months' time, another £3,000 if it becomes a book-club choice in the USA, and 5% of producer's profits. If I'm lucky, I'll gross £15,000 or so. But of course there's Ogden's 10% and Cape's 10% and tax. What I don't know is whether I should have held out – it was a gunpoint offer, of course, as Ogden admitted: 'I wish I could say fuck you, you s.o.b.'s.' He sounded soundly American.

---

[1] During the Cuban missile crisis, the philosopher and anti-war campaigner Bertrand Russell had sent a telegram to the Soviet leader Nikita Khruschev appealing to him not to be provoked by the United States' 'unjustifiable' naval blockade. Khruschev then made the Soviet Union's climbdown public in the form of a reply to Russell's message.

[2] i.e. Christopher Woodhouse, the then conservative MP for Oxford and a Joint Under-Secretary of State at the Home Office.

[3] *The Isle of Saints* (Arthur Baker, 1962).

1 January 1963
We saw the New Year in with Gerry Mansell. Alone with them in their
Hampstead Garden Suburb house. A house of the dead. Perhaps the
snow made it worse. He has become an even more insufferable dullard;
his egotism gets more astounding, his anecdotes longer – endless,
endless, he makes the hours. His neo-Panglossian (not 'This is . . .' but
'Mine is the best possible of all worlds') is wearing thin, not that he has
the humanity to let one see it. He is still the most successful and
important man he knows. But poor Diana isn't successful, can't get a
second child, and fills the room with a sort of stillborn-calf atmosphere.
Numbing and white.

He, ostensibly very decently, drove us home through the ice and
snow. Terrible how such people revel in the fun of unpleasant conditions; he did it only to show off, to run a negligible risk, to be a know-
all. Absurd.

He hates me. When Eliz pointed to a novel and said 'John's literary
agent wrote that' he asked no question. Neither of them asked me a
single question about myself the whole evening. I think it is largely
personal, but he has a loathing of graduates. Just as he's a Jew who won't
ever admit he's a Jew, he's a culture-and-learning snob who won't ever
admit he has none.

Memo: ask Jennifer Ardagh whether he knew about *The Collector*.

8 January
Kohn and Kinberg, the two Yanks who have bought *The Collector*.[1] I went
to them in Wigmore Street. In grey cardigans, earnest, sincere, and
slightly obtuse men, I am afraid. They have their fixed view of the book,
and I could see they wouldn't be shifted. Principally it was that the
ending must be happy – the girl must not die. I said, 'That's unmar-
tyring the martyrs. Taking the nails out.' 'But wasn't Christ resurrected?'
said Tweedledum (even Archie Ogden doesn't know which is which).
'She'll be resurrected in people's memories.' Negotiations broke down
here and we returned to initial opposing positions.

10 January
The Collector brings many anxieties with it. I suppose it is already, five
months before publication, a comparative success. I've got a lot of money
for it (for a first novel) and a lot of praise from those who've read it.
But I sense that the professionals think it's a freak, a flash in the pan.

---

[1] John Kohn and Jud Kinberg were two American screenwriter/producers who
ran a production company in London called Blazer Films.

One big problem is whether I should leave St G's in the summer (May) or not. If the film money comes through, I'd be mad not to leave; if it doesn't, I'd be mad to leave. I've got an accountant, and he advises my employing Eliz to dodge taxes; and to claim for expenses for ten years back.

I find the whole thing makes me restless, unable to concentrate. All the waiting. The indecision about what to write next. The problems of meanness – what sort of presents we should give to people who know we're 'rich'. Are we being generous enough? Problems of how to talk about the book with other people, whether to talk about it.

And all this makes anxiety.

2 January

Dear John,

I have read your novel, maybe more quickly than I should have done, but I knew Mother was waiting on the doorstep. It must be years since I read a novel, and for that reason amongst others I must be a pretty useless critic.

The difficulty for me is to get away from the meticulous character writing of the Victorian novelists who never allowed their people to change from the original portrait right through a long story. I suppose after this came the biographical, sociological brand of writers, bursting now into the psychology of Freud. We have broken from the sententiousness of our fathers, but it means learning a new language for some of us. This comes easily to modern writers, such as yourself, and the science of inventing terms to carry the meaning of sentences is no doubt necessary to cope with the amazing flow of ideas in the context of readable events.

You have a very good plot, although you may not like the use of this word. Dramatized it would require two, if not three top class artists, and as a film you would have to be prepared to let the hyaenas maul the carcase. I should let them do it. They know their job.

So far as your people are concerned, Ferdinand[1] holds throughout and is psychologically drawn in a way that helps to bring light to the hazy understanding by rational men of the world of phantasy dwelt in by their unhappy brethren. I don't understand the girl, and I doubt if I ever should do so even if I lived in

---

[1] JF's father – doubtless thinking of *The Tempest*, in which Miranda and Ferdinand are brought together on Prospero's island – means Frederick Clegg, the 'Collector' who kidnaps the art student Miranda Grey.

a cluster of her breed. This does not mean that I doubt her existence in any way, and for this reason some of us should be grateful for the insight disclosed in your story. The artist fellow is a type of historical nastiness, and I despise him to the extent of failing in lavatory language to express my views.[1] But he exists and no doubt thrives, like many gods whose perceiving eyes probe deeper than their souls.

Good luck. May the book go well. And have plenty of Eno's ready for the belly-aching critics.

Glad to say Mother is feeling better, and I sometimes feel well myself. See you soon.

Love to you both,

Father

18 January

Pan Books have bought *The Collector*. £3,500. This is an English first novel record, it seems. Of course I get only 50% − 5% = 45%. I owe it to Tom Maschler, who seems to have amazed even Kinross. I haven't changed my mind about them (since Oct 24th). Maschler came here for a drink the other evening. He thinks I'm naïve, I 'think we're all hostile to you'; Ogden 'is an alcoholic'; 'Look, we'll be your agents and we'll want 10% for American deals, not 20%.' So I am a simpleton with him and to him, and find out what he feels and thinks. Poor Kinross suffers; we both attack him. TM gets angry when I say I feel sorry for Kinross, but I do. He gets a lot of money for nothing, but I'd never like to be alone with TM in business. He talks about literature and his love for it; but he is a pathological salesman. He even sells you his contempt for selling.

27 January

Spending. All this money tends to leave us completely unchanging; not unchanged. But it is like too sudden a change to a warm climate from a cold one − we still wear the clothes of the winter of our discontent.

It isn't really for certain yet that I am become richer. I have handed in my notice to St G's; and so far the book has earned £150 + £1250 + £1000 + £1750 (£5900), of which I shall eventually get £3,510 (− tax).

---

[1] The 'artist fellow' is Miranda's mentor, George Paston. Following his advice to live an authentic, committed life, Miranda breaks with an aunt over her failure to appreciate art, a gesture that recalls the sort of impatience that in real life JF felt for his mother.

But this is only two years' salary (if E doesn't work), with no allowance for a car, buying a cottage, and so on. On the other hand, there is a lot more money that may come in.

So this last week we have been spending:

Overcoat and suit for me	£32		
Suit for E	£12		
Camera (second-hand)	£20 Retinette IIA 83963 (cost price £38)		
Pottery (all New Hall)	£16		
Coffee-table	£ 7	10	
Chairs (second-hand)	£ 4	12	6
	£92	2	6

Eliz thinks the pottery a waste; but it's neither a waste in terms of pleasure to look at nor as an investment. Such things can't go down in price. For £14 I got from Pilgrim's Place three New Hall teapots, two in perfect condition (one splendid fluted one, unused owing to a fire-crack) a slop-bowl, a jug, two saucers (one a Liverpool copy), and a Worcester fluted cup decorated at New Hall.

Montaigne, Essai XIV. His wisdom on the subject of money. The three biographical paragraphs on the three stages in his own attitude to it: perfect.[1]
     Two nice howlers from the English girls' essays:
     'Some people say Shakespeare was a *homme de plume.*'
     'I felt full of flustration.'

3 February
The Collector. The three sources. One. My lifelong fantasy of imprisoning a girl underground. I think this must go back to early in my teens. I remember it used often to be famous people. Princess Margaret, various film stars. Of course there was a main sexual motive; the love-through-knowledge motive, or motif, has also been constant. The imprisoning,

---

[1] For the first twenty years or so after childhood, Montaigne had no fixed income and was dependent on the help of his friends. What spending he did was all the more enjoyable for being fortuitous, and he found his friends were generous because he was always scrupulous about paying them back. The second stage was to have money. He laid by reserves and tried to insure against every emergency, but there never seemed to be enough money for all the emergencies he could imagine, and he found the more he accumulated, the more he worried. The third stage was to make his expenses match his receipts. He contented himself with having enough to meet his present needs, realizing that he would never have enough to ward off all the ills that fortune can bring.

in other words, has always been a forcing of my personality as well as my penis on the girl concerned. Variations I can recall: the harem (several girls in one room, or in a row of rooms); the threat (this involves sharing a whip, but usually not flagellation – the idea of exerted tyranny, entering as executioner); the fellow-prisoner (this is by far the commonest variation: the girl is captured and put naked into the underground room; I then have myself put in it, as if I am a fellow-prisoner, and so avoid her hostility). Another common sexual fantasy is the selection-board: I am given six hundred girls to choose fifty from, and so on. These fantasies have long been exteriorized in my mind, of course; certainly I use the underground-room one far less since *The Collector*. Two, the air-raid shelter incident. Three, Bartok's *Bluebeard's Castle*.

Simone Jacquemard, *Le Veilleur de Nuit*. This won the Prix Renaudot last year. It's based on the same idea as *The Collector* – on the same news story, I should guess. Anyway, a peculiar earth-worshipping young man who imprisons a girl in order to make her dig for him, and doesn't have any sexual relations with her. She keeps a good deal closer to the original than I do; which doesn't help her. But she really kills her chances by using a high old alembicked style and shoving in pages of earth-mystery and dark-force purple patches; pages also of Robbe-Grillet descriptions; a general Woolfishness (or perhaps it's Proust). The general effect spoils the nice clean fantasy of the real original; such a weight of symbolism that the poor book is bursting at its seams.

8 February

Kinross rang me up to say that Little, Brown are, it's believed, doing a first print of 20,000 – the biggest since *Goodbye, Mr Chips*. And the paperback figure has now gone up (potentially) to 35,000 dollars.

22 February

We've just sent some poems to Kinross and Maschler. Sequence Four, the series of thirty about various sexual perversions and disasters; the breakdown of love.

I'm working on another sequence – another minor-key one – *Testulae*. A few poems I wrote in Rome last summer; and a few more now.

These last two months I've been revising *The Aristos*. I think I'm going to recall it 'Propositions'.

25 February

Reach for Glory.[1] Kohn and Kinberg's other film. We saw this at Richmond. Much better than I expected. It's sincerely liberal and fails at a fairly high level; perhaps because the story is rather far-fetched. I was the same age as the boys in the film and at the same sort of school and at the same point in history, and it wasn't like that.

Sequences of poems. A series of interstices on some 'inner' world. I don't mean by this that the inner world pre-exists and the interstices merely open on to it. The interstices are the inner world. That is, I create a world by deliberately choosing to look at it *as if* through interstices.

17 March

Down at Leigh. Auntie Tots (Dorothy) died last week, so we went down to look over the loot; the leavings. Some surprisingly good furniture – three fine early tallboys, one Queen Anne, an early American wall-clock, several pieces of some value. A pathetic life she led, this Auntie Tots; very womblike, enclosed in the small world of her private nursing-home,[2] with its decrepit patients, her cats and dogs, her mania for Dickens, for literature, *Literature*, her being dominated by the fierce, floridly dour Harrison. It ought to have been a lesbian relationship; they died within a week or so of each other; probably was, in some obscure, unspoken way. Tots was a gentle, myopic creature with the usual Fowles talent for dreaming and failing; and the obstinacy. We found her diary – a weird day-by-day jumble of quotidian trivia, quotations, rather touching strivings after something better. 'This damned diary is a hell of a nuisance,' she wrote one day. We've put down for some of the things, but F is insanely worried about keeping to the law. He followed us round the house, groaning as we picked and pocketed things. He has a mania for legal rectitude that I find about one quarter admirable and three quarters obsessive; but Hazel, M and Eliz found it absurd. 'If we don't take it, the workmen will.' I think he wants money; it infuriates him that we should want to buy the good things at probate valuation off the estate, where we might sell them at auction and get more money that he can invest.

Very odd, this vulturine rummaging through the chattels of the dead;

---

[1] Set during the Second World War, the film was adapted from John Rae's novel *The Custard Boys*, about a gang of jingoistic teenage boys who play a series of brutal war games and long to be able to fight in the war before it ends. One of the members forms a friendship with a Jewish refugee boy who has been ostracized by the gang.

[2] Together with her companion Harrison, Aunt Dorothy ran a nursing-home in Westcliff-on-Sea.

vultures must lead happy lives, since the activity is extraordinarily pleasurable, a real treat; the mystery, not knowing what is going to turn up
next, the exposures of the past, the windfalls of the present. The true
paradise, perhaps: being given the keys of the house of a dead eccentric.

24 March
Evening News – one version of the truth.

LUCKY FEW

A recent gloomy report from the Society of Authors confirms that
most writers earn less than £500 a year.

For the lucky few, however, there's always a pot of gold at the
end of the typewriter ribbon.

A Hampstead schoolmaster, John Fowles, has just sold film rights
in his first suspense thriller, *The Collector* (Cape, May, 18s.), and
this *before* publication.

It sounds original and exciting.

A young clerk turns from butterfly hunting to kidnap a pretty
art student outside Hampstead Town Hall.

What follows is told by kidnapper and victim almost like a police
report.

28 March
Italian rights sold for £400.
    French rights sold for (we hope) £600.
    Now we are waiting to hear about an extract being published in the
    Sunday Times; still in the balance. (March 29th – no go.)

This Sporting Life. A good British film. But mainly because it is a bit more
'real' than all the others.[1] The English film-makers have fixed on closeness to reality as the great yardstick. This film is terribly close; like Zola.
And somehow it seems to lack all poetry, all complexity, all sophistication. Another little French film we saw – Truffaut's *Vivre sa vie* with the

---

[1] Directed by Lindsay Anderson from David Storey's novel, *This Sporting Life*
starred Richard Harris as Arthur Machin, a professional rugby player who falls
in love with his widowed landlady.

adorably cool and pretty Anna Karina – seemed to me a ten times better film: more moving, though that wasn't the purpose, as it was in *TSL*; far more contemporary; and far, infinitely far, more poetic.[1] What those *nouvelle vague* directors have, and especially Truffaut, is a dazzling lightness of touch, a simplicity; and that, especially the latter, seems of the essence of the cinema. All the greatest films have it. Simplicity is to the cinema what the metaphor is to the poem.

London, March '63

All Hail, hatcher of plots!

Should you remember a flying shuttlecock, a pattern of stars, a see-saw tree, a zany zoo-ramble, and an innate Admiral and yet earnest weekend culture-vultures, ceramic dogs (spotted as the minds that made them), ghost stories in crypts, 'Edward', birthday strawberries and cream, lessons on wild flowers, an elusive badger seen at the witching hour, then phone TEM: 4343 Ext 697 and ask for the British Sportsman's Club Secretary and come to lunch. Should you remember none of these things, tant pis! But should you remember . . . oh what jollifications.

Another disagreeable foretaste of things to come; the appearance of ghosts. When I got this I didn't know who it was from, Sanchia or Sally, and had to read it several times before it became clear it was Sanchia; so many things, details, become blurred in my mind. I remember spirit, mood, not exact details. But when I read the diary for that time out to E, there were references to everything mentioned. My instinct was to pick up the telephone and say no, no, no, keep art; then to keep silent; then to write and exorcize. The telephone rang last night and E answered, and a girl said 'wrong number'; and now we think that was her. I shall have to meet her. But I want her back there, in that strange other-world at Ashridge; as in a glade in a beech-forest that can never be returned to. It seems a pity that the museum has to be a living-room again; especially as it seems she hasn't changed. And I have.

When you receive a letter in 1963
Which seems to bear a postmark 1954
Why do you cry No, No, No!
Why this sudden fear?

---

[1] *Vivre sa vie* chronicles the day in a life of a prostitute. JF misattributes the film to François Truffaut. It was in fact directed by Jean-Luc Godard.

Life has its meaning
In the moment
Beyond the present nothing
can exist.
Reality we hold –
Is here.
Not back in time
Or times that are not now
Then why this sudden fear?
The figure on the skyline
Waits.
One day you'll doubt
Look up and see
That reality
is never held
But only imagined when it's
past.
So why this sudden fear?

Elizabeth, March 1963.
'There's a sting in the tail.'

10 April
My last day at St Godric's. I took in six bottles of sherry and there was
a sort of party. The Loveridges have given me a carriage clock; the staff
the *Shorter Oxford* and a soda-maker. Speeches, kisses, everyone being
human and well-wishing.

I leave without any regrets whatever; I think this is because I so want to
write, not because I am cold-hearted. I've always liked being in the stream
of youth, the warm current of the foreign girls; their prettiness, their
subdued sexuality, their groping through the forests of their upbringing
and their wealth to some sort of humanity. And I've liked most of the
people I've worked with; their unpretention and their communality, their
determination to set up some sort of community. And I've liked (since I
became Head of the English Department) the sort of relationship established on both fronts: the elder-brother one with the students and the
rather withdrawn one with the other teachers; for I haven't wanted to be
too superior with the former or too identified with the latter.

The wilderness was it. And one gets an affection for even the worst
wilderness. When I look back I feel I've done more useful work than I
ever expected, and perhaps precisely because this wasn't an academy one
could be proud of. All one could ever do in it was a job of work – I mean
there was no striving to be done for promotion or academic prestige. But
simply each day's work, and that done, all to do with the place was done.

Now, too, I am a professional existentialist solitary. I can't make friends with people; they all bore me, even when I like them; even when I like them very much. More and more I listen, or want to listen. I seem to remember that in my twenties I wanted always to talk more than I ever did or could. But the only people now I can talk to are very old friends and I have to lump most other people in the Many – *not* contemptuously, but regretfully. Their minds don't work like mine, they aren't 'free' or 'authentic' in the senses I use those words. I don't blame them. They are victims; conditions, or born that way. I don't want to cut them (I'm talking of the people at St Godric's) out of my life; but nor do I want to keep them in it.

Tom Maschler. Ringing up – worried that I am writing short stories for money, that Kinross is 'milking' me. It is absurd that he should give me this advice. He may know all about selling books, but I know all about the ideals of writing. The most absurd is that he does not even realize this 'advice' is atrociously insulting.

12 April

Being 'free' is nice; like virtue rewarded. We continue to spend too much money, but then we have had so many years of not being able to spend any money. I have pangs of conscience about not giving anything to charity. I must do that; but as with everything else I like to store these decisions up, to (neologizing by mood) constipate them.

Today I went down Fleet Road and bought some books. Fitzgerald's *Literary Remains* (1889) in 3 vols;[1] Ovid, *Works*, in 3 vols; Petronius, and some other Roman filth, in another volume; Thomas's *Lawrence of Arabia*;[2] Wyndham Lewis's *Childermass* (1st edn) and Barbellion's *Diary* (1st edn);[3] also, 1830 New Hall cup and saucer; a Staffordshire transfer blue bowl; an album of Edwardian postcards (a new collecting mania) of Hampstead and musical comedy beauties; a Dresden cream-jug; £2.

*

---

[1] The *Letters and Literary Remains* of Edward Fitzgerald, most well known as the translator of the *Rubáiyát of Omar Khayyám*.
[2] *With Lawrence of Arabia* (1924) by Lowell Thomas (1892–1981), the American journalist who met T. E. Lawrence in Jerusalem in 1917. In his dispatches from the Middle East and lecture tours after the war he was responsible for building the legend around Lawrence's exploits and was the first to dub him 'Lawrence of Arabia'.
[3] 'Barbellion' was the pseudonym of Bruce Frederick Cummings (1889–1919), who wrote two volumes of journals which chronicled his struggle with an illness diagnosed as 'disseminated sclerosis'.

I am devoting some of my freedom to writing my name in all the hundreds of books I have bought these last ten years. 'John Fowles 1963' in each one.

14 April
Barbellion. He should be more highly rated, both as a writer in the Jefferies/Lawrence tradition of describing natural England,[1] and as an English social phenomenon: the sharply empirical odd man out. He's really one of the first 'angry young men'.

His feeling a secret Gulliver among the Lilliputian world around him; his loathing of Bible worship; his reading old diaries and having forgotten so much of them; his swinging from the scientific to the aesthetic, and back, in his approach to nature; his embroidering of the trivial: all these define me too.

I spent almost all my 'intelligent' childhood from ten to twenty walking alone in the countryside, watching birds, looking for flowers, butterflies; I suppose I would be a better writer if I had been reading more, and learning to write at that age, instead of in my thirties. But that love-affaire with nature – is it all waste?

16 April
Writing a piece, hypothetically for *Encounter*, about *The Collector*. In it I've said I've ceased to have the Bluebeard fantasy since the acceptance of the book. This is true, but it's been a gradual trailing-off. One reason I haven't mentioned in the article is the leaving St Godric's; that is, I am being cut off from the most fertile source. I think that once I used to 'kidnap and imprison' generalized girls – archetypes. But for many years it has had to be someone I know – students.

Sunday Times, 14 April 1963.

The Late Developer

John Fowles gave up his job as a schoolmaster in Hampstead last week. He is thirty-seven and has been teaching since he left Oxford. For fifteen years he has spent his spare time writing. He completed two books and started, but never finished, another twelve. He considered himself unpublishable so he sent nothing

---

[1] JF is thinking of D. H. Lawrence and Richard Jefferies (1848–87). Jefferies wrote several books on the countryside and, most famously, the children's novel *Bevis: The Story of a Boy*, which drew on his memories of growing up in rural Wiltshire. Bevis lives on a farm, and plays games of make-believe with his friend Mark, turning the surrounding meadows into jungles and deserts.

off – until last year, when he sent a novel called *The Collector* to an agent. Jonathan Cape snapped it up.

It doesn't come out till next month, but five months ago the paperback rights were sold for £3,500 and it was bought by Columbia, who have already finished a shooting script. Overseas rights have been sold in America, France and Italy and Cape have just started a second edition. So far, the book has made £12,000. Which is why John Fowles – 'I suppose I must be a late developer' – gave up his job last week.

He hasn't allowed Cape to tell anybody about him up to now because he was slightly worried about the impression which might be created at his school – a well-known girls' college.

The book is about an inarticulate clerk who kidnaps a student from outside her home in Hampstead. He locks her up in a cottage, but never assaults her. Cape thinks it is a remarkable feat of disquieting suspense.

Fowles says the situation is an archetypal male fantasy. 'Psychologists call it the Bluebeard fantasy. I'd own up to having indulged in it myself.'

'And he seemed such a nice young man.'

Sanchia. I went to meet her in the Press Office of the Savoy. A rather coarse-looking foreign clerk typing, two supercilious PR officers; and Sanchia, still with a girl's face, but with grey hair among the black (she's twenty-nine, I asked her later); with her same odd easy-formal manner, as if we'd last met yesterday and not ten years ago. She got me a whisky, fiddled about with place tickets for some dinner, helped the coarse-looking foreign clerk to type an envelope, whereupon he kissed the inside of her wrist in a very foreign way, shook hands with me, and left.

'That's Christoff,' she said. 'He's the bane of my life.'

'Christoff?'

'*The* Christoff.'

'The singer?' And it seemed it was;[1] he is lecherous off-stage. Then a vivacious foreigner passed through. That was Amelia Rodriguez, the Portugese fado singer.

Later, I got her out of the Savoy and we went to the Heneky's at the end of the Strand, and there I forced her to drop her isn't-life-fun mask. Slowly it came off, and in the end she told me everything that had happened to her in the intervening years. Five years in Africa, then this last two years in Europe: in Paris, in London, doing odd jobs, a

---

[1] Boris Christoff (1914–1993), a then popular Bulgarian opera star.

sort of cheat poverty, because her parents will always help her if she's absolutely lost. So she slums in the rue de la Huchette in Paris and as a waitress in Cambridge. This is a common situation among middle-class women – they want to be independent, they want to prove their independence; and yet they can't, quite, ever, with that money behind them.

She still has the *princesse lointaine* charm I associate with her; only now I look through binoculars at it, so to speak, and feel pretty sure that it would disintegrate rapidly, this charm, if I ever came in closer contact with it. Because it is very largely based on a refusal to face up to reality, physical or mental. I dragged out of her the details of a relationship she has now 'with a married man'. They speak always in terms of allegory. They live in India (where neither of them has ever been), S up a tree; the man comes hunting in her 'domaine'; sometimes she speaks to him, sometimes she withdraws 'so high' that they can communicate only in the third person, by means of a heron. 'The heron says . . .'

'It's so bloody childish,' I said in the end. But for her it was 'wonderful': 'We say things that can't be said in any other way.'

Then she talked for hours about her family, her wretched, possessive, insanely insecure mother. 'I can't marry,' said S. 'I've got to have some escape. Every marriage for me is like my parents'.' She said she had lived for five years in South Africa with a German, an ex-SS man. 'He was very hard, but he taught me to be independent.'

She talked on and on about herself. I should have made an excellent psychiatrist. A certain category of woman, thirtyish, failed in their ambitions, ratted on by men (Jennifer Ardagh, Lorraine Robertson), find in me the ideal father confessor. In S's case I asked for it, because I kept on asking her the sort of questions she hates but (I suppose) knows she needs: that is, she needs cornering, her evasions admitted.

It was very curious, the evening. We walked up and down the Tottenham Court Road, at the end of it; I had the old feeling of sadness – that I shouldn't ever be close to her (like a mountain I shan't ever climb, a country I shall never go to) added to a feeling of sadness *for* her – sympathy and pity. She was trying to express the same thing, in her usual very oblique way – making a tiny direct confession of emotion, then immediately retracting it, covering it up under some triviality.

I think, really, that I like her because she is unique, unique in her behaving, her looks (without being a raving beauty), and in her approach to life and in her extraordinary mythomania. I can see now clearly her faults, the pathetic nature of her evasions, her feyness, her swathing herself in ambiguities, her obstinate refusal to listen to, or even respect, male reason. ('I hated *La Peste*,' she said. 'I hate the way he says what he means.') She reminds me very much of the sort of young woman one reads about in Peacock – a sort of late-eighteenth-century amalgam of shrewdness and snobbishness and femininity – Fanny Burney and Jane Austen. That's it. She's Jane Austen-like, in her way.

My whole feeling for her was, is, and always will/would be literary. Not real. Eliz is reality; and I long ago chose that. So much so that I can't say that I had even the ghost of a shade of Kierkegaardian anxiety – there was no choice to be renewed.[1]

19 April

Sunk in *The Magus* again; I mean creatively plunged. I have the skeleton, the symbolisms, the implications, so clear. It's the putting of the flesh in all those big and little bones. The destinations, and the days getting there.

Sources: *Robinson Crusoe* and *The Tempest*. As in *The Collector*, but different, more direct aspects, this time.

The Conchis–Lily relationship is Jullié–Micheline at Collioure – my situation vis-à-vis them. Alison = Kaja.[2] Perhaps that summer at Collioure is inherent in the psychological situation. It is not Spetsai at all.

23 April

Copies of the book. One to Denys, one to the Porters, one to the Loveridges, one to home, one to Sanchia (in which I wrote a properly cryptic 'Dig the orchard' and left it at that); two that I shall keep.

25 April

Fuss with Tom Maschler. I have written a piece called 'Some Notes: The Collector', in which he figures as a brilliant young salesman. He is hurt; nobody ever wants to be what he is. He wants to be director of conscience, guide, protector, all. We had dinner with him the other evening, and I liked him better. A house full of modern paintings; but even those, one felt, were bought because they were good investments, though he tried to keep that hidden. He has Midas fingers. Everything he touches turns to gold; but I like him because I think he does want some of what he touches to turn to something human.

An interview with a young lady from *Books and Bookmen*, a magazine I'd never heard of before. A nice kid, but a ninny; and it suddenly became ridiculous to talk seriously with her.

---

[1] The Christian philosopher Søren Kierkegaard (1813–1855) held that a necessary state of anxiety preceded the choice to make the leap of faith into Christianity.

[2] See introduction, page xiv.

2 May
The Magus. I am working on this all the time. Conchis's running away
at Neuve Chapelle.

3 May
Curious dream. I was at a window looking down a façade at right angles.
Various figures appeared at other windows in this façade. I knew they
were ghosts – or 'visitors', as I am calling them in *The Magus.* I felt no
fear, but a burning desire to make them look at me. I could feel my
eyes bulging out of my head with the intensity of this desire. Yet their
eyes carefully avoided me, as if I (the living) were the one who did not
exist. I interpret this dream in three ways:

1. It is simply an extension of *The Magus.*
2. It is something to do with the elusiveness of created characters.
   They have a life and will of their own, etc.
3. It is a dramatization of my having to face the critics (of my anxiety);
   the first reviews will be out on Sunday.

5 May
First reviews. The worst in the paper where I would rather have the best
– *The Observer.* By the egregiously dilettante 'man of letters' Simon Raven,
who would manage to make *War and Peace* sound rather ordinary. But
clearly I can't complain.[1]

7 May
First swifts.

I spent three hours today down in the West End Lane library, reading
The Times for January–March, 1915, and *Punch* from September 1914 to
March 1915. I have been doing that part of *The Magus* for some time.
At first, intense interest; then irritation. I wanted to get back to my ima-
gined, simplified 1915.

9–11 May
Bad days. I get no pleasure from reading the reviews of the book – what
reviews there are. There were none in the weeklies and papers I hoped
might have something to say. 'Quite a little masterpiece of suspense'

---

[1] In a review of faint praise Simon Raven wrote:'This book has two merits. There
is, first, an intriguing study in warped sexuality . . . Secondly, there is some
cunningly worked suspense... An entirely plausible ending further recommends
this tale.'

seems to sum up the general view – the 'immensely unimportant' sort of judgement. This last week has made me very jumpy and I wish to God now that I had cleared out of England – alone. Eliz doesn't seem to understand what this is doing to me. On top of everything else I have got into a bad patch with *The Magus* where I can't see whether the trouble is simply authenticating Bourani[1] or the sheer impossibility of authenticating it under any circumstances – I wonder whether the patch is beyond my powers, beyond any powers.

We went to Sudbury on Friday, to look at a house – part of a Tudor manor house at Glemsford. But the experience disconcerted me completely; as we caught the train to Marks Tey, changed on to a sideline and ambled through Victorian stations and green fields under a wet grey sky, the whole business became unreal; and more unreal, going in a taxi through Long Melford, up an endless village street and round by some council houses into a lane.[2] The house was very fine, beamed, gabled, lopsided, like an illustration in a Dickens novel. Nice old rooms and staircase, a pretty orchard. But I knew at once that I could never live there. Not at the end of an ugly village, with council estates going up all around. We saw another house at Little Waldingfield, and the next day another at Lavenham,[3] one with a fine Jacobean staircase, a splendid piece of design; but the house in foul condition, so damp and dilapidated that I couldn't be bothered even to pretend to the owner that we were interested. This whole area is much too conversion-conscious, too professionally 'country' to interest me. The villages are pretty, Sudbury is a nice little country town, but this is not what I want. I realized that my ideas about what I want in the country are so vague that it is ridiculous to make any decision until we have seen more of England and of possible houses or cottages.

I see now that I need 1. not less than an acre or so of ground; 2. either a very modern house (designed for me) or a Georgian one – Tudor is out – too dark, too introverted; 3. seclusion – I don't want to be overlooked or overheard; 4. water – the sea or at least a stream; 5. an orchard – the Tudor house at Glemsford had a fine little one on a slope behind the house; 6. a hilly landscape – combes.

---

[1] The name which JF gave to the character Conchis's villa. It was modelled on the Villa Jasmelia which JF used to visit when he was teaching on Spetsai. See note 3 on page 258.

[2] Sudbury is a small market town situated on the River Stour in Suffolk. Getting there by train from London required JF and Elizabeth to change at Marks Tey. Glemsford is a small Suffolk village to the north-west of Sudbury situated on a hill overlooking the River Stour.

[3] Two more villages in the South Suffolk countryside close to Sudbury.

But besides all these limiting things I still don't know whether I really want to live in the country or not. There is that Chekhovian sadness that hangs over all sensitive people in the country; that terrible loss of proportion we call local pride; that sameness, or lack – lack of incident, lack of choice; and there is still that old, old Tory view of life, Tory in the eighteenth-century sense, which lingers in the eyes of all educated people – I heard it in the estate agent's voice, I saw it in the manner of a sad-genteel, cultivated hotel proprietress, in the curator of the Gainsborough Museum's eyes.[1] (Atrocious, the Gainsboroughs – his 'Ipswich period' is totally without genius.) A world with an unhealthy respect for money, property, family, tradition. Where the world is still squires and peasantry – older than that even. Chiefs and tribesmen.

Eliz suddenly lost her temper in the middle of the night when we got back. Quite unexpectedly. Whatever else was a failure at Sudbury, our making love wasn't; something intensely aphrodisiac about hotel rooms. But my collecting of china irritates her – I think unreasonably. She was deeply offended when a stupid girl reporter came here the other day and asked me questions about the china and the books. I hate the collecting of living objects, but I just cannot see any harm in that which I do. Collecting is bad when 1. the objects cease to exist as objects in a collection, 2. the collecting is done purely for investment, 3. it is so expensive that it unbalances the rest of one's life. Eliz keeps on accusing me of having nothing but these motives, although she has read and heard me say a dozen times what I think constitutes legitimate and illegitimate collecting. In Lavenham we saw by chance a New Hall teapot in a cottage window – and it gave me quite as much aesthetic 'kick' as collector's excitement. I think this pottery is English with exactly the Englishness I admire and love. And as for the books, I collect them for reasons that would make most bibliophiles spit in disgust – because I want to read them, plunge back into the past. Not because they are rarities, in fine condition, and so on. My mistake has been – because I find it impossible to communicate the joy I feel in a New Hall milk-jug, an obscure eighteenth-century play – to boast of prices, of bargains. The silly girl reporter wanted to know 'how much they're all worth'; and this age reduces one to that – 'how much they're all worth', in money. It shocks me often that Eliz thinks all money spent on non-practical things is 'a waste', is in some way 'wicked'. This bread-alone view of life is a hangover from our poorer days; but it is also characteristic of all our friends, for whom collecting, in even the very humble way I do, is totally 'out'. They are like the Porters, who buy the odd bit of bric-à-brac

---

[1] The Gainsborough Museum was opened in 1961 in the house in Sudbury where Thomas Gainsborough (1727–88) was born.

because it is 'amusing'; like the Sharrocks, who like to be able to 'live from one suitcase'. And over all hangs the interior decoration mania. If there is a blasphemy of the object, that is it.

Eliz attacked me, too, much more reasonably, for watching a girl in a house opposite through my telescope. It is sheer curiosity, or almost sheer, much closer to ornithology than voyeurism. But of course one is meant to be deeply ashamed of such instincts. Even if I was a voyeur I don't think I'd be very ashamed.

The row is made up. The wonder is not that we had it, but that living so close as we do, and so isolated from other people, that we don't have them more often.

Archie Ogden. A nice man, in spite of the fact that the demon Alcohol has him in its claws. He's in torment without a glass in his hand; though once he has one, he doesn't drink hard. Just happily sips. I think it's high time we talked of New World courtesy – he has eighteenth-century good manners and graciousness, like so many educated Americans.

That lovely (pure American) joke about Philadelphia: 'I spent a week there last Sunday.'

14 May
A wet afternoon. We have suddenly decided to go to Greece. To camp and hike through the Peloponnesus.

Hudson, *Green Mansions* (1904)[1] I have never read Hudson before. I think I've even had some vague sort of contempt for him, not really as English. Whereas he is intensely English, of course; *Green Mansions* is quite as English as *Robinson Crusoe*. I found it, for all its feyness, a powerfully and truly sad work. I think I like it because I can feel exactly how Hudson was obsessed by his idea, by the idea of Rima; in books like this the imagination goes flaring through the dark spaces, the void of all the countless imaginationless, obsessionless books. It's a pity he made Rima talk, though that last 'Abel, Abel' down into the flames almost justifies it; and whenever he describes her physically an Arthur-Rackhamish, James-Barrieish quality creeps in; while the sex is that odd misty half-ethereal, half-physical ballooning-out of emotions we call

---

[1] Born in Argentina of American parents, William Henry Hudson (1841–1922) lived in England from 1874, where he published novels and several books on nature. *Green Mansions* (1904) tells the story of Abel, who, fleeing persecution in Venezuela, travels into the jungle, where he falls in love with Rima, a girl of the woods. The novel ends with Rima being captured by Indians and burned on a pyre.

passion – the word has a pejorative sense now, of course; although if any book could tell us of the Sex Age, what we have lost by existing in it, it is *Green Mansions.*

The book fascinated me because I have just come to the part in *The Magus* where Lily 'enters'; and because it has precisely the quality I think needs putting back into life and into the novel – mystery.

Hudson's pantheism and his rejection of the idea of an interceding God – of course he is right. The latter requires the former.

17 May
A peculiar, very disagreeable day. I'm not feeling well, but it was something more than that. It started well enough. We went down to Dorset Square to see a maisonette flat Eliz had seen advertised. But very rapidly I had a feeling, still with me as I write, so like existentialist nausea that I can hardly believe it – though it is here and real. As we looked round the flat it began to seem at two removes. As if in a film. The nausea was not at the otherness of the objects we saw, but at their remoteness, as if they had nothing to do with me, as if I was seeing them in a film – in a film I didn't want to see, moreover. Sitting afterwards in a coffee-bar – Eliz likes the place, she wants to move in – this nausea became worse, the sharpest attack I have ever had. A girl walking outside, other customers, Eliz, my own queasy stomach – everything only quarter existent. As if I was dying. Walking about the Baker Street area, arguing about whether we should take the place or not. One of 'the boys' who was in the flat took us in his car to the estate agent's, just by Holborn Viaduct. Weird griffin-like creatures painted maroon and g(u)ilt (Freudian: guilt for gilt); an endless climb up past the gilded mesh of a non-working life. Down a long top-floor corridor; a clerk with a stutter. The whole building seemed empty except for this one Kafkaesque creature, who knew n-nothing. Eliz felt car-sick, and stood reading letters in the clerk's tray. Quite openly. All my self seemed shifted out of me; it was as if only my body and the bodily sensations were left. As if my persona had blown up and there was nothing left except fragmented perceptions of coagulations of phenomena. We wandered about Holborn afterwards like two people in limbo. But with Eliz it was just a physical nausea. I felt, and feel, ontologically dislocated; as if there has been a break in the course of my life. It would be alarming if it were not so strange: that things one has read and written become so physically real.

It is not the otherness of things that is terrifying; it is when they lose their otherness, when they lose all intrinsic value, all ontological meaning. They are, but are not. They no longer reflect one, so one's personality is no longer contained and 'fixed' (in the navigational sense) by them; it disperses through them out into psychological space, into the *néant.*

19 May
We took Jane and Bert Saunders to see the Dorset Square flat. Thank God, their good solid urban ex-Bohemian common-sense rejected the place at sight.

22 May
Awake at five with indigestion. Sitting in the long room, facing one of the small windows in the east wall. It was just light. And suddenly a huge ripe persimmon floated up over Highgate woods. I watched it through glasses, round, trembling-edged, orange and huge. Some odd distortion made the lowest part reach out, as if still attracted to the skyline, like an inverted droplet. On its right shoulder a black mole; the still drowsy sun, hanging over the cool grey banks of the dawn trees. A most lovely colour, a most lovely shape; and the moments full of silence, only pigeons cooing, no traffic, no men, pigeons cooing and swifts flying between me and the sun, all power, all nature, very mysterious, trembling there like a pregnant woman, more beautiful than anything I have seen for many months.

28 May
Off to Greece tomorrow. Crowded, these last days, tense, empty, nervous, dull; but at last we feel some of the joy of going. This morning I went to St Godric's – a roomful of foreign girls with books to sign. Nice gentle, eager creatures, treating me and the book as simple, healthy things – as if we were a mother and child; so much better than the nervous miasma that surrounds the being an author in England.

6 August
American reviews are coming in – mostly very favourable. But the book is so often misunderstood – no one will take it as a parable, as the Heraclitean sermon it is meant to be.

The film treatment of *The Collector* from John Kohn – so bad, most of it, that I read it with a sort of stunned incredulousness. Changes in the story, the happy ending and all the rest, I'd accepted. But to find characters totally changed, motivations changed, worst of all, my ideas changed – that's what I can't stand. And as for some of the Americanisms they've put into the mouths of my poor English characters . . .

9 August
We've got out a huge list of objections; and I composed a letter.

Dear John Kohn,

This is going to be a very difficult letter to write, and to read.
But here it is: even when I allow for all the demands of the box-
office and the change in art-form, your treatment seems to me in
many places hopelessly inadequate.

Please don't think I'm dismissing all the work and thought I'm
sure you and Stanley Mann have put in on this job. I like some
of your visual inventions very much, and – one key thing – you've
by and large jettisoned the characters and situations that need
jettisoning.

Can we for Christ's sake not now get together on this script? I
understand that you feel I'm not competent to help you, but surely
you need on the screen, with a story like this, as much consistency
and authenticity, in visual detail, in motivation and in dialogue, as
you can get. And if there is one word that can sum up my criticisms of your treatment it's this: it is implausible, it just doesn't
make realistic English (or any other) sense.

Let me end by saying that my disappointment would not be so
great if you hadn't done such a good job on *Reach for Glory*.

There it is. Forgive, if you can, all the harsh words (my 'urgent
reaction') in what follows; all my criticisms come from a desire
to help achieve something better. You want to have a good film,
I want to have a good film. Must we come at it from opposite
directions?

But Archie Ogden thinks they've got me in the contract 'by the short
hairs' – they could tell me to go hell. And would, if I sent the letter. So
he will speak to them, and try to convince them that they have me in
to clean things up. He thought, anyway, that it was a good job – they'd
beaten 'a really tough problem'. Part of the difficulty is the gulf between
the English and the American imaginations. Even an American intellectual like Archie seems to me so unsubtle, so surprisingly content with
clumsiness and obviousness in the script. It's not a matter of intelligence, but taste – they like all their shadows lit, all their ambiguities
elementary, all their symbolisms pushed down the audience's throat.
Understatement here, overstatement there. (Lecture over.)

14 August
Two days down at Leigh – miserable ones, full of a sort of choked nausea.
I get more and more of this vile nervous rage at the stupidity of the
environments I am condemned to – my parents. M irritates me so
intensely that within a few hours of getting down there I find myself
unable to look her in the face; F at least I have some pity and sympathy

for, though his views on books and writing are so idiotically Victorian-suburban that I have to keep a tight hold on my tongue.

Leigh, though, was probably no more than an irritant on an already ulcerous situation. Because I feel myself at a crossroads, torn by so many anxieties and nauseas that concentration is impossible; all the American success means nothing – at any rate, brings me no pleasure. I am sick to death of *The Collector*, really, and the thought of having to plough all through it again (writing a film script) makes me wonder if I shan't end up on the couch. I have forgotten what relaxation and peace of mind are – and the holiday in Greece has done me no good in that way. It was two months in a vacuum; now reality begins exactly where it left off at the end of May.

One major cause of all this mental ulceration is my feeling of frustration over the poems and *The Aristos*. Getting them published seems no more feasible now than it did before *The Collector*. I feel misinterpreted, misunderstood, belittled. Of course this is arrogance – the preacher in prison. But more and more I feel myself slipping out of control – that is, the ship won't answer the helm of reason. I am what my obsessions and deep drives demand, not what my reason says I should be. Behind the façades, dark corridors: the commands come from the shadows, not the brightly designed surfaces.

A curious moment of peace at Leigh, when Eliz and I had escaped for an hour or two. We sat in the public library gardens overlooking the mild estuary. Feeling I was great enough to outlive, to *outbe*, all this period of neurotic worry about success, about being understood, about writing something else as good. But it was a glimpse of something far away, something that flashed past.

All the weight of this falls on Eliz, here and at Leigh. Sometimes she seems like a wall between me and my madness, my disintegration, the shattering of my coherence, exhibiting all the sanity and patience I once had, and she hadn't – like some peculiar transference, this.

A hedgehog in the garden, at Leigh. I wanted to catch it, and in the end hurt the poor beast, which was stuck under a fence. It wouldn't roll up, wouldn't run, but lay half on its side, one pink paw out, its dull black eye staring reproachfully from among the bristles. I cursed myself for having used so much force – for being trapped by the old hunting maniac. The next morning it had disappeared; but I must learn this lesson.

20 August
Tom Maschler: 'Mary Hemingway's[1] asked me over (to America) to do

---

[1] i.e. Mary Welsh (1908–86), Ernest Hemingway's fourth and last wife, whom he married in 1946.

something with Poppa's manuscripts. She doesn't trust anyone else.'
Absurd: like a grasshopper assessing a Stravinsky. Not that Tom doesn't
say 'God only knows why' and all the rest. We like him a little bit more
each time we see him: his restlessness, his meanness with his praise –
the Jewish oil and vinegar.

These last four or five days I've been fighting the battle of the film script
– two long sessions down at Wigmore Street, and three days on my own
here (Eliz in Birmingham). Strange days – eighteen hours each day
completely rewriting all the worst bits of dialogue (i.e. those not taken
from the book), and suddenly having the trio Paston, Miranda and Clegg
alive with me again. That odd state in which one's creations seem so
real that it becomes a bore to stay at the typewriter when one can walk
round the room, and hear and see them.

After that I had to meet the other (and less real) trio at Blazer Films:
John Kohn, a liberal, perhaps, but under such a crust of Hollywood-
mogul crassness and with such a natural lack of sensitivity that the liberalism dwindles to near nothingness; Jud Kinberg, a nice, easy man, but
a bit of a deadweight; and Stanley Mann, a slim stick of taut nerves,
obviously intelligent, but a non-creator, a slick cutter-down of originals
to the required size. Mann's more or less on my side; Kinberg's on the
fence; Kohn is violently against – he wants gimmicks, suspense, two-
dimensional characters, a happy ending.

I read out my bits of dialogue. Some they liked, some they didn't –
Kohn almost always not. The language in these script conferences
becomes peculiarly tense and obscene: 'OK, he wants to lay the fucking
broad, but she's a fucking little cockteaser, she won't let him'; 'Look,
you got this goddam virgin fucking around . . .' And so on. It reminded
me of *The Naked and the Dead* – some war novel. It's blasphemous; and
in a way it has a sort of authenticity – they've thought about the film
so much, tried so many possibilities, that you feel the characters have
become really battered and shapeless, like things in war.

Both Kinross and Maschler think I'm wrong to have anything to do
with them – especially without having got any financial terms settled.
But on things like this I know I'm right. If they take only half the changes
I got them to accept yesterday, then it's worth it. I know the Devil when
I see him; and he's not going to walk over me.

Billy Liar. There's a girl in it – Julie Christie – they're screen-testing for
the part of Miranda. She has the face – better than I expected. They
won't beat her for looks. Clegg is to be Terence Stamp. The director
should be John Schlesinger, but they sent him the script.

29 August
Trying to find a house in London. Eliz is out looking most days. I don't really know where I want to live – in London or abroad or in the country. Nor, at present prices, do I feel happy about the financial side. The cheapest houses, all in tatty areas, are about £10,000. Nothing under £15,000 in Hampstead. We'd have to borrow at least half the purchase price. And I think of all those writers who lived all their lives in a miserable state of debt.

Whiting, *The Devils.* A very fine play.[1] A touch of genius, that rare, rare thing in modern literature. The idea of a mosaic of short scenes – yes. If I write a Robin Hood, this is the thing to keep in mind.

Genius: recognizing in another an achievement one could never have achieved oneself in the given situation; and which one would have liked to achieve. With this, always, a shock of delight. Because the curious thing about genius is that it destroys envy.

4 September
Little, Brown want me to go to America for a week, to help publicize the book.

Golding, *Lord of the Flies* and *Pincher Martin.* The first is the better, though that ending is wrong. Ralph should die, and the earth be given over to darkness.[2] The second is a *tour de force* of physical description; but the flashbacks are horribly weak.[3] I think I have the following main criticisms of Golding: 1. he treats of extreme situations expressionistically, he comes from the Kafka (Rex Warner) line – expressionism and extreme situation do not go together, the one trips up, weakens, the other; 2. his dialogue is weak; 3. his prolonged descriptions of physical sensations and actions end up cancelling each other out – in practical terms, one skims them. Rule: the more extreme and fantastic the situation the more realistic (camera-eye) and sober the descriptions and dialogue. Examples: *Robinson Crusoe*; *Darkness at Noon.* Corollary: the

---

[1] John Whiting (1917–63) based the play on Aldous Huxley's book *The Devils of Loudun,* which dealt with a historically documented case of demonic possession in seventeenth-century France. The play opened at the Aldwych Theatre in 1961.
[2] In *The Lord of the Flies* (1954) Ralph is hunted down after the failure of his attempts to organize his fellow-schoolboys into a civilized society on the island where they have been stranded, but is finally saved by the arrival of a navy ship.
[3] In *Pincher Martin* (1956) the narrator is a British naval officer who has been shipwrecked on a rock in the mid-Atlantic. As he struggles to stay alive, he recalls details from his past life.

more ordinary the situation the more exotic and fantastic language and dialogue may be. Examples: *Ulysses, Mrs Dalloway.*

The Collector is now third on the *Time* bestseller list.

Flying to America. This frightens me. Statistics mean nothing. It feels like a 50–50 chance. Not that death means anything. I wouldn't mind dying now, in some strange way. In spite of the incompletion of everything.

14–23 September
Like most people who call themselves socialists I went to the States for this first visit with my suitcase stuffed with a lifetime's prejudices against the place, prejudices softened by a good deal of liking for American literature and for a few beautiful American expatriates I'd known here and there in Europe, but aggravated by almost everything else. Somehow I have to explain how I came back a week later still a socialist (in my fashion) but also hopelessly in love. The faults are there all right, as plain as the eczema on an adolescent's face; but nobody ever told me how forgivable and lovable and good-looking the poor child is. And so, at the risk of having all my friends tell me I've gone soft, this will largely be in praise of America. Just for a change.

One comes in over Boston, inferiority complexes on the *qui-vive*, one lands. A collection of scruffy one-storey buildings, a dirty corridor, peeling distemper, windows painted coarse brown with bizarre shapes scratched in them by idlers outside – spiders of light behind the immigration officials' heads. It would be a national disgrace in Europe, but here it is human, unassuming. But ah, I think, the dreaded Boston Irish, now we shall see. I go up to the most unpleasant-looking official. He stares at my form. Tears it up, takes another and carefully fills it in again for me. 'They oughta make it clearer,' when I mutter an apology. 'There,' he says, 'and I hope you have a really happy stay with us.' From then on I am permanently off-balance.

Ned Bradford, Little, Brown's editor-in-chief, a quiet, intellectual-executive type, met me. Glasses, sizing blue eyes. The bits of Boston we went through looked tatty, too – human. Because this is what one comes into the States expecting not to find – dirt, rust, tattiness, all the usual human failings of old civilizations.

On the expressway out south down to Marshfield, passing the English names – Weymouth, Braintree, and then the lovely-sounding Indian names mixed in with them – Nantasket, Cohasset, Scituate. Then Plymouth. Then Cape Cod.

The biggest shock is the beauty of the domestic buildings in the New England countryside – the Cape Cod and Colonial cottages, barns and houses. The lovely sober colours they're painted in. White mostly, shutters and details picked out in grey, steel-blue and white; here and there a sober maroon house, window-frames and door in white. And the spacedness of the houses. America is where space is cheap, and things like this alter a nation's psyche. Round here you have to buy at least an acre if you want to build.

Atmosphere of the Bradford's 1780 house – of total informality tinged with gracious living (using that last term without most of the pejorative associations it's accreted to itself). Simply living with easy grace, with pleasant things around one, and space, lawns, a lake, woods. 'We just want to live on our own,' says Pam Bradford, 'and in our own way.'

This seems to me to be one of the tragedies of America, that the combined pressures of conformism and an only superficial consumer-goods paradise drive the decently intelligent into a nostalgia for isolation (shades of Thoreau) and the indecently intelligent to sex, alcohol and the headshrinker's den. It is easy to sneer at the neuroses of wealth. I've done it pretty often myself. But socialism dismisses this aspect of the American adventure at its own peril. In this, as in so many other things, they're pioneering for all of us.

Pioneering spirit. There's an old stove in the kitchen. 'When there's a hurricane we have to cook and do everything by that.' It seems incongruous, beside all the apparatus for modern living. Incongruous and deeply appealing, of course. That is another not so obvious charm of this country. The close proximity of sophisticated gadgetry to the aboriginal wild. The trees that end nowhere.

Monday morning, into Boston in the rain. It seems a terribly ugly city, coarse and dirty, even though the area round Beacon Hill has a certain charm. 'This is really nice,' says Ned. But it isn't. There's very little urban architectural charm in the place. Some pleasant built-out bow-windows and Colonial doors, but mainly vistas of heavy Victorian-Edwardian brownstone ugliness. And the tired jams of long-tailed cars. The way American men drive their huge cars. Even miserable old wizened sheep try to look toughly relaxed, virile to the grave, in the driving-seat. They have a pathetic lack of dignity.

Bob Fettridge. He's Little, Brown's chief publicity and promotion man, and I owe him most for the success of the book, so everyone says. 'He kind of looks like a store detective,' says Ned Bradford. But he's simply a shy, nervous little man, with a shrewd, intense face. I like him. There is a big lunch for me in a private dining-room of the Union Club – the two Arthur H. Thornhill's, Senior and Junior. Senior a crusty old boy, but with a nice old pride in his imprint and a hatred of publishers who print books to catch the pornography market (such as Scribner's have recently with *Fanny Hill*). Junior is the college-boy executive, rather English and slightly ludicrously top of the pecking order. All the various heads of department were around the table, distinctly nervous, angling for the right remark, the right moment to be sincere, the right moment to make a 'sick' aside (to get a laugh). All nice men on their own, all liberals, yet this organizational pattern is very disagreeably present at such reunions; and once again the pattern is basically power.

Power – this is America. The neurosis of power; the application of power; the poetry of power; the psychologies of power. The long cars, the great flowing expressways and flyovers, the huge buildings, the size and the space. Everything here, from the simplest conversation – all that has size, has energy, has space – is a symbol, an emblem, a metaphor of power.

To New York. In clouds all the way, but then we came down and there was the Hudson and the East River and the Statue of Liberty and the great cluster of scrapers in downtown Manhattan. We picked what Bob Fettridge said was the most typical New York taxi-driver he'd ever seen: a guttural, glottal Brooklyn accent – Thoid Avenoo – incessant talk, offers to take us round Greenwich Village – 'I was a cop in the Vice Squad, I can show you everything.'

The University Club. Very staid and proper. No women allowed, and as like a London club as could be, even to the serried ranks of old fossils in the reading-room. But I have a nice big room, a splendid bathroom. Very solid comfort. I look over the Museum of Art courtyard, and Fifth Avenue is ten yards away.

The poetry of New York – under cloud, the skyscrapers losing their tops. Sunlight, the windowed cliffs floating in the blue sky, heavenly cities. The long vistas have an almost Claude-like peace. And the sunshafts catch little bits of green. New York is cool, zesty, young. The girls in bare-armed dresses.

Meeting Naomi Thompson, the LB publicity girl in New York – a short-sighted Scandinavian American of fortyish, plump, bossy, scatty in a deliberate sort of way, full of publicity raves and gimmicks. She lives on her nerves from moment to moment, sucks up and utters literary gossip like an alcoholic barman. A nice homely Nordic woman deep in her somewhere.

The pace of New York. Whip in and out of taxis, from one date to another. It's not nearly so neurotic as one would think (or the natives like to make out). There's a great lack of fuss. One slips into a studio, shakes hands, tests for sound, talks, shakes hands, is out. None of the empty exchanges of London life, which wear out one's nerves so.

The Americans interview much better than we do, much more relaxedly, much less anxious to needle and much more anxious to find out what you really believe, why you do things, who you really are. I have a job explaining existentialism, still inextricably confused in the American mind with beatniks and that notorious New York folk villain

Norman Mailer. I was needled once or twice on the Profumo affaire, but in general people realized that the thing was no more than a boil, and needed lancing; in any case the way Western sexual mores are going no country can afford to laugh at another over a Profumo affaire. 'Oh, we laugh,' said one New Yorker. 'And keep our fingers crossed.'[1]

Days flow in and out so fast that things seem to go by as in a dream. Wednesday. Up at 7.30 to meet Norton Mockridge of the *World Telegram* for breakfast. He's an avuncular type (it seems he's the city editor, and hasn't done such an interview for years), with a freckled bald head, and the bluff NY urbanity the older men have. Very agreeable, this American man-of-the-worldliness. Long serious talk. But the breakfast interview is a bore, really. On at 9.30 to an interview with Mitchell Krauss, a type I can tell a mile off. Nervous, phoney, as treacherous as a shark and as 'authentic' as a plastic mouse – an odd blend of harmfulness and harmlessness. All through the interview he was glancing anxiously round, fingers trembling. I realize my apparent stolidity worries the less experienced (and genuine) interviewers. And I'm glad.

Then a riotous three hours with Marguerite Lampkin, the star Condé-Nast 'culture' interviewer. A slim girl with dark glasses and neuroses worn like the best French scent and a Louisiana accent like one long caress – as she well knows. I went with her and Bruce Davidson, the ace *Vogue* man, very offbeat, simple, 'genuine', the James Dean type. Almost inarticulate, like a shy boy. Yet he's the highest paid man in the highest paid magazine in the States. Somehow we seemed to strike up a sort of New Wave rapport, the three of us, and there were absurd posings in front of the Seagram building. Marguerite had worked with Tennessee Williams, lived with Isherwood, knew Freddy Ayer. All this bubbled out in her sweet-acid way.

'Mah second husband was so clevah. You don't know. We had cleverness all day all night long . . . and my . . .' Her absurd indefinitely drawled 'my'.

'Come of it,' I said, 'you're putting on that accent.'

'Ah'm not.'

'You bloody well are.'

She wrinkles her pretty nose at me, as phoney as a bit of Fabergé.

We went to the Central Zoo, we all hate zoos. Dozens of shots of me in front of the polar bears. We wander out in the park and I insist on an Antonioni series – ridiculous posings and standings and idle -

---

[1] The Profumo scandal had dominated the headlines since March, when the defence minister denied in Parliament that he had had any improper relations with Christine Keeler. In June Profumo admitted that he had misled Parliament and resigned. In August Stephen Ward, the society doctor who had introduced Profumo to Christine Keeler at Lord Astor's Cliveden estate, committed suicide after he had been put on trial for living on immoral earnings.

walkings-about. I am Mastroianni and she is Vitti. Davidson gets all excited, dances about like Ariel. People on the sidewalks look at us standing rapt and alien and stand themselves looking puzzled and a bit shocked. This was great fun for me. We didn't say a serious thing and it was so light, so presto, after the heavy stuff about what did I mean by this and by that.

Got to bed about half past one and up again at 6.15 for the big thing of the week, the TV interview on the most serious programme of the day, the seven through nine *Today*. This is coast to coast, and has huge audience raitings. I was on between Saarinen's wife[1] and Bobby Kennedy, so LB are happy. I felt relaxed, no blocks, although we didn't get in as much as I would have liked.

Interview with Lewis Nichols of the *New York Times*. A stout, flabby man with the face of a huge pug-dog. He had the usual NY sour wit in its most concentrated form. I like it, this sour deflation of everyone and everything, this turning of everything naïf into something sick – the Albee syndrome. He got slightly drunk and was evidently in a bad temper with life in general. I too began to go over the edge and for about an hour we did a minor *Who's Afraid of Virginia Woolf?* – he and I, that is.[2] I became as 'vicious' about the Americans as I could. 'God, how I hate the English,' he kept on saying out of his Charles Laughton mouth. On that narrow tightrope, a well-beaten path round here, between bottle-smashing venom and don't-really-believe-me-I'm-only-kidding. However, in the end we pulled ourselves together and ended more amicably.

My book is a sort of 'in' book in New York. Everywhere I went I met people who wanted to argue about it, about what I meant – and all because one of its themes is that of impotence: sexual, physical and psychological. *Who's Afraid of Virginia Woolf?* is the same. It *obsesses* people because it is about power and impotence; not because of all the other things it is about. 'All American women want to be locked up underground,' said one lady. 'We're all in love with that monster of yours.' All this line of talk surprised me; that effect of the book was totally uncalculated. But Americans won't believe me when I say so.

Friday morning. My stomach gave out – too many clams, snails, bourbons, cigarettes. I took two overdoses of chlorodyne, and drifted most of the morning, not really aware of what was happening.

---

[1] i.e. Aline Saarinen (1914–1972), a celebrated commentator on art and architecture who was the widow of the Finnish architect Eero Saarinen (1910–1961).
[2] In Edward Albee's play, which had opened on Broadway some weeks earlier on 13 October 1963, husband and wife George and Martha drink into the early hours and, in the presence of their late-night guests fellow-academics Nick and Honey, become brutally frank about each other's failings.

Gloria Vanderbilt. Ever since the girl-woman expressed a desire to see me, eyes have gone green.[1]

'Vanderbilt!' they say. 'Good God.'

Gracie Square, an opulent tenement, up a lift that lets you straight into a hall. Round a corner. A very slim girlish creature, with greying black up-ended hair and crinkles round her dark eyes – these two things humanize her at once. That her hair isn't dyed and that she has lines of suffering. In her den, panelled in Gothic wood, a bad painting in one corner (her own) and a french window out on to a terrace. Champagne and a heap of caviare in a huge glass bowl of ice. Three editorial men from *Cosmopolitan*. The two under ones were nice quiet fellows, but the editor was too fly, too talkative, balding, glasses, eager to impress Gloria-darling. We drank champagne – every half an hour she'd slip away and bring in another magnum – and talked and gradually a sort of warmth grew up and I played the let's-be-serious game and shut the editor up a little. Gloria kept on jumping then and saying yes, yes, yes – she's plainly a woman starved of authenticity, of seriousness she can believe in, starved of being able to believe in anything, in fact. We discovered we both liked Katherine Mansfield.

'Oh, you must come and see what I have in my bedroom.' And I noticed this remark, which anywhere else in New York would have got a wisecrack over the head almost before it was finished, passed. You don't laugh at *her* naïveties. I smiled. Gloria told a story about Salinger. A friend of hers wrote to him to say that she wanted to kill herself by cutting her wrists. His answer was, 'Cut deep and hold under cold water. The blood runs faster.' She's still alive. Another story about a girl who wrote him long inarticulate letters. One day he wrote back, 'I don't think I want to know a girl who writes as badly as you do.' A few years later out came *The Catcher in the Rye*. Ever since the girl has gone around wailing, 'But they're my letters!'

She talked about Truman Capote and Oona Chaplin, her 'best friend' – she is that kind of American society girl. As a matter of fact, Vanderbilt seemed to me just about the least affected and most secure person I met in New York. Of course (to give a New York answer), boy, she can afford to be secure. Poor thing, she's only the richest girl in the world. But meeting her I found it difficult to establish a correct socialist response. Anyway, I liked her so much as an obviously sincere admirer of what I tried to do in *The Collector* (which she knew backwards) that I was off-balance from the start. We also seemed to have all the same views on art and writers.

[1] Heir to the huge Vanderbilt fortune, in 1934, aged ten years old, she was famously called 'the poor little rich girl' in a custody suit between her mother and aunt.

I had to get to the Albee play at eight, but she kept on holding us back and taking us round the apartment. More like a small palace than anything else. Upstairs to her roof garden, a film set, high over the East River, long white chairs, shrubs, statuary, and all New York spread around. Everyone struck rather silent. She put her arm through mine and pulled me round the back. 'This is where I'm a voyeur. I've got field-glasses.' There were apartment blocks all around. So we found another curious link. Then we went down to look at the lower terrace. Tugs tied to huge lighters, like insects with monstrous geometric parasites. A river of cars going along a riverside road below, a pulsing flux of bright light. All still up where we are on the terrace, almost Tibetan in its withdrawn peace. A room with a huge mantelpiece made of Louis Quinze and Seize gilded brackets, each one holding a rare pot – oddly like an interior decorating shop wall, really. Didn't come off. Round the walls hung her paintings, children standing with flowers in their hands, staring out into the room with wistful, hurt, ambiguous eyes. Like her own brown eyes. Canvases much too large, she'd get twice the effect if they were cut down. But the pastel colours and the ambiguity of the faces had a certain Matisse-like charm. They were rather better than I expected.

Then we went into her bedroom and there on her mantelpiece was a 'unique' photo ('I bought the negative') of Katherine Mansfield, looking very serious, straight, black eyes staring with a faint troubled beadiness into one's own. Gloria stood beside me and said, 'I've put these beside her because she liked them so much.' Two bits of Dresden, shepherdesses against a wall of flowers.

At her door, she takes both my hands in hers, and the others are rather embarrassed, but I know what she's trying to say, in spite of everything, in spite of everything.

Outside, in the taxi, we treat her as the famous American phenomenon she is. Or rather the others do. All these victims of too much money want to flutter out of the gilded cage for a while, and I know how to hold the door open – as have most writers ever since time began. We can liberate them for a moment and they all want to be liberated for at least a moment.

The *Cosmopolitan* boys are obviously exploiting her, and she's already stopped them putting her face on the front cover. But she wants to be a writer and I'd say she's using her name at the moment to get herself into print; is unhappy about it, but can't resist.

As if all her life she's been Cinderella at the ball. I too have felt like Cinderella all this week. A play could be written on Cinderella at the ball; and not have a child's line in it. But all glitter and anxiety. The wind suddenly blowing through the curtains, a sudden wind through the room. Then foghorns from the river below, very loud, very close. A sudden shyness, inarticulateness, she had.

Idlewild,[1] the Tati-like magic of the doors that open automatically as you approach them. In the BOAC hall, a group of three English business men, all with pipes, in brown woollen suits, all jovial. One hears a joke, roars with laughter, turns, walks away for four steps, then turns back. Such silly *little* people. I hate the aggressive virility of some American men, but this mousy-goaty insularity of the English male is nauseating. They sat in front of me all the way back, these three, making eyes at the air-hostesses, asking them unnecessary 'funny' questions. 'Is it raining outside?' (Of course at 35,000 feet it can't rain.) The hostess gives her mask smile. 'Shall I go out and see, sir?' Haw, haw, haw. Big joke with the girls.

You leave Idlewild, last light of the day, at 8 p.m. Then four hours later the dawn begins to rise over Ireland. The whole flight took just over six hours. Back at 28 Church Row, the strangeness of realizing that only nine hours before I was walking down Fifth Avenue, that it's twice as quick to get to the heart of New York from here than to travel to Venice, say, by train.

The flatness, the lack of accent in England. This is my first impression. A sort of deflatedness. America is erect, England seems prone. I am talking architecturally, really. Then the lack of power – the current's turned off suddenly, the tempo falls, the pressure goes, superman becomes man, power hardly matters, social prestige and caste take its place.

Going with Eliz to see a house she liked in the Vale of Health. I don't think I could have stood it at the best of times, but to have to see it after this experience, with its cramped rooms, its boxiness, its present petit-bourgeois décor, its whole invitation to a quiet, small life. I was feeling tired of this before America. But I know now, deeply, that I need openness, I need space. It is not England that needs to be conquered, but America. From England, but living closer to America, closer to power, to energy. We must, within our means, get some kind of décor in which I can operate as a writer in that way (to use American language). To say that the English are living in and on their history is a cliché; but this is what I felt intensely coming back here. That America and the Americans are in some obscure (and even noble) way facing up to the size and dimensions of twentieth-century man and the colossal complexity of his problems. I imagine one would have exactly the same feeling in Russia. This has nothing (in this context) to do with the size of the countries, but simply to do with the extent to which the countries are obliging the individual to face up to the problems of modern

---

[1] New York's airport, which had been built on the site of the Idlewild golf course, would shortly afterwards be renamed John F. Kennedy International Airport.

existence. This business of a living décor is not very important; but one is conditioned (I am) by the spaces one lives in. It's the rocket thing. One has to probe a wider space.

Part Ten

Escape to Lyme

30 September–4 October 1963
Cheltenham. We are in a hotel near the Town Hall, a hotel stuffed with elderly fossils, retired schoolmarms and gents, with minds of the twenties and thirties themselves embalmed in the seventies and eighties of the last century. So slow seems progress here. Cheltenham's a town of façades and nature tamed, good trees and vistas, black scrolled ironwork on fawn and beige surfaces.

The other writers here – Freddy Raphael, a voluble Jew, very like Tom Maschler, dewy-wet with intelligence, with being brief and simple, with having nothing to do with stuffiness, pretention, talk, *idées reçues*; one can't help liking this sort of bright young Jew – their caustic humanity, their impatience with mere Englishness. There's a certain throwing-out of the baby with the bathwater, of course; they dismiss too much, see too much dead wood in the past, in England.

'Gabriel Fielding',[1] also voluble, but in a pathologically extrovert way – his Catholicism breeds out of his need to confess himself. Out of any five minutes with him, four will be in the confessional, and one understands how priests get bored with even the most interesting sins. By profession he's a prison doctor. Thomas Hinde, quiet, a little self-involved, and his wife Susan Chitty, too well-named;[2] an insipid chit of a girl, really, with bright small ideas; and too much in love with names, as they all are.

For the opening panel, the state of literature today, Iris Murdoch and John Bayley joined us. Bayley was with us in Aix in 1949,[3] a frail-looking, balding, myopic man with a stammer. I remember him always glancing off on his own, a solitary, a man without blood in his veins, only the gentlest milk. The marriage with Iris Murdoch must surely be *hors de lit*, one of affection only. She is prim, rather schoolmarmishly precise, with (she implies) slightly daring opinions. 'I love Italy,' she advances, coyly,

---

[1] Gabriel Fielding was the pen name of the poet and novelist Alan Barnsley (1916–86), who had the previous year won the W. H. Smith Award for his novel *The Birthday King*.

[2] Thomas Hinde and Susan Chitty were pseudonyms too – for Sir Thomas Willes and Susan Glossop.

[3] Bayley was a contemporary of JF at New College, where he had read English. The trip to Aix was actually made in 1948. See introduction, page xiii.

like an ugly schoolgirl presenting flowers. I sat next to her at dinner, which the wretched Jolly Jack Priestley 'chaired'. He made all of us (except the Bayleys) feel sick – an embittered old man with no care for anything but getting the programme over as soon as possible. 'We're not going to discuss other writers, or publishing, or reviewing,' he said. 'It's not on.' And somehow we all meekly followed his lead like lambs, said our pieces, round once and round again, all very cold-fish; nothing got defined, people agreed and disagreed with what had not been said in the first place. All futile. He brought the programme abruptly to an end, without any discussion; a few silly words about our needing 'more love, more hope, more admiration' in literature.

I'd come with the intention of attacking Murdoch, among others, less for themselves than for the position others have hoisted them to in the temple of fame. Murdoch is in fact a gentle creature, with a good clear mind. And of course I couldn't attack her to her face. None of us attacked anything, in fact; we just talked in vague generalizations.

At the dinner Murdoch felt herself vaguely hostess. In a break in the conversation she suddenly announced, 'The greatest living woman philosopher was trodden on by a horse last week.' There was a puzzled silence. Was it a joke? A tragedy? 'Elizabeth Anscombe,' said Murdoch, with her prim smile, ambiguously.

Going round the antique shops with Raphael. I can get on better with this sort of person than the purely English writers. We agree that the good of such festivals is nil. They are pointless. I suppose some meeting with other writers is good for one, but we are all basically alone; together we aren't things I would want to write about.

Long talk with Wolf Mankowitz in the Ellenborough after the lecture he gave. Freddy Raphael was there, bubbling his ideas out. FR is like a sort of young Isaiah Berlin, a powerhouse of ideas and opinions that come rushing out. Very quick to burke, to take umbrage in a brisk intellectual-Jew's way. Mankowitz is really rather a pathetic creature underneath all the curt disparagements, the sour-sweet wit, the professional selling of himself as a success.[1] A Roman character who has to have his tongue tickled by a feather (his weaknesses revealed in such sessions – we sat around till 3 a.m. in the brown leather armchairs of the morgue-like hotel) in order to go on being a success. I said his life seemed so rich (in the bad sense of 'rich' food) that I couldn't understand how he managed to live. Then he began to spew out gobbets of regret. How he hadn't written a single thing he really liked, was always

---

[1] Wolf Mankowitz (1924–98) had made a reputation for himself as a novelist, journalist and playwright but also as a much sought after screenwriter.

doing jobs for the sake of the job. I have six islands, he said (two or three real ones and two or three houses in which he walls himself). 'And you hate bridges,' I said. 'And I hate bridges, God how I hate bridges.' He and FR (a ten times more intelligent person) both share this strange sublimation of the successful Jewish writer – a love of names, of being 'in' in the London literary and film world, of getting the best figures and having the best agents; a love of 'credits' in the film sense of that word. They both said that they were continually insecure, they don't trust anyone. I said (this is what I feel about the Americans as well, in a way), 'But it's wonderful to be a Jewish intellectual, you're free, you belong nowhere.' They like to feel rootless, of course, because Jews want always to be pitied. Later Nathaniel Tarn the poet (also a European cocktail Jew) said, 'This is the century of the Negro, the Jew and the Asiatic.'[1] I feel this. Of the rootless, the dispossessed.

Thomas Hinde. He's rather pathetic, in love with understatement and discretion, and has the typical Wykehamist love of being perversely normal, of defending the ordinary man's point of view, even in the situation where the ordinary man's a fool – nothing wrong with television, with novel reviewing, with Butlins' holiday camps. A slight man with a hunched head, like a thin grey bittern. He and his wife are poor. 'I go to bed early because Tom can't afford to buy me the drinks I like.' I felt I ought to pass over a fiver. We think it nice that he shrugs away success; and don't like her because she has a complex about it.

I 'chair' a lecture by Diana Rigg – my favourite young actress. She was Cordelia in the Scofield *Lear*.[2] A bright and sincere young woman, off the stage what she seems on; gripping my hand behind the scenes before we went on stage. 'I'm so nervous.' But she was charming and frank, and I managed to show how much I liked her. Eliz thought it was the best thing of the week. Rigg's not a pretty girl. A flat face with a snub nose, but beautiful brown and eager eyes.

Tarn (Michael Mendelson) joined us the last day there. Very 'green' about publishing, about life, really; but a wise young man, a sort of 1963 version of Thomas 'Pussy' Eliot. He writes a dense sort of throbbing poetry and leads (one feels) rather a dense sort of throbbing inner life. By profession he's an anthropologist at London University. Tall and quiet

---

[1] Born in Paris in 1928, Nathaniel Tarn spent his childhood years in Belgium, until the outbreak of the Second World War caused his family to seek refuge in England.

[2] Paul Scofield and Diana Rigg (as Cordelia) had appeared in Peter Brook's 1962 Royal Shakespeare Company production of the play at the Aldwych.

and slow to laugh. A whiff of the dandy about him, but this is pleasant.

Oxford. The Fieldings drove us over to Podge's. There, the old astringent world. The assumption that if you succeed you must have sold out. I like them to run me down, to take me down a peg or two. A furious argument between Podge and Eileen about Cathy, who's going round with a group of young 'beats' – 'poets without poetry' Eileen says. Podge thinks they're contemptible because they're irrational and politically nil. The other teenagers call Cathy's group the Pseuds, Cathy's group calls the middle-class others the Bloodies.

Podge insisting on paying for a meal out to which I'd invited them. I can see it makes him happy, he'll having something to complain out.

Murdoch, *A Severed Head*. Everyone, including myself, is forever running her down, but this is really a very funny book, a bit of Freudian *marivaudage* that comes off perfectly.[1] Something of the abstract about it, cool and geometric and even poetic in a way. An artistic triumph, if not a literary or human one.

11 October
Bad days. Eliz in despair because we can't find another place to live, me the same because I'm right in the mood to go on with *The Magus*, but I can't – not when everything is unsettled, undetermined. We've seen two or three possible ones among a host of impossibles. I think I'm hardening towards a house in the country, mainly because at least one has space there. Eliz fancied a house in Canonbury – 15 Canonbury Road – fine in itself, but the road is used by the long-distance lorries, and it seems insane to me, to choose such a position when one knows one will be at home all day – and trying to write. It enrages her that my priority isn't the getting of a house, it enrages me that her priority isn't giving me the time (or peace) to finish *The Magus*. So we live at cross-purposes.

18 October
Another house – perhaps. 44 Southwood Lane, Highgate. It's a 1780 peasant's cottage, very small, but pretty. £7,500.

---

[1] Murdoch's 1961 novel, which was adapted for the stage by J. B. Priestley in 1962, took a satirical look at middle-class morality. Wine merchant Martin Lynch-Gibbon has been having an affair with a young academic for some time, but is none the less shocked when his wife tells him that she wants to leave him, having had her own secret affair with her psychoanalyst.

22 October

Going round Hampstead with Jud Kinberg. Looking for locations. He's a nice New York Jew, expatriate: 'I live in limbo.' Takes hundreds of photos, mostly at the wrong angles, for the director, to see. Coming home, we saw a sturdy little woman carting a heavy suitcase down the other side of the road. It was Iris Murdoch. I went over and said hello: 'We met at Cheltenham.' She flushed a little, absurdly gauche, as if she had been caught smuggling marijuana. 'It's my college, I've got to sit for a portrait.'[1] 'We've read *A Severed Head*,' said Eliz. 'It was meant to be funny?' 'Well, mm,' said Murdoch, going red again, 'half.'

The way we drift – getting up and going to bed (and making love) when we like. This seems to me the only decent life. *Sans* programme, *sans* routine.

24 October

'Tarn' comes in sometimes nowadays. He really is rather humourless; more than a shade precious. Too self-serious, in short. Suddenly today he said, 'My name's not Mendelson, really. It's Stavrogy.' And then a little later, 'There's a possibility that I shall come into a peerage. I may have to change my name again.' Sometimes I find him hard to believe. He admits that his parents and in-law parents (all Jews) are rich, and support him 'in kind, thought not in cash'. At the moment he 'can't work, can't think' and has fainting-fits. 'I may seem quite normal with you,' he said, 'but if I go back to work on Monday, I shall probably not be able to face it.' He spoke as if the delicacy of his own mechanism was really rather a miracle.

Eliz and I are a sort of unpaid, unhallowed pair of Catholic priests. People who come here seem to start talking about themselves automatically. Without our even asking questions (not that we aren't expert at breaking through people's façades anyway, now). There's evidently something inherently confessional about us.

8 November

Lovely dawn. A fierce north-westerly gale, torn grey rags of cloud and rifts of very clear white, lemon and tawny sky. London a vast sparkle of light, orange and blue, pearl-towers, diamonds; the tall blocks shadowy, the downs and hills around all visible, the wind had swept things so clean. The whole dawn city sparkling and as lovely as a young woman in the new light and wind.

*

---

[1] Iris Murdoch was a philosophy tutor at St Anne's College, Oxford.

If I had been Adam I should have enjoyed the Fall. Discovery is always a release.

A novelist is a kind of charlatan, and his science is like alchemy.

9 November
The Magus. It's been lying in the land since May. It will go, though I must cut down the philosophy. Nothing like that craft-joy – the plunging back into one's own unique world, one's people, one's words. Conchis, Lily, Alison, Nicholas Urfe, they stand in the book and watch me. I have this strange feeling – they are mine and yet I am theirs. If I do certain things to them, they cease to be mine. A critic, a non-creator, might say that this is simply the logic of characterization. But the relationship *is* emotional; there are things one cannot do to one's characters for logical reasons; there are also things one cannot do to one's friends.

19 November
Weekend in Ashtead with D and M. They live in a sort of limbo; a grimly trite suburban house full of furniture not theirs, of objects so ugly that they scratch their nails down the optic nerve; a vista of other such houses, wet leaves, grey skies; only the television between one and insanity. Eliz thinks that M is essentially suburban; certainly she seems rather aggressively to seek this sort of life. Whether out of obscure pique against life (that it hasn't let her be an actress), out of hatred of 'southern' pretentiousness; or whether because they've overspent so in the past and lived in a dreamworld, it's difficult to say. It still seems a dreamworld in many ways; their driftingness, their very weak sense of time, leave me feeling always a day behind. I want to stand up and walk briskly somewhere, pulling them with me. Denys remains his parfit, gentle self. He'll arrive a minute late on Judgement Day, but put up the best performance of us all.

On Sunday night we came back to Chelsea to go to a party at John Kohn's, for all the American film people in London. It was empty, void, because all the 'important' people there were empty and void. Wyler[1] looked grey and harassed, shifty-eyed, mouth full of clichés. I was introduced to Sam Spiegel, the mogul of moguls. 'A great book you wrote,' he said, and went back to what he was saying. Stanley Mann was there being hurt (as always) by my rejection of this world. He keeps on talking about *Mr* Wyler, as if he's Eisenstein, Griffith and René Clair all in one.

---

[1] i.e. the Hollywood film director William Wyler (1902–81), who had won Oscars for *Mrs Miniver* (1942), *The Best Years of Our Lives* (1946) and *Ben Hur* (1959), and would soon direct the film version of *The Collector*.

They're Egyptian, these film people, totally unable to question rank, power and money.

The big trouble now is that Frankovich, head of Columbia over here, wants Samantha Eggar to play Miranda. None of the others want her; but they think F will have his way.

Jud's an island of sanity in this world, with a nice Jewish sourness about himself and the rest of us – a sourness that seems to come out of a fundamentally well-balanced character. He goes with the Hollywood view of life, of course, in many superficial things, but deep down he manages to live with it and see through it. We also like his wife Suzanne, who once acted in Jouvet's[1] company. When she 'auditioned' for him, he sat and watched her put herself so much into her role that she cried. He went up to her and looked at the tears on her face; then sneered. *'C'est l'assistance qu'il faut faire pleurer. Pas vous.'*

I made a whole series of mistakes with this film business: selling too soon and too low; not retaining rights; not getting Stanley Mann off the script (which I might have done if I'd been ruder); and continuing to be involved in it. The film is dead, before it's been born.

22 November

Assassination of Kennedy. The shock, of course, is the shock of death; not the shock of the death of the 'leader of the Western World', not all the pious things the officials of the world are saying. It amazes me that there are not more such assassinations. Kennedy stands for success in a capitalist society – for money, happiness, power, all apotheosized in one man in a world obsessively orientated towards those things; and in a world largely without them. The secret desire to shatter the dream, or the few who have realized the dream, is ubiquitous. It is a desire to exhibit basic equality: I = you. It is more than Kennedy who was killed – these war-brokers in the brain of capitalism, of the agora society. His own society pulled the trigger; not Lee Oswald.[2]

26 November

I'm revising *The Aristos* for publication – submission, anyway. The Kennedy business confirms so many things in it. I feel a kind of mournful rage that I can't explain it all in public – the gag across my mouth, since no one will publish anything I say.

Newspaperman (1960): 'Why do you want to be President?'
Kennedy: 'Because that's where the power is.'

---

[1] i.e. Louis Jouvet (1887–51), the celebrated French actor and theatre impresario.
[2] Kennedy was assassinated at 12.30 p.m. on 22 November. His suspected assassin Lee Harvey Oswald was arrested later on the same day, but murdered two days later by Jack Ruby while still in police custody.

John Wilkes Booth (before he assassinated Lincoln): 'I must have fame
– *fame*!'
Ruby (Oswald's assassin). His sister said of him: 'He's admired every
President so much. That's been the trouble.'
Jackie Kennedy: 'I want the funeral to be as Lincolnesque as possible.'
(How much this says of the American sickness!)

29 November
The penalty of being too realistic. With *The Collector* I've suffered because
I gave Miranda too exactly the language and ideas of a girl of her age
and background; whereas most, even 'realist', writers cheat. They speak
themselves through their characters, and *sans* mask.

6.15 p.m. I think I have finished *The Aristos*.

Le Grand Meaulnes.[1] This is the first time I have read it. A strange experience, Crusoe-like, seeing those footprints on the sand, knowing that
after all one is not the first on this island. Because the green ghost behind
every line in *Le GM* is brother to that I want in *The Magus*. Fournier's
work is conceived in aquarelle terms, mine in cinematic ones (not *of course*
that I'm writing the book for the film of the book, but it's absurd to
pretend that the cinema, especially the fantastic-romantic-poetic cinema
– Cocteau, Bunuel's *Crusoe*, Antonioni, and the rest – can't influence one's
writing deeply); but the purpose is the same. Mystery, pure mystery. A key
to *Le GM* – its being based on a solid peasant-village background.
  The secret of its force is that the symbolical psychological truth is so
great that it carries all the surface improbabilities. It could have been
even more fantastic than it is; and we could still have believed. This
gives me courage.

3 December
The Aristos. Now Eliz and I are delousing it. That is, removing priggishnesses,
pomposities, preachings, what she calls 'platforms'. The tone of voice I
want is a sort of ageless, unvoguish one; pure independence; and I'm
prepared to risk accusations of pretentiousness to get it. Because in this
benighted and malicious age to claim independence is to be pretentious.
I also want this to be an international book, a pamphlet for no one country;
and so I have tried to avoid being English for the sake of English critics.

*

---

[1] In Alain-Fournier's 1913 novel, the seventeen-year-old Augustin Meaulnes
discovers a mysterious *'domaine perdu'*, where he falls in love with the beautiful
Yvonne de Galais. But once he has left, he is unable to find the *domaine* again,
although he spends the rest of his life searching for it.

Evening with Bob Parrish and his wife at Egerton Crescent.[1] They have rented the house, which is full of antiques and yards of oil painting. It was quite a nice evening. A Mr Goldstein, who had a yacht in Malta and the quiet calm Buddha-like egomania of the Hollywood mogul. 'My father was called No-gun Goldstein,' he said. 'I was born in Arizona. You had to carry a gun there.' A wistful little man as he said it. His spectacles pushed up on to his bald forehead. He was trying in an over-mogul-like way to lay Sarah Miles. A pretty, pert creature, with a large white dog. 'My mother would never let me have pets.' A coarse, gargling sort of laugh a sort of heat cased in steel and porcelain. Neil Paterson, some scriptwriter,[2] and his Scots wife. We like Bob and Cathy Parrish, and Sarah Miles seemed a nice enough kid. She was an early candidate for Miranda – not my idea of her, but she could have made something of the part, I think. 'I look naked' – some scene in *The Servant* – 'but actually I had something stuffed under the towel to make my poor little tits stick out.' That sort of dry-hoarse, faintly vicious tone, is most her 'personality' probably. The truth is that all these 'stars' are soiled by the film world so young that only an unknown could possibly play Miranda.

Later, Paterson and his wife took us up to their suite in the Hilton Hotel and the nice evening turned sour. He'd already seemed to me a sold-out man and I disliked the way he tried to sell a film idea to Sarah Miles: 'I'll be honest with you, Sarah . . .', 'Listen, Sarah . . .', 'I'll write in something you can get your teeth into, Sarah . . .' He'd never met her before.

Somehow over the whisky in the Hilton we got involved in 'professional writing' ('All I care about is doing a good story') and 'committed writing' ('What the hell right has anyone [i.e., J. Fowles] to get a message over'). He seemed to be a fuddled, warm-hearted, embittered Scot. Vague talk about Truth and Beauty and 'broad-based radicalism'. He was deeply shocked and hurt that I should not see he was a 'liberal'. I was 'intolerant', because I said I could never be really friendly with a Tory or a Christian. 'Of course I'd never put my writing above the human relationships around me.' I said I would. 'But being a writer is being kind to the people around you.' I said I loved humanity, but most of the specimens of it around me made me sick. Eliz was wisest, and never said a word: 'I felt too sick.'

Home at 4.30 a.m. The nice simplicity of the taxi man; quiet and tired and just a workman. The film world stinks.

---

[1] Robert Parrish (1916–1995) was a Hollywood editor who became a director and worked mostly in Britain during the 1960s.

[2] Paterson (1915–) was most well known for writing the script of *Room at the Top* (1959), for which he received an Academy Award.

3 January 1964
These last two or three months I've been reading mostly Emily Dickinson.
LB sent me the *Complete Poems*. She is beyond any doubt or competition
our greatest woman poet. (In the language.) I find she constantly
humbles, first by her firmity of purpose, second by her skill with words.
One gets in her that acute ivory-working kind of creativity that is so
touching and admirable in Jane Austen – these two make such a fine
pair. I find her rhetoric very magnetic, too; the apophthegms and new
coinings and abuses of syntax, the neat skewering of subtle perceptions.
Her 'difficulty' is exaggerated. I've read Johnson and Chase on her,[1]
but one needs only a very elementary command of her 'vocabulary' and
catalogue of symbols to understand; and in the end one seems to understand her rather better than any other woman who has ever lived – to
know her better and to sympathize with her better. For me she is very
like Catullus, in this proximability. One can't imagine knowing her any
better – however many trivial details about the life might be discovered
– and one can't imagine any art but poetry giving this knowledge. She
proves poetry, in fact. Finally, in the context of the (our) fullest humanity,
there is only poetry. The other arts fall off somewhere below. We have
to spend most of our lives below, so this is no dismissal of the other
arts. But they can be burnt off poetry; and poetry can't be burnt off
them.
A diminishing essence in her quality – her genius for first lines and
a good deal less than genius with last ones. All her poems, almost all,
taper away, end with a sort of semantic whimper. Of all the chains that
shackle her the ghost of the Really Bad Woman Poetess is the most
sinister – not just the flat-arse smacks into stock Victorian piety and the
waftings into whimsy, but the way her basic material, words, simply won't
stand the twisting and compressing she gives.
An analogy no one seems to have used with her is that of quilt-work;
but all her poetry seems patchwork-quilted, bits sewn together, sometimes with ravishingly fresh and subtle effects, and sometimes lament-
ably botched and *criard* in the matching.
'Kinsmen': clear foreshadowing of the noösphere. So much in her
foreshadows – technically, philosophically (pure existentialism, some of
her thought), and emotionally. I'm timeless, she manages to hint
(though never directly says), because the thing is the battle between me
and my predicament and the exact features of my predicament are only
my imagery, not my truth. Her imagery is the most improbably attractive, to me; it consists mainly of beliefs that I find absurd, and yet, and
yet, again and again she gives it some twist that makes it unimportant

---

[1] Thomas H. Johnson, *Emily Dickinson: An Interpretative Biography* (Belknap Press,
Cambridge, MA, 1955); Richard Chase, *Emily Dickinson* (Methuen, 1952).

whether her Christian beliefs mean anything or not – what matters is what *she means* in her situation.

I haven't felt so influenced for years.

12 January

We now own Southwood Lane. It has some charm, especially the narrow sloping garden between brick walls and the ground-floor garden-room with its Adam fireplace and carved wood. The plumbers have found a lot of woodworm – inevitable, I suppose, in a house that old.

15 January

Podge has sent me a copy of *Marxism Today*. And I've just read Carew Hunt's attack on the creed – a very impresive one. The obviousness of what is silly in Marxism is only equalled by the obviousness of its virtues. Has there ever been a philosophy so *clearly* good and bad? I suppose a lot of *The Aristos* counts as Marxist – or will be counted so. But there are several impossibilities, for me, in Marxism: alienation theory, dialectic theory and ethical theory (or absence of it) being the great unswallowables.

The dull job remains the dull job, whatever socio-economic aim or framework it is given. It is not the capitalist who finally exploits the worker; it is the work itself. Of course man is alienated; and for many of the reasons Marx gives (so also his remedies, or recommended alterations of the present system, are good); but to suggest that anything can alter the fundamental situation of a man faced with the necessity of doing unpleasant work is ridiculous.

The dialectic – a dialectic is like an infinity. To suggest that there is a perfect state, an end, to which the dialectic points, is logical suicide. Of course reality is dialectic (or can conveniently be assumed – relatively, man-wise – to be so), and of course it cannot suddenly become adialectic. This utopianism again.

Ethical theory (Leninism): Communists place themselves here in the same sort of strait-jacket as Christians who defend dogma.

But the worst strait-jacket of the lot is surely the language Communists find themselves obliged to use – all that clogged, soiled jargon that clings round basically simple and clean ideas.

There's a key article on alienation in the January *Marxism Today*. 'Common ownership restores true human relations in industry so that all the faculties and powers of the individual are developed.' But the job won't change. The *thing* won't change, whatever the climate of society. 'The essence of man is "the ensemble of the social relations", concrete man in society, and not isolated but living in fellowship.' But this is rampant anti-individualism, both in terms of what actually is (man must always be an island in many ways entire unto himself) and what the Marxists would like to be (man forced to be 'concrete in society').

26 January

Dinner with the Kinbergs. Wyler was there, a wizened, worried man, hopelessly bad at explaining himself. He doesn't know whether to use a happy or a sad ending or not, and gave me a long and gratuitous spice about what dictated the choice: 'My art is working in the limits of what the public will pay to see.' He ran down *Ben Hur*, thank God. I like his indecisiveness and self-frankness; and that everyone else feels affection for him. Apparently Goldwyn once said of him: 'He needs a daddy.'

Story about Wyler. He did forty takes of one small sequence of a boy walking through snow. 'For God's sake,' said his producer, who was watching, 'they're all the same.' 'I'm waiting for him to trip,' said Wyler.

Dinner at Claridge's with William Wyler. It wasn't very enjoyable, perhaps because Wyler himself is a bit too complex and untypical to be dismissable as just another Hollywood megalomaniac. We were the only people in the restaurant, and sat surrounded by a dozen or so waiters, wine-waiters and an all-sorts mixture of *maîtres d'hôtel*, who stood in a semi-circle about fifteen feet away and solemnly stared at us. As Wyler is deaf in his right ear and has to be almost shouted at, our meal was about as private as a *coucher du roi* at Versailles. The flunkification of life at a hotel like Claridge's is absurd, of course, and one has to suspect the sort of person who stays there of far worse things than mere wanting to throw money away. It's the décor as much as the bill for the décor that reveals the way of life. Wyler is full of these ambivalences – as confused as the pettiest petty bourgeois over ordering wine, diffident about all sorts of things, groping his way through life, but then suddenly arrogant, 'big' in the traditional Hollywood style. A soft, muffled kind of arrogance, but unmistakable.

Apparently he's not happy about the film treatment, and wants me to look at it; but I suspect Jud Kinberg and John Kohn would prefer me not to.

'What's the girl die for?' he kept on half-moaning. 'That audience is just going to say, "What happened, why'd she die?"'

He has a creased face, and soft hazel eyes, lugubrious, probing, as if he's starved of reassurance, perpetually in doubt.

The night before he'd had dinner with Princess Margaret. Apparently she said that she liked Wyler's film *Roman Holiday* – which was based on her affaire with Townsend – and that she especially liked the happy ending.

Wyler: The happy ending, ma'am?

M: The way she got her man in the end.

Wyler: But excuse me, they never saw each other again, ma'am.

M: Oh yes they did. I remember very well.

'I didn't argue any more,' said Wyler to us, with an aren't-royals-sweet smile. 'She saw it her way, and her man was sitting right opposite.'

My anti-royal feeling irritates him, as it does most Americans. I suggested a little scene in the film, Clegg would put up cheap coloured photos of the Queen and Philip Glucksburg[1] in the cellar, which the girl, of course, would remove as soon as she saw them. 'Oh, no,' said Wyler, 'what d'you think people would say when this horrible man put a photo of your queen on the wall and it's the girl who takes it down?' Poor Tom Paine, he must turn a lot in his grave these days.

4 February
A fascinating little pamphlet on Hardy by his ex-parlourmaid (*The Domestic Life of Thomas Hardy*, the Toucan Press, Beaminster, 1963). The unrelieved gloom of Max Gate in the last years has to be seen through such obviously truthful eyes to be believed. *Per ardua ad atra!*[2]

Whenever I am on a bus, in a train, I have extreme-situation fantasies – I see myself locked up, stranded for eternity, with the people around me. This is why I dislike other people so much. It is a mechanism that I can't rid myself of. Just as I reduce sexual fantasies to exactly the same situation, the cellar, the desert island, the car in the snow.

5 February
Curious winter – every day for days now has been almost cloudless, the weather like late March more than anything else. I did 'our' walk alone from Wendover through Hampdenleaf Wood to Missenden. A cold wind, but out of it, it was warm enough to sit and read. Not that I did, the only words I had with me were this month's *Encounter*; as diastrously stuffy and silly a number of it as I can remember. The intellectual-literary scene in this country is desperately sick – played out, small beer at best, and now flat small beer into the bargain.

But the country was very clean, very clear. Sad how the birds have gone, after last winter's disaster.[3] The corvidae and the blackbirds have come through well. Two or three flocks of chaffinches, one at least a hundred strong. I heard greenfinches. One pair of great tits. One coal tit. But plenty of blue tits and, surprisingly, marsh tits – I saw seven or

---

[1] Until he renounced his Greek royal titles and became a naturalized Briton in 1947, Prince Philip's family name was Schleswig-Holstein-Sonderburg-Glucksburg.
[2] 'Through hard work to the depths!'
[3] The British winter of 1963 had been one of the coldest in living memory.

eight. No long-tailed – they will take years to recover. Plenty of hedge-sparrows. One nuthatch heard. But no woodpeckers at all. No goldfinches. No larks. No pipits. No hawks. No pigeons.

A cock bullfinch on top of a hawthorn bush, biting the buds, toppling, against the clear blue sky. An intense soft carmine against that intense soft blue. Breathtaking, such moments.

I watched a man burn a field – a great bow-shaped sheet of orange flame eating into the beige stubble, with the dim green-blue hills behind, the white-grey smoke drifting up and the fiercely eager sound of the fire-crackle. I could hear that sinister crepitation long after I had disappeared into the trees.

In the deepest part of the woods, a hare.

I walked all day, saw hardly a soul. Then London at five in the evening, all the people going home from work, the office blocks, the buses, the neon lights, the urbanity of things. No other age but ours will know how strange the leap between this world and that world of the ageless winter trees.

28 February

The Aristos. Still with Cape. Anthony S says that the other MS hasn't arrived in New York. It 'seems to have got lost'. I despair.

Larkin, *The Whitsun Weddings.* Larkin, thank God, is an English poet, not just a poet in English. I recognize in myself, without much liking, the same deep-dyed melancholia; surely still an intensely climatic thing. And a pleasurable thing too, of course – the lovely dark dinginess of the English provinces, the backstreet blues, the pervasive palpable futility of existence. Larkin's characteristic 'spine' is: Things are bad; but (last stanza) not so bad as I've made them seem. This is very English. The scorpion-tail in our pessimism.

2 March

Tom M 'quite likes' *The Aristos.* He thinks Cape will publish. The loss of the MS sent to America, and the luke-warmness over here, is depressing. It is long past the time when I ought to have been getting on with *The Magus,* but I feel too stale to do so. This last winter's been a drag; mild and interminable. And working for oneself has all sorts of complications – moodiness; lack of exercise; literary doubts; isolation; no discipline. We go to bed at all hours, get up never before ten, usually later. *The Collector* keeps on coming back into my life, which irritates me. I've just spent two days on the latest 'treatment' from Hollywood. Much better than the one I saw last August. But I loathe having to get involved in all that again.

10 March

Jud Kinberg telephoned from Hollywood. They want me out there for a fortnight. I fly on Saturday.

The Aristos has arrived in New York. Bach is enthusiastic.[1]

America, 16–31 March

Los Angeles. Silver-pink towers in a honey-coloured evening air. Palm-trees. Tall trees, a sprout of leaves, and 'beards'. The great flow of power up and down the freeways, easy and controlled and fast – everywhere this characteristic American mode of moving, a sort of inherent jet-age tempo that you see in the way a young man crosses the street or a chair is designed – even static objects have this laconic muscled flow.

Jud Kinberg is his usual nice warm Jewish self; he pours words about Wyler and his 'junta' (special advisers), the script battles, Samantha Eggar's troubles and their troubles with her.

I am luxuriously ensconced in a hotel on the Sunset Strip, with a view south over the whole of LA. The night view is very beautiful, a spill of endless jewels glittering in limpid air, as in clear oil; green, red, blue, yellow, white bursts and chains and towers of light that stretch as far as one can see. This is the mad, rich woman America; with the courage of her convictions, her rich madness.

The hotel room is in mustard-yellow and Louis-something imitation furniture. A sliding glass door leads out on to a patio-balcony with a sort of Maltese-cross-fretted balustrade, blue breeze blocks walling it off from the other balconies. A basket of fruit, compliments of the management. A radio let into the bedside table; a television set; air-conditioning; a bathroom with countless buttons and handles. This environmental comfort of living is sickly overeasy; at the end of twenty-four hours it becomes irritatingly necessary-seeming, like a whore who has one by the senses only.

Morning. Waking up early to the sound of birds, like thrushes, but super-thrushes; the voice of the girl on room service, as mechanically sweet as a saccharine tablet ('Thank you for calling room service and please consider yourself welcome to call any other time') – all responses seem learnt by rote – or tape-recorded, like the singing birds. A sparrow's chirp comes as a kind of pleasant reassurance.

Breakfast. The thermoserver coffee-pot; and the drip-cut honey-pot.

Going up alone to SE's room to meet her. She's a slim creature, pale green eyes, no make-up, nice red hair (natural); not very pretty, because

---

[1] Julian Bach was JF's American agent.

she totally lacks any life. I expected someone much brassier, but this
lifeless creature really made me feel rather sorry. Some mysterious incident took place at Peter Sellers's last night (I've just learnt) – Sam was
'badly treated'. Certainly she behaved like someone suffering from colli-
sion shock.

I walked round her room while she sat on a couch and watched me
in a manner halfway between fright and boredom. Exchange of polite
nothings. A roomwaiter brought a Pimms for her and a lager for me. I
sat by her and tried to thaw her out; but it seemed impossible.

She is so remote from my conception of Miranda – or anyone else's
– that I can't imagine Wyler doing anything with her. The essential thing
– life, intelligence, an eager thrust – she seems to lack completely, both
in looks and mind. But various aspects of her past suit her casting: her
parents are separated, daddy's a brigadier, she had two years at art school
(father wouldn't allow the stage), she's had an affaire with a much older
man – but the vital spark isn't there.

The two things that are wrong with Hollywood: the too much money,
the enormous surplus that has to be wasted; and the belief that showbiz
is the same as art.

There have been fires all night and the Santa Ana, the local mistral,
has been blowing; this morning a great pall of smoke lies over the city.
It has a sinister pink-grey colour, though it smells nice, of brushwood
and aromatic shrubs. Thirty-one houses have been burnt and a telly
pundit talked a lot of rubbish about Los Angeles still being a frontier
city and Californians a frontier people. 'We may not carry guns and
wear the buckskin jacket any more but . . .' This kind of cant is very
American. The idea that this is a frontier city is hilariously silly.

All day there are ashes in the air; people's eyes smart. I listened to
Jud's secretary at the studio talking to a friend over the phone: 'Gee,
the fires are bad this morning. They really made my eyes bug out.' John
Kohn had heard about someone who had 'slipped all the silverware in
the swimming-pool' – normal practice out here, it seems. Like living in
a permanent Pompeii.

John Kohn took me down to the studio through an endless area of
tall palms, parking-lots and bizarrely exuberant cinemas and amusement
places. The studio is rather tatty; like a factory, in feel. A lot of machinery,
a lot of mechanicals; no room anywhere for art. When we finally went
into a large studio and came on the set for *The Collector*, built in the
middle of the huge floor, it seemed a very small kernel for such a big
nut. It's the only current Columbia production here.

The cellar they've built looks like the crypt of some thirteenth-century
chapel – wildly implausible. And they've furnished it out with a sort of
queasy attempt at luxury that may be a parody or may, one feels, be
Hollywood's idea of what a nice furnished cellar ought to look like. I

went round it picking out faults. Nobody really listens to criticisms, for two reasons – a sort of instinctive trade unionism, a deep Hollywood belief that each man does his own job and never interferes in anyone else's, and a sort of inability to concentrate. Everyone works under pressure or likes to give that impression. The absence of leisurely amateurism, from which all great art finally springs – that is, an insistence on taking pains, not compromising and the rest – is the most frightening thing here. Terry and Sam said on the way back tonight: 'We'd be shooting by now in an English studio. We'd be on the floor.' They meant that this aimless mulling over and pressuring of simple operations is really constipating, not liberating.

We sat round a long wooden table in a corner of the studio. Willie Wyler, Sam, myself, Jud, Bob Swink the editor, John Kohn, Terry. Terry is splendid, a lovely quick-thinking and highly articulate Cockney lad, sensitive and aggressive. After the first scene I said I thought he was too aggressive and he immediately read it through again with a wonderful dead monotony. He keeps on flashing out ideas about the part, trying out lines – he has absolute command of his voice, in contrast to poor Sam, who reads like a high-school understudy. Terry feeds her so well that he ought to be the easiest man to do dialogue with. But she constantly hits false notes, gets wrong emphases, and the one quality we're all looking for, a sort of warm eagerness, just doesn't appear. Instead of flashing genuine anger, she has a sort of debby petulance; instead of genuine sorrow, a B-feature pathos. This is the sad fact: she's a B-feature starlet, as she is. Terry completely outclasses her – she keeps on looking at his exuberant explosions of ideas and mimickings with a sort of little-girl admiration.

Willie is the biggest kerfuffler. He doesn't hear half of what we say and keeps on cutting into discussions with a remark about the discussion before. Many of his 'feelings about the script' are absurd. The girl must be kidnapped by day, must walk in the garden by day. 'I'm not going to do any night shooting.' Kohn shoots hot blue glances round the table when Willie isn't looking – you see, you see, this is what I'm up against. Bob Swink, part of the Wyler junta, nods, laughs, says, 'I agree'; and contributes nothing. Wyler's method isn't all loss; I see that he is a kind of cross between Rumplestiltskin and Socrates – he worries sleepily at things and sometimes he makes a point. And he's good at cutting the dialogue right down to essentials. Sam and Terry get very restless; Sam looks bored and tired, Terry begins to guy the whole thing, putting on a Tommy Steele accent and staring at Wyler with an absolutely straight face as he says lines absurdly.

After the day's session I sat with Terry in Sam's car and we had a long talk. The more I see of him the more I like him. He talked about Sam ('She and I used to live together. She was always trying to correct my

English, that's what's so funny.'). He wanted Sarah Miles to act with him. 'I did the same scene with both of them for their tests – Sarah was wonderful, Carl Foreman told Frankovich so, but he wouldn't listen.' He also thought Julie Christie could have done it.

An evening with Jud, looking for an apartment for Suzanne. I have to tell him that Sam hates Suzanne and mistrusts him. A painful business, as he takes it rather hard; but everyone lives in a mist of misconceptions about one another here. They're mostly centered on Sam, whose coldness and mistrust and fear of everyone and everything around is really rather alarming. She has a strange way of looking at you absolutely without expression, as if she's damned if *you*'re going to get a response. She does it with everyone.

Terry's current mistress; a very charming little French girl, Annie Fargé, a leading soubrette on TV here; he treats her outrageously in his style and calls her my 'fucking French bit' to her face, and she wrinkles her monkey face and kisses him. Terry has created a sort of dream lifestyle for himself. He says whatever comes into his head, does what he likes, lives like a sort of Hamlet without neurosis, eternally white-shirted, open-throated, thrusting, on the crest of the wave.

The awful American-English language problem. Anything that wouldn't be comprehensible to the average American moron Willie objects to. Today we cut 'An ash tree a foot tall is still an ash tree.' All long words are taboo. We had the line (Paston's): 'I did it to exorcize you from my life.' 'Exorcize, exorcize,' said Willie. 'Who's ever going to be able to say that – we need another line.' 'I did it to get you out of my system,' I suggested. Yes, that was fine. But Willie kept on saying it over and over again. 'Out of my system, out of my system, OUT of my SYSTEM. That sounds kind of peculiar.' About twenty minutes later, we ended up with 'I did it to get you out of my mind.' Everything has to be mish-mashed to a smooth banality.

Phone call from Boston from Ned Bradford. He will publish. A publicity man from Columbia wanted to know about this next book. I had to spell existentialism for him. 'Jesus,' he said.

Phone call this evening from New York. Julian Bach. He was nice and enthusiastic about the book, about everything. East Coast Americans seem delightfully sane and fresh and European after this town of can't and never saying what you really mean.

I've just read the latest script. It has a lot of rubbish from the past re-incorporated. Far worse than the one I read in February. It is this insane tacking from bad to worse to better to even worse that makes one doubt the seriousness of everyone here. They discuss so much that nothing is allowed to stand; perpetuum mobile.

Sam took me in to the studio this morning, as John Kohn had to go in early to see Wyler. Her car wasn't waiting for her when she came down. She flew into a sudden filthy temper: 'In future I want my car out here when I say.'

'I'm sorry, lady,' said the car-fetcher, 'there's a jam at this time of day.'

'I don't care what there is. I want my car out here when I say.' And she slammed the door in the man's face.

I gave her a look and said, 'Relax.'

But she didn't. On the way there she talked about Terry. 'He won't talk to me, he hasn't said a word to me for a year now.' He's badly cast, she thinks. 'So many people tell me I'm ideal for the part.' I threw her a startled look at that; it seemed too much. But she won't admit that anyone else knows what's wrong. 'This part is so terribly important for my career.' She looked prettier today, but as human as a mannequin in a shop window.

Wyler explained to me at length – every sentence, however short, takes him about a minute to get out – why he wants to change the ending. Now it's the 'Double Cellar' (the sequences have names – the 'Statement', the 'Aunt Annie', the 'Whitcomb' – which people hurl around like chunks of rock). 'That girl's got to hold the gun over the boy in the end. People feel angry if they don't see the man with the gun disarmed at the end.' Basically Willie's mind works on the Western level: Shane must triumph.

Willie has a Punch nose and soft hazel eyes that search continually, like some small animal, a marmot or something, first for your encouragement and then for your betrayal. Every so often he spits out, gets petulant. At first sight he seems to avoid the homage and awe directors of his stature inspire in all the lesser men in the hierarchy; then every so often he uses it to get some victory. He reminds me slightly of Queeg in *The Caine Mutiny* – a sort of half-mad, half-inspired captain who one day is going to get court-martialled.

So far the film has cost two million dollars; that's about one and a half million more than it should have done.

Terry on the set is rather alarming, as he dances around inventing 'business'. He acts very Method-style, like a Cockney James Dean, and makes the boy impossibly appealing and charming at times. Most girls would give their all to get in a cellar with him.

John and Jud and I had a script conference all afternoon, constantly interrupted by props men, costume men, an actress to play Aunt Annie, Uncle Tom Cobbley and all. I try to get some sense into the sets and décor, but it's hopeless. All the electrical equipment is madly un-English; the furniture is flagrantly American; the clothes the same. The English art director, John Stoll, is a wash-out.

John Kohn dominates all the script conferences – he shouts and argues and pours out his ideas. He's like a sort of pipe of power; his voice and energy never tire, while Jud has awful moods, and they keep on snapping at each other. However, ghastly as the script conferences I had with them in London seemed, here they are comparatively creative. One actually gets things written and decided. Of course Willie will probably shoot them all down tomorrow. Both of the boys have wild ideas – wildly implausible, and I spend miserable hours shooting down their 'ideas' – not that I say much, but they have to explain their point of view at such gigantic length, as if I might not have understood what was obvious in the first place.

There's a sort of calculating machine feel about all script discussion; things are shifted round at such fantastic speed that I am often left hopelessly behind. At first this is very impressive, but then one realizes it comes from a complete dissociation from the characters and the story as a living organism. It's as if one group of people treated flowers as flowers and another, as machinery.

When Willie has some particularly doubtful point to make he turns to the editor, Bob Swink, and says with gusto, 'Right?' and Swink shouts back like a bouncing ball, 'Right!' Kohn takes a deep breath and Willie turns to the next page.

Willie, looking at the work of various art students, candidates for Miranda's drawing work: 'Aw, what the hell, let's get the one with the big tits.' The only thing that lets one know he is teasing is a mischievous monkey grin that comes two or three seconds later.

'We've written a new scene, Willie,' said John Kohn very earnestly the other day. 'Yeah,' said Willie. 'Got a new director too?'

Terry on the set, muttering to me. 'If they change the fucking end I'm off. That'll be the end all right.' He told me in strict confidence that he nearly didn't come here. He only signed his final contract last Friday, and had already booked an air ticket to Greece. 'I was going to fucking well disappear. This film's such a fucking bore.' Like all Cockneys his 'fuckings' are without venom; just the equivalent of the middle-class 'terrible'.

Terry blames it all on Mike Frankovich. He got Sam. He got the film made out here. He got it done in colour. 'It's all his fucking fault.'

Sam's clothes. The wardrobe mistress has no taste. They're all trite Technicolor get-ups to accentuate her bust and her femininity. Her bust doesn't need accentuating; and when they use 'femininity' out here, read 'figure'. Sam is very fed up about this; and for once I don't blame her. I at least got them to agree to use the old faded pants and cardigan she was wearing on the set today for one sequence. But not the actual clothes: 'We'll get some like that made.' One gives up.

Phone calls. John, Jud and I sit in an executive office these days and go through the script. But the interruption of phone calls is absolutely non-stop; and every tiny point has to be gone over and over again. Where the idea that Americans got things done fast sprang from, I just don't know. They sound fast and look fast, but they talk and they talk *and* they talk.

Dinner at the Wylers, in Beverly Hills. A palatial house, rather like the Loveridges' in some ways, except the Wylers have four or five Utrillos on the walls, a fine Renoir, a Rivera, a Kisling, a Boudin. Willie is much nicer on his home ground, more French and more human altogether. Mrs Sam Zimbalist (Ben Hur killed her husband as they say) was there, and the George Axelrods (the poetry of Hollwood names), Terry and his sweet little French monkey Annie Fargé, and some other producer and his current starlet 'best friend'. Champagne for aperitifs; I sat alone with Willie and we argued about the beginning of the film. He has just this one very primitive idea about what people need for entertainment, but he knows this domain very well, and he's difficult to budge on it. A very formal dinner, for these parts. I sat between Mrs Axelrod, a glittering white lady with predatory nose and eyes, and Willie's wife, generally agreed to be the most charming woman in Hollywood – with which I wouldn't disagree. She'd make a nice progressive duchess.

Terry turned up in a pink open shirt and for the first time the boy looked a bit ill-at-ease. But thank God, he doesn't put anything on. If he's uncomfortable he just looks it. His voice remains Cockney, and his attitude Cockney-aggressive. After dinner we played pool, pretty clumsily; then Terry strolled up and executed three or four brilliant shots. 'Christ,' I said. 'Oh, I played a bit back home,' he said, and strolled away again. He even had the nerve to blush.

Willie took me round all his paintings – he's unashamedly rather proud of them. One of the Utrillos is a beauty; two others are very poor, of the postcard period, but one has a message from Maurice himself scrawled over the back. Willie said they went to the Utrillo house one day to see him. Madame Utrillo took them in to her own large studio and said, 'All these paintings by me are for sale.' 'Well, we came really to see Maurice,' said Willie. Eventually the wretched woman took them to Maurice in a tiny dark room tucked away in the basement – that was *his* studio.

I drove home with Terry and Annie. She sits perched (she can't be five feet) at the wheel of the huge car. Terry sits slumped back and talks about how he must learn French. He only knows three phrases at the moment – *oui, bon jour,* and *bon soir,* but he has them perfect. He even has a very authentic flat Parisian-Cockney *ouai* for *oui.* She and I try to shake him into reading *Le Grand Meaulnes.* 'Is there a part for me?' says Terry. 'I'm not going to read any fucking literature that hasn't got a part for me. That fucking book by what's his name – Stindle? I got fucking halfway through it before I realized there wasn't a part for me.'

Annie collapses deliciously into outraged giggles. 'It's a bit much, isn't it?' says Terry to me. (He was talking about *Le Rouge et le Noir*.)

Robin Zaccarino. I've met her twice more, in the studio. Her warmth and just ordinary intellectual-human intelligence seem weirdly out of place there. There is a human equivalent of my concept of the Few. I can smell them a mile off.

Late last afternoon I had a violent argument with Willie's silly little brother – about the Paston flashbacks. 'You've convinced me, you've convinced me, Mr Fawles,' the little monkey shouted, and rushed off to see Willie, who was notably unmoved. This morning the monkey brother came up and said, 'My brother is convinced you are right.' I said, 'Like hell he is. I had dinner with him last night and he spent half an hour proving I was wrong.' The monkey fell back, amazed. 'Wait, wait, there is some mistake. Off he rushed again. The result was that I had to have a tête-à-tête lunch with Willie, who said again how proud he was to have me here. I must say whatever I felt, if I wanted a secretary, etc, etc. As soon as I could I got off the film, because it's a waste of time arguing at length with Willy. He's one of these people who change their minds by some slow interior process. He's fundamentally an Alsatian peasant; he doesn't buy anything without letting a decision grow turnip-slow in the field of his instinct.

I got him to talk about himself. His past. His father spoke German, but his mother French. He was born at Mulhouse. He remembers having changes of occupation troops a dozen times during the 1914–18 war. 'You never knew who you ought to cheer, so you ended up by cheering everybody.' Then he said: 'The only difference was that the Germans always put the town hall clock back an hour when they arrived. So we kids decided that that was what the war was about – what the time was.' He wrinkles his Punchinello nose: 'Isn't that nice?'

Willie is a Democrat, of course. I asked him if he had trouble in the UAC days. 'I nearly left America,' he said. 'I nearly went back to Europe. They suspected me and put me on the list, but they talked like this: "That Wyler's a Commie all right, but he's so goddam soft and silly he doesn't count." And I was working for Paramount then, under contract. Paramount had pressure put on McCarthy.'

I tried to sell Willie the idea of getting Sarah Miles, who's in New York, and sacking Sam. But he think's Sarah's 'kinda dirty, kinda not pretty. No boy's going to follow her around.'

Sam doing the illness scene. The make-up man came up and asked me if she looked sick. I said, 'She always looks sick. 'You English,' he said. 'You're just so unkind.' He's a nice sour-salt New York Jew.

Sam did a 'test' take with Maxwell Reed, a forty-five-year-old 'rugged' masculine lead, who looked to me like six feet of tired intestine. He's supposed to be English (on the strength of having once been married to Joan Collins). He spoke throughout in a strong American drawl, adlib-bing some lines. 'I'm never gonna see you again, baby' was one English-Midlands gem. Willie thought he was great; but I exploded, and I think I cooked Mr Reed.

Terry came up to the office and blew his top this afternoon. I think he must have rehearsed it as he put up a magnificent fifteen minutes' solo performance of mingled rage, frustration and brilliant mimicry of Sam on the set. Jud, who normally never laughs (out here), was bellowing with laughter, tears running down his face. These sudden moments when grown men dissolve into giggles are very characteristic – and sympto-matic – of Hollywood.

Terry: 'We're all in the fucking soup. It's the film I've turned down a dozen fat Hollywood parts to do. It's the film that's going to make you boys (John and Jud). It's his fucking first novel. I mean all this arsing about. It's fucking ridiculous.'

Outside he said to me: 'It's incredible. I'm a serious actor, I know I'm going to be bloody marvellous one day, and here I am – stuck in the one fucking situation I've fought against all my life.

'There I am doing the big scene, shouting at her, doing my fucking nut, telling her she's never going to get out, and she's sitting there like a sow who's just had a full breakfast.'

A letter from Eliz full of what seems remote and curious emotional scrabbling on the other side of the world. I rang her up to get perspec-tive back. To hear the quiet silence of the hall at Church Row almost as much as her voice. I mean her presence in the flat; and normal humanity and things that matter.

I took Sam out this evening, to hear Segovia and to try to get to the bottom of the mystery of her nothingness. We drove miles across Los Angeles to the concert-hall, finally stumbling on it by chance. She drives fast, in bare feet, singing to the radio, and I felt like Seneca locked up with Poppaea . . . or something. A pretty corrupt Seneca, as I have done my best to get her the sack these last days; and like everyone else have indulged wholeheartedly in the favourite sport on the Columbia lot – making fun of her behind her back. She is an astoundingly gauche young woman. From certain angles very pretty indeed but only as a still, not as a motion. She sat bored through the concert, and then we drove fast home to the hotel. She's at her best in a car, younger and gayer. And then I took her to the restaurant downstairs, and finally forced her to listen to words of wisdom about her coldness ('I know people think I'm cold, it's because I can't be bothered to make friends') and her ghastly harsh upper register ('I have voice problems'). I don't think anyone has spoken to her so directly for some time, but I really had very little effect. I shook her hand in the lift and said 'If I can help you with the part, for god's sake ask me.'

Jud is frantically phoning to New York and to London to try to get

Susannah York or Sarah Miles. Susannah Y wants three hundred and
fifty thousand dollars for the role; they think Sarah has just been signed
for another film.

'I've thought of how to sack Samantha,' says John Kohn. 'I go up to
the broad and I say, "Sam, dear, owing to circumstances inside my
control . . ."'

I feel this film is like a car running out of control. Jud has seemingly
ceased to worry about the budget. At any moment there's going to be
a crash and the whole thing will disintegrate.

We sat all today in John Kohn's house, a UCLA professor's house he's
rented, and beat at the script, shouting and pleading and bellowing and
walking away and let's-try-this-ing. So mad. Outside there was a pleasant
garden with camelias and hibiscus in flower, and a blue swimming-pool.
But we stayed at the same table from ten till seven. The script is their
life, the characters ten times more real to them than the people around.
John Kohn bawls at his five-year-old daughter: 'Get outta here!' The
little thing trots off. 'Wow, wow, wow, I'm getting out.' His violence with
his children and their indifference to it are comical. Everything he says
is pitched at the same tense level of energy, so that in the end one can't
take him very seriously. 'Answer the phone, goddam you,' he bawls at
his wife. Then ten seconds later, 'Honey, we want lunch.'

Every day a vast stream of conjectures flows round and about; mostly
about Willie and Sam. Whether they'll be on the film still next week,
whether Willie's going to change the ending – all discussed like matters
of life and death. Endless speculation and fantasy.

Copulation imagery – it dominates every sentence here. 'Screw the
film.' 'He makes like he's going to lay the broad' (= he kisses her but
no more). 'I told Uncle Willie go fuck himself' (= I disagreed with his
point of view).

'Sue York's wonderful. But 350 G's is a lot of wonder.'

All Saturday and Sunday at John Kohn's house, battling at the script.
It gets a little better as I wear them down, line after line, into some sort
of sense – or realism. They are geniuses for finding melodramatic
gimmicks, out of which they have to be coaxed and pushed and argued
interminably. I am also preparing a long blast at Wyler to try to get the
beginning and ending problems solved.

A new star is in the air for Miranda's part – Yvette Mimieux.

The horrible monotony of a city where you turn and look when you
see someone walking down a pavement. Everyone has a car, the buses
are as rare as rainy days. There is nothing but this flow of people isolated
and insulated in their individual tin boxes and sweeping from point A
to point B. One doesn't have to say goddam a city without walkers; God
has damned it.

'God, Jesus,' said John today, 'you and I ought to write a script.' He is full of wild ideas and flagrant corn, but he has a sort of flair for what will make a movie work. All the subtleties are beyond him, but he knows the craft. I come slowly to realize this. He hammers out how scenes must link, and then I go through them picking the lines to pieces. Now we begin to realize each other's fortés: his is construction, mine is dialogue.

I have a choice of thirteen TV channels in my room. All those books about automaton-humans of the future seem real here. It becomes less and less necessary to think.

All the walls of the main office building on the Columbia lot are covered in photos of stars; they stare out with an inane grey and white glamour. Their ghosts haunt the dry corridors.

Kohn, Kinberg, Wyler, Frankovich – all Jews. A lot of the tone of the Hollywood world can be accounted for by the ubiquitousness of Jews. They still don't quite belong to this country, and yet they have their hands on the taps of one of the richest oilfields.

John Kohn: 'Hell, Frankovich, who was he, an athletics major at UCLA, and he started on the schlock side in the industry and just because he spoke a couple of other languages he becomes the goddam big man – and he couldn't tell a good actress from a knackwurst.'

'He's a schmuck.' A favourite word.

Today (Monday 23rd) has been 'getting the star' day. I have taken a leading part. I wrote a long report for Wyler over the weekend slamming Sam. Willie pretends that it was his choice, but everyone believes he was pressured into it by Frankovich. Terry and I have both been selling Sarah Miles like mad – I had lunch with Terry and John Kohn, and let Terry do the talking. Sam played into our hands by forgetting her lines and having a row with Willie on the set; and then the rushes from Friday came through. I sat next to Terry in the projection room and watched her play a scene with him and one with Maxwell Reed, then one of her alone, being ill. The last was hilariously funny, and the session suddenly dissolved from all seriousness. 'Frankenstein,' howled Terry. Jud and John Kohn just walked out in despair.

At half past five Willie called the three of us in, and admitted defeat. 'The girl makes me feel I never directed a film before. I don't know anything any more.' We all in turn attacked Sam. Jud started talking about some brilliant coach he'd heard of, so I gave a somewhat vehement version of my evening with Sam – she was empty, there was nothing to coach, and so on, and so on. I got Willie to promise that he would look at *The Six-Sided Triangle* to see Sarah again. I told him he would like her, Terry liked her, everyone liked her, and so on, and so on. It was strange, the four of us and Bob Swink in Willie's palatial office, the crisis of the production; and what never seemed possible suddenly seeming very possible. 'It's my fault,' said Willie. 'It's all my fault.'

I began to feel sorry for Sam about then; she's really, in a merciless world like this one, a victim of the machine. She ought never to have been cast, and she plainly (to me) begins to know it. She walked round the set this afternoon and no one would talk to her; but everywhere there were little angrily discussing groups – Willie and John Kohn, Bob Swink and someone, Willie's brother and me. Sam walked like a Renaissance princess among all the courtiers who know she's going to be poisoned for state reasons at dinner that night. Terry was outrageous on the set, upstaging her and clowning, suddenly starting to laugh when she forgot her lines for the tenth time.

Mike Frankovich flies in from New York tonight. He's the great unknown quantity in all this imbroglio.

'Who's going to tell him?' asked Jud.

'I'm going to tell him,' says Willie, 'and I mean tell. Not ask.'

But John Kohn says, 'Willie talks big tonight. Let's see how he sings tomorrow.'

John Kohn: 'All my life I've been playing small league and hating it. Now I'm playing big but real big league and I hate it. Why do I hate it? Because the big guys are all schmucks like the small guys.' I get this hatred-of-Columbia stuff from John and Jud all day long.

Today my loathing for this place reached a climax, and I have been five or six times on the point of catching the next plane out. The one reason I don't is that I feel someone should be here to record all that's going on. At 10 it was said that Willie had not chickened during the night. At 12.30 a conference was called for Willie, John Kohn and Jud with Frankovich. Meanwhile I went out to lunch with Sam and Terry. At 2.15 Sam was called up to Frankovich's office and given the sack. At 4 Terry was called to Wyler's office and we heard him shouting through the door. At 5 Frankovich rang John Kohn to say that he had Sam with him and that she had something important to say.

Frankovich won't look at Susannah York, who once refused to go to bed with him or something. He wants Audrey Hepburn, the best thirty-five-year-old twenty-year-old in the business; or failing her, Natalie Wood.

This morning while I was waiting out front for Terry, Sam came up. 'You going out to lunch? Can I come?' I knew Terry wanted to hear the latest on Sarah Miles (who's starting her film in May, so is 'out'), but I couldn't dodge it. He suddenly appeared. We walked solemnly down a block or two to a restaurant, Terry two or three steps in advance, refusing to speak, look or take any notice of Sam. The script-girl joined us, which made things a bit easier. Sam was, or was trying to be, pleasanter than usual, and even managed to look like a freckle-faced kid of twenty-four once or twice – innocent in a sort of way. On the way back to the studio she manoeuvred me on one side and said, 'Terry's making it impossible. I'm going to Mike this afternoon to tell him so.' Then a bit later: 'Terry spoke all his lines this morning to the script-girl.' And 'I know why Mike wants to see me, Wyler's told him I'm not into the part yet.' Then she asked me a couple of things about her lines. It was horrible, trying to find something to say. Jud got angry when I said I was sorry for her this afternoon: 'For Christ's sake don't get emotional!' But he said it pretty emotionally himself, and the fact is that none of them has any innocence in this thing. Willie ought never to have hired her, John and Jud ought never to have let him hire her, Frankovich ought never to have played his part and made this the film that is going to help make Hollywood a world centre again.

Robin, as we walked through the lot today: 'I hate working here. It's so inhuman.' Then she said, 'They'll never make good films again in Hollywood. They don't understand the spirit of the age has changed. Our generation don't feel like this any more.' I told John and Jud. 'I'd like to fuck her,' said Jud. 'Whadyya talking about? An ugly broad like that – she ought to be a maid, have her round the house like a maid, clean your shoes,' said John. I keep on calling her Hollywood's only human being and it makes them angry. She really is a terribly nice person, very robin-like to look at, about thirty, dresses badly, really isn't pretty at all, but somehow makes Sam's 'glamour' look the synthetic thing it is.

Wyler's monkey-brother rushed up to me in a corridor. 'We must get Seberg. She is the answer.' I said, 'She's intelligent.' 'More than intelligent, Mr Fawles, brilliant.' He scuttled off to tell Willie.

Frankovich apparently said, 'Sam, I've got some terrible news for you.' 'Only time I ever saw her face go soft,' says John Kohn.

I am very much left to my own devices, as they say, in the evenings. Palatial as this bedroom is, it begins to bore me; even the view begins to bore me.

7.15. I tried twice to ring Terry to find out what happened at the studio after I left, but he wasn't in. Then John Kohn rang to say that after Sam had gone on her knees to Wyler he promised to give her one more chance tomorrow.

'Oh God,' I said.

'It's nothing. Willie's not chickening,' said John Kohn.

7.20. I rang Sam's room. Could I help? Yes, please would I come up? She stood telephoning for drinks and watched me cross the room. I went and stared out of the window. She put the phone down. 'Willie told me you think I'm no good. I was amazed. You said on Friday that I could do the part.' 'Well look,' I said, 'I thought you could do the part if . . . you know, it's this business of . . . I'm a writer, you know, I have a sort of ideal . . .' It can't have been very convincing, but the poor kid (and to give her her due she looked a poor shocked kid this evening) was too overwhelmed to notice a few prevarications. Apparently Willie wasn't present when the axe fell. 'He told Mike he didn't want to see me again. I couldn't believe it. He sacks me and he hasn't even the courage to look me in the face.' She did get to Willie in the end. Then she flew round to Terry 'to have it out with him' – 'he's hurt, it's because we were once so close, I was the first girl he ever took out (Sam's a great one for the euphemism) and I taught him a lot and he's never forgiven me.' I said, well, I'll try to help, so we played a couple of scenes together, I doing Freddie and directing her.

She ordered up a whole lot of drinks. 'If I fail tomorrow I'll have a departure party. If I succeed, I'll have a staying-on one.' She didn't give her little whinny-laugh all evening. As we went through her lines, I kept on saying, 'Your voice is so harsh, so debby, so hard . . .' Then I said, 'I wish you could have heard yourself bawl out the car-fetcher the other day. You sounded such an utter young bitch from Belgravia.' 'Oh God,' she said, wide-eyed and with a great thought bubble ('Thinks back') emerging from her tawny hair, 'Did I?' Sometimes she looks almost Pygmalionable.

The irony is that Wyler forced Terry to coach her for an hour late yesterday afternoon, and then I 'coached' her for an hour this evening. If by some nightmarish miracle she suddenly started acting in this great final test, the two people who most want her out would have got her back in.

The climax day. Terry came tearing in to the office from the set at 12.15: 'He's going to fucking well take her!' Consternation and alarm. We went off to lunch with him, and he poured out the details of the morning. He and Sam had been alone on the set with Willie. 'She was so bloody frightened she was almost good, weeping all over the fucking place and all the rest. I could see old Willie swallowing it all.' He urged Jud and John to walk out; he said he would walk out. We were all scared stiff that Wyler would tell her during the lunch-hour that she was back on the production.

2.15. John and Jud and the monkey-brother Bob Wyler. Violent discussion, a feeling that the whole thing must be decided in the next hour. The monkey-brother rushed off to phone Tally, Willie's wife, to get her on our side.

'I don't know what she's got for her except a lot of red hair.'

'She was sixty per cent better this morning,' said Bob Swink.

'Yeah,' said John Kohn. 'Sixty per cent of nothing.'

2.30. Willie came in and marched up to me. 'You ought to be directing this film. That girl's much, much better.' John and I began arguing all over again. I said she hadn't any voice, any technical skill, any heart, any conception of the part. Mike Frankovich kept on ringing through. 'Tell him I'm not here,' said Wyler. He paced around the room. What did I think of York? He wanted York. . . So I sold York, beautiful, passionate, virginal, brilliant York.

2.45. We hear Terry shouting at Willie through the wall. It goes on for about an hour. I rang up Terry later back at home and he said he'd done the same as us, sold York, attacked Eggar. 'I told old Willie I wanted to make a great film and I tell you one thing, John, he's a fucking sight more excited about this film than I ever realized.'

3.30. John and Jud are called to Frankovich. Eggar is to go. Apparently Frankovich was very angry against everyone – he even managed to include me – that writer's a hypocrite, coaching the girl like that and then trying to get her the sack. 'Jud lost his temper,' said John. 'He told Mike you were only being humane.'

4.00. They went down to tell Sam she must go. Willie funked it, and refused to see her. She went out slamming the door, it seems: 'I wish you luck with your next leading lady.'

'You got a bit o' bird, John?' asked Terry. 'What do you do for a fuck here?' I explained my theory of fidelity, which must be becoming as strange and incredible to Columbia ears as Einstein's theory in the 1920s was to the ordinary physicist. He said, well everyone does it, don't they? I said, it's not what happens outside, it's what happens inside. The nice thing about Terry is that he didn't, and I knew he wouldn't, give a flip answer (he'd just been going down his own incredible roll of bed-battle honours) – just a nod, as if he thought I was mad, but believed I meant it. Through all his insane bragging there shines this strange sensitivity he has – not only faultless timing of words and obscenities, but faultless timing of emotional response. That's why he will one day be a very great film actor.

He has the cruelty of genius – of the genius of his trade, acting. The irony is that he is so obviously of the Few (what Miranda should be) as Sam is of the Many (what Freddie should be). Of course he sensed this at once, though he never put it in words.

Actresses' names have been flying round the lot all today (Thursday): Natalie Wood heads the stakes, but then there's Mimieux, backed by John Kohn and me. Inge Stephens, Hope Lange, Susan Pleshette, wild talk of getting Sarah to break her contract with MGM, and many others whose names I've never heard of. All depends on Wood now. She is said 'to have loved the book', but no one knows whether she will love the script. If she's as good as they say she is, she won't. Her name is spoken with bated breath; the star system isn't dead.

Sam, it was said, had flown to Palm Springs to nurse her wounds. But she rang up at eight and asked me to go to her room. Her boyfriend from London, the actor Tom Stern, was there. She wanted to pump me, in fact. I kissed her hand, and said she was a brave girl, which I think she has been. She is furious against Wyler: 'He's been such a hypocrite.' She's a very innocent creature: 'Terry hates Sarah, I know, he told me so the other day.' When I explained the real situation, she looked at me with hurt eyes. Tom Stern evidently infatuated by Sam. 'Sam's a great actress,' he said. 'They'll never get another like her. The smartest thing they could do is re-hire her.' He said, 'I read the script. That girl in the cellar is Sam. She doesn't have to act. It's her natural self.' I looked appropriately of the same opinion. He said, 'Sam and I are very close – we were on the front page of the *Evening News* together.'[1]

A last morning. We did the Aunt Annie scene one last time. I said goodbye to Willie: 'I want you to come to a party tomorrow, all the stars will be there.' I said, 'Too late, I'm flying out.' I spent a last ten minutes trying to get him to drop Reed and take Kenneth More, but he was as slippery as ever. 'We'll see.' Robin came in and I signed a copy for her: 'Robin Zaccarino, a human being in a town in need of them'. She talked about her husband and her teenage daughter; a sweet woman. I've made her promise to send me a drawing of LA.

My last morning. Jud took me out to Marineland with Suzanne and Stephen. Down the endless San Diego freeway, through the wastelands of Redonda, car-lot on car-lot, red and yellow flags fidgeting in the hot air; a hideously artificial red and yellow. 'Sharp' say the car-lot signs (sharp = cheap). But things got better at Palas Verdes, with the sea and the eucalyptus trees and pretty shingle-roofed houses covered in bougainvillea. Marineland is built on a bare clifftop, a splendidly Roman place, a lovely circus tossed to the masses. Tiberius and Nero would have approved of the idea; and made it more 'interesting' by substituting sharks for dolphins, and living slaves for dead herrings. The most impressive thing is the degree to which the dolphins, whales and seals have been trained. Training animals is the Roman skill; loving them, the Greek. To a 'Greek', all this anthropomorphization of the poor beasts, this teaching them to play baseball, to kiss, to run races, is as nauseating as the silly commentary. Not that any obvious cruelty is involved – the dolphins especially display a sort of enthusiasm, a joy in their tricks, that must be more than a mere desire for reward. Jud went all Pavlovian, but I thought the animals enjoyed the leaping and diving and playing as much as the humans.

I bought Stephen a baby turtle in Farmer's Market the day before. He insists on carrying it around everywhere with him in a small paper bag. It irritates me that Jud and Suzanne don't forbid it. But they let Stephen do as he likes. If a child does something wrong here the parents keep quiet and send him to the analyst to be 'repaired'. 'Correcting children is a skilled job – they send the children to the man skilled at the job.' Suzanne said this approvingly of Californians the other day; I don't absolutely disagree. But it's an easy get-out for parents.

Jud told me the latest on the film. Frankovich has turned down Natalie

---

[1] Samantha Eggar was re-hired and, for her performance in *The Collector*, went on to win the Best Actress awards in the Golden Globes and at the Cannes Film Festival, as well as being nominated for an Oscar.

Wood, who has decided she wants to do the film. She has asked for 400,000 dollars and ten per cent, not an exorbitant price by Hollywood standards. But Jud says F is still furious that they have turned down 'his' girl, and is determined to put Jud and John out of business. 'We're never going to do another film with Columbia. That's sure on both sides.'

I had a last drink with Jud and Suzanne in the airport, then caught the plane up to San Francisco. Columbia had booked me in to a much plusher hotel than I would have chosen, but even that couldn't spoil the town, whose humanity and complexity strike one immediately like an oasis after the desert further south.

Over the States to Boston. A taximan took me right across Boston to a hotel down by the river Charles – an old-fashioned place, where I was delighted to see that the hot-water tap ran cold, and vice versa; tatty paint and the carpets worn. I went and had a hamburger and a beer in a friendly bar, and it was like being back in England after the West Coast. Boston isn't beautiful, but nor is it slick or modern or emancipated from all pasts.

The next morning I went up to Little, Brown's and after lunch with Ned Bradfield and a tour of old Boston, we went out to Marshfield. The same quiet austerity ruled in the house there; Ned's refusal to allow modern America to enter his home life. We talked about *The Aristos*, some things he did not like about it. He said a lot of it was too difficult for him, and plainly he wanted things simplified down to the wrong sort of level; but he liked the book, thought 'it will sell, slowly but surely'. We went to bed at nine, but I couldn't sleep. It was full moon, and bitterly cold – there are still snow-patches on the ground; and there is something strange about this house. It seems poised on the brink of the wilderness, I don't know why; but one's foothold in America still seems a precarious thing here. A keen and beautiful sense of isolation.

Julian B flew up from NY and we met in the Ritz-Carlton bar to discuss what we should say to Ned. J was suavely business-like, and over lunch the two of them discussed my future as if I was a Beatle, a property, not a human being. We decided to write a new contract; LB will pay me ten thousand dollars a year from 1965 on, against the Dell money, *The Aristos* and the second novel. Ned thinks they will publish *The Aristos* in October. He fills me with a sort of quiet confidence; something neither Sheil nor Tom Maschler ever do.

A last drink with Bob Fettridge and Ned in the Ritz bar, then home in an almost empty plane over a vast sea of cloud under the moon, with Isosceles and Cassiopeia on the black wall to the north; breakfast in brilliant sunshine – and then a vile plunge down through thousands of feet of cloud. We came out finally only just above ground level, and landed at once. Cold, dank rain and wind, the temperature 35, added injury to the eternal insult of England's small scale and miserable inadequacy as a twentieth-century society – the traffic crawl, the mean housing, the cramped appearance of everything. It's like a punch in the face, that descent down back into England.

1 April

No sooner back at Church Row than there is a phone call from Leigh. F has had a heart attack, is in bed, can't attend the wedding.[1] M treats it all lightly, her voice gleams a sort of madness. If Armageddon started tomorrow, she'd still see Hazel married in due pomp on Friday.

Coming back to Eliz is real, a sort of childish relief, like getting 'home' untouched in a game of 'prisoners'. She has a good sort of cool suspicion of me, too; sniffing to see how much I've changed, how badly America has got me this time. We collapsed straight into bed in the afternoon – total sex succeeded by total exhaustion on my part. I hadn't slept for forty-eight hours.

2 April

Down to Leigh, through the insufferable drag of the North Circular, the infuriating stopping at lights, the choking of heavy lorries. I dream of freeways in the sun.

F is in bed, muttering and grey-faced. 'He's putting on an act,' says M, and it's true that he half-enjoys this descent of doom. He likes to retire to a cranny and watch cautiously out. Undoubtedly it's mainly the class worry that's sent him to bed, the insane concern that everything shall be *comme il faut* (or *comme il fallait* fifty years ago). Dan goes through it all with a sort of breezy innocence, M talks, talks, talks, Hazel looks frightened, Eliz and I disapprove.

3 April

The wedding day – appropriately enough, the coldest April 3rd for a century. Togged up in hired morning clothes, I took Hazel to Old Leigh Church, stood and froze outside for the photographer, then marched with her down the aisle to the priest. 'You looked so bloody grim,' said Eliz. The vicar was ginger-haired and mean-eyed, intoning the marriage service pompously and looking at us suspiciously through his green slit-eyes, as if we might burst into laughter at any moment.

Then a mammoth reception at the Overcliff: the O'Sullivans from the upper middle class, and the Fowles from the middle and lower middle class, all rather uneasily mingling, soon to separate. I wandered about trying to remember who people were, dodging the relations I can't stand and sticking to those I can.

---

[1] JF's sister Hazel was about to marry teacher Daniel O'Sullivan.

We stayed on two or three days, endlessly dull and depressing. M drives us both wild with rage; she has a sort of active, preying stupidity that will not let one's patience be. The day after we left she collapsed – with complete exhaustion, the doctor said. As ninety per cent of the exhaustion is of her own making, it's difficult to feel sympathy.

Eliz has had intense platonic friendships with Podge and Tarn in my absence. One day she had coffee at eleven and tea with Tarn, lunch and dinner with Podge 'without either of them knowing'. She has a sort of Astarte-like charm for them both.[1] They've both discovered her genius for seeming intelligent as (because she is, of course) they are without actually having to say anything or feeling the need to say anything to prove it. Tarn came in to take her out to the theatre yesterday. His dandyism bores me; something curiously provincial about him. He drives me on to the wrong tack, the hard thrusting commercial literary tack; all this fiddle-faddle about getting a guinea's worth of poetry published.

13 April

The Leopard. Visconti's film of the novel – a travesty of it, in this version . . . in any version. Dreadful to see one of the last expressions of true aristocracy so whored about and betrayed. Visconti calls himself an aristocrat. But all his actors look like people from some Hollywood Western – and dreadful dubbed American voices. Like hearing the Goldberg on a cinema organ.

The Carpetbaggers, Harold Robbins. Possibly the nastiest book ever written, certainly the nastiest I have ever read. It might have been written by a computer set to calculate what is most likely to appeal to the worst instincts of the American masses. The calculations are very accurately done. It is also interesting as a demonstration of the importance of the concept of power (and sexual potency) in the American psyche.

I've spent the last week doing final corrections for *The Aristos*, and reading the French translation of *The Collector*. The latter isn't very good – dozens of mistranslations, and Miranda's part sounds much too stuffy and explicit.

17 April

Dear John,

　　I received a letter from Anthony Sheil yesterday suggesting terms

---

[1] Astarte was the Phoenician goddess of love.

for *The Aristos*, assuming we would want to go ahead even if we lose the Canadian market. Of course we would, and though the advance of £400 which he proposed may turn out to be in excess of the book's earnings, we are happy to accept it.

I say that the money may be in excess of the earnings not from any lack of enthusiasm for the book, but rather from what I fear may be a realistic view of its reception in England. I am sorry if you felt earlier that I was not as enthusiastic as you had hoped; that was not because I did not appreciate the book, but rather because I feared – and still do fear – that its reception here may not come up to your expectations.

Yours,

Tom (Maschler)

LB are giving me a $2,000 advance; will publish in October. There's been a row over Canadian rights, which I want to give to LB. Cape (Tom) are hurt – some vague patriotic line. English authors should give all 'Empire' rights to English publishers. The economic hard truth – that, on *The Collector*, LB Canadian royalties would have amounted to more than the total actually received Cape royalties – is brushed aside. But I think I'm having my way.

30 April
We moved to Southwood Lane today. Yesterday the carpet was laid – not the green we ordered. Urgent phone calls – but it turned out later that Eliz was misinformed, and ordered wrongly. The house is all right, but noise is a problem, after the strange perched-on-high silence of Church Row, where no one could knock on the side-walls. Here there are voices, the traffic, a maniac beat couple in the next house, whose records blare out over the peace behind. The little green gardens running down the hill, and the wooded Essex hills in the distance, are nice. We felt oddly indifferent about leaving Church Row and I feel oddly indifferent about coming here. Place doesn't matter much any more.

Ronnie and Betsa have moved to a house round the corner – 7 North Hill, grander than this, but under the shadow of Highpoint.[1] I envy them the space, though; and going there gives me doubts about the narrowness and noise in Southwood Lane.

---

[1] A high-rise block of flats.

14 May
The house. It has a sort of capricious effect on us. Irritates us mildly one hour, charms us the next. Usually charms in the morning, all sun, the little brick garden running away downhill with its wild sprout of forget-me-nots and lilies of the valley. The rooms have a sort of terrace-cottage elegance, and if they look ugly, they make one feel wrong. We can't be ugly, they say, we have elective grace; and since this was first a terrace for dissenters, appropriately enough. The houses sit very prim, drab-fronted; all the charm and uncorseting takes place behind the scenes, facing the rear. Eliz has organization neurosis, the house must run; and I have writing neurosis, I must write. The three of us all jangle together; and we haven't learnt to settle down as yet.

27 May
The Magus. I've been working on this for a week. I've agreed, in the new LB contract, to have it finished by January 1st, 1965. I cut everything that stands in the way of the narrative thrust; anything that lapses beneath a certain state of tension. Because this seems to me the essence of the novel – the exact harmony between subject-matter (symbolisms, intellectual and stylistic aims) and narrative force (simple old readability). The words on a page have got to lift it over. Narrative is a sort of magnetism.

Cuts. Some good cuts are as satisfying to perform as good passages.

25 June – 25 July
Norway.[1]

23 August
I have been back on *The Magus* this last fortnight; and I feel full of writing ills again. The really enormous *physical* effort of writing a long novel – the psychological and imaginative effort I do not mind at all. Even the indigestion, the piles, the sleeplessness, the collapse into flabbiness.

Writing in the first person. I cannot imagine any other way of writing a novel. But it seems to me that it is also a sort of cowardice. Perhaps I ought to force myself to write a third-person narrative one day. I mean that I have always regarded third-person writing as old-fashioned, unreal; and now I wonder. Perhaps it is a pleasure to experience?

An envelope stuffed full of cuttings about sex and cruelty. It was

---

[1] JF had been commissioned to write a travel piece about the country by the American magazine *Venture*.

addressed to me care of Jonathan Cape. There was also a three-page letter with a list of sex books; and an enclosure asking why I didn't 'do a movie called *The Death of a Sadist*'. This is the first ugly one of the thirty or so letters I have had on *The Collector* from England and the USA, though there was an odd specimen from a mental hospital in Berkshire. I don't mind the obscenity; but the undersmell of hate is intolerable.

The next day a Totteridge girl, Margaret Harving, disappeared. A polar analysis of a fantasy (by which I mean a narrative situation that springs from the unconscious) about this event: in this fantasy I assumed that the writer of the obscene letter had kidnapped the girl; I hand the letter to the police; the police track the man down and release (save) the girl. The pleasure in the fantasy came from the idea 1. of my book causing a man to act in this way; 2. of my 'good' action and the publicity attached to it. I got no pleasure at all from any sexual aspect of this – all the details of the fantasy concerned dialogues with the police, my examination in court, and so on. At first sight this fantasy seems unhealthy, but although such a chain of events would give me pleasure, I am of course certain how I should act if I could in any way have a device of stopping in motion or preventing such a sequence of real events. If I could in fact prevent a kidnapping, of course I would. The conventional moralist would say that even to imagine cruelty and evil is to weaken the moral will. But I suspect this imagined counter-situation to the real situation – a 'real' imagined crime against an 'unreal' hypothetical prevention of a crime – is in fact a source of *moral* energy. There are situations in which the constant (and at first intentionally innocent) toying with the idea of a murder might lead to the actual murder; but in nine cases out of ten, in every case when the person is not a murderer, the imagined counter-situations affect real behaviour in the real situation – the way the person lives. I see the same mechanism in fidelity. The imagined counter-situations (affaires, adulteries, brothel scenes, perversions and the rest) underlie and suppose the real situation of fidelity. And I suggest the most unfaithful husbands are unfaithful through lack of imagination rather than through excess of it. A full imagination creates an ideal world, a fantasy world that feeds the real one – the dungheap breeds roses; in terms of conventional horror of 'perverted' fantasy and admiration of 'normal' behaviour. I think it is only in this last year that I have become completely free of guilt about my own (I presume) abnormally rich fantasy life; now I indulge it and cherish it because I am convinced that it (in the sexual contract) keeps, among other things, my fidelity 'healthy' – in existentialist terms, fresh, constantly re-chosen. This is a form of sublimation; but a sort of homeopathic sublimation – a using of the primary (amoral) desires to create the adult moral attitude.

7 September

One thinks one has grown up, by which I mean that one thinks that all one's attitudes, proclivities, and the rest are finally hardened beyond remoulding, but then I came back from Norway feeling very depressed. Superficially about the tourist rape of Europe, more profoundly by the permanent mystery of my life since *The Collector*; that I don't feel in any except one way happier or more fulfilled. We have money enough now, freedom to live where we like and do what we like. I have one of the great blessings of life – no one is my master, I am completely my own. But I don't feel happier.

There are one or two obvious (using Heidegger's word) *Dasein* (being-in-history) reasons. These last two or three years have seen a strong conservative-fascist-selfish swing in the West; the decline of the intellectual approach to life and the rise of the visual; the predominance of what its defenders call an amoral (healthily free), pragmatic attitude to living – enjoy it while you can, buy as many pleasures as the affluent society and you yourself can afford – and its attackers call immoral (blindly uncommitted to anything but selfishness). So I feel what many must have felt in the 1930s, a being swept on in the direction I do not want to go. The usual metaphor is of being swept in a sea-current. But this is more like a current of wind. I walk one way, and the world blows the other.

Always, too, I am haunted by my own lack of any practical application of the ideas in which I believe. I never give anything to charity, rarely bother to contradict people who talk rubbish, never march, never protest, never act. I defend this through the argument that the writer is a sublimated doer (enactor), and the best thing to do is to concentrate on your integrity (literary and politico-social) as a writer.

For all that, I feel out of social and communal life; beside it.

Then we can't make up our minds about this house; whether we really want to live in it or not. Sometimes it seems too small. It faces the wrong direction, and anyway do we even want to live in London? The other evening Betsa and Ronnie were saying they felt they were in their new house 'for good', and 'This is us', and all the rest. And though there's a counterpole of relief for me when they said it – to be *so* settled smells of stagnation to me – there was that old feeling of the need for roots, for finding some corner in the world which will be the permanent base. The place where one plants bulbs and knows one will see them come up next year. I have a sort of morbidly obsessed interest in gardening at the moment – with propagating plants, with seeing them flower next year. A symbolic thing, of course.

All this doubt in me has rubbed off on Eliz, who goes through recurrent crises of depression. In her usual erototropic way she derives all our to me geographical doubts about the house from a failure of love between us. Which I can't take seriously, which really irritates me by its irrelevance. We have assumed each other far beyond the sort of point where anything is to be got except petty misery and dissension from doubting the assumption. It's like the mouse teasing the lion; it can be done, but it can't alter the basic fact that our lion (our assumption) is infinitely greater than the mouse (her doubt).

I said 'except one way'. There is one way in which I feel happier. That is in writing – because I feel I am at last beginning to know clearly what I must write and (perhaps more important) how to write it. I mean I know my (using the word in the old sense) genius, my specific technical powers as well as my specific aims. The craving I used to have for the limelight, for a sort of publicity, has diminished a great deal. More and more I have a sense of immortality, of what will last and what won't, in contemporary literature. I think acquiring this sense of what is durable in art is an essential, perhaps the essential, criterion in creating. It is a much more important one than, say, the sense of what will appeal to one's contemporaries, of what is technically well or ill expressed (flair with taste and flair with words).

In fact, this sense of always anxious but not neurotic literary well-being really dominates all my other worries and neutralizes them. One cannot feel one is creating well (whether objectively one really is not) and be unhappy. That is why, finally, the It smiles, the All smiles.

The Magus. I am now on Chapter 54. It will be very long. The thing I have changed is the relation between Nicholas and the 'magic'; in the original mid-1950s draft I tried to carry on the 'psychic' pretence far too long. Now I am abandoning it very early on. The audience knows the magician is tricking them; but they still watch.

The symbolism between Alison (reality) and Lily (imagination) is now absolutely clear in my mind. But it's worth recording that I didn't put Alison in the book at the second rewriting last year for symbolic reasons at all. Just a feeling that another girl character, sex interest, was needed in the first part. She herself built herself up – because the way characters develop seems organic, from outside my own invention – into the real heroine of the book. In a sense she personifies my own now hard decision that reality and reason (the one in literature, the other in philosophy) are my faiths. This needs amplifying. I am not, of course, 'against' all unreality and unreason; but I am against the *unnecessarily* irrational elements in existentialism (despair and Angst – which are constituents of life, not *the* fundamentals) and illegitimate (artistically unjustified) uses of non-realism. Of course my opinions in these matters are, ultimately, subjective. I 'choose' them 'blindly'.

12 September

Curious boiling-over when writing is really going well – a point when the excitement of invention in the book spills over into invention in life. Scenes of praise, 'rave' reviews, and the rest. Before *The Collector* I made some sort of attempt to check this Walter Mitty complex; but now of course it's hopeless. I laugh at it; and go on doing it.

28 September

Sheila and Nat Hopkin came for the evening. Podge came last week and told us that he had had a row with them – they all went together to Poland this summer. Sheila and Nat had travelled by train and met Podge in Warsaw, but after three days had parted from him – a good deal of acrimonious feeling on both sides. Some of it rather comic; but a touch of tragedy in it all. As Podge presented the business it was stuffy old Sheila and her yes-man Nat who took ludicrously exaggerated umbrage at his briskness and the rather full programme he had organized.

Sheila and Nat's side is much more convincing. They say Podge and Cathy laughed at them throughout the days in Warsaw; Podge seemed totally bound up in Cathy, even sleeping in the same room as her (she is seventeen now); he was neurotically restless; rude to them; totally inconsiderate, even though he had argued them into coming in the first place. Cathy sided with Podge, Eileen remained neutral.

After we had discussed it all for some time, Sheila suddenly burst out with a confession. Eight years ago, just after she and Nat were married, Podge had seduced Nat's daughter Linden. 'He gave us free tickets to *The Drop of a Hat* and then came to the flat and seduced her. She was mixed-up at the time, her mother had died just a year or two before, she was ready to get into bed with anyone.' One day Nat had had a serious talk with her, telling her she was going around (sleeping) with *variens*, and she had said, 'What about Podge?' Podge then confessed and tried to justify himself in a series of letters by the misery of his home life – and by the fact that Linden was more or less nymphomaniacal at the time. Sheila said, 'It nearly broke our marriage. Nat was magnificent. He forgave Podge.' Nat was crying as she told us this. They'd both drunk rather a lot of whisky.

She kept on saying, 'I love Podge, I love him, I've know him since I was three and I shall be fifty next birthday.' I was really as surprised that she should have told us as that Podge should have done such a thing.

I had a grim Oedipal dream during the night in which Podge did not appear but where he plainly haunted the situation – in which I felt betrayed by the father-figure. Podge has always represented a sort of substitute father for me, of course. Our very first meeting in Aix in 1948 involved us sharing a room together; and my first envy of him was when he came and said, 'Do you mind letting me have the room for an hour this afternoon – I want to talk to a girl alone?' Also he kept on saying how much he was looking forward to getting back to Oxford and 'having a good fuck with my wife'. I see (only now, sixteen years later) that all the elements of an Oedipal relationship were there, before I fell under the spell of his intellectual qualities.

The 'truth game' he introduced us to at Nice (Faith, Ronnie, he and me) was also semi-traumatic. We all had to say exactly what we really thought of each other. I seem to remember that I accused him of sadism and voyeurism – probably not in those words, but by implication. I also from the beginning had strong feelings towards Eileen, which I now see were mother-identification feelings in an Oedipal situation. I have also always had feelings towards Cathy with guilty effects. Probably in recent years partly sexual, but also partly a transfer from former feelings about Eileen, and also partly feelings of envy towards Podge. I have always treated this as an envy of his having a daughter, but it is symptomatic that I envy no one else their children. Increasingly, and with more than a little reason in view of the actual unhealthily close relationship between Podge and Cathy, I have come to see Podge and Cathy as man and wife – in other words, as my own father and mother, with all my suppressed love going to the latter and my outward love to the former (as in fact with my real contemporary relationship with my parents). In short the Porters have served as a substitute family for me, perhaps because it is one in which the suppressed love is more easily manifested – certainly more easy to fantasize about. I can't fantasy-marry my mother, but I can (and some years ago several times did) fantasy-marry Cathy, as formerly I fantasy-fucked Eileen.

Intellectually, too, of course, Podge conveniently filled in the defects in my own father. His Marxism, cynicism, his mechanistic view of life, his Voltaireanism, all supplied wants in the original father-image.

Other symptomatic events – at the peak of the crisis in the affaire with Eliz, I turned to Oxford. Podge found us a room, gave advice, acted as conscience, and so on.

An occasion during that period when we went punting and were late meeting Podge and Eileen, who were joining us in the Parks. He went off angrily after waiting for some time and we arrived at the rendezvous to find Eileen alone. I felt ashamed and angry with him.

The first fiction I wrote and tried to get published. I sent it to Podge for his opinion. He wrote back a critical but very tactful letter; a model handling on his side, in fact, which made me realize my weakness as a writer but also gave me the incentive to go on. This contrasts with his later reaction to *The Collector* and *The Aristos*, which he has damned by implication, by saying nothing.

For at least five years now I have been fully aware of a change in our relationship – one in which I have been increasingly disillusioned by him, increasingly in disagreement with his judgements (especially in their erratic flippancy, his boredom with art). A key incident here was when I was with Ronnie Payne and Sam White, the *Evening Standard* correspondent, and I mentioned his name once too often – because I attribute to people like Ronnie the same relationship towards Podge as I have myself – and Sam White said, 'Who is this man? He sounds a fucking bore.' I felt angry and at the same time was aware that the remark was in context justified.

The final disillusionment was when he tried to get Eliz into bed while I was away in America, and I realized that I was no longer his credulous admirer at all, though of course I retain a very strong affection for him.

Furthermore I have been aware for some years that Podge envies me; he expresses this by malice, often concealed as teasing, and irony masked by sudden bursts of wild overpraise. I think this partly explains his attraction towards Eliz. She is something to be defiled as well as seduced – once again, something he wishes to reduce to his own situation. He wants to spread guilt around him.

Undoubtedly the relationship between the three of us is coloured by the fact that both Eliz and I have superimposed a father-function on the real Podge; which he has used and at the same time resented.

Podge as he is – a series of questions and some answers. The new fact I take into consideration is the deep feeling of guilt he must have over Linden and probably other affaires.

Why has Podge changed intellectually? He no longer seems to believe in anything seriously. Guilt – the effort of keeping up a façade of public righteousness (his CND work, standing as local councillor, etc) over an inner feeling of moral wrongness and sterility.

What went wrong between him and Eileen? I find it difficult to believe that any death of sexual love, however cruelly executed, could result in the present state. There has to be some additional twist to the dagger.

Podge's infidelity? Compensation for some much deeper frustration – more than sexual. His overaffection for Cathy would then be an attempt to stifle infidelity as an outlet. Cathy becomes the outlet.

Sheila spoke of his paranoia. 'Because we forgave him, he thinks we are masochists, and he can trample over us.' She meant that he felt they were persecuting him with their forgiveness. I remembered how Podge always sticks up for Nat, though he was bitter last time about how 'Nat always does what Sheila says'. But his attitude for many years has been 'There's a lot to be said for Nat.' Obviously he would resent this debt paid by his conscience and drawn on his real feelings of unsolved guilt.

Another symptom of his guilt. He said to me only last weekend: 'What use is analysis? It only tells you about the past. It doesn't help over the future.' Associate this with his debunking of the man he saw last year. The psychiatrist who went to sleep 'as I poured out my soul'. Which obviously he did not.

6–15 October
Our little tour of the West. On the 6th we drove to Winchester, and stayed in the new international-anonymous hotel there. Such hotels seem sinful to me, less because of their high prices than for the unreality, the remoteness from ordinary living, that they disseminate. Sensitive Romans must have felt the same when they did a stint in savage Britannia; while insensitive ones must have been very like the young executives with which the hotel was filled – aggressively pleased to be able to afford more civilization than the indigenes.

On the 7th by an old Roman and pack road to King's Somborne,[1] over chalky downs. Dense yew-woods, the dark green branches rich with berries; very pretty berries of a glowing coral-pink, each cupping a stone. I ate one; bitter-sweet. The woods were filled with thrushes and finches of various kinds, some 'recording'. June-evocative music out of the green shades; and a little further on, the real season, lapwings on the ploughed downland, and a cold wind.

Stonehenge, which is now ancient-monumentalized out of its true nature. As in Greece, the old harmony with the environment has been destroyed by the wire fences and the tea bars and the explicatory notices and entrance fees. We can never more *come on* Stonehenge; it is a *gone-to* now, the visitable.

An old coaching inn at Shaftesbury.[2] The unchangingness of the small provincial town is a shock: the streets without lights, the rural accents, the incestuousness of it all. In even the smallest town, though, we met the strange new young, who might – accents apart – have come from any country in Europe. Boys with Jesus haircuts and black leather coats and loud voices, girls equally without charm; the roar of unsilenced motorbikes and scooters.

It's not much better inside the hotels, where the English middle classes whisper through their meals and then go and gawp at the screen in the TV lounge. Outside the yobboes shout, inside the last of the *ancien régime* cower over their dying way of life and the protocols of an insipid gentlemanliness. Nothing in our lifetimes will break this great window between the two Englands – the 'gentry' and the 'labouring classes'.

But the country dies hard. Billhooks and rabbit snares in an ironmonger's; and out of the towns the emptiness of the countryside is extraordinary. We try to use lanes wherever possible, and down them we drive for miles without passing other human beings or cars. I think

[1] A Hampshire village on the River Test, about seven miles west of Winchester.
[2] A market town in North Dorset built on a hilltop 750 feet above sea level, the 'Shaston' of the Thomas Hardy novels.

this is owed to modern agriculture. There have never been fewer farm-workers; and those that remain fight a sort of rearguard action against the town. But we are the last generation to know this old England. The population of 2064, with their three-car families and their autostradas and helicopters, will kill the England I love beyond all hope. And they won't even be able to imagine how lonely and peaceful much of it still is this year.

Dorset. Green valleys and straw-coloured downs – less straw-colour than the pale dun of dead grass that takes its colour from the weather. Almost grey under rain, almost golden under sunlight.

East Compton. Fine gargoyles round the church tower. Dorset 'goes in' for gargoyles, just as it 'goes in' for neolithic monuments, barrows, tumuli.

I feel full of envy for Hardy, during our days round Dorchester. Having such roots, such a rich humus of land and local history to suck from and retreat into.

10 October
I walked up before breakfast on to a hill behind Abbotsbury; looked down over the Chesil Bank to Portland Bill; a grey and blue landscape under an intense pale light.

The Hardy monument on Black Down.[1] We walked a mile over some fields to the Kingston Russell stone circle.[2] A view there, right down to Dartmoor. We could see Hay and Rippon Tors quite clearly.

Through Bridport and inland to Beaminster, where I went to see Stevens Cox, the man who does the Hardy monographs.[3] A woman in an antique shop went to get him. A scruffy little man in a beard, with manic blue eyes. 'I'm an ex-policeman,' he said, 'I don't much like Hardy, but I love getting at the truth.' He talked like a fountain, so fast that one lost trace of who his 'he's' and 'she's' meant. But I liked his wild enthusiasm for exposing the great, despite all its neurotic undertones. He confirmed that there is a lot of dirt to be had on Hardy; hinted at an incestuous love affaire with Tryphena, a 'buried

---

[1] This stone monument, built on a hill 770 feet high, is a memorial not to the poet and novelist Thomas Hardy, but to Vice-Admiral Sir Thomas Masterman Hardy (1769–1839), who was flag officer aboard *HMS Victory* at the Battle of Trafalgar. It is situated five miles south-west of Dorchester and a mile north of the village of Portesham, Dorset, where Admiral Hardy lived from the age of nine.

[2] Located on a high ridge, the circle was built about 4,000 years ago and consists of eighteen slabs.

[3] Under the imprint of the Toucan Press, Cox was responsible for the publication of a series of booklets on various aspects of Hardy's life.

child'.[1] The first marriage was a disaster from 'the very beginning to the very end'; the second was 'just Hardy being decent'.[2] All is rooted in Tryphena, it seems; the secrecy and the tragedy of Hardy's books, his poems, and his life. The real mystery is why Hardy became such a great writer; not the facts of his life, which can only be facts about motives; not facts about genius.

Broadwindsor, Whitchurch Canonicorum, Lyme Regis. We liked Lyme very much, far and away the best resort on the south coast, with its steep contours, old houses, the sea light, the beautiful harbour – the Cobb, the cliffs. We get into another Ionesco hotel, full of elderly Frederick Cleggs and their wives, whispering, nibbling their bad food genteelly, quarter-existing.

At breakfast a 'lady' said: 'Of course it is extremely hard to follow a popular vicar.' The gentility of such places.

11 October

To Charmouth[3] to do a little ransacking of the lias in search of fossils. We found a few ammonites, but a man came along with a sack and produced a beautiful vein of them still set in the grey rock and made us look silly with our broken bits and pieces.

12 October

A Hardy day. Bockhampton,[4] a gloomily set cottage under high beeches on the fringe of Puddletown Heath. A dark, maternal, womblike sort of place; Hardy never left it. Then we walked along a little stream, very pretty, to Stinsford church; also gloomy, dark, womblike.

Over Moreton and Galton heaths and through Winfrith Newburgh to Lulworth. We climbed round to Pepler's Point and had lunch there. All beyond that to the east, almost to Swanage, is military ground. They keep it lonely and deserted. The choice is vile: the military horror or the bungalow horror. Probably it is best as it is.

We drove on to the desolate bay at Kimmeridge, where strata of beautiful golden sandstone layer the great stodge of sepia shale. On the beach, ammonites and beautiful lemon-yellow winkles. A razorbill dived close inshore. A desolate place.

---

[1] In the monograph *Tryphena and Thomas Hardy*, which the Toucan Press published in 1962, Lois Deacon argued that Hardy had once been engaged to his second cousin Tryphena Sparks. In a later book, *Providence and Mr Hardy* (Hutchinson, 1966), she claimed that the two had had an illegitimate child.
[2] Hardy married Emma Gifford in 1874. Two years after her death in 1912, he married Florence Dugdale.
[3] A town two miles eastwards along the coast from Lyme Regis.
[4] The village near Dorchester where Hardy was born.

To Corfe, where we stayed at a pub and had the best meal since we left London, mainly because it was simple and the food tasted fresh. As we ate, the curfew rang. Corfe seems tradition-conscious and lives in the shade of the romantic castle, very much a self-conscious eighteenth-century ruin (in spite of its much greater age),[1] a kind of gentle English attempt to make a Schloss-on-the-Rhine.

12 October

We left Corfe and drove to Wyke Regis via Lawrence of Arabia's cottage,[2] a mournful place in the middle of the tank training-grounds. It is extraordinary how one kind of English writer (Shaw, Lawrence, Hardy) apparently rejoiced in liking such ugly houses and places; almost as if it was a need.

A long drive north. Buckland Newton, Sturminster Newton, Gillingham, Mere, the Deverills, Chitterne, Tilshead, Devizes. There, a good old coaching-inn hotel, the Bear, though the bedrooms have been brothelized.

That evening we listened for a few minutes to an election meeting – the Liberal candidate's. To my no doubt oversensitive ears, all modern electioneering is sham. There is a hollowness in the voices, a spew of clichés that drowns all feeling. No one is excited, no one cares, because the politicians themselves lack all vigour, all life, all real conviction in anything but their own careers. Two nice men got up and spoke at this meeting; some nice people applauded. Sheep meet sheep.

14 October

Devizes,[3] a market day. It's a fine little town, beautifully arranged around its market square. People in town for the day, greeting faces they haven't seen for weeks, perhaps months. Broad accents, fresh produce, local cheese and butter.

Avebury stone circle. Pottery decorated by impressions from blackbird femurs. Bowshere heads. The museum is rather touching; the first dawnings of human features in man. A pot with a first attempt at decoration, a line of holes pricked under the rim. Roads traverse the circle, houses are built across the middle of it, but it stands greater than them and more enduring and far more in tune with the landscape around, with the bleak long hills and openness to the sky.

Four hours later we were back in London; but London seems four centuries away from much of what we saw. I felt very little love of London this time. A purpose we vaguely had in going to Dorset was to prospect

---

[1] Corfe Castle was built in the eleventh century from local Purbeck stone on the site of a ninth-century wooden structure.

[2] T. E. Lawrence lived at Clouds Hill, just outside the village of Bovington, from 1923 until his death in 1935.

[3] A small market town in North Wiltshire, by the Kennet River.

for a house, and I came back feeling that I could now face the plunge into the past that living in the country represents; and clearer in my mind about the kind of fire one wants to leap into – something remote, something facing south-west and shielded by hills to the north, something before 1830 but not before 1700. And perhaps most important of all, something that is for good; that need not be left till the coffin journey. Perhaps this last reason is why I am so slow to make up my mind. I want – too much – a perfect house, almost a country house, large grounds, water, sea, a perfect aspect. I can't afford such a house, though I think one day I may be able to do so; and this thought of what I might buy then makes choosing a house now seem nearly impossible.

Hardy, *A Pair of Blue Eyes*. Difficult to deduce Hardy's town from this novelette, though it is by any standards a magnificent period piece. But two things distinguish his very immature genius here – the power of his imagination (both the events of the narrative *and* the power of its onwardness – its readability) and the occasional vivid phrase or simile: 'The world today smells like the inside of an old hat.'

It's also clear, of course, that Hardy was dominated by archetypes – by the Tryphena image.

15 October
Voted Labour.[1]

23 October
In a male-dominated society – enormous skill needed to remain a woman.

Women judge by relationships; men by objects.

All artistic creativity, all the arts, all paradigms of the essential act of creation in nature (not, of course, an act of *first* creation, but an act of continuous creation). All arts are tenses of a fundamental infinitive: *poein*, to create. Poetry is the more human art because it is an attempt to *understand* the creative process.

25 October
The relationship between character and dialogue. There are three degrees of skill here. In the first, the discord between what seems to be the writer's conception of the character and the character's dialogue is

---

[1] It was the day of the General Election. The Labour Party won the election by a tiny majority of four seats, bringing to an end thirteen years of Conservative rule.

offensive; in the second, there is harmony – we say such a writer has 'a good ear'. In the third, the writer in fact reverts deliberately to the fault of the first – that is, he gives out-of-character dialogue to firmly established characters, and it is this out-of-character dialogue (and actions, of course) that gives the character that special quality of uniqueness and human credibility that we associate with great novelists. I suppose Dickens is the test case here – he is a master of the second degree, for all his great characters belong to the third. Jane Austen's are almost all in the third. Trollope's (and C. P. Snow's), in the second. Thackeray's, in the first – for me, Thackeray sneaks into the category of master novelist partly on this one trait – the ability to create out-of-character dialogue, and get away with it. Waugh and Greene can do it, among twentieth-century writers. This is a very vital part of the craft.

Art – the great natural preserve of mystery. The function of science is to demolish mystery; of art, to preserve it.

7 November
The Magus. First complete draft finished.

27 November
Sunk in the rewriting.

Cape party. Better than last year's. This time I met my fan Hester Chapman, a white-haired cocotte's face, very mannered, both visually and linguistically; spiky mascara'd eyebrows, rouge, blood-red lipstick, but good, intelligent, humorous eyes. I suspect the first Queen Elizabeth would have given one, in her private moments, the same impression. She is very kind about *The Collector*. 'You know, my dear man, to us older people' – she really meant her chum Rosamund Lehmann and herself – 'you have written a book in the great English literary tradition.' She wants us to meet Angus Wilson. 'Such clever dialogue, he could mimic us each so well, yet as soon as he tries to describe the relationship between you and me, me and her, he's lost. That is because' – a Firbankian flutter of the eyes – 'he is a homosexual.' She pronounces it like an Irish-French name: Homme O'Sexual.

Tarn and Arnold Wesker being Jewish together – Wesker's a little black-eyed birdlike creature with the curious brimming eyes very small men sometimes have: inquisitive, both malicious and suspicious. I sat by him and asked him how Centre 42[1] was getting on. 'I want half a

---

[1] The organization established by Arnold Wesker in 1961 to bring the arts to working people.

million,' he said, with a monkey grin. And that ended the conversation; his monomania and my rejection of it. Of course the entertainment of the proletariat is important; but it seems to me unimportant in the context of world starvation. He and I disliked each other on sight. I sense anti-Aryanism in him, and he assumed anti-Semitism in me.

At the end, Edna O'Brien. We sort of reach for each other as human beings across her Irish self-mockery and my English self-importance. She talks in non-sequiturs, in comparisons where both terms are obscure, voice trailing away.

'Are you happy?' I ask.

'You don't know me. You have no right to ask me that.' But she sort of leans towards me as if she is going to burst into tears, wraps the confession in her Irish brogue: 'No . . . no . . . I'm not happy.'

I say she can't really be unhappy, being the writer she is.

'Och, with all copper pans in a window – do you know that shop in Wardour Street?' And then, 'What have I got – just this empathy with people.' As if it's all a cross. The persona she has developed is half mother-goddess, protector of the lame, and half wounded waif; all carried off with a maximum of complexity, of thorny, prickly fences erected against any man's getting at the truth of her. As she goes, she presses my hand convulsively, in the mother-goddess role, exchanging courages. I see Tarn's wife looking suspiciously at our half-hidden clasped hands; wondering what the weird gentiles, Celts, are up to.

Earlier, Edna and I held our hands out side by side. Equally white, weak hands. 'We're maimed,' she said.

Hester Chapman on Angus Wilson. 'I'm supposed to be Mrs Eliot in *An Afternoon with Mrs Eliot*. Or something. Of course that's who he thinks he is. George Eliot. Rather a lot to live up to, don't you think?'

28 November

We went to have a meal with Edna in her Putney human zoo; a house obscurely full of children and people, chicks under her hen-wings. She is really as (consciously and unconsciously) Irish, rural Irish, a person as one can meet, a lovely blend of warmness and amused melancholia about herself; added to which is her percipience as a writer, her seeing through English façades, and judging by the heart. Like so many Catholic-educated novelists she tends to talk in anecdotes, in descriptions; by parables rather than principles. She is a bit like a favourite church, too; is visited by everyone, knows everyone, doesn't much like going out, stays and receives.

Stanley Mann was meant to be there, but characteristically failed to turn up. The little film actress Rita Tushingham and her husband came.

She looks about sixteen, a peaked, bright-eyed face; a 'nice kid' who happens to answer the age's need for a lowest common denominator heroine, an epitome of chirpy lower-class unpretentiousness; a figure they can 'feel' with; identify with, in the jargon. Her grocer's daughter, shopgirl, no-nonsense manner disguises a pretention, of course – to reduce the cinema and theatre to a matter-of-factness, an ordinariness that it may be in need of, but can never be made of. She is the anti-actress, the anti-star; a little frightening. Not in herself, but as part of the fierce current against rhetoric, breeding, imagination.

We sat till four, after they went, in Edna's kitchen, drinking whisky and milk. She sits with her plain pink face, already more matronly plump than girlish, her smudged brown eyebrows, saying 'yout' instead of 'youth', being angry about Tom Maschler's sadism, trying to understand her husband Ernic's bitterness, complaining about her mother ('She writes and says, "I pray that we shall both be buried in the same grave." Would you believe it now? The woman's impossible.'); remembering her sister 'standing in the window' – she had had an affaire and an abortion – and telling Edna, a little girl then, 'I'm sterile, I can't ever have any babies.' Edna tells this sort of story, of human cruelty – with a kind of gently scalding incredulity; as Phaedra, say, might have reflected on her own myth.

14 December
Some vile virus; it makes my head swim and ache, and I can't write, which depresses my already existent depressions. Lie in bed, sweat and stink and read Genet.

16 December
A vile dream. A dark black body, male, forty or fifty – or two such bodies? Situated at Bourani. In one way he was death, in another Genet, in yet another Conchis. Part of the horror was the feeling that he represented vast changes and rewritings in *The Magus* – this is the second night running I have dreamed inside the book. Inside the domaine. All-pervading sense of death, of my mind's being fuddled, blanketed. No narrative element in the dream; simply the squat figure.

Still in bed. The constant headache destroys will. Wait and waste.

23 February 1965
We took the last part of *The Magus* to be typed. It's very far from the end of the book, of course, but it feels like a sort of end; a relief, and a more pregnant doubt. I alternate between anger and pleasure at it. But these last few months I have grown so close to it that I can no more judge it than a mother in parturition the baby coming down between

her legs. On the whole I like this gestation period; I suppose I would have made a good, aneurotic mother. Trust that the child has a life of its own?

Last week Willie Wyler was in town with a copy of the film. Lunch with him at Claridge's. He is delighted with it, in love with it. At last I meet Frankovich,[1] pink-faced and white-haired, with that humourless glint of amusement in his eyes that men of power carry with them like a warning light. 'I'll be nice to you, but you'd better be nice back.'

A story of Willie's – about Max Ophüls. 'One day he did a moving shot so complicated that when it was over they couldn't find the camera.'

His hatred of 'gimmick' directors – directors who allow their own inventions, or their camerawork, to come between them and the story – is professionally his most endearing trait; and also the best aspect of the film. It was no better, and not much worse, than I expected: Technicolored and glossied and blunted out of all contact with the book, so that the lies I told afterwards didn't come too hard on my conscience. One can judge it only as a Hollywood movie; and as a Hollywood movie it rates an honest beta. Edna O'Brien, who was there, wrote and called them (film people) 'all tasteless bandits' – and Eliz hated it. If an Antonioni or a Bergman or a Truffaut dictates one's comparisons, then of course it's a bloody monstrosity.

Sam Eggar was really the surprise of the evening for me. A moderate performance; but much better than I expected. Terry Stamp says she has had to dub her part six times. In a way he disappointed me. But the whole film has been made to flatter Sam – flagrantly so in some of the cutting.

I hate being dragged back into that world. My world now is *The Magus*, and *The Collector* is ended. Down with yesterday.

Writing: putting oneself into a position of isolation and rejection.

The death of Churchill. Odious recrudescence of the Red-White-and-Blue Britain. A whole country mourning its ugly past. Shall we ever get over the trauma of 1941?

9 March
MS of *The Magus* to A. Sheil.

15 March

Miserable cross-currented days, windless above and seething below, waiting for the first reactions to *The Magus*. Tom Maschler came the other night and took away a typescript of it. As usual, he was full of himself, of the excitement of publishing – but full less in a natural than an aggressive way. Some strange drive in him forces him to humiliate, to depress the writers he comes in contact with – Edna O'Brien said the same thing the other day. As if *you* are the writer he mistrusts, has no confidence in. Instead of joining his writers, he isolates them.

Anthony Sheil came to lunch today. He has been reading the typescript in bits all through the week, as he has to fly to the States tomorrow. 'It's superbly written and I'm sure it will be a success, but . . .' and there followed a long list of criticisms. I don't doubt he means them sincerely, I don't doubt, even, that quite a lot of them are valid, but no one realizes the ludicrously tender state of the writer *at this stage*. One is the shorn lamb, and even the warmest breezes cool. And then too, as soon as one enters the literary world, all motives are suspect. Tom M would never say good of the book, because it might prejudice the buying price. A. Sheil has his agent's prerogative to protect – his right to 'guide' and 'criticize' – and in our age inability to find fault is almost synonymous with lack of intelligence.

Meanwhile my nerves jangle. I don't lose whatever fundamental confidence I have in John Fowles the novelist, but I lose all confidence in novel-writing as a significant activity. I feel like giving up that side of writing, of concentrating on poetry, think-pieces – even learning to paint.

Partly this is because I have a fascinated horror of the showbiz side of writing (rather, a horrified fascination). The other day we took Edna O'B, and Terry Stamp and his girlfriend, Jean Shrimpton the model, out to dinner; and then the next evening we went to a party at Edna's, where she has a sort of microcosm of All London – all artistic London, anyway. Kingsley Amis and Elizabeth Jane Howard and Mordecai Richler and Wesker and the film directors Clayton and Donner and Desmond Davies. Edna thrives in all this glitter of names; this demi-paradise of celebrity. And at one level I feel envious of her (though I like her as well as any writer I have met). But I distrust intensely that drive to be in the limelight, in the okayest current of the age: where the cinema and the novel meet. Everyone in this world is driven frantically to destroy his or her nemo; all the talk is half vainly of one's own prospects, or half enviously of other people's. Who has an option on So-and-so's book, who will direct this, who will act in that. All this must be inimical to good writing, let alone good living.

Eliz stands through all of this like the rock of ages, telling me to have confidence, not to be shaken, to be patient. It's true that they all want another *Collector*, they want something small and assignable to current ideas of what the novel should be. That being a writer is really writing what you think fit, not what anyone else feels fit – and finally not for literary reasons (since as often as not the advice and the criticism will be valid by the best *literary* standards) but for existential ones. One's duty is one's freedom of choice, even to the point of the faults that freedom leads one into.

Robert Shaw, *The Sun Doctor.*[1] I suppose this is the sort of novel they want. Clean and quick and smooth, good for the season, and removable by next year. I know, as if I were a disinterested third person, that *The Magus* is worth a dozen such books. And this kind of knowledge is nothing but pain. *Not* satisfaction. If only the outside world could understand that about writers: that the knowledge that your book is better than some is as bad as knowing it is worse than others.

I'm reading a good deal of John Clare[2] at the moment; besides all the historical sympathy and pity one feels for him, there is something more frightening, a sense that all of us who write are John Clares, all victims both of what we write and of the world that handles what we write. Isolated by the one and tyrannized and abused by the other.

20 March
Strange dream: in which I am told Edna O'Brien has been killed in a car-crash in Jerusalem. Someone said, 'There were nails, that was what killed her.' I had an image of a shoulder pierced by nails (long clouts, a recall of those in the artisans' chapel at Coventry Cathedral). This seems a suppressed-envy dream; a wish to crucify. Though the impression in the dream was of shock and horror. On a Freudian level, the phallic symbolism of the nail in the flesh is obvious; and Edna O'Brien's charm is a distinctly maternal one. She is the original lame-ducker. Perhaps our sadistic pleasure in pain always has this incestuous undercurrent; it is always partly a metaphor of the one totally forbidden act.

*

---

[1] The second of Robert Shaw's five novels, *The Sun Doctor* won the Hawthornden Prize for 1962. Shaw (1927–1978) enjoyed a separate career as a well-known film actor.
[2] Of peasant stock, John Clare (1793–1861) worked as a labourer. He wrote poems that celebrated nature, but also mourned the passing of an unspoilt countryside, which with the onset of the Industrial Revolution became scarred by enclosures, drains and new roads. Feeling increasingly dislocated and suffering from frequent bouts of depression, he was certified insane in 1837, and spent most of the rest of his life in a lunatic asylum. JF has spoken elsewhere of his 'astonishing folk relationship with nature', calling him 'much more important than Shelley'.

Shrimpton, whose aloof, vaguely sad face fills every women's magazine. She is bored with modelling. Her affaire with Terry: 'It's nothing, just a physical thing.' Underneath the surface glass, there's a sort of simple shepherdess *de nos jours*; a Marie Antoinette feeling. One pities this doomed return to a nature that has rejected such returns – returns in that context, anyway. Crucified, really, by her own prettiness.

Terry was claiming, humourlessly, that each of the Rolling Stones (a pop-singing group) lays nine girls a day. And she laughed at him; his green virility and Cockney absurdity.

28 March
We are both ill, Eliz with bronchitis, myself with some unidentified virus that makes me feel sick all day; a lovely warm day, the first of spring. We are both full of bile, spleen, melancholia. I don't really want another summer in this house. They are building on the plot at the bottom; people invade from all sides. And I can't get over its facing the wrong way.

Telegram from Tom Maschler (24 March 1965): 'Was greatly entertained, intrigued and very very impressed by *The Magus*. Congratulations.'

29 March
Ned B telephoned from Boston. Likes the book – never read anything like it before. But he seemed worried about the symbolism after the Trial scene. 'Who or what is Lily de Seitas?'

7 May
The Magus has now been read on both sides of the Atlantic, and the general reception is good. 'Rave' reports from the Americans. This end, there are still lots of doubts. I always underestimate the ability of people not to understand symbolism. Nobody seems clear what the two girls stand for. They are bewitched by Lily, and Alison is a sort of intrusion, they can't believe in the ending. I am more or less committed now to making fairly big alterations, especially in the third part. No one in England likes the Highgate Cemetery sequence – too melodramatic, they say. Of course it was intended to be that, to contrast with the last dialogue. But in a novel like *The Magus* the reader becomes a slave to sensation . . . and I don't know myself. Except that I am exhausted with the book and wish to God it was in print. Behind me.

19 May
Cannes. Columbia send a car to take us to the airport. Sam and Tom Stern are there, Sam slightly pregnant and slightly more relaxed than usual, her *'grand athlète de mari'* (as one Cannes paper called him)

dancing discontented attendance beside her. Husbands of film stars are half valets, half gigolos. Some kind of spiritual impotence must be involved; and this gives rise to their characteristic style – hints at their own project hopes ('I'm working on a project with . . .' = 'We had half a minute's conversation the other day because he couldn't reach my wife and felt sorry for me'), their cantankerousness with servants (the major-domo role), then moments of glittering-servile euphoria. Everyone here thinks Stern is so uncouth the marriage will blow up. I still feel sorry for Sam, and so do most of the other co-haters.

The taxi-driver to the airport. A perfect stereotype. 'Of course I know all the special double backs.' ('Double back' seems a new synonym for 'short cut'.) 'You remember, madam, when we left your *résidence* . . .' He used his sir's and madam's, his obsequiousness, like a weapon, to tyrannize. They become menacing in the end, those perfect servants.

At Nice, Sam is met by the publicity people – and standing behind her in the crowd, we brace ourselves to re-enter the world where the star is all, the creator nothing. But at least this writer is give a fine penthouse room in the Majestic overlooking la Croisette and the port, with the Esterel beyond. The stars and giants mostly live in the Carlton, but there is a constant *va-et-vient* between the Martinez, the Majestic and the Carlton. The scene from our room: palm-trees, flags, posters, the blue diamond sea, yachts, all animated, trembling, quivering in light. Dufy Cannes.

Along the Croisette the *ambre solaire* floats up from the beach with the brine. Starlets pose, photographers perform their sighting, angling antics, the ordinary world stands on the promenade and watches. Some old men, frank voyeurs, bring their field-glasses.

The first day we are left alone, feel hurt. Publicity is an addictive drug, and paranoia the withdrawal symptom. We wander down to the old port, to France. Because the Croisette seems more Californian than French. But even the *pétanque*-playing sailors in the port seem like film extras. Here all is contaminated.

20 May
Carlton. A millionaires' bazaar. All the film world wander between *terrace* and *plage*. 'Projects' float from table to table. No one relaxes, and the contrast between the sea and the neurotic need to do business is like Jewish cooking – sour-sweet.

Frankovich rises to greet us. Then the Kohns, then Willie, as sly and deaf as ever. They all think (with absurd innocence) that the film has an excellent chance of winning first prize. It is Columbia's favourite child of the moment. Not that it is any better a film than it ever was; but it seems remarkable by Hollywood standards. Talk of Suzanne and Jud.

They are coming after all. We sit in the beach restaurant, a press lunch; and they arrive, Suzanne as prickly as ever, Jud jumpy and neurotic.

I put on a white tuxedo and we go to the showing of *The Collector.* Flashlights, celebrity. I liked it better, but it is soft at the edges artistically. At the gala dinner afterwards I listen to Willie pressuring Crerenne, the Festival Director of Publicity. *'Il faut expliquer aux jurés que . . .'* on and on . . . What the film means, why the press conference was a failure . . . Crerenne nods, a rubicund little man with eyes like sharkskin, dark grey and merciless.

The gala dinner. Suzanne walks out. Jud runs after her. And we are left among the champagne and strawberries.

At the showing I was introduced by Willie to the Begum Aga Khan. *'L'auteur.'* She examined me, searched for words, then said, 'Ah.'

21 May

Robert Hossein wants to produce, and act in, *The Collector* in Paris this winter. He is a slim, treacherous-looking young man with lively black eyes. Yes, I say. Everyone thinks it is a good idea. Hossein is a power, a force, they say.[1] But I like him because I see in him the meanness of a Clegg.

Nicholas Ray. Will I script the Dylan Thomas piece, *The Devil and the Doctors,* about the anatomist Knox and Burke and Hare? Ray is a tall white-haired man, atrociously hesitant and uncommunicative. After his first 'good films' he has had a decade of bad ones. He explains, with nervous drawings that mean nothing, his idea of mixed shots in one frame, to tell, say, three stages of a story simultaneously. But he is vague, so vague, about Knox. I have glimpses of what he intends – something expressionist, historical, Bergman-like. But his sentences taper off into silence. He stands, sits, lies on his bed with half-smoked stubs of maize-paper Gauloises in his mouth. His blue eyes glitter reflectively behind screwed-up eyelids. Long silences invade the room.

'He's a difficult man to work with,' says Jud.

I sit till two in the morning reading the Knox synopsis, which plunges from good to bad and back again. I can't decide, it is so far from decency. Another meeting with Ray in the morning. More indecision, more hovering silences. He'll ring me from Madrid on Tuesday.

---

[1] Hossein (1927–), who had worked as an actor/director with the Théâtre Grand Guignol in Montmartre, made his début as a film director in 1955 and also appeared, usually cast as a villain, in a number of crime dramas. When JF met him, he was riding high on the commercial success of the swashbuckling romance *Angélique, marquise des anges* (which would spawn several sequels), in which he had played the heroine's lover, the comte de Peyrac.

22 May

To St Tropez with Jud and Suzanne. Days with them are conducted so fast, so wastefully, that all pleasure soon disappears and indigestion, both literal and metaphorical, sets in. A peaceful lunch at St Aygulf,[1] where I could have spent all day. S and J want only to leap from town to town, from one half-eaten meal to the next, one lot of expensive shops to the next. They are not happy doing this, or only transiently happy. Jud is ever articulate and American-Jewish about it, constantly knocking this spending neurosis.

Tahiti-Plage.[2] Even the mattresses cost 7/6 each to hire. Stephen gets three or four francs – six or seven shillings – to buy sweets. He comes back a minute later.

'Buy your sweets, Stephen?'

'No, I lost the francs in the sand.'

'Where?'

'I dunno.' He shrugs, they shrug.

'From sand to sand,' says Jud.

'You must spend,' says Suzanne. 'You must learn to order and leave most of what you order.'

A splendid meal in St Tropez – *bouillabaisse.* Eliz squeezes a crab and scatters saffron-yellow juice all over the next table. C. P. Snow and wife. So much for the English literary establishment. This restaurant was rather stuffy, full of people off the opulent yachts. S and J strike a hard, harsh note, an American note, which I like. E and I tend to sink into an abashed conformity. Their hackles stridently rise.

Many beautiful girls and women – and men – at St Tropez. But this whole coast is now a gilded sewer. Not the Côte d'Azur, but the Egout d'Or.[3]

At the showing. Ursula Andress. An Aphrodite dress split down to the waist. Her eyelashes charred, as if the green-blue eyes have been fired in a crucible, and the blackened despoit still clings to them. She reached out a hand to Sam. 'Simply marvellous.' The tinkle of ice.

Mike Caine. A Cockney boy made good – Terry's friend. He can't act, but takes himself very seriously: hot for birds, for the *dolce vita*, for prestige. Very ugly, these new ultra-hard young princes of limelight.

The real absurdity of Cannes is that it is based on such an evanescent medium – even the best films last two or three years at most. Nine out

---

[1] A village on the Riviera midway between St Tropez and Cannes.

[2] A beach at St Tropez.

[3] 'The Golden Sewer.'

of ten will be forgotten this time next year. It is essentially as frivolous as a bubble-bath, superficially as self-serious as Versailles.

A world dominated by appearances. By images. By expendables. The need to spend money – Freudian fear of constipation. A permanent diarrhoea treated as a state of normality.

Most of all, this film world approaches Versailles. Though there isn't a Roi Soleil, there is everything else. An intense, incestuous interest in their world; none in any other. Endless intrigues. Vicious overspending on follies. What it needs is less its novelists than its Saint-Simons. He was lucky, he had it all concentrated in one place.[1] Not in a dozen cities and festivals.

16 June
The Magus. At last we sent the revised version off to the publisher's. I think the new ending is better; is certainly more consonant. In the first ending I fell into the Lily trap. Was seduced by imagination.

13 June
First reviews of *The Aristos*. A malicious one in *The Observer*.

Pensées manquées, by Francis Hope, *Observer*.

1. John Fowles wrote a highly successful novel, *The Collector*: now he has published a book of *pensées*.
2. Numbered, like Wittgenstein's *Tractatus*; arranged in groups, covering politics, science, education, humanity, art; sub-titled 'a self-portrait in ideas'.
3. In tone, pretentious; in outlook, existentialist-socialist-humanist (ho-hum); in grammar, frequently lacking.
4. Some entries are sensible enough – the small change of any intelligent mind. One or two are even worth remembering: on the new intellectuals – 'visuals', as he calls them; on the spread of knowledge and its trend to equalization; or poetry, or on the appreciation of art. These would make up, perhaps, 10 pages. Of the rest, most are self-evident, and not very elegantly phrased. A few are sheer wind: –

> I.117.   All objects have a non-self. Our belief that an object is, is assured by the fact that it has a non-existent non-self.

---

[1] In his *Mémoires*, Louis de Rouvroy, the duc de Saint-Simon (1675–1755), provided a brilliant and vivid account of life at Court during the later years of Louis XIV's reign.

II.262. The more absolute death seems, the more authentic life becomes.

5. Some might even have crept over from another, more personal notebook. In the middle of a discussion of morality we find: '36. Prolong the time before ejaculation.' A recommendation few would quarrel with; but of a relevance many would question.

6. Heraclitus: a heavy debt is acknowledged. But the fragments that fascinate when they are all that remains of a classical thinker are irksomely self-important in a contemporary. Logan Pearsall Smith's *Trivia* were at least no more presumptuous than their title: the incoherent form of Cyril Connolly's *The Unquiet Grave* was in some ways also its subject. Who is Mr Fowles that he should save himself the trouble of construction, arrangement, order? Or that we should pay attention to his random thoughts on everything from Fascism to adultery.

7. An unset jewel must be a jewel.

8. The heroine of *The Collector* seen through the demented eyes of her captor seemed indeed a paragon. When we were allowed to read her diary, she seemed nothing but a half-educated Hampstead girl. I am afraid she would have liked *The Aristos*. I liked *The Collector* (the first part especially) and regret this book.

9. One can be a good novelist and a poor thinker.

10. To invite comparison with Pascal is unwise. To compare this book with Pascal would be unkind.

None of these reviews review the book; but the manner of it, or the writer. It's useless to protest; apart from anything else one ends by hating the book oneself.

Clearly the form is wrong. I could have said the same things in essays, and had much better reviews. It was wrong to let Cape photocopy the American edition, wrong to publish so soon – and so on. But it has established my position in what Robbe-Grillet calls the *vie politique* – that is, the life a writer can't afford to incorporate into his creative work.

They isolate, the bad reviews. Podge was here the morning of the *Observer* review; read it and made no comment. And even with him, it's something of a shock to see how transparent the revenge of envy can be. He wants failure in others (as do English 'men of letters' – men far too urbane and sensitive not to know they have failed, that the nemo has scooped out their hearts and hopes) and especially failure in me, one of his oldest friends. The same thing comes from Anthony Sheil and Tom Maschler: pleasure, really, that they have me down, even though their livelihood depends to a certain extent on my being up.

I too have my perversities. In a way it is refreshing, after all the over-praise of *The Collector*, the loathsome hyperbole of the film world, to go through this. Writers, even more than fruit-trees, need pruning. There's too much in the English literary world that is nothing but hatch-etwork, as opposed to scientific pruning, and it has become so voguish to be acerbic that there is forming a soft-and-kind counterpole whose only effect can be to prolong the acidulous malice of the very tendency it's trying to counter. As always when the will to do good that springs from the ashes of war loses impetus, our whole time is set towards triviality and frivolity. The problem is to attract customers; and justice of any kind, let alone fair reviewing, is uneconomic in weekly journalism.

For all that, it comes at a wrong time. As usual, now *The Magus* is finished, I feel empty; one goes through the motions of childbirth long after the baby's out. And nothing new has been conceived. Meanwhile the one before is murdered.

7 July

I don't know how people sustain a life of being *désoeuvré*. I can settle to nothing, work at nothing, concentrate on nothing. I have it vaguely in mind to try a play on Robin Hood, *The Outlaw*. But we saw John Arden's *King John* (called *Left-handed Liberty*) the other night. Historical plays present insuperable difficulties of language. If it is too modern, it jars; too antique, it bores. Miller managed the tightrope in *The Crucible*, though; it can be done.

I could start writing the F tomorrow.[1] But a novel is like a mountain. It's useless to attack it without preparation; without time; and without drive, the need to climb.

26 July – 3 August

Looking for a house in the West.

To Bath. The smell of wet barley, rotting corn. It is peppery, not unpleasant.

The amber-grey walls of Bath. We buy some antiques, which puts me in a good temper. It is very bad that it always should, but it does.

Into the Mendips. Dyer's Greenweed,[2] a few forlorn Marbled Whites.[3] And then to Wells, almost like an Italian city for tourists. Nowhere to park, hordes drifting aimlessly nowhere, the place itself finally nowhere.

For two days we hesitate over a house at Stawell, called Abbot's Grange,

---

[1] The working title of this unrealized project was *The Fox*. It was the story of a member of the English aristocracy who sets about killing members of the middle and lower classes.

[2] A spineless grassland shrub.

[3] A distinctive black and white butterfly.

two miles north of Sedgemoor.[1] The garden is nice, the house an old tithe house, though it's been done up, and the ancient features are buried under the comforts of modern living. The country between the Mendips and the Quantocks is very agreeable, flat watermeadowland, silvery, rife with thalictrum and marsh valerian; cows, distant grey and blue hills, the leas sheeted, this wet summer, with water – a little Dutch, a little French.

Cattle lowing in Wells.

A farm in the remote Quantocks, at Spaxton. The woman was a neurotic, and wouldn't let us in. 'I've told them again and again that no one can view except on Saturdays.' Unhappiness breeds around her. As we get back into the car we hear her screaming tiredly at her child. 'Edwina! Edwina! Don't do that!' The child stands sadly in a window, patting a dog. Later we hear that the husband was one of the two survivors from the *Hood* in 1942;[2] has money in the Argentine, but 'can't get it out'. Edwina must be after Lady Mountbatten. Poverty, one smells, and social ambition; and lives as sour as the sourest hay. We strike up an acquaintanceship with a spaniely publican – yet another axed officer, we suspect – in a pub near by. 'The woman's barmy,' he says, of Edwina's mother. 'We've had people staying here a week trying to get in.'

Lunch at the Squirrel, Wellington. There is a little waitress of fifteen or so, with myosotis-blue eyes, blonde hair, a Somerset accent, and a heavenly – literally heavenly, angelic and virginal – smile. Very slow, and very wide, a perfect crescent. She is so shy and gentle that she is useless as a waitress. But she is the wayside vision the knights had when they fell from their horses to their knees. We go on and see various houses between Tiverton and Barnstaple. But they are all too remote, too sad, too lost in the uplands, Victorian parsonages which still smell of cabbage-water and the village fêtes of yesteryear.

At Barnstaple we get involved in the dreadful lemming-rush from the industrial north to Cornwall and Devon. No rooms anywhere. It pours with rain. The bed-and-breakfast signs are all shrouded in sackcloth. At last we get a room in Torrington, in a dreadful hotel with bright red carpets and glass engraved with fishes.

The next morning we see another sad rectory; then at Fremington a real joke of a place, the remains of a lovely Georgian house bought by an amateur odd job man. He calls himself an 'accountant', but we suspect he's a clerk. He insists on showing us everything, every cupboard, every window, every nook and every cranny, and he talks in a flat, equable

---

[1] A tract of land in West Somerset encompassing the Mendip and Quantock hills.

[2] HMS *Hood* was actually sunk by the *Bismark* in May 1941, and there were three survivors.

flow. It's a house full of conversions he has started, and abandoned. 'I was going to make this into a separate bedroom'; 'I thought I'd put a bathroom here'; 'I never quite finished the papering'; and so on. His taste in colour and wallpaper is hilariously bad – like his taste in language, for he's an old RAF man. 'That put the kibosh on that,' he keeps on saying of his 'schemes'. I ask him whether the jets fly over often. 'Never notice them myself,' he says. 'They're only doing circuits and bumps. And never at the weekends.' But the strangest thing of all was that the house was full of black babies. He and his wife look after African students' children. The kitchen was full of them, fat black pickaninnies with beautiful dark eyes. The boys especially have a way of surveying one with great chieflike dignity; like noble animals, though still so young. Eliz and I become the 'new uncle and auntie'.

Then a cottage miles away in the woods. But too many miles away, we decide. So we plunge south through Tiverton again and back over the Blackdown Hills to Ilminster; then on the next morning to Yeovil, where we set ourselves up with another sheaf of particulars and orders to view. House-viewing is really a very enjoyable way of spending a holiday. Rather to our surprise we find people like us. Without wanting to, we draw them out and they talk and pour out their troubles; and then there is nothing nicer than being allowed to poke round strangers' houses without having to be polite, as one would on a visit. In fact it is polite to stare and take note, it shows interest.

We see in turn the wrong house with the right garden, then a good situation with the house too bijou, then an Elizabethan manor house run to rack and ruin, Victorianized and dead, irredeemably past, in a hollow with only a church and nest of mewing buzzards up a nearby combe for company. Then a ramshackle cottage near Membury. A once pretty woman with a painted face, a very marked type this, the Vivien Leigh species; her husband a retired MFH,[1] a general, we think, booming and amiable in a pair of belted corduroys, dressed impeccably like a country labourer, as only the very best county people know how. 'Got a dog, need a dog,' he booms. We murmur something. 'Old Joe up the road, he's my old huntsman. Isn't a thing about dogs he couldn't tell you.' This is evidently a selling-point; as other people point to central heating or mains sewerage. They stand on the road and wave us goodbye, apparently almost as sorry to see us go as the mad clerk of Fremington.

By this time we had abandoned hope of actually seeing a house we would want to buy, but then we arrived at Underhill Farm, near Lyme Regis, down a long unmade road. An ugly house, with a litter of chalets

---

[1] Master of Fox Hounds.

and chicken houses lying about it; but beautifully set on the cliffs, three hundred yards from the sea, with its own fields running down to the cliff-edge and the water. The house is old, set uphill from a square high-walled garden. A fig-tree, strawberry beds, the sea beyond. I have that strange feeling I wrote about in *The Magus* – of meeting onself coming the other way in time. This is the place, something will be lost for ever if one avoids the encounter. The owner, a peculiar man in shorts and black boots, like one of the German prisoners-of-war who used to haunt the English countryside years after they could have been repatriated, takes us round. He cannot imagine anyone not living as he and his wife have lived there, selling teas, letting rooms, running a chicken farm. One senses he has been there too long, has lost all sense of perspective. He makes the house ugly, and offends Eliz especially. But there is a ghost of a beautiful house in it still, a ghost I can seize on. Floors with ammonites in the flagstones. A ghost. 'She's called the Grey Lady, we've never seen her, but we don't tell most people – old Miss Bowditch she was.' The wife, organizing, busy, the cock of the roost. The husband is definitely peculiar, says suddenly in the kitchen, 'Jane Austen used to come here to drink syllabub.' So what with the ammonites, and Jane Austen drinking syllabub, and the fig-tree full of fat green figs, and the bullfinch I hear whistling at the garden-end, and the sound of the waves on the reefs below, and no house within two hundred yards, a private road, and nothing to the west but six miles of nature reserve, badgers everywhere, and the deer in winter, I know I have met my match.

Back in Yeovil we get in touch with Jane Richards' father-in-law-to-be, a Mr Hulburd, an estate agent in Lyme, but he is gruff – and a sub-agent for the sale, won't say anything either way.[1]

In Lyme the next morning another estate agent tells us the road may subside any moment, the house is overpriced, all woe. Eliz veers one way and then the next, but I feel certain – the sort of certainty, I recognize, one has only when one is in love. In a way I like the house being a Circe, a dangerous temptress, its being so literally on dangerous ground, England's most notorious landslip area. It gives me a strange sense of freedom, of health, of not being contaminated by the English disease of our day, that craving for security, the safe investment, the 'good buy', and all the rest.

Eliz weeps at night. It is madness, she can't face it. But I can feel my Cornish obstinacy as stiff as an iron stake inside me. In the morning we go again, and chance on the workshop of the potter David Eeles at Mosterton. His old Cockney mum and dad strike up talk, show us round

---

[1] Jane Richards was JF's cousin and by coincidence happened to live in Lyme.

their house, swear blind by the country life, and we can feel the spirit of this corner of England, sunnier, slower, more genial, at work on them. Like tired old house-plants put out in the rain, one can sense the green working.

We walk along the shore under the cliffs of Underhill. Slabs of hardstone layer out of the grim grey lias; it's the water in these hardstone layers that makes them slip slowly seawards. The lower part of the fields, by the cliff-edge, are dense jungles of high bracken, eight feet or more. But further along there's a way up to the house, over a mud moraine where yellow-wort grows.

We go to Axminster on the Monday and find a surveyor. I make a second offer. On Sunday he refused £11,000; he will take £11,500 only. 'We'll sit and wait till we get our price.' And it's obvious they will. They're not exactly grasping, but unable to think except in terms of profit and loss; and afraid to move. I know they must be bought out.

So there it is. The survey may be so bad that we cannot go on. They are quite capable of wincing back from the outside world when actually faced with it. Strutt kept on talking about 'the old dog'. 'We really wanted to stay on till the old dog died.' Mentally they are as fossilized as the ammonites in their floor. So though I have sent a deposit, it is still remote. But wanted.

5 August
Cable from Boston. Literary Guild have made *The Magus* their January selection. A $35,000 guarantee.

Tom Adams' cover. Pomfret has insured it for £2,500, as a sort of publicity stunt.[1] It's very good, a nice English feel about it – the Englishness of Palmer and authentic Gothic overtones. I wish it had a little more of the feel of Greece, a touch of Greek blue somewhere, the space and light. But I am not complaining.

Hazel. A son. Jonathan Neil.

10 August
Ronnie Payne. We took him and Betsa to see *Thark* the other night. A miserably silly farce, made even worse by his suddenly blurting out in the interval, 'I was in tears in the taxi on the way here, I was bloody well in tears.' Betsa had already hinted that all is far from happy between Ronnie and the *Sunday Telegraph*. He wants to leave, they want him to leave, but he won't resign and they won't sack; and a whole hidden reef

---

[1] Virgil Pomfret was an artists' agent. He represented Tom Adams.

of unhappiness swells up beneath the placid, happy surface of their life.
R wants to write, but lacks any real drive; Betsa nags him in her delicate nibbling way. She's told Eliz that she has masses of money, R needn't
work, but feels he must – bloody ridiculous working-class thing, says E.
But it's Non-conformist really, his minister father working in him. And
he's impotent in some way and they are condemned to childlessness.
He's a man racked by impotence of several kinds, in fact. And I find
his predicament as painful as the sight of a raw wound in another body;
of course it's the pain one can also feed on, since he preserves an aggressive façade of control, of having done quite nicely for himself. But the
mask is transparently thin. We spend hours with Betsa trying to think
how we can coax him into doing something more solid, but he retreats
before charity. Sometimes the English mask ceases to be an amusement;
becomes a damnation.

16 August

Dinner-party at Virgil Pomfret's. Quite the most vacuous evening we
have had for some time; a uniformed maid, silver candlesticks on the
table, the ladies leaving the gentlemen after the dessert. Perhaps
everyone lives like that in Cadogan Square, but such upper-class living
must be confined now to a small Knightsbridge circle. It seems colos-
sally futile and provincial (in the way life at the Hameau[1] in Marie
Antoinette's day must have done). A very with-it party of young people,
all ten or so years younger than ourselves. A with-it young dress designer:
'What I find about the Ad Lib is that I get release – you know? – I mean
all the music just blasts everything out of your brain – you know? – I
mean and what's so fab it's just you, you just dance for yourself.'[2] A with-
it photographer and his TV-model wife. Mark Collins, the publisher's
son, a lanky wet drawl of a young man-about-town, whose natural habitat
is the carpet – sprawled thereon and evoking a world of Christian names
and Old Etonian nonentities. All the talk is about the Ad Lib club, pop
singers, glossy magazines, the eternal silly small chat of the European
rich. I think this began at Versailles, since it is intensely of a world withdrawn from reality, in love with withdrawal, with its own vogues, personalities, vocabularies. The basic cause is lack of intelligence, of course; if
one cannot be intelligent, one is reduced to being fashionable. Eliz is
silent, I gently, much too gently, tease and contradict them.

*

[1] The make-believe peasant hamlet that Marie-Antoinette had built in the
grounds of Versailles.
[2] Situated on the top floor of the Prince Charles Theatre in Leicester Place and
a favourite haunt of the Beatles, the Ad Lib was one of the most popular clubs
in 'Swinging London'.

Underhill Farm. We are going ahead with the buying of it.

17–22 August
Cornwall, Mawnan Smith.[1] Five days with Denys and Monica. They are both going grey, have gone grey during this last year in Nigeria; though nothing else about them changes. Denys is still a writer *manqué*, Monica a woman aggressively in search of a separate identity, as thorny and prickly as ever to live with. Of course they are envious of us, impatient of our grumbles. One morning in a pub Denys came out with a sort of *apologia pro vita sua*: how he (and of course Monica) felt no sense of vocation, how they were aimless, largely unhappy (they loathe Nigeria). Monica the evening before had been maintaining – against the three of us, in her contra-suggestible way – that there was nothing humiliating in being a waiter or waitress, it was a job with a mask like any other; and Denys that morning said to me, 'I've worn the mask of the conscientious teacher so long it's beginning to deform my real self.'

One feels that acutely with him now. Once one could believe in the revolt behind the mask, but slowly it is the revolt, or semblance of it, that has become the mask. What was once the convention has become the reality. As usual I nagged at him to write, but he said, 'I've got nothing to say. What's the point of writing if you've got nothing to say.' But two breaths later it was: 'I'd give all the textbooks in the world to write one decent book or play.' Monica evidently nags him as well, but he will not budge, will not try; as if he is proud to be so paradoxical and complex.

Like so many other men I know (Ronnie, Jud) he has a curious inability to drive or walk slowly. Any delay between two points is unbearable; but as soon as he has arrived he is restless. As if the surface of the world is uncomfortably hot and he has to keep hopping off somewhere else. We went one day to a deserted cove near the Lizard,[2] a lovely green-blue sea, the turf full of flowers, sunshine, where even the most anti-rural mind could have passed a day. But we hadn't been there an hour before Denys was off, a long walk up a mile or more of cliffs, then a drive of several miles for a pint on his own. Just as Jud one day on the beach this spring at St Tropez suddenly got up and said, 'If I don't have five minutes on my own I'll go mad.'

The angel from another world in all this troubled limbo is Michael, as innocent and charming a ten-year-old as one could easily imagine – the kind of child, brimming with gentleness and enthusiasm and affection, that has never been common but nowadays seems almost frighteningly

---

[1] A village two miles south-west of Falmouth.
[2] A peninsula whose tip is at the most southerly point of Great Britain.

strange. Though Denys and Monica bring him up with a healthy and sensible strictness, his parents don't really account for Michael. He is a Blake-like creature, a tiny fragment of the divine; and especially in his fascination for V-bombers, warships, soldiers and all that world that is the very antithesis of his gentleness. He must become either a saint or a homosexual; or perhaps the actor or writer his parents dreamed for themselves.

29 August – 5 September

Anna staying with us. It upsets Eliz, who overmothers her, overloves her, but the miracle is really that she is not in the least a problem child, has not turned into the neurotic guilt figure we all promised ourselves. Roy and Eliz obviously still upset each other far more than either worries Anna herself. The only conflict that I can see now is between Roy's regression into a sort of working-class way of life and our very different mode of behaviour. But even there Anna seems quite capable of living both worlds – I think she is essentially that common but rarely described type, the happy schizophrenic. My own type, really; to whom balancing the bad and the good and coming to believe that both are necessary becomes second nature.

We took her down to see the farm, while I did some 'searches' at Axminster. Eliz is upset about the farm, too, move and change again. But to see it, to see the sea stretch beyond the old garden walls, reassures me. We forced our way down through the jungle to the shore and swam, and then climbed back from Pinhay Bay.[1] The wildness of the woods there is strange, almost subtropical. And certainly ecologically primeval in terms of English history.

16 September

I have begun a new novel, called provisionally *The Orgiasts*, set in Turkey; to be a variation of *The Magus*, though the echoes will be tenuous and remote at first reading. 'Turkey' (violence, lust, Moslem views of women) as opposed to 'Greece' (reason, morality, love, etc.). I was going to write *The Fucker* (or *The Exterminator*) next; but the implications of it are too black, in a way too frightening.[2] I want it to be a short, hard book, and they are the most difficult to write – take more time; and I need to screw up courage to write it. It can of course be written without courage; in a sense finding the courage to write it means finding a way to carry it through. Not only facing the ordeal, but first arranging it.

---

[1] A bay to the west of Lyme Regis and a short walk from Underhill Farm.
[2] *The Fucker* was an alternative title for *The Fox*. See note 1 on page 633.

18 September

Denys and Monica have just spent the night with us, and gone, and now Eliz, after hours of bitterness, has gone too. Something sour always comes among the four of us. Eliz says it is me: last night I was boorish, crass, bored, insulting – I made the evening impossible, and so on. It didn't seem as bad as that to me, though we were all tired, and it grew tiring towards the end; but we know each other well enough surely not to care about yawns and silences. Even so my wretched books do lie between us, the three of them and the one of me, in an ugly way. I'd like nothing better than to discuss both the problems of writing books and the specific books I write – but that is as forbidden a topic as a dirty joke in a monastery. If I start, and nowadays I always start very modestly, cautiously, obliquely, if I start to talk about literature or being an author, I can see Monica bridling, Denys putting a defensive veil over his eyes, Eliz ready to pounce and protect them from my dreadful vanity, my boasting. Really the choice is quite simple: either one keeps absolutely quiet about all the serious side of one's life as a writer or one prepares to lose the only friends, the old ones, one wants to keep. So at one minute I get out a pamphlet and scribble *To Denys and Monica with love, John*; and ten minutes later I push it away because I feel I can't risk giving it to them, i.e. alienating them.

And now, over this last few months, Eliz has been contaminated by the same poisonous virus. She has told me six hundred times that I am an egomaniac, I am self-actuated, I am full of romantic illusions, I think of no one but myself, which is of course exactly what one's old friends would like to say in this situation. They say it, in a way, by never mentioning or praising anything one has written. And this too has contaminated Eliz – as the closest of my old friends, so to speak, she couldn't in fact forgive me anything even if I were the best writer in the country. But by beginning to seem to her 'just a romantic novelist' (her words) I am adding insult to injury. Not only self-actuated, but with second-rate, or *on* second-rate, success.

So I live surrounded now by a kind of resentment: all right, I've not done too badly financially, but I'm a failure in everything important and I ought jolly well to behave like one. And I even subscribe to the myth, because dismissing is easier than boasting.

Eliz is on better ground when she complains of loss of identity. I don't believe all the feminist argument (Betty Friedan's) about unfulfilled women. There are just as many unfulfilled men, because fulfilment is a comparative thing. But of course for both man or woman, proximity with fulfilment (assuming, ludicrously, that I am fulfilled) is the glare of the sun – it spotlights non-fulfilment. All E's complaints run on the 'Look at you and look at me' line. It's no use pointing out that she is looking at herself in the distorting mirror of me – her old masculine

protest again. Of course it *is* difficult to look anywhere else. But I hate
the way she seizes on this twisted reflection and uses it for whipping up
her anger and despair.

20 September

Difficult to know all the reasons that drive me to this move. But it is
identified in my mind with the need to write poetry again; and to do
things with my hands again. For three or four years now I have lived
with the assumption that my time was too precious to waste on menial
and manual tasks; in fact the only thing I can do now in that line is to
type. And suddenly the idea of having to cut grass, mend walls, paint
and strip paint, and the rest, is attractive. Frost was so bad a farmer that
he thought geese roosted in trees, and apparently immortalized the
frightful howler in an article he wrote for an agricultural magazine; I
should be just as bad, if I took to farming, and I don't intend to be a
good householder or to let any household thing stand between the typewriter and me. One can be sure Frost never let anything on his farm
stand between him and a poem.[1] The 'return to the land' is a dangerous
myth if it is taken seriously; on the other hand it is as capable of forming
a constituent in a pleasurable life as any other. As long as one always
makes believe; and never actually believes.

29 September

Completion day for Underhill Farm. We now own it.

Dropped *The Orgiasts.* Began *The Accountant* four days ago.

1 October

Day of misery. Eliz and I have some throat infection. I've had it for
weeks now, can't swallow comfortably, can't smoke. To the Television
Centre in Wood Lane: I meet Melvin Bragg, an earnest young man with
floppy black hair and pink cheeks. He and Julian Jebb are putting me
in some cultural programme they are starting – *The Collector* première
is on October 13th. Jebb is a little blond bird of a man, gently queer,
excitable and mimicking; fastidious, ready to peck and pounce but seemingly not so malicious as most of his kind. We sit and savour each other.
I remember his fine review of *The Collector*, and seeing him, so light and
young, rather tarnishes it; and seeing me, a lumbering, mumbling old
bore, must have had something of the same effect on him. Bragg wears
a black leather jacket, a grey polo-necked sweater; nice and quiet on his
own, on his guard against being corrupted by the gloss and swagger of

---

[1] i.e. the poet Robert Frost (1874–1963).

the Centre. The place is full of important-looking, stylishly important middle-aged men; as if TV is some wonderfully daring and avant-garde art instead of the stodgy old hash it is.

Then in the evening to Roger Burford's in Park Lane. Twentieth Century Fox have offered an option deal on *The Magus*. Ten thousand down, sixty-five more on exercise, escalators that would bring the figure up to a hundred, and five per cent of the picture. Perhaps if we wait we can get more, twice as much; perhaps not, the book may fade. I try to explain that I am too tired, too messed up by worries over selling the house, to care – money ceases to have meaning beyond a certain point. One is not talking about anything tangible in the end, but about prestige. I would really be content with the 75,000 dollars, I just don't want to worry endlessly about the price I deserve, the price I might chisel, the price I can gamble on if I wait.

Then home – and a telephone call from Stephen Winkworth, the boy who wants to buy the house, to say that his mother (who is finding the money) and her solicitor have decided that the road-widening scheme is too much of a risk. They will not buy. Although this has been hanging over us for two or three days, it falls like a hammer blow. A great wave of depression hits us. It is comic, really – to have 'success', the interview on television, the large film offer, and to end up feeling near suicide. On top of that I feel in the mood to write, and things could not be more impossible. Success is like a wall; it keeps one from one's work.

An odd dream, after our evening of woe. Monique was in it. I have not dreamed of her for many years. Perhaps it originated in *Monica* Sharrocks having been staying with us for several days; and then leaving yesterday. I wanted her to leave, really, so the dream can spring only from the fact, not the desire.

I was on a cruise liner. I had shared a cabin with Monique, but I can't recall any incident from the sharing, except the strong feel that it had no sexual incidents whatever.

It was not clear where the cruise was, or where to. But there was a sense of arriving at a port of destination – passengers leaving the ship. Monique is standing near the head of the gangway, with several books clutched to her breast – a picturebook or two, I think also some Penguins. I went up to her because I wanted to ask her to return books of my own I suspected she had taken (by mistake?), but when I saw her face, which was turned away in profile, down-looking and infinitely sad, I felt obliged to change the question. I asked, 'I hope you haven't any books I bought for the ship's library there?' She did not answer, but not answering implied 'no' very clearly. She had a *mater dolorosa* face, profoundly sad – something for ever lost. Beside her was standing another unrecognized woman or girl, in a sort of supporting role – two womanhoods shrouded in grief, the one totally sunk in it, the other watchful that the grief shall not be intruded on.

I turn away, aware that my question is meaningless. She is going somewhere I shall never go. It is a separation for ever, which is why it is sad for me. But her grief has nothing to do with me. I do not exist for her.

The essence of this dream was loss. In some strange way she seemed to symbolize the passing of time.

Perhaps my dislike of Monica S, which is now far more historical than real – in fact I now rather like her briskness and independence, her courage, really – is based on a subconscious rejection of Monique as a Circe (Lily in *The Magus*) figure. In this case 'subconscious' means 'unconsciously conscious'; I mean I have rejected such figures consciously. Monica S is not consciously a Circe figure to me; but I reject the implications of the pun.

4 October
Today we shall know whether TC Fox have accepted our counter-offer: another 25,000 dollars. Last night we heard that the Winkworths will definitely not buy. Now we will see if the bank will tide me over till next spring; I would keep this house and let Dan and Hazel have it at a cheap rent. And we have asked Monica S to come with us to Lyme for five or six weeks. This last idea is so obvious that I can't think why I didn't work it out before – or I can think. The vile Iago in the subconscious.

Two small girls bouncing a transparent blue plastic ball up a grassy hill; into sunlight, the sun singing in the edges of their hair, their twinkling trepidant feet; and the ball a third being, like a spherical water-blue dog. They ran up the hill into the oblique sunlight, very small on the wide green ridge, turned, ran down again, as innocent and ageless as the sun itself, shimmering with light, fragile and shimmering. Then they see us both standing and staring at them, go silent, stare back as they trot past, and the sun is suddenly on their backs, and they are just two trite little girls. Very odd, this being intensely beautiful, angelic, poetic, in the sun's eye; and then banal when the sun's behind us.

5–7 October
At Underhill Farm. We camped out. Extraordinarily mild weather, like Greek weather, making the already poetic place even more so. Eliz is still battling it, though she has conceded defeat on the garden front. The fig-tree had still some luscious last figs on it; the sea rushes gently against the Cobb far below; curlews and oystercatchers cry. The

Michaelmas daisies are dense with butterflies and day-moths. In the morning we went and picked mushrooms. Eliz hates the building – it's all 'mess'. I like the old parts of the house – and the others I can tolerate. We lit a huge log fire one evening. The smell of wood smoke. Flames.

A Mr Wiscombe comes round to see about doing alterations. His father got 'old Bowditch' into the farm, and he was a great friend of one of the sons. Originally the farm belonged to a Mr Philpott, who let it to a gamekeeper, who used to pay his rent each year from the rabbits he caught. The farm went to rack and ruin. It was the Bowditches who worked like niggers and turned it into a dairy farm. 'Old Emma, she made the best cream and butter for miles. That was where the old copper was. Then here' – in the dairy – 'here were slate slabs and she'd have ten, fifteen copper scalding-pans in a row. All day and all night, she worked.'

London is dull and concreted, afterwards. The farm is a world apart. A domain.

17 October

I accept the Fox offer. $7,500 for the option, $92,500 on exercise, $10,000 for a treatment; escalators of $5,000 on each 5,000 copies sold above 25,000, up to 55,000; of $5,000 for one week at the top of the bestseller list, $10,000 for two, $5,000 for any four weeks in any position; of $5,000 if the paperback sale is over 50,000, $10,000 if it is over 75,000.

19–20 October

We move into Underhill Farm. The bad throat I have flames up into acute pharyngitis; I can't swallow, can't think, and all is miserable. I spend the days in bed. Monica and Liz brush, clean, make their nest. A nice old Scots doctor looks at the throat, gives me yet one more antibiotic. The weather is fine, balmy as spring, and I chafe, chafe, chafe.

A weasel dancing round and round the garden trying to escape us. Flinging itself at the stone walls, then rushing for the strawberry beds.

Brown owls. They hoot all round us at nights. Lovely cool sounds – mystic oboes.

The sound of latched doors.

The silence here at night. The house creaks and murmurs in it. No cars, no passers, nothing.

23 October

1. The novel. Digging out one's character, as if they had been long

buried under the ground. I mean they are there, but one never knows what they are till they are excavated.

2. The novelist. Really a storyteller, a figure in the corner of the bazaar. I think there is a deep shame, a humiliation, in being a novelist. Deep inside us crouches a man on a ragged carpet; and the real world rides by.

3. Dialogue is the most difficult thing in the novel. That is why so many TV plays fail. Their writers can't afford decent dialogue, because it needs time, patience, endless revision.

The sea hushes and strishes on the reefs below.

Every night there are curious running yaps behind the farm; rather frantic and desperate, as if a dog has run off the edge of the world and is falling, falling through eternal space.

Depression, reading an article on subsidence. The whole farm may slip into the sea. And then those constant joys, because the place is like a huge, complex poem. The impossibility of it, and the poetry of it.

The light in the bedroom. The window is ridiculously small, but it fills the old room with light, because of the mirror of the sea.

25 October
In the conservatory, the sky like lapis lazuli, a blue totally clean, without sweetness, softness, that turquoise opacity English skies so often have.

I picked two ripe figs.

Mr Chichester. He owns the fields to the east, a cousin of Frank Chichester, the ocean-crosser. A brisk man of splendid transparency and rudeness and inquisitiveness. 'My father's the fourth senior living officer in the Royal Navy.' He keeps on probing at me. Who am I? What am I? How dare I buy his farm? The Strutts warned us that he regarded it as 'his' farm – the one he was going to retire to. 'My wife will never come here again. She told me, "I'll never go near Underhill again . . ."' Of course he gave me first refusal. I told him his figure was monstrous. I was damn rude.' Then he said, 'I'm a bank clerk. I know the value of money.'
    Later he said, 'They got it for £6,150.' And his eyes flashed daggers of envy at me. It was absurd, really; he was like a small boy, so eager to sour the possession; so unconcealedly envious. 'I'll be back,' he said, at the door. Poor man.

The joke is, we have a letter he once sent Strutt, offering £11,750 for the farm.

26 October

I felt better today. We lift potatoes, but it's too late, woodlice, wireworm and slugs are in each. Still, a heavy crop. I use the axe, but we need a circular saw for the logs. And a thousand other things. Its thousand-other-thing aspect is one of its pleasantest, really. All days are too short here.

5 November

A cold east wind, which brings noises out of Lyme. The crackle of fire-works, a red-and-green shower over the skeleton of a hedge. The moon glitters on our sea meanwhile.

Monica left today, to go back to Nigeria. She has saved us, these last weeks; just by being here, not that she hasn't worked hard, harder than anyone we could have hired would have.

Beautiful days, these last – clear blue skies, a sharp wind, but we miss most of it. The farm is warm, a secret place. Butterflies today, one of the pears in blossom; the workmen eat lunch in the garden.

Yesterday I walked along the beach for two or three miles, saw not a soul, the sea a clean blue, the beach littered with driftwood; plucked some lovely cress at Pinhay – the best cress I have ever eaten. Lazy waves coming in; the seaweed caught in the inner arch of them, swallowed up, reddish-brown and sepia in the cool green aspic of the water.

9 November

Full moon near midnight. On the waves, a grey that holds a ghost of green, the light is so clear. At a certain point there is a magnificent glint of pure silver; a lovely liquid, gliding lump, so silent, mysterious, graceful. The sea is the beauty here. Ships do not spoil it. The sea, the sound and shape it makes as it touches land, rapes land, caresses land.

10 November

Today old Bowditch, who lived here for fifty years, came to see us. A purple-faced old man with a curious double-bridged nose. He's a whisky-soaker. 'Old Jack wouldn't walk a yard to pick up an egg,' said one of the builders, 'but he'd drive twenty miles through six feet of snow for a bottle of whisky.' All his life he'd obviously, transparently, preyed off his stolid, solid wife. He has charm, uses Dorset dialect beautifully, a Raleigh-like burr and elegance.

'The land courts the sea here,' he says. And ''Tis sidling land.' I could have embraced him for that first splendid metaphor.

'It was all sward, all to the bottom beaches.'

'Now, Mr Fowles' – he says my name as hissing soft as silk, no one has ever said it less awkwardly – 'now, Mr Fowles, keep open drains. Don't have no pipes. They clog. Keep open drains, nice, clean open drains.'

We've had two ceilings down. In one the joists are right off the wall. Even the builders whistle. But in the hall the timbers are old ship ribs, curved and beautiful.

27 November

I plod on wearily through the film treatment of *The Magus*; a job that both bores and disgusts me. If I didn't so need the money I should have refused to go on, weeks ago. But we are in a mess financially – for the simple reason that the house in Highgate won't sell. An agent has had it for a month now, without even an offer being made. So I have an overdraft of £5,000, and all the expenses here.

Here is good: the sea as doorstep, sea and light and the silence of the nights. I still wake up at times and see the whole place slipping into chaos. But in daylight it sits in its little cradle of land, and scorns disaster.

Index